THE WAY
IT WAS

THE WAY IT WAS

An Oral History of Finance: 1967–1987

The Editors of Institutional Investor

William Morrow and Company, Inc.
New York

Copyright © 1988 by Institutional Investor, Inc.

Portions of this book previously appeared in the magazine *Institutional Investor*. The book was also published under the same title in a special limited edition.

Library of Congress Cataloging-in-Publication Data

The way it was: an oral history of finance, 1967–1987 / [compiled by]
    the editors of Institutional Investor.
        p.   cm.
    ISBN 0-688-08005-7
    1. Finance—History—20th century.   2. Investments—History—20th
century.   3. Institutional investments—History—20th century.
I. Institutional investor.
HG171.W33   1988
332'.09'04—dc19   88-9679
                                                                            CIP

Printed in the United States of America

First Edition

1 2 3 4 5 6 7 8 9 10

BOOK DESIGN BY MERLIN COMMUNICATIONS, INC.

CONTENTS

6

7

8

INTRODUCTION

"The management of money is one of the oldest of the arts and one of the newest of professions. As a profession, it is changing continuously, so much so that it bears little resemblance to the same field only a generation ago. Perhaps at one time it was easygoing and social; today it is fiercely competitive and intellectually challenging."

With those words, I launched *Institutional Investor* in 1967. We started with some ambitious dreams of chronicling, analyzing and perhaps even influencing the changes that seemed destined to sweep the financial world. This book is a reflection of how we succeeded. Based upon *Institutional Investor*'s twentieth anniversary issue, which was published in June 1987, it tells the story of the most extraordinary twenty years the financial world has ever experienced.

Back in 1967 institutional investing was in its infancy. Even the subjects we were writing about then, looked at in retrospect, seem redolent of an era that has long since vanished: "performance" investing; "gunslinger" money managers; the "age" of block trading. In rapid succession, the go-go years went, the high-flying stars fell, scores of fabled old Wall Street firms disappeared from the scene, and the New York Stock Exchange itself almost collapsed.

But soon there was a host of new topics to grapple with: ERISA, the pension reform act, which revolutionized the way retirement funds were invested; "Mayday" and the end of fixed brokerage commissions, which obliterated the price umbrella that had protected the brokerage world for more than a century; the rise of new quantitative investment techniques, which reflected a growing belief that if you can't beat the market you might as well join it.

11

Those developments merely scratched the surface of the changes of the period. Investment banking saw a shift from long-standing relationships with clients to a preoccupation with transactions, getting the deals done. The takeover boom in mergers and acquisitions brought fear to corporate boardrooms and a new breed of corporate raider and tactics such as greenmail to the fore. A host of new financing instruments changed the way and the pace at which corporations raise money.

At the same time, the backdrop against which this drama was being played exploded. In the late 1960s a typical day on the New York Stock Exchange might have seen trading volume of 10 million shares. By the middle of 1987, volume averaged an astounding 185 million shares a day. Money managers' jobs have been transformed; now they can be found in front of their computer consoles as they let their buying and selling programs do their talking for them. And, for better or for worse, many of the firms we were writing about then don't even exist anymore—and those that do are part of much larger organizations into which they were folded.

To recount what happened during two tempestuous decades and to dramatize those events, we have produced an "oral history" of the period. This approach, telling the story entirely in the words of the key players, has been used successfully in other fields ranging from sociology to sports. But never, to the best of our knowledge, has it been applied to the world of finance or, for that matter, to the business world in general. We found this approach compelling for a number of reasons, not the least of which is its reaffirmation of *Institutional Investor*'s long-standing conviction that the essence of high finance is the human element.

We talked not only to the people who are the leaders of the financial world—the Rockefellers and the Wristons and the Rohatyns—but to those whose fame is more narrowly rooted in their specialized fields: block trading, money management, research, pensions, M&A and the like. And we also sought out the unsung players—ranging from a veteran retail salesman to cops who pound the Wall Street beat to the vicar of Trinity Church. In the end, 116 people participated.

The selection process was only the beginning. The oral histories, undertaken between late January and early May 1987, involved all of *Institutional Investor*'s editors and writers. Most of

12

the sessions ran for two hours or more, and some were done in several installments. The histories were taped in conversations with our staffers, transcribed and then edited into these running commentaries, which remain in the subjects' own words.

The editorial effort was overseen by Editor Peter Landau and Executive Editor Cary Reich, who first suggested the oral history approach. They had the help of Editorial Assistant Elisabeth Mason in handling the avalanche of tapes, transcripts and edited copy. Keeping this mammoth project on track was a major task; the transcripts alone amount to a pile that is more than three feet high. Copy Chief Laura Gilbert, Copy Editor Richard Cunniff and their staff worked tirelessly to see that all the pieces came together.

The results of all these efforts are in the pages that follow. Some of the reminiscences are reflective; some are delightfully anecdotal; some are confessional; some even anticipate the stock market crash that was to rock the investment community a few months after these words were spoken. And all of them provide an inside view of the world of high finance that few people ever get to see, and an introduction to the powerful personalities who have shaped—and are still shaping—that world.

Return, now, with the editors of *Institutional Investor*, to the way it was.

—**Gilbert E. Kaplan**
Editor-in-Chief
Institutional Investor

THE WAY
IT WAS

Walter Wriston

Former Chairman CITIBANK

Few chief executive officers can look back and say they wrought revolutionary change—not only in their companies but in their industries. But Walter Wriston can. His time as Citibank/Citicorp chief spanned most of the twenty-year history of *Institutional Investor* magazine, and during that period he guided his institution to new heights of power and profit. Even more significant, Wriston—more than any other individual—aggressively sought to redefine what a bank is and isn't, and in so doing lit the flame of the financial services revolution. Today he is a director of nine corporations, including General Electric.

I had just been made president and CEO of the bank in 1967. George Moore was chairman, and we were just dreaming up the idea of the bank holding company.

We were looking for a way to survive because it was clear that the banks, with their current product lines, were losing their advantage. I remember we had an offshore policy meeting in the Bahamas, on Paradise Island, and we sat around for two days and debated the question of whether we should form a holding company. Some of the most senior guys in the bank were against it. The debate was just about even, and George Moore was on the sidelines. He was thinking about something else.

Then the phone rang; it was Aristotle Onassis inviting us all to his yacht for dinner.

Everybody got charged up about what fun that would be. George woke up and picked up the argument and came down on the side of forming the holding company, and the thing passed our policy committee by a small margin. And one of the ironies of history is that I still believe that, if Ari hadn't telephoned at that time, who knows how it would have come out? Because it interrupted the discussion. It energized George, who had sat through a whole day—which was unbelievable for George—saying almost nothing. And then he got all excited: "We're going to go see the yacht tonight. Isn't that terrific? What's the issue we're talking about here, fellows?" And that was it.

In '67 we were professionals with other people's money, and we were amateurs with our own. We had no budget in Citibank. We had a historical society: At the end of the year we'd sit around and say, "That wasn't bad." We had no formalized salary scales. We didn't have the general tools that modern corporate management requires. We had no management information system.

And so, in order to figure out where we should be in ten years, we hired a think tank by the name of Tempo, a subsidiary of General Electric.

That went on for almost a year. And at the end of that period they came in and briefed us for several days, and then we put together a corporate plan. We set targets for where to go, and we bet pretty heavily on technology.

And I think that it's fair to say that the Tempo study was a catalyst in getting that vision out. The vision was very simple. It was to supply any worthwhile financial service anywhere in the world, where we were permitted to do so by law and where we could do so at a profit. And, so far as I know, that still holds. So that vision was extremely clear.

It was around the same time that we came up with the 15 percent annual earnings growth target. We were growing at about 6 or 7 percent at the time. And we sat around at one of the offshore policy meetings and looked at all these ranges of numbers and saw that the top range of corporations then was around 15 percent. We decided collectively that that was a good number for a target. One of the interesting things is that it sort of became embedded in an analyst's mind: If you didn't make it one year, it was a terrible failure, and if you went over it—as we did for several years—we obviously set it too low. The usual can't-win syndrome.

Did we always make it? No. Might it have been 16 or 12? Yes. But the real question, to me at least, is: Did it serve as one of the motivators to move the corporation to where it is today, the greatest financial institution in the world? Or did it not? And I would argue that it did.

One other thing on the 15 percent, just historically, that might interest you. Arthur Burns used to come and see me to talk down the interest rate. The interest rate got up to some wild number like 6 or 8 percent. And he would come and sit in my office and say, "Walter, you're wrong to have an earnings target." And I would say, "Arthur, you keep saying we ought to have more capital. I've got terrible news for you. In order to sell my stock in the marketplace, we have to have as good an earnings record as General Motors or IBM or anybody else because it's a tough, competitive world out there." He said, "But banks are different." I said, "Tell that to the portfolio manager of the pension fund." And we had a long debate. And what fascinated me was that I was at an Institutional Investor conference in Cannes a few years ago and Arthur and I were on the same program, and he looked at me at dinner and said, "You know, Walt, you turned out to be right. Banks have to earn money in order to sell capital."

Hallelujah.

Getting back to the subject of interest rates, you may recall that Arthur, as well as the president of the United States and other players, kept beating up on the banks, saying that interest rates were too high, they were slowing down the progress of the world, etc. It's the oldest argument in the world.

So we looked around and we kept saying, "Look, the prime rate is a market rate." They kept saying that it isn't, it's an administrated rate, whatever that means. So we looked around for a way to make it crystal clear that it was in fact a market rate, and we came up with the idea for a floating prime rate.

It took us quite a while to make a decision on it. I remember we were out in California—[then Citicorp president William] Spencer, [executive committee chairman Edward] Palmer and myself—and we continued this debate standing in the lobby of the Fairmont Hotel, waiting for our wives to come home from a dinner party. And we had been arguing about this thing for a year. We were getting all kinds of political heat about holding the rate down. So we finally said, let's do it.

And we said, gee, if you do it, you can't do it without informing

19

the powers that be. And it happened that the secretary of the Treasury was coming to address that conference we were attending. But I was going to the Philippines the next day, and Billy was going to Japan. So we told Palmer, "Why don't you go out and meet John Connally at the airport, ride in the car with him and lay it on him?" And that's precisely what he did. And Connally said: "I don't have any objection to that. It is a market rate. Go ahead and do it."

It was nothing more or less complicated than trying to focus the attention on the market and not on the venal bankers. That was the object of the exercise. I think it made it more difficult for them to bludgeon us. And I think history will bear out the fact that they couldn't make the same argument and that argument died.

We went through our share of crises; there's no doubt about that. One was Penn Central. At one point we were their lead banker, and, I have to say, we weren't totally surprised by the collapse. About six to nine months before the balloon went up, the fellow who handled the account came in to the senior credit officer, George Scott, and said: "The company is going to hit the wall. I've taken all these numbers apart, and it's going to go bankrupt." And he was 100 percent right. The chief financial officer—I'll never forget it—asked for a meeting of the banks, and we had one at 399 [399 Park Avenue, Citicorp headquarters]. Before the meeting, Scott brought him in to see me, and the CFO said, "I'm going to get up and ask for X million dollars." And we said, "There's no way. You don't have any assets. You're down the slippery slope." He got extremely indignant and he said Penn Central does not give collateral, and so on and so forth. He got up on his high horse, and Scott sat there and said no way. Scott said: "I will give you the use of our hall. You can talk with the banks, but you can forget it as far as we're concerned."

And so he went down, and he made his speech and that was about it. It was clear that when nothing happened at that point, we were on a downhill slope. The last hope was for a so-called V loan: a government-guaranteed loan for the transportation of military supplies. That was to be approved on a Friday afternoon. And my phone rang. It was about 6:00 on Friday, and it was Dave Packard, deputy secretary of defense. He said, "Walt, we have disapproved the loan." So I said, "We're in a tank." He said, "You're in a tank."

On Saturday I was up in the country; we were building a house and we had sort of a foundation and we had a phone. I got on the phone around 9:00 in the morning and hung up at 4:00, and we had Burns, [Transportation Secretary] John Volpe, [Treasury Secretary] Dave Kennedy and every once in a while, I think, Jim Lynn, who was a general counsel.

And the issue was that Penn Central had a bunch of commercial paper coming due the next Monday; my memory of it is it was $300 million. So the argument was: What's going to happen to the market? And I kept saying to Arthur: "What you have to do is call all the Federal Reserve banks, all twelve of them, and tell them to call all the dealers and the banks and say, 'The discount window is open.' And then nothing will happen." And he said, "Well, you know the banks know that." And I said, "I have terrible news for you. There are reserve banks like the one in Detroit and the one in Atlanta that aren't about to lend any money. And there are others like New York and San Francisco." He said, "They're all the same." I said, "Please believe me." We argued about this all day long. And I said, "If you do that, the market will absorb this whole thing."

I got a call about 10:00 Sunday night from the chairman of the New York Fed saying the discount window was open. I said, "Thank you very much." And no bank borrowed from the discount window the next day. The market took the $300 million. It was one of the reasons why I believe in the strength of markets. The debate between the Fed and the market is always whether the market can sustain it, and those of us who believe in markets believe it can. And it turned out that that was right, even though we all took tremendous hits and got back very innovative Mickey Mouse paper, one of which was even a lien on a lawsuit.

Then we had the New York City fiscal crisis. The city was selling this paper, and people weren't paying all that much attention. It's like somebody challenging the figures of the U.S. Treasury Department. How do you know what the national debt is?

But what happened was that we had a fellow named Jack Friedgut, who was an urban economist, and he came in one day and said the city is going down the tubes. And I said, "It is?" And he said, "Yes. And you're going to sit still and listen to me while I tell you why." And I said, "You got my attention."

When he got through, it was clear he was right. And so the next fellow who came in—I forget who it was; maybe it was still Jack—said they're going to run out of cash this week. So I got in a cab and went down to see [New York Mayor] Abe Beame, and I said, "Sir, you guys are going to run out of cash." He said, "It's a total lie. It's not true." And I said, "Well, that's what I'm told by my folks." Then he brought in [Deputy Mayor James] Cavanaugh, and Cavanaugh also said it's totally untrue. So we came back, and I looked at all the numbers again; Jack Friedgut was right.

And so I said, "What do you then do?" I talked to my partner Billy [Spencer], and I concluded that we couldn't do anything except to alert people. *The New York Times* doesn't know there's a crisis because they're worrying about the Middle East and you can't get their attention.

So I called the senior senator from New York, Jack Javits, who was an old friend of mine, a remarkably wonderful man, and I said, "Jack, the city of New York is going to go bankrupt." And he said: "Yeah, it's very interesting, Walt. I'm on my way to Russia to free the Soviet Jews, and then I'm going to stop in China. When I get back, I'll call." I said: "Jack, you don't understand what I'm telling you. I'm telling you that the city is going broke." He said, "I'll remember what you said," and he left.

And I said, "Now what do we do?" So I called Jim Delaney, who was the head of the New York congressional delegation, and I said, "Jim, will you get the New York delegation together? I will send down Jack Friedgut with a dog-and-pony show to explain why the city is going to hit the wall." And he said, "That's very interesting, yes." And Ed Koch's book opens with that conference. But the only people there were Elizabeth Holtzman, Ed Koch, Jim Delaney and one other. Four guys showed up. Holtzman called Beame and said, "Citibank says the city is going broke." Beame said, "They lie."

So we could not get anybody's attention. And it was one of the most frustrating things in my life.

What finally happened was that they couldn't sell the paper; the syndicate that was going to flog the paper quoted an interest rate that was totally unacceptable to Beame. And there was some lawyer working on the prospectus—I can't tell you who it was now—who wouldn't go along with it. And that was the end of the ball game. Then [New York newsman] Gabe Pressman was down at the 399 lobby, running around looking for the man who took New York bankrupt. That was me. And then my friend [labor leader] Victor Gotbaum turned out 10,000 pickets. The media then shifted from saying it was our fault to saying we were imprudent because we had too much paper and *we* were about to go bankrupt.

And so I finally said to the boys: "The hell with it. Let's publish how much city paper we've got." So we published it. And then finally all the banks did, and the world didn't stop. And then the governor stepped in, and, as they say, the rest is history.

It was around the same time that we started to get some attention with our consumer strategy. We began by looking at the fundamentals, and that was that the demand deposits of the clearinghouse banks in New York didn't increase for ten years in nominal terms. You don't have to be too bright to know that with the nominal GNP increasing every year, we're out of the game.

So the CD was invented and gave the clearinghouse banks another couple of years of life. But there's a finite limit to everything. And the next thing was holding companies issuing commercial paper. That gave them another ten years of life.

What do you do after that? The answer is you have to go, as Willie Sutton said, where the money is. And the money was in the consumer's pocket. We did a little study that showed how many households there were and how much money they had, and it was perfectly clear that that's where the money was.

Second, the first rule of thumb of banking is to diversify both assets and liabilities. And while you could buy money in the market for your Euros or whatever, the more you had in consumer deposits the steadier your institution would be, whatever wind blew in the future.

And then the question is, How do you do it? And we really didn't know. We had a good branch system in New York, but it wasn't really making any money on a fully loaded basis. We had some Mickey Mouse accounting that said it was, but no one believed that. And so we formed a little task force and put a fellow called Reed [John Reed, now Citicorp chairman] in charge of it and said, come up with a vision and a strategy and a plan on how to get from nowhere to someplace. And we went to our board and we explained the rationale, and they said, "Okay, we'll go with you."

Well, there were two years when nobody got an IC [incentive bonus] payment. Walking down the hall was not the greatest experience. And we took some enormous hits—lost lots and lots of money—and took a lot of ink from our friends in the media on how dumb we were.

I don't think we ever doubted it would work. I think that we had moments of thinking about the price we were paying. I'd go in and talk to my partner Billy, and he would say, "Do you realize that this is the biggest goddamn risk we've ever taken?" I understood that, and it was tough, very tough.

We took some big hits on our credit cards. The credit card was a chicken-and-egg deal. You go out and tell all the restaurants you've got a zillion cardholders, and you tell all the cardholders you've got a zillion restaurants. And then one day none of the above is true. What you've got are a lot of deadbeats.

The changes were enormous. You needed an incredible computer system. You had a whole different culture based on marketing. All the guys from General Foods who were shlepping coffee were now dreaming up Citidollars. The cultural shock was enormous.

I guess the people whose tails were on the line were Spencer and I. If the thing hadn't worked, I think I'd probably be somewhere else. The new folks coming in probably would have sacked Reed, too, I suppose, but that's all subjective stuff. The fact is, Wilbur, it did fly.

Meanwhile, on the international side we were dealing with the recycling process—which was, I suppose, one of the greatest successes in the history of international finance, especially when you consider some of the nonsense we heard at the time. When the Arabs went from two bucks a barrel in two stages to $30, Bob Roosa wrote a piece for *Foreign Affairs,* saying the Arabs would own the world in a few years. You had people warning that, quote, the Arabs would pull all of their dollars out of America and we'd come crashing down. When that surfaced, I held a press conference and explained that you couldn't take dollars out of America except in a tin box, and that's not many.

The world adjusted extremely well, considering the shock to the system. What nobody knew was that Volcker was going to lock the wheels of the world. And when he threw the U.S. into the deepest recession since 1933, it spread to the whole world. And that's what started the, quote, international debt crisis: Export ratios that looked very good the month before he took office looked like a disaster a year later.

Now, you could say that we should have known that that would happen. We didn't. In fact, I recommended to [President Jimmy] Carter that he put Paul in there because I told him that if anybody was in there who was a name the Europeans had to learn how to spell, we'd be in trouble. But then one day he just locked the wheels. And the fact is, that's what caused the international debt crisis. It wasn't the recycling or the rest of it; it was the fact that the growth which the world had been enjoying was suddenly stopped.

I said at the time that no American bank would fail because of it—which turns out to be true—but that many would fail on good American real estate and oil. That turns out to be true, too.

But that's not very exciting. People would rather talk about my comment that LDCs don't go bankrupt. Well, they don't.

And the facts are—if anybody reads that article, which, of course, nobody does—what I said was that the infrastructure doesn't go away, the productivity of the people doesn't go away, the natural resources don't go away. And so their assets always exceed their liabilities, which is the technical reason for bankruptcy. And that's very different from a company.

Would I have done anything differently? In the recycling process, probably not. Once again, none of us, I particularly, thought that the Fed would throw the country into a depression. I just didn't believe that was going to happen. I was wrong. They did. And that's what caused the whole damn problem.

I realize there was a lot of talk about my management style when I was at the bank. People get characterized as confrontational or needling or whatever, and there's a certain amount of truth in all sides.

Was I exacting? Sure. Was I occasionally sarcastic? Of course. On the other hand, good people knew that if they had a real problem, personal or otherwise, they were going to get dealt with fairly.

But the stories still go around—like the one about my supposed

25

edict when we were building Citicorp Center. [Wriston reportedly was so annoyed by the pornographic bookstores and massage parlors surrounding the building site that he demanded they be evicted at any cost.] You know, in the great echo chamber that is the media, you get a story like that and it's on my Nexis data base out there forever.

The facts are that *The New York Times* said that I went to my window in my office and I pointed and said, "Get rid of that massage parlor." Well, as you probably know, my office faced Park Avenue and the massage parlor turned out to be on 53rd Street, between Lexington and Third. So all I could have been pointing at was the George Washington Bridge. But it's been immortalized, even though it's totally untrue, because it makes a terrific story.

Of course, it's been a great disappointment to the media that the management team I left is still in place. A great disappointment. I remember that during this great competition [the horse race to succeed Wriston] I had a very famous former government official come to call. He said: "You've got these three vice chairmen, and what's going to happen is what happened to the First of Chicago with Bob Abboud and Dick Thomas and all of these fellows. The only way to solve this problem is to bring in somebody from the outside—like me."

And I said: "Well, thank you very much. It turns out that these folks all work together pretty well. It's a pretty big outfit. And we think that it may just work." And he said, "You're making a terrible mistake, and the whole bank will self-destruct." That was sort of typical of what went on. What really went on was what you now see.

Today I'm happy and employed and have more to do than I know what to do with. People ask me if I'm disappointed that I haven't been tapped for public service. No, I'm not. The train's been through the station a few times, but that's the way it goes. You know, you make your decisions on the basis of the known facts at that time, and you sit with them the rest of your life.

When I left, I decided that I wouldn't want to stay on the board. You see, I'm one of those folks who walk out the door and don't look back. I believe very strongly that there's nothing worse than staying on. If you say something, you're messing around in the new guy's yard. If you don't say anything, you're kind of useless. So what is your function?

Billy and I gave it our best shot. We made mistakes; we also didn't do that bad. It's a pretty good outfit. No regrets. So now it's yours, fellas. And we're not going to mess around with it.

Editor: Cary Reich

John English

Chief Investment Officer FORD FOUNDATION

John English is vice president and chief investment officer of the
Ford Foundation, whose more than $5 billion in assets is both in-
ternally and externally managed. English assumed his post in 1981,
after 26 years at AT&T, where, for the last six years of his tenure,
he was director of pensions for the Bell System's giant, pre-divesti-
ture fund.

I graduated from the University of Iowa in 1955, on a Saturday,
and on the following Monday I became a management trainee
at the Illinois Bell Telephone Co. My career ambition was to
work 43 years for the telephone company like everybody else did.
You started when you were 22, you retired when you were 65, you
joined the Telephone Pioneers of America and you moved to
Florida, and that was my life. Then on January 1, 1966, I was
transferred to the treasurer's office and I really thought that was
the end of my telephone career, because the action was in the
operations side of the business. The treasurer's department was
then the elephant's burying ground.

But at that time, the Bell System had decided that each of the
telephone companies should take its portion of the pension fund
and bring it back home, which was one of my first assignments.
Indeed, in my time at AT&T, the pension funds were shifted
from being consolidated at the parent to going out to the operating companies, and then, when the Bell System switched from
local bargaining plans to national bargaining plans in 1980, the
plan assets were again concentrated in the parent. We pushed

them out, we brought them back in, and then, eight months to the day of my taking the job at the Ford Foundation in 1981, the Justice Department dropped the neutron bomb on AT&T and broke it up into bits and pieces.

In 1972, I was promoted to AT&T as director of banking relations. I was named director of pension fund administration in 1975, a propitious time since it was the year after ERISA was passed.

To me, one of the most significant things about ERISA is that it made corporate America aware of how important the pension fund really was. In the years before ERISA, the pension fund was really thought of as a sideline. But the attention that the funds received increased the awareness of corporate America of how important this area is. When ERISA was passed, the board of directors at AT&T established a committee on employee benefits, and I was required to meet with this committee quarterly, to review investment results and to tell them what happened to the market.

I also got involved with a strange breed of people called actuaries. An actuary is described as an accountant without personality. I don't think that's true. I also got very involved with attorneys. Because ERISA had so many legal ramifications, I spent hours, days, weeks with inside attorneys and outside attorneys trying to figure out the strange Form 5500 and what it meant.

Throughout all this, a major part of my job at AT&T was to try to get 23 telephone companies, Bell Labs and Western Electric to agree. The Bell System then had a very federalistic system where AT&T owned all of the stock of the 23 companies, but the companies were run in a very autonomous manner. We would make a proposal to, say, increase equity exposure or to do something in real estate, and it seemed to me at the end of the meeting set up to decide these things that we would get eleven companies to agree and eleven to disagree and one would abstain.

When I took over as pension administrator, I was somewhat overwhelmed. At that point the Bell System had 111 money managers managing about $38 billion located all over the United States. I thought, "Gee, if we meet with them four times a year, that will be 444 investment meetings." As it turned out, we didn't, because of divestiture.

Anyway, we discovered that with 111 managers, our performance in the aggregate was no better than the S&P 500's, minus fees and commissions. So we eventually created in-house index funds to manage some of the assets. I've learned a few things in the business, and one is that large pools of funds are market-driven. If the markets do well, the fund is going to do well. If the markets do poorly, the fund is going to do poorly.

But the first thing I decided I should probably do was meet some of the major players. At the time, I thought there were maybe 200 money managers in America. Little did I dream that there were then 2,000 and that each of them at some point would come in and pitch me on what their firms could do.

One of the first telephone calls I got after being named director of pension funds at AT&T was from a person named Dan Breen [former director of marketing at Fayez Sarofim], who said he wanted to welcome me aboard and said that he and Fayez Sarofim were coming to New York and could we get together. I then flew to Houston, because I like to kick the tires and look in the trunk, and I remember how tremendously impressed I was with Fayez's office.

It looked like the Metropolitan Museum of Art, with beautiful statues and pictures. I also remember that it was about 106 degrees in Houston, but in Fayez's office it was 55 degrees. I think Fayez, growing up in Cairo where it's always hot, decided that he'd been hot long enough and wasn't going to be hot anymore. I remember I shivered in that office because I had a summer suit on and he had a winter suit on.

Fayez needed Dan more than he ever knew. Dan was the guy to make the customer comfortable. You know, a customer might say to Fayez, "Why do you have these energy stocks?" and Fayez would say, "That's a stupid question." And Dan would say, "What Fayez means is that we are overweighted in the energy sector because of blah blah blah." They had a great symbiotic relationship.

I think I have been pitched by just about everybody in this business. I've seen every investment pitch known to man. The thing that is most interesting to me is that every one of the managers is able to give me a chart that shows me that he was in the first quartile or the first decile. I have never had a prospective manager come in and say, "We're in the fourth quartile or bottom decile."

Money managers have become more sophisticated. The first ones I met were all balanced managers, and most of them came out of bank trust departments. The pitch was that they knew when to switch between equities and bonds. That didn't turn out to be true.

Some of the investment managers seem to have an investment process that really holds together and makes sense, and the very best investment managers that I have met know how to listen. An amazing number that come to see me don't know how to listen. It's like they've been wound up and they have rehearsed this proposal in front of a mirror and, come hell or high water, they're going to take me through their three-ring binder.

I've met some great turkeys. They're going to come in and tell you about their low P/E strategy. And I say, "But I'm interested in large-cap stocks." And they say, "And with this low P/E approach, we can do this and the other thing." These are the people who don't listen.

But then, I could not deal with the kind of rejection these men face. They have 99 people in a row slam the door, and the next day they land a $50 million account. I would absolutely come apart. I couldn't do that.

You know, the really superior managers, they have a process that makes sense. I mean, they don't just wing it. And even the best investment managers do not always have great results. There is no man for all seasons in this business. I try to think of the really outstanding investment people that I have had the privilege of getting to meet and to know, people like Claude Rosenberg, Bob Kirby, Dean LeBaron, Dave Williams. All of them have one thing in common, and that is that they are superb marketing people. They know how to sell themselves, they know how to sell their firms, because of their sincerity, knowledge and inner confidence. I don't think many of them think of themselves as marketing people, but they really are.

But, you know, it's so competitive—even with people who have more money than they know what to do with. This morning I had a very successful money manager in this chair. He must have an incredible amount of money, and he is over here hustling me. I think to myself: "My God, don't these guys ever give up? When is enough, enough?"

It used to trouble me that the money that we were putting into the fund was going to be paid out in the year 2022, and yet we would meet with the money managers every 90 days to find out how we're doing. Maybe you don't need to meet with them annually; maybe it would be better to meet with them every five years. Part of that quarterly performance way of thinking stemmed from the development of the art of performance measurement, and that occurred twenty years ago. I don't think anybody really knew how well or how poorly funds were doing until, in 1967, we started quantitatively measuring the Indiana Bell pension fund versus the Mountain Bell pension fund. It introduced a spirit of competition that, looking back, I'm not sure was a sound thing to do.

I switched from the corporate arena to the not-for-profit sector on November 1, 1981, and it was a very difficult decision for me to make. I really agonized about the move. I was a lifer at the Bell Co. I do have a Bell-shaped head, and if you cut me, I bleed Bell System blue.

But on June 15, 1981, I got a call that changed my life. It came from Korn Ferry International, the executive placement people, and the next thing I knew I was at the Ford Foundation meeting with the president, Franklin Thomas. We engaged in conversation that went on through June, July, August, September, October and November.

All through this I really thought they wouldn't offer me the job and I wouldn't take it anyway. Then one evening at home I got a call from Thomas, and, I'll never forget, he said they had had a special meeting of the board of trustees that day. And I thought to myself: "This is really class. He's calling to tell me they picked somebody else and to thank me for my interest." Instead he said that they had reviewed the 112 candidates for this job and they had decided on me.

Then I did something that I wasn't sure I had a right to do. But I said, "Mr. Thomas, could I bring my wife in to meet you?" And he said, "Yeah, why don't you come in and have lunch?" So I turned to Ann and said, "Forget the paddle tennis, forget the bridge tournament, you're going to come to New York and meet the president of the Ford Foundation, who has offered me a job."

33

The blood drained from my wife's face, and she said: "Is this a joke? I thought you were going to work 43 years for the telephone company. Don't you realize we have two daughters in college?" But she came to lunch and met Franklin Thomas, who swept her off her feet, and at the end of that lunch, we agreed that it would be a good thing to do.

I was absolutely terrified, but it's turned out to be the best thing I ever did. You know, in my 26 years with the Bell System, I made many, many trips to Cleveland, Milwaukee, Omaha and St. Louis. In my five years plus at the Ford Foundation, I have been to Nairobi, Cairo, New Delhi, Katmandu, Mexico City, Bogotá, Lima, Rio, Tokyo. It's absolutely changed my life.

At AT&T our single biggest problem was what to do with the new corporate contributions to the fund, which were coming in at a rate of $1 million an hour. When I first came to work at the Ford Foundation, I convened the investment group and, though I knew the answer, I said, "Do we get the contribution from Ford Motor Co. on the first business day or the last?" One brave employee said, "Mr. English, the last contribution came in 1947." And I immediately knew I was in a different atmosphere.

I came here in 1981 and the Ford Foundation portfolio was about $2.5 billion, and I thought, if I work here fifteen years, maybe I can get it up to $3 billion. I never dreamed we'd get to $4 billion, and we recently went through $5 billion.

My mother taught me that you should divide your life into three segments. In the first third of your life, you should learn. In the second third, you should earn. And in the third, you should serve. When I came here, I entered the service portion of my life, and if the Ford Foundation is willing to put up with me, I plan to make this the rest of my career.

Editor: Julie Rohrer

34

Bernard Cornfeld

Former Chairman INVESTORS OVERSEAS SERVICES

In the late 1960s, Bernard Cornfeld sat atop a mutual fund colossus in Geneva, Switzerland. From modest beginnings investing the savings of U.S. military personnel, his multibillion-dollar Investors Overseas Services and its flagship Fund of Funds tapped the talents of the best of the performance managers of the day. But then a devastating bear market, overaggressive tactics and problems in the public market toppled the firm and its chairman, who was replaced by now-fugitive financier Robert Vesco. After a spell in a Geneva jail, Cornfeld's once-playboy lifestyle is now somewhat diminished, but he still maintains residences in a number of countries as well as a mansion in Beverly Hills, California.

At the height, we had a total of eighteen funds with something over $2.5 billion under management. We had offices in 100 countries. We had 25,000 salesmen, virtually all of them full time. Toward the end, we had positive cash flow of between $15 million and, on one particular day in the middle of a sales contest, $100 million. Those numbers may not seem so large now, but at the time the whole U.S. mutual fund industry was less than $50 billion.

When we had company conferences, we had a United Nations setup, with earphones and translations into eight or ten languages. And there was a camaraderie that made the company unique, mostly because of our stock-option plan—which permitted everybody, from salesmen to ladies that served the coffee, to buy company stock at a fraction of what might be considered a realistic value.

In a way, though, the stock-option plan led to our demise, because it became necessary to do a public offering. We couldn't maintain a plan where we were buying back option shares based on a formula that kept going up, because it related not to actual cash on hand but to book value, which was substantially higher. So we had to permit people to sell their shares outside the company.

A few things happened at the time of our public underwriting. One is that we created 143 millionaires in the company, some on paper, some in cash. No one except retiring shareholders sold more than 10 percent of their stock. A lot of people that suddenly discovered they were very rich decided to retire. That not only weakened the company but substantially weakened *my* position because it included some of our key board members, people I could count on for support.

Anyway, one day some German banks began a program of selling the stock short. Now, in the United States you've got to cover your shorts within seven days. This wasn't true overseas; they were simply bookkeeping transactions: They didn't have to deliver the stock. We knew it was short selling because in the underwriting, only six months earlier, no individual stockholder received more than 10,000 shares. So if a block of 500,000 shares hit the market, it had to be a short sale.

The stock went from something like 18 to 12 in the spring of 1970. Ed Cowett, who headed our banking operations and was also president of IOS at the time, went on a trip to Japan and left instructions that we were buyers at 12. He had put together a pool, just after the underwriting, of people who were prepared to buy at that price. I committed to $300,000. John King [head of King Resources], some of his associates and some other people I don't remember were in the pool. They were people Ed had contacted just in case we needed some support in the aftermarket.

When Cowett got back from Japan, he discovered that $11 million of our stock had been purchased. He told them to stop, and tried to raise money to cover the shortfall. He raised some by utilizing the money of the IOS Foundation, but we were still about $2.3 million short. So Ed borrowed the money from our bank and took down the rest of the stock in his family trust, for which he was very much criticized afterward.

Ed had a very serious flaw. He thought the market in any stock—including ours—could be manipulated. Just as soon as we stopped purchasing, the stock really began to drop—going from 12 to 2, when it recovered slightly. But within the company there was total panic. Individuals who one day were worth $28 million, the next day saw they were worth 25, the next day 23, the next day twenty, the next day sixteen. By the end of the week, they wanted someone to come in and save them. They had a choice between the Rothschilds and John King. They chose King, primarily because the Rothschilds were very arrogant and, in exchange for lending credibility to the operation, really wanted control, which they weren't particularly prepared to pay anything for. King, on the other hand, offered to pay back any monies that he had borrowed, lend the company $8 million and do all kinds of other things.

I think just two of us opposed King. The board voted for him and the contract with King called for my resignation as chairman, so I resigned. But eventually the SEC indicated that if it went head, they would stop U.S. trading in the stock, so King had to pull out.

Now, it was June or July 1970, and sales, strangely enough, continued to be good. But morale was very bad, particularly with our large stockholders, who were also directors and key people in the company. Now, Harold Lever, who had been a member of Parliament for many years and whose family owned a bank in Switzerland, he offered to lend the company $5 million at commercial rates with the proviso that I resume my post as chairman. And then there was Robert Vesco. He went around to the board and promised to cover their losses in tax shelter deals. One director was promised $50,000 a year for life as a consultant. Vesco beat Lever by one vote. A lot of the key people now indicate that there was a sort of hysteria then and that they don't know how they could have supported Vesco.

When it became evident in about 1972 what Vesco was up to, I flew down to the Bahamas, where he lived at that time, but he just wasn't taking calls from me. I knew that Jim Crosby, chairman of Resorts International, had a direct line to Vesco, because Vesco wanted to purchase Resorts' operations in the Bahamas and go into the casino business. Crosby thought it would be awkward to give me Vesco's number since they were in the middle of negotiations—though he did call Vesco and Vesco assured him that he would be contacting me. Crosby and I played backgammon for a couple of hours and eventually he had to go to the restroom, and I promptly jotted down Vesco's number from his address book, which was by the telephone.

I called Vesco and said, "Look, Bob, I've come all the way down here to see you, and I would appreciate your cutting out this screwing around and getting together with me." And he said, "Okay, I'm going to the casino tonight; meet me there at 7:00."

He came to the casino with his mother, his father and a handful of bodyguards, and we went off to a corner. And I said: "Bob, I get the impression that you're involved in something that's kind of crazy. Do you want to go through life as a fugitive?" And he said, "Well, if I'm going to be a fugitive, I'm going to be a very rich fugitive."

I said, "Yeah, that's great, except that some of the money that you have comes from people where that's all they got." And he said: "Well, they've got their problems. I've got my problems."

I said, "Bob, if you're not interested in anybody but yourself, hasn't it occurred to you that one of these people is going to become desperate enough to come around and blow your brains out?" And he said: "Bernie, they're not going to blow *my* brains out. They're going to blow *your* brains out. You're the one who sold them the funds."

In a sense he was right, because he didn't go to jail. I did.

I was arrested in November of 1973. One of Vesco's henchmen wanted to discuss IOS matters in Geneva. As a precaution, I called an attorney and asked if there was any problem with my coming to Geneva, and he said, "No problem at all." Later I learned that he called the authorities—and really caused me to be arrested—because, I suspect, he figured he would make more fees if I were in prison.

I was held without bail until the beginning of April 1974, when they finally set bail at Sf5 million—the highest in Swiss history at that time. The jail was a converted sixteenth-century monastery in the middle of the old town of Geneva. It didn't really feel like jail, although it had bars on the windows. The bed was just about the size of a chaise longue, a little longer, barely wider. It was all right. I didn't have problems sleeping.

There were four of us, maximum, in the cell, and it was about 15 by 35 feet.

I had some interesting cell mates. One was a retired banker who was acting as an agent on a piece of art that turned out to be a forgery. Another was a man who bought jewelry with bad checks. He only worked on Saturdays. One of his stunts was that he had a gold pen worth a couple of thousand dollars so that the jewelers would think that no one would write a bad check with such a valuable pen. Another was a second-story man.

Jail gave me a tremendous opportunity for reading and for writing letters. Perhaps it's surprising, given all the mythology, but I didn't particularly miss sex. You really weren't sex-oriented in prison. There's nothing very romantic about the setting. What I missed most was the phone.

———✥———

The trial wasn't until 1978. My then-attorney said that he felt that there wasn't any question in his mind that I was not guilty, but he said that I would be judged by a "jury of my peers," which consisted of hairdressers and taxicab drivers. And he told me that they wouldn't understand what really happened at IOS, but there were a few things they would understand: one, that I was a foreigner; two, that I was wealthy; three, that a lot of people had lost money; four, that I was Jewish; and five, that I was a playboy. And all of those things are actionable in terms of the Swiss mentality. So, he said, it was perfectly conceivable that I could be found guilty, and financial crimes in Switzerland are treated on a par with murder and mayhem, and he felt that I would get the maximum, fifteen-year sentence.

Well, the choice was between going through life as a fugitive, which I could have done if I decided not to leave the United States, from which I couldn't be extradited, or returning to stand trial. And I decided to take my chances. The trial itself was extraordinary—by the time the government got through putting on their witnesses, they were all so favorable that I hesitated to put on any of my own. One after another said that they hadn't ever had a work experience that compared to IOS, that I was very generous and concerned about my employees and that I did everything to create a climate in which work was a joy. They only put on employees because they dropped all the charges except the

39

charge of having incited my employees to buy company stock with the full knowledge that the company would collapse.

When it came time for the prosecutor to sum up, it took about three minutes. And what he said was that trials were not like tennis matches. It matters not who wins or loses, as long as justice is served. And as such, in all good conscience, he couldn't ask the jury to bring in a verdict of guilty. Everybody was astonished. My attorney told me that in his experience this had never happened before.

The trial lasted a few weeks, and every day there were headlines in the Swiss papers and one of them was *"Cornfeld, l'Americain décontracté,"* which means "Cornfeld, the relaxed American." If I seemed relaxed, it had to do with Dilantin, the drug that [Dreyfus Corp. founder] Jack Dreyfus thinks everybody should be taking. Not only has Jack taken it for years and years, but he feeds it to his dog, and he created a $40 million foundation primarily to study the drug, which equalizes the electricity in the brain and allows you to concentrate. Every time I saw Jack, and I saw him quite often socially, he would hand me bottles of Dilantin, so I took it throughout the trial. I actually haven't ever taken any drugs except Dilantin.

My really great selling job came fairly recently, however, when I argued a case for myself in tax court in April 1986. The IRS decided that I did not intend to make a profit on an aircraft I had purchased in 1969, and if not, then I had no right to depreciation and losses. With penalties and interest over the years, I would have owed the government $12.5 million just on that particular situation. At the trial I felt how unevenly matched we were. I had an attorney who was brilliant and articulate and charming and probably making $3 million a year; the government had an attorney who could hardly speak English and was perhaps making $25,000 a year. In a way, it's kind of unfair.

As we walked out, I was congratulating my attorney on what a beautiful job he did, and he said that I couldn't have been a better witness. And three months later, I pick up *The Wall Street Journal*, and it says, "hard to believe that Bernie Cornfeld purchased an aircraft without an intent to making a profit, but that's what was decided in the Federal Tax Court in Washington." And I was clobbered with this decision. We were congratulating each other on what a wonderful job we had done, and I had lost.

When we appealed, I decided if I had nothing to lose I'd go and

40

argue the case *pro se*. I took the Red Eye to Washington and got there before the courthouse opened. I had a couple of hot dogs for breakfast from one of those hot dog stands with an umbrella, although I've been a vegetarian for years.

When I was through with my presentation, one of the judges asked the government attorney, "Do you think Mr. Cornfeld would have been upset if he had made a profit on this transaction?" And the attorney said: "No, but I don't think that's why he bought the aircraft. He bought it as a tax shelter." And the judge said, "Well, what's wrong with a tax shelter?" I could have kissed him. I won.

I'm not really as rich as I'm reputed to be. Still, life is pretty comfortable. Since IOS I've worked on several projects. One of the first was going to be a film-making community in Palm Springs, but, before the project got launched, Dart Industries offered to buy the land at an attractive price. Now we've developed a health products line, Better Living Enterprises, which took a long time to get to a point where I was happy with it. It looks like our first sales will be in Germany.

I'm chairman of a company called Suprex, which has developed an automated supercharger for auto engines, and of a gypsum mining and marketing company. And I'm involved in a little film production company that's doing a video on how to become a model.

Ultimately, I'm going back into the mutual fund business with an international fund of funds [the original FoF invested in North American securites]. In the U.S., where the business has really changed dramatically with the increase in option buying, indexes and so forth, there's a lot of expertise that just doesn't exist outside the country, and to the extent that we can provide it overseas, we get to be in a ballpark all our own. I would work with John Templeton, who used to be one of our directors and who is an old friend, and I've talked to FoF manager Fred Alger; he hasn't said yes or no.

An old business associate, an American who is offshore, seems prepared to put $100 million into kicking off the fund. We would manage this $100 million for him and he'd be a principal of the company. At my suggestion, he's invested over $300 million in Fidelty and a couple of hundred million in Dreyfus. So I said,

"Look, you're in the mutual fund business already; why not get involved in the other end of the business as well?" And he said: "That sounds like a good idea. I can put together a few of my friends, and among us we can put up $3 or $4 billion." And I said, "I don't really want that much, because I can't go public with a vehicle that has half a dozen investors with $3 to $4 billion; I'd just like $100 million." He said: "Fine, you've got it. Put it together." So we're going to do that.

God, I miss Ed Cowett [who died in the mid-1970s]. When we drove somewhere together, we'd sing in harmony. He had a beautiful voice; he had wanted to be a cantor. We were complementary. I need someone like him to get this off the ground.

Editor: Heidi S. Fiske

John Whitehead

Former Co-Chairman GOLDMAN, SACHS & CO.

The son of a New Jersey telephone lineman, John Whitehead put up his life savings—all of $5,000—when he was invited to join the Goldman, Sachs & Co. partnership in 1956. He served as personal assistant to the firm's legendary leader, Sidney Weinberg, and then went on to spearhead its investment banking effort. When Weinberg's successor, Gustave Levy, died in 1976, Whitehead and John Weinberg (Sidney's son) were named co-chairmen. One of the securities industry's most thoughtful and articulate spokesmen, Whitehead served as chairman of the industry's trade group, the Securities Industry Association. In 1985 Whitehead was named deputy secretary of state.

One of the great challenges we faced at Goldman Sachs twenty years ago was the transition from the leadership of Sidney Weinberg to Gus Levy. For one thing, there were the corporate client relationships; Sidney was the principal figure that 90 percent of Goldman's clients looked to. He once had 30 directorships—although that number is a bit misleading because some of them were of subsidiaries. Fortunately, we had a plan for the maintenance of those relationships, with a No. 2 person assigned to each of the companies. We made an effort to show these companies that Goldman Sachs was more than just Sidney Weinberg. And my recollection is that Goldman Sachs kept as clients every one of the companies that he had been personally responsible for.

Gus and Sidney had each come up through different sides of the business, so they each had different sets of talents and different backgrounds. Sidney was in many ways a business statesman, with influence far broader than just that of an investment banker. He was a very close personal adviser to five presidents, starting with F.D.R. He was not a highly educated man—he never went to school beyond eighth grade—but he had an instinctive ability to make the right decisions.

Sidney had come through the dark days of the Depression in the role of managing partner of Goldman Sachs, and the difficulties that a banking firm faced in just staying alive during that period had made him very conservative. He was very cautious financially and very cautious with our reputation. And he was very reluctant to do new things or to do things differently. Gus, on the other hand, was less interested in being a broad statesman than in being a banker, and he was aggressive and ambitious and creative, and eager to see Goldman Sachs grow and develop. More growth occurred during his period of leadership than during Sidney's period of leadership. Sidney saw to it that the firm survived and that its reputation reached a high level; but it was Gus who saw to it that the firm had the thrust and drive to grow during this period.

Gus was in touch with everything. There were very few things that went on at Goldman Sachs that he didn't know about. And he operated successfully in a great variety of arenas: not only in Goldman Sachs but in the affairs of the fifteen or so companies that he was a director of. Every CEO used to say that Gus Levy was his best outside director. Well, it's easy to be the best outside director of maybe one or two companies, but to be the best outside director of all the companies whose boards you're on is really quite remarkable. And yet that's what people said he was. Then he had a whole further life in the world of nonprofit organizations, particularly Mount Sinai Hospital, where he was the active president and chief executive officer for a long period of years. There were also fundraising activities, political activities he was involved in. But my memory of him is of him sitting in his office and opening up that sliding glass door and shouting out an order to the trading room to sell something or buy something at the same time as he was carrying on a conversation about a completely different subject.

44

If there was a fault in his management style, it was that he was not a very good delegator. And Gus was not a planner; he was a day-to-day operator. I say this with great fondness and kindness rather than as a criticism, but to Gus short range was what's happening this morning and long range was what's going to happen this afternoon. He felt that investment banking was a constantly changing profession in which it was hard to plan, maybe almost impossible to plan. You just sort of took advantage of the opportunities when they appeared; it was a sort of trader's instinct that created success. And so others of us, rather than Gus, were the ones who thought in terms of looking ahead and planning, and what activities we should go into.

Those of us who were doing the planning were concerned at that time with the structure of the partnership. Being a partner in those days did not mean you were in charge of a particular department or division or activity. When you became a partner, you were sort of above everything, and the organizational structure was down there somewhere. And once you were a partner, you were free to do almost anything you wanted—and most partners did. So we tried to bring about a division of responsibilities, and make people responsible for doing the kinds of things they did best and not have them cross over into things they weren't very good at.

The managerial style changed again after Gus died and John Weinberg and I took over. We recognized that the big and very simple secret of whatever success Goldman Sachs has had has been that it spends an inordinate amount of time attracting very outstanding people coming out of the leading business schools. And there was a pool of tremendous talent that was basically underutilized at the time because the responsibility hadn't been pushed down to them. So we did a lot of pushing down of responsibility, clarifying authority, departmentalizing, segmenting the business and creating profit centers all over the place.

If we had tried to operate with the same style of dominant, single personalities, we never could have grown the way we did in the ten years that John and I were chairmen. It was only by spreading the responsibility and delegating authority that we were able to accomplish that.

Of course, as the firm was changing, we were also seeing changes in the structure of the investment banking business. Back in the old days of the '40s and '50s, these historical syndicates were taken terribly seriously and were considered to be absolutely sacrosanct. Once a firm was in a particular syndicate as a major, it was a major for life. Changes came very rarely. I can remember resenting bitterly the fact that Kuhn Loeb and Dillon Read, which I considered at the time to be a bit old-fashioned and not up to Goldman Sachs in their talents, were in a bulge bracket that Goldman Sachs was not in. Nobody was willing to face the reality and change these historical structures.

Client relationships in those days were all-important. The cultivation of clients was an extremely significant thing. There was very little shopping around for different investment bankers. And almost no price competition. You didn't have somebody bidding against you for an issue. What price competition there was was self-imposed. Your pride was at stake. If you underpriced an issue, you would subject yourself to great embarrassment with your client, so you were very careful to see that that didn't happen too much.

There were hardly ever any changes in investment banking relationships. We would evaluate our performance on how many clients we added in a year and how many we lost, and we would be up three or up six or something like that. And the triumph for a year would be that we persuaded some company not to use Lehman Brothers for some issue and to use Goldman Sachs, or to add Goldman Sachs as a joint manager in addition to their historical banker, Morgan Stanley. That would be a great, fantastic achievement.

All of us used to try to take advantage of being the traditional investment banker with our existing clients. We'd say to the new CEO who had just come into his new office: "Oh, sir, you wouldn't think of changing your investment banking relationship, because this is something that has gone on for generations before you came on the scene. You'll be CEO for a few years, but the relationship between Goldman Sachs and your company will just go on forever." We tried to inculcate that tradition with our clients. But with other people's clients, of course, we talked a very different tune. We talked the tune of, "Who does Morgan Stanley think they are, to claim that they own you? You are an independent

46

company. You ought to be able to pick your own investment banker based on whoever you think is the ablest, and not be bound by past history."

All this began to change in the '70s. Companies wanted more than one banker, and they began to take in joint managers. More and more, the banking community lost its captive clients. I guess the landmark issue, in that sense, was the IBM issue [in 1979, IBM replaced its traditional lead manager, Morgan Stanley, with Salomon Brothers and Merrill Lynch]. It reflected the fact that the power of the investment banker was no longer determinant and that companies were, for the first time, completely free to choose their own investment bankers and not be dominated by historical circumstances.

Then you had Rule 415 [on shelf registration]. I do believe that Rule 415 did represent a sort of a milestone. But, on the other hand, the trend that brought it about was already existing and practices would have changed even without Rule 415.

At the time, I was fairly outspoken against the rule. I was afraid that the elimination of the whole process of the investor studying the details of a prospectus and the terms of an issue—which took place from the filing date to the offering date, a period of 21 days by law—would lead investors to buy things they didn't understand and would later live to regret. That was the aspect of Rule 415— the disappearance of that waiting period—that caused me to be against it.

I don't deny that there might have been some selfish motivation that caused me to have these public-interest concerns. I think it's fair to say that when Rule 415 came in, there were a handful of special-bracket firms that managed most of the issues. But those firms felt a responsibility for the markets. We felt obligated to protect the system, not in our own selfish interest, but just to have it continue to work successfully. We were the whole capital-raising machinery of the United States—indeed, of the whole world.

Now, it turned out that those who thought the structure should be opened up were right; the system wasn't damaged the way we feared. But I think our motivations were good ones rather than selfish ones. It was not a matter of protecting a monopoly, because, Lord knows, the business was already extremely competitive. It was just a fear that the system might somehow be damaged by these changes.

47

After Rule 415 came in, you heard a lot of firms talking about the need for capital. They acquired capital and they have all grown, but I would raise the question of whether it was all necessary. I think the desire to cash in was what caused the public offerings of investment banking firms, not the "need for capital." And I've also felt that a shortage of capital is not necessarily a bad thing. It forces you to make choices as to what businesses you engage in and don't engage in. Any business that has all the capital it could possibly need is in trouble, because nobody is there making choices as to how it uses its capital.

The fact that Goldman Sachs was private and did have somewhat limited capital forced us to choose whether we would make markets in, say, bankers acceptances or not. If we had had more capital, surely we wouldn't even have stopped to think. We'd have said: "Sure, everybody makes markets in, say, bankers acceptances. We'll make markets in bankers acceptances." But with limited capital, you have to analyze and make choices, and you pick the most profitable businesses to be involved in. Therefore you do better than if you have access to unlimited capital. At Goldman we had a study going every year about whether or not we should go public or whether we should raise capital in some other way. But there was never any serious feeling that we needed to augment our capital very substantially.

I think maybe part of the reason why I felt the time had come for me to step aside at Goldman Sachs was that the business had changed so much from what I was used to, particularly the change from a relationship business to a transactional business. I worried about whether I was really with it anymore. After all, I was a relationship banker, and I thought that that system was better for the clients than this wild bidding system in which the relationships counted for nothing. To have a company rely on your advice—to say, go ahead, do the issue now, or do a bond issue instead of a stock issue—well, that was a very responsible job. But when you're only asked to decide whether to bid 7.22 percent or 7.24 percent—that didn't quite seem important to me anymore.

When I decided to retire, which I did three years ago last November, I thought I would have a busy life of a lot of nonbusiness activities; I was beginning to write a book about the social responsibilities of business. Then one day George Shultz called up and asked me down [to Washington]. To make a long story short, I said yes, even though I really didn't seek the job. I had never wanted to work in Washington, because I thought I would be frustrated with the difficulty of getting things done. And I always thought that if I did come to Washington, it would be in some place like the Treasury or the World Bank or the Fed. It never would have occurred to me that I would ever come to work in the State Department.

The transition wasn't as difficult as I had feared, not as difficult as Don Regan said it was for him when he went from Merrill Lynch to Treasury. I remember he said that when he was at Merrill, if he asked someone to jump, the only question was how high; at Treasury, he was told, "Well, first we have to have an environmental impact study, and then we have to check with the congressional subcommittee, and then. . . ." The difference was that the command structure I was used to wasn't like the one Regan had at Merrill Lynch. At Goldman Sachs major decisions were always made by consensus and by persuasion. So the structure really wasn't very different.

When I look at what's happening on Wall Street today, I think of something that Gus Levy once said, that he was "long-term greedy, not short-term greedy." He wanted to do what was right for Goldman Sachs in the long run and didn't deny that he was greedy for that, but he didn't want to be greedy in the short run if it . . . well, you can see what the phrase implies. There has always been a certain amount of greed, but somehow it's become more common in the last couple of years. I remember how hard we had to work for small rewards; now it's there on a silver platter for everyone. Profits have become so *easy*.

As I look around at the individual firms, I think generally speaking they are all very well managed. But they haven't always been managed with a dedication to integrity and a feeling of responsibility. If the downfall of Wall Street ever comes, it will be because these aspects of integrity have been ignored.

What happens, unfortunately, is that the competition between firms becomes so very intense that when you hear that some other firm is doing something that lowers their standards but allows them to compete more effectively, you are tempted to lower your standards to match them. So you get an escalation of lowered standards based on too intense competition—the "we have to do that in order to survive" kind of thing. That's a very dangerous thing to have happen.

Anybody who alleges that Wall Street is rotten I just don't think understands Wall Street. I think it's a remarkable system that still works effectively at the heart of our free-enterprise system. But if we are going to avoid sweeping government controls and regulations, then it is incumbent on the system to clean up its act.

The people who are in charge of these big organizations should be spending their time thinking about how they can protect the system against these few rotten apples. They should look at it as an attack on the system by a few rotten people who have somehow infiltrated it, and they should feel a responsibility to root that out.

I wonder whether enough is being done by the leaders. I haven't been out of Wall Street long enough to start criticizing those who followed me, but I wonder if enough is being done.

Editor: Cary Reich

Robert Kirby

Chairman CAPITAL GUARDIAN TRUST CO.

Robert Kirby has been a money manager for over three decades
and is a pioneer in pension management. Capital Guardian Trust
Co., a subsidiary of the mutual fund holding company Capital
Group, opened its doors in late 1968 and was instantly flooded
with major pension accounts formerly managed by sleepy bank
trust departments. Over the years Kirby has been an outspoken
and pithy critic of investment fads and pension funds' focus on
short-term performance—a philosophy that met its real test in the
early 1970s, when his firm stuck by value investing in the midst of
the Nifty Fifty madness and clients deserted in droves.

The $64 billion question that haunts me most is whether
money management is really a business at all. Or is it like
other strange things that have come and gone—the lost
cities of the Toltec and the Aztec, for instance, where they find
these empty buildings and they can't figure out why anybody left?

After all, there isn't much history yet. "Money management"
didn't really exist until the late '60s; it was all custodianship, really.
The big banks had all the money, and their charge was to be
careful and produce an income. They didn't have to beat the S&P
500 or anything else. I blame the creation of this whole business
on Jack Dreyfus, because he was the first guy who publicized
investment returns—known today as "performance."

In the late 1960s the lion began to tell everybody what return
Dreyfus had gotten. And so some director would stand up in a
company's board meeting and say, "How big is our pension fund?"
And the response came back, "$300 million." And everybody

gasped and said: "My God, that's equal to the net worth of the whole company. Does anybody pay any attention to it?" And the answer was no. And somebody said, "Well, then, why don't we call up the bank and ask how they've done with it?"

And, of course, the CEO of the bank was one of the directors, which is why the bank was the trustee of the fund. So somebody called him and said, "Joe, how is your bank doing with our pension fund?" And he said, "I haven't the foggiest idea." So there was a great scramble, and they found out that the money was 75 percent in bonds, and the bond market had been going straight south for fifteen years. So the performance was terrible, to put it politely. Then somebody said: "Look what this Dreyfus Fund has done. My God, if we had been there, we'd have four times this much money."

General Mills started the avalanche that followed when they hired a bunch of bright-eyed, bushy-tailed Harvard Business School guys in the mid-'60s and told them, "Let's have our money managed in a more innovative, imaginative, and so on, way." All euphemisms for, you know, "Let 'em roll the dice." And so these guys looked at the records of people who had been managing money for a while to find the best records, and the mutual funds of the Capital Group showed up. They called us up and asked, "Would you be interested in managing a pension fund?" And we said: "Gosh, I don't know. We never thought about that."

I had been hired from Scudder in 1966 specifically to set up an investment counseling arm—kind of a Scudder-type business, but concentrating on large portfolios—but we thought that would be mostly high-net-worth individuals or hospitals and colleges in southern California. We really didn't think IBM was ever going to hire us to run their pension fund. So General Mills said, "Well, would you talk to us about it?" And we said sure, and they hired us in late '67 or early '68.

And all of a sudden—whammo! In no time at all every big company just said, "If that's good enough for General Mills, that's sure good enough for us." You know, big corporations are the ultimate run-sheep-run guys. We went from *nothin'*, like a rocket ship, to a billion-and-a-half dollars under management. We got approached by people we never made a presentation to.

One day I was in [the late Capital Guardian Trust president] Ned Bailey's office when a call came in from Phillips Academy in Andover, Massachuetts. And the caller said, "Our finance committee met today, and we'd like to talk to you about possibly managing a third of our endowment." And Ned said: "Gee, that's wonderful. What are the circumstances?" They described everything and concluded, "And it's $12 million." And Ned said: "Well, gosh, I'm sorry. Our minimum account is $20 million, and we can't do this." There was a long pause. Then this very indignant guy on the other end of the line said, "Do you realize this is Phillips . . . Academy . . . at . . . Andover, and I'm telling you as chairman of the finance committee at Phillips . . . Academy . . . at Andover that we're thinking of hiring you?" And Ned said, "Well, this is Ned M. Bailey of the Cleveland Union High School, and I'm telling you that you don't meet our minimum."

Our second big early pension client was L.A. County. Right after the California legislature allowed public retirement systems to buy common stocks, I got a call from the L.A. County treasurer, whom I knew. "You're perfect for us," he said. "Please bid on our fund." I told him, thanks anyway, but to forget it. "There'll be guys in there with fees that are literally one tenth as high as ours," I said. "You simply won't be able to hire us." Well, months went by, and one day the treasurer called again and asked me to come and see him in his office. When I sat down, he gestured behind him and pointed to three flags—one for L.A. County, one for California and a U.S. flag. "Look at the U.S. flag," he said. It was red, white—and purple. "That's what competitive bidding got us," sighed the treasurer. "Now, please, bid on our account." And we bid at our usual rates, and, by gosh, we got it.

You know, we really thought we were magic. We all felt like World War I fighter pilots. You know—daring young men off pushing out the frontiers. We spun in from nowhere and were eating the big banks' lunch. It was the thrill of victory more than anything else. At the time, we felt that we were doing things that mortal men would never dare to do, and succeeding: running all-equity portfolios and buying stocks that didn't have "General" in the name and unbelievable stuff like that. We went from managing $100 million to $1.5 billion still in crazy stuff like Mohawk Data Sciences and bizarre Brand X junky companies.

We were crazy to allow ourselves to grow as rapidly as we did. But how can you say no when somebody says this is Whirlpool or Armco Steel or Merck calling? We were hiring people left, right and sideways. A guy would get hired, and before he found out where the men's room was, he was managing $300 million. And Smith managed money this way and Jones managed it some other way, and there was no coordination. Anyway, we did everything wrong that was conceivable to do.

So during the adjustment phase in 1970–1974, our numbers were just awful. In mid-1974 ITT invited a lot of institutional investors on a tour where we were running around so frantically that I hadn't looked at anything for two weeks. When we got back, I couldn't believe how much prices had changed. When I punched out my portfolio on the Quotron, I turned to Ned and said, "Gee, look at that: All my stocks split 2-for-1 while I was in Europe." We went from $1.5 billion down to something like $600 million, helped partly by the crash of '73–'74 but helped a lot more by clients departing at the speed of light. We were in a terminal power dive where you expected Spencer Tracy to cry out, "Buffeting! Buffeting!"

I discovered during that period that I'm a fatalist. I gradually became numbed to the whole thing and just walked woodenly into the office every day to take my medicine or out to the airplane to talk to clients and have them say goodbye. One of our most harrowing meetings was with Ford Motor. They have this routine where they put you in a dark room and have a prepared slide show reviewing your record. And a guy drones on in a monotone about the particulars in your portfolio, and then a slide flashes on the screen, showing where you come in: "outstanding," "good," "satisfactory" or "unsatisfactory."

So he went through our portfolio for the past two years, and at the end the slide went up, and it said, "*un*satisfactory." Then they did the whole thing for one year: "*un*satisfactory." Then for six months and for three months: "*un*satisfactory." And Mike [Michael Shanahan, now president of the Capital Group] leaned over to me and said: "All they're going to do is fire us, for crissake. Why don't they just call us in L.A.?" But they didn't fire us. In fact, Ford is one of the longest and best clients we have. Still, after that meeting we got on the plane in Detroit, and we staggered off in California so drunk that we left our car and took a cab home.

Another good client was Inland Steel, where we dealt with then-treasurer Bob Greenebaum—a really nice guy and very supportive. One day he indicated that he couldn't support us to his committee anymore, and I said, "What about this as a last chance? I'll pull the guy off the portfolio and manage it myself, and I just know I can get it turned around." His finance committee said okay, so I got all the research people together and said, "I want every one of you guys to come up with your one or two really red-hot ideas."

We turned over the portfolio about three quarters as a result of this meeting. And, lo and behold, the portfolio took off like a rocket ship for about 90 days. And then the wings fell off. I now think that if you take good research people and ask for a stock that will do it *right now,* you end up with a missile whose power is gone, and all it's got left is momentum and soon it will crash. That was when Greenebaum called up and said: "Only an idiot would try to catch a falling anvil, Kirby. Send the money back."

Our nadir was June 30, 1973. At that moment we had one account, the Kettering Foundation, for whom we had under-performed the market by 32 percentage points in eighteen months. That doesn't get you into the bottom percentile; it gets you into the bottom *decile* of the bottom percentile. One benefit of your numbers getting that bad that fast is that some clients say: "There's no way we're going to fire them now. We'll only ever get back to where we started if we keep the yo-yos and hope they keep their crazy portfolios." By that time we had long since given up our Mohawk Data and Recognition Equipment and were buying the cheap stocks, which were Exxon and Du Pont and AT&T. Everyone else owned Xerox, Avon and Polaroid.

The issue became the two-tier market, so when an *Institutional Investor* reporter asked me what we were going to do, since it looked as if, continuing on our present path, we might be going out of business, I said: "Well, yeah, maybe we are. But I can tell you, the one thing we are not going to do is fade back into our own end zone and throw a Hail Mary pass, hoping that somebody's going to catch it and save our bacon. Sooner or later people aren't going to pay 80 times earnings for a Polaroid while they pay six times for International Paper. And if we've got any clients left when that happens, they'll be okay."

55

Nineteen seventy-three and '74 made everybody in the world say, "We've got way too much of our pension fund in common stocks. Nobody told us they could go down 45 percent in 24 months." And so the business began to mature. Standards of prudence began to develop, and the business grew because of the market and an enormous ongoing flow of money out of bonds. And we had a chance to flesh out as an organization.

Still, I wonder if this is really a *profession*. You probably need ten years to distinguish skill from luck, and we've only had about fifteen, and the market's been going up most of the time since the wild, wonderful rally of 1975. As far as I'm concerned, there's really only one thing we need to do to be more professional, and that's focus longer term. It seems to me that most of the guys who made what Barton Biggs calls "a unit"—100 million bucks—invested in a few well-chosen companies and stayed there. The investment business is one of committing your clients' capital to quality growing companies and leaving it there until the company changes or gets grossly overvalued. You ought to have to disclose whether you're in that business or the screwing-around business.

The basic question facing us is whether it's possible for a superior investment manager to underperform the market for three years in a row. The assumption widely held is no. And yet, if you look at the records, it's not only possible, it's inevitable. If you focus on a meaningful time horizon—ten or fifteen years—every manager runs into a three-year-plus air pocket somewhere. If there's a logical explanation for why the world doesn't see things the way I do, I think it's because the whole thing is so damn new.

Money managers have created their own nightmare by saying, "Boy, look at the February we had." They call about March 3. And this creates an awesomely short-term focus on the client's part. You could have a really great ten-year record, but about the time you underperform the S&P three percentage points two years in a row, the client begins asking: "What's wrong with you guys? Lost your touch? Taking too much vacation?"

The thing I find deplorable is money managers' telling prospects, "We can produce a 600- to 800-basis-point advantage," and the prospects' buying it. It's nuts. Look at the audited, real-life, for-sure records of older mutual funds. (We can't use those of money managers because they're on the honor system, unaudited.) I had the research guys whip up a list of mutual funds that have been around 30 years or more. There are 71 equity funds that qualify, and only 22 of the 71 have beaten the S&P 500: That's less than one third. Templeton is off the charts, but if you take the next five, they have beaten the S&P by a little less than 200 basis points on average. So the client gets a one-in-three shot of beating the average, and if he hires someone in the top 10 percent, he's not going to beat it by much more than 200 basis points, no matter what.

So what do we tell our prospects? Naturally, I wouldn't bring this up if I couldn't say the following: Nos. 3, 4 and 5 on that mutual fund list were from the Capital Group.

But could we point to the same results in the trust company? No. When my ship comes in, I'm going to fund a study of the relative performance of mutual funds and comparable pension funds. The guys who manage mutual funds spend roughly 100 percent of their time focusing on investment decisions. If a pension manager is lucky, and few of us are, he spends 50 percent of his time on the portfolio and the rest talking to the clients. That's a problem in itself, but the nature of the conversations makes it worse. Because the client focuses on the 3-W list: What Went Wrong? Our Ford position was the classic example of all times. We started buying in the low 40s at the end of 1979 and were still buying down around 16, 17 at the end of 1981. We must have owned 6 to 7 million shares of the stock; it was in every client's portfolio. It takes maybe six quarters to build up a mistake of that magnitude. Every time it goes down, the client says: "You bought more Ford? What is wrong with you?" And you say to yourself: "I could solve this problem really easily—namely, write a sell ticket. He'll never ask me that question again." It's like canceling an appointment with your dentist for a root canal.

But it's not the right thing to do for the client. Remember the Kettering Foundation, for whom we underperformed the market 32 percent points in eighteen months? It only took two-and-a-half years more to where, over the life of the account, they were ahead of the market. One of my favorite sayings is that a sick portfolio is like a sidewalk burn: If you keep picking at it, it will never heal.

And someday a broad awareness among institutions is going to develop. And they're going to stop hoping to beat the averages by the 600 or 800 basis points that marketing people are promising them, and they're going to stop paying 1 percent fees based on that hope. I think fewer and fewer people are going to hire active managers.

I read someplace that there are now 5,000 registered money managers, and of the 5,000, 4,000 of them must have made a million dollars apiece last year. (I don't think anyone in our shop has ever made a million in a year.) And when you look back at the whole twenty years, the overwhelming feeling that hits me is: Never have so many people made so much money by achieving so little.

We've contributed a negative result in the aggregate, and we've been paid like Croesus for it. You'd think, in due course, retribution or regression to the mean would reel us all in and, of the 5,000 firms now in business, 4,500 would go off and do something else.

Editor: Heidi S. Fiske

Will Weinstein

Former Head Trader OPPENHEIMER & CO.

> Will Weinstein built Oppenheimer & Co. into a block trading pow-
> erhouse in the late 1960s; for a time only Salomon Brothers and
> Goldman, Sachs & Co. surpassed it in trading clout. In 1976, com-
> plaining of early burnout, Weinstein dropped out of Oppenheimer
> and Wall Street and moved his family to Ketchum, Idaho. This
> semi-reclusive phase lasted only a few years, and by the early 1980s
> Weinstein was in San Francisco as managing partner of Montgom-
> ery Securities. In 1986 Weinstein became a key aide in the Pritzker
> family empire.

I came to Oppenheimer in 1962, just before Black Tuesday; I wondered what the hell I was doing. The trading depart- ment began in late '64, early '65. There were two people in the so-called over-the-counter department and two or three or- der-executing clerks. That was Oppenheimer's trading depart- ment. I had come to the firm from graduate school in psychology; I didn't know the first thing about Wall Street, which I suppose uniquely qualified me to try whatever they wanted.

I started out trading over-the-counter stocks, trying to get us some wires to firms like Merrill Lynch. You held your breath when you said Merrill Lynch in those days. Getting a wire from your department around the corner to theirs was a major accom- plishment. I remember I did an enormous amount of negative trading. I'd buy 25,000 shares of something from Bache at 11 and sell it to Merrill at 10⅞ just to show both firms that we were a real factor and intended to make a big market. It was a cheap eighth to lose because it got us the recognition we needed. There was a tremendous amount of that.

I think in the beginning it was research that opened the doors for us, and then it was a question of what leverage you could gain once the door was open. I remember being told by a major institution that we were being taken off the research list and how proud we should be. Proud? I thought the world had come to an end because it was a major institution. And then it was explained to me that brokers who were on the research list had a minimum but they also had a maximum. And they could only be paid X number of dollars because they were research brokers. We had achieved the status of executing broker, they told me afterwards. It meant we could do an unlimited amount of business with this institution, which we virtually did. It was a major breakthrough for us, but who knew?

Initially, Salomon wasn't really a factor. It's hard to know if we would have gotten to where we got to if Salomon had already been there. We actually achieved the status of being No. 2 to Goldman for some period of time. We probably realized we were one of the big guys when Salomon was chasing us—and it didn't take very long for Salomon to catch us, although there was some speculation that it would have been cheaper for them to buy Dow Jones than to buy the position on the inside back page in *The Wall Street Journal* every day in the "Abreast of the Market" column.

I think the competition was healthily intense. We had a lot of respect for each other. We all, of course, had enormous respect for Gus Levy and for Cy Lewis. And for Bob Mnuchin and Jay Perry and Boyd Jefferies. What you did was you competed ferociously, but you also knew you had an opportunity to be responsible to your fellow block traders by not killing them or letting them kill you. Institutions were feeling their way around this new thing called block positioning, and from time to time it got mean. I think we did a good job protecting each other. We certainly didn't hold hands but also didn't consciously allow each other to be hurt. If you could stop it—if you could warn Jay or Mnuch—you did that in a gentlemanly, polite and efficient way. You'd say, "Don't buy the first 100, there's 400 behind it"; or "there's 200 sellers away that I'm looking at"; or "if you put a print on at 35, you're going to have to take me out, too." That kind of thing. Things that were not collusive but were just honest attempts to protect each other.

On the other hand, the competition for that business was just ferocious, particularly during Salomon's ascent. That was also during the advent of hedge funds, and there were some practices going on at that time that today would not be countenanced. A lot of selling us 25 or 30,000 of something and then turning around and selling another 50,000 to someone else, just laying your position off to all the block traders on Wall Street. And in those days commissions were so big that even though you didn't like it and thought it was an unethical practice and screamed and hollered, you stayed in the game.

You can probably describe me in a number of ways, but one of them wouldn't be uncompetitive. I was extremely competitive with Jay. And very friendly. I was very much aware of what Salomon was doing. I felt they could afford to do it and they were intelligent people, and there wasn't a whole hell of a lot that any of us could do about it. Now Goldman could compete with them, and Goldman was very clever in picking the spots where they chose to compete. They didn't compete just because they had egos. An ego in this business is a dangerous thing.

In the beginning, I took it personally every time we lost a piece of business to Salomon, but I fairly quickly realized what was going on. Often I felt holier than thou; I was protecting the holy profitability grail. I felt this was an unprofitable transaction, and I didn't give a damn if Salomon did it. In fact, more power to them; the way I saw it, the more unprofitable transactions they did, the more there was a possibility they'd get out of the way and stop screwing up the business. So I had mixed emotions about it; I didn't like getting beaten but I didn't mind getting beaten, because I felt what they were doing sometimes was beating themselves. And, in fact, they were, but they were accomplishing their purpose. Jay was absolutely brilliant, in my opinion, in getting done what they decided they wanted done—to be the home of the big print, to buy their way into a position that was competitive with Goldman. And Jay did it with flair and with brilliance.

I had a number of incidents with Salomon where they would call me and say, "We're getting a call on so-and-so, and we see you've had a dominant role in the stock. What should we do?" And I would say: "Under no circumstances should you buy the

61

stock at that price; it's totally ridiculous. In fact, if you want to do that, you've got to buy 275,000 from me." And Jay would say, "Listen, I know you're right, but Billy [Salomon] wants to buy 'em." And I'd say, "Jay, why do you want to commit suicide?" And they'd put it on and they'd buy my stock and the client's stock and everybody's stock, and the stock would go down $3 and Jay would be screaming and hollering. But the truth is, they had accomplished the biggest print of the quarter: They were buying the airline business. Whatever they were doing, they were quite successful at it. And why not? If you're an institutional trader and you're saying to yourself, "How can I get the best price for my fund or my end user?" you'd have been foolish not to go to Salomon. You might allow Oppenheimer or Goldman to compete, and you certainly couldn't do all your business with Salomon. But it was tempting for a while, because they did anything that went in the door and often at prices that were outside the normal pricing mechanism.

The specialists had a wonderful deal—and we came along and screwed it up. We made real markets. We embarrassed a lot of them. The concept of fair and orderly markets with some specialists was their credo, but with others they couldn't spell it. They didn't make a market at all. I remember in a manufactured-housing stock I put a 350,000-share block on the tape down $3 or $4 from the last sale. And when I got a report from the floor, I said, "How many did the specialist take?' and the answer was "none." He didn't buy a single share, down $4. He was right, but that's not the point. The question was, Did he or did he not have some kind of affirmative obligation to that market? And his attitude was, "To hell with it. You guys are taking over, let's see how smart you are."

Specialists could kill you. Ultimately, if you wanted to get into a real war, you could take it out of town and you could do all those kinds of things. But you know if you get into a war, you lose sometimes, and even if you don't lose, you win but you're bloodied. You'd rather not be in a war; you'd rather be helping each other. We had that with some specialists, but in the beginning it wasn't the norm. They resisted as hard as they could.

We ultimately had the upper hand because we had the clients.

You knew you would win ultimately, but it was often a very expensive trip to the altar. In those days the specialist could play when he wanted to. It's not entirely untrue today, but mostly. There were no real measurements of excellence like there are today. Allocations were based on who you knew, not what you knew.

Going back as far as 1962, I remember that Oppenheimer had a major position in one of John Coleman's stocks. And on that day in May, it was very important for Oppenheimer to get that stock open, down fifteen, down twenty, down anywhere. And Coleman refused to open it; he opened it on the closing bell on 150,000 shares, down twenty. And in response to some threats that some of my partners made about taking him to the SEC, he said something like, "The hell with the SEC. If they don't like the way my stocks are traded, let them come down here and trade them with their money."

They tell that great story about Julie Marcus's father, the Senior Barracuda—about him and Lehman, in the early days when Lehman had no floor brokers because it was beneath their dignity. And one of the senior partners of Lehman—it may have been Bobbie Lehman himself—called, I think it was Morty Marcus, and said, "Dear Mr. Marcus, this is, ahem, So-and-So at Lehman Brothers. We have both a buyer and a seller of Litton Industries, one of the stocks you make a market in down in the uh, ahem, New York Stock Exchange. And we were wondering what the procedure is for executing this transaction."

So Morty Marcus said: "Well, we have a public outcry system here, Mr. Lehman. The procedure is simple. You have your broker—you do have a broker." "Well, we don't have a broker, but we have a partner here who is a member of the New York Stock Exchange." And Marcus said: "Have Mr. Member come down to the floor, and have them ask for me. They all know where I am, and have him come into my crowd. Now what do you have to do, Mr. Lehman?" And he said, "Well, we have 200,000 shares to buy at 61, and we have 200,000 shares to sell at 61." So Morty Marcus said, "Well, you have him come into the crowd and say, '200,000 at 1, three-quarters for 'em, take 'em,' which means there's an offering, a bid, and the bid steps up and takes the offering."

Mr. Lehman thanked Mr. Marcus for his advice and counsel, and sent their partner, who happened to be a member of the New

York Stock Exchange, down to the New York Stock Exchange with the specific instructions. The guy walked into the crowd and he said, "Is this where Litton is traded?" And someone said, "Yes, it is," and he said, "200,000 Litton at 61," and Morty Marcus said, "Take 'em." And he bought the 200,000 in front of Lehman's buyer. When the guy said, "You can't do that, why did this happen, this isn't what you told me," Marcus said, "You forgot to ask me if I wanted any."

Has it changed? I think a lot of it has. I think there is much more potential for abuse at that level than at certainly any other level, and I think there is occasional abuse. I'm not highly sanguine that all of it is either caught or dealt with. Any time you have a single entity with a franchise, you run the risk of abuse of privilege. And while I don't think it happens very often, I've seen a number of occasions where it does, and there really isn't any recourse. What are you going to do? Call the New York Stock Exchange and complain?

In the evolution of buy-side traders, there were certainly some institutions that felt you could get away with hiring somebody for $15,000 a year who had no education or sophistication and wasn't very smart or analytic. But my recollection of the guys like Frank Mullin and Joe DiMartino and Bill Devin and countless others was that those guys were smart as hell. They understood the game, and they figured out ways to make us perform for their institution. And there are a number of those people still around today. What really changed was when they were called into meetings, when they were allowed into the investment process, when they were consulted about the apportioning of the commission dollar. When they were taken seriously by their institutions, they became real forces on Wall Street. Of course, there were some jerks. But they weren't the majority. And every sell-side block trader wasn't a genius, either.

We did a lot of business in '74 and '75. We were concerned about the advent of negotiated rates, and we were "preparing ourselves," which who the hell knew how to do that? What you really did was set up a series of defensive maneuvers to try to forestall the inevitable. I made a decision to leave Oppenheimer at the end of '74; I didn't actually leave until June 1975. So for me personally that was an anxious period in many ways. No one had any way of knowing what was going to happen. Thinking back on it, I remember the term "nonevent." For me it was a major event, because I remember the day after Mayday I woke up, and I went to a candy store that sold newspapers. I remember walking in and buying a newspaper and the guy saying to me, "Hey, you're on the front page of *The New York Times.*"

I think it's fair to say that I was much too optimistic about the result. While I didn't think or say it was a nonevent at the time, I remember a day or two afterward some shocking things happening. A large New York bank came into us with 100,000 shares of a $100 stock for sale. I bid him 99 and the question was, What's the commission rate? And I said some very tiny discount off the old rate. And he said he would only do it for 10 cents a share. And I said no way. And he went out and sold the stock all the way down to 95; he only sold 80,000 shares of it, but he did sell it for 10 cents. I was shocked at the idiocy of the whole thing. And the guy's explanation—he was a friend of mine—was that "the legal guys were standing over me." He had no choice. If the legal guys were going to find ways to cost their clients five points on 100,000 shares of stock, all the legal guys should have been tossed in the Hudson River. They weren't, and for a long period of time they dominated that kind of thinking.

Enormous sums were wasted. And we all resisted it, when we should have just gone along with it. And ultimately, that's what happened. And many less-than-first-rung firms felt that since they were getting screwed on rates, they were going to screw the clients. So they'd run ahead of the clients and do all kinds of things. From '75 to '80 or '81, there was an awful lot of that stuff going on.

I was pretty crazily idealistic in those days. It was certainly a factor, an underpinning in my decision to leave Oppenheimer. It wasn't strictly a function of the fact that the business was changing; it was a function of the fact that I had become a member of the executive committee. I was starting to take on more responsibilities and starting to feel, as I put it then, burned out.

Three years after I left Oppenheimer, the firm was sold for what I thought then was an incredible amount of money. I was one of the largest partners of Oppenheimer when I left, and I could probably have made a great deal of money. I looked at it and laughed and said to myself, here I am in Idaho, I'm alive and well and happy and I'm doing something that's productive and fun and I have no reason to look back. And I'm pleased for everyone who made all this money. I'm very fortunate to have had these experiences in different roles doing different things. Certainly, what I'm doing now is the most exciting challenge I've had. I haven't figured out yet exactly what it is, but it is a very thrilling challenge.

Editor: Cary Reich

Saul Steinberg

Chairman RELIANCE GROUP HOLDINGS

Saul Steinberg was one of the boy wonders. He was a pioneer in the computer leasing business when, in 1961, he started Leasco and built it into one of the raging successes of the decade. Seven years later he acquired Reliance Insurance Co., which he has used as a base for aggressive investments in a wide variety of companies. His hostile attempt to acquire Chemical Bank in 1969 earned Steinberg the badge of the first modern-day corporate raider. Since then, many of his big investments—including a raid on Walt Disney productions in 1984—have put fear in the hearts of corporate managers who have shaken him off with greenmail.

The whole conglomerate movement happened in the '60s. The reason was, in those days everybody was concerned about antitrust. No one was concerned with the U.S.'s competitive position in the world. I mean, I started my business based on the consent decree that IBM signed [a 1956 antitrust settlement that in part opened up the leasing business to third parties]. There were people in this country, including professors at the Wharton School, who wanted to see IBM broken up—because it was too competitive. It didn't do anything illegal. It just tried harder. Maybe the greatest company that has ever been built—and people in this country wanted to tear it apart!

The entrepreneurial scene was just getting started again. In other words, the industrialists of 1900 to the 1920s were all dead and gone, and we had a whole new movement in the '60s of owner-managers. I think it was easier for the second wave, if you will, than the first, because you could accumulate capital faster in a service business than you could in, say, making steel.

The most exciting thing for me was the esprit de corps that existed in Leasco. It must have been like what the Marines knew: We felt we were the best of the best. We just felt we could do anything, accomplish anything. Whatever goals we set, we achieved them and surpassed them. It was a phenomenal time.

In the beginning I was in the business alone, for maybe four years. There was no competition, and we were able to write leases that really were riskless—that is, we could get back our cost of equipment and interest. We had no capital. We had to borrow 103 percent of the cost of equipment. Banks used to laugh at me because I'd say I need 3 percent for operating expenses and 100 percent to pay IBM.

After we went public, which was in August of 1965—it wasn't very long after that that a lot of companies started to copy what we did. And since we had no real proprietary anything, except an idea, many of them were willing to charge less and then less and then less. By the late '60s, companies were begun—it may not sound like a lot of money today, but then it was quite a lot—with $50 million in capital and $50 million of subordinated debt and hundreds of millions of dollars of bank borrowings available to them. And the competition forced the profit margins to be very, very small. So what was a riskless business became quite a risky business. It was too risky for my taste. I was already, in 1967, looking to ease out of computer leasing and search for a business that would be around for the rest of my business life.

But we continued to do better than I anticipated. The fact of the matter is, we did better than anyone else. I thought it would be over by the early '70s, maybe the mid-'70s. But, in fact, the last of Leasco is being closed down in Europe this year.

Harold Geneen was a model, and I met with him a few times, by my own request. He let me sit in on one of his famous meetings. I was very impressed with him. I would say that Geneen gave me a sense of how important it was to have really great financial controls. So I really bent over backward to see that Leasco had the best we could afford in the financial area.

Among my peers in the '60s and '70s were Carl Lindner and

Larry Tisch. I was the first to go into insurance. I probably influenced Carl and Larry to some extent, because they came to me and asked me about the insurance business. I had known them for years. People like that all seek each other out. I mean, it's very lonely, and you need a kindred spirit to commiserate with from time to time. I was the kid, you see. There must have been other kids, but I didn't know them. Most of the young financial successes of my era have disappeared.

In the late '60s I thought deregulation of the financial markets was just around the corner. At that time all of the banks were forming one-bank holding companies. In the holding company they wanted to do leasing and consulting and other things that they were not allowed to do in the bank. I thought that whatever made sense to the consumer would happen—ultimately. And my concept of "ultimately" was in a few years. So I thought that Reliance could acquire Chemical Bank.

My plan was that we would offer insurance, consulting, leasing, mutual funds—the nonbank activities that were financially related—and the bank would run the bank. This was my proposal to Chemical. They could have a majority of the board. We thought Glass-Steagall would be repealed. We were early. Okay, we've been early before. What's different about then and today is, I think today you could do whatever makes economic sense. I believed you could then. I was wrong.

I would say 1974–75 was the toughest period of the last twenty years. The insurance industry went through, up to that time, the worst down cycle in its history. Nixon was resigning. I remember it was August of '74. He was resigning every day, and every day he didn't resign, the stock market hit new lows. Interest rates were only 12 percent, but there was no money, because the Fed put such limits on the growth of money that you couldn't borrow money in the United States. So you had to borrow money in Europe, and the Eurodollar rate was 21 percent. That was the real cost of money.

We had our first loss ever, our only loss. That was quite a blow to me. I'll never forget that our statutory surplus, our net worth in the insurance business, went down to about $50 million in August of '74.

I wasn't even involved in investments in those days. We had an investment department. I used to run around the country trying to get excess cash flow to the investment department so they could invest it. Then I discovered in August '74 that they were very human and they lost it. We were investors in the traditional insurance company sense—that is, we owned all the Dow Jones stocks. And when the market went down, we looked like everybody else.

And then the board, almost to a man, decided that we should sell all of our equities. If we wouldn't have sold at the bottom, we would have been within points of it. Really. I was astonished. I mean, suddenly it hit me that all these older, wiser men who I relied on had panicked. It was a terrible time for me. I felt vulnerable for the first time in my life. I felt alone. And I said to them: "Hey, guys, I'm not selling. I'm a buyer here. And I know we're in deep trouble, but, you know, I own 20 percent of the company. I'm the chief executive. I've been listening to everything you've told me to do, and it's all *wrong*. I mean, you're like the public."

I took control of the investment department, and no longer did they sit there and buy municipal bonds all day long. All the old concepts were reappraised, all the raisons d'être that they had. For example, we had a guideline: We keep $50 million in cash in the insurance company at all times. And I said, "By the way, why do we keep $50 million in cash?" "Oh, it's the guideline." And we looked and went back maybe fifteen years, and one time, maybe in 1960, the insurance company had a negative cash flow in the first quarter, because of a very bad winter, of like $35 million, and so they said we're going to keep $50 million. And no one ever looked at that again.

I'll tell you what led to the presence of so many corporate raiders. There were tremendous values in a lot of companies that shareholders weren't getting. So smart guys went out and said, "Hey, if they won't realize these values, if these guys won't do the job, I'll do it and make the money for myself." Today it's much harder to do, because the movement in the market, the change in multiples, will cause a tremendous downturn in takeovers. And then one day, sure as we're sitting here, the market will go down for certain, and the phenomenon will start again.

I think that the corporate raider has a very, very valuable place in the business history of this country. The corporate raider helps to keep management honest. And I say "honest" in the sense that they give shareholders a fair shake. There were some manage-

70

ments—à la General Electric—that always worked for the best interests of their shareholders. But not all. Many managements thought they owned the company, that the company was run for their benefit. Many companies—not even giant companies, but mid-sized companies—had shooting lodges and apartments all over. They were like kings.

I think that Boone Pickens is doing a phenomenal job of getting shareholders sensitized. We've tried to do it. We've been, in my opinion, very unsuccessful. I tried to organize the shareholders in Penn Central—all institutions—when Penn Central was going to acquire Marathon [Manufacturing Co.] in 1979. It was a dumb deal. I told them it was a dumb deal. I begged the management not to do it, but if they were going to do it, don't do it the way they wanted to. The board did *nothing*. I went around the country and spoke to the leading institutions. I think I spoke to nineteen institutions. I think I got *one* to vote with us. And I will tell you, every one of them privately agreed with me—every single one— that the management of Dick Dicker, then head of the Penn Central, left a lot to be desired.

I mean, he sat in my breakfast room in my house and he said: "I have a great idea for raising money. I'm going to sell the real estate on Park Avenue." And I said: "Dick, if you find yourself the head of a company that owns from 42nd Street to 59th Street, much of the land, and every twenty years it's revalued, and you get a rent of 6 percent—*nobody* would sell. That's the center of the universe as far as we know it. You don't sell that." This was in the late '70s, and a lot of those leases came up in the early '80s. He sold it. This is what bad management's all about.

I think, I hope, that institutions are going to be more and more involved as shareholders. I thought that was happening in the late '60s and early '70s, and I was totally wrong. I think more of it is happening now.

Most of the money *we* make on our investments is not from getting bought out or anything like that. They are tough situations that we see intrinsic value in, and they're not easy to turn around. So we get involved with the management, whether we get on the board or not. A la Tiger [International]. We had to fight to get on the board of Tiger [in 1985]. If we did not get on the board of Tiger, the company would be bankrupt today. And it's my belief that you're going to see Tiger have a tremendous resurgence now. We've got new management. We're refinancing everything. You'll just see. But it took fighting to get on the board and really doing some of the difficult things that nobody wants to do. But that's what I think responsible large shareholding is all about.

I don't have a mission like Boone Pickens to acquire a major oil company. In my case, I really was an investor. I would have made just as much money, perhaps more, if Walt Disney didn't buy me out, because I understood what Walt Disney could be. I bought my investment and they said, "Leave us alone." You don't have to do that. I would tell every one of these managements, "I just would like to be able to make suggestions to you, and you tell me why it's a bad idea." That's all I ask. I mean, by definition if you own 10 percent or 20 percent of a company, the chief executive should at least meet with you.

These managements pay greenmail because they don't want any large shareholder: not because the large shareholder's going to take over the company but because by definition a large shareholder spends more time on the investment, on the company, asks more questions.

I guess we've been bought out as much as any single investor has ever been bought out. We have never once asked to be bought out. Companies have always bought back their own shares from large stockholders, usually at a premium for a large block. That's been going on with us for years. It was not always a dirty word. I think it became a dirty word when the term "greenmail" was coined and became popular in the press.

Frankly, I've always believed that all shareholders should get the same offer. But you almost always have to accept greenmail. The offer is usually coupled—I'm basically giving you my experience—with a threat. The management of XYZ Co. says to you, "Listen, we want to buy your block." And you say, "Gee, if you want to buy 10 percent of the company, why don't you make an offer to all shareholders, like they have to do in England, and we may or may not sell part of our block." And they say: "No, we want your block. And if you don't do it, we're gonna do the following." It depends on how serious you think the threat is. In the case, for example, of Disney, they threatened to make an exclusionary tender offer to the extent that there would have been no net worth left in the company. It would have been an empty shell.

72

In the takeover phenomenon, Drexel and Mike Milken—a genius—took advantage of the opportunities that existed, and they built their business the way Salomon Brothers did in the '60s and '70s, the way J. P. Morgan did at the turn of the century. Drexel played a role, with its junk bonds. But Morgan Stanley played a role, and Kidder, Peabody played a role and Goldman Sachs played a role. They *all* played a role. Wall Street's an awfully competitive place, and Salomon Brothers and First Boston and Shearson Lehman—these guys are jumping right in.

I never worked on Wall Street, but I must tell you that I'm a fairly sophisticated person, and I am astonished by the insider trading cases. I don't understand what's happening. This is not how we operated. It's beyond my reasoning. I mean, you just didn't cheat. Let me give you an example.

In 1971 or '72, my general manager in Europe came to me and he said, "I can get us this contract in Iran. We'll make"—and I want you to know this was money we needed at that time—"we'll make between $10 and $20 million a year for three years." And I said: "Terrific. What do we have to do?" And he went through all this: We have to move 200 people to Iran. Fine, fine, fine. And then he said: "We have to make a small payment—but it's added to the price—to this company in Geneva, or Zurich. To a bank account." And I said, "Wait a minute, that sounds like a bribe." And he said, "Well, no, that's how it's done." But I said, "That sounds like a bribe, and we're not gonna do it." Now this guy was so incensed, he said, "Saul, I want you to take this to the board." And I did. And I tell you that two or three of my outside directors said, "What's wrong with that?" I was astonished. I said: "But it's wrong. We just mustn't do it. It's illegal." And we didn't do it.

Takeovers have increased the leverage in corporations today. In the '60s when mergers were made, they were made with stock, mostly. There were not so many cash deals, so that didn't add debt. The leverage came in the '70s, when the stocks were under-valued and managements didn't want to use undervalued stock, so they started to borrow money. The trend is irreversible. We live in a world economy, and the fact of it is that if you think *we* have leverage, the Japanese think nothing of six-to-one leverage for industrial companies. I think that we're going to learn to live with more leverage. Managements clearly have learned to manage with cash flow. In the '60s nobody looked at cash flow.

By the way, in the '60s we also heard a lot of talk about leverage. I think every period looks like it's too leveraged, until you look back, and you say, "Gee, the good old days—nobody was really leveraged in the '80s."

When I look to the future, my greatest single fear is that we're going to have significant trade restrictions. I think the sentiment for protectionism may be too strong to stop it. And I'm afraid that we will have a global recession or depression that is going to be very significant. And the stock market, from my experience, won't follow in kind. It will lead.

Editor: Hilary Rosenberg

David Rockefeller

Former Chairman CHASE MANHATTAN BANK

No banker played a larger role on the world stage than David
Rockefeller during his twelve-year tenure as Chase Manhattan
Bank chairman. Although some critics felt he spent too much time
outside the bank, his globe-trotting was an indispensable element
in Chase's international expansion. Indeed, no one would gainsay
that his impact on Chase—and on the image of banking around
the world—has been profound.

Looking back over some four decades of banking is enough to
give anyone pause. So many changes have occurred so
rapidly—and have been so interrelated—that it's quite a
trick to pick out what really has been pivotal.

Moreover, I don't think we can any longer put too much faith
in the infallibility of even "20-20 hindsight." Too many of what
we once thought were accomplishments in finance or in the
world at large have turned out to have produced seriously adverse side effects. It seems that conclusions drawn from experience are not always correct the first time around, or even the
second.

Yet one must continue to try to learn lessons from history, and
I would like to think I learned at least a few during my career at
Chase. These cover quite a spectrum of activity, but let me just
touch, somewhat randomly and sketchily, on such subjects as
management, the internationalization of the world's economy
and, last but not least, corporate responsibility in the age of the
"fast buck."

Management as a science is taken for granted today, but it was very remote indeed when I joined Chase in 1946, after World War II. It was only that year, for instance, that the bank started its first "management training" program, which really only focused on credit analysis. Interestingly, Bill Butcher, who now chairs Chase, was a member of the quite successful second program in 1947.

The direction of "personnel," as it was then called, was largely given to credit officers who hadn't quite made it as successful lending officers, and there was no concept of a professional human-resource manager—not to mention professionals in such fields as planning, marketing, product development, communications, technology or even budgeting.

Personnel practices were also very paternalistic, and it was the rare exception for anyone to be fired unless they had committed some sort of crime. In one way, this engendered loyalty, but it also meant that less capable or energetic people were retained but were shunted off to areas then considered less important but that later were to prove very important. Needless to say, putting people considered less good in departments already treated as second-class only compounded the problem.

Given my personal education, experience and instinctive interest in management and organization, all of this bothered me from the outset of my career. In overall terms, I felt that we should apply at least as rigorous standards of management to ourselves as we did to the companies we were lending to. I also felt that there were other skills important to successful banking in addition to commercial credit analysis, and that we should reach out for top-notch professionals in such areas as human resources, planning and marketing.

I worked hard on these issues from 1946 on, as well as on my primary interest in internationalizing the bank—achieving some success but still short of what I believed desirable. Indeed, the continuing split in perception between the "old" guard and the "new" guard about the proper course for the institution remained quite evident even in 1960. At that time, following the retirement of Jack McCloy, the board named George Champion and me co-chief executives of Chase. George became chairman, and I became president and chairman of the executive committee.

To the best of my knowledge, there have been few—very few—situations in which this type of arrangement has worked out well. Usually it only does when there are two people with a common vision but different, though complementary, interests and skills. In the case of Chase, however, I have to say that I don't think the arrangement worked particularly well. From 1960 until 1969, for almost a decade, we had two chief executives who had quite different visions as to where the bank should go. This caused us pretty much to stop dead in the water.

George Champion felt strongly that Chase should continue its traditional emphasis on major domestic customers, and that overseas activities were there to serve the needs of these U.S. customers and should be serviced primarily through our correspondent banking relationships. Indeed, he and others felt that an extensive international branch network would endanger our extensive and valued network of correspondent banks.

I felt quite differently. Given the growing multinational activities of U.S. corporations after the war, as well as the growth of major corporations based in other nations, I was convinced that Chase needed a strong international presence of its own in order to maintain its leadership position. I saw that others, such as Citibank, had long since established a solid international branch system, which began to pay off handsomely after the war and by 1969 had become an increasingly large source of their earnings. For us, even with unanimity on the need, it would be a long and expensive project to build a comparable international branch system.

I did not think that Chase could or should remain the way it was when I joined it. Things had begun to evolve quickly from a 1940s atmosphere in which the manager of our Paris office could pride himself on the fact that he could not and would not speak a word of French and saw no reason why this was important.

These conflicts about management practices and basic corporate mission were quite fundamental, and they created a situation in which it was much easier to stop innovation than to carry it out. This was not widely perceived by the outside world, since Chase continued to do fairly well from its core businesses, and both the bank and I personally received much good press. To some people, the Rockefeller name implies an aura of mystery and almost magical powers of getting things done. In fact, this is generally nonsense. I would come down firmly on Ernest Hemingway's side in his famous exchange with F. Scott Fitzgerald. As I recall this,

Fitzgerald said, "The rich are very different from the rest of us." And Hemingway dryly replied, "Yes, they have more money."

Indeed, internally at least, the press attention that my name helped to attract sometimes compounded the difficulties, since it stimulated more resentment and resistance from the traditionalist camp within the bank. Later on, in addition, I suspect that my name helped fuel the vigor of the bad press we received when some lingering problems began to surface. I guess I shouldn't be surprised that many publications, including *Institutional Investor*, long ago concluded that the Rockefeller name in any context is good for circulation.

One thing that George Champion and I did agree on was that Herb Patterson would be the best choice to succeed me as president when George retired and I finally became the sole chief executive. Herb was a highly competent credit officer who had run two or three important departments successfully. Though somewhat shy, he also was a very nice and attractive person who got on well with people. I had hoped that he would take on substantial control for day-to-day operations of the bank while I focused more on strategy, planning and external relations, which were my strongest suit.

Unfortunately, Herb seemed unable or unwilling to assume the full responsibilities of the new position. I suppose it is not uncommon for someone who is very good in certain areas to be overwhelmed in others, but I had not expected this in Herb's case, and I probably waited too long to realize it and fully act on this realization. When I did tell Herb that I thought it was time for him to resign, I think that he was actually relieved. I was never aware that he ever expressed resentment publicly or privately.

The resignation of Herb Patterson was quite a shock to a number of people, since I was often viewed as too nice a guy to make tough decisions and who didn't have the stomach to let people go who weren't meeting standards of excellence. I certainly tried to be gentle in bringing about change and never practiced the insensitive brutality that some other corporate leaders seemed to actually relish. Nevertheless, especially after Bill Butcher took over as president, we put in place an increasingly rigorous management evaluation system, which led to the departure of a significant number of senior people. At the same time, we began to recruit the best people we could find outside the bank to fill critical positions in which we did not have existing talent.

Bill and I also quickly established the rapport and balance of duties I had been seeking between the president and the chairman. He handled day-to-day operations, and we worked closely together on questions of policy and strategic planning. At the same time, I was more able than previously to focus on building the strong international network I had long believed essential.

Even though we were relatively late in the game compared to some others, this effort proved to be quite successful, and Chase became and today remains one of a very small number of banks that have truly international banking networks. To some degree, at least, I believe that our international expansion benefited from personal relationships I had cultivated with people around the world, starting even from the time when I was overseas in the Army during World War II. I always have believed deeply in the importance of people and personal relationships. I still am as convinced as ever that successful long-term financial relationships are far more a matter of personal knowledge and interpersonal relationships than of just supposedly "objective" numbers and technology.

This aggressive international thrust required a great deal of time and travel on my part, however, and that in turn engendered a flurry of negative press—especially in the mid-1970s, when the real estate recession and the New York City financial crisis hit and created serious problems for our bank. Such a public reaction was not particularly pleasant, and it didn't make running the institution any easier. Some suggestions were made in its time that I should "fire" myself, and frankly the dire predictions of internal critics might have come true had it not been for the really wonderful support I had from our board of directors, as well as from a number of very able associates. I also was confident in my own convictions that we were taking the right steps and that our problems would be worked out. I was convinced that we were establishing a stronger foundation for the future.

I remember one young woman from *Institutional Investor* who was particularly aggressive in her questioning about my management of the Chase. Finally, I suggested: "You come back and see me next year. I assure you I will be here, if you still have *your* job." Happily, I was.

Happily, also, Chase continued to put in place a broad and sophisticated international banking network that recognized that Chase was an active part of an ever-growing interdependent world and that we were an international bank that happened to have its head office in New York.

This interdependence offers many new opportunities for institutions such as Chase, but it entails very real risks and responsibilities as well.

An example of both risk and responsibility is the so-called debt crisis that faces banks and others today. In retrospect, it's self-evident that some developing countries borrowed too much and that banks loaned too much. What is not so obvious to many, however, is the web of circumstances that led to this and the very constructive role that the banks played.

The two oil shocks—in 1973 and 1979—created a totally new situation in the world's economy. Nations such as the U.S. that had benefited greatly from low energy prices in building up their industrial bases suddenly suffered, and this created a very disruptive situation throughout the world, especially for oil-importing nations. At the same time, oil-exporting nations, particularly in the Middle East, suddenly had huge sums of money, far beyond what they could spend or invest in the short run. Since payments for oil were generally made in dollars, this left a massive amount of dollars that had to be placed somewhere—and that somewhere was with the major international banks.

The banks in turn used a good portion of these funds to help finance the oil imports of nations that needed energy and other essentials for their development. At the same time, banks extended large credits to some oil-exporting developing countries, such as Mexico, that had created ambitious development plans based on income projections from high oil prices. Then, when the oil prices dropped, everyone was left with a great deal of very onerous debt.

This leaves a very difficult situation for borrowers and lenders alike, which demands the rigorous implementation of a series of new growth strategies as well as patient assistance from the developed world's nations and creditor bankers. In the process that led to this situation, however, I think that the banking system did a very creditable job of recycling the so-called petrodollars and thus helping to avoid a very severe disruption and probably a deep global recession. So far, at least, the banks and the industrial nations, as well as the IMF and the World Bank, have been working relatively successfully to avoid catastrophe and gradually to bring back order.

A lot more needs to be done, and the debt problem will be with us for many years. We have a tendency, however, to do straight-line projections from the present that often aren't borne out in the future. I remember one projection in about 1970 at Chase, for instance, that predicted that everyone in New York City would be on welfare by 1990! Just five years ago, many were fretting about the size of the U.S. current account *surplus*. Today that is hardly the case, but any present deficit will not go on forever, either.

I think that financial institutions have responsibilities to do what they can to help not only in major financial shifts, such as those caused by the oil shocks, but in many other ways as well. Social responsibility was a major theme of Chase's for many years, and it was one on which I placed particular emphasis. I felt that we had an obligation to pay systematic attention to the concerns and well-being of our customers, our staff, our shareholders and the public at large. Aside from a deep moral motivation, I felt that we would have no marketplace unless there existed a healthy social and economic environment in which we could function.

Chase Manhattan Plaza was an outgrowth of this philosophy in a sense, although the project was actually begun when Jack Mc-Cloy was still chairman. Social responsibility touched many other bases at Chase, and eventually involved all of senior management in one way or another. Beyond a strong push to increase the hiring and promotion of minorities and women, projects included training programs for the disadvantaged and help for public schools (both of which George Champion helped to initiate). We also became quite active in promoting through the New York Clearing House affordable housing. This led to the creation, along with other commercial and savings banks, of the Community Preservation Corp., which has now helped renovate over 17,000 units of affordable housing in New York City.

Much of this was not without criticism, as had been the case with the creation of our art program to complement the building of Chase Plaza. I believe most of that has passed, however, and that the majority of corporations view art collecting and social responsibility as good things. Indeed, many are involved in the New York City Partnership, which I have chaired since shortly before my retirement from Chase. Interestingly, Walter Wriston played a major role in getting me involved in this undertaking, and Citibank has been a major supporter, as have the other New York commercial banks.

An area of special concern to me at Chase was ethics, and here I fear that the financial world is not doing very well these days. Unhappily, the vast sums of money and accordingly high fees involved in the recent rash of mergers and acquisitions have created an atmosphere in which some of the financial community are acting like sharks in a feeding frenzy!

Aside from insider trading and blatant theft, a more fundamental challenge seems to be the conviction on the part of some people that a fast buck today will assure a good tomorrow. I am old enough to remember the giddiness of the 1920s and the gloom of the Depression—and I know that any philosophy based on short-term selfishness just doesn't wash in the long run. Moreover, when such a house of cards collapses, it takes down not only its proponents but many others as well.

Purely financial deals in mergers and acquisitions add no value to society and generate no new productive capacity. A strict emphasis on belongings and the trappings of economic success soon leads to very empty personal lives. An enormous and burgeoning national debt only assures the poverty of our children and future generations. Trade wars and protectionism, allowed to run rampant, can all too easily escalate into conflicts of an even more serious nature.

All of these developments give me at least as much pause in looking ahead as in looking backward. Nevertheless, I am heartened by some signs that the current mortgaging of the future for the present may be causing a period of serious and constructive national and international reflection. I see it at meetings in Washington. I see it at meetings of bankers and private sector leaders around the world. I see it in my own children, family, friends and associates. I saw it in a class of fourteen-year-olds I met with recently at a public school in Brooklyn. The subject of the class was personal values. That is a subject I think we grown-ups would do well to reflect on as well.

**Editors: Gilbert E. Kaplan
and Cary Reich**

Alan Greenberg

Chairman and Chief Executive Officer BEAR, STEARNS & CO.

Alan (Ace) Greenberg started out his Wall Street career in 1949 on the arbitrage desk at Bear, Stearns & Co. and over the years helped build it into one of the Street's most aggressive, opportunistic and successful trading firms. At the death of founder Cy Lewis in 1978, Greenberg became chief executive and since then has overseen Bear Stearns' diversification into other areas of the business. Here he recalls his early days as a trader, working with the legendary Lewis.

I remember very distinctly that when I started in Wall Street the volume of the New York Stock Exchange was less than a million shares a day and there were more firms than there are now. I'd been here about a week or two when I figured I'd be back in Oklahoma in about four months, because the people who were in the business weren't making a living, so how was somebody going to start off and make a living? I started out at Bear Stearns as a clerk putting pins on a map where oil wells were being drilled in Texas and Canada. After I left my clerkship behind me, I went right to the arbitrage desk.

Risk arbitrage in those days basically depended upon the bankruptcy proceedings of the railroads. There were also some public utility holding companies that had been terribly enmeshed in bankruptcy proceedings that were coming out of those proceedings. And the consensus was that after these things came out, there'd be no more arbitrage business. There really wasn't much; there'd be a merger announced every two or three months. That really wasn't enough to have a whole department, so they let me handle it.

And then, of course, it started just absolutely exploding, till by the late '60s it was very, very active. By then there were many takeovers, and the conglomerateurs were getting tremendous heat because they were issuing paper that people were very suspicious of, just like they are now—only it was called Chinese paper instead of junk bonds. The establishment resented these men coming along and making bids for their companies, so they put pressure on the New York Stock Exchange, which passed a rule: They would list the preferred and common of the conglomerates, but not the junk bonds. It seems to me that the bond has got to be better than the preferred or common—but they did it.

The late '60s really saw the origin of junk bonds. Drexel Burnham did not invent them. The companies issuing the bonds were the companies trying to do the takeovers, and Bear Stearns was active in trading and arbitraging them. Larry Tisch, Charlie Bluhdorn—they were all issuing warrants and bonds. They worked out very well, and all the dire predictions did not come true. Later on Drexel and Bear Stearns started issuing low-grade bonds for corporations for cash, instead of as an exchange medium, and the proceeds went to the company.

I was on the desk at Bear Stearns when block trading got its start. In those days, if an institution called and said they'd like to sell 10,000 or 15,000 shares of stock, you'd call the stock exchange specialist in that stock, and if it was late in the day, he'd say, "We're not going to trade it today. Call me tomorrow." Like it was the law. Because the specialist was the boss. So Cy [Cy Lewis, Bear Stearns' chairman] said, "Well, if you don't want to buy it, I'll buy it." And then the specialist was coerced into buying some of it and Cy bought the rest. So block trading really came about for two reasons: the institutions wanting to sell something and get out of it and get their money and go on.

When Cy and Gus [Gus Levy, chairman of Goldman Sachs] started doing blocks, they would, if you'll pardon the gambling expression, lay off enough of the risk so that after taking into consideration the commission they would come out all right, even if they took a point licking on their position. That was fine and good. The problem came when negotiated rates came along in 1975, and people who continued to try to do block trading found out that the percentages were now against them. It was just a losing, losing proposition, because the commissions were sliced so much that the vigorish was gone. So now if you lost a quarter of a point or a half a point on what you had left, you lost money overall.

I realized very quickly after May 1, 1975, that block trading was a losing proposition. It was perfectly obvious to me. The problem was that some people who had been doing it for years, and didn't know anything else to do, didn't want to give up. And, frankly, Cy was one of those people. I told him it was just silly to try doing it the way we used to, and I would have taken all the money and put it in arbitrage. But because he'd done it for so long, Cy felt that he was capable of picking the right ones and holding our losses to a minimum while recapturing the commission dollars. But that was wrong and will not and did not work. Anybody who says they make money in block trading is, in my opinion, either joking or not telling the truth. If you want to say you're losing a lot of money but overall—considering the corporate finance business that you hope to get or are getting—it's worthwhile, that's okay with me. We look at it that way here. But we call it by its real name.

I don't blame the institutions for the fact that rates went down so far after Mayday. It was our competitors that did it. And I was never mad at them. The morning of May 1, some of the firms that had a small share of institutional business immediately cut rates, thinking this would increase their market share. And it probably did for a short time. What was the client supposed to do, pay us 25 cents a share when somebody else said they'd do it for 10? I didn't blame the clients—never did. The traders at the institutions did their jobs and did them well.

There isn't any question that Cy put the firm on the map and gave us an identity. He was tremendous about giving people opportunities and letting them do what they wanted to. His problem was that he'd been kicked around very badly when he first came to Wall Street by certain firms and people, so he had a real chip on his shoulder and was constantly trying to show them up, make them look silly, make them look bad. And that doesn't endear you to the competition. Another problem was that he didn't like to be wrong, and if he told you something and it turned out the way he said, then he'd keep rubbing it in if you had disagreed with him. And if it turned out the way you had said it would, he kind of disliked you because you were right. But he couldn't help that. He was tough to work with, very.

I'm not sure Cy wanted to sell a stock at all, once we had a position. He always thought if he bought it, it was going to come back and make a profit. I explained to him that the stocks don't really know who owns them and they don't care. I just went ahead and sold. There weren't any arguments. And Cy got used to it. He didn't like it, but he got used to it. That was the deal we made. Otherwise, we'd have no firm.

Just before he passed away, unfortunately, Cy bought a big block of American Telephone from somebody. It started going down, so I said, "I'm going to sell it." And he said, "You can't sell that, that's Telephone; it won't go down much." I said: "What do you mean it won't go down much? It can go down plenty. It is still a stock." He said, "Don't sell it." So we had an executive committee meeting, and I said, "We bought Telephone, it's down, we have $12 million tied up in it, our capital is only $35 million, and we have got to sell it."

And so one of the other partners looked at him and said, "Well, Cy, shouldn't you sell it?" And Cy said, "Well, I want to make some money for you guys." So one partner said, "Well, if it goes down, you're not making money for us, are you?" So then Cy said, "Okay, go ahead and sell." He was like a little puppy dog that had been spanked. As it happened, the stock went down considerably. I think it went down twelve points from there. But that's beside the point. He wasn't feeling good. He was just a shadow of his former self, and he was trying to hold on to something that said, "Look what I did."

Editor: Nancy Belliveau

Michael Starkman

Senior Vice President PRUDENTIAL-BACHE SECURITIES

Michael Starkman has been a retail broker—his firm prefers "registered representative"—for 30 years, 28 of them with Prudential-Bache Securities in its Beverly Hills, California, office. For ten straight years he has been a member of the Chairman's Council, his firm's exclusive club for its biggest producers.

I started at Merrill Lynch, in their Hollywood office, in 1957, just out of UCLA. I was 22 years old and wasn't a broker yet. I had all kinds of jobs—menial jobs, like chalking up hourly movements on a blackboard. Two million shares was a big day then. I remember when 5 million was a benchmark. And then there was the day Kennedy was assassinated. I think volume that day ran around the 30-million-share level, and the tape ran three hours after the close. Now they handle that the first hour in the morning.

The business looked absolutely fascinating to me, so I decided to give being a broker a try. After I got my license, I started at Merrill for $300 a month, which, by the way, was just great then. At the end of the year, I figured out that on a commission basis somewhere else—everything was salaried at Merrill—I'd be making $600 to $700 a month, so I went to the manager and told him I'd like more money. He offered me a $25-a-month expense account. So I looked around the city and saw the name of Bache & Co., whose office was on Roxbury Drive in Beverly Hills, about three doors up the street from where we are right now. That was in March or April of 1959, and I've been with Bache ever since.

We were given lists of cold calls to make, and that, I think, is still pretty basic. The younger brokers still obtain those lists. But the customers were less sophisticated than they are today. It's because of the media. I mean, you have television programs in the morning, afternoon and evening. We have more publications—new ones like *Money* and *Investors Daily*. There used to be two pages in the business section of the paper; now there are six or seven. The market is the topic on the tip of everybody's tongue.

But that's better. The customers that come in are more serious now. In the old days they would come in to buy 100, 200 shares of stock. A lot of them were just gamblers, some of them kooks. Nowadays they come to you with a sum of money and seek your advice in placing it. You function far more as a counselor.

In the old days, too, you would build relationships on social contacts, the golf course and so on, and you did special favors for big clients. I remember years ago a broker left and an account was turned over to me of a famous movie producer, Mervyn LeRoy. The first thing Mervyn did was to ask me to make sure that when his plane arrived in New York that we have a car waiting for him. I was astounded, but that was not the exception to the rule then. But that's all a thing of the past. The business has changed. The times have bred more serious investors.

LeRoy, by the way, was a wonderful guy and became a good friend of mine. Being in Beverly Hills, I have had my share of celebrity clients, people like Burt Lancaster, Danny Thomas, Steve Lawrence, Shecky Greene and some others. And Joe Di-Maggio. He's the greatest. He is sensitive, and he is polite. I'll be on the phone with him, and some other phone will ring, and he'll say, "Mike, that's okay. Put me on hold and get your other client."

A big difference between then and now is that we were trained to open monthly investment plans of, say, $50. We were taught that a $6 gross ticket meant something. There was no such thing as a minimum order. Now retail brokers will take small orders, of course—I do it, we all do—but they are difficult to service. If I have a client call to buy ten or twenty shares of stock, I advise the person to save up money until he's got enough to invest properly, unless he wants to buy ten shares of IBM and accumulate it through the years. That's a different type of thing. And I've tried to lower the commission greatly for the little guy like that. We have the freedom to negotiate commissions now, too, of course.

The '60s were good years, and by the end of the decade I guess I was ranging about $150,000 gross a year, which was satisfactory enough then, and then something happened to change everything. First we had the '70 break. We were getting our clientele back after that, we were beginning to breathe again, and the '73–'74 break came, which I understand, proportionately, was more severe than '29, and I can believe it, because I had a stack of margin calls from my clients that was almost as big as the Beverly Hills telephone book. It literally wiped clients out and rubbed brokers out of the business.

As far as I was concerned, after the dust settled there wasn't much left. The phones were quiet. We were literally playing gin rummy here during the day. Even if you had an idea, people were soured on the stock market. Bonds weren't yielding that much. There were no special products then like there are now. I had five days out of eight that I did not write a ticket. My monthly gross before then was averaging about, we'll say, $10,000, and my gross one month after was a little more than $4,000. I was looking at other businesses, maybe real estate. But I had already been in the business fifteen or sixteen years, and I hated to give up my experience.

People who came into the market in those years literally made a fortune. My brother started out with $1,000 in 1974 and amassed a fortune of over $3 million by pyramiding on margin— which I don't recommend. I have the records to attest to it and have showed it to some New York Stock Exchange auditors. He's been written up in magazines.

I was his broker, but I had nothing to do with it. As a matter of fact, at $100,000 I strongly urged him to unload and take his profit. He knew nothing about the stock market, but he was a commercial artist for various companies in the entertainment industry, including 20th Century Fox and Warner Communications. That's how he came upon the idea of buying 100 shares of Warner at $10 a share in 1974 when they brought out *The Exorcist*. The stock went to 12, and he bought another 100 shares. When it went to 14, he didn't have any more money, so he put his existing stock on margin and bought another 100. Then it went to 16 and he bought another 100, and then the market broke badly and the stock deteriorated and came down to the $6 level, at which point my brother begged, borrowed and did everything to hold on. I even had to lend him $100 one day to help him meet a margin call—though I didn't know where the money was going.

He also began to accumulate 20th Century Fox. He bought it as high as 6 or 7 and as low as 4 and a fraction. The stock was eventually tendered to Marvin Davis at, I think, $70 a share, which is the equivalent, after a 2-for-1 split, to something like $140 a share, so he made quite a coup. He followed up by buying shares of Columbia Pictures, which became part of Coca-Cola. He bought Columbia at around $3 to $4 a share. For every 100 shares of Columbia you had, you now have something like 650 shares of Coke, valued now at about $30,000, plus all the dividends paid through the years. And he still has his Warner. In fact, he is an investor in Warner almost daily via options. Every time one of the calls expires, he takes his profit and buys the next quarter's calls. And Warner has been an outstanding stock.

As far as I'm concerned, there are only two ways to make money in the market. One is like my brother. If a person is able to come up with capital—and not necessarily a lot of capital—and accumulate shares in a company he knows is strong in its industry, that guy will come out on top. But those are people difficult to come by. And there are very few people who make fortunes in the market.

The other is the fellow who looks to hold on to his capital. He is conservative and never goes hog-wild in the market. He will have his money in several areas—short-term instruments, blue-chip stocks, high-yielding stocks. And if he wants to take a small percentage and go for the gusto, then he can do that, too, with maybe 10 percent of his funds. There's no genius to that. It just takes someone who understands the pitfalls of the market. He's not a great client, but he's steady. I enjoy that client, because when he comes to me, he comes to me with some serious business.

And as evangelical as it sounds, I know that I'm doing good for him. If a hard-nosed trader comes to me, I know that I'll make commissions and we may have a little fun, but that's the guy who just doesn't make it, never can and never will, in my opinion. I've seen traders make a vast sum of money, but they lose it, because the thing in their system that enables them to trade and make money eventually works in reverse. And by the way, though some brokers may be at fault for overtrading, and clients may blame their brokers, it mostly occurs because of the clients' directives. Clients' needs are generally met by brokers, and if clients want to trade, that need is met.

I finally qualified to buy Bache stock—it wasn't publicly traded then—in 1968. The next year, I believe, both Harold Bache and Charley Schwartz, who was instrumental in building the firm, passed away, and a great amount of their stock was turned back to the firm. I was told I could buy a large amount, so I arranged a loan with some New York banks to purchase the stock, and, believe it or not, I was arranging for a loan to buy a million dollars' worth of stock.

I was then told by a very smart banker friend of mine that if I did that, he'd never talk to me again. He'd been through a lot of near-tragedies in high-leverage deals. Well, he scared me so much that I cut back to purchase $100,000 worth of shares. The stock came public at 14 in, I think it was '71. The stock went to 15 or 16. I had no intention of cashing in. Then came the market debacle of 1973–74 and the stock dropped as low as 2¾. It was then the banks nudged me to sell. I hadn't the capital to hold on. Two thirds of my stock was sold at around $3 a share. If I had bought my million dollars' worth, I would have definitely been wiped clean.

I then spent the next ten years, through a Bache profit-sharing program, buying back just a few shares a month, at as low as $3.50 a share. When Prudential took over the company in 1981, they purchased my shares for $32 a share.

I think the firm has changed for the better under Prudential in so very many ways. Prudential is in a position to do a more qualified job in real estate programs, limited partnerships, leasing deals and, of course, insurance products. And there's no question, the firm is better run today. I see so many differences. I think we have a tremendous research department today, for example. That's another thing that's changed, by the way. We used to be able to pick up the phone and get an analyst's opinion. But we've got too many brokers now. We have liaison people on an information desk we can call, we get updates on our screens, and a squawk box lets us know when there's a change of opinion. The research people in New York can't be continually bothered or they wouldn't be able to do their job, so they really are unreachable, even for someone with as many years with the firm as I've had.

George Ball runs a very tight ship. He rewards competence and loyalty, but he won't tolerate rudeness or incompetence. When we go to the Chairman's Council meetings, he asks all of us about our problems, our complaints, and when he hears from a number of us about someone who has consistently caused problems, you can bet your life that person will not be there when we come back. George is very approachable. You cannot write him a note that you won't get an answer to, and I've called him on many occasions during the day—maybe a problem, maybe just to let him know I appreciate some service I've had from someone in the firm—and he'll be right there for me as long as I want. If he's not around, he will certainly return the call. I think he has changed attitudes within the firm dramatically.

But beyond all that, we've always had a credibility problem in this firm. And the Hunt silver scandal created a very serious credibility factor. When Prudential took over, that whole image changed. It has really done a lot toward bringing confidence in here.

If you had told me ten or twenty years ago that my mix would be what it is today, I would have just fallen over. In the old days, stocks were the way you made a living. After 1973–74 everybody's business dried up. Then, when interest rates got very high, you couldn't beat CDs and money market instruments offering 13, 14, 15 and 16 percent. It was foolish even to try.

And the advent of negotiated commissions made a huge difference, too. In the old days, if 100 shares at $50 was a $45 commission, 1,000 shares was $450 and 5,000 shares was $2,250. Now the rate is lower, and any sophisticated investor is going to ask—as much as you service them—for some type of discount, so on an order like that for 5,000 shares at $50 a share, you may end up with around $1,700. I could not have survived if I hadn't attached myself to the new products in every way, shape and form.

I do not presently work in insurance and I'm not licensed to. But I probably did 20 percent of my business last year in the mutual fund area. I've done an incredible amount of business in the Pru-Bache in-house funds, particularly their government funds. I did business in CDs and limited partnerships. And I've worked in the options market ever since they started trading on the CBOE. Clients usually turn to me for help, because they feel that I know what I'm doing. Mostly the last two years my strategy's been what you might call a risk arbitrage program. Without going into details, it involves S&P futures versus S&P options. I have a computer setup where I weigh potentials, and I think I'm pretty good at it. And I'm in touch with my clients on, really, a daily basis to keep them up on what I'm doing. It's a monumental change for me, almost as if I'm in a totally different business from where I started out.

But a lot of this business hasn't changed. There are no geniuses. I believe the reason a client does business with you is because of his confidence in you and his belief that you understand his needs. I can't do business with people that I feel don't trust me, and yet I know it's a natural thing in this business not to trust your broker. And it's service, service, service. It's that simple in any retail business—in any business at all, forget retail.

It's a very tough business. You can never forget it. There's not a second of the day that goes by that I don't know who I am, what I am and the responsibility that I have. The market is on my mind 24 hours a day, wherever I am. I cannot get away from it. I will try on a vacation, but it's impossible. I was in China. I put in calls, whatever time it was, and sometimes it took hours to get a call through.

You live daily with a lot of tension and stress, so there's a very fast aging and erosion of one's mental and physical powers in the business. As I see it coming on, I try to get away from the office more often, come in a little later. But I do like to work evenings and weekends, because the stress of market hours is off and there is no telephone ringing. I come in every Saturday; it's one of my pleasures. I come in about 2:00 and work for four or five hours. But still, I've got to pay attention to other things. Maybe I could make more money, but I want to enjoy the fruits of my labor. I see too many people that become 100 percent wrapped up in the business and fail to live and smell the flowers.

Editor: Everett Mattlin

Frederick Whittemore

Managing Director MORGAN STANLEY & CO.

During the 1960s and well into the following decade, Morgan Stanley & Co.'s client list was uniquely blue chip, consisting of America's biggest and most prestigious corporations. As head of the syndicate department during this golden era in corporate finance for the firm, Frederick Whittemore got to exercise almost dictatorial sway over which firms participated in major underwritings and—practically as important—where they appeared in the accompanying tombstone ads.

In the late '60s the syndicate man had the responsibility to commit capital all by himself. Today firms have inventory positions in bonds or stocks that may be made or operated in the syndicate man's position, but very frequently they're made on the trading desk or as part of an overall inventory. And we have an entirely different capital structure today to support it. We also have a lot of hedges, which we never had in those days.

Syndicates then were, in today's terms, sort of naked positions. When you took down $50 million, it was a big event. Communication wasn't like it is today, either. Syndicate business actually meant putting on your hat and going to meetings. Syndicates, too, were stylized affairs, all wrapped around a registration statement, all done with long-standing habits of client relationship. And in those early years, syndicates were formed by people getting on the phone and actually individually inviting each firm. Nowadays the deal gets put on a screen, and everybody knows about it in fifteen minutes.

What you got paid for in Wall Street in those days was your origination. And origination was a relationship business. It was unconscionable for someone to buy business. Yet Salomon Brothers would go around—John Gutfreund was good at it—and call up Dillon Read in the middle of one of their bond issues for R.J. Reynolds, and would say, "I would like to give you an order for 25 or 50 million bonds." "Wonderful, John, who's it for?" the Dillon Read banker would respond. "It's for Salomon Brothers." And Gutfreund would take the bonds down at the public offering price without necessarily getting a selling concession or anything of that nature. Then he would sell and distribute the bonds for a modest profit or virtually no profit. And two weeks after the deal, he would go to the company and say: "Now you've got a manager who has no distribution. Look at what we did. We did 20 percent of your issue, had to take it down as an order, because the syndicate system is too rigid. They're trying to preserve the business, and it's not in your own interest to do it in that manner. You really have got to have us as a co-manager."

Very effective. This was how John got Salomon Brothers really moved up. Salomon at that time didn't have a very strong corporate finance department. They got themselves into underwritings through their trading skills and their distribution business. And that made the market much more diversified. Today you have to be able to fight for having securities that can really perform for you. Therefore, a lot depends not just on which companies you underwrite but on how those companies perform.

During the late '60s and early '70s, the block trading desk became enormous. This was the time of the go-go boys, the secondary trading in equities and all the rest. Salomon Brothers in the early '70s decided they weren't going to just be a bond house—they were going to be a major equity house. The Jay Perrys all paraded around Wall Street and contributed a lot of volume and great areas of revenue. So the syndicate man receded, not just as a matter of Rule 415, but because the revenue stream of his firm started to become much more diverse.

In those years the actual bulge group was Morgan Stanley, First Boston, Kuhn Loeb and Dillon Read. So, therefore, the players and the syndicate people of those firms were important people.

Morgan Stanley had modest capital, but our position in the Street was to really be the investment banker for large corporations. This gave our syndicate department an ability to command a lot of decision making—more than just figures and league tables. The '70s were more a decade of league tables than the '60s.

So Morgan Stanley *insisted* upon being in the bulge. We wouldn't go into an underwriting as a major. But the bulge had to change, and we'd go to Dillon Read and Kuhn Loeb and we'd say: "Sorry, fellows, it's in your interests to have a bulge, but you're no longer in it. We insist there be one, however, and frankly it's going to be First Boston, Salomon, Merrill [and Morgan Stanley]." Then Goldman came in after Salomon and Merrill. Salomon and Merrill got in based on massive distribution. Goldman was just horrified by all that—couldn't stand it—and leaned on Morgan Stanley [to include it] because we'd had this relationship where Goldman has always supported Morgan Stanley. Shearson didn't get in until after they merged and bought Lehman Brothers.

Morgan Stanley had a policy then of refusing to appear [in a tombstone ad] unless it was first. And it refused to have co-managers. Subsequently, that got us into the great debacle of IBM: We refused to have Salomon as a co-manager, and we ended up being out of IBM's business for years. I participated in that decision—a watershed decision—and I thought we were right, but obviously we were wrong.

First Boston, interestingly enough, had a policy that said that they could only appear one position away from the manager. And Morgan Stanley, of course, would not appear in anybody else's syndicate; we might accept the underwriting role, but we wouldn't actually show up in the tombstone. I know it sounds sort of sappy now, but as a practical matter we took those things terribly seriously. Morgan Stanley had a history of keeping meticulous records on other firms' performance—we actually had large yellow cards that we posted for every issue.

We would decide where firms would rank in underwritings. I can remember talking to Dean Witter. I called up the senior man and asked him to come have a visit on a business matter. He gets the syndicate guy there. The senior guy didn't really understand the business, but he was Witter's lawyer on the East Coast; therefore, he was president of the firm and the senior man in New York. I spent twenty minutes explaining that we were adding some managers and we weren't going to have Dean Witter, and his syndicate guy—Jimmy Burns—kept getting very nervous because this fellow thought we were promoting the firm. He didn't get it: that the nice words I was using meant no, not yes. Finally, Burns had to interrupt and tell him.

There was a time, too, when Lehman tried to demote Loeb Rhoades. I can remember sitting on a couch in one of our rooms with tall, spare John Loeb. He was saying he found it very offensive to have to come to Morgan Stanley for help but that [Lehman] was about to demote them. And he felt that, considering the long Wall Street relationship [between Loeb Rhoades and Morgan Stanley], Morgan Stanley should preserve their status as a major firm.

Well, we did—not because we loved John Loeb, but because it was in our interest to weaken Lehman Brothers. Lehman tried to make Street policy of what it did in its own business, but it didn't have enough business to be able to make the habit stick. If you're going to dictate where other firms will appear, you've got to have a lot of business to make it work.

We were careful when we promoted Reynolds and E.F. Hutton. We were worried about Goldman, Kidder and Lazard. We made sure we did it at a time when there were going to be three or four issues—all announced within a two- or three-week period—so that it was like a machine gun. If they bitched the first time, they'd get it again two days later and they'd get it again three days later, and by the time the second week rolled around all the reluctant dragons were back on their perch.

Syndicate business was not just a matter of firms. It was a matter of personalities. One time we met with Lazard because they were dropping from our bids. André Meyer thought I was a young whippersnapper, so I saw the next guy and told him that Lazard really didn't do very much bidding and they weren't going to be promoted [in the syndicate]. The next day André came over to see John Young, our senior partner, and John, with good grace, had me sit at the end of the couch and listen to André's bitch. He and John were the same age and had known each other for years.

Meyer said, "Well, John, John, with the great long history of the great firm of Lazard and Morgan, you have embarrassed us, insulted us." And John said: "But, André, you never want to bid.

100

You drop out every time." He replied: "Well, we aren't here to just buy things. We're here because of the prestige of being seen to be a major firm." This went on and on and on, and John kept saying, "André, there has to be a reason to do things and not just do them on the basis of our so-called position." André had a habit, when he was trying to be persuasive, of almost sounding like he was crying. Now he was really whining—he had this little pinched voice—and he said, "John, John, how can you do this?" And John told him: "André, come on now, you don't really have to cry. I haven't seen you cry like that since you sold Bill Zeckendorf the last building and made him go broke." After that, André became much more friendly with me.

I remember one time when we were in a World Bank financing with First Boston and Salomon Brothers. It was the first deal for Bob McNamara as president of the bank. McNamara was an imposing and intimidating kind of a client, and in this case he didn't like our price recommendation. And Larry Parker, who was negotiating for us, said, "Well, I've got to go and consult my partners," and he got up to leave. Then John Gutfreund said, in a whimsical way, "Well, I guess I'll have to go and consult my partner, too." Then he paused and said: "Well, she's always said yes to whatever I want to do. I guess we'll go along." It's putting a hell of a lot of pressure on the other guy when John in effect says, in a cute fashion, "I'll do what you want, McNamara, and we'll make First Boston and Morgan Stanley follow it." But the business of syndicate one-upmanship was all part of the law.

The 1977 British Petroleum offering was the watershed—the one that launched the learning curve for international equity deals. It was the first issue where we had to create a way to sort of mold a securities act registration on top of an English system offering. Basically, we [in the U.S.] announce something, sell like hell and then price it. The British announce their underwritings as a surprise and then try to accumulate applications later, having priced and underwritten the issue at a big discount. And we put the systems together in a sort of innovative way, and we got a lot of co-managers involved. In the end, we had to sell our stock at a higher price than the British investors got for their stocks. We also had to get the SEC to accept a registration statement where the principal market was somewhere else. And they also had to accept the leadership of the British system and realize that we were a small add-on to that.

When you had a complicated issue—for instance, Southern Co.'s issue of 7 million shares at a time [1971] when utilities were just beginning to negotiate their deals and the investment climate was hostile—instead of just calling the usual underwriters' meeting, where people sort of meet for due diligence purposes and to ask innocuous questions about the prospectus, we had a sales meeting and urged all of the major salesmen of the firms to come. The chairman of the company and I got up and explained what we were going to do. We told how difficult the deal was going to be and honestly 'fessed up to the fact that none of the southern states wanted to increase utility rates to support Southern Co.'s debt and common stock.

And the chairman had to get up and cross himself and hold his hand to the sky and say, "I shall continue to pay the dividend, no matter what." And I was able to put my hand on the chairman's shoulder and say: "And we are going to compensate Wall Street very generously. And that means 8 percent, at the beginning. Your grandmother said, 'It's time to take cookies when they pass cookies.' It's *cookie* time. Go out and sell the shares, and you will be paid."

After the early '70s recession, the bond market improved down to 8 percent and 9 percent. Chuck Marshall became AT&T treasurer, and the chief financial officer was Charlie Brown. We got them to buy in all their cushion bonds at 112 or 113 and refinance them at 8¾ percent, which made a 50 basis point or so difference. We actually did one big tender where we had something like six or seven regional-firm issues—all announced at the same time. We had a huge, colossal conference phone call. You know, this deal was made for the telephone system—they had everybody all over the country plugged into that big conference room.

Marshall was nervous as a cat. Like most telephone people, he was made treasurer without ever having been a financial man before. The telephone company does these funny things. I can remember going over the presentation with him and then being with him when we made the presentation to Charlie Brown. He was afraid that Charlie Brown would say, "You mean, you're going to do what!" That kind of thing. Charlie sat there and listened to it and listened to it. And then he said, "Well, that's a

102

damned good idea." Marshall just went. "Ooh." All of a sudden his career was not going to be ruined.

There was an assumption once that all the wire houses and all the little ladies in tennis shoes were buying bonds, because they were 12 percent and 13 percent bonds. Then we came to find out that institutions owned 85 percent of them. So from a syndicate point of view, to hell with you, Bache and Reynolds and E.F. Hutton and all the rest. You guys didn't help out in that recession anywhere near as much as you said you did in getting individual investors to buy bonds. We used information [from the AT&T deal] to reconstruct thinking in the syndicate business to the effect that it's basically institutional distribution that was running the bond market. And that is true today.

In terms of the heyday of Morgan Stanley's power on Wall Street, we were probably more powerful in those days when we were smaller. But firms needed to measure each other in terms of their power in a way that's different today. We're all big businesses. When you have firms that are earning several hundreds of millions of dollars and you're in as many businesses as Salomon or Goldman or Merrill, you're an entirely different structure.

I have shared and helped in that, and I like that. I like the idea that the firms today are strong, that they're far more diverse. As an owner of the firm, I am much more comfortable in the Morgan Stanley of today, because it's got so many different businesses. And they're powerful businesses, and they're far more profitable than they've ever been. And that's true of all the significant firms, really.

It's been very rewarding for those of us who have been able to survive. I mean, I put a modest amount of money in Morgan Stanley at the end of 1966, and it's worth a lot of money today. But the old business was a fun business. It had a different origin, function and style. Life was simpler. You could shout and yell at each other. You could win or lose. I had a great deal of fun as a younger man playing the world of Wall Street. I had a chance to shape things and to play a role that would be hard to define in today's world—it doesn't exist. But on the other hand, as a business, and as a productive business, we're better than we used to be.

Editor: Tom Lamont

T. Boone Pickens Jr.

Chairman MESA LIMITED PARTNERSHIP

Behind most legendary oilmen is a major discovery of untapped
reserve. In T. Boone Pickens's case, the truly momentous discovery
was that Wall Street, rather than the Texas Panhandle, was the
best place to go prospecting for crude. Recognizing that buying oil
companies for their reserves was a lot cheaper, and a lot less risky,
than drilling for petroleum, the chairman of Mesa Petroleum Co.
(now a limited partnership) embarked on a contentious career of
raiding the majors, including Gulf Oil and Phillips Petroleum, that
shook up the entire industry.

They call me a corporate raider. Well, that's exactly the way
I see management. Why did oil companies—large oil
companies—sell at a deep discount to the appraised value
of their assets? The marketplace is pretty damn accurate in looking at these situations. The price identified managements that
were not going to do anything for the stockholders. I saw that a
long time before anybody else noticed. I saw that back in the '60s.
We acquired a company that was twenty times our size [Hugoton
Production Co.] in 1969. I hadn't given up on exploration, but at
the same time I saw that acquisitions would bring cheaper reserves than exploration. I was trying to upgrade the value of the
assets. Damn sure make some money out of it—I'm not kidding
anybody. I'm not altruistic to the point that I'm just out there
working for somebody else. But there isn't one time we left the
stockholders out in a deal. Now, how can you identify that as a
raider?

For all the bad things anyone's ever said about me, there's not one of them that will debate me. That's got to tell you something. I think this issue cries out for public debate. And none of them will debate it. Sure, you can call somebody a son of a bitch, but, I mean, to stand up in front of a crowd and say, "Let's debate the issues," that's another thing. Fred Hartley [chairman of Unocal] has been the most vocal. He said I was a Communist, and he said I was a crook and things like that. I mean, you can say those things, but you're gonna have to back it up with facts. None of them back it up. If I'm the rascal they say I am, why don't they get me out in front of a crowd and really just absolutely kill me?

Listen, there were three huge deals in '84: Chevron-Gulf, Texaco-Getty and Mobil-Superior. There was a common denominator in all of them, and that was a large stockholder that was unhappy with management: Gordon Getty at Getty, Howard Keck at Superior and us at Gulf. We didn't propose to sell the company; all we said was, "Share part of the cash flow." That's all. Now, with Gulf we finally got ourselves in a spot where we had to make a partial tender offer to get everything off high center. But Keck sold out the company to Mobil—took his cash first—and the other stockholders got cash and debt. And Getty, he just put Getty Oil up for sale and sold it to the highest bidder. And the only difference between Getty, Keck and myself was one thing: how long I'd owned the stock. Keck and Getty had inherited their stock 30 or 40 years before; we'd owned ours for three months. That's the only difference.

People used to say to me, "You should go out and drill because you're in the oil business." That's ridiculous. I mean, if it isn't economically sound, you're a fool to do it. I'd be a sap to go out and try to find oil at $15 a barrel when I could buy three barrels for the same price. It didn't take a financial genius to figure all that out.

The only change of mind I had in the early '80s was that the better values were in the bigger companies. They were more deeply discounted. The investing public believed smaller companies were gonna do something, and so consequently they were selling at or near the appraised value of the assets. But it was clear that size protected the big ones. You'd sit down and talk to investment bankers and say, "Look, here's Cities Service. The assets are appraised at $100. Do you agree with that?" They'd say, "Yes, we agree with it." You'd say, "The stock price is $35." They'd say, "That's right, we agree with that, too." But then they'd say, "You can't get there because of size."

Now, a lot of people say we were the ones who kicked everything off. We weren't. Dome [Petroleum] was ahead of us on Conoco. They were gonna buy enough Conoco stock to swap for Conoco's Canadian assets—Hudson's Bay—but Conoco's management said, "Screw off, fella, you ain't big enough to handle this deal." Well, Dome then made a partial tender offer for 20 percent of the company, and they got over 50 percent. Du Pont got Conoco in the end, but it didn't take people long to realize, "My God, this is a new game. You can tender for 20 percent and get 50."

It was about that time that Cities made the offer for us. They thought we were coming after them first, but we couldn't get our partnership together. But once they made the offer to us, we had to do something. So we did a partial tender offer for 15 percent. That was with all the money we had, which was $600 million. Reporters never ask, "What are these guys really up to?" The real reason for a bid in some cases is because you were being forced into it. With Cities Service we had an average price on our stock of $44, and the stock was selling for something like $36. I was afraid we'd get out and have an eight-point loss. That was $30 million. I didn't want to take the loss, so I had to force something to happen.

I also knew that if I started selling the stock and if anybody found out about it, the price was gonna tumble *real* fast, so I was gonna have a much bigger loss than $30 million. So here I'd gotten trapped into a deal. I had trapped *myself* into a deal. Even so, I said, "The values are there, the company is worth probably $90 a share and it's selling for $36, so maybe we can figure out some way to force the management to do something to realize values."

Now, in the end, Gulf made its $63 offer, which knocked our $45 offer out. But that was all the money we had. We were looking for another partner and we just about had Occidental lined up when the $63 offer came in, and out the window it goes. Then Gulf pulled their offer, and Occidental came back in and bought it for $53.

107

We had had our eye on Gulf for a long time, probably since 1981. We had looked at Gulf and realized that it was the really big one with the worst record of all. And we had to make some money because we had put $1.8 billion into the outer continental shelf, believing that that was really the last place to build an oil company. We bet a ton of money on that, and we were wrong. We found some stuff that was pretty good, but we paid too much for it. Because of that disaster, we were looking at probably somewhere between a $400 and $500 million loss, which we could not stand.

So it meant that we had to quickly do something else. I called my guys together and I said, "Fellas, the single or double won't work now. We need a home run." And that was Gulf Oil. We believed that we could take that big position in Gulf, show them how to restructure the company and enhance the value of our stock along with everybody else's. That was it. We were not trying to acquire them. We told them straightaway, "We don't want to go on the board of directors." Frankly, we didn't have the size for it. There was no way we could take over Gulf. All we wanted them to do was to share a part of the cash flow with the stockholders through a royalty trust.

You didn't get to where you are talking about how you could finance one of these things until the Gulf deal. Halfway into the Gulf deal one of our partners, [Canadian investor] Sam Belzberg, suggested that we talk to [Drexel junk bond king] Mike Milken. Now, I really didn't put much faith in the meeting. It was just kind of, well, a partner asked me to do it and I went along. We met for 35 or 40 minutes, and Mike said, "Well, let us go back and see if there's something that we can do to help you on your financing." And that was it. David Batchelder [then Mesa's chief operating officer, now president of Boone Co.] worked with them. I didn't.

I still thought that I could convince Gulf to go along with my royalty trust spin-off. See, I probably can identify a dry hole quicker than most other people can, but I'm optimistic and a bit of a dreamer at times, and I want things to work. The trust made so much sense to me. It left the company intact. It didn't disrupt anything. It was simple. Those kind of things are the easiest for me to understand. David said, "I don't think you'll ever talk them into doing it," and he went to work with Milken,.

They devised a plan that was very loose and they explored some ideas, but nothing ever came of it. Even so, we said: "Hey, these [Drexel] guys are not playing games. They're really seriously trying to figure out a way that could finance something." [Then–Gulf chairman] Jimmy Lee truly believed that we could raise the money through Drexel to make an offer for him, and I kept pursuing the royalty trust idea. Our next ploy was to make a cash tender offer for 15 percent of the company—for $65. Our plan was to beef up our ownership and challenge them at the spring stockholders' meeting and put people on the board.

Gulf had some paranoia about us going on their board, and I had to assume that they had things that they didn't want us to learn about the company. They could see the handwriting on the wall—that we were gonna go after them in a proxy fight and we were gonna have a hell of a lot of stock when we did it. When we did that, well, that put them in serious negotiations with Chevron, which bought Gulf, and that was the end of it.

We really wanted to buy Phillips. That was our next deal. I realized they were undervalued, and that management had really not ever done much for the stockholders. And I knew Phillips. I used to work for them. I'm a native Oklahoman and my wife is, too. I went to Oklahoma State. What made me move was, I was watching the accumulation on Phillips and I said, "Somebody's buying Phillips." And I said, "If Phillips is taken out of Bartlesville [Phillips's headquarters], the town will just collapse." And Phillips is the largest company in Oklahoma.

So I said, "Well, why don't we go in and make an offer for Phillips and just put it on a basis that this is just for corporate control is all it is, that everything else remains intact." We even said, "We'll move to Bartlesville." I mean, that's how pure we were with the idea.

But I could never sell that. It was an absolute disaster. It wouldn't sell. In the Gulf deal we were perceived as the underdog, people were on our side. In the Phillips deal, because of the high profile we developed in the Gulf deal and what we caused to happen there, some people believed we were bigger than Phillips.

We were hung up early in the Oklahoma courts. They did the kind of job we supposed would take place in Oklahoma courts, but we were plowing through that pretty good. And then we won in the Delaware courts, and our offer was about to come alive when they said, "Boone, let's talk."

So we sat down in New York with them on the weekend before Christmas and worked out a deal on a restructuring of Phillips. It wasn't greenmail. Phillips actually offered me greenmail in the very first telephone call, and we turned it down. We were offered greenmail by Phillips at least five times. They were the most aggressive in offering greenmail. The problem you developed on Wall Street was, when you restructured Phillips, you had a big drop in the price of the stock. I think it was trading for around 52 or 53 and dropped to 46.

Unocal, which came next, was kind of a fluke. We were watching Arco, Phillips and Unocal and trying to figure out which one had the best chance of being restructured. This was in the summer or late fall of '84. The company we should have played was Arco, because they're the company that did restructure voluntarily. We took Unocal and Phillips down to the wire, though, and decided to make the offer for Phillips. But we still had the Unocal position. We either had to get out of Unocal at that point or it would be revealed, even though we had less than 5 percent at that point, in a 14-F filing. So we said, "Well, if that's the case, we'll just go ahead and move forward."

We weren't gonna try to take over Unocal. We thought that Unocal was gonna restructure the company. We were there as an investor. We just made a mistake and bought the wrong company is all. A very aggressive chairman [Hartley] started changing the bylaws and making public statements about his new largest stockholder. They finally did force us into a corner where we had to make an offer. They just started arbitrarily taking away rights of stockholders—and we were their biggest stockholder. They were after us, is who they were after, and they were ultimately successful in the Delaware courts, though the decision was later reversed by the SEC.

We lost; we didn't get the company. I've never said otherwise. But our aftertax gain was something on the order of $80 million. But if I had it to do over again, I think that we would just probably not have done the Phillips and Unocal deals. The funny thing is, we've never used Drexel's junk bond financing but in one deal,

110

Unocal. But they did raise the $3.5 billion for us in four days, which shocked the hell out of Unocal.

When I first started talking about restructuring in the early '80s, some people called me a radical. They said that I was really against traditional values and things like that, that I was fooling around with stuff that I had no business talking about. I saw undervalued assets in the public marketplace. My game plan wasn't to take on Big Oil. Hell, that's not my role. My role is to make money for the stockholders. I just saw that Big Oil's management had done a lousy job for the stockholders, leaving an opening to upgrade the value of those assets. The opportunity was there for us *because* management had done a poor job. Otherwise the stock price would have been at a level that would not have invited somebody trying to upgrade the value. We took advantage of management for what they had done, and we made them pay for it. The investment bankers and the lawyers working for management did the same thing. I mean, they took advantage of them, too, and made them pay for what they had done. Management doesn't understand that to this day, that everybody was there because of their poor record. It's the only reason *anybody* was there.

Fortunately, the stockholders did prosper by what we did. Eight hundred thousand stockholders made $13 billion. Nobody's argued that point. Not one person has said: "Hold it. This son of a bitch is lying." These 800,000 stockholders made $13 billion, and our part of it was less than 5 percent. We took all the risk, paid all the money, did all the work and got less than 5 percent of the profit.

But management won't admit that. Look at the Business Roundtable. They were lobbying on Capitol Hill in the '70s and the early '80s and saying, "Leave us alone—acquisitions are just the free-enterprise system working at its best." Then along came Milken, and that's when you found out that the little company could get the big company. And that's when those guys went back up on the Hill and said, "The big one getting the little one is free enterprise; the little one getting the big one is un-American."

I think we've had a big hand in restructuring corporate America, and that's gonna make this country competitive again. It hasn't been completed yet, but it's on the road, it's on the road. The more ownership you can get in the hands of management—

and all the employees in a company—you'll get a better performance. That's all there is to it. See, I don't differentiate between management and labor. It's all labor. I'm a laborer at Mesa just like everybody else. We've got to get away from the adversarial relationship in labor and management. That's not the enemy. The enemies are the Japanese and the Germans and those that are taking away our market shares. Eventually, somebody else would have done it if I hadn't. It would have had to have happened. See, that's why the Dow's above 2,200. I don't think that anybody will argue that it's not because of restructuring, whether it's takeovers, mergers, acquisitions or just pure restructuring. Certainly, the managements haven't performed to the level that would cause the Dow to be above 2,200. It's been forced on them.

Editor: Gregory Miller

Mohammed Ali Abalkhail

Minister of Finance and National Economy SAUDI ARABIA

Sheikh Mohammed has been minister of finance of Saudi Arabia since 1975. A quiet, unpretentious man, Abalkhail has grappled with the kingdom's budgets since 1967—from its meager totals to the surging surpluses of the late 1970s back through the dramatic fall-off of the mid-1980s. Along with Sheikh Abdul Aziz al-Quraishi, former governor of the Saudi Arabian Monetary Agency, Abalkhail was the key Saudi overseeing the kingdom's massive influx of petrodollars, which was to become at the time the largest international investment portfolio in the world.

We didn't really realize the consequences of the oil price rises at first. To a certain extent, Sheikh Abdul Aziz [al-Quraishi] and I were surprised by the size of the surplus. It was a big responsibility, especially after the second big increase. There was no question it was something you had to be worried about. Working on the budget and the development programs and managing the surplus meant that the hours we worked lengthened: from 7:00 or 8:00 every morning until 9:00 or 10:00 at night. We practically lived in the ministry building.

Many people said, "Let us give a chance to any projects, to any idea, as long as we have the resources. We are a new country, and we badly need so many things, from A to Z, from the small school to the big power stations." We stayed up through many nights trying to put things together and to decide on the priorities.

There was a maximum effort to coordinate with the planning agencies and other ministries. But we were all under the pressure to go as fast as possible.

Prince Musaid [bin Abdul Rahman, minister of finance until 1975] was a real leader; he was very efficient in the way he handled things. He would always like to go directly to the heart of an issue in a no-nonsense approach, even if it meant the people involved made harsh comments. It was useful for everyone to speak so frankly; it made for good coordination in economic policy.

Prince Musaid was the right leader in the economic sector at the right time. We have continued in this fashion, so in a sense his legacy has continued at the ministry. Instead of just behaving in a happy-go-lucky way—because we have the increasing revenue and therefore can expand in this way or that—we looked at each suggestion or proposal to consider the pros and cons. We at the ministry knew that not everything was so rosy and that there were problems with the increasing oil revenues.

⬥

The foreign media in the United States and Europe were talking about our development in a different way, and they were not all in favor of just going ahead. There were *enormous* comments on the possible consequences of increasing foreign labor in Saudi Arabia, what it meant politically, socially. For our part, we didn't see any difficulties. It was a unique situation; I don't think there was any other country in a certain stage of its history that had such an increasing number of workers coming over in such a short period. This movement of labor was a movement of experience, the transfer of technology. We didn't feel that what people said on the outside really reflected what we were facing, but it was, I guess, a good thing in a way because it made us much more aware of certain directions.

Saudi Arabia was under enormous pressure in the way it was watched so closely by the foreign media. I do not remember another country that was watched as carefully as Saudi Arabia. They would say, "Never in history has such wealth come to a country." The media role sometimes had a positive effect, but I can say that we were in many cases upset, that we hurt from inside. In some cases, what was written up was completely false.

114

Articles told us what we should do and what we should not do. But maybe more than any other country, the influence of the international media on our development program was often useful simply because we didn't have enough experience at the time. The media coverage influenced us to a degree in being even more cautious.

We were not happy with the way the media and other circles talked about petrodollars. They just looked at the negative side or talked about "this one small country with such a huge amount of money." There was so little attention on the positive way we were managing our assets. We were not trying to use our investments to gain influence here or there. It was never political.

Without the prudent way Saudi Arabia's assets were invested— by our specifications, between institutions, banks and currencies, available for investment in different parts of the world—I do not think certain developing countries would have been able to achieve what they have in their development. It was clear to us that we should not—we could not, really—lend directly to the other developing countries. We did not have enough experience in this. How could we? We didn't have developed institutions. We really felt it was in our interest, and in the world's interest, to go work with the specialized institutions. When I sit and talk with Sheikh Abdul Aziz about the things of ten or thirteen years ago, we really feel that we went through the right channels.

We always felt the IMF should expand its role. It is much better for the developing countries to talk and deal with the big countries within the framework of an international institution. It gives them a say, a better position. Look at what Saudi Arabia and the other Arab countries did when they had the surplus, cooperating with the international and regional institutions in recycling the surplus funds or the way we established our own development fund. As far as I know, it was the first time that a country dealt with them from such a strong position but in a very nice manner. We respected their experience, and I think they respected our way of dealing with them.

Compare this with what the other surplus countries are doing now. Japan, for instance: They have a huge surplus, much more than we had in the past. They are a rich country; but when we had a surplus we were at the beginning of our development, and our need was great for everything. But still we faced the moral re-

115

sponsibility to other parts of the world. The other surplus countries are not doing now what we did in the 1970s.

A lot of people were also saying we should have made more direct investments like our Kuwaiti friends. But from the very beginning we thought this was not the way for Saudi Arabia. We would talk with [Kuwaiti Finance Minister] Abdul Rahman al-Atiqi and Khalid Abu Sau'ud [director of investments at the Kuwaiti Ministry of Finance] about this. But we never really saw their way as a realistic approach for Saudi Arabia, simply from the management point of view. We didn't have enough people. From the beginning our priority was always on the domestic side. We didn't want our people spending their time and efforts with some company somewhere or participating in management or having a man on the board. And, besides, we felt that this was not the role of the government. The government should take care of its own economy. If someone in the private sector wanted to make foreign long-term investments, that was his own business.

There was an idea that if you invested in a company outside the country, you would be able to use and benefit from its experience and technology, to develop it inside your own country. But to have done so would have limited our ability and choices in investing. There was some debate inside the Council of Ministers about this, but I can say it was not really that extensive. That kind of idea came more from the outside than inside. It was rejected from the beginning.

We also always felt that the surpluses had a very temporary nature. They existed only because our absorptive capacity inside was not fully developed yet. But our absorptive capacity was always growing, so the amount of our investment outside would decrease. And that is what happened. We never wanted to keep investing outside forever. I was never taken in by the idea we would be rich forever. This is related to another issue. From the beginning we never felt it was good for the oil-producing countries—and especially us—to push oil prices up and up and up. This was one of our basic policies. We wanted an oil price to be reasonable and to be sustainable. So when the price shot up, it was against our way of thinking, our strategy. Remember, we

116

stayed for one year and more at $30 to $32 while the others sold for much more.

We are by nature a cautious people, and when we entered this new, challenging period, we were cautious enough not to take in all ideas. And second, we worked hard. We selected the right advisory sources—I mean people who are not of show, are not boastful. They just sit down and talk and get the job done. It was immediately clear that the most important thing was to concentrate on the good management of the assets and to find good, low-key people.

The idea of using oil as a political weapon was not, and up to now is not, a strong idea in Saudi Arabia. Nineteen seventy-three was an exceptional case. If you look at Saudi Arabia, look at the people, the leaders, we have always been a moderate people. It is our nature. I can remember many media stories saying that Saudi Arabia, the Arabs would buy up the United States, all its real estate, its companies. But really, we never had any idea to do so. If we had a surplus, it was temporary, and we had to keep it in a way that would be ready for investments inside as our absorptive capacity grew. Equity or real estate were never really attractive to us; it was always under 5 percent of the total. That was a very rigid rule.

But we were very, very careful in trying to build a good long-term business relationship with some of the developed countries where we invested our surplus. The leaders of the central banks and treasury people, the bankers, they all understood what we wanted. There were a lot of exchanges and visits. We always made them very discreetly, very quietly; it was a successful approach. And when the accumulation of assets grew, there was an increasing coordination and understanding in that circle. We were selective and were reasonable with the ones we chose, letting them know our policies. If we wanted to move into a certain currency or investment, we contacted the central bank of that country.

I was always impressed with Karl Otto Pöhl, the president of the Bundesbank. He is among the people whom I really like; I respect him. I also liked working with [Manfred] Lahnstein when he was head of the office of [former] Chancellor [Helmut] Schmidt and then finance minister; he was really a good person. In the United

117

States, I worked much with Bill Simon during the days of the increasing surpluses. I remember that Simon was on the board of Citibank at the time, and he played a good role in helping with the negotiations with them when we wanted to Saudi-ize the bank in Saudi Arabia.

Some banks, like the Dutch, made the response immediately, but Citibank was very resistant to the idea. I also met with Walter Wriston several times. I like him; he is direct, serious. [Then-Treasury] Secretary [G. William] Miller had this ability to cooperate with others. And Paul Volcker was the same. He visited us in Riyadh when he was president of the New York Fed. He was very impressive, very astute.

I also enjoyed working with [former Swiss National Bank] president [Fritz] Leutwiler. I remember once Sheikh Abdul Aziz and I went to Zurich just to talk with him and hear his analysis of the present situation. It was just general questions but with someone who you know is an expert. We just called him on the phone and said, "We would like to visit you." We went there and had lunch and talked for a while; it was as simple as that. There was so much responsibility in those days, but it was enjoyable to work with these kinds of people and to talk on that sort of level.

I can remember when President Carter froze the Iranian accounts in U.S. banks. We didn't think it was the right thing. But the reasons were obvious; there were more than 100 Americans kept in Teheran. One could see it was an extraordinary situation, and any government in that situation has few options. I got a phone call from Mr. Miller at the U.S. Treasury a few hours before the announcement, and Sheikh Abdul Aziz got a call from Paul Volcker to warn us that the United States was going to take this action and to explain why. But in principle, we were against it.

When Mexico had its problems and the debt crisis began, neither we nor the commercial banks in Saudi Arabia had any direct investments in Latin America. It made us feel that the way we diversified our investments, by currency, sovereignty and institution, was right. It took much time to devise that strategy. We had much help from Baring Brothers and Merrill Lynch. They were honest, and their role was very useful; we got very professional services, no question about that. And we never really encountered much resistance from other countries when we were implementing the diversification of our assets.

The decline in oil revenues and the surplus happened in a way that was not only unexpected but very difficult. It was impossible for us to make a very short-term focus in our investment strategy. All we could do was to shorten the maturities of some of our investments and to get ready for drawing down some of them. It fell much more quickly than we imagined possible. We tried to take the uncertainty into consideration, to be conservative, to reduce the forecast of the Oil Ministry to be on the safe side. But we were still surprised. I was working with Sheikh Zaki [Yamani, the minister of oil] a lot then. We were working with the same uncertainties. It was beyond the control of anyone in the government. The hours were unbearably long.

But one point to make about this most difficult period was that it came when we were about to finish everything. This is one thing we can thank God for. It also proved my point that it was right that we pushed to implement a lot of programs, increase internal spending and finish everything in a short period.

The main question in our minds when government spending declined and the infrastructure was in place was whether the private sector was ready to expand to fill the gap left by the decline in the role of the public sector. With the private sector increasing its role—in the way they deal with the government as contractors, gaining experience and accumulating assets—they can then expand, benefiting from the infrastructure built by the government. But the slowdown took the private sector by surprise, too. So what we are trying to do now is to encourage the private sector. But you know, the long-term strategy of the government, regardless of the slowdown in spending, was to level off and reduce government spending and encourage the private sector.

I am fairly satisfied with the way things have come out. If the private sector can expand, Saudi Arabia can maintain a good rate of growth, and prosperity will continue without any interruption. The fundamentals of Saudi Arabia are sound. We have good financial assets, private and public; we have a good infrastructure. We have a good banking system, we still have the largest reservoir of oil and we have good business relations. This is a good record. I am not talking in a purely nationalistic sense. I really mean it.

I can look back at when I was working on budgets of only Sr30 or Sr40 billion, even less. I used to remember every figure in the budget, how much we allocated for this ministry or that. I always had a knack for memory. From that to working on a budget of Sr260 billion and more—and then again to the smaller numbers now, when there are no surpluses at all.

The most satisfying thing about this whole experience for me is to be from a Saudi generation that lived in the old way of life. My generation was lucky to have this opportunity to start from where we did and see all that is going on now. It was unique. There has been no generation like this generation in Saudi Arabia—in any place in the world or history that I know of—that has witnessed this. In the United States it took hundreds of years, in Europe, even longer. It gives me a lot of satisfaction.

Editor: Kevin Muehring

Helmut Schmidt

Former Chancellor FEDERAL REPUBLIC OF GERMANY

Except for a brief period in the early 1960s, Helmut Schmidt was a member of the West German Bundestag from 1953 to January of 1987, when he decided not to stand for reelection to a tenth term. During those three decades, Schmidt, a student and protégé of former economics minister Karl Schiller, served as minister of defense (1969 to 1972), minister of finance (1972 to 1974) and chancellor (from May 1974 to October 1982). Together with former French finance minister and, later, president Valéry Giscard d'Estaing, a close personal friend, Schmidt is credited with launching the European Monetary System and instigating the Western economic summits, which have been held annually since 1975.

Good personal relationships play a much greater role in government, finance and economics than the press understands. I first met Karl Schiller in Hamburg in 1946. I was a rather belated student of economics; I was already 27 when I started to study, having been a conscripted soldier for more than eight years. Of course, the relationship between students my age, having gone through the whole war, with professors at that time was quite different from the normal student-professor one. We were grown men and found it difficult to take seriously a professor who would arrogantly play up his so-called science, whether it was economics or philosophy.

But Schiller was unique because of his knowledge of modern Anglo-American economics. He was one of the very first to teach Keynes in Germany. He had an overview of Keynes, Samuelson and Schumpeter, and although I did not take my studies very seriously, I listened with great interest to Schiller. I became his personal assistant when he was minister of economics in the Hamburg state government, later his department head for economic policy, then for transport. Then, in Bonn, both of us were deputy leaders of the Social Democratic Party faction in the Bundestag, and in 1972 I succeeded him as federal minister of finance and economics.

George Shultz and I first met when I became minister of economics and finance; he was secretary of the Treasury under Richard Nixon. We quickly became good colleagues, cooperating rather closely. Partially, it was thinking alike on matters of finance and economics, but I think more important was the personal chemistry. We liked each other. It was exactly the same thing—economic rapport and personal friendship—with Arthur Burns at the Fed. [Valéry] Giscard [d'Estaing] and I met when we were both ministers of finance. It was a coincidence, but a very lucky one, that two years later we came to office [Giscard as president, Schmidt as chancellor] in the same month—May 1974—and therefore had a time of close personal and political cooperation for a full seven years, until May 1981. We met and talked by telephone maybe 24 times a year; we had a great number of private meetings.

I still believe, as I did then, that fixed exchange rates, in many respects, are preferable to floating rates. But in 1972 and '73 it was already quite clear that America had ruined the position of the dollar as the foundation of the Bretton Woods system by financing the Vietnam War. They had started to terminate exchangeability of dollars and gold in '68 and were still going on as if nothing was happening. On the other hand, Nixon was unwilling to take the appropriate measures in fiscal and monetary policies to restabilize the dollar. Several attempts to reestablish fixed exchange rates at lower levels for the dollar—the most outstanding example was the Smithsonian agreement at the end of 1971, of which I was not a part—had failed. So Giscard and I saw no other way than to let it go. We were fed up with those ridiculous, dramatic resettings of exchange rates every half year or once every quarter.

Yes, I envisioned the complications that have resulted; I even expected them to be more serious. What I did *not* foresee back then was the first oil price explosion, which would never have attained such enormous economic importance if the dollar had not been depreciated half a year earlier by free floating. I wouldn't call the present system a system: It's a floating nonsystem.

The Americans, having been liberated from fixed exchange rates, felt no inhibitions about producing federal budget deficits that could no longer be fully financed by the American capital market. The net *foreign* debt of the U.S. on Reagan's last day in office in January 1989 will be on the order of half a trillion dollars. If you calculate that at a modest 8 percent interest, they will have to transfer $40 billion per year to the outside world. None of the presidential hopefuls seems to have understood this; at least nobody has the courage to talk about it. The new president, whoever he is, conservative or liberal, Republican or Democrat, will find it very difficult to embark on a totally different course of economic, financial and monetary policy. It is going to be a very hard time. Because once he starts to change the direction, let's say in late 1989 or early '90, the foreign debt will already be far beyond $500 billion.

But let me go back to autumn 1973 and the quadrupling of prices for imported oil. Remember that Germany imports 95 percent of its oil. Of course, we saw the threat of inflationary pressures; anybody could have seen that. But we did not then take refuge in deflationary monetary policies. I thought it would be wise to let some inflationary move happen and to try, after some time, to redress the money supply and also get the fiscal policy again under control. By 1977 or '78 we had, at least in Germany, totally overcome the repercussions of that first oil price explosion. We were not able to achieve the same thing after the second one. But after two years we were able to redress our current account deficit by taking fiscal and monetary measures, and by 1982 our annual balance of payments was in equilibrium, though at the cost of deflationary measures that normally bring about some degree of unemployment.

I don't know who exactly cooked up and tried to foist on us the idea that Germany should play a "locomotive" role to the world economy. I seem to recall that the main speakers were American, especially Jimmy Carter. Actually, we didn't do anything that we wouldn't have done anyway in accordance with our interpretation of our national interests. But at the Bonn economic summit in 1978, we presented it as being a response to American and also British pressure in order to get something in exchange from the

123

Americans—which we got: liberalization of domestic American oil prices in order to bring down the American consumption of petrol. Then we said we would be willing to, as the British incorrectly called it at the time, "reflate" the German economy by 1 percent of GNP. But I had already decided to do this before the meeting. Of course, neither Jimmy Carter nor the British had the slightest [right] to ask us to play the locomotive role. What nonsense that was.

The idea for economic summits came from Giscard and myself; we needed some time to convince the others. The last bit of convincing was done at the Helsinki Conference in the summer of 1975 during a meeting between Jerry Ford, Harold Wilson, Giscard and myself, and, though reluctantly, Ford bought the idea. From the beginning, Giscard and I thought it was necessary to have a meeting not only between these four Western powers but with Japan as well. The Americans agreed to that readily.

We each appointed a personal representative to make the arrangements in order to avoid having the whole thing spoiled by eager and ambitious bureaucracies. My representative was Wilfried Guth of Deutsche Bank. We had the first summit in Fontainebleau at Giscard's invitation, and he also invited France's Latin sister, Italy. Before the second meeting in Puerto Rico, three quarters of a year or so later, Ford decided to invite his Canadian neighbor.

The first two summits weren't all that bad. In Fontainebleau there were just six prime ministers or presidents, six foreign secretaries, six finance ministers and a few interpreters. The press didn't have a chance to interfere, and government press spokesmen had no chance to run out every half hour to tell the press what their great chancellor or their great president had just told those other six idiots. This has deteriorated; nowadays it is a meeting of the mass media, on the fringes of which you also have seven prime ministers or presidents. No decisions of importance are taken anymore. Still, I think it's valuable that they meet; to enforce upon them the necessity to listen is very important.

Of course, it helps for the heads of government to have some knowledge of economics and finance. If they don't, they don't make much sense, but even for them it's important to listen if there is at least one in the group who does make sense. In our days there were always at least two people who understood these matters—Giscard and myself—and two years after the first meeting there came a third, Takeo Fukuda, the Japanese prime minister, who also understood. And British prime ministers [James] Callaghan and [Margaret] Thatcher always had good economic sense.

This close relationship between Giscard and me is also what brought about the European Monetary System and the ECU. Fixed exchange rates impose a certain economic discipline on the behavior of governments. With fixed rates you want to avoid devaluing, because if you do you are criticized by your trade unions and consumers for increasing the prices of imported foodstuffs and other imported goods. You also want to avoid revaluing, because that will get you criticism from both the trade unions and industry, because both of them fear that they will lose exports. So, in your fiscal and monetary behavior you try to avoid such acts and you try to keep within the margins.

Giscard and I were deeply concerned in 1973 when we had to go to free floating of our currencies. And a few years later, in one of our private conversations, the idea sprang up that we should try to bring about fixed exchange rates at least for the greater part of our exports and imports, namely among the Europeans. I think we told our European colleagues that we were undertaking this in 1978. Again we steered it without too great an involvement of our bureaucracies on either side.

We installed a first phase of EMS in '79 and envisioned a second phase, but [French President François] Mitterrand and [German Chancellor Helmut] Kohl and others are just too timid to carry it on. The ultimate goal—and we declared it in 1979—was to arrive at one European currency, a parallel currency in all of our countries that, in the course of time, would become more important than national currencies.

The ECU would then have needed a central agency of West European central banks to manage the ECU money supply. This central agency would play the role within the European Community that under Bretton Woods had formerly been played for the world at large by the IMF. But this second phase has not been brought about, mainly due to Mitterrand and Kohl coming to

125

office and their reliance, as laymen, on what they are being told by their central banks and Finance Ministry officials. The central banks and finance ministries dislike the whole thing because it would mean shifting some of the competences they enjoy to a centralized European monetary fund.

I certainly would rather see the ECU as a reserve currency than the deutsche mark. I resent the idea of the deutsche mark's having become the second important reserve currency in the world, as much as I resent Germany's having become, behind Japan, the second-largest creditor to the world. That's political and psychological nonsense. The world may accept it for a couple more years, but not for eternity. It will not bear a situation in which those two countries, which were most responsible for World War II and lost it totally, should become the greatest creditors to the rest of the world.

I also saw the EMS as playing an integrating factor in Europe, politically and psychologically and, more important, economically. Just as under Bretton Woods, so under a "European monetary fund" European governments would have to exert more disciplined monetary policies to prevent depreciations or appreciations of their currencies. It would have brought about—and even the first phase has brought about—a greater degree of harmonization of economic policy within the EEC. And over the past ten years the ECU has proven to be the most stable currency.

Now, despite what I've said about central banks and their resistance to an EMF, I really have nothing to complain about the Bundesbank during the period that I was finance minister or chancellor. I do have some complaints about the time after. I especially had nothing to complain about as long as Karl Klasen was president of the Bundesbank [1970–1977], and no complaints when [Otmar] Emminger [1977–1979] and [Karl Otto] Pöhl [since 1980] were chairmen. Until 1982. I don't recall ever being in real conflict with the Bundesbank or with Pöhl. Maybe we were at odds over a quarter or half percent of interest once, but it didn't matter much, and it happens in many countries from time to time.

But, of course, all central banks in the world have underestimated a number of new developments. Number one, they did not see that they were losing their grip over the markets when they allowed commercial banks to establish offshore affiliates. Second, they did not detect that the so-called recycling of petrodollars, only to roll over the credits every three months, was building up what nowadays is called the debt crisis. Third, they did not observe and prevent all these new financial instruments from coming about, which nowadays have made the international financial markets almost uncontrollable. In the fourth place, despite what they think of each other, they are not really cooperating closely enough to prevent the internationalization of financial flows without an international controlling agency. Nowadays you have one worldwide stock exchange. Nobody is controlling it. You have one worldwide money market. Nobody is controlling it. The central banks are still living in the world of the '70s—some in the '60s.

Of course, some central bankers are more prudent than they are allowed to show, because there are various kinds of central banks. There are those which are, practically speaking, just appendages of their ministries of finance, as in France. Some are more independent, like the Federal Reserve. Some are really independent, like the Bundesbank, the Dutch central bank and the Swiss National Bank. These are the ones that love their independence and would not give away any competence to a joint central bank of Western Europe, an EMF, which, in my view, should be constituted to be a totally independent central bank of national central banks.

I've been asked, looking back over fifteen to twenty years to the time when I was finance minister and then chancellor, what I might do differently in the economic and financial sphere if I could do it over again. Well, I don't want to give the impression that I feel I was right all the time, but I find it hard to come up with any answer that differs substantially from what we have actually done—not much, really, not much. Had I remained in office longer, I would certainly have completed the EMS and thereby made Europe a little more cohesive, created a higher degree of harmonization of economic policies without saying so, without making great declarations on the subject, but just by the push of exchange rate discipline. This would have created a somewhat greater autonomy of the European countries vis-à-vis the American deficit policies.

It was also a great mistake, and I was part of that mistake, not to bring about a worldwide energy conference in 1974, after the first oil price explosion. We tried to bring about such a conference in early '74. [Soviet leader Leonid] Brezhnev was willing to participate; the Americans were not. Instead, they called for a Western energy conference, which ended up as a total failure because [French President Georges] Pompidou did not send Giscard, who was then still finance minister, fearing he might be too American-ophile. The conference led to nothing. It was not tried a second time, which was a mistake for which I also have to take some responsibility. It's still a mistake that some such thing does not exist, because the third oil price explosion is sure to come. I would put it in writing that before the year 2000 we will see oil prices of $50 per barrel. The economic repercussions of that—whether it's an explosion or a gradual increase of prices doesn't really matter—will be enormous.

Editor: John Dornberg

Valéry Giscard d'Estaing

Former President REPUBLIC OF FRANCE

Valéry Giscard d'Estaing, president of France from 1974 to 1981, was the youngest man to hold that office and the youngest head of the French state since Napoleon. But it was during successive tenures at the Ministry of Finance and Economic Affairs from the late 1950s through the early 1970s that he made perhaps his most important contributions to French and international financial and economic affairs. In 1971 Giscard d'Estaing accompanied President Georges Pompidou to the Azores mini-summit with President Richard Nixon and Paul Volcker, where the decision was made to devalue the dollar for the first time since World War II; he would later participate in the Smithsonian negotiations, which resulted in the system of floating exchange rates. In response to the 1973 oil price explosion, Giscard d'Estaing moved quickly on three fronts— to impose a strict anti-inflationary policy, launch an ambitious nuclear power program and create a network of overseas borrowing facilities that both introduced France to the Euromarkets and established the French signature as a benchmark for international creditworthiness.

There was never really a "Nixon shock." The destabilization of the Bretton Woods agreement had been coming over a long period; it was a slow process. There was a kind of dogma by which we lived, the dogma that the dollar was as good as gold. We thought very early, with de Gaulle around '64, under the pressure of some theoreticians like Jacques Rueff, that this structure would not remain stable forever. We decided, remember, to bring back some of our gold reserves that were stored in Fort Knox. This was resented by the Americans as an unfriendly gesture—which it was not, because it was perfectly normal for any central bank to have in its own vaults its own reserves.

But the idea of having unlimited convertibility between dollar and gold for central banks could not last for long. So when we had destablization of the international monetary situation in the '70s, it was not a surprise for us; it was really what we expected. Not what we hoped for, but what we expected, due to the imbalances.

There were two aspects: One was the flotation of currencies, and the other was a change of parity of the dollar. The man who was pushing for floating currencies was Karl Schiller, the German economics minister at the time. And when we had the devaluation of the franc in July of '69, we had a debate with the Germans. It was a question of how we would maintain future parities, and they said they would let the D-mark float; they didn't want to play the game of fixed parities anymore. So for us, the movement toward flotation started in Europe.

After that we had a long debate with the Nixon administration about the devaluation of the dollar, which ended in a meeting in the Azores attended by Kissinger and Volcker on the American side, President Pompidou, myself and our foreign secretary on the French side. We thought that the overvaluation of the dollar should be corrected. There were two ways then: One was to float, the other to devalue. And President Nixon accepted the idea of devaluation, which showed that, at that time, the American leaders were able to decide on very important and difficult issues. It was the first devaluation since the war.

I still recall a very curious document, which was the decision to devalue the dollar. We drafted the paper with Paul Volcker and submitted it to President Nixon and President Pompidou. They asked for some modification and they themselves wrote on the paper, altering some wording. After that, we gave the paper to be typewritten, there was a formal communiqué, and then we left. So the original document was just left sitting on the table. It is now in the French archives.

What was significant was that this devaluation didn't succeed in stabilizing the situation. And there was a second round, the Smithsonian agreement, which was, in fact, the beginning of the new monetary era of flotation. We—the French—opposed it. Our idea was to have a new set of parities but to keep a fixed-exchange-rate system with adequate changes. And probably we were wrong, because we did not anticipate the oil shock and the extraordinary magnitude of capital movement that was created in the mid-'70s. It was impossible to deal with this movement with fixed parities. So at that time we tried to maintain an orderly system which was fixed but with adjustable parities, and we created certain bodies—the Group of Twenty—to propose some structure for that. But history went another way.

Our attitude was not similar to the German one. The Germans had to revalue from time to time due to the surpluses and due to speculation, which was pushing the D-mark up all the time. And they were tired of the endless disputes about the revaluation of the D-mark, because every time you had to choose a new parity, you had to draw conclusions about farm prices and all that. So it was the Germans who really wanted a floating system, not us.

Our position was different—and, in the French tradition, dogmatic. We had favored for some time a system in which the central, ultimate value would be gold and not the dollar; we thought that the dollar was linked to the monetary policy of an important country with a huge economy—but, of course, a country with its own national concerns and national policy. And so it was better to have gold at the center of the system.

As long as we believed that there could be real convertibility between gold and the dollar, there was no problem for us. But we saw very early that it could not work that way. And we had to create an additional credit system—the SDR—which the French proposed in '63 in Tokyo at the IMF meeting. Even this was not enough, because the additional liquidity was not meeting the demand and there were still the imbalances between the dollar and gold. Our idea was to have a system in which the network of fixed parities would be adjusted vis-à-vis gold from time to time when needed, every three or four years. So flotation was not the system we had in mind, and I would say that the first devaluation of the dollar by President Nixon and the Smithsonian agreement were more the Germans' concepts—that is, "We cannot handle the economic or financial imbalances with fixed parities; we have to have a floating system."

131

No one could have anticipated the oil shock—I just state a fact—no one. There was some logic to the oil shock, because it was very clear that it was a rare, valuable commodity. But the problem was that the real price, the fixed cost in Saudi Arabia at the time, was very low. Very farsighted people could envision that it would go up—as we can again now—but there was no perception by the economic leaders of the world that a price increase would come soon and with that magnitude; it was triggered not by the economic events but by a purely political event, the embargo. We were, with Japan, the largest importers of oil among all the countries relative to our GNP.

We had several reactions. On one side was to embark on a very large nuclear power program to try to disentangle us for the future. Today, due to that program, in France more than 65 percent of our electricity is nuclear-powered, so we are in the best position in Western Europe because our energy costs are the lowest of all. Now, with the relatively low price of oil, the situation is more or less in balance. But with any increase we would have significantly lower energy costs than, for example, West Germany or Italy, which have practically no nuclear power.

The other side was economic policy. At that time, the overall situation of the French economy was tightly regulated because of the long-standing pressure of administrative policy, due to the war and to the dominant theory of the time. We reestablished price controls, at least for prices of chemicals and other products derived from oil. Then, since we could not absorb the entire shock by a movement in prices, we had to create a counterpart to the shock. And the idea was to borrow the cost, or a part of the cost, of the shock, which we did. The figures are difficult to quote because the value of the franc, of the dollar, of everything, has changed. And compared to the magnitude of the present situation, it's not enormous. But it was enormous at the time.

So we arranged a network of borrowing facilities to be able to pay for the additional cost of imports. In fact, we used it very little; it was a precaution, and we were able to absorb a larger part of it than we expected. But the error, the mistake we made overall, was to try to absorb the oil shock not through the prices people paid but through forecasts of the value of the economy. We

132

created two major imbalances. One was in the companies; prices were frozen but the costs were increasing, and the pressure on their profits was very strong. And the other aspect was that people expected that they didn't have to pay for the shock, so they kept the same demands for wage increases from '73 to '78. Everyone expected their income to go on increasing, so this created a second imbalance in the economy. And the result of that was pressure on our foreign trade in the years '75 and '76. People accepted politically that we had to organize a counterpart for the shock, but they did not realize their own resources would have to support it also. We could have done this at the time through the movement of prices, as the Germans did. But if we had let prices of gasoline or oil go up, then the customers would have had to pay a large part of the bill. But we didn't, and later we couldn't.

As for foreign borrowing, we had repaid all our debts, we had practically no foreign debt. I can remember very well. I was very young, a junior minister, and I went to the United States to pay the last part of our war debt. I had a check which I brought to President Kennedy, and I handed it to him; it was a political gesture to indicate that we had gotten rid of all our war and postwar debt. And the reason we weren't eager to see the French Republic asking for foreign loans again was that the problem was not an imbalance of the *state;* it was an imbalance of companies. The French state didn't buy oil; but Electricité de France and several other groups of big oil consumers did, so it was better to have the companies borrowing by themselves. And it was also good to let some French agencies go into the international market to get accustomed to it. So it was not because we were afraid of a state loan, but because it was not required.

We had just a few gold-linked bonds at the beginning, before the oil shock. The French people were never very secure about the quality of loans. The French signature is very good because we have always met our commitments, whatever happens, but at times, due to inflation, investors were ill-protected. So when we used a gold reference, it was to give some security to people as the prevailing rates were changing from fixed to floating. And we didn't use it for foreign loans; we did it just for domestic loans. And, in fact, the state had a rather large gold stock. It was a no-risk situation, because what we had to pay to investors we had as a counterpart in our own public stock.

This was also the period of the growth of the Euromarkets. At the beginning, French banks were at some disadvantage. The Euromarket developed purely for American motives; it was a question of regulations, of restrictions on the way to borrow and to issue loans. And it was easier not to use the domestic market. It was located in London and at the beginning was only a Eurodollar market. Our banking system is very large, and at the time it was probably the second in the world, after the U.S. So it was abnormal for French banks to have such a limited part of the Eurodollar market. When the Eurocurrencies started to develop—but this was later—then the French banks were active. But, of course, business was done more by foreign subsidiaries than by the banks, and I think it's better to have the banks themselves involved and not through some Luxembourg or London-based companies. More flexible regulation on our part was certainly needed. We started it; the new administration is doing it again, and I think that's good.

The next market in which we want to be more active will be the ECU market, and I hope that the French banking system will move speedily enough to be very active in promoting financial operations in ECUs. But at the moment, the size of the market is still too limited, in my view, and I hope that it will enlarge. The SDR never became a currency; it is a unit of account for credit in limited IMF operations. The ECU, curiously, started to be a currency without anyone telling it to do so. We started by using the ECU as an intervention instrument for central banks; now it is used as a currency for operations, accounting, settlements. I think the maneuver for the next few years will be to let or to encourage this development of the ECU as a currency and also to develop a structure which will develop official use as an intervention instrument. The two movements must be parallel yet meet at some point, because we cannot have two ECUs—official and private; they must be one and the same.

So we must act on the institutional side, for the official use of the ECU, by creating what I call a central bank of the central banks. It's not exactly the American system. We have a network of central banks which will go on issuing their own currencies, at least for the time being. But we need to have a central bank of the central banks for the administration of the ECU system, and I

134

hope it will be decided upon sometime next year. At the same time, we must review all the offsetting conditions that should be improved to facilitate the private use of the ECU. One is the acceptance by all the countries of the ECU for the denomination of deposits and loans; this is a question for Germany, but I think they will make the decision. The second condition is to have free movement of capital all over Europe.

The agreement to use the ECU as a central bank intervention instrument was drafted by the heads of government. I had a meeting in Bremen with Schmidt and Callaghan and people from the other countries. In fact, the heads of government had been finance ministers before, particularly Schmidt and myself. And it became a formal agreement in '79. So there was a kind of old-friends' network during all that period—[George] Shultz was also our partner all the time; we had a personal relationship. It's always an important question to know if personal relationships matter, and certainly they do. They do not change attitudes or solutions, but they help you to communicate. And we had a very easy communication. We called each other quite frequently and unofficially, and when we had a problem or difficulty, the instinct was to call each other to know how we were reacting, what was being prepared. I think it was very helpful. But it is dissolved now.

Editor: David Cudaback

Gerald Tsai

Chairman PRIMERICA CORP.

Gerald Tsai was one of the "performance" money managers fea-
tured on the cover of the second issue of *Institutional Investor* magazine. It was a style he personified at both Fidelity Management &
Research Co. and the Manhattan Fund, which he launched in
1965. It, in turn, was sold to CNA Financial Corp. in 1968, and
five years later Tsai left CNA to head up his own brokerage firm,
G. Tsai & Co., which soon bought a small insurance holding company, Associated Madison Cos. Tsai expanded Associated Madison
into a financial services company, then sold it to American Can Co.
in 1982. Tsai joined the company as executive vice president and
in 1986 was named its chairman. American Can was rechristened
Primerica Corp. in 1987.

In 1967 I suppose my mind was totally on equities, the stock
market, looking for a hot stock to buy and relative performance against other funds. I went to see all kinds of companies
and came back and bought some stocks or sold some stocks and
that was about it. So I would say that even though the stock
market is a broad subject, because you're looking at all kinds of
businesses, today, looking back, it's pretty provincial, pretty narrow, basically. I wouldn't do it again.

Nineteen sixty-seven was a very good year for the Manhattan
Fund; we were up 58 percent, as I recall. I think among the big
funds, we were best. So I must have been feeling pretty good that
year. Not the following year. The following year felt lousy. The
stocks that did so well in '67 did not do well in '68. Either I
overstayed, or I had the wrong stocks. But I think the press has

been very unkind, because Fidelity Capital started in 1958, so you might say that from 1958 to 1967 we were always on top. We had one bad year, in 1968, and I've been killed in the press ever since. Like a ballplayer, right? If you have ten good games and one lousy game, you're a bum. I don't think that's fair.

Of course, we also had so much money coming in that it became a big subject the year before. Then you follow that with bad performance and a lot of people felt, "He made a lot of money selling the fund to CNA and I didn't make any money; I lost money."

We sold the fund to CNA in April 1968. I became the largest stockholder of CNA, and what I hoped was that they would diversify. The press said that I was looking to go to Chicago to work, the implication being that I was looking for the top job and didn't get it. This is where sometimes I really get upset at the press. They don't look at the facts. I was just building a big house in Greenwich at the time, so why would I be going to Chicago? I can't say that I had the ambition to have the top job at CNA, whereas when I got into American Can, I did have great aspiration to be CEO—though I absolutely did not go there with that promise. We began to talk about it when I was made vice chairman in June of 1983.

I didn't learn much from dealing in the CNA environment that was useful in moving into the top job at American Can. The lesson I needed to learn for this job was patience, how to deal with people, not to do everything yesterday. Accept frustration from time to time, but keep your eye on your same goal. But age taught me that; I didn't begin to get good at it until ten years ago. What also taught me patience was what I did after I sold my CNA stock and resigned in 1973—running G. Tsai & Co. It wasn't easy to run a small brokerage.

It was a tough period. The market was bad. We were a small institutional firm. I didn't want to build a big brokerage business because I kept reminding myself of Ira Haupt—you remember, they went bankrupt. We didn't take positions unless I wanted it for the firm. If Dreyfus called and said will you take on 50,000 U.S. Steel, that's the kind of business I didn't want.

I had always been on the buy side, and now I was on the sell side. Big difference. Customers are customers, so when you're on the buy side and dealing with institutional brokers, you pick up the phone and they jump, right? Now it was the reverse. I tried to do my best, but it was frustrating. A small example: I was used to getting brokerage reports from the whole Street because I love to read them. I still do it today. But at that time who was going to send them to me? So every Thursday for many years, I sent a driver to Larry Tisch's office and got them. Larry doesn't want to be bothered to read them, you know, so he piles them up.

It was the period in which I was operating on a small scale. That didn't feel too comfortable. But it was okay, it really was. For one thing, G. Tsai was always very profitable. I don't think we ever made less than 100 percent return per year. But there was no glory or anything.

In 1978 I found a little insurance company called Associated Madison. I bought control and kept G. Tsai for a number of years, but I decided to use Associated Madison as a base to build a financial services company. It was a tiny little nothing. I think their earnings were $800,000 and the stock was $4.

The reasons to build from an insurance base are simple. Even a small insurance company controls a lot of assets that you normally wouldn't be able to control. So that's No. 1.

Number 2, the securities gains that you make out of the portfolio go into the book value of the company, and insurance companies are sold at two times book. So if I make a dollar buying and selling IBM, that's all it's worth. But once it's in the insurance company portfolio and you sell the company, you sell it for two bucks. I don't know any business that good. And then you have tax advantages; a third of the earnings are deferred.

We built Associated Madison through acquisitions, and people have always said that I overpay for companies. They're wrong. I'll give you just a couple of examples. Just two years ago we bought Berg Enterprises for $125 million. Earnings were $14 million. This year they're going to earn $40 million. So I overpaid? That's what they said. On the day of the closing, the discount rate was reduced and our portfolio went up $14 million that same day. When we bought American Capital in 1983, everybody said, "That's ridiculous—Jerry Tsai paid three times book." It had $3.3 billion in assets under management. It's now $17 billion. We paid $38 million, and we have gotten $75 to $80 million of dividends out of that company. We sold 17 percent to the public for $90

139

million. And we have a leftover market value of $450 million. I'll be delighted to go through every one of them, so I'm not just picking the good ones. The reason I was willing to overpay was because I was analyzing them like stocks. I still think of myself as a securities analyst, you know. Nobody pays 100 times earnings for Xerox unless you think you know what Xerox's earnings will be five years out.

But I didn't have the capital to buy all the situations I wanted. Then on April 8, 1981, there was a very interesting story in *The New York Times* in which Bill Woodside said he was going to sell off a fourth of American Can's assets to go into service businesses, and perhaps financial services. So I wrote him a letter, saying: "I would like to come and see you. Perhaps we can have some kind of joint venture."

When I finally met Bill, he had no jacket on. Generally, he works in his shirtsleeves. He was very warm, quite direct and open-minded. And he didn't say, "Well, I'll talk to you again." He didn't leave it in limbo. He just said, "It sounds interesting. Why don't you go back and put your thoughts down on paper?"

I had all that in my head for years, so it just took me a weekend to write it. I made out a table of ten specific companies, some public, that were the kinds I thought we should buy. One of them was Dreyfus, because it's a great company and it was a very cheap stock at the time. Fidelity? I can't afford it. And it couldn't be bought anyway. No, no, it's going to go to Johnson the fourth, the fifth, the sixth. Of those ten, we now own quite a few. I can't remember exactly which were on that first list, but before Associated Madison was sold, I mentioned to American Can people that we ought to buy four names [Penn Corp., Transport Life, Voyager Insurance and Triad Life], and we own all four.

After my memo, we continued to talk from May to October about American Can buying 20 percent of us. I was not interested in selling more. But during June, July and August, I lost several opportunities because of lack of funds. And I got sick of it. You know, I got tired. So then I decided, well, maybe if I join American Can, I'll have the capital to do certain things. So finally in October we arrived at a different solution. American Can would buy 100 percent of Associated Madison.

At the same time that this was going on, our company was 24 percent owned by Lincoln National, so I was kind of torn as to whether we should do business with American Can or Lincoln. They're both big companies, right? But I felt, if American Can really wants to be in the financial services business, at least I can be fairly important. At Lincoln National, they're full of insurance companies and investment people, and so I'm just one of hundreds of people out there. And there were several suggestions that I gave Lincoln in the financial services area during 1981 that they were not willing to pursue. So I called Ian Rolland, the chairman of Lincoln National, and said, "Do you have any problem with this?" And he was an absolute gentleman. He said: "Well, we like our investment in your company and we think it has a lot of potential. But on the other hand, if this makes you happy, we certainly will go along with it." They also made a lot of money, so Lincoln wasn't exactly crying.

It took a year from the day of my letter to Bill to the final papers. I have my letter dated April 8, 1981, and the company's press release announcing the acquisition on April 8, 1982, together in one frame. It was a long time, wasn't it—one year? Was I impatient? There were moments. . . .

When we made our agreement, Bill and I had lunch. And at the end he put his hand on my back and said, "Jerry, I'm making a billion-dollar bet on you." So I said—at the time we were earning about $8 million—I said, "Bill, on your 65th birthday I will deliver to you $100 million of earnings." And I remember Bill said, "That's a pretty ambitious statement." And I said, "It'll be there." So Bill turned 65 in January 1987, and in 1986 we had delivered close to $300 million of earnings. So I feel that I've done my job.

You know, he was very supportive. A very early acquisition was Penn Corp. I met Bill on top of the escalator one day. He said: "Where were you the last couple of days? I didn't see you." So I said, "I went to Los Angeles." He said, "Working on something?" I said, "Yeah." So he asked me what the company was and "How much is it going to cost us?" I said, "300," and he said, "Million?" And I said, "Of course." We laughed. At the time, our market value was $500 million. And we bought that company.

And so with his help, with the company's money and, I think, with my hard work, we built something here. So I feel very attached to the man, because if he hadn't given me the opportunity, I would not be where I am today, although I have worked hard. Everybody is supposed to work hard, but you have to have an opportunity. The same opportunity Mr. Johnson [Edward Johnson II, chairman of Fidelity when the Capital Fund was launched] gave me. If Mr. Johnson had said the first time, "Jerry, I'm not going to let you go be a portfolio manager; we won't start Fidelity Capital Fund," I guess I wouldn't be anybody. I don't know.

So when Bill retired, I spent a lot of time on his goodbye party. We had 342 people. I planned the menu and I picked the wine. Dom Perignon was the bar champagne, and the first course was beluga caviar. After dinner we had a video on which people from different areas of Bill's life said things about him. And I gave instructions that I didn't want this crazy music of today's generation that we can't dance to. We had a seventeen-piece band, and we concentrated on big-band music of my generation. I used to play the clarinet, sax and piano, and I love that music.

And then in my speech I said, "Bill, you served the company well for 37 years, and it is now my pleasure to present you with a gold watch." And I gave him a Tiffany box, but inside was a bright-red toy convertible sports car and a set of keys. And then the curtains opened, and the picture of the real car was on the screen. I know it sounds pretty lavish, but after what he did for the shareholders, they should want to give him ten sports cars! Then [American Can board member and Dewey, Ballantine senior partner] Joe Califano presented him with a gift certificate announcing that Dewey, Ballantine would defend him on all his speeding tickets. Bill likes to drive rather fast. Afterwards everybody called me. They thought it was the warmest retirement dinner. Everybody was dancing.

Now I have eight years to run this business. I think my role at American Can is much broader than what some newspapers seem to think. I changed the style. The corporate headquarters staff is down more than 50 percent. Corporate organization has been simplified, and the incentive program is much more aggressive. I work with the guys every day, whether it's the comptroller or

M&A or corporate finance or human resources. And I formed a president's council three years ago, where once a quarter all the division CEOs in the financial services sector come to New York. We spend two days together. It's like my family. These are my buddies. We talk about who's doing what to whom in the industry, what new products do we have and how will Division A hook up with Division B. That's the fun part. These are my guys. I had dinner with them when I was just made chairman of the company, and the guys gave me a little Casio piano.

So I'm interested in three things: in managing, in growing the company internally and, of course, in making acquisitions. Because through internal growth, let's face it, unless you're a scientific company, to grow much more than 15 percent is not easy. So if I want to go from $4 billion in sales to $20 billion by the time I retire, don't you think we have to make a few acquisitions along the way? You got to. I have eight years. I'd better be plenty brilliant.

There were many days in the last five years when by 3:00 in the afternoon I had no idea whether the market was up or down. That's not the impression people had of my life 30 years ago. I think the fact that I don't look at the stock market every hour is very helpful, and the fact that I don't look at the relative performance of Putnam vis-à-vis Manhattan vis-à-vis Keystone, etc. Because you can't manage a portfolio as if you're running a race every five minutes. That's stupid; it really is. So if I were starting my life all over again, 25 years or so of managing portfolios, I wouldn't give a hoot about the relative performance of other funds. And the same is true at American Can. I don't care what other people do. If General Motors is selling its mortgage business and if we have a mortgage business, you can't influence me one bit just because GM is selling, whereas in the old days I might have been tempted. I might think, oh, I'd better get on board. That is the main difference today: I'll do what I think is right, and I don't care what somebody else is doing.

And here's where patience comes in. Suppose there's a major acquisition in front of me today that is heavily involved in the financial services business. I may not do it today, contrary to ten years ago, because I say to myself, "Well, 1982 was the bottom for financial assets. And we bought Transport Life and Penn Corp., and then a couple of years later we bought a mortgage origination business. But the financial cycle was right." But now you say to

143

yourself: "Hey, 1987 is five years out from 1982, and long-term rates are down 700 basis points. In 1982 we bought insurance companies with bonds at 68 cents on the dollar. Today they are above water. So maybe this is not such a good time to buy another financial services company that's interest-oriented. Wait. Either wait for the stock market to go down or rates to turn." So you say to yourself every day: "Gosh, I'd like to do that one. But damn it, I'm not going to do it." Now, I think that's quite different from twenty years ago, because it takes a lot of discipline and patience. That is a major difference that I can see in myself.

Editor: Heidi S. Fiske

Muriel Siebert

Chairperson MURIEL SIEBERT & CO.

The year 1987 marked a twentieth anniversary for Muriel Siebert:
In December 1967 she bought her own seat on the New York
Stock Exchange. She was the first woman to do so. From July 1977
to May 1982 she was New York State superintendent of banks.
She resigned that post to run for the U.S. Senate, coming in sec-
ond out of three candidates in the New York State Republican pri-
mary. At the beginning of 1983, she returned to her firm, Muriel
Siebert & Co.

It was Jerry Tsai who gave me the idea to buy a seat on the
exchange. That was during an era when a lot of people would
not let me work for them in their research department and go
out of town representing the firm. That was the Street at that
time. They just didn't have women going out representing them
and they weren't going to.

I was in Jerry's office and I said to him, "Jerry, where can I go
where I can get credit on the business I'm writing?" And he said,
"Why don't you buy a seat?" And I said, "Don't be ridiculous." I
knew there were no women on the exchange. And he said, "I
don't think there's a law against it."

So I took the exchange's constitution home. You had to be over
21, you had to have a business purpose, and you had to be able to
finance it. He was right. There was no law against it. But until
Jerry mentioned it to me, I had never thought about it. And that
idea became a challenge.

There was some hostility when it got out what I was doing. A lot of people were *very* unhappy. I couldn't get sponsored by anybody that was a member on the floor. Mine were all upstairs people. The people that I had asked, when the time came, they just ran out the door.

But Ed Merkle, who ran Madison Fund, was super when I bought the seat. He tried to get me a couple of sponsors. Jim O'Brien, who was an upstairs partner at Salomon Brothers, became one of my sponsors, and so did Ken Ward, who was one of the deans of the analysts at Hayden Stone. And they each told me that they were called over during interviews and asked, "Gentlemen, what do you know about Miss Siebert's personal life?"

So I learned you can't break a tradition that was 175 years old and have everybody love you. It's got nothing to do with me as a person. People just like things status quo. One governor of the exchange said to me, "And how many more are there *behind* you?" Like I was gonna lead a doggone parade onto the floor.

And twenty years later, where are they? I was determined. But I didn't run down to the floor 'til I was a member a year, year and a half. I was a trainee and I had to wear my square little badge, and I had to have my sponsor with me every time I executed a trade. I wanted to prove to people that I had bought the seat for business purposes, not for publicity. Then I passed the floor test. That meant I could execute any order that I wanted to down there.

Now *that* made a lot of people angry. They thought I shouldn't work the seat. I could own it, but they thought a man should be executing the trades. I had a couple of people come up and tell me that.

And some of it . . . some of it was not nice.

You just had to stand there and cry. All you could do was cry.

And yet for every one of those, there was somebody who was super nice. You know, there's always this balance. While you don't expect somebody that you know to turn out to be a real bastard, there's somebody that you don't know well that turns out to be a special, super person.

Thank God there's a balance. It would have been too much.

About the time I decided to buy a seat, [the advertising firm of] Albert Frank Guenther Law had bought a whole-page ad in *The*

146

Wall Street Journal, saying, "We've lost our biggest account, Merrill Lynch, and we're looking for business." So I called and said, "I'm buying a seat later this month, and I'm not Merrill Lynch." They sent me Jack Penninger. He said, "We'll use your picture." I said, "No. No member of the stock exchange has ever done anything like that." And he said, "You're *different* from other members of the stock exchange." So there was a picture. That was the Meet Miss Muriel Siebert ad.

But what really made people mad was the hundred-dollar-bill ad.

I went into Mayday very professionally and silently. But about a year later, I put an ad in *The Wall Street Journal*—it was Jack's idea—a full page of me cutting a hundred-dollar bill in half. When we first shot it, he didn't like the expression. He said: "Mickey, you have to look like Ginnie Sweetest. You are cutting the bill, you are cutting their commissions." So I said, "Okay. Girl Scouts of America all the way."

But Wall Street didn't like it. Hey, it was a rough environment at the time. Not everybody loved it. But a girl's gotta make a living.

But, you know, when you have X dollars, you don't need X dollars more. I don't understand the people walking around with a suitcase of cash. I have a Mercedes, I have a Chrysler convertible, I have a home in East Hampton. I live in the best building there is in New York, or pretty close. What am I going to do? I need a third car? To do what? I mean, there are yardsticks. There is a group downtown, their only sense of accomplishment is, are they worth more money this month than they were last month. I don't understand some of these people. I feel sorry for them.

In politics it isn't just money. You can make a difference. I remember when Governor [Hugh] Carey first came to ask me to be state banking superintendent. I had been on the New York State Economic Development Board, and as I got to know the reality of politics, I realized I was a "twofer"—I was a Republican and a woman. Because, you know, you've got to have one from Column A and one from Column B. I'd only met the governor once or twice. He was very honest. He said, "I'm looking for a woman." In this case, I was a beneficiary of the women's movement.

Being banking superintendent was one problem after another. That's why I stayed so long. Because if it's a meet, eat and greet job, then you're wasting your life being there, then you've got only the worst of the bureaucracy. You need the kick and the thrill. With all the aggravation that I've had, I know that I accomplished something.

Our first real problem was the Municipal Credit Union. The MCU was a $135 million institution in trouble and we took possession to rehabilitate—the first time it was ever done in the state. We got a lot of flak for that and a lot of respect. The *Daily News* had gotten ahold of the problems there and made it a front page. So I stood in line at the place one day, and I was very sensitive to the race problem—I shook hands with a white person and then a black person, a white person and then a black person or a Hispanic. And I'd say, "Your money's safe, it's insured." And the answer was, "I don't care, lady, you look honest, but. . . ."

I was sued when we put it back. I had said that anybody that was on the board when we took possession should not be allowed to go back to the board again. I was knocked out by the judges in New York. They said I had to prove charges against each director. I said, "Wait a minute, why should you tell me I have to retain the people who brought me Pearl Harbor?"

But the main thing is, the institution's doing well. Sure, I was embarrassed and I lost, but I saved it.

The Iranian banks were fascinating, too. You know, every once in a while you have a lucky little angel on your shoulder. What happened was, the hostages were taken the day before election day. And state employees do not work on election day. That must be the eleventh or twelfth commandment: "You shall not work, you shall go in the voting booths." So I was watching the television news in the morning and I saw the hostages. I knew we had charters for four Iranian banks. And I knew that banks could wire out their deposits. You can wire out your assets in a half hour. So I called the deputy in charge of the examiners, and I said, "Get into the Iranian banks."

I didn't know what was going to happen, but I knew there was trouble. I knew we were their prime regulator. I just felt there was something. And he gave me a hard time. So I said, "I'm telling you, I want examiners in the four Iranian banks tomorrow morning." And we got in there. And we watched every telex going in and going out for a week—banks they were loaning money to, banks they had deposits with.

I started calling some of the banks personally, the big ones. I remember I called Bob Abboud at First Chicago. He said, "You're in there?" I said, "Yeah, I just want a call if there's any unusual activities in your accounts." And he said, "Good for you." I called the head of Bank of America, and he said, "You have no right going in there." But I just felt that as their prime regulators, we had an obligation.

Then we had the Marine Midland problem. Now, when Hongkong and Shanghai Bank came in originally and said they wanted to buy it, I thought, "What a good idea." And then I started to think. First of all, contrary to belief, Marine Midland was in good financial condition at that time. Before we considered a decision, we sent an examiner in there that was so tough, he would classify his mother. They were not earning what they should have been earning, but this was not a case of a bank going broke.

The second thing was, we could not get the information we wanted out of Hongkong and Shanghai. We wanted a list of stockholders. They said, "None of your business." I said, "But we get it from every bank that we regulate." They said no. Also, I said: "You want to come and you want to buy a bank that is No. 1 or No. 2 in the state, big in Rochester, Syracuse, Buffalo? You will continue to support these communities?" "Oh, no." And they didn't. They changed charters. They went from a state bank to a federal bank, and the deal went through.

The governor was not happy with my position on this. That was the only issue where we had serious problems. They tried to fire me. But it blew over. And we became friends again when I was fighting for the savings banks. The savings banks is where I saved the system.

I worked so hard on that. I came home, dropped my clothes, fell into bed. Lord, what day is it? But I worked with Howard Baker [then senator from Tennessee], and when you work with the best in the country, you know you're doing it for a reason. You're not doing it because you're going to make $59.29. You feel that you can make a contribution.

What had happened was very simple. The usury rate had been 8.5 percent in the state for years. They had all these twenty-year mortgages lying around that they were stuck with. All of a sudden the rates went up. So people took the money from the 5.5 percent day-of-deposit, day-of-withdrawal account, and they shoved it into 12 percent six-month certificates. So you've got income coming in at 8.5 percent and you're paying 12 percent for the funds.

I knew that this was a major problem. At that time, according to the constitution of the state of New York, all savings banks had to be mutual institutions. It was not in my power to sell them to a commercial bank. That was later changed. We would have had to take possession of the institution, declare it to be insolvent and sell the assets. You can do that if you have one bank that's going broke. You can't do that if you have an industry. Because the public won't take it. You'll get a run. You'll do it once, you'll do it twice, and then you'll get a run.

I sent the governor a memo, and I made the rounds. I had private meetings with Senator Baker and a meeting with Mr. Garn [Jake Garn, then Senate minority leader and head of the banking commission]. They looked at the list, asked me questions. [Senator Alfonse] D'Amato was just in office. He called me up because he wasn't at the meeting with Baker and Garn and their AAs. He told me, "How dare you see these people without my permission?" I mean, I got an industry that's going broke!

Then Baker said to me, "Who are you seeing next?" I said, "I'm seeing Senator Proxmire." That was one of the nice things about politics. I walk down the hall, Prox is standing there, opening the door, "Come on in, Mickey." They finally passed a bill in Albany to help us so the banks could use FDIC paper as capital.

When I left the state, after I made my bid for the Senate, there were problems when I got my firm out of its blind trust. But they're over now. I still get a thrill out of doing things that are connected with the business, but do I get a thrill out of writing 500 tickets a day as opposed to 400 tickets a day? The answer is no. But when I make a step like the Conrail deal, the answer is yes.

When the Conrail thing got started, we found that people were calling us: "We saw the stock's coming up, can you get us some?" So I definitely had a business reason for going into that deal. And I said to myself, if I got into it, I was going to perform. And I have been all over the country and I have been calling the accounts, and I've talked to people I haven't talked to for a while and I did my homework.

And at the same time, I realized that the black firms, God bless 'em, were going to get a law passed saying any sale of government assets must have minorities. And I realized I had to take a stand.

I'm gonna make sure that the women are included. Because if I don't do it, what constitutes a minority? Blacks, Hispanics, Eskimos, Indians. American Indians, Aleutians, Guam, Mexicans, Pakistanis, Japanese Americans, Chinese Americans? And I say, what the hell, nobody's ever done anything for me. Nobody's ever done anything for any woman. So I said, just deal me in.

I still think it's a great business for women and I still encourage young women to go into it. Wall Street is still the place where you can make more money. I am a feminist, but in my own way. I've gone through a lot of not-niceness. After I was a member, on a visit to England I became the second woman to go onto the floor of the London Stock Exchange. The queen was the first. They had reciprocity with New York, so that's how I got in there. And they were shocked. They took me around, in their hats and tails, and then I started talking to a couple of specialists, and they were surprised, because I knew what I was talking about. Look, there was a period when that was not considered nice for a woman.

Still, there have been strides. Women are coming up, 'cause they're making money. But it's very late. I've been outspoken about the lack of women partners on Wall Street. Some of these women are making three, four, five hundred thousand a year, but they've been passed over. I think the litmus test is going to come when some of these gals have a million bucks in the bank, and they realize that they have as much money as they need in this world. And will they then pound the table and say I want to be a partner or I'm leaving? There have been too many of the women that I knew that have gone out on their own, and if you start questioning them, it's because they did not have equality. They'll give you other reasons, but when you get right down to it, that's what it was.

Editor: Amy C. Pershing

Joseph Perella and Bruce Wasserstein

Co-Heads of Investment Banking FIRST BOSTON CORP.

When an ex-accountant named Joseph Perella joined First Boston Corp. fresh from business school in 1972, the firm had no M&A department and, what's more, had cause to look askance at all merger activity. From that unpropitious beginning, Perella managed to fashion First Boston into an M&A powerhouse that today has a staff of more than 160 merger professionals and an annual deal volume of $75 billion. He could not have done it, however, without the help from his co-head of M&A, Bruce Wasserstein. Hiring the gifted deal maker in 1977 was probably Perella's own greatest deal.

JOSEPH PERELLA

Way back in 1973, right at the time the firm sent out its broadcast that I was going to be put in charge of mergers and acquisitions, Felix Rohatyn was on the cover of *Business Week,* and I remember reading about all the fees he had collected working on deals. I was so impressed. I said: God, this is really a great business to be in. You don't use any of the firm's capital—at least you didn't in those days—and you make all these nice fees. You know, this is a *great* business. It wasn't like underwriting, where you actually had to take a capital risk. So I was very inspired by seeing Felix Rohatyn on the cover of *Business Week,* and I said to myself, "Well, you know, someday if I work hard, I'll be on the cover of a magazine." I thought of that as a sort of fantasy, never expecting it to really happen—though it did.

The entire M&A department at the time I was put in charge was one person: me. I didn't know it at the time, but First Boston was in the throes of a monumental lawsuit, which was later to become a famous Supreme Court case: *Bangor Punta* v. *Chris-Craft*. First Boston had advised Piper Aircraft on a takeover defense against Chris-Craft and later helped Bangor Punta, the white knight, get control of Piper. I think First Boston earned $10,000, or maybe $40,000—some small amount of money. The firm got sued by Chris-Craft and lost the lower court case and was on the hook for principal plus interest of around $38 million—this at a time when First Boston's capital was less than $100 million. Luckily, the verdict was overturned by the Supreme Court, which said basically that the only people that had standing to sue over a registration statement [Bangor Punta had inadvertently published false financial data in its prospectus] are those who've made an investment decision based on the statement and not the loser of a takeover fight.

The suit had cast a pall over the department—M&A was a dirty word at First Boston. I spent 1973 to 1975 just building up my own credibility with the managing directors. Then in fall 1975 a great turning point came. That was when George Shinn left Merrill Lynch and joined us as chairman and CEO. First Boston was at the time in a decline, though the rest of the Street hadn't really caught on to the fact. It didn't have a clear vision of the future.

Before George arrived, we had made some progress in M&A. There were a good number of merger assignments in the early 1970s that came from the house accounts. In December of 1973, after I'd been at it ten months, we represented Cargill in a raid on Missouri Portland Cement. It was a hostile raid, and that was a year before Inco bid for ESB, when the so-called blue-chip raid was made famous. I guess the only reason ours wasn't considered a blue-chip raid was because no one knew who Cargill was. It was a grain-trading, private company in

Minneapolis, but it had a net worth of a billion dollars, and that made it pretty blue chip for us.

After Shinn had spent nine months studying all the different departments of the firm, he made a presentation to investment banking and said: "First Boston is like a sailing ship. It's easy to change directions, but we really need some auxiliary power and, Joe, we're going to get you help." In his opening line he singled out mergers and acquisitions as an area that needed a lot more resources. So with that mandate, I was really able to recruit people, both internally and externally.

We soon started doing more business. In '74–'75 I got to work with [Morgan Stanley's Robert] Greenhill [on International Paper Co.'s acquisition of General Crude Oil], and that was a great experience. Bob had been doing M&A for a while, and I really got to see the personality of the M&A person—the force, the perseverance and staying power it takes to be successful in the business. I had certain role models at First Boston, and I'm not saying that they were bad—they were models of professionalism and, most importantly, integrity. But they weren't merger and acquisition role models. Greenhill was different from a lot of the people I had been used to working with around here. I didn't say better, just different: much more aggressive, much more persistent—dogged—in pursuit of the client's objective. And *very* tenacious. Investment bankers tended to have a softer touch.

Late in 1976 we were hired by Combustion Engineering, the potential white knight, in a situation involving Gray Tool. Skadden, Arps [Slate, Meagher & Flom], which I'd been working very closely with, had a conflict, so I called up a lawyer I'd heard a lot about named Sam Butler, and hired [Cravath, Swaine & Moore] for the deal. We—myself and Tom Hill—went over to a meeting [at Combustion Engineering's counsel, Shearman & Sterling], and Butler showed up with another partner and this young associate named Bruce Wasserstein. I don't think I was at the meeting more than twenty minutes before Bruce had virtually taken charge. He was telling everyone the way the deal should be done from the lawyer's standpoint, and I said to myself, "Holy mackerel, this guy is unreal." It was one of those moments in life where I knew I had met a rare individual. Bruce had the ability to take what he knew about the law and translate it into action that was going to accomplish the client's objective.

155

We went down to Houston; we represented Combustion, the white knight; and we came away with the prize, Gray Tool. I got a chance to work with Steve Friedman of Goldman Sachs, who, again, personified to me what was the best about the merger and acquisition business.

After the [successful completion of the deal], I called up [Butler] and said: "Sam, I've got to tell you, I was so impressed with the job Cravath did. I'd like to figure out a way for us to work more closely together, maybe giving you an exclusive on our legal advice or whatever. But I've got one condition." Over lunch I told him my condition was that Wasserstein be permanently assigned to First Boston. He said: "Oh, you don't understand. I can't do that." Bruce was supposed to transition off of Butler's M&A team and go to work on Cravath's municipal bond team. I said, "Oh, my God, I can't take the time to understand this Byzantine structure at Cravath."

One day not long afterward—it was in April of 1977, I think—Harry Gray's United Technologies raided Babcock & Wilcox. And there I was, doing every function in the merger group. I was reading the tape; I was dialing for dollars, as we say; I was the new-business calling effort; I was doing everything. I called up Cities Service and said: "Have you ever thought about getting into the power end of the energy business through Babcock & Wilcox? You know, they're probably looking for a white knight." And they said, "Gee, that's interesting." So they hired First Boston to study Babcock & Wilcox.

We needed a lawyer if Cities was going to be a white knight, so I called up Wasserstein. I said, "Bruce, do I have to call a partner to hire your firm, or can I call an associate?" He said: "Gee, no one ever asked me that. I'll get back to you." And he called me back and he said, "No, you can hire an associate." I said: "Fine, I'm not calling Butler. I'm calling you to represent me. Our client is Cities Service in the Babcock & Wilcox affair." So we took two trips to Tulsa in the spring of 1977, and it was during those trips that, in addition to talking about the client's problem, I vented my frustration at trying to get the Cravath M&A team to include him.

I said: "You know, Bruce, why don't we cut through all this BS of trying to negotiate something out with Sam? Why don't you just come to work for us?" And he said, "Gee, I hadn't thought of that." Bruce came by the firm a few times, and I introduced him to some of the managing directors (at the time I was a vice president) and we negotiated a title—he was going to come in as a vice president—and established his starting salary, I have forgotten what it was [$100,000]. In summer '77 Bruce joined the merger group at First Boston.

We were now in a growth mode as far as staff but not yet in terms of revenue. Then in late 1977 we had two fortunate developments: We got hired by Combustion Engineering again, this time to go after Vetco, another oil service company, and we also got hired by Kennecott to go after Carborundum as a white knight after Carborundum had been raided by Eaton. I was involved in soliciting both of those pieces of business.

We continued to add staff, and in 1979 I felt we were really ready to break out. The rest of the Street also realized there was going to be a lot of M&A activity, and those firms that didn't have the necessary expertise, I knew, wanted to just go out and buy it. I felt sure Bruce could be the head of a group somewhere else on the Street. So I went to see my boss [then–investment banking chief] Jack Hennessey, and said, "Jack, look, I want Bruce to have the psychological equivalent of having his own group, and I'd like you to call him into your office right now and make him co-director of the M&A group with me." And he said, "You sure you want to do this?" I said: "Yeah. This'll work because I'm imposing it on *myself*. You're not imposing it on me." He said okay.

That was April 1979, and Bruce and I have been co-directors ever since. Then last February we were asked to head up not only M&A but all of investment banking. So it's been a really rewarding relationship. It's a *unique* relationship on Wall Street. I don't think either one of us could have ever accomplished separately what we did together, and I mean that. It takes a lot for any two people to share something and to work together at something—it's almost like a marriage.

What we like to think of as our crowning achievement was the Du Pont-Conoco takeover. Du Pont, which we represented, was perceived as a sleepy company relative to Mobil, Texaco and, of course, Seagram—all of them vying for Conoco. But First Boston achieved victory for Du Pont, mainly because of the deal's complex structure, the so-called Big Rube, after [cartoonist] Rube Goldberg. We nicknamed it the double-barreled two-step: We had a tender offer for 40 percent of Conoco plus an exchange offer, using Du Pont common stock, for 60 percent. It was an offer for 100 percent of the company, which was unique, and the structure, combined with a mistake by Seagram, enabled Du Pont to get control of Conoco.

We were now able to go out and market our track record. We said we do the difficult deals better. And look what happened. In 1982 Cities Service, which traditionally used Lehman Brothers Kuhn Loeb, brought us in as co-adviser on defense—that was our first big battle with Boone Pickens. American General, using another banker, attacked NLT. NLT counterattacked, and American General then brought us in as adviser—and the other banker dropped out—after we had made a presentation on how we could help the company.

When it all hit the fan, we got called in. Bill Agee of Bendix raided Martin Marietta; Martin Marietta counterattacked Bill Agee; United Technologies counterattacked Bill Agee. I made a presentation to Agee before United Technologies showed up, and I said: "Bill, your problems are bigger than Martin Marietta. You need help." When he did get counterattacked, I don't know where I was, but Bruce went over and followed up my presentation with his presentation. So we got brought in as adviser to Bendix after they'd gotten into the soup, and we arranged the deal with Allied.

I am very distressed to see what's happened to our industry as a result of the transgressions of a small group of people. There are thousands of people who work at First Boston, Goldman Sachs, Morgan Stanley and other firms who come to work every day and make an honest living. They're not crooks, but their futures are threatened by the acts of a few people who I think ought to be thrown in jail and given the stiffest sentences possible. But in the end, as long as human beings are involved, there's always going to be an ounce of corruption somewhere. It started with the Bible, right? Isn't that the story of the Garden of Eden?

BRUCE WASSERSTEIN

From the date I arrived at First Boston in the summer of 1977 through the following Thanksgiving, we had no business. We didn't have *one* deal. But we did do a lot of work on long-term strategies to differentiate First Boston in mergers from other firms. We realized that we would not be competitive at arranging deals on the golf course. Therefore, we tried to figure out whether we could be effective through the elbow-grease route, and what we saw was an opportunity to *professionalize* the M&A business. We said we will be more knowledgeable as to the conceptualization of transactions, the analysis of transactions and the implementation of transactions.

That was our strategy. What we next needed was to develop tactics to implement it and make ourselves competitive. On the conceptualization of transactions, we wanted to have, if you will, a creative group. We turned to an acquaintance of mine—Bill Lambert—who was a research analyst, and asked him to introduce us to people on Wall Street who might be good conceptualizers. We went through a group of people introduced by Bill—each worse than the former. They began getting so bad, we would stop going to the interviews. Finally, Bill said he had one more suggestion: possibly himself. The more we thought about it, the better the idea became. In fact, Bill turned out to have a unique talent for conceptualization.

On the analysis side, one of Bill's obligations—and ours—was to professionalize our whole system. At the time, people worked out mergers on the back of envelopes rather than through the management-consulting-type, by-the-pound analysis that's fairly standard now. We tried to go beyond computer printouts to get a *qualitative* analysis of companies, and that differentiated us.

We realized, though, that we had to go [even] deeper, to have some real understanding of companies. So we came up with this concept that our people should specialize by industry rather than cover everything. And we said, "Let's figure out what industries will be important [for mergers]," and identified two of the most obvious: financial services and energy. So all of a sudden we were transformed, on a knowledge basis, from being a noncompetitor to being a real competitor, if we had an opportunity.

The best example of how our merger approach had been

transformed was IC Industries' purchase of Pet in a hostile takeover [in 1978]. That deal combines the analysis elements— the evaluation elements—and the specialization. But it also demonstrated the third prong of the strategy: implementation skill. We were able to get a hostile deal done for a client [IC] that other people had considered too difficult to do. It was a surprising victory, with no white knight and only a small increase required over the initial bid.

We were building overhead, but whether it was because a rising tide lifts all boats or because of luck or because of some degree of skill, our bets did pay off with a little bit of patience. The key to this was the patience and support of [then–First Boston chairman] George Shinn, who was willing to invest and allow us to increase personnel at then-unheard-of rates. The buildup took us from ten transactions a year in the late 1970s to over 200 now and from four people in M&A to over 160.

We knocked on a lot of doors in the early years. I remember well going down to Houston nine years ago and saying that we were from First Boston and being asked by people, "How's the weather in Boston?" At the time, our wedge into seeing a CEO was to say, "We have an idea for you." People would listen to the idea, though they were rarely interested. But it would be an opportunity to build a bond or a relationship or an acquaintance-ship. What was really important [in drumming up new business] was the second-order effect. For example, getting the business in American General [in its takeover of NLT] was the proximate cause of our getting all the other Texas business.

The Du Pont acquisition of Conoco was a fascinating experience not only in the deal sense but also as a sociological insight into America. I remember thinking about the deal on the beach, trying to understand the second-order implications of the SEC rules [since changed] on multiple pools. But it was a deal of such complexity that it would have been very difficult to figure it out on an intuitive basis. *The New Yorker* ran an article about how complicated it was, that it was difficult to understand, and they were absolutely right [the deal involved an intricate double-tier bid].

We were also very pleased with the Marathon deal [in which First Boston fended off a takeover bid for the oil company by

Mobil and arranged its sale to USX]. In part that's because we got along as well as we did with the people we met in Findlay, Ohio [site of Marathon's headquarters]. I spent a lot of time out in Findlay, Ohio, and I know it well. The peculiarity of that deal at that time was that Marathon actually had the opportunity *not* to sell to [the then] U.S. Steel. The board was looking for ways to resist the offer, and in the end [the directors] realized that Marathon had an antitrust basis for fighting Mobil.

They had two proposals before them. One was from Gulf, and it had a provision that if the Mobil deal was blocked for antitrust reasons, Gulf would go away. What was very interesting to me was that the board decided to select the alternative U.S. Steel bid, which involved definitively selling the company. They felt it was a better home for Marathon and a better idea and a better price than staying independent. It's one of the few times that I remember a board making that sort of decision—it's obviously very unusual to have that freedom of choice.

The Campeau takeover of Allied Stores is the demarcation of a new era. What we tried to do [representing the Canadian retailer] was conceptualize how to become competitive on the financing side of acquisitions. We came up with this idea of a bridge loan, really an extension of what we did in the leveraged buyout of First Brands. We provided $1.8 billion in financing to Campeau to buy Allied shares, of which only $900 million was actually funded by us, because the banks provided the rest during the one week period [it took Campeau to complete the transaction]. There was a swirl of controversy around this deal. Our competitors were passing around stories about all the difficulties we were having. But there *never* were any difficulties as regards the bridge loan. Things went according to plan.

Within the M&A industry, the people, as you get to know them over the years, are quite impressive. I'd say that generally about our chief competitors. It takes a certain persistence and dedication and skill to have survived for ten years and to be perceived as saying something worthwhile to chief executives. Of those I admire, there's Felix [Rohatyn of Lazard Frères] and, as you go down the firms, [Robert] Greenhill and [Eric] Gleacher of Morgan Stanley, Steve Friedman and Jeff Boisi of Goldman. But I'd have to put Joe Flom [of Skadden, Arps, Slate, Meagher & Flom] and Marty Lipton [of Wachtell, Lipton, Rosen & Katz] above all of us. I think maybe I aspire to be at the point to be their equals when I reach their seniority—but that's an aspiration rather than an achievement.

To succeed in M&A, one has to be willing, certainly, to be dedicated, to work hard, to enjoy the business—otherwise it makes no sense at all. I personally enjoy deals. Unlike some people, who feel that they're getting burnt out or really don't like the deal business but would rather be painting or something of that sort, I genuinely like the process. It's quite deep within me, and I think it's not only fun but meaningful. I don't find it stressful.

To succeed, you also must be persuasive, have something to say of some value—otherwise, in the end people will see through you. And, ultimately, you must care about people, because clients sense whether your concern is genuine. The other characteristic I'd add is a high tolerance for failure. Certainly, in our experience at First Boston in the early years, frustration was almost a certain by-product. I would also argue that high tolerance for change and for ambiguity is very important. But in the end, the one common characteristic is, I think, the combination of tenacity and some modicum of common sense—which is surprisingly lacking and surprisingly important.

In terms of what I've tried to do, I'd say there are three things. One is to be the ideal doer and business getter. Second is to be a planner, to think where the industry will go, to anticipate it and to anticipate where the tactics will go. And third, I've tried to be a leader to the people I have to deal with here and also a friend to them and to the clients. What I'd like to think of as the hallmark of a Bruce Wasserstein deal is that the client got good advice: whether that is saying they should not do a deal or that they should do it and pay a dollar more. In the long run they all appreciate that.

Editor: Firth Calhoun

Joseph Fontana and Theodore Madsen

Police Officers NEW YORK CITY POLICE DEPARTMENT

> Joseph Fontana, the head of community affairs for Manhattan's
> First Precinct, which takes in Wall Street, has covered the financial
> district's beat for the past ten years. He and another veteran po-
> liceman, Theodore Madsen, the precinct's administrative lieuten-
> ant, share their observations.

The First Precinct starts at Houston Street and reaches to the west side of Broadway—all the way to the river. We do the Staten Island ferry, and we cover east and west of Chambers Street, also down to the ferry. Wall Street is a big part of it. It's a very nice, clean precinct to work in. You see the financial types, the three-piece suits. Everybody's nice-looking. Everybody's well dressed to go to work.

It's very busy. We're the fifth-busiest precinct in the city, believe it or not, all five boroughs. We do have a lot of peddler problems—box vendors—the same type of problems they have in midtown, the kinds of problems that have been going on for years. And, naturally, narcotics, like any other precinct, is a part of ours. The financial district is no different.

Mostly, we have a lot of marijuana and low-level drug dealing, which has increased over the past ten years. Anybody and everybody in the area is involved—from the messengers right on up to the top. It's not unusual at lunch hour to see three-piece suits out there—let's say people in their mid-40s, people in some type of supervisory position, managers—people who, instead of having a drink or two, have a joint or two.

163

Most narcotics areas, you have to go in at night to buy drugs. But here they do it in the daytime. We don't have coke or crack, just marijuana. The better-quality people, if I may use that term, are more intelligent. They're not into the heavy-drug-type scene, like crack. They're out there for the leisurely hour or hour and a half at lunch, especially when the good weather rolls around. And they prefer marijuana over beer or Scotch or anything.

There's going to be a new system down here now. We're going to concentrate on the buyers, because concentrating on the sellers doesn't seem to be helping us. So we've decided to try and scare away the buyers and make it not good to be out there smoking. Generally, plainclothes personnel are brought into the area; they observe the violation and make the arrest—put them in a truck, bring them back to the station and go out and get another group. Yesterday we totaled 31 arrests in the Water Street area, people ranging from kids to the executive level.

People are afraid of cocaine, and if that happens, it happens at night, and it's not purchased on the street. It's brought in. Maybe the executives are getting it. Maybe they have their own little office space upstairs. It's not the street-level stuff.

The drug scene has not expanded that much at night. The night scene here, you're dealing with computers and, of course, the cleaning services. Those people are usually in the buildings, and if they're doing anything, it's probably inside.

There is some office crime. People there are not very security-conscious. People feel once you walk into your office, you're safe, so they get lax. They leave things around. Like a wallet in a jacket, which becomes lifted. Nobody seems to see the guy with the coffee looking for this or that. Or the old UPS or Federal Express scam, where a guy comes in and says, "anybody order a package to be picked up?" and while somebody's looking around for a package, something else is lifted.

There are very few people robbing a runner who's carrying around a lot of money. People in the Wall Street area are dealing in millions of dollars in stock every day, and any individual carrying a lot of money could be robbed, but it just doesn't happen. That's astounding, isn't it? These are small, petty street thieves. What are they going to do with a million-dollar bond?

There has been some violent crime. We had that stockholder shoot his brother over his father. Recently, there was a fight in front of Job Lot. One guy bumped into another guy and stabbed

164

him to death. Job Lot is an institution; everyone knows to shop at Job Lot.

There was Nicholas Deak's murder. That woman walked in and killed the secretary and Deak. When the press showed her arrest on the news, they said she surrendered. She didn't surrender. When the cops got there, she had the gun in her hand and was going to escape. She was trying to walk out when the police walked in. And they grabbed her and made the arrest. What you read in the paper, that she waited for the police to arrive and surrendered, was wrong. The report wasn't even close.

Duane Street Park isn't very far from the financial area. It used to be a primary drug location. Last summer we devoted a lot of manpower and hours and cleaned out the little park. So the drug problem became dispersed. It went around the block, up the block, down the block, everywhere but the park. The base population around the park used to be people on the loading docks, truck drivers that were coming in and out. Now it's all condos and apartments. You can't even get near the place without spending $150,000, $200,000 for a one-room apartment.

The whole area is growing in leaps and bounds when it comes to residential population. This is the fifth-busiest precinct in the city, and it's going to get busier. There's Battery Park City and, of course, there's Manhattan Landing, which will be a combination of apartments, offices, and, I guess, stores, shops.

Many places that are just landfills right now will eventually be completed as housing developments—like the northern end of Battery Park City, the north cove, which is still nothing but a beach. This is going to bring in a lot of big-dollar-type persons— most likely working couples that will never have children, because they can't afford to pay the rent.

Many of these places will have their own security systems, but we'll still have a lot of calls for services. If they need an ambulance, for example, the police have to respond. Even with 911 emergency calls, traffic is a big problem. We get 3,300 radio calls for service a month, and our cars can't get there because of the traffic. We're trying to go to scooters, but they're dangerous, and nobody wants to be out on them when it's raining.

We have a million-and-a-half people coming in here every day, and the streets never get any wider. And the tractor-trailers get bigger. They can't make room for deliveries; they can't make turns; and everybody's dropping something off or picking something up. There's double parking. Let's see, we gave out about 68,000 parking summonses and 13,000 moving summonses last year. And the Department of Transportation gave out another 500,000.

You got to remember the skyscrapers being built. You got the World Trade Center, right off the bat. That's a monstrous location. They made provisions to take in deliveries and things like that, but the amount of traffic that goes to the Trade Center still has to use the public streets.

The past couple of years, the Borough of Manhattan Community College was completed, so now that's brought a lot of kids into the neighborhood. In the same area as the college, another condominium, Greenwich Court, is now under construction. At one time that location was nothing but two- and three-level warehouses, storehouses, little butter and egg and cheese places, like where the old market used to be. Remember the old market that was down here before the Trade Center?

Now all the construction that is taking place is bringing in more construction trucks, equipment, steel, the iron, the concrete. That's constantly on the go in the area of Chambers and Greenwich. On the other hand, the Maiden Lane area, underneath the highway here, we've got 180 Maiden Lane, a brand-new office building that is going to be about 35 or 40 stories high at least.

Another thing that's made this precinct so busy is tourism. People come from all over the world. The exchange has a visitors' gallery. That's all part of the tour package. We have a lot of history down here—Fraunces Tavern, for one. The tourists bring this place alive on weekends. The place is hopping on a weekend now—all day long.

You can spend an entire weekend down here and not see the same thing twice. You can go to the South Street Seaport, bounce from there to the Statue of Liberty, see a few things in the park itself. Robert Fulton is buried in Trinity churchyard. You walk by and see some stones; you loiter there for a half hour.

Editor: Julie Rohrer

Bennett Kaplan

Executive Recruiter BENNETT KAPLAN & CO.

In the past decade or so, securities analysts have shucked off their image as the brainy but somewhat boring professors *manqué* of Wall Street and become glamorous, high-paid superstars of stock research and the 7 o'clock news. As a longtime specialist in wooing securities analysts, executive recruiter Bennett Kaplan not only observed firsthand the analyst's apotheosis into a Street celebrity but he also helped bring it about through his recruiting practices.

If you look back fifteen years, the dominant institutional research firms were boutiques. They were in one-product businesses with one revenue source: commissions. The boutiques, pre-Mayday, were the firms that had special identities and cultures. Factors such as pride, loyalty, ownership and prestige were very important. That's changed totally today. Research is now probably as heterogeneous a function as any on Wall Street, and the small number of research boutiques that survived have specific market niches that command good trading volume and produce a differentiated product.

Starting in, let's say, 1974, when it became clear that the unfixing of rates was going to be totally destructive to many boutiques, analysts changed jobs because of fear. Suddenly, the game was going to change, and they had to make sure they were with a company that was going to still be in that game when the war was over.

During 1974 to 1976 you began to see the emergence of the investment banking firms as voracious acquirers of analysts from boutiques. Indeed, the primary historic change in this business has been the evolution of the investment bank as the primary research vendor. Every firm in the bulge bracket except for Shearson Lehman is in the top ten. And of the balance of firms in the top ten, only Paine Webber is not an investment bank of significance. Institutional research has changed from a for-profit business to *part* of a for-profit business.

Merrill Lynch single-handedly changed the way analysts are hired. If Merrill Lynch had not done what it did, analysts' compensation would be much less than it is today—and my fees would be smaller as well. Our greatest appreciation of your publication was the first issue of the All-America Research Team, and our second greatest kudo was for the man who decided to capitalize on it—Arch Catapano [then-head of Merrill's research department]. Thanks to Catapano, Merrill made the discovery that, for the mere investment of $50,000 to $100,000 more per person than the analysts were being paid, Merrill could advertise that it had become the No. 1 research firm in the world.

When we were engaged by Merrill Lynch, we didn't have a position description. We didn't have salary restrictions. Nothing. It was very simple: Get one of those AART people, preferably high on the list. It was easy recruiting, because not only did Catapano want them, he was willing to pay whatever it cost. He was the only guy who ever did it successfully on a major scale.

What were the pivotal dates for the important decisions by firms to commit a lot of money to research? If you run through the top companies, you will see that they are all dated six months to a year after Merrill Lynch started hiring AART members. Merrill was a catalyst in overpaying, and it was a catalyst in changing the way analysts looked at their work. The external value the market would place on them would be more of a factor in governing their earning power than the quality of their work, which is less measurable.

Merrill Lynch invented "the hammer." The hammer is executed by the firm that cannot hire. It combines two elements: The first is that the firm makes a significant compromise, either in the length of experience or the standing of the analyst. Very often this method is used with young analysts or long-experienced analysts who have slipped. You find a person making $125,000 a year who is fairly priced at a mediocre firm and offer that person $250,000 to join your firm. By contrast, in the early '70s increases in compensation were measured in thousands of dollars—$5,000, $8,000. The hammer is typical of wire house recruiting. You pick up the newspaper and read that a third-team AART person just left a major firm and went to a secondary factor in the institutional business—you know the hammer was used.

I'd venture to say that Merrill Lynch probably caused more career dislocation by its buildup methodology than the next five firms combined. I did work for Merrill Lynch in the early years of their buildup. We had instances of people meeting with Arch in the morning and getting an offer in the afternoon. You cannot learn in an hour or two who you're recruiting, what their needs are going to be or whether their product is going to fit. Today's methods are much more careful.

A good number of people were hired into environments that they ought not to have joined. People who were adept at stock selection, who had built a reputation for their ability to move securities—were joining firms where the product strategy was very intensive, top-down research with lots of company coverage and industry coverage.

The large wire houses did attract a heck of a lot of boutique people because they looked safe. These firms were publicly owned, and you didn't have to worry about whether the firm was going to be in business unless conditions became catastrophic. But when you look back, a lot of people who moved to wire houses have made at least one subsequent move. In many instances these turned out to be parking spots.

From the analyst's side the situation was reactive. Whoever bid the most aggressively prevailed, provided you saw stability. That was much more important than what sort of research you'd be doing. Today you'll find that analysts are more focused on being successful security analysts—they understand what they need to do to succeed institutionally. And the more mature the analyst, as long as he or she is on an uptick in their career, the less greed is a factor. The younger the analyst or the further a senior analyst has passed the point of maximum impact, the greedier the analyst.

For the top-of-the-line analyst, the next dollar earned is not nearly as important as the predictability of continued high earnings. At age 50 your sights are more on: "Can I continue to earn this extraordinary quantity of money for a decade?" I don't think the primary psychological mind-set of the security analyst is greed. I think they fear losing this relatively rare opportunity in American business. Where would a security analyst earn a half-a-million dollars if they had to do it in a function other than security analysis? Beats me.

A lot of movement in the period from 1970 to 1980–81 was candidate-initiated. Today people aren't looking for opportunity. Today you've got to dig them out. The single biggest problem in prying loose security analysts is in identifying the factor that differentiates the firm you're representing from the firm the candidate is working for. It's become increasingly difficult for the top firms to recruit among themselves.

There are always exceptions, of course. You will always run into a candidate whom you'd never expect to move, but something has occurred within his company that's critical to how he perceives his ability to do something he wants to do. We just finished a search in which a candidate had built an extraordinary capacity to develop new business. A couple of years before, his firm had committed itself to strengthening its investment banking capabilities. But they didn't do it. When I started the search, I looked at his name and said: "That fellow's not moving. He's a shareholder. We know his income level, and he's turned down six calls in ten years." I called him nonetheless for the seventh time and caught him when he perceived that he wouldn't be able to get what he wanted—real investment banking capability. We had a viable candidate.

The primary method of defense when an analyst resigns is to match or exceed the cash offer. Firms have even started to involve their chairmen in retaining analysts. Step two is to expand the position or commit to hiring additional support. Most firms don't wait. Smart firms preempt receptivity in the first place. A lot of senior analysts are running groups or may be responsible for some segments of research—international, for example—or a specialty product, such as special situations research. These are serious titles. Or they've been delegated one or another managerial function—training and developing, college recruiting. Another example is encouraging analysts to initiate corporate finance business. This is meaningful job enrichment.

For a recruiter, if you're attentive to the probability that there's going to be a counteroffer, you line up an alum—preferably one who is with the acquiring firm—to help convince the candidate. But the primary method of preempting a defensive move is to provide the candidate with an irrefutable explanation of why he or she should leave, provided it's true. It's never money; it's never title; it's never prestige. You seek to structure the offer to put in something that cannot be addressed by the losing firm.

We had a case where, although the candidate loved the research environment at the acquiring firm, he wouldn't have gone just for that and the dollars. We used five investment bankers in that candidate's area of expertise, and every one of them legitimately loved the guy. They were seeing dollar signs float through the air, and he could see them seeing the dollar signs. When he walked in to give notice, he didn't tell his boss about the big raise he got. He told them, "The firm I'm joining is committed to doing the kind of investment banking business I have the ability to do." What you're really doing in this case is disarming the donor company. This was that candidate I called for the seventh time in ten years.

Firms are working harder not to lose people, but it's less effective. The impression I have is that a candidate who accepts an offer and then takes a counteroffer doesn't last much more than a year and a half before he goes. No research director is going to make two counteroffers.

Sometimes your client, though, turns out to be the monster. Who's not for real as a client? The fellow who is running a very small company, who has not ever looked for a job or looked for a job twenty years ago, succeeded and started his own business. He doesn't know what it feels like to be a candidate; he's totally internalized the value of association with his company. So he consistently makes offers that are too low. Close to three quarters of my business—in any good practice—is repeat business, and the nonrepeaters always tend to be little firms run by rich guys and major departments run by rich, long-tenured people.

If you look at the reality of what executive recruiting is, it's simply allocating the rational use of resources in a capitalist system. And by the way, I don't see "headhunter" as pejorative at all. It's literally what you are doing—you're hunting. In fact, I tried to get the word "hunter" for the plates for my car; I ended up with "black ink" (as opposed to red ink). You know, it's not all that difficult being a headhunter. If you can identify a group of people for whom a 50 percent or more increase in pay makes them happier than they ever dreamed of being, and the opportunity to advance is high, it's doable.

Reseach directors did not have the kind of publicly visible personalities in the early years that they do today. They aren't just pencil pushers and proofreaders anymore. In most of the large companies, an awful lot of the grind work has been delegated, and research directors have a lot more freedom to stimulate production, to motivate people and to get out there and sell the company. The external role of research directors has been enhanced considerably in client relationships, in selling, in being spokesperson for the firm in many cases and in executing portfolio strategy. In addition, to whatever degree analysts are involved in corporate finance, research directors are much more involved in investment banking, particularly in firms' capital commitment functions. How often do you see Leon Cooperman [head of research at Goldman Sachs] quoted? Burton Siegel [head of institutional equity at Drexel Burnham Lambert]? A fair amount. Bob Salomon [head of research at Salomon Brothers]? Quite a lot.

Research directors are very solid citizens. They're sober people, smart people. They've run very complex operations for a long period of time and probably have the best overall view, from the equity distribution side, of securities pricing and placement. In a lot of firms they have as good a view as the head of syndicate. And if you look at the personality profiles of research directors, *ex* one or two, they tend to be very fatherly people.

But when there is a supply overload—as when firms merge— there is no group of people more vulturelike than research directors. Everything stops while they attack. The classic was Shearson merging with Lehman. They both had good-sized departments and therefore tremendous redundancies. It took an extraordinary length of time until they sorted out who was doing what. Nobody knew where they were going to land, so everyone was available.

There used to be analysts whose spreadsheets were on the backs of envelopes. But the perception was that they knew what they were talking about. No one wanted to see their numbers. They moved stocks. Now I think you see a more fully rounded job. You see a demand that the analyst conduct pretty rigorous research that is published regularly, albeit not at the same length as before. You're seeing more stock recommendations. You are seeing shorter action reports and more of them. They're being marketed by strategists and research directors as well as by analysts. The market has changed, too. The primary commission allocator for a good number of years has been the portfolio manager, not the buy-side analyst. Buy-side analysis is evaporating.

But even though the analyst's job has evolved over the years, some of the age-old standards can still apply in recruiting. We were doing a search for the senior partner of an investment adviser—an extremely high-quality firm. All the partners there wear white shirts, dark suits, cuff links. They are nice people, but they have a particular style. I found them a genius—the candidate is dead perfect. But he wears plaid suits and a paisley tie to the interviews. This is a pretty sensitive issue. After the second interview I tell him: "You know, you're perfect. But listen, did you once have a bar mitzvah suit?" He said, "Sure, but I don't fit into it anymore." I press him and he thinks he's got a charcoal-gray suit somewhere. I suggest he start wearing it.

Three or four interviews later, I called up the client. It was about time for the company to make a decision. The client is one of these very dry, reserved, unexpressive kinds of people. Finally, after a long pause, he said, "The suit." I said: "Don't worry about it. I'll call you in a day." I called the candidate and asked him to meet me at the Madison Room at Barneys. He's been shopping at Bond's all his life. We get to the Madison Room. They look at the guy; they almost drop dead. I tell them we need a Hickey-Freeman navy blue, a perfect shirt and tie, some shoes. And we need them to be wearable in two days. The candidate's not saying a word. This guy was really well off. He'd socked away a ton of money and invested it well. But he'd never spent a penny on himself. I said: "I can't believe you almost blew it. You're going to triple your income and become a partner in one of the most prestigious money management firms. You have to start looking the part." He got the job.

Editor: Margaret A. Elliott

173

Felix Rohatyn

Partner LAZARD FRERES & CO.

Felix Rohatyn was probably the first of the superstar investment bankers: someone whose deal-making prowess and public stature catapulted him to the covers of magazines. The premier merger maker of the late '60s and early '70s, Rohatyn's career began assuming larger dimensions when he chaired the New York Stock Exchange crisis committee at the time of the paperwork crunch. But his greatest renown came from his work as chairman of New York's Municipal Assistance Corp. during the city's fiscal crisis. Still very much in the public eye—thanks in part to his frequent speeches and articles—he is often mentioned as a possible U.S. Treasury secretary.

In 1967 I was a relatively young partner in this firm, doing merger work. I think '67 and '68 were the years I worked on a couple of large deals for other clients, who then became quite prominent. One was the acquisition of Lorillard for Loews and Larry Tisch. I think that was the first time—maybe it was the second time—that I got up the nerve to ask for a million-dollar fee, which our younger partners now look upon as small change.

The merger environment then, compared to what it is today, was like comparing a Mozart quartet to Mick Jagger. First of all, there were very few people involved when you did a deal in those days. In the ITT deals, I worked with Harold Geneen and a senior vice president, Stanley Luke, and their general counsel, Howard Aibel, and that was it. I worked pretty much alone. I would do the numbers on a spreadsheet myself.

They were practically all friendly deals. The notion that somebody would top your bid and interfere in the merger wasn't something you thought about very much. The ITT takeover of Hartford [Insurance Co.] was a bear hug, which was a new thing. Most of the deals were negotiated mergers. They were done with equity, and the arbitrageurs were hoping that the deal would close, because they were short one stock and long the other, instead of what they do today, which is to hope that there is a bidding contest, because they are mostly all cash deals today.

I did a lot of work with Geneen in those years, and it was an extraordinary education. First of all, he was very stimulating intellectually because he was so enthusiastic. He really loved making deals. And when he was determined to make a deal, he was a powerhouse in terms of determination. He had an extraordinary capacity to analyze a business and then to charm the chief executive of whatever company we were trying to buy, because he knew more about the guy's business, usually, than the guy himself. He was also perfectly truthful, although quite incapable of ultimately carrying out the wonderful visions of collaboration that he painted to whomever we were acquiring. He would take some chief executive up the mountain and show him the promised land and say, "You and I are going to conquer the world together." Then, after he acquired the company, this chief executive would try to call Geneen to say, "Let's go conquer the world together," and he would get a call back from the ITT vice president for personnel.

I always felt I owed Geneen a great deal. He put me on his board when that was a daring thing to do. In those days you didn't put a young, nonestablishment, Jewish investment banker on your board when you were a big white-shoe company, which ITT was at the time. In fact, André Meyer wanted to put a more senior and more established partner on the board, and Geneen wouldn't hear of it. He was really a very good friend. When I was chairman of the New York Stock Exchange crisis committee in '68–'69, and was struggling with what seemed like impossible problems and numbers that didn't make any sense, Geneen would walk around the block with me at 1:00 in the morning and give me advice on accounting. He would take the time to do that, which was terrific.

The crisis committee was really my first public exposure. It had a little of the New York City fiscal crisis drama—not as much, but it had some. The paperwork crisis seems very unreal today; I mean, the notion that you couldn't cope with 10 million shares a day! It's like the Wright brothers. And we were talking then about firms that by today's standards seem minute. Yet I remember how we feared for everybody's life when it looked as if Hayden Stone was going down or Glore Forgan or Francis I. DuPont or Goodbody.

It seemed to a lot of us that there were enough possibilities of something really going wrong and of the whole system becoming unraveled that you just didn't want to take a chance on it—just as with New York City, we didn't want to take a chance of finding out what a bankruptcy of the city would do. I remember going down to the White House for the swearing in of Bill Casey [as SEC chairman]. Somebody introduced me to President Nixon, and one of the first things he said to me was, "Well, I'm glad to hear that everything's under control at the stock exchange." I said: "Mr. President, I don't think anything is under control. I don't want you to have any illusions." We were right in the middle of, I think, Goodbody at the time. I said, "I don't really think it's better than 50-50 that this is going to work." And he was obviously very troubled by that, really very worried.

I learned quite a lot from dealing with that crisis that I would later put to use in the city situation. For instance, I would always go back to one of the things I learned from Harold Geneen; he had a rule that said, "Don't ever try to get 100 percent of the facts, because by the time you get them, it will be too late for you to act on anything. Get as much as you think you need, and then move on." And that's what we did at the stock exchange, because the numbers were always suspect.

The other thing I learned that was important to me in the stock exchange crisis as well as in the New York City crisis was to try to deal as frankly as possible with everybody and not try to play games with people. You can make a one-sided deal once or twice on a relatively small scale, but you can't do it on a large scale with public companies or institutions. You couldn't outsmart the labor unions in the New York City situation, nor would I try. Or the banks. Or Senator [William] Proxmire. Or Mayor [Abraham] Beame.

You also have the dichotomy over the question of how much you should disclose. If you let people know how serious the prob-

177

lem is, then they can try and cope with it; on the other side, the disclosure about how serious the problem really is may create a runaway crisis that you can't deal with anymore. I found that the latter rarely is a danger, that you don't trigger a crisis by telling people the reality of how bad things are, and that disclosure is worth doing. And if you don't, it leaks out anyway, so you might as well do it.

When I first got involved in the city crisis, I had no idea I was getting into a long-term situation. I was at a stage in my life at the time of being single, I had been through the very difficult ITT-Hartford case, and I had just been called for jury duty. I was contacted by [New York Governor] Hugh Carey, whom I had never met, who asked me if I could help the city stay out of bankruptcy. I had been, quite coincidentally, talking with Scoop Jackson [Senator Henry Jackson], who was running for president at the time and whom I was trying to help, about some kind of legislation to guarantee municipal obligations for certain types of cities that couldn't finance themselves. So I had done some homework on it. I said to Carey: "Look, governor, I'm happy to help you. If you will get me off jury duty, then I'll help you for 30 days, or whatever the jury duty period is"—never thinking that this was going to be a long-term commitment.

So then we started, and I must say that it was very heavy going. First of all, I love the city, I really do, and as a refugee [Rohatyn had fled from Nazi-occupied Europe with his parents], it's probably more meaningful to me because this is my last port of call. At the same time, I was pretty battered and scarred from the whole ITT-Hartford affair. I was somewhat at loose ends because I was alone. And it was also an opportunity. I never thought of it that way at the time, but it was clearly, in retrospect, a way to distance myself from André, to have an identity of my own.

I got a great deal out of the whole experience. I could see from within what happens in the New York State legislature or in the New York City Board of Estimate or in the United States Senate or in the White House. And when you go out to speak—and I started speaking a fair amount around the country, first of all to sell MAC bonds and then to get political support for the kinds of things we were going to need in Congress—you get a different

178

perspective. It's different than going and working on a merger in San Francisco or Boston or on Wall Street. I think it ultimately makes you a better investment banker. It also makes you, probably, a more complete person, and it's very satisfying—I mean, if it doesn't kill you.

I believe it's true that the prestige I acquired because of my involvement with the city probably helped the firm. But I truly don't think that's why I got involved. On the other hand, I was always able to justify doing it by the knowledge that it was not hurting our business. If I thought it was doing us harm, I wouldn't have done it, or I would have taken a leave of absence. And, I must say, it's to the credit of the firm that I wasn't forced to take a leave during this period. André could well have said, "Listen, you want to play marbles with the city, then take a year off and call us when you want to come back, and in the meantime we'll give your percentage interest to the other partners." There was never even a suggestion of that, although there were clearly people here, including André, who were very nervous about my public involvement, thought it might be bad for the firm—and thought it might destroy me.

André was nervous about my city involvement on several counts. First, that it would take me away from business and therefore that the firm would lose business. Second, that being involved in public life is a dangerous thing, that I would get in trouble personally, and that if the city went bankrupt, I would have a problem. Third, that I would get to like it so much that I would go into public life 100 percent. And fourth, deep down *he* wanted to be on the front page of *The New York Times*.

Up until the New York Stock Exchange crisis, to some extent, and certainly until the New York City crisis, he was clearly the dominant person here, both in the firm and publicly. After the New York City crisis, it changed. First of all, he was much older, and his health was failing. But also, I was by then a much more visible and important figure in the public sense, and also in the business sense, in that I played a larger role in the total business that the firm did. So our relationship became much more of a relationship of equals—in fact, equals going in somewhat opposite directions.

There were other things that troubled him about my involvement with the city. One was that I had to take positions that antagonized the banks; in fact, I still believe it cost us the account of a major bank that was a good client here. But, again, I must say, André never interfered. He kept saying to me: "God, this is going to kill you. How can you do this? You must be a masochist."

Actually, I was able to do a lot of business while I was working on the fiscal crisis, probably because I was able to ration my time a lot more intelligently. For instance, [Colt Industries chairman] Dave Margolis and I worked on a deal while we were negotiating with the pension systems on New York City investments, because there was simply no time to do it otherwise. Sometimes, though, it was a little difficult to shift gears. I remember once going on a Saturday night from a very difficult labor negotiation to Marty Lipton's office, where I was being deposed on some takeover litigation. I showed up there unshaven, in blue jeans and a turtleneck, and I gave the deposition while a camera crew was waiting outside to talk about the city crisis.

As far as the resolution of the crisis is concerned, the person who deserves the most credit is Hugh Carey. He had the vision to decide that bankruptcy for the city was unacceptable. He was able to gather around him people from the private sector who were very competent. People like Dick Ravitch, who was running the Urban Development Corp., and Peter Goldmark, who was the budget director. And he was willing to go out on a limb on our advice and support us in very, very hairy situations. Situations like freezing wages of city workers, which was unheard of. Or putting in tuition at the City University. With a cautious governor, or a governor who was really concerned about his image, it couldn't have happened.

Carey was probably more generous in giving me, and other people, credit than any politician I've ever seen, and was also more willing to take the blame than any politician I've ever seen. I remember one time Peter Goldmark and I thought we had made a deal with the banks early in the crisis on a refinancing, and it took an enormous effort on the part of the governor to twist the mayor's arm to go along with it. And then the deal blew up because Goldmark and I had misunderstood the banks' position. Carey had a press conference and had to tell the world that although we had thought we had a deal, now we had no deal. A reporter said to Carey, "Well, Governor, don't you have egg all over your face?" And Carey said, "Well, I'd rather have egg all over my face than the city all over the floor," or something like that. But he could have said: "Listen, here's Rohatyn. He's an investment banker. He should have told me that this thing wasn't going to work." He never did. There wasn't a second's hesitation on his part. I thought that was pretty elegant.

I was credible, credible to the unions and to the banks and to the legislature and ultimately to the Congress, and I kind of give myself a B+ on that, maybe an A−, but no less than a B+. But the real credit for saving the city, that goes to Hugh Carey, without any question on my part.

I really had a limited decompression from city affairs, because over the last few years since the fiscal crisis I've remained chairman of MAC. I now spend about 75 percent of my time on business and 25 percent on my public life. If I had to really go cold turkey and do nothing but business, I would not be happy doing that.

I've been asked to run for office a few times, but it's clearly not something that I will do or could do. And there's always a recurring theme that I want to be secretary of the Treasury. But the truth is that it's just not a burning ambition for me; it's not something that I'm yearning for. Obviously, if a president asked me to help him in any capacity that I felt competent to deal with, I would certainly consider it and probably do it, because I think anybody would. If anybody who thought he was competent had the opportunity of serving in a high position in government, I can't conceive of his not doing it, simply as a duty and a challenge. However, I feel strongly that this is something that either happens or it doesn't happen. You don't chase it, and, as in everything of this kind, I would probably have very mixed feelings if it really happened.

I recognize that there may be some jealousy about my public profile. But what can I do about it? I can give up my public activities or I can give up speaking out on what I think is important, and then people won't be jealous. By and large, whatever jealousy there is is more than offset by the people who come up to me on the street and are appreciative about my work for the city and the state, people I run into in elevators or in airplanes or in restaurants. Now that may sound corny, but that really is nice.

Inside Lazard, Michel [senior partner Michel David-Weill] sees my public activities as an advantage to the firm. And I would have to say, it takes somebody very secure to be the senior partner in a firm in which there is someone with as high a public profile as I have. But Michel is totally secure.

Michel and I have the most delightful and satisfying relationship. I wouldn't say we were trainees together, but we do go back 30 years together. We both bear the scars from the lashes of André Meyer, which is like having been in Guadalcanal together. We complement each other. He runs this firm absolutely, and there is no question about it in my mind. At the same time, I am a very senior partner in his mind. I don't think Michel would ever think of doing something critically important without our being in agreement on it. And in all of the years that we have worked together, we have not had one harsh word with each other.

Michel is really entitled to an enormous amount of credit for the performance of this firm, which was in a state of, I wouldn't say crisis, but clearly stalled when André got really sick. When the question of succession arose, the only solution always seemed to me to be Michel. He had the family aspect, the sense of the tradition of the firm, and he wanted to do it. Not only did I not want to do it, but I couldn't do it without hurting the business of the firm, because you can't run a firm and really be in the front line doing business every day.

It was very difficult for Michel in the beginning. André gave him a very hard time, as he would anybody who succeeded him. But Michel prevailed, diversified the firm, expanded our existing businesses and made major moves in personnel and in new businesses. We were about 300 people when André died; now we're between 500 and 600, still very small compared to our competitors. But our earnings are ten times what they were then. We are probably by any standard the most profitable firm, even more profitable than Goldman Sachs in terms of return on capital, return on investment—whichever way you want to look at it. Michel deserves an enormous amount of credit for it, much more than he has gotten.

He takes risks that André wouldn't take on people and on getting us into other businesses, our capital markets group, for example. Also, the LBOs we have done have been done because Michel is pushing. And the fund that we set up with Lester Pollack to do capital investments is Michel's direction. Michel is much more of a risk taker than I am; he'll take more risks with his own capital. My capital is all in the firm and Treasury bills and in stocks of companies that I'm on the board of. Other than that, because of the work that I do, I haven't bought a stock in twenty years. I'm not going to make a huge effort to build an empire. I've told my children that when I die and when my wife is gone, they'll have whatever is left—if there's anything left.

Not too long ago I gave some testimony to Congress about takeover abuses, and I talked about greed in our business. I talked about the cancer of greed. One business magazine took me to task for it; they wrote an article called "Good Greed" and said who is Felix Rohatyn to talk about greed? Well, if the worst that ever happens to me is that some magazine attacks me on the notion that I'm against greed and they're for it, then God bless them.

I'm not being moralistic. It's just that I grew up in this profession when it was an honorable business, and now it is not perceived as an honorable business. Yes, there were some dishonorable things going on 20 or 30 years ago, but they weren't systemic. I remember carrying André's briefcase when we'd go to Bobby Lehman's office. Now, they were tough people, and I'm not saying that none of them had ever heard about inside information; I'm not naive. But deal making wasn't a way of life, like it is today, in which the only standard is whether you win or lose, whether you've made the deal or not made the deal and whether at the end of the year you've made $100 million personally.

There's a lot of macho in these deals on the part of the investment bankers, the lawyers and the executives. I think one underestimates the impact the lawyers have had on these deals. I think the big, big differences between the deals today and those of the '60s is, first, the big hostiles have created the ability to mobilize huge amounts of credit almost instantly, whether by using a highly confident letter in a junk bond raid or by just going to the banks and borrowing $3 billion in a weekend. So that's one thing. The second is the way the legal tactics and the advice of the lawyers drive these deals much more than the advice of the investment bankers. In some cases you're never really quite sure whether as an investment banker you're just the Charlie McCarthy to the lawyer who is Edgar Bergen.

It seems very easy to be a financial expert. Lawyers love being financial experts and pricing deals, and telling you at what price you should buy a company and at what price you shouldn't. So it's very easy for a lawyer to begin running the business side of a deal, while it is clearly not possible for the business people to run the legal side of a deal.

I guess the deal that most represented to me how much things had gotten out of hand was the Bendix–Martin Marietta battle. It was anarchy let loose all over the place. Here was Bendix making a bid for Martin Marietta, and the defense of Martin Marietta was to make a counterbid for Bendix: the Pac Man approach. In the middle of this, we represented United Technologies, which wanted to acquire Bendix.

At one time there came a moment when it was clear that the logical thing to do was for everybody to call time out and go home and to stop the investment bankers and the lawyers and just forget the whole thing. But Bendix pulled the trigger, assuming that Martin Marietta wouldn't; then Martin Marietta pulled the trigger.

Here you had a situation similar to the story of the scorpion and the camel swimming across the Nile. The scorpion is asking the camel for a ride, and the camel says, "But you're going to poison me," and the scorpion says, "Don't be ridiculous. Why should I do that?" Then in the middle of the Nile the scorpion stings the camel, and as the camel is going down, he says, "How could you do this to me?" And the scorpion says, "Well, this is the Middle East."

I suppose this Martin Marietta thing is similar. People just pulled triggers and then said, "Well, this is the new Wall Street." And as a result of this, Allied came in and picked up the pieces and [Bendix chairman] Bill Agee had an untimely and premature end to his business career, and a lot of people looked very, very bad. It was one of the most appalling things I've seen in terms of people playing with companies as if they were Monopoly sets.

I feel sorry, in a way, for a lot of the younger people. They work brutal hours and they work under brutal conditions. And they feel themselves under the gun competitively in a way that I didn't when I was their age. I didn't feel that I had to produce all the time, that if I didn't close X deals a year I would be passed over. In those days there were no winners and losers. You either concluded a merger or you didn't, and most of the time if you didn't, nobody knew, because it was never announced.

Today it's all win or lose. And the thing that's ironic is that many times the people who win will wish they'd lost two years later, because they've bought bad businesses at crazy prices. But there is this aspect of winning and losing, and show biz, and a compensation structure that is based on that. You can say as many times as you want to younger people, "Look, don't think you're going to be judged by the number of deals you close." They don't believe you—and you don't believe it yourself.

Editor: Cary Reich

Barton Biggs

Managing Director MORGAN STANLEY & CO.

> The career of Barton Biggs closely parallels the evolution of *Institutional Investor* magazine. A hedge fund manager in the late 1960s, he joined Morgan Stanley & Co. in 1973 and built up its formidable research effort. Long regarded as one of the Street's top portfolio strategists, he also helped guide the firm's move into asset management and then, in the early part of this decade, spearheaded its move into international research.

Gunslinger isn't a pejorative term any more. I think the gunslingers are viewed as some kind of antique that no longer exists. It's like the old cowboy pictures on the wall. They're no longer relevant. But for someone who once was a gunslinger, who is always described in the press as "a former gunslinger," I think he really likes it. It shows that in his youth he was a real cowboy. He was one of the gunslingers of yesteryear—those people with the smooth, placid faces and the faraway looks in their eyes. I always had the feeling that they were a little spaced out from looking at the tape for too long.

Fairfield Partners, which I started with Dick Radcliffe a few years before *Institutional Investor* magazine was launched, was really the third hedge fund. The first one was A. W. Jones; the second was City Associates, with Dean Milosis and Carl Jones; and we were the third. Dick was working for A. W. Jones at the time and I was a special situations analyst at E. F. Hutton and ran a model portfolio for Jones. We decided to split off and form our

187

own hedge fund, and since we both lived in Greenwich [Connecticut], it was natural to locate it in Greenwich.

You can almost chart the rise of the bull market with the number of hedge funds that were started in the late '60s. That was really an ebullient period—the rise of the young, go-go performance money managers. But what people forget was that those guys really got wiped out in 1970, in the 1970 bear market, because a lot of those stocks never came back from that bear market. I'm talking about the real go-go things, the National Student Marketings, the things that got to 200 times earnings. Then from 1970 to 1973 we had a last, final high-quality institutional bull market. That ended in the 1973–1974 bear market.

Fairfield Partners had grown very rapidly, and we were in a dilemma. We had this fund and a couple of pension fund accounts. And some of our hedge fund partners were less than thrilled that we were being diverted by other investment activities. Were we going to concentrate on the hedge fund and stay small? Or were we going to become a much broader-based investment management firm? That was what I really wanted to do. But the economics of it were such that the right decision was for Fairfield Partners to remain a hedge fund. There's no way you're going to make more money than through the hedge fund.

Actually, Fairfield Partners did fine—it still exists—but somewhere in 1971 we were approached by Morgan Stanley to do an offshore fund. And in the course of doing that, I got to know a lot of people at Morgan Stanley. The firm was then grappling with the issue of its future. Dick Fisher and Bill Black really came up with the concept that the firm had to switch from being an underwriter of high-grade securities with no distribution capability into being a much more broad-based firm. The first step of that was to have a research capability, and so they began talking to me about building it for them.

I was somebody they knew, and they thought it was a logical choice for me to build their research for them. And in 1973, I think it was in April, Frank Petito, the chairman of the firm, made me an offer that was hard to refuse to come in to Morgan Stanley. I think I surprised him because I accepted right on the spot. I was the first person they ever brought in as a partner.

My decision was really more of a lifestyle decision. I was 40 years old. I had gone into this lifestyle—I moved out of New York and back to Greenwich—when I was 31, and I wanted to try something else. We were basically running money for 85 or 90 very rich people. And I said, "Am I going to be out playing tennis at lunch three times a week for the rest of my life?" It was a pleasant, lovely rut, but I'd rather have been mixing it up a little bit more. It was just like that Kipling phrase: Life's like a book, but no matter how good the page is, sometimes you've got to turn it and get on to the next one. I sort of wanted to get into the bigs again.

When I moved to Morgan Stanley, it was a classic situation. I sat in this space with a nice view of the harbor. The other offices were all empty. So it was pretty clear what I had to do. But it wasn't really hard to fill those offices. Morgan Stanley was a great name, and once you told the analysts the story, and convinced them that Morgan Stanley was serious, it wasn't hard to get them to move.

My first big hit was probably Barry Good, who came from what was then Laird. I'd known Barry for a long time. I saw him at some dinner and I said, "Barry, I really want to talk to you." He said, "Gee, I hoped you were going to say that." I'd always had a good relationship with Barry, and it was reasonably easy—although it caused a pretty big splash when it happened.

In terms of identifying who I wanted to go after, I'd been on the receiving end of Wall Street's research for eight years. And as I recall, the *Institutional Investor* research team at that time was really in its infancy, and I used it to see who was good. But I had a good idea of who the strong people were and I went after them.

You have to remember that 1973 was a relatively tough time, so you really didn't have to step up [the compensation] that much. If you gave the guys a reasonable increase, they were ready to move. We took John Wellemeyer from Faulkner Dawkins and our computer analyst, Ulrich Weil, from Lehman. Shortly thereafter we got John Mackin from Drexel Burnham, Ben Rosen from some other place that doesn't even exist anymore, and Walter Loeb, who came out of the retailing industry.

At that point our aim was building a research department that was of high quality and one of the five best in the business. We never set as a goal trying to outspend whoever was trying to be No. 1 or 2, because that was just a numbers game and didn't make sense. But we wanted to be in the 3-to-5 category. And up to about

1980 we were on a steady rise. I guess we got as high as second or third or something like that in the *II* surveys, though at that time it was a lot less competitive than it is now. By the late '70s, we basically had between fifteen and twenty core analysts.

We always tried to have the dominant analyst in these industry groups. Our argument was that an average analyst was worthless because in order to achieve the averages all you had to do was to buy an index or buy a sector fund. So the only way you could hope to have an impact was to have either a unique insight or a really exceptional analyst. All our analysts, we like to think, were exceptional in a different way. I mean, Ben Rosen was never viewed as a stock picker but he was viewed as a great mind on the way the electronics industry was evolving. Barry Good was really a stock picker and great conceptually—on the rotation in and out of the oils group. Each guy that we hired was different, and you had to have somebody that people were willing to pay to talk to.

That was the goal, but in recent years it's become much more difficult. You have the merged firms and these periodic ego trips where somebody wants to make a run at the *II* team. Someone spends tremendous amounts of money to hire the honorable mention savings and loan analyst to jack up his totals. It just has never made any sense for us to try to do that. And so we've really stuck with our basic case—although now we've probably got 50 analysts around the world.

In the mid-'80s, it became clear that Morgan Stanley and all the major firms were becoming global. We saw an opportunity in the international equity business. It was a non sequitur that we had strategists and research in the U.S. but we didn't have it—no major U.S. firm offered it—internationally. Clearly, there was a developing interest in international securities. And I think we were fairly alert in perceiving that the dollar was going to peak in early '85, that there was gonna be a powerful wind behind international investing from a declining dollar. And so we got positioned for that at the right time.

I really turned over the direct management of the domestic research department to Dennis Sherva in about 1982, though I still had overall responsibility for it and was doing the strategy.

Then this international idea came up, and I really got involved again in the recruiting and developing of analysts. We basically decided that there were a couple of key areas. The European markets had to be covered out of London. We wanted a European strategist and country analysts with some industry responsibilities in those markets. So we went out and began recruiting them. The same was true in the Far East, except that Japan was such a big market that we immediately knew we had to have a Japanese strategist and Japanese analysts who really were industry analysts. And that's what we've been building over there.

Now we've got about eight analysts and a strategist in England and eight analysts and a strategist in Japan. And I think that in both cases we're only about halfway to where we're going to be. In each case we've got a research manager in those countries who is directly responsible for the recruiting, and Dennis Sherva is in charge of all our research activities. I make strategy presentations as to what we think the attractive areas of the world to invest in are, and when I travel I'll go out with the analysts and call on companies in countries where we've got some research recommendations.

Another area I got involved in at Morgan Stanley was the buildup of an investment management business. We really started that in the mid-'70s, but the firm was reluctant to go all out at it until about 1980. We started out very low key, with just a couple of guys. Initially, we were not involved at all in the ERISA, big-account business. Then at a planning meeting in 1979 the firm decided to really grow that as a major business line.

It actually was a traumatic moment for me. As I recall, it was at the River Club, down in the basement, and the partners spent a whole day down there. This was a big decision, and there was a lot of opposition to it from some of the older and retired partners. They really felt it was a big mistake, that it was a conflict of interest. The firm was an investment banking firm, and they always had this horrible fear that some investment banking client was going to turn its pension fund over to Morgan Stanley Asset Management, who'd screw it up. And they'd lose the banking relationship for a four tenths of 1 percent fee.

As soon as we made a decision, however, we started to really

191

gear up—in terms of hiring marketing people, more portfolio managers. And we went after all kinds of business, fixed income, ERISA and so on. A very important addition was that I talked Peter Nadosy into joining us on the fixed-income side. Our fixed-income business under him has had spectacular growth, and that was a tremendously important business addition for us. In any event, once we got Morgan Stanley as a whole really supporting us on this effort, we've had very, very strong growth—now probably up in the area of $16 billion or so under management.

Clearly, I suspect it was the right decision. And now that we're publicly owned and asset management earnings are viewed as more stable and worth the higher multiple, it makes sense. When you look back on it, though, it sounds easy. And we obviously made a lot of bad decisions on people in the course of building the research department and building investment management, too.

When you're building businesses and you're growing very rapidly in terms of employment and hiring a lot of people, you're going to make a lot of mistakes. And oftentimes the people that you thought had the highest potential don't work out. And some of the ones that you weren't quite as convinced of but went ahead with anyway turn out to be the real stars.

You have to be humble when you think about all the people mistakes you've made. The firm also had to deal with a culture problem. It was very hard for an investment banking firm to understand what the true market worth of analysts was. One of the great tragedies was [the loss of] Ben Rosen, who was just a superstar, who understood the electronics business and who had connections in the electronics business like no one else in the country. Somewhere back in 1981 we didn't give him an extra 100 shares of stock or something at a promotion period. So he went off on his own and started his own venture capital business, which has been very successful. But we should have promoted Ben Rosen to whatever he wanted, because over the next two or three years alone the amount of business, new-issue business, he would have brought into the firm would have been absolutely staggering. We would have dominated the technology equity markets forever with Rosen there. I did make that argument but it really sort of fell on deaf ears.

I'm a creature of the stock market. So my big successes are in getting secular swings in the stock market right. I think we've gotten some good ones. I was certainly right on the end of the inflationary period of the '70s and the end of the oils. That felt good. I got a lot of abuse in May 1983 for turning bearish. It turned out that was only a month early, but in that month the technology markets had a big move. That was tough. Still, the next couple of years were pretty slack. In retrospect, when we started writing our research reports, the first couple that the analysts put out were devastatingly wrong. But somehow we managed to live through that.

It's like being in the entertainment business. You're only as good as your last call. And when the employees of a financial service firm, your fellow employees, think you've made a wrong [forecast], they tend to turn on you fairly quickly. It can be snide comments in the elevator or the salesman looking at you with a fisheye. It happens.

There are some things we'd have done differently. I think if we'd known then what we know now, we would have gotten into the mutual fund business five years ago. The philosophical truth is that to really grow a business you've got to have the secular wind at your back. When I started at Morgan Stanley, there were something like 275 employees on two floors. You literally knew everybody who was at work every day, everybody at the firm. Now we have more than 5,000 employees. And while it's really been fascinating to see a business grow the way this one has, it makes you appreciate, when you're looking at emerging growth stocks, how perilous the whole thing is.

If Morgan Stanley had started its [research] buildup in the late 1960s, we'd have had a lot of overhead in place during 1973–1974's devastating bear market. The S&P declined 50 percent; the Value Line was down 82 or 83 percent. So the firm would unquestionably have retreated. And we might have been so scarred that we wouldn't have made the initiatives we made in the 1970s. Getting started in 1973 was very fortuitous because we just scooped it at the bottom of a bear market and then we had the wind at our back.

On the other hand, I suppose that we'd have been a lot better off if we'd decided to go into the asset management business in a big way in 1975 rather than waiting until 1980. In about 1976 or 1977 we were really thinking about it, and it was just a question of getting a very strong guy to run it. We were very close, but it just didn't quite work out. That's too bad. Because instead of having $16 billion, we'd have $25 billion now.

Editor: Peter Landau

Herbert A. Allen

President ALLEN & CO., INC.

Herbert A. Allen, better known as Herbert Allen Jr., the son of
Herbert Allen and the nephew of Charles Allen—two of Wall
Street's greatest investors—has made his own mark on the Street
over the last twenty years. Under his leadership, Allen & Co., Inc.
(a sister firm of the elder Allens' partnership) has scored big as a
venturesome investor in the likes of MCI and Columbia Pictures
Industries. The Columbia investment was Allen's claim to fame in
more ways than one: His confrontation with Columbia president
Alan Hirschfield over the handling of studio boss David Begelman,
after Begelman was charged with check forgery, made nationwide
headlines and was the subject of the bestseller *Indecent Exposure*.

Certainly my father and my uncle provided me with an
inestimable advantage. They allowed me as a young man
to go out and do things; I was free to go out there and
make stupid mistakes if I wanted to.

I think the biggest mistake you can make is to move forward
when you don't understand what you're getting into. Correct that:
If you don't *think* you understand what you're getting into. On the
other hand, very often, after you've had a failure or a success, you
realize you didn't understand what you were getting into to begin
with. I think when I first got involved in Columbia Pictures I
didn't understand what I was going into, but it worked.

I went into the Columbia investment because I had nothing else
to do. It was a time when there was very little going on, when it
didn't seem as if there was an awful lot to lose. I figured we might
make some money on the stock, and we'd be investment bankers

195

to the company. And it was show business; it was more interesting than heavy metals. But I never expected to end up in control of the company. Today, if somebody buys 5 percent of a company, he's deemed to be moving forward toward control. In those days, if you bought 5 percent, everybody else quit and you ended up in control. And that's what happened to me at Columbia. Virtually all the directors quit once I got involved.

The company then had roughly $6 million of equity and about $175 million of debt, with no foreseeable means of paying it off. So we formed an executive committee made up of Matty Rosenhaus, Alan Hirschfield, Leo Jaffe and me. Then, separate from that committee, I got involved in choosing the management. I chose the head of the company, the head of the studio, the head of the television division. I was much more involved than I expected to be or even wanted to be. But there was nobody else there.

I never got involved in any creative decision—except once. Alan Hirschfield and I lobbied very hard that we should not make a certain movie. We met with David Begelman, who was then head of the studio, and I spent a total of four hours trying to talk him out of making the movie. The movie was *Shampoo*. It turned out to be the second-biggest picture in the history of Columbia.

In terms of the Begelman business, I think we were caught up in a series of events and a post-Watergate morality. It was very hard for us to get our story across: that Begelman had been fined the largest corporate fine in the history of the country—a million-and-a-quarter dollars—that he had been turned over to the district attorney, that he had been stripped of his titles, that we had been cooperating with the SEC from day one.

There never was a question about Begelman's guilt, but I think the board acted in a humane way. I wouldn't have changed anything that we did with Begelman. The general concept that he got away with something was false. It's just not true. I think he was unfairly hounded by the press. I would imagine that the people who wrote some of the stories about it at the time, if they were to read those pieces today, would have a lot more to be ashamed of than anybody else involved with the case.

I think the mistake I made was with the management; I should have fired Alan Hirschfield the first day I found out that he was negotiating with Jimmy Goldsmith to take over the company. But

I didn't want to; I had known him too long. I was too soft on him. In those days I think I was easier to push around.

A number of people made offers for Columbia. At one point, when the stock was $28, [MGM owner] Kirk Kerkorian bid me $50 a share for my stock alone, which was a very fair price at the time. But I've always felt that one thing that a large shareholder should *not* do is take himself out at the expense of other shareholders. If you're in a position to command a premium for your block of stock, I don't think you have the option of taking the premium. I don't think you use your muscle to gain profit over everybody else in the deal.

We ended up getting $72 a share in Coke stock when we sold it [to Coca-Cola]. The people who bought the original Columbia stock when we bought it would have paid between $3 and $5 a share. And that Coke stock today is worth about $130. That was the best deal we've had.

Another good one was MCI; that was a deal Harold Wit did here. We put up some early money, and then they needed to raise $8 million to make some bank payment. So we did an underwriting for them, a unit deal: I think it was four shares of common and four warrants at 8. The only problem was that the deal fell completely apart. I'd say 80 percent of it was bought back by us. And it ended up being a bonanza because we stayed with it for quite a while.

The deal that gave us the best return on investment was Northwest Energy; we put up nothing—we owned an option—and we made $30 million. There were also a lot of little deals. There was one, Allegheny & Western, another Harold Wit deal, where I think the initial investment was 75 cents. No, it was less than that—40 cents. And the stock is trading at $26.

The worst investments we ever made were in airlines. One was a commuter airline, Washington Airlines. We chose the wrong airline, the wrong route, the wrong time and the wrong management. We probably were the only people in the history of aviation to own a plane called the Dornier Sky Servant. We invested in three of them to fly from Washington to Dulles Airport and to Baltimore. Originally, we were supposed to break even—I remember the figure because it was like the beer—at 3.2 passengers per plane. And each week the break-even point went up until we finally got up to something like twelve, and the plane only carried eleven. I just called them one day and said: "Let's close this thing down. That's enough."

The other one was something called British West Indies Airlines. On that one, the money was gone by the time I signed the check. It was something that Dick Pistell got me into. He had helped start Frontier Airlines and had made a lot of money in Frontier. Dick was a great visionary as well as a great character. He made and lost, in the time I knew him, three separate fortunes. He told me the country the airline operated out of was going to forgive the airline's debt—but the country never did, and we were $30 million in the hole before we started. Ironically, the people we brought in at the end to help us as advisers were an outfit called Lorenzo Carney. I think it was the first big deal Frank Lorenzo ever worked on.

A lot of the deals we did came about because of personal contacts. I was introduced to John MacMillian of Northwest Energy, for instance, through a fellow named Yuri Arkus-Dontov. Yuri was a Russian refugee who left Russia in '23, went to Germany, left Germany in '33, went to France, ended up in the Foreign Legion, serving in God knows where, and then came here in '45 as an aeronautical engineer. I believe Howard Stein gave him a job running money at Dreyfus, where he did well, and then he went on to Equity Funding, where he managed the money there. And, of course, when that house of cards fell, he was out of a job. Not only that, but because of the scandal, it was very hard for him to get work. So he came over here, and I liked him and I gave him an office. And he introduced me to MacMillian.

I prefer not to be on the boards of companies in which we've invested, and I prefer that most of our people not be on boards. It's all right if it's a large company, like Coca-Cola. And if Stan Shuman [an Allen & Co. managing director] is on the board of Rupert Murdoch's company, News Corp. of America, that's fine. But in small, speculative companies, if you're on the board, you tend to overmuscle it a bit. My experience watching the people here is that they tend to get too involved with the company in its fledgling state. You should let the management make its mistakes; either you

198

survive and your investment grows, or you write it off. After all, what do we know about computer chips and biotechnologies?

With Columbia, I came from such a strong belief that you don't get involved with management that I think I oversold myself; I think I overlooked too much, and I don't think I acted as responsibly and quickly as I should have. When Begelman was out of the company, the balance was lost. A couple of the deals they wanted to do early on were just ridiculous—but rather than take those deals as indicative of what management's competence was, I just dealt with the deals themselves and killed them. I didn't put the pieces together early enough.

But if you're a speculator—and certainly that's a major part of our business—you have to accept the fact that you're going to get burned and you're going to make mistakes and you're going to be fooled and you're going to be defrauded. If you get so cynical or hardened by being defrauded or fooled or burned that you say, "I'm not going to do this anymore," then you might as well buy government bonds.

On the whole, it's more fun to believe in people than to constantly assume they are inherently evil and are out to take your cash and return nothing. I think you have to remain open and receptive. It's a little bit like dating: You may go through an awful lot and be disappointed, but it doesn't mean you go to a monastery. You stay in the game.

On the other hand, you can't be foolish. I had four people last year who wrote to me that they wanted $50,000 a year for life because they were nice. Somebody wanted money to play his flute in Nepal; somebody else wanted to be the roller-skating champion of Wisconsin. They felt that because they were good people, they deserved financing, and that because I obviously had more money than I needed, they should have part of it. I understood the logic. I just didn't necessarily agree with the premise.

When you're sizing people up who come to you, you're not looking for great characters and home-run hitters. You're looking for a guy who is just constantly out there making an effort and who is flexible enough so that when his or her original game plan doesn't work, they change it. Because that's one thing that you know for sure: The original game plan for a business almost never works.

199

In today's market I wouldn't do many start-ups because there are so many stocks selling for under $5 that have already been through the experience of moving from the garage to the plant. They've gone through some of their original cash; they've gone through their second round of financing. They've got a little bit of experience. Rather than go through all the growing pains yourself, why not buy something in the market that's already public and where you can buy a decent position?

Looking back on my career, I'd have to say that the greatest successes I've had have been mostly luck, unbelievable luck. Look at it this way: The great growth at Columbia came from the day that Begelman got into trouble. The stock was selling for, give or take, $16 or $17; five years later we got five times our money for it. Begelman stole money, so I was able to reorganize the management, take out what I considered to be an inefficient management and put in an efficient one.

Then Coca-Cola came in. I had nothing to do with that, nor did anybody else on the board at Columbia. Coca-Cola had made a choice between the ethical drug business and the entertainment business, and they didn't want to change the size of their company, so they decided to buy Columbia. Now what did I have to do with that?

We were also lucky that Kirk Kerkorian didn't take control of the company. He owned 20 percent of it, and he very well could have taken it over. So what took place to drive him out? You could say my tenacity in fighting him. But you could more logically say his hotel burned down; some of his allies were involved in the silver markets, and the silver market broke. If that hadn't happened, could he have taken over the company? The answer is, probably.

There was luck in MCI, too. If the underwriting had gone very well, we wouldn't have owned anywhere near as much stock as we ended up owning. We took advantage of the opportunity, but we didn't plan for the underwriting not to go well. There was tremendous luck in that. And in Northwest Energy: We didn't plan for somebody to come along and pay us $30 million to get us out of the way. Now, you could say that it was very smart to position yourself and all that stuff. But essentially, the payoff was due to luck.

There are two sides of the business that we're in now. One, the investment side, is the same as always. You put up your money; you take your chance. The second is the corporate finance func-

200

tion, where you have to follow up, where you have to prepare the brochures that everybody else prepares on Wall Street—things that we don't necessarily think have great value, but if you're going to be competitive, you have to do it.

There were instances where companies in which we invested ended up taking their underwriting business somewhere else— not many companies, but some. And I think it was instructive for us. When we lost Bill McGowan and MCI, it taught us that we had to increase our ability to deal with the customer. And I think we're a lot better at it now.

The competition with the rest of the Street is very tough and, I think, in some cases invigorating. I think it has helped rub the arrogance off the people around here. It's knocked us out of our ivory tower. There's a tendency here sometimes to talk down to people. When you're an investor and you've had a reasonable record, there's a belief that you're right and that the rest of the world doesn't know what you know. And then somebody comes along and knocks you out of your roost, and you wake up and say: "Wait a second. I better get competitive. Maybe I didn't know so much, because if I knew so much, how come I lost MCI?" I think that's very good for us.

Looking ahead, one thing I'd like to do more of is merger and acquisition business. We've done quite a bit of it, but we'd like to do more. With the fees that are being paid now and the level of knowledge you need, why not? My God, people are paying you $5 million and $10 million to put something between two leather-bound things and produce 60 pages of computer printouts.

You know, all they're doing is paying you millions of dollars to pad the rear ends of directors against lawsuits. That's all. In fact, I don't know why a responsible board needs investment bankers at all, except for the decisions of the courts. I mean, everybody's in cahoots on this one: The courts say you have to have due diligence, you prove that you've done due diligence by hiring an investment banker, and so what's the function of a director? The directors should be doing that stuff.

I'm not sneering at any of the people who give us the business. I think we do a superb job, and I really think that we give value in relation to what's paid in the marketplace. But you don't create anything. You don't create any jobs. All you do is build padding for the rear ends of directors. That's all.

I remember when I was in Laos in 1971, and there was an ambassador named Godley there who always reminded me of a lead duck because of the way he walked. They had a State Department walk at that time that looked like they all had problems with their rear ends. He was walking along in the embassy with about eight guys walking behind him. And every time I see investment bankers with their staffs, it always reminds me of Godley and all of these guys walking around, all of whom were doing absolutely nothing. Whenever I sit in a room as a director or when I was chairman of Columbia, seeing these guys parade in, all I can think of is Godley and the ducks behind him. I wonder whatever happened to him.

Editor: Cary Reich

Edward Johnson III

Chairman FIDELITY INVESTMENTS

After 31 years in the mutual fund business, Edward Johnson III says the various aspects of his job still fascinate him. Ned Johnson inherited Boston-based Fidelity Management & Research Co. from his father and nurtured it into one of the powerhouses of the financial services industry. Johnson began his career at Fidelity as an analyst in 1957, managed the Trend Fund from 1961 to 1965 and became president in 1972 and chairman in 1977.

The Trend Fund was the first fund I managed, but then for a short period of time I managed Magellan. It was very small. I can't remember, but it had a half million in assets, whatever it was. It was just starting off.

Jerry [Tsai] started out with me as a teacher, and we ended up as competing portfolio managers. I always thought he was an excellent teacher. I learned a great deal about the stock market from him. He had then and has today an extraordinary energy. At that time there wasn't a company listed on the New York Stock Exchange that he didn't know the quarterly earnings of and a projection for.

I think he would have liked Fidelity to become a public company. We're very happy to remain a private company. I think there are great advantages to remaining private. Most important, the profit we make goes to the people who are doing their job, and all of those jobs have to be done very, very well. It's absolutely essential, and we feel we can motivate people better as a private company.

I assume Jerry wanted to run the business. My father and Jerry were, I always felt, very, very good friends, and I knew my father had extraordinary respect for his skills. There was obviously the question of whether he was going to run the business or whether the family would maintain control. Jerry was, and is, a very successful, very capable person, and it was really just a matter of two different self-interests conflicting.

Jerry had created a tremendous amount of goodwill for Fidelity and created a wonderful name for himself. A lot of investors went with him [when he started the Manhattan Fund], though that didn't really injure Fidelity. In fact, he was good advertising for Fidelity. And he had a chance to build something the way he wanted to build it. And I think the whole process was a very healthy process.

It was back then, about '67, that we went into the leasing business. We were paying very high tax rates and thought leasing, with its obviously favorable depreciation implications, would cut down our taxes and increase our cash flow. We had ambulances, we had an engine in somebody's boat, we had a Lockheed Electra, we had some machine tools—I'd say we had about anything and everything. But we just came and went in the business. We spent some money, we lost some money, and I think we lost enough so that we never made a penny of profit.

It was also about that time that we set up Fidelity International. It seemed to us that some American companies would diversify abroad, and obviously a lot of European and Japanese companies would be very successful and eventually major markets would develop for their securities. Now, as to when all that would happen, I would be the first to say that we had no idea; the general public's tremendous interest in foreign securities in the last couple of years was unpredictable. We knew it would happen sometime, but the timing, to put it mildly, was inscrutable. The important thing, obviously, was to be in a position to be ready whenever it happened.

I remember in those go-go days that when I saw Bernie Cornfeld on the front page, in color, of *Der Stern* magazine, with his favorite cheetah and in his velvet jacket, I knew we were in high territory. In fact, we became quite bearish at the firm in the late '60s, early '70s. The trouble was, we got sucked back in the '72–'73 advance. The Nifty Fifty just tore everybody's guts out, but it was a performance game, and if you didn't own the Nifty Fifty, you were behind.

We may be going back into that now, but instead of its being the Nifty Fifty, it's the Nifty 500, whatever is in the S&P. All of the geniuses have figured out that the best way to have a glorious party is to all join the index, and, needless to say, the consultants recommend it, the clients feel comfortable with it, and the only problem is that all of the money is flowing into a limited number of securities and the index is no longer an index. It's making its own market. What will happen? Come back three years from now and I'll tell you.

After the 1972–74 decline, most equity investors had very substantial losses and there was zero interest in equities or equity mutual funds. That was the first, the only really major correction since the Second World War. And none of the other declines had been accompanied by the enormous negative reaction of the general public and, for that matter, a lot of investment professionals.

Companies that were great at 30 times earnings in Nifty Fifty days no one would touch at eight times earnings. There were good stocks at three and four and five times earnings. They really whetted the appetite. When looking at the attitude of the public, though, and our ability to sell them stocks, it was depressing. We issued a lot of prospectuses and we talked to a lot of people, and we made practically no sales.

The other side of that coin was, if the public didn't want to buy common stocks, they seemed to be interested in money market funds. We thought we could provide a really good service by providing access to the money markets. We could give people a much better deal than they were receiving from their local savings and loan or bank.

Reserve Fund was the first money fund, in 1971. Dreyfus started in 1972, about a year before we did. Dreyfus spent a lot of money on promotion. I don't know what the numbers were, but Dreyfus was taking money in by the bucketful. Dreyfus basically was winning the game by doing a first-class merchandising job. We felt that since we were coming later, we wanted to come in with something that was better. We came up with a lower management fee and offered check-writing service.

The time spent on the check writing, looking at it with the power of hindsight, really didn't pay off. We could have started out the same time Dreyfus did. Instead we wasted a year engineering the check, which was wonderful for the client but it meant that we were not in the marketplace for one year when the market was burgeoning. There were a lot of shareholders just waiting for the service, and they would have been happy without the check. We never spent as much money on promotion as Dreyfus, and you might say it won the lion's share of the market.

I'd say the only lesson learned there was that, if you have something really good, if you don't really promote it, it doesn't matter what the price is or how good it is, you won't gain market share.

When negotiated rates came in about that time, and obviously commissions were going to come down, we were worried about whether we were going to get good research, and we were *very* concerned about whether brokers would ever bother to sell any mutual funds. Brokerage houses find sales organizations very expensive, and here their commission income was going to be cut way back. We had a real question about whether the brokerage industry would ever come back to selling mutual funds in quantity.

We were a company without any distribution at all. If we let things run that way too long, there would be no company left. We had no idea how we were going to create a direct relationship with our customers and sell on a cost-effective basis to them. We knew that developing specialized sales forces just to sell mutual funds was a very, very expensive process. A lot of companies had gotten into financial difficulty trying to do that. IDS was able to do it because they had insurance and savings certificates as well as mutual funds, so they could support an independent sales force.

And that's why we focused on the use of the telephone and the printed page to sell our mutual funds. We thought this would probably be a cheaper, more effective means of distribution. Advertising in the '70s, when nobody wanted equities, was a waste of money. But when we tried again, in the '80s, it began to work a little better. All I can say is, thank goodness it worked. I don't know what we would have done if it hadn't worked! We wouldn't be here today.

Nobody had really ever set up a complete telephone-based information service that allowed you to call up and find out anything about your account or place an order—a complete facility working through the telephone. I think we started out with about six people in a room, and they made a hell of a lot of noise. First we had six-button telephones, and then we got the 25-button units. Oh God, I remember that wonderful feeling of going down and looking at that room and seeing all of the lights lit up.

But it was a wonderful feeling only up to a point. Then you realized that some of the calls weren't being answered on a timely basis. That led to our interest in the use of automatic call switches. There was no way that we could afford to spend more than a few thousand dollars. So we went to a local inventor who was going to build his own switch. We were his first installation.

I remember this closet of about 150 square feet, and there were shelves all around the room. Sitting on the shelves were telephones—no people, no desks, no anything. Each of the phones was wrapped in a kind of T-shirt, so when its bell rang it didn't make a hell of a racket. There was some kind of sensing device and timer on each one of these phones so when it started to ring, it was put on hold, and the switch put all the calls in a queue. I don't think it ever functioned the way it was supposed to.

My interest in technology goes pretty far back. When I was a kid, I liked gadgets. I used to have an intercom system running between my room and the rest of the house. I can remember one time when I was around twelve or thirteen, my sister was beginning to have a stream of boyfriends coming through the house, so my friend and I lowered a microphone outside the window. My sister and her boyfriend were sitting there when all of a sudden they heard a bump . . . bump . . . bump outside their window and they saw this big microphone.

In the late '50s, early '60s, I'd say Fidelity was as far behind in technology as you could possibly be. I think we had some of those mechanical calculators that whenever you pushed a button, they made a hell of a racket. I think the first electronic calculator was in the trading room. It was a Wang and it had a great enormous cable, about three eighths of an inch thick, that went down to a tremendous box that sat under the desk.

We used an outside service bureau for the accounts. Shawmut Bank did our account processing. Then we decided we would be mavericks and have a little competition for our outside transfer agent, so we brought the State Street Bank in, and it subsequently became the largest independent transfer agent.

But we always had a problem [with outside processing services]. When something was wrong, the shareholders would always call us up and blame us. We'd suggest they talk to the Shawmut Bank or the State Street Bank. They would say: "Well, you know, you sold us the account, you straighten it out. We don't know who the hell the Shawmut Bank is."

And there was always tension back and forth between the bank and ourselves. The bank was very interested in building up its balances, but it was hard for it to have the same attitude toward our shareholders that we would have toward them. After all, you can't think of any commercial bank that has grown to a tremendous size that goes to another bank or independent demand deposit manager to do all of the bookkeeping on their deposits. They may clear through another bank, but they deal directly with their own customers. So we thought if we're gonna have really good service, we better provide it ourselves.

So in 1970 we purchased a computer system [for shareholder accounting] called Valhalla. We spent $2 or $3 million on it, but it never ran for us. It spewed out a paper tape, and then all these paper tapes were all meant to be run through a paper-tape reader that fed all the data into a mainframe. It was slow and just didn't work efficiently.

Well, we didn't want to admit defeat or we just didn't have any sense, one or the other. We decided that if that system didn't work, we'd canvas the country and find the best one available.

We ended up choosing Data-SysTance [now DST Systems] software, which turned out to be excellent. It ran on an IBM machine, so we had to buy one. The whole thing ran the first weekend that they put it on the computer. To put it mildly, we were amazed. Even today we are still on exactly the same system.

Most of the hardware we bring in here lasts, on average, about three years. But it really depends on how fast you are growing, because if your business is growing at 20 percent a year, it's possible that certain parts of your computer operation can be growing at 40 percent a year. That, of course, is caused by the development of new applications, which keep taking more and more computer power.

All during the '70s, though our equities under management were going down, we kept the size of the investment department the same. Consequently, I think the quality of the investment research greatly improved between 1975 and '80.

As the bull market began in 1982, fortunately most of our managers were paying more attention to the value of securities at the time, rather than trying to second-guess the direction of the stock market. We were in what at that time appeared to be the cheapest securities.

I remember being very skeptical about the start of the bull market in 1982, asking the technical department, "Has any bull market ever started in this way?" I don't think I got an answer back from the technical department for about four months, when it was obvious what the answer was.

The money didn't start coming when the bull market started. It was almost a year lag, between six months and a year. It was one of these things that started slowly.

The job I have, really, is to work in the parts of the business that need strengthening, where the company itself needs to have a greater understanding of what it's doing. I also think that the person responsible for the organization has to know something about the newer parts of the business, like marketing and the computer area. And so my first ten or fifteen years in the business were spent more on the investment side and then on administration, then into marketing, then into servicing and then in the computer operation. You're always working on that part of the business that needs work the most.

The nice thing about our business is all of these areas are fascinating, whether it's dealing with public relations or dealing with stock market decisions or what role Fidelity ought to play vis-à-vis the companies we invest in. Because clearly, today in America too many large corporations are the property no longer of shareholders but of management and investment bankers. Together they're having a ball and sometimes clearly at the expense of their common shareholders. They've sort of forgotten who

209

their owners are. We don't think there needs to be a great revolution, but we think that maybe shareholders, such as ourselves and pension funds, shouldn't take a totally passive role and just say, "Hey, if they're a bunch of idiots, sell it out." We have to be more activist.

This is going to cost money, this is going to take time, and this is going to mean companies like ourselves are going to have to develop new skills. I think that we have to have a separate process for voting proxies. We don't believe we should force our analysts to get into these issues; that isn't what we hired them for, and it isn't where their expertise lies. It really has to be separate from the investment process, because the skills needed are very specialized skills, more management issues than valuation issues. So it has to be done separately. And I think if it is done separately, we can have an influence on some of the companies that we invest in. We have lots of ideas about it, but they change every day. I think at this point the only thing we would say is that we will be moving cautiously in the direction of more involvement in—what shall I say?—shareholder issues.

Editor: Larry Marion

Henry Kaufman

Chief Economist SALOMON BROTHERS

When Henry Kaufman talks, the stock and bond markets listen, and the impact of his bullish 1982 prediction is already part of Wall Street lore. The Street's most famous economist talks about what goes into his predictions, and how he came to be called Dr. Gloom.

The last twenty, 25 years have been a period of very significant change in financial markets. When I came to Salomon Brothers in January of 1962, the structure of the markets was far different from anything today. They were highly compartmentalized. There were credit market demarcations. Institutions more or less understood what they were supposed to do and what not to do. There was a kind of cyclical rhythm to economic and financial life.

The bond business was a very stately, quiet business. The three-month Treasury bill rate in 1962 probably was at around 2¾ percent and fluctuated maybe five basis points a week. The long government bond at the time probably was around 4 percent and fluctuated maybe one-half to one-quarter point a week in price. And we were still in the period in which we did not have the auction system in anything except the bill market. The bonds that were sold were sold on a rights offering. It was a different world, really.

There were no real bond analysts around that were writing in any way, but Sidney Homer, who was my mentor and under whom I worked for quite a number of years, was an individual who had an enormous grasp of the bond market. He was able to put that grasp into an analytical framework, which no one had done heretofore in the fixed-income markets.

I had come from the Federal Reserve Bank of New York, and Homer said, "Well, you ought to do a weekly commentary in-house on what the Fed is doing, and you ought to track the U.S. Treasury." Today you have legions of people who are tracking every nuance of monetary operation, but at that point there were very few who were really monitoring the Fed on a day-to-day basis: What's the Federal Reserve going to do? Is it going to buy? Is it going to sell? Is it going to do repos? How is it going to operate in the market? And what is it targeting?

And so I did this, and I did the same thing for Treasury financing requirements. I wrote for a while an in-house commentary on the weekly banking statistics, and that gave birth to the "Comments on Credit."

Now, there was an event in 1962 that people didn't pay that much attention to. It was the year in which Citicorp issued the first negotiable CD. It was the beginning of the liberalization of the Regulation Q ceilings on time and savings deposits. It was, I think, the birth of the restructuring of the financial markets, because it was then that the banks started gradually to bid for funds; previously, people just went into the bank to deposit.

In that period of the early 1960s, the balance-of-payments problem also started to emerge, as did the need to deal with it under the Bretton Woods agreement. And we had, therefore, Operation Nudge and Twist, with the Federal Reserve trying to hold up the short rate and hold down the long rate. And then we got into a period of monetary restraint, the first credit crunch in 1966, and it shocked participants to see the tautness in the marketplace. I remember the '66 credit crunch quite well. It occurred when the three-month Treasury bill rate in August–September–October of that year hit 5⅝ percent, and Standard Oil of Indiana, a triple-A industrial, came to market with a 6 percent coupon—unheard of. We were over at 60 Wall Street, and, I must tell you, when that credit crunch occurred in the summer of that year, conditions were more taut than when the prime rate hit 21½ percent in the early '80s.

In '66 the pressure on the thrift institutions was extraordinary because disintermediation in real size came along for the first time. I think it was Sidney Homer and I who coined "credit crunch," and I believe it was in the summer of that year that this word, "disintermediation," came into being. We ran a little campaign in the "Comments on Credit," asking for substitute words for "disintermediation." It's a terrible word. And people wrote in the weirdest things: "circumfiduciation," for example.

That was the first real shock in terms of functioning in this new environment. That was the beginning of change, and Regulation Q was liberalized some more. We had a mini-recession the spring of 1967, and the credit crunch eased. But then the Vietnam War heated up, and the economy rebounded and the markets flared back exceedingly quickly.

I remember being down in Washington in the summer of '68 and visiting with Art Okun, who was then chairman of the Council of Economic Advisers. Congress had just approved a request by President Johnson to raise taxes, and Okun got the call as I was sitting in his office, and he said: "Oh, Congress just approved some increase in tax. Now we can ask the Federal Reserve to become somewhat more accommodating. Here's the trade-off."

But the market had been anticipating a cut in the discount rate, and when the Fed finally gave in, it was the low in yields for that cycle. After that, the market just went straight against everything. Even though the Fed held the short rate, long-term and intermediate interest rates just started to move up. And then the issue was: How high is high?

I sensed as we moved into that '68–'69 period that there was something changing in the financial system where we were removing all kinds of impediments to interest rates. And we were also gradually removing constraints for markets, for financial institutions to be in different types of businesses. And I felt that this was going to eventually have its impact on the interest rate structure, that we could not look back historically and say, "This is a high level of interest rates, and this level of interest rates is going to cut away economic activity."

As we moved through the 1970s, I always thought that interest rates would move higher than generally anticipated for the very simple reason that interest rates weren't restraining early enough. The financial institution had become part of the mechanism that was pushing credit and would allow the system to operate at a higher level of interest rates. Heretofore the financial institutions really were part of the braking mechanism. They got squeezed and suffered losses when interest rates went up.

But I sensed this was not occurring this time around; it was gradually being abandoned for the very simple reason that, first of all, institutions became buyers of funds; they bid. And then they looked out to see where they could acquire an asset, either a loan or an investment, that would have a higher yield than the cost of the liabilities. This was the beginning of spread banking, and you changed the institutional arrangement as a result. You allowed institutions to protect themselves against changes in interest rates.

And then, of course, we had the advent of floating-rate financing, which helped you structure the maturity of an asset and the rate of return on an asset and have it spread against the liability side. So you were able to take the interest rate risk out of many a financing arrangement for a financial intermediary, although the financial intermediary kept the credit risk. All that, to me, suggested that there was a change and that interest rates were not going to behave anymore like they did in the 1950s or in the early 1960s. I've held that view ever since.

The other thing that I sensed as we were starting to move through the '60s into the early '70s was that attitudes toward credit were changing in the United States. A generation that had been adversely affected by the Depression of the 1930s, that generation was diminishing in influence and power, and the new generation that was coming on-stream in the decision-making process was not working in the 1930s environment at all; they had only heard about it, and they weren't tainted. And I sensed that a more aggressive group was coming into being.

And I remember meeting in the late '60s, early '70s with banking clients. One prominent banker came in and I said, "You're going to have to pay 8 percent if you want to put long money on your balance sheet as a source of funds." And he said, "I'm not going to be the chief executive officer that's going to be identified with an 8 percent coupon."

We moved through a number of squeezes and crises. We had the '66 crunch; '70 was Penn Central; '74 was Franklin National and City of New York; then we had that period of '79, '80 and '81, where we had Penn Square and Continental Illinois. The level of interest rates seemed to suggest that these stringencies were very severe. But in terms of market perception and requirements, it took higher and higher levels of interest rates to have markets recoil.

In November of 1973 the business cycle reached its peak, but I did not change my mind on interest rates. It wasn't until October of 1974, after we had been in a recession eleven months, that I changed my mind. I had attended the World Bank/IMF meeting and I listened to the terrible complaints of every finance minister that spoke officially, and every central banker that I saw unofficially, about the serious problems in the economy and the financial system. That induced me to go back to my room in the hotel and to reassess and to think about how far we had come and how much more risk there was of a rise in yields. And I concluded that I could only be a couple of months wrong, if I was going to be wrong, and therefore I went back to New York and I wrote a memorandum and said that we were very near the cyclical peak in interest rates. And it was very fortunate that interest rates peaked a month later, which was just an accident.

I held that view about declining rates until October of 1976. Then I changed my mind. I became very bearish and didn't change my mind until 1982—except temporarily in the spring of 1980, when President Carter imposed selective credit controls. The reason I became bearish again is because I saw not only the economic revival but the willingness of market participants to ignore old credit standards, to accept the liberalization of credit terms, to expand and utilize debt. And I saw this was going to heat up the economic momentum, so I turned bearish in October '76, and the market bottomed out three months later.

I think that reputation I picked up of being Dr. Gloom came into being because I had these bearish views during relatively long periods in which the bond markets acted adversely. I never felt good about being called Dr. Gloom, but I never worried about it, either, because I think you should try to say it as it is. You're not in a popularity contest here. You try to say things that are in the best interests of the country, and it's better to be forewarned and

215

try to make a change than not to be forewarned at all and to take the adverse consequences.

Starting in about 1974, whenever I've taken a position contrary to the previous one, I have written it down on paper, for a lot of reasons. First of all, I want to meet all of the regulatory requirements. I don't want to front-run anything as such, and if I get misquoted, I want to know the quote that I made. I mean, if somebody misquotes me, why, that's the way it is, but I know, at least, what I've said. So when it came to October of '74 or October of '76, or 1980 or 1982, I wrote out those views and the rationale for them and then disclosed them to the firm and to clients.

I remember the Volcker shock in 1979 quite vividly, because I had been in Europe for a week or two, and when I was about to come back I was told I should go from the airport right up to Armonk with a group of my senior partners to visit with IBM. We were at that time trying to get some of the IBM business. They were about to come into the market for the first time to do a debt financing. This was in September, and the question was, When should they come to market? And I said, "Well, you should come as soon as possible because the backdrop continues to suggest a tightening in the credit market." Inflationary momentum was very strong and very heady, and there was bound to be additional restraint put into the system one way or the other in order to deal with the problem. There was also pressure from a number of countries for us to begin to do more to stabilize the American economic and inflationary situation. Well, they did proceed with a considerable amount of speed and brought their issue to market. And it was the day afterward, as I recall, that the Federal Reserve anounced the change in its operating procedure, the targeting of the monetary aggregates on a more near-term basis. And, of course, that immediately put that famous issue underwater, and we took a loss on the financing.

When the Federal Reserve announced a closer adherence to monetarism, it was clear to me that, first, financial markets were going to be much more volatile than heretofore because the Fed was going to target the growth of money and not pay attention to the movements of interest rates as much as before; and, second, this ran the risk under the new financial setting and environment of interest rates ultimately going much higher than had been generally anticipated, because it freed the Federal Reserve in its own strategy from an interest rate constraint. The Fed just said,

"We're going to provide a certain amount of funds; whatever that will do to interest rates, it will do."

This, of course, occurred against the backdrop of a market that now had floating rates in it and adjustable-rate mortgages, a prime loan rate that was floating, the advent of floating-rate financing in the Euromarket, the beginning of leakages of funds—that is, from one national border through another national border; if you couldn't finance here, you could go to the Euromarket and so on. All of that meant a substantial escalation in the rate structure.

We reached about 21½ percent on the prime rate, and we reached 17¼ percent on the bill rate in the early 1980s. The peak of long-term interest rates was reached in October 1981, when long governments hit about 15¼ percent. I only sensed in the third quarter of 1982 that the economy was not about to get back on its feet very quickly, and so, finally, in August '82 I became bullish. And, of course, that day when I turned bullish, the stock market had the biggest gain in history; on that day bonds rallied dramatically—and in some ways I remember that now more vividly than I did at the time.

We were going into an executive committee meeting for the firm at the Waldorf. I had written the night before a two-pager, indicating that I thought yields would go down quite sharply and my rationale for it. And I'd given it to my driver to deliver to my secretary so she could type it up and put it into our machine, on our screens, to be shown to our traders and salespeople at the same time—oh, around 8:45 or 9:00 in the morning, before the markets opened. I then went to the Waldorf where we had eight people from the executive committee. I got a call from my secretary asking me to explain something that I had written because she was typing it up—I had written in longhand—and I think it was John Gutfreund who said, "What are you on the telephone for?" And I said, "Oh, I just dictated a memo." Somebody said, "What about?" And I said, "Well, I've just changed my view on the market." And they said, "You've changed your view on the market?" Well, by that time it was going on the screen, and then the market went wild.

What then, of course, materialized was the advent of the new administration in Washington, and what bothered me was the budgetary explosion. I'm not against tax cuts; I think that's a wonderful thing to have. But we have tax cuts and big increases in defense expenditures. And it seemed to me unlikely that we could control the budget deficit under those circumstances. I was critical of that. I think that decision laid the foundation for a structural budget deficit that now is causing us problems. And we've been unable to resolve it.

One of the remarkable things that happened in the 1980s was this further sharp explosion in debt, way beyond any historical benchmark. It is way beyond anything that you would have expected relative to GNP, relative to the monetary expansion that was taking place. But it came about, I think, as a result of freeing the financial system, putting into being financial entrepreneurship and not putting into being adequate diciplines and safeguards. So that's where we are.

Editor: Clem Morgello

Karl Otto Pöhl

President DEUTSCHE BUNDESBANK

> When Karl Otto Pöhl took over as Bundesbank (West German central bank) president in January 1980, he was, at 50, the youngest person ever to hold the job. But the breezy, informal Pöhl already had a lifetime's worth of experience in international monetary affairs: As state secretary and a key adviser to former chancellor Helmut Schmidt, he helped negotiate the transition to floating exchange rates and the creation of the European Monetary System.

Frankly speaking, I have to admit that it was one of the very few jobs in my life I really aimed for. I wanted it and I got it, and when I got it I said to myself, "After this I cannot be promoted to anything else, and so I will do everything I can to do this job as well as I can, up to my limits."

The president of the Bundesbank in this country has, how should I say, a very good standing. He's really independent. But it's not as easy as it looks. You have a lot of internal problems to solve because it's a very decentralized system. It's like the Federal Reserve System, I suppose, in that you have eleven central banks from the states, and they get together every fortnight with the members of the executive board. They form what is known as the "central bank council," and I'm the chairman of that council. If I want to reach decisions, I have to aim for majorities. I have to convince people; I have to talk to them. Maybe this is something which some people underestimate.

You know, I started out as an economic journalist. In 1967 I was still an economic journalist, in Bonn. But I always had the feeling I should do something more operational, and in 1968 I became a managing director of the Federation of German Banks. But I didn't do that for very long, because Karl Schiller, who was then economics minister, offered me a job in the ministry. So my career in government began in 1970.

I always had great admiration for Schiller, but when I came into government I learned he was more an economist than a politician. He stuck to his principles; I always admired that and still do. But in May 1971, when he decided to let the D-mark float against the dollar, he did it in a very unpolitical way. He just let the D-mark float, and then he informed people afterward. And so everybody was upset about this decision, which, I think, in substance was entirely the right decision. But it was very badly prepared. I learned from this that it's not only necessary to have the right convictions and the right analysis, but you also have to think about how you are going to implement them.

When Schiller decided to resign, I thought that would be the end of my career, because everybody thought I was very close to Karl Schiller—intellectually, that is, not privately, not personally, but intellectually. But to my surprise, and to maybe everybody's surprise, when Helmut Schmidt became finance minister after the election of 1972, he offered me the chance to be his state secretary. I accepted it, and we had a great time.

We had enormous speculative flows at that time, if you remember. And Schmidt dealt with this turmoil in the exchange markets in a completely different way than Karl Schiller. Schmidt was much more a politician than an economist. Schiller had already had this idea of having a European monetary system, but he didn't succeed in implementing it. Schmidt handled it in a much more clever way. He arranged the system of floating against the dollar but having relatively stable exchange rates within Europe, and so we had the European Monetary System, which he and Giscard d'Estaing can take credit for.

Another thing which started at the time was the Group of Five, the informal meetings of finance ministers and central bank governors of the leading industrialized countries. We called it the "library group" because it all started in May 1973 in the library of the White House. There was a group of only eight people at the meeting: George Shultz [then secretary of the U.S. Treasury], Giscard, Schmidt, Tony Barber, Volcker, Claude Pierre-Brosso-lette, Derek Mitchell and myself. When Schmidt and Giscard became chancellor and president, they thought it would be a good idea to continue this kind of meeting on a higher level. Schmidt said, "We want to keep this very informal, and so every head of state or government should appoint only one personal representative." I was asked to do that job on the German side. Raymond Barre was on the French side, Shultz on the U.S. side. We also had the so-called Group of Twenty, in which Emminger [Otmar Emminger, Pöhl's predecessor as Bundesbank president] and I represented the Federal Republic. I was a newcomer in that club, which had all these experts like Emminger, Volcker, Bob Solomon and others.

I remember somebody saying at one of these meetings, "Floating rates—that's no system," and I said, "Maybe it's the system of the future and we have to live with it." I was in favor of floating—in contrast to Helmut Schmidt, who never liked it very much. He always thought that floating is anarchy and disorder and what have you. I have a much more positive assessment, even today. Of course, we have seen enormous fluctuations of exchange rates, which were very harmful in many respects. On the other hand, I don't think we would have overcome the oil price increase and other shocks during the last fourteen years with a fixed exchange rate system. And without floating exchange rates in the '70s, I don't think we in Germany would have been as successful as we were in avoiding inflationary pressures.

When Karl Klasen decided to retire as Bundesbank president in 1977, Otmar Emminger, who was deputy president, became president, and I became deputy president. But everybody knew that Otmar wouldn't serve very long because he was already 66 when he became president, and he was appointed for only two-and-a-half years. When he retired, there was a long debate on who should succeed him. I was not the obvious candidate. I was regarded as too close to Helmut Schmidt. Everybody knew that [Deutsche Bank co-chief executive] Wilfried Guth was Schmidt's favorite, and he certainly would have been an excellent president of the Bundesbank. But finally the government decided to appoint me and not Wilfried. I think it had something to do with the fact that there had already been a Deutsche Bank chairman [Klasen] as president, and, after all, Wilfried was not so interested in

221

it at the time. I don't know all the details, and I don't want to elaborate too much on that.

As soon as I took over here, I had to deal with a change in the performance of the German economy. After so many years of surpluses and appreciation of the D-mark, for the first time we had this current account deficit, an acceleration of inflation, capital outflows and downward pressure on the D-mark. This was a very new experience, but the government didn't recognize that—at the beginning at least. In 1980 we had the highest current account deficit any industrialized country had ever had: $15 billion. So I thought we had to do something about it, and we raised interest rates step by step. Of course, the U.S. Fed had started this policy already, so we had to follow suit to a certain extent. But I also had the feeling that the D-mark was approaching a crisis of confidence.

We decided on this very spectacular increase in interest rates in February '81. And that was when I had my confrontation with Helmut Schmidt; he was really angry about that. There was a conflict between the Bundesbank and the government, and it was a conflict he could only lose, because in this country the Bundesbank has a very high reputation and the government had at that time a very low reputation. They had a high budget deficit and were criticized by everybody, and so we had public opinion behind us. And looked at from hindsight, it becomes very clear that we were right. The climate changed dramatically. We got a decline in inflation; we also got a recession, but it was a very short one, and we had a turnaround in the economy already at the end of 1982.

A little later, we had the beginning of the international debt crisis. I remember it was September of 1982 when Fritz Leutwiler [then president of the Swiss central bank and the Bank for International Settlements] called me on a Saturday afternoon to tell me that Mexico was close to default and that Paul Volcker had requested the support of the BIS, which could only be provided with the backing of the leading central banks. We arranged the emergency loan to Mexico within 24 hours that weekend; it was there on Monday morning.

I had a slightly different view on the way to deal with this crisis than, say, Volcker or Gordon Richardson had. I was a little more relaxed. They were more nervous about its leading to a world financial crisis and so on. I was not so nervous about that. My attitude—and it was also the attitude of Leutwiler and other European central bankers—was that we should first of all insist on the debtors and creditors dealing with this problem themselves, before involving the BIS and the central banks. I was also against this arm-twisting of banks. I told our banks here in Germany, "Look, it's your debtor, and you have to be interested in keeping your debtor liquid. If you want to maintain your business relationship with a country like Mexico, I think you have no choice. But it's your decision." I'm still convinced this is the right attitude, at least under German circumstances.

Yes, to a certain extent we were arm-twisting the banks in the case of Schröder Münchmeyer [the German bank that came close to collapse in late 1983 after making excessive loans to the IBH construction machinery group]. In that situation we thought it was appropriate and necessary, and it was necessary for only a few banks. All the big banks knew what was at stake.

This thing was pretty terrible for me personally because Ferdinand von Galen [then head of Schröder Münchmeyer] was a close friend of mine. I had known him for many years, long before I became president of the Bundesbank. When he came to see me to tell me what had happened, I was terribly shocked; it was like a lightning bolt out of the blue.

It was suggested that all banks that had deposits of, I think it was Dm10 million or more, had to change these deposits into capital. Two or three banks made problems about this; it was ridiculous because the money was lost anyway, so they wouldn't lose anything more by doing this. So we twisted them a little bit, and finally we got what we wanted. This thing was isolated and kept under control. The deposit insurance fund of the Federation of German Banks stepped in and provided some Dm100 million to cover the losses. So, legally, the Schröder Münchmeyer bank has never gone into bankruptcy.

The Schröder Münchmeyer case was not like the Herstatt thing, which was a kind of bushfire around the world. We learned from the Bundesbank's experience with Herstatt, and we tried to avoid the mistakes they made at that time.

We have had enormous shocks in the market over the past twenty years: the oil shocks, the debt crisis, the collapse of the Bretton Woods system. Yet today I would say we are again facing a very difficult situation; in a sense it is maybe even more difficult than it was in 1980 and 1981, because at that time it was very clear what we had to do. The tightening of monetary policy was very easy to justify. But today's problems are more complicated for central banks. We are expected to stimulate economic growth, keep interest rates low, exchange rates stable and at the same time avoid a revival of inflation. This comes close to squaring the circle.

Looking back, I would say that my greatest accomplishment here was how we handled the 1980–81 situation. That was very, very difficult for me, taking into account that Helmut Schmidt had brought me into this position and was a man I admired very much. I think that was the main achievement. And I take some credit for myself for that, I must say. But I was also lucky during this period. As Frederick the Great once said, a general needs to know his profession, but on top of that he needs a little luck, too.

Editor: Cary Reich

Johannes Witteveen

Former Managing Director INTERNATIONAL
MONETARY FUND

By his own account, the International Monetary Fund was an institution in search of a raison d'être when Johannes Witteveen, a
former Dutch minister of finance, took over as managing director
in 1973. Indeed, the end of the dollar's convertibility and the collapse of the Bretton Woods accords had rendered the IMF's articles of incorporation completely irrelevant. But less than a year
after his arrival at the fund, the world was reeling from the first oil
shock. Under Witteveen's leadership, a suddenly revitalized IMF
provided relief in the form of oil facilities (one of which bore his
name) and embarked on a whole new era with its precedent-setting
loan arrangements, based on strict conditionality, for Britain and
Italy.

Today we have become accustomed to muddling through, and we know that monetary reform is very difficult. But when I came to the IMF in 1973, the United States had only relatively recently stopped convertibility of the dollar, so that the basis of the old Bretton Woods system was taken away. And that was a shock. The international monetary community was engaged in a very intensive debate about reforming the system, and there was the Committee of Twenty, chaired by Jeremy Morse, trying to design a blueprint. It worked on very ambitious schemes for what was called "stable but adjustable exchange rates." That was the aim.

In order to achieve that aim it was necessary to have rather close cooperation among the different countries, and there was a discussion about which countries would have to take certain measures and so on. All this implied, of course, strong discipline for all countries, including the United States. There were differences of views about this, about how it should be developed. But I think as discussion went on, governments became more and more reluctant to accept these rules and this discipline. And then when, at the end of 1973, the first oil crisis started, there was an argument that said, "Well, now we face such pressure and such difficulties that we can't accept this monetary reform, although we believe in it for the future. We hope in the coming years to achieve some elements of it, but for the time being we can't continue." And the Committee of Twenty was disbanded.

The urgent thing at that time was how to face the oil crisis. We had a meeting in January 1974, the last meeting of that committee, which I think was at that time very successful. Because at that meeting I proposed the first oil facility of the International Monetary Fund to cope with the problem of these oil deficits, to enable countries to finance these deficits short-term, with relatively light conditionality. There was very widespread support. Mainly the United States and Germany were reserved about it, but these reservations were later overcome and that oil facility was established. That was one thing. The other was that in that meeting we also agreed on a new valuation of special drawing rights. It was a small but necessary element of reform; after the dollar was no longer convertible, the SDR couldn't be tied just to the dollar anymore.

The central banks were not ready—and still are not ready—to give a major role to the SDR in their reserves. That is, of course, related to the legal restrictions that still limit the role of the SDR. Central banks are much happier with dollars and other currencies which they can trade every day in the market; that's what they need. So in all the discussions about the role of the SDR, there's always resistance on the part of the central banks of the main creditor countries. They didn't really consider it a sufficiently attractive reserve asset. There was a kind of competition in the debate between dollars, gold and SDRs. And I remember a personal discussion with Mr. [Bernard] Clappier, the governor of the Banque de France at that time, who said we had these three racehorses, and he was afraid the dollar would win. He would have liked gold to win, perhaps, but he certainly didn't expect the SDR to win.

At the end of my term I made a suggestion to create a substitution account. Dollars were being accumulated all the time; the dollar was very weak then, people were fearful there were too many dollars and didn't want to hold them. So I started some thinking in the fund about a substitution account where countries could change their dollars for SDRs. The SDR's characteristics would have to be improved in order for it to be usable in the market, and there was quite a debate about this after I left the fund. Proposals were worked out, but finally they were not accepted.

It was a very interesting idea. That would have been a real change in the monetary system, away from the kind of multiple-reserve currency system that we now have to an SDR system. That was always the intention—for the SDR to become the main reserve asset. But, of course, there were complications in it; guarantees by governments were needed, and in the end nobody was sufficiently interested. The governments didn't see a real need, no real pressure to overcome the difficulties. In the end they preferred to accumulate dollars.

But the main discussion at that time was about how far governments should intervene in exchange markets. And the feeling in the United States was that it should not be done at all. Instead, there should be "clean floating"; all intervention in exchange markets was called "dirty floating," and the United States was opposed to that.

I remember quite well that in my first address to the annual meeting in Nairobi in 1974, I advocated some management of exchange rates. I felt that now we had floating exchange rates, but at least some management was very desirable. And there were some differences on that with the United States. So that debate went on, and in the amendment of the articles of incorporation of the IMF it became an important issue. They had to be amended because of the system of floating exchange rates. The articles were not relevant anymore, they were not being obeyed.

So what should we put into the articles now about exchange

rates? There was a strong difference of view, mainly between the United States and France, so that in the end a kind of group of two was created. This problem was finally negotiated between only the United States and France—Ed Yeo, the under secretary of monetary affairs, traveling to Paris to see Jacques de Larosière, who was then head of the French Treasury, and Larosière traveling to New York. So they worked it out together. And I remember quite well that when they finally had agreed on this, they told us, "This is such a difficult negotiation you can't change it. It has to be accepted as it is."

The French felt it was good for the IMF because the role of the fund was clearly formulated; there would be—and this is a very strong term—"firm surveillance" of exchange rate policies by the International Monetary Fund. But, of course, this had to be discussed in the executive board. I brought our lawyers to look at it. Sir Joe Gold, our legal counsel, of course could point out that the idea might be all right, but it was not drafted in a legally correct way. And when it was discussed in the executive board, some other directors brought in some better formulations, so in the end it was changed to some extent. But the main elements remained as those two had negotiated it. To amend the articles, you need a rather large, qualified-majority vote. (You know that member countries have different votes according to the size of their economies and so on.) It's quite a difficult and time-consuming process. There was a very long negotiation that was finally concluded in a meeting in Mexico City in 1976. So, in a way, that concluded the debate on monetary reform in that period.

It legalized floating under certain rules of surveillance by the fund. Then the question was how that surveillance should function. And I think it has been disappointing. When the amendment was adopted, the staff of the fund felt that this was really giving a very strong position to the IMF. I was always more doubtful about it because I felt it would be very difficult for the fund, especially with respect to the major countries, to have an influence on what happens to exchange rates or the policies they follow. Because as long as these countries don't have to come to the fund for financial assistance, we really have no power, no sanctions. And it is always a matter of judgment whether certain policies are more or less desirable. So I thought it would be extremely difficult.

In fact, when I had the first discussion with Ed Yeo and some of

228

his staff about this agreement he had reached, I suggested that in order to make this firm surveillance function it would be very desirable to have regular meetings between central bankers and ministers of finance of the main countries, together with the managing director of the fund. The fund could be involved in the discussions and the debate which comes before actual policy decisions are taken. But Yeo rejected that. He said: "No, that is not the idea. The fund should be the judge, and it should come in *after* we have taken our decisons." Now that was very nice to put it like that—the fund as an objective judge. But, of course, in practice it's very difficult to make that effective. And as you know, this is all still in flux. Some time ago the Group of Five decided there would be meetings about changes in policies in which the IMF would participate. But I don't think it has happened very often.

The large industrial countries are more inclined to make their own decisions. It's difficult enough for them to consult each other and to coordinate together—the Germans, the Japanese and the Americans—and they are really reluctant to let the fund, even the managing director, in on very sensitive policy discussions.

Another interesting aspect was the role of gold. In the articles of incorporation there was an official price of gold. This was not realistic anymore because the market price had moved up much higher. So we needed also some amendment with respect to gold; the role of gold in the monetary system had to be reduced. It was a difficult debate because many central banks still attached great value to their gold and wanted to keep an important role for gold in their reserves. I proposed that the fund sell part of its gold in order to help the developing countries, especially the low-income developing countries. This was finally decided, and the fund sold 25 million ounces of gold, which was a very important assistance to these countries. And the same amount of gold was also given back to all the member countries. That was a kind of compromise decision.

I think it was a much better situation at that time. The fund is not meant to be an institution specially designed to help developing countries. It is meant to help all its member countries when their balance-of-payments situation requires some assistance. The

229

IMF played a crucial role in restoring some equilibrium to Britain and Italy. These were very important and interesting negotiations, in that the fund had considerable influence on the policies of these important industrial countries. And that strengthened, in a way, the position of the fund in its negotiations with developing countries. Because they were looking very carefully to see whether the same strictness and the same conditions were applied to these important countries as the fund applied to the developing countries.

That is what made the negotiations with Britain so difficult, because the British wanted to get the maximum support. They came to the fund saying, "Our policies are all right, so now we want to draw the full four tranches from the fund." And it was a very considerable amount of money for that time. Of course, we didn't agree that their policies were right. We felt their deficit was much too large and the public sector borrowing requirement was much too high. We felt it should be reduced by cutting expenditures. That was mainly what the negotiation was about. The negotiations lasted for a few motnhs, and in the end I came to London myself at the critical moment when the British cabinet was debating it.

I talked first to [Chancellor of the Exchequer Denis] Healey and his officials and then with [Prime Minister James] Callaghan himself. And it was decided. I still remember that Healey was very relieved after the discussion with Callaghan, because apparently that was the first time that Callaghan as prime minister had expressed a view on the whole issue. He had always remained kind of neutral, not supporting the chancellor on this, and that made it very difficult for Healey to get any kind of decision out of the cabinet that would be acceptable to the fund.

So that was a crucial discussion. And I think it was very successful. After that the pound strengthened considerably, and that restored the confidence of the market and restored equilibrium in the British economy. But it was also a *test* for the fund, because the British had really tried, in various ways, to press the IMF to accept their drawing with no or inadequate conditionality. They had been pressing the Americans and the Germans to put pressure on the fund to be somewhat easier. And if we had made it easy for Britain, then it would have been very difficult to maintain conditionality for developing countries.

Now I must say the Americans didn't give in to this pressure; I wouldn't have given in in any case, but they didn't press me to be easy. In fact, Arthur Burns, who was chairman of the Federal Reserve Board, was very supportive. He called me on the telephone one evening to tell me that he was behind the fund's position. He put it like this: "We have to keep to the rule of law." He considered fund conditionality a kind of international rule of law. And I think that was quite right.

In the Italian case, it was not necessary for me to come to Rome to finalize the negotiations. It was all prepared by the staff. But at the end, Mr. [Gaetano] Stammati, the minister of finance, came to Washington to talk about the difficult final issues. And I'll never forget I had to discuss the whole afternoon with Mr. Stammati the details of indexing wages in Italy. We wanted some elements, I think some public tariffs, to be taken out, and that was the sticking point. Finally, I reached an agreement with Mr. Stammati. I think that was a very, very extraordinary case of influence of the fund on rather detailed aspects of the policies of an industrialized country. Because sometimes even governments of industrialized countries seem to need some kind of external pressure to do what is really necessary—and what the minister of finance himself very clearly saw was necessary but couldn't get accepted by his colleagues or the labor unions or Parliament.

But that was a special case. It was not a situation, as we have today after the debt crisis, where many developing countries have very serious problems. In fact, during this period when I was at the fund, the problem was that the banks were so easy in lending to these countries. In cases where a country got into difficulty, the banks were supportive of the fund. They didn't want to lend any further unless there was a fund drawing—in the case of Peru, for example. But before that, they had been lending so much to Peru that an enormous disequilibrium could grow. And those developing countries who were considered generally to be creditworthy could borrow so easily from the banks that they didn't have to come to the fund at all. It was mainly the poor developing countries which came to the fund; in the case of Peru, disequilibrium had grown so large that they came to the fund too late. There was a discussion at that time: How can we bring about a situation where countries come to the fund at an earlier stage, before such

231

an enormous disequilibrium develops? Because it is very painful and difficult to restore equilibrium. So that was the situation at that time.

There was a change around 1976 in my position, in the fund's position. In '74 and '75 I felt that these very large oil deficits had to be financed, because if all countries had tried to adjust immediately to these deficits it would have pushed the world into recession. So some time was needed to adjust. And I said in my speech at the annual meeting in Manila in '76 that now the policy should shift toward adjustment. But that wasn't done sufficiently. I think at that time countries, especially the developing countries that were borrowing so heavily, should have adjusted more and the banks should have become more reserved. But they were still in their big lending spree. They felt there was no sovereign risk and it was a marvelous thing to do—the expanded lending with nice margins and so on. So it just went on.

The main thing the banks were pressing for was to get more information from the fund; that was the main issue. That was impossible for the IMF because much information was given to the fund on a very confidential basis, and the staff was afraid that if it were given to the banks we wouldn't get that information anymore. It would make the consultations between the fund's staff and these countries much more limited. Nevertheless, in general terms, information was given to the banks. They were told in informal discussions and telephone calls and so on how the fund judged the country. So there was, I think, a good working relationship between the fund and the banks.

At the same time the developing countries began to press the fund a little bit for easier conditionality. But we never gave in to that; we always explained that this was really what was needed. [The pressure] was not as strong as it is now; the situation was not as difficult, of course. The world economy was still growing, and real interest rates were still very low.

As for the achievements of the fund, I think the various facilities which I created were the most important—the oil facilities and the supplementary facility later—because it was the first time that the fund organized such a facility, borrowed money in the market in order to lend it again to different countries. I think it worked very well at that time, and it was a step toward giving the fund a more active role in financial markets. It was also an efficient and fast reaction of the fund to a change in the world situation. I'm still somewhat proud of that. Very quickly after the oil crisis came about, by the second half of December of '73, the fund had correctly estimated the consequences for balance-of-payments situations, and in a meeting in January of the Committee of Twenty, we had a complete proposal on the table to cope with that difficulty. That was really very efficient for an international organization.

In fact, I feel that if the main countries would have given more support to the oil facility at that point, the present debt problem would have been less serious. The influence of the fund on these countries would have been stronger, there would have been better adjustments, and the role of the banks would not have been so large. The position of the industrial countries, but mainly the United States, has been, however, that these deficits should as far as possible be financed through the markets, and only in cases where they couldn't be completely financed through the market was there a role for the fund. That, of course, kept the oil facility limited and maximized the role of financing by the banks.

And I think that if another position would have been taken by the main industrial countries at that time, many oil-exploring countries would have been willing to lend a much larger part of their surpluses to the fund. The Saudis especially were very positive about the fund at that time. The oil-producing countries had confidence in the fund, perhaps precisely because they were not so very sophisticated. It was a very new task for them to invest enormous amounts of money, and I think they felt that lending to the IMF was a very safe investment. And it was also positive international cooperation; they liked that. It was a very good relationship.

I traveled to all these countries and discussed it with their governments. The Iranians and the Saudis were the most supportive. There was in the beginning some reluctance on the part of the Kuwaitis, who felt that they would in this way be supporting the United States or the industrial countries. And I explained to them that this was not the case; on the contrary, I said, the United States was not so very happy about the oil facilities; this was more a help for the developing countries. This helped convince the

233

finance minister at that time, [Abdul Rahman al-] Atiqi, to support it.

It was interesting that they gave that support to the IMF and didn't make difficulties about the fact that Israel could draw on the facility. The Saudis only asked that the fund should not use their currency but rather another one. So we used Venezuelan bolivars for Israel's drawings. The Saudis were very reasonable in that respect.

Eventually, I overcame the initial opposition of the United States. And in the later facility—the supplementary facility that was sometimes called the Witteveen facility—I must say I had very strong support from the United States. [Former Treasury secretary Michael] Blumenthal and [then New York Federal Reserve president Anthony] Solomon felt that this could be very useful in a world economy where deficits were still large and could develop still further, and they supported this very strongly.

There was a kind of competition at that time between the IMF and the "safety net" proposal at the OECD. This was meant for industrial countries; they got into financing difficulties because of increasing oil prices, and the OECD said they should create a safety net. That would have been a very new development for the OECD, which is mainly a consulting and advisory body; it would have called them into the financing role in competition with the IMF. So I think it would have, to some extent, weakened the position of the fund. But it didn't come off; the U.S. Congress was against it and, more or less instead of that, supported the supplementary facility in the IMF. What was important was that after very extensive negotiation, it was the oil exporters and the industrial countries that together financed this.

In general, I think in these years there was positive spirit with respect to international cooperation. It seems to have become less later on. There was also more understanding of the need to cooperate in policies, supporting effective demand: for example, discussions with Germany and Japan about stimulating their economies. They were much more open to doing that at that time than they are now. To some extent the attitude has changed because West Germany and Japan felt pressure, I think, in '77, to stimulate and felt this was responsible for the revival of inflation later on. My feeling is that this is exaggerated, that it was largely because of the second oil crisis that inflation accelerated. But there was a generally good cooperation about what countries should do.

Cooperation on the debt problem has had very limited success. The whole fund approach was always short-term adjustment, and generally, in a normal world economic situation, balance-of-payments problems can be overcome in two or three years. But that became impossible. The great disappointment was that when the first adjustment took place after '81—an enormous, very successful balance-of-payments adjustment—what should have happened is that the commercial banks would have been willing to lend again. That has not come about. They were frightened, and they did not want to increase their lending on a voluntary basis. That made the problem a long-term problem because these countries had become completely used to capital imports. For developing countries, it's normal to have certain capital imports; now suddenly you have to do without. You have to pay much higher real interest rates and repay in a difficult world economic situation.

So what can the IMF do? It doesn't have the funds to provide more support itself. The banks are unwilling. So you have to propose rather tough adjustment programs. Today the feeling is, I think correctly, that this adjustment has often been too painful and too tough. But what can the fund do? Neither the commercial banks nor governments are willing to provide more financing. *That* is the main difficulty, that the main industrial countries have been unwilling to provide, in some way, additional finances. It has even been very difficult to get a normal quota increase for the fund; a capital increase for the World Bank is still difficult. And central banks don't do anything. The official export credit arrangements are cutting down their credit availability; they behave just like the commercial banks. It's all very fair to criticize the fund's conditionality, but the real problem is the lack of finances and an international climate which is difficult for these countries.

There has been a remarkable change in philosophy. There has been a shift to much greater emphasis on bringing down inflation, the feeling that all this lending to developing countries has been too much, that it has been badly used and so on, and that now it shouldn't continue. And as you know very well, there is the feeling in the United States that commercial banks were stupid to lend so much and that they shouldn't be bailed out by the government or by central banks. And that sort of climate is very difficult.

Behind this is also a shift from a more Keynesian philosophy to monetarism. That's a very fundamental shift in thinking, which now I think is beginning to turn back, because it's very clear that monetarism doesn't work; that fashion is over. But it was very much behind this negative attitude toward providing more financing.

Recycling by the banks was a useful function. But they overdid it in certain cases. I'll never forget, I was visiting one of the poorest developing countries that was very much in need of some adjustment—it had very bad policies, really—and we were hoping to get them to accept some kind of an IMF program. At the same time, there were bankers visiting the capital offering big loans without *any* conditions. And I thought that was quite wrong. Now, the country was sensible; it didn't take these bank loans and went to the fund, and the policies were improved to some extent. But it was typical for the atmosphere at that time.

I think the crisis, if not prevented, at least would have been much less serious if the banks would have been willing to cooperate much more closely with the fund in their lending at a much earlier stage, requiring IMF drawings and consulting the fund about how much the country really would need. But they were not at that time willing to do that. Which I can understand; I mean, they wanted to be independent and have their own policies. It was a profitable business and so on, and it's always easy to say these things with hindsight. Nobody expected at that time the sudden shift in the whole situation, with interest rates going up so much and the world moving into a recession. It's still difficult to foresee what will happen. But I felt at the time it would be better if they would bring in the fund at an earlier time. I often said that to the banks and to the countries.

Of course, countries are always reluctant to do that because they have to take unpopular measures. It's never a very nice thing to do politically, so if you can borrow without conditions from the bank it's much more attractive. There was also in many cases some corruption involved—prestige projects, commissions on these investments and so on. There were the consultations with the fund, but you could never touch such things. It was always macroeconomic; we couldn't tell a country, "You shouldn't spend so much money for buying airplanes; spend more for something else." That was not considered to be the fund's field, which I think is correct.

As an international institution you have to limit your interference as much as possible to what is essential for the purpose of the institution—balance of payments, the monetary system, credit creation and exchange rates. The result was, of course, that the fund required a reduction of the deficit, and a government did it not by reducing military spending but by reducing consumer subsidies. Then there were riots in the streets, and the IMF was blamed for this policy. That is a difficulty for the fund; it often has to press for unpopular policies, which in some cases could have worked better if the government had followed the fund's advice more fully.

But the fund always felt that it could not defend itself publicly against criticism; the fund is silent. It's crucial for the fund to have very open and confidential discussions with governments; there must be cooperation. That makes it very difficult to start a public debate with the government. So then there's criticism in the press, and once the fund starts to take positions against that, it's delicate. But it is certainly a factor behind the unpopularity of the fund at the present time.

It was a great task to bring together the different views of the different governments within the IMF, to create a consensus on the basis of which we could carry out a policy. Because the fund always works by consensus, and I think that this has worked very well. This always struck me very much coming from Europe, where I had, as minister of finance, been in many discussions of the EEC Council of Ministers; these were always very long, drawn out, very difficult, because there had to be unanimity. I came to the fund, to the executive board, where decisions can be taken by voting, but in practice there is always an attempt to reach a consensus. Of course, the fact that in the end a vote is possible makes all the executive directors much more reasonable, because what they aim for is to influence the consensus. To do that you must be persuasive, you must not be unreasonable. It created a very different climate, much more effective decision making. The task of the managing director is to formulate a consensus, to bring the different points of view together, to create some constructive policy out of what in the beginning are always very different views.

The IMF managing directorship has always been a European appointment, and in 1973 the European ministers had agreed that they wanted me to be managing director. There was also some support from developing countries. I had a good relationship with them, and they knew something about my personality. The Netherlands was very much an aid-giving country; that may have been a factor. And the Indonesian IMF executive director, whom I knew, was also playing a role.

I hesitated at first and said no; then I began to think about it again. Then [former French finance minister Valéry] Giscard [d'Estaing] invited me to Paris to talk about it. I asked what the alternatives were if I didn't do it, because for personal reasons it didn't come at the right time for me. He said that, of course, there were other candidates, but he felt it would be more difficult with the developing countries, or it certainly would not be as good. Then I said, "Yes, all right, I'll do it."

At that time, there was no candidate that was supported by a particular government—so very different than now. It was much less a political prize than it is now. [The contest in 1986 between Dutch Finance Minister H. Onno Ruding and French Treasury Director Michel Camdessus] was a different situation, a kind of public debate and very unfortunate, I think. In fact, in 1973 the whole monetary system was in disarray. There was debate about how it should be reconstructed, and it was not at all clear whether the fund should be in it at all. Today it's very clear that the IMF is an extremely powerful institution. That power began to be built during the time that I was at the fund; and when I left, the position of managing director was considered much more important—and for the developing countries, extremely important—than when I came.

Editor: David Cudaback

Eugene Rotberg

Former Treasurer WORLD BANK

> Eugene Rotberg has never ducked controversy. As associate direc-
> tor for regulation of the Securities and Exchange Commission's
> trading and markets division in the mid-1960s, Rotberg fought to
> break down the New York Stock Exchange's commission rate
> schedule and set in motion the forces that ultimately led to Mayday
> in 1975. But by the mid-1970s Rotberg was involved in a new chal-
> lenge: expanding the resources of the World Bank. Under his
> leadership, the institution became the largest and most innovative
> borrower in the world, tapping new markets with new instruments
> at a breathtaking rate. Rotberg left the bank in June of 1987 for
> Merrill Lynch.

My career at the SEC started in the early '60s, and at that
time a friend of mine, Fred Moss, and I were somewhat
puzzled that stocks would double in price within minutes
of coming to market. So we stuck a name on that—called them
"hot issues"—and tried to figure out, quite unsuccessfully, why a
stock price would double. We wrote a short memo to Barney
Woodside, who at the time was director of corporate finance, and
said we wanted to do sort of an investigatory study of hot issues.
At about the same time, another colleague, Dave Silver [now
president of the Investment Company Institute], was doing a
study of what was going on in the American Stock Exchange with
Jerry Re. Our studies progressed to a point where we were opening up things that hadn't been opened before. We began to write
memoranda; and then that led to the special study of securities
markets, which was a two-year study of perhaps nine volumes that

opened up a lot of issues that are still with us—automation in the over-the-counter market, member firms going public, the un-fixing of commission rates, to name a few.

In all fairness, I think the driving force behind the resolution of some of these issues was really the staff at the SEC. Manny Cohen and Irv Pollack at the commission level supported it, but it's hard to think of any others. The staff at the SEC recognized that regulatory agencies, particularly the SEC, were not likely to make fundamental, structural changes affecting the competitiveness of an industry. And that is why we felt that the way to implement change was to let basic industry competitiveness work.

It was quite a group at the SEC in those days: Milton Cohen, now an outstanding lawyer in Chicago; Ralph Saul, who subse-quently became president of the American Stock Exchange and the head of Cigna. Fred Moss was there—he subsequently became president of the Boston Stock Exchange and later a principal at A. G. Becker; Bob Birnbaum, now president of the New York Stock Exchange; Art Fleischer of recent merger and acquisition fame; and Harvey Pitt. I hired Stan Sporkin. I feel somewhat self-conscious naming them simply because there were so many others who were of similar caliber.

The theory we all held at the time was very straightforward: The only way to regulate an industry as strong and effective and with so many bright people as the securities industry was to let com-petition work, as distinguished from regulation. We basically were not comfortable with regulation; we didn't trust how it could be turned or corrupted. We also thought we had better learn as much or more about the way the securities business operated as those who were actually in it. So we spent days, months, cross-ex-amining people in private: "Tell me what you do in the morning and how you do it." In the end we had a reasonably good under-standing of how the markets worked.

What we were doing was no great secret. We said: "Look, fel-lows, you have a system going. We're going to see how we can change it, and then you're going to change it for us." When I left the SEC, people said: "My God! He's ruined the securities indus-try. What's he going to do to the world's financial system?"

I wrote the chapter in the special study on the over-the-counter market and the "issue" chapter. One problem was how to handle the volume of paperwork and the recording of the transaction. This led me to recommend a whole series of changes which in effect led to the creation of NASDAQ. Before that was done, however, the industry was able to make presentations. I'll never forget the presentation made by the law firm representing the National Securities Traders Association. They said that the opening line of the first printout of the first trade would state as follows: "This transaction, this opening quotation, will record the death knell of the over-the-counter market." They believed any computer system that would tell you what your bid was and asked was—let alone the best bid and asked—would so narrow spreads that it would make the business quite unprofitable.

Well, it was right after those public hearings in 1968, after Nixon was elected, that I left the SEC. Nixon had issued a letter to Wall Street saying he was going to get rid of all these young, Kennedy-type lawyers, and I, for some strange reason, thought he was talking about me. So I left and came to the World Bank sometime between the time he was elected and inaugurated. I had intended to go to one of three firms: with Don Regan to Merrill Lynch—heaven knows where I would have been if I had done that!—with Leon Levy at Oppenheimer or with John Gutfreund at Salomon Brothers. One of the first people I talked with about whether I should go to the World Bank after my initial interview there was Gutfreund. He suggested, not entirely facetiously, that he was willing to make a switch—I take his job and he comes here. Now *that* would have produced an interesting scenario.

The World Bank approach started when I got this strange call from [then World Bank head Robert] McNamara. I had not known him before. He said he had heard I was leaving the SEC and asked me if I knew anything about international finance. I said no. He asked me if I'd ever studied accounting. I said no. Finance? No. I'd studied for the most part English literature and history; I was a trial lawyer and far more adversarial than I am now. He then asked me what I thought about investment bankers, and I told him the truth—which was that I was trying to indict most of them under the Sherman Act. He asked me what I thought of commercial bankers, and I said I thought they sailed around in little ships on Long Island Sound in the summertime and wore white buck shoes. He asked me what I thought about problems of poverty, and I said it was one of those things where one could spend one's life and not succeed. Then he asked me if I wanted to be treasurer of the World Bank.

I came here essentially because I have always believed in public service, first, and second because the job as described by Bob McNamara was very rewarding in the sense that you knew that the lending operations of the World Bank could make a difference in people's lives: higher caloric content in the food they would eat, more schools, more electricity, higher standards of living, a sense of survival—and with that, hopefully a more stable world. He said he had come here to lend for high-quality purposes. He said he needed someone to find where the wealth existed in the world and to get it.

I haven't the vaguest idea why he chose me, although I suspect that he didn't want anyone who was excessively burdened with too much knowledge of how difficult it might be. Not that it turned out to be all that difficult, but if you wanted to lend $1 billion, you had to borrow $1 billion. And the bank hadn't done anything like that. Nor was I particularly burdened with great knowledge of the traditional forms of borrowing money. So in that sense I was at a great advantage, because when deregulation, competitiveness, and a breakdown of international barriers occurred, I was not— and my staff certainly wasn't—locked into traditional ways of tapping the world's flow of wealth.

In the first week or two, when McNamara said, "Do you think we can raise $1 billion a year?," I said, "Sure, why not?" We now borrow $10 billion a year. We were fortunate because both Germany and Japan had begun to develop very substantial foreign exchange reserves and were therefore able to export capital. Then OPEC began to develop substantial resources, and we were able to attract those; we borrowed several billion dollars—$6 or $7 billion—rather quickly.

Bob always had very clear objectives. He would set those out and say, "Borrow the money we need at as low a cost as possible, because any mistakes you make will be borne by the poorer countries in the world." As a result, I found myself going to Japan very frequently in 1969 and 1970 with the expectation that Japan would have explosive growth and would maintain a high savings rate. They had no bond market, but we had lent Japan very large amounts after the Second World War, and therefore emotionally they were prepared to allocate those savings through the opening up of their markets to the World Bank.

I had been told that in negotiating transactions in Japan there's a lot of ritual, that everything's very formal. I knew the cost of borrowing was going to end up at about 7 percent, and I didn't want to spend two months drinking tea until we got down to that point. I started off the meeting by saying: "Look, I know we're going to end up at 7 percent—that's already been decided by our betters, the Ministry of Finance. So let's just shake hands, say you've been delightful, and that's it." There was this impassive response: "Come back tomorrow." The next day, I come back and I'm told: "We've heard very much what you said; we know you don't want to negotiate or bargain. We know you believe that rates are arbitrarily set in Japan and we respect that. We can assure you that it's a fair price. The cost is 12 percent." I said, "Fine, we can pay 4 percent." Two weeks later, after a lot of tea, we ended up at 7 percent.

OPEC members are among the most professional I have ever dealt with. They made a clear policy decision in the mid-'60s and later that as their financial resources were increasing they would not take those resources and recycle them to countries in deficit. They would put them in the hands of strong intermediaries— money center banks—or lend them to very high-quality issuers, like the World Bank. Those funds are still in our debt portfolio. The terms and conditions were always on the market. I did not see them demanding or asking for better-than-market terms. Indeed, I found myself going to Iran and negotiating transactions directly, and to this day we still pay interest on those loans to Iran. And to this day, Iran still pays the World Bank interest on the loan we made them in the early 1970s. And Lebanon, too. Lebanon in recent times has been in great turmoil. Their central bank does its best to meet its obligations. The world doesn't stop functioning because of changes in government.

I have been involved in private placements in the past where McNamara asked to break off the transaction where the cost to us was too low, where unexpected changes occurred between the agreement and the actual signing. These were transactions that were adverse to the other side and beneficial to us. We've always believed—under [former World Bank chief A. W.] Clausen as well, and I'm sure Mr. Conable—that the only transactions that are worthwhile are those where, at the end, all parties feel it's a reasonable deal at the time it is done. And that's it.

Our investment banks give us very, very effective, expert service—service in the best sense. They tell us where the market is vulnerable or fragile, where on the yield curve it's strong, where the buying power is coming from. And it's rare that we get investment bankers more than two basis points apart from each other. No one is fooling us; no one is saying that they have something when they don't. Nor do firms give us suicide bids—knowing the market's 8 percent for a given currency but telling us, "Say, look, Gene, we'll do this for you at 7⅞." There's a lot of mutual respect. We don't deal with people who either don't know where the market is or do know but want to lose a lot of money.

What one must focus on is who has wealth, how fast it is accumulating and what kind of instrument do the controllers of wealth want in order for you to take it. Do they want equity? Do they want to be liquid? Long? Short? Leveraged or not leveraged? Fixed or floating? That is essentially what every government, private corporation and quasi-public institution has to figure out worldwide. And once you know that, creation of the instrument is child's play. All you need to do is ask what the market wants and can you afford to pay it. The stuff in the middle—investment banking, merchant banking, commercial banking—is simply the vehicle you use to tap into that ultimate saver or investor.

Ninety-five percent of our borrowings are at fixed interest rates. Although our loans are floating, they are floating on the basis of a pool of fixed-rate loans. When interest rates dropped from 14 percent to 7 percent, we became almost 100 percent a fixed-rate borrower for twenty- and 30-year maturities. We do not believe that the way to cope with high interest rates is to borrow at floating rates. The way to resolve high interest rates is not to borrow. The way not to borrow is to have $20 billion in cash, then let it drop until you get through the cycle. A floating rate is society's proxy for discontent; it means, "I don't want my future to be fixed." So short-term borrowings at floating rates are not bad per se; they simply reflect the unease of a culture. We borrow at fixed rates and borrow more than we have to, because when the fixed-rate market really and truly disappears, you can have a breathing space and not borrow at all if you have liquidity.

I think I helped create an environment where my colleagues could raise $100 billion for poor people and where we could attract those funds from institutions that do not ordinarily lend, directly or indirectly, to that constituency. And we were able to do so through the formation of a very sophisticated institution, using the most sophisticated financial tools, by building the bank on the asset and investment side so that they would have confidence in leaving their funds with us. Otherwise, we would not have been able to attract private sector funds.

I guess I once said that Robert McNamara is Martin Luther out of the Harvard Business School. And that's meant to be a compliment, a pretty strong one. He is a great humanitarian—driven, committed, a very vulnerable human being. It is simply a great pleasure to talk with someone who, at the age of 70, retains the motivation, the drive and the liberalism that he still does. Clausen and Conable are quite different from each other and quite different from McNamara. They both have great skills—excellent analytical skills, personal skills and management skills.

I think Tom Clausen got a bad rap and unfavorable publicity simply because the world expected this institution to be a magic one that could resolve the debt crisis or at least prevent the world from having one. That's an unfair burden to put on him or the institution. It's a complicated world out there, and there are many things that occur which are outside anyone's control— let alone one institution that functions out of Washington, D.C. We might have a great deal of money and a great deal of wisdom, but you can't prevent earthquakes from happening or high interest rates or a recession in the West or protectionism. Yet these are variables that will affect the way the world is held together. It's a little naive to think that the president of the World Bank or the bank itself can intervene to move things or prevent these things from occurring. And the better part of wisdom—and I think both Clausen and Conable have that wisdom—is to understand that while we are an ethical spokesman for what *should* happen, we really can't make major changes or prevent the untoward. There are a lot of constitu-

245

encies in the world, and we're just one of them. What we have that the others don't is objectivity. I hope we can retain it.

The rhetoric will change; the bank will not. There will be changes in the margin of the kind of lending we do. But the bottom line, when you cut through it all, is, What kind of advice can you give to facilitate a country's growth? And will that occur within one year, two years, ten years? External capital flows into these countries are beyond our control. Our job is to try to raise the level of comfort and confidence. But ultimately, the country has to decide the way it's put together.

This is an apolitical institution. I hope it remains one. That's one of its beauties. And as McNamara said when I came to the bank, "This sure beats the hell out of selling automobiles."

Editor: Margaret A. Elliott

Denis Healey

Former Chancellor of the Exchequer UNITED KINGDOM

Oxford-educated, as well as a former member of the Communist
Party, Denis Healey has carved himself enormous stature as an intellectual powerhouse within Britain's Labour Party. From 1964 to
1970 he served as defense secretary and confronted crises in eastern Suez and the Persian Gulf. When Labour returned to power in
1974, Healey then became chancellor of the Exchequer, master-
fully administering during a period of horrific U.K. economic
strife.

In a sense, the first year I was chancellor was very much a
learning year for me, as I think it is for most chancellors.
Obviously, one is learning the whole time. I hadn't studied
economics, which I think was a good thing, because people who've
studied economics, when they're in government, have a vague
memory of what some professor taught them twenty years earlier
about the situation twenty years before that. Economic training in
the academic sense can be very misleading, because the world
changes from country to country and from year to year—at least
economic behavior does. For my part, I think I'd gotten a pretty
clear view of what I wanted by the middle to the end of 1975.

The big mistake the first year was attempting an expansion of
the British economy when all our trading partners were restrict-
ing theirs. So we were bound to run into a balance-of-payments
crisis. Another weakness was that I tried very hard, my early
months as chancellor, to persuade my colleagues to organize some
sort of international, official scheme for recycling the OPEC sur-

pluses. But the Americans, particularly, were very hostile to this idea. Basically, they didn't believe in government mucking around in what they thought should be the role of the private sector. They would leave it all to the bankers, who were licking their lips at the thought of what they would get out of it.

There were also two other immediate problems. The first was selling enough government bonds—gilts, we call them—to finance the amount of money in circulation without going to the banks. But persuading the financial institutions to buy gilts then often required me to raise interests rates higher than would be desirable from an internal economic point of view. And more important at the time, we had a net cost in developing North Sea oil while we were getting no benefits from it. We only got the first oil out of the North Sea when I was about halfway through my period as chancellor.

So we had enormous problems on the foreign exchange markets. These were masked the first year because the Arab OPEC countries, which suddenly found themselves with enormous unspendable surpluses, chose to keep them in London. They kept sterling afloat until Easter of 1975. But as they became more used to the opportunities available all over the world, they started putting money into other countries, and we had a major sterling crisis in 1976.

This was the most difficult moment for me, without question. We had a hiccup in August. It's a very odd system, ours. We finance a government deficit, or should finance it, by selling gilts to the nonbank public. But the nonbank public goes on holiday in August. So in August of '76 we weren't selling any gilts. But, of course, spending goes on, as it does every month, and revenue is what it is. The crisis was developing. It was obvious to me and my officials and to Gordon Richardson, who was then the governor of the Bank of England, that we would have to raise interest rates in order to sell gilts. The governor persuaded me that we needed to raise interest rates to 15 percent, which was unheard of in those days, in order to sell enough gilts to get money under control. But I was also persuaded by him that we could then get them down again within a year to 12 or 10 percent, which was roughly the level of inflation.

248

So we raised interest rates, and almost at the moment we raised them, we started selling gilts, and we didn't really have any more trouble with the domestic markets. The big crisis came a month later: the foreign exchange crisis. It turns out, we now know, that we were publishing unnecessarily pessimistic figures then about the likely size of our domestic and external deficits. Anyway, people started taking their money out of sterling.

The pound went into a free-fall on the day I was due to leave for meetings with the IMF and the Commonwealth finance ministers in Hongkong. About every quarter of an hour, the pound dropped another cent—that's nothing these days, but in those days it seemed like the end of the world. I was on my way out to the airport with Gordon Richardson. In those days there was no way of communicating when you were in the air. So I was going to be out of contact with my advisers for seventeen hours. I decided in the airport lounge that I couldn't afford that. I thought it would have been very dangerous to arrive at those international meetings under these circumstances. The IMF annual meeting is a hothouse of rumors. All the commercial bankers in the world as well as all the governments meet there and talk about each other, and these rumors do terrible things to economies. I thought, if I let the pound slide, then go there and nothing had been done, we could be facing a very serious crisis—worse than what I already had to deal with, anyway. I turned around and went straight back and had a meeting that evening.

We had gotten a very handsome standby credit fixed from the central banks and commercial banks in July, but it was conditional on going to the IMF if we needed more. In light of events, when I got back that Tuesday evening and met with my officials, I decided we must apply for IMF support. When I went up to our Labour Party conference, I was booed by one half of the hall and cheered by the other half. And then we had a very odd panto-mime. The prime minister was very nervous about the political consequences of bringing in the IMF, so he kept the IMF team, who'd come because we'd gone to them with our cap in our hand, hanging around their hotel for a week or two before he would allow any Treasury officials to talk to them.

When we finally started the negotiations, they were difficult. Johannes Witteveen was in charge of the IMF. I got on well with Witteveen—a mean, crusty, typically obstinate Dutchman, but, you know, with the welfare of the world at heart. He had a very

249

good deputy named Alan Whittome, who still works for the IMF, and he was in charge of negotiations on the ground. But Ed Yeo, who was an ex-Marine, the type we have gotten to know well, masterminded the operation from the U.S. Treasury in Washington without really understanding it all. And in the end he persuaded Witteveen to ask for much tougher lending conditions. I told Alan to tell Yeo—what was the word I used? Oh, yes—to take a running jump! That's right. And he did, actually.

To be perfectly honest, I never sit on feelings of vindication, because you're always dealing with the next problem, aren't you? I think there are three things a chancellor has to do in the management area. First is to get domestic expenditure and revenue into a close enough relationship that if you want to borrow money to bridge a gap, you can do so without stoking up inflation. The second big job is to do the same with your external accounts. If you have to run a deficit, it's got to be one which you can finance by borrowing in foreign currencies, again, without stoking up inflation or adding intolerably to interest costs. Finally, and what I didn't succeed in doing, was producing a lasting answer to the problem of wage inflation.

The thing that ruined us was being overambitious on pay policy in our last year. If we'd said we wanted settlements in single figures, we'd have finished up with probably an average increase of 12 percent, which would have been perfectly possible to handle economically—and I wouldn't be talking to you now because I'd be leading my second Labour government.

I think what you could roughly say is, I'd gotten the domestic and external accounts into balance by '78, and for about fifteen months before the election we had both the unemployment figures and inflation going down slowly. Once we'd been to the IMF and it was clear that we were getting a surplus on our balance of payments and getting our domestic deficit under control, well, I think it was *Institutional Investor* magazine, actually, which named me as one of the five best finance ministers in the world. As all the others named were finance ministers in dictatorships, I thought that was high praise, because it's not difficult to control the economy if you can use electrodes applied to your opponents' tender parts to get your way.

When I really knew I'd succeeded in my domestic job as chancellor was when we had a Commonwealth finance ministers meeting in Barbados, which I think must have been in '78. The Reuters man came up to me with an ashen face and said, "Look at this, Denis." It was a telegram from his head office saying, from now on you'll be paid in dollars.

It paid Reuters, you see, to pay him in a weak currency rather than in a strong one.

Editor: Michael VerMeulen

Leo Melamed

Former Chairman CHICAGO MERCANTILE EXCHANGE

> No one has been more instrumental in fostering the growth of financial futures than Leo Melamed. Melamed created the first currency futures contract fifteen years ago when he headed the Chicago Merc—and helped revolutionize global finance.

Innovation happened at the Merc because we were hungrier, because we had much more to gain with success than an institution that was already very successful, such as the Chicago Board of Trade. The Merc was on the make. And so when you have that kind of institution and you have a brand-new idea and you have a membership that is willing to follow you and you yourself are capable of being a leader, you've got a mix of dynamite and innovation. And so, in 1967, I was swept onto the board of the Merc on the need for reform.

The first thing I did was to ask that the rule that discriminated against women being employees or members of the exchange be dropped. And there was a big argument on the board because the question was, How much above the knee should the skirt be allowed on the floor?—in case it would give the members problems, you know, distractions in this very, very businesslike atmosphere we have on the floor, God forbid. You know, with the tumult, nobody cares if you are a woman, a man or a guy from Mars.

At the time, I suspect a lot of the older members thought this young turk was going to bring down the Merc with all these horrible innovations or experiments. Anyway, the first stage of the innovations was this organizational effort to redo the rule-book, change the rules, modernize them and stop the corners and the squeezes. The membership felt they had very little say in the process of governing the exchange and that the exchange had done some very dumb things that the members felt hurt their future, such as the onion debacle of the previous decade, when corners and squeezes allowed that market to go down the tubes.

We traders lost a lot of money over the course of time, and clearly all of us felt victimized; we felt that the institution was being raped before our eyes. It gave the Merc a bad name. Unless you're on the inside, you don't know what is going to happen tomorrow, because the market seems to go contrary to the dictates of supply and demand. It goes up when you know everything dictates that it should go down. It's hard enough to be right just on the basis of supply and demand in futures. And if you add to that the element of corners and squeezes, the public wouldn't have a chance. Anyhow, I represented a lot of people who felt the governors of the exchange were too lax and seemed to turn their heads away instead of confronting the issue. This is not to say they were in on the manipulation. I don't know. I never knew and never really cared. I gave teeth to the business conduct committee so that it could deal with corners and squeezes, and that was the first step of what I did for the exchange.

The second step was diversification, and that was in 1971. The rulebook was now in place; we were successfully doing the meat business; we were growing. But I had learned during my forma-tive years on the exchange that if an exchange becomes overde-pendent on one line of business, like it had been on eggs, and if anything happens to that line of business, then you are out of business. And let me tell you that in terms of agriculture, we had hit the limits. I mean, the CBOT had grain and all the grain by-products, so we were locked out of that. We already had meats and we were doing well, but, I mean, where could you go with that? You can't invent another meat.

So now we were all meat, and I said we must diversify. You cannot depend on meats. In my mind was another idea, entirely different: not agriculture, but currencies. I saw finance as a uni-verse that was totally untouched, completely open and the sky was the limit. I recognized this would be revolutionary, but it was there. I had my ear to the ground. I had attempted trading through the banks. I recognized that while Bretton Woods was in existence, currency fluctuations, at least in the open, weren't likely—except on nights when finance ministers got together and devalued 2 percent or 5 percent or 10 percent and suddenly you have this giant move overnight and the rest of the time it's fixed.

I and some friends used to talk about these things. We focused on the fact that the British pound was overvalued. It was well out of line, and either the British government would go broke trying to hold it (which it almost did) or it was going to have to let it go or devalue. So the key to making money was to find some way to be short sterling. And, of course, there was no way, because the banks would literally not take your money. So if Bretton Woods would indeed come apart, then my idea for a currency futures market could work. This fit diversification, and it fit the world that I thought was coming.

I was interested in economics, and Milton Friedman's name and writings attracted me like a magnet. I even visited his classes at times. I became more enamored of his ideals and his ideas about free markets. They fit exactly. Here was a man saying exactly what I was thinking. Only he had the credentials to say it, which made me feel real, real good. If Milton Friedman's view that Bretton Woods would indeed come apart in the near future was anywhere near correct, then my ideas for a currency futures market could work.

So the president of the exchange, Everett Harris, and I met with Friedman and asked him what he thought of the idea. Well, he loved it. He embraced it instantly. So we asked him, "Would you give us the benefit of a feasibility study?"

In December of 1971, when the gold window was closed, I knew we were on the right track. And we were all ready. All we had to do was do things quickly now, and we did. We set the date for May 1972. I said to the board: "You don't launch currencies from your back pocket and say to the world that we are doing something in Chicago that isn't important. If it is meaningful, then we ought to advise the movers and shakers of the world." I wanted people to salute it.

In those years, from 1972 to 1976, I crisscrossed the country so many times I can't count them. In seminars, speeches, one-on-ones, all over the country trying to preach the idea of currency futures and that the idea was the right idea at the right time and that it was going to work and that one more thing: the Chicago Mercantile Exchange was an okay place to do business. And the International Monetary Market, the IMM, was created as a separate organization that sold its own memberships to the world. I said to the traders of the Merc, "Look, you've got to leave your cattle pit, your hog pit, your belly pit; you've got to come help us launch currencies." And they came and did it. But I also knew they had to make a living. These people would give me their time, but for how long? I knew I needed a captive constituency of traders that would concentrate solely and only on the currency markets.

There was a tremendous amount of money to be made. When we launched the IMM, it was when the Swiss franc was selling, I recall, for 28 cents to the dollar. It went from that over time 'til 1979, when it was something like 79 cents. So there was big money to be made. Also, there was something else. You couldn't squeeze and corner the currencies. Nobody was worried about some people getting together and saying, "Hey, let's corner the deutsche mark tomorrow." You knew it was economics that was going to dictate the market. Supply and demand was going to determine the value, nothing else. Oh, sure, government intervention was popular, but we viewed government intervention as just another big player. They were entitled to their view, and they could deflect the market for a while. But we knew the market was bigger than they were.

Morrie Levy was one of the great protagonists of the currency futures. He and his brothers were spreaders in the meats. Spreading, as you know, is just a technique, arbitrage, that you can do anywhere. Right. They recognized that very quickly. He knew there was a connection between the deutsche mark and the Swiss franc and maybe even with the others. So, therefore, he could spread one against the other, and he learned how to do that.

With very little training, you can translate and transfer your knowledge as a trader in one commodity to another. There are stories of people who have never seen a pork belly, and they have been trading it for years. There is an old saw that goes, "A real good trader walks on the floor and listens to where the noise is coming from, and that's where he goes to trade." It doesn't matter what it is, because markets go up and down on the basis of supply and demand. And if you are a pit trader, all you want to do anyhow is go with the flow.

Pit trading is a seat-of-the-pants game. It's go with the flow, and the years haven't changed it. If you are an upstairs trader, like I am now, you trade from the screens, and I trade differently than I did in the pit. But now the market has moved dramatically. The volatility factors have changed. Why? Because the computer has married the telephone, and now everybody has instant access and instant information, and these changes create more and more volatility. You need more capital to stay in business, but by the standards of world capital, it still isn't that much.

At the Merc, we never were looking for vindication, but we sure were looking for business. But if I had to pick a date when we *were* vindicated, I would pick September 1, 1976. That was the day the Mexican peso was devalued 50 percent and the entire world was all shook up. Nowhere could you get a forward price in Mexican pesos—except where? At the Chicago Mercantile Exchange, our market was right there. It opened up. It never had to sweat. A hundred million dollars changed hands, and we were safe and secure. And the world took notice that the Chicago IMM stayed in business and continued to trade Mexican pesos. I think from that day forward, it really started to move fast. Our market represented a viable force in currency forwards, so we often led the direction of market change. And that is still true today.

Sure, we made mistakes. The mistake we made the first day was trying to launch—imagine—seven currency contracts at one time. We'd never do that today. Today it would probably take an entire year. You don't launch seven in one day. But at the time we organized the contracts, we did not know enough not to listen to the bankers. So we created contracts that were far too large, and we couldn't get the public to participate when they had to put up this large amount of money.

Also, I would clearly have preferred to have the long bonds at the Merc. I would have done that differently, but I was talked into doing a four-year note. Our economists made the case that the world was going to the middle range of the interest rate spectrum rather than the long range. So we went with the four-year note in 1977 when we should have gone with the long bond—obviously, a big mistake. But economists sometimes make that mistake. Interest rates was the next stage, and then came probably the most important new product of recent vintage—no question about it which is—equity futures.

Stock market futures were not a new idea. I remember as a kid on the floor being cornered by Elmer Faulkner, a little guy who wore spats—that was the thing I remembered about him. He smoked a big cigar and he used to spit in a spitoon that was on the floor. He said to me, "Of course, the ultimate future is the stock market futures." And then he'd spit into a spitoon and say, "But you'll never see it in your lifetime." Well, we wouldn't have if we couldn't have convinced the CFTC that cash settlement was something they ought to experiment with. And it took us four years to convince them—from 1978 to 1982.

The first cash-settled contract was Eurodollar futures, launched in 1982. And once they approved the idea of cash settlement, we all went scurrying about for the stock market of our dreams. All our analysis indicated that the portfolio manager, who we felt was going to be the one that will eventually drive the business toward us, measured his performance on the basis of the S&P 500. We went after that contract because the S&P 500 is the way the world measures performance in stocks.

But we had to launch six months after the other exchanges. We had to put on a hell of a marketing effort to succeed. We immediately overtook the others after the launch of the S&P 500 futures. But then, three, four weeks later, we were behind them. Jack Sandler [then chairman of the CME] and I were in London. We got on a plane and relaunched the S&P 500 with a pretty famous marketing plan called 15 Minutes, Please. We urged every member of the exchange to stay 15 Minutes, Please, in the S&P pit. We turned it around in a couple of weeks, and we were off and running.

We have always gotten more response out of our membership at the Merc than any other exchange. But I caution you: I don't know that this is the way the world can always work, because you get beyond a certain number of people and it probably doesn't work as well.

Futures has always had a sordid history. Not just at the Merc; it was true at all the exchanges. It's misunderstood; it's little understood. It looks like a gambling casino, and therefore it is used as a scapegoat. When anything goes wrong in the world, it is easy to pick on futures and say it is their fault. We have proved time and time again that it isn't our fault. They have had soybean examinations. They blamed their recent problems on program trading and then, when it is examined, you find out program trading had very little impact on the recent volatility in the stock market.

But we represent an odd and difficult world. Where else can you, in the same day, lose the kind of money you can with futures? It sounds like it's Vegas; it's colorful and noisy and all that, so that's odd for a business arena. It's not a bank-looking place. I grant you, the New York Stock Exchange doesn't look all that different, but the New York Stock Exchange has this long history of respectability. After all, it's the pillar of our financial world, and it is where capital formation occurs. So what can be wrong with that?

But I think we've established our legitimacy now, partly because of who we are; we are no longer the pork belly and cattle traders only. Look who is among our ranks: Salomon Brothers, Goldman Sachs, Morgan Guaranty. We recognize that their entrance into our world will give us the legitimacy we've always thought we deserve, and why should it bother us that maybe they came a little late?

Now we are in a transition stage, and transition stages are very hard. We have brought in a whole new clientele, a whole array of new markets, and they demand different technologies. Their way of doing business is different. I think we have to experiment with the technology without endangering the open-outcry system, because I don't think technology can create liquidity the way a competitive arena does it, eyeball to eyeball—a bunch of people, each competing for a price. It just doesn't happen the same way in the sterile atmosphere of your office.

Our way works. It's an open fishbowl. A lot of business does happen here, and there is an honor system among the traders. There are some bad apples in every barrel and we've got our share, I am sure. But overall, the community is an honest one.

The reason our traders carry business cards that say "capitalist" is that they are conscious of what they represent, and they are proud of what they represent. They've been to New York; they've been to Singapore. They've been all around the world, and they know what they've got in Chicago isn't anywhere else. These markets do represent a last frontier in a way.

People have tried to mimic what we have here, and sure, there is a little bit of Chicago in Singapore, a little bit of Chicago in London. But in Chicago, you've got the real thing.

Editor: Henny Sender

Donald Weeden

President and Chief Executive Officer WEEDEN & CO.

In the era of fixed brokerage commissions on Wall Street and the New York Stock Exchange's monopoly over stock trading, Don Weeden was a strident voice for change. The head of the leading firm trading off-board in listed securities, he was the most vocal advocate of competition and unfixed commissions, which had a profound impact on Washington and probably speeded up the reforms of the period by a number of years. In a bitter twist of irony, however, the changes he sought very nearly brought his own firm down.

A lot of people say that the third market—and Weeden & Co. in particular—was the catalyst for much of the change that has taken place in the last ten or fifteen years. I think, to a great extent, that is true, if catalyst is understood as a stirring up that caused much larger things to take place.

The New York Stock Exchange's argument was that it was the best, most responsible, most organized market in the world and that to do business away from it was detrimental to the public interest. On the surface that's a very straightforward, easily accepted concept. But what it really meant was, don't do business with our competitors, even if they have a better price. Now, that was an old argument, like Mr. Rockefeller might have made in trying to concentrate all of the oil business in Standard Oil.

Still, there was enough business out there, and there were people who saw the advantages of dealing with Weeden & Co. and were willing to ignore the entreaties of the New York Stock Exchange. Institutions were becoming larger and larger buyers of listed stocks, particularly among the industrial stocks, and they were desperately looking for ways of buying in amounts that were not always available in the auction market without price changes.

A proportion of our business came from members of the New York who found that we were willing to buy a block of 1,000 or 1,500 shares at a better price—net—than the specialists on the floor of the NYSE. And so they went off-board and sold to us because it was in the best interests of their shareholders to do so. By 1968 it had gotten up to 8 percent of the total amount of business done in listed stocks on the New York.

We got the name—the third market—from the Securities and Exchange Commission's special study [of 1963], which became aware of this funny market called the off-board market in listed stocks. They called it the third market, the first being the listed market, the second being the over-the-counter market and the third being this hybrid. Now, we're only talking about one aspect of Weeden & Co.; it was part of a larger mix of dealer activities, but it became the most visible and the most controversial.

In any event, while there were occasional customers who would come to us and say that it was not in their interest to do business with us, we had no way of pressuring our customers to challenge the position that the New York was taking. But then, in the early '60s, something came to our attention that concerned us. There was a firm in Texas that depended on direct lines to a number of NYSE firms and the availability of the ticker tape. And the NYSE ordered their members to withdraw those lines and took the ticker tape out—which they had the authority to do because of the agreement that anyone who wanted the ticker tape had to sign.

We were concerned about that because if the New York Stock Exchange could do it to someone, they could do it to us. We did not want to pick a fight; we just wanted to get along and do our business. We were not trying to change the world. We were not necessarily protective of our role. We merely wanted to compete.

I happened to have an opportunity to run for Congress in 1968, in the nineteenth congressional district of New York. I was out for about six months until I lost. And that was the first time we went public with our thoughts. We said that as a market maker, we wanted to be in a position where we could make a market to anyone in the industry, including members of the NYSE. We argued that anything that prevents competition or creates monopolies is not good. And Rule 394 [the NYSE rule, later changed to 390, that prevented member firms from trading off-board] was one of those things. Then someone would come along and ask what we thought of fixed commissions, and we would say that fixed commissions were as much a violation of antitrust laws as was Rule 394.

We felt that you could only have it one of two ways, and we would prefer to have an open, highly competitive market than to have a marketplace with these artificial constraints that prevented us from doing some of the business that we would otherwise be able to do. As for fixed commissions, we said that we didn't have fixed commissions in our end of the business and we were able to survive and prosper. Therefore, the argument that you needed fixed commissions to survive and prosper was not right. Municipal bonds, corporate bonds, government bonds—none had any fixed commission structure. So why was it necessary in this case?

I think we took a perfectly logical position. We said we thought there should be a reduction in commissions because of the larger size of orders. The commission was structured on 100-share lots. And because there are efficiencies of size, monopolistic profits were being made in our industry. Those would be eliminated with competition. If everybody was able to negotiate his commission, certainly the institutions would benefit. But our opponents argued that if that happened it would be at the cost of the individual, because the individual price would have to increase in order to make up for what the firms would lose on the institutional business. Well, you know what *really* was happening was that the institutional business became so profitable that everyone started turning his back on the individual investor.

We never wavered in what we thought was right, what we philosophically thought was valuable to the public. We felt that unfixing of commissions would allow every firm to price its services according to the costs involved in the providing of that service. Yes, there might be cases where individuals might be charged more, but it would be a competitive environment. Those arguments annoyed people on the Street, but we were drawn into this battle reluctantly. There was no hard charging because we felt there was a moral or economic issue that we had some God-directed responsibility to go out and advocate. But the New York Stock Exchange became increasingly concerned about what we were doing. And they increasingly made use of their power and influence to try to dent our impact.

The report made by William McChesney Martin [in 1971] was, we thought, part of a well-thought-out strategy to counteract the growing influence of the third market. Among its recommendations was one that called for the elimination of the third market. In just those terms, it recommended elimination of the third market. This was presented to the SEC.

I guess we were kind of pulled into this fight because the New York Stock Exchange's antagonism intensified in such ways that we could no longer stand back and not come out and tell the public what our position was. We didn't know whether it would be the Congress saying that we've got to preserve the central marketplace so let's legislate the third market out of business, or whether it was the SEC that would legislate us out of business.

You know, someone can go into a bar for a drink, or someone can go into a bar looking for a fight. We weren't that. I wasn't looking for a fight. But if you're pushed around enough, at a point you say you're either going to get out of here or have to start fighting. Certainly, I was of the character, or whatever it is, that I wasn't going to be pushed around. My role in the firm was to convince our management that we could no longer sit back and try to resist this effort in a quiet, behind-the-scenes way.

My brother, who was in charge of municipal bond trading, would get reactions from friends of his who asked why Don was doing that. Why couldn't he lay off? Why did he have to be so antagonistic, obnoxious even, in his remarks about the exchange? But I don't think we ever lost business. And the fellows on the floor were in two groups. Those who knew us knew that, while we would argue with them, we would put our money where our mouth was. We took positions. We took risks. We were not just taking advantage of the stock exchange's market and pirating off what it was creating. They knew we really performed some service.

On the other hand, the exchange also knew that all of these other securities had in the past been traded on the exchange floor, where the exchange dominated them. As they became institution-oriented, they moved off the exchange. These fellows knew that if there wasn't something that prevented the process, that would also happen to the industrial stocks listed on the New York.

Of course, they couched all of this in public interest terminology, and they did a fairly good job. I can remember, later on, going down to Washington to make my pitch. And before I would go in, there would be this group of people coming out who were representatives of the New York Stock Exchange. I would go in and make my pitch, and when I would come out there would be this body there representing the Association of Stock Exchange Firms, going in right after me.

We were a fairly lonely voice in Congress and the SEC. But our arguments were good arguments. They had the value of not being self-serving. We didn't take a different position on fixed commissions. We said, nope, we can't justify, and we don't think the industry can justify, keeping fixed commissions, even though it would hurt us. We said we think we can survive and we think, on balance, that it would do us some good, even though there were uncertainties.

Our articulation, which was good, was very influential in the thinking that developed in Congress and in the SEC. And here *Institutional Investor* played a valuable role as another catalyst in the process of change. The magazine was of enormous significance in that it was the ideal forum for the exposure of different points of view—that and the conferences the magazine sponsored. These did two things. They brought controversial ideas together. And they also brought together people from all over the country, who had been living in isolation, to learn how other people were doing it. They learned responses to the presidents of their banks, who said they didn't want to trade with anyone other than members of the New York Stock Exchange.

After the market downturn in 1972 and 1973, we made a very calculated decision to diversify. We expanded our dealing activities into many more and different areas of dealing. We were considered one of the larger and more powerful municipal bond dealers; not that we got so much publicity, but we were co-managers in what they called a guerrilla group of more aggressive, more risk-taking underwriters. We would go out and break away from the traditional underwriting syndicates and narrow it to a few of us who were aggressive, on top of the market, quick to react and willing to take larger positions.

From 1974 to 1977 we expanded considerably. In fact, one of the problems we had was that ultimately we got into so many dealer activities that required, because of our style of dealing, that we carry enormous amounts of inventory relative to our capital. But one of the worst mistakes Weeden & Co. made was that we did not make use of our outstanding position in making markets, secondary markets, in corporate securities and listed stocks and go into the investment banking business more aggressively. We were not oriented toward that kind of business. It took different talents, different experiences and personalities than the Weedens had.

I guess the other mistake we made was that we let the firm get out of control and put it in the hands of someone else to run in the middle '70s. That was for a number of reasons that concern what we felt was important. I concentrated my time down in Washington and away from operations. My brother Alan was away doing something else. We put the firm under the direction of someone outside the family, and that proved to be disastrous.

Finally, of course, we found out the problems that we had, which came quickly at the end of '77, and I took over as chief executive officer in the last week of that year. But by that time, our firm was already in a death spin. We had enormous inventory, great leverage on our capital, more than we should have. It was an accelerating spin. And as you cut personnel or divisions or offices, you cut profitability. But fortunately, we managed to right the wings just at treetop. And by the end of 1978, we were very lucky to find someone who wanted to take over our assets and liabilities: Moseley, Hallgarten & Estabrook.

If I had to do this over again, instead of trying to save as much as we could in the process of correcting the company, instead of being somewhat tentative in our decisions to cut back, I think we should have been more dramatic and decisive. We had been decisive in liquidating Wainwright Securities [which Weeden had acquired in 1976 and liquidated some six months later]. If only we had made two or three other decisions like that early on. Maybe we should have said, Let's get rid of corporate bonds, government bonds and these various offices we had developed. We'll cut back

50 or 60 people. We'll take a $10 million loss. Bingo! But we didn't do it.

To save Weeden & Co. was a challenge that took all my energies and talents. It was the most enervating time in my life that I can remember. The emotional effects of trying to save a company that meant so much not only to me but to everyone who worked there and to the family was very, very trying.

One of the most significant things I did as CEO during that very difficult time—we were strapped for capital during that whole period from the beginning of '78 until our merger—was being an interested investor in Instinet. If we hadn't put that money into Instinet, it would have gone out of business. That became important to Weeden's shareholders when we merged with Moseley Hallgarten. Moseley did not want the Instinet stock, so we distributed to our shareholders 2.3 shares of Instinet for every Weeden share they had prior to the merger. So despite what happened to Weeden, the Weeden shareholder, if he held on to his shares, would have gotten out of that Weeden investment with a very, very handsome profit.

Now [since the Weeden firm has been reestablished on its own] it's the same old Weeden. We have a friendly, informal, relaxed atmosphere. We work hard. We play hard. And we believe we're very professional at what we do. But it's a much narrower focus than the old Weeden. Mostly, the new Weeden is a dealer-oriented business that will concentrate on trading equities and doing a little venture capital business.

If you look at the retained wealth of our family, it comes primarily from venture capital investments, and it's one area I have a particular interest in. When you get right down to it, the one real contribution Wall Street makes is bringing risk capital together with new ideas, new products and new groups of people. I'm risk-oriented and therefore I don't mind taking a risk when the rewards will be commensurate. In fact, we've just developed Weeden Capital Markets, which will probably remain small and niche-oriented.

Besides the role I played in righting our wings, I think we did a pretty good job against enormous odds to convince the SEC and the Congress both to allow and encourage the changes that have taken place in the industry. And I'm pleased with that because I think everybody gains. I always thought that our product was price-sensitive, like every other product is price-sensitive. Lower the price, and you sell more of them. Lower the commission, and the more trading you'll have. And that's exactly what happened.

If I had it to do over again, I would be more careful in some of the things I said about Wall Street. People thought that sometimes my use of words was a little bit snarly and uncalled for. And looking back, they probably were right. I don't think they served any particular purpose, and, being a little older and just a little bit wiser, my being critical in that manner didn't help bring about the changes that I thought were important. It probably hurt me, personally, to have said those things. Yet I've been kind of surprised at the support we got from the Street when we reestablished Weeden & Co. Wall Street is a forgiving place.

Editor: Solveig Jansson

Michael Steinhardt

Managing Partner STEINHARDT PARTNERS

Michael Steinhardt is one of money management's legends. Since forming the hedge fund Steinhardt Partners twenty years ago, he has generated one of the industry's best long-term track records, in part by employing an active trading style that has made him one of Wall Street's most sought-after clients. His firm currently runs about $1 billion in both private and institutional assets.

When we started this firm twenty years ago, I was 26 years old and thought that I, along with a couple of other guys about the same age, could do a better job of managing money than people substantially my senior.

I had come from Loeb Rhoades, where I inadvertently became the hottest conglomerate analyst on Wall Street. I had been asked to visit a company that was nominally in the auto-parts business but was growing by acquisition. And growing by acquisition was a dirty word in the mid-1960s.

In any case, I visited this company and I had a remarkable experience, because the guy I met was a very rigorous, bright guy, with an accent, who cursed and sputtered and became easily frustrated. But he was so persuasive and so charming and so unusual that I recommended his stock, which proceeded to double in four or five months—or maybe triple. An extraordinary move. And the name of it was Gulf & Western Industries.

After that, someone else asked me to see another company that had the same characteristics. So I went down to, I think it was the Carlyle, and I met this guy who had just come from Litton. Litton was considered one of the premier industrial companies of that period.

So I went to visit this guy, who looked you straight in the face with these bright, twinkling blue eyes and who had just come to run a company a few months earlier that was the sleepiest company in the universe, that had a few dollars in cash and owned a couple of buildings in New York and not much else. He came in and said, "I'm presently negotiating with 58 companies that have total sales of $7.3 billion and earnings of $427 million, and I'm sure I won't be able to buy them all but I'll be able to buy some of them."

And he did. And that was George Scharffenberger, who was running City Investing, and I recommended City Investing and the stock went through the moon. It tripled in a short period of time. Everything I touched in that period turned to gold. It was remarkable.

So I thought, when we started up our company, I could compete effectively with older people in the business. Youth believed in such things, because we had grown up in the '40s, '50s and '60s and saw extraordinary technological innovation. We saw the jet plane and television and then color television—all sorts of new things, terrific innovations in a host of areas. And some of the stocks we made our greatest money on were companies that were really a function of wonderful stories that were largely based on technological innovation.

One of the best analyst groups, perhaps the best, which I helped found, was called the Concept Group, based on the notion that the way you made money in the stock market was through concepts. Concepts related to all sorts of things that had "onics" at the end of their names and were really little garages in Long Island where some guy was working on some sort of new chip or new transistor or God knows what. It was a period where billions and billions of dollars were being bet on technological innovation.

People who were in this Concept Group were Howard Berkowitz and Bob Towbin and Bob Wilson and Ed Hajim—it continues to this day, you know—guys who could weave the most remarkable stories. And some of them were great pickers of stocks that went from 2 to 300 and back to zero—you know, crazy sorts of moves.

Stocks like King Resources, where we made, in a period of less than a year, more than eight or nine times on our money. If anything, that's conservative. I think within a year of our selling, it went bankrupt. There were plenty of them like that.

There was a great deal of euphoria in that peculiar period, largely based on the perception that you could think about things long term, and if the concept made sense, it was likely in this period of innovation—assuming management was good—to be justified. If you searched the libraries of the various brokerage firms that were around then, you'd see a different kind of brokerage report. You'd see brokerage reports where research people were far more comfortable than they are today in extrapolating long-term estimates on things like how many hamburgers McDonald's could serve.

Part and parcel of that confidence was the ultimate heights reached by the Nifty Fifty. Avon Products had grown at 10 to 15 percent a year for some extended period of time and it was going to continue to do it, as were Polaroid and Memorex and Xerox and IBM and Merck. Stocks like Polaroid had a cult following. I mean, the word "cult" was often associated with certain stocks at that point. No more. There are very few cult stocks today. Genentech is one, but I can't think of very many whose evaluation has so much—well, an extraordinary amount of expectation in it as to be explainable only by something other than financial logic.

The big difference now is that people no longer have faith in the long term. That sort of faded after the debacles of those two fairly major—quite major—bear markets in 1969 and 1973–1974. You know, we had our worst relative year, I think it was 1971 or '72, because the multiples in those stocks got so high relative to the rest of the world that we shorted them and we bought some lower-multiple company in the same group. We'd short Sears at 24 times earnings and buy this other company at eight times earnings, and the other company would go to six times earnings and Sears would go to 30 times earnings, and we got killed.

I'm tempted to say that I've probably shorted more stock than anybody alive in these last twenty years. It would surprise me if there was anybody even close. I should readily add that it's a dubious distinction. I mean, I ain't gotten rich necessarily in shorting stocks. Right now, for example, we have a large short on

271

a stock. It's a pain in the ass, a tough position we have lost a lot of money in. It's certainly easier to be with the crowd.

You know, the original hedge concept came out of A.W. Jones, and I'm not sure anybody seriously followed it from the late 1960s, and certainly nobody to my knowledge follows it today. The concept evolved from the same longer-term view. Short term, the stock market was subject to too many variables to make it subject to easy predictions.

Therefore, if you wanted to be a sophisticated investor, it was sensible not to deal with the market but to analyze, say, the automobile companies—there were only four then, since investors hadn't even begun to think internationally—and carefully choose among them. If you went long a dollar of General Motors and short a dollar of Chrysler, you had zero exposure to the market. That was the original idea of the hedge fund—to reduce the impact of the market and to emphasize stock selection.

Over time, people have lost faith in the long term. And for me, personally, the first bear market, which was in '69, '70, really changed my role in the business from that of an analyst to that of a trader. It became increasingly clear that in order to survive, as many hedge funds did not in that 1969–70 phenomenon, there had to be a shift in focus on our part. We couldn't be only long-term investors, and I became much more involved in trading, because trading really became a far more dominant issue in surviving during a period when long-term conceptual stocks were going to the floor.

Back then, opportunities in trading were created because there were relatively few people on trading desks who had very much in the way of flexibility. There are far fewer opportunities today.

For instance, people talk about first calls. In the '60s and the '70s, first calls had meaning. Today they have very little meaning. People say to me I get first calls. I don't get first calls. I don't even exactly know what a first call is anymore. Then, if you knew Baker Weeks was going to change its view on some gamey growth stock and say, was going to "unrecommend" it, it was really terrific to know that first, because you knew there would be an extraordinarily uniform, homogeneous reaction, and you could make a lot of money.

Now there's nobody that has that sort of research impact. Research is disseminated far more evenly and with far less intensity than used to be the case. There aren't the same heroes. There aren't the same powerful personalities that were involved in the research aspect of the business then. Or firms that had influence, like Baker Weeks, Faulkner, Dawkins & Sullivan, Donaldson, Lufkin & Jenrette.

So who are the heroes today? They're the raiders, the arbitrageurs—some of them now tarnished heroes—basically the people who make money by making short-term judgments. You know, Sir Jimmy Goldsmith, Carl Icahn, Boesky until recently.

The thing I don't quite understand is why so many people think I might be involved in these insider trading investigations. I have the sense that a lot of people think I am. I mean, there was once an article done by some guy from *The Wall Street Journal* where he talked about some trade I had done on "fancy information," a clever expression I used, which he happily repeated.

If you trade as actively as I trade, you can be involved in anything. For example, John [Lattanzio, head trader] walked in earlier and said he heard someone had bought 100,000 shares of a deal-related stock. Knowing that this guy bought 100,000 shares is not inside information. It's not irrelevant either, because he apparently owns—I don't know exactly—4 or 9 percent of the company. That suggests that he's still interested. I already have a big position, so I bought more.

Now, if today I am an active buyer and tomorrow this guy makes a tender offer, I'll get investigated? I guess. I should tell you I have not been investigated. I have not had an SEC inquiry in years, but it really bothers me a little bit why people ask. But the net of it is, I'm not part of that circle.

You have two interesting things about inside information. One is the ethics of the business, yes. And the second is the lack of clarity about most situations. It's my belief that some levels of inside information are part and parcel of the normal activities of many of the participants in this business. It's part of, you know, somebody seeking out the best possible information in order to make a judgment, in order to properly do his job. It's a gray area, and there are a trillion examples.

The question of ethics—what's right and what's not right—is a major issue. In the years 1983, '84, '85, '86, you had to be deaf, dumb and blind not to see what was going on. I used to rant and

273

rave at [financial columnist] Dan Dorfman and tell him to call those putzy friends of his at the SEC. Every day a stock goes up two points and goes up three points the next day, and then they announce a deal and nothing happens? It was like the SEC disappeared. It was embarrassing. I mean, what's happening now is nothing compared with all that stuff. That was a flagrant joke.

The fact that four or five guys finally got arrested, it's not even so interesting, because these cases are all black and white. But the SEC hasn't remotely dealt with the other, gray areas, which is where the bulk of the stuff goes on.

If you're going to be a long-term investor, maybe it doesn't matter much, but you should know that the world ain't simple and pure and we don't all come on with the same weapons. When people talk about inside information in Boesky terms, they're missing the point—because Boesky is just a thief.

As you get older, you don't have the same enthusiasm about meeting new people and getting to know them well enough to determine whether or not you should rely on their input. I was at a Goldman Sachs party recently at the Metropolitan Museum to see the van Gogh show. I've done business with Goldman Sachs for twenty years, and at the reception I looked around at the people and I suddenly realized that I was older than the average person there. I said, "Oh, my God, through most of my life I've generally been in environments where I was one of the youngest people." At that party, it was clear that it's different.

If I'm going to get a new salesman at a certain brokerage firm, he's probably going to be ten or fifteen years younger than I am. And I don't know if I'm going to be able to invest the time and energy to figure out which of these younger guys are smart and which ones aren't, and if I'm going to have the patience to listen to them.

I remember, back in the late 1960s, going to a Bob Brimberg dinner at a restaurant—I think it was called Le Pavillon, run by some man named Henri Soulé—and I sat next to a man named Jerry Tsai, who I didn't know then and I hardly know now. But I remember him. Jerry has had some high periods in his life and maybe one or two low periods, and this, I think, was a low period. And I was very effusive, because we were knocking them dead in all these what proved ultimately to be gamey, speculative, concept stocks.

And he said to me then that money management is a young man's game, that you probably shouldn't do it for more than ten years, because it requires an ability to deal resiliently with change. And most people can't do it for most of their lives, because the emotional impact is too great.

Well, I've managed so far to do a fair amount more than ten years, but I know what he means. And when I look around at the people who are competitive money managers, with some few exceptions, I think most people don't do it for all their lives, or they do it in more mundane, traditional and less demanding areas.

Sometimes when I think about what I do, I have a problem in that I don't feel what I do is profoundly virtuous. The idea of making wealthy people wealthier is not something that strikes to the inner parts of my soul. I've made enough money so that my lifestyle has changed to a degree that makes me comfortable, and incremental money has very little, if any, application in a practical sense to my life. So why do I continue to do the same thing? I have never had a good answer to that question.

I mean, the simple answer is, I do it well. I probably do it better than anything else I'll do at this stage of my life. A more complicated answer relates to power, self-image—I'm not sure. I think the power, for me at least, is in the sense of doing something exceptionally well, and my sense is that I have managed money as well as anybody has managed money in the period I've been doing it.

But I lose that sense very quickly when even for several weeks I'm wrong and getting banged around in the market. I don't have the ability to say, "Listen, over these twenty years you've had plenty of bad weeks and plenty of bad months and maybe even a couple of bad years, and therefore you should have a certain sense of equilibrium about that sort of stuff." But the fact is, I don't. I can't quite do it. As much as I think about it, and as much as it bothers me, and as much as I've even gotten help about it, I can't do it. I can't be reasonable about the bad periods.

I have a wonderful family life, and I really feel pretty good about myself. But if I have two bad weeks in the market, those things

275

somehow, you know, become tertiary. They hardly exist, so much of my sense of self is tied up in doing this well. And there are elements of disappointing the important people.

The people around me who love me say: "Jesus Christ, what's the matter with you? Quit. You got all this money, what's the difference?" Why do I worry that something of great magnitude might happen if I stop staring at the Quotron for fifteen minutes? I don't exactly know. Maybe it's that I'm less secure than other people.

I'm almost tempted to conclude that a necessary part of doing this job successfully is the suffering. However, if you start out as a macro-oriented money manager, in some sense the macro is made up of a lot of little micros. Part of my inspiration comes from watching the market evolve. Maybe other people might get that inspiration from sitting at home and reading Shakespeare.

So I keep asking myself, in the great world does it really matter? Do I know what I'm talking about? Is it applicable in this instance? I don't exactly know. Who knows? But that's part of the challenge you feel.

Editor: Julie Rohrer

Joseph DiMartino

President and Former Head Trader DREYFUS CORP.

There is no better advertisement for how far the institutional trading game has come than the career of Joseph DiMartino. Head trader at Dreyfus Corp. from 1973 to 1976, he rose to the No. 2 position at the company in 1982. During his tenure on the trading desk, he both witnessed and played a key role in the transformation of buy-side trading from a backwater at most money management organizations to a powerful and respected function.

My first experience with trading was when I started managing money at the Chase in 1970. I was doing convertibles, and they said it was probably a good idea to spend a day at the trading desk at Goldman Sachs with Goldman's convertible trader, Eric Sheinberg. So I go to Goldman, and in the morning I meet Eric and I sit on the trading desk in the old 55 Broad Street building. Eric is here, and Bob Mnuchin is there, and Gus Levy's office is in the corner. And I'm watching Mnuchin. Mnuchin is standing up—I'll never forget this—he's got no belt on, and he's got the top button of his trousers unbuttoned. He's standing up, with this cigarette hanging down from his lips, talking into two phones, and everybody's yelling at him.

"Mnuch, pick up the garage," "Mnuch this," "Mnuch that." He's trading a piece of Parke Davis at the time, and he's getting on the system, saying, "Come on, fellas, we got to do this piece of business here, let's go, let's get going on this piece of business." And all day long I can't get my eyes of Mnuchin. I mean, I'm talking to Eric, but I keep watching Mnuchin. It was, I guess, what a taste of narcotics must be like. I got a taste of it and I never forgot it, and I said, "Someday that's something that I would like to try my hand at."

But when I came to Dreyfus in 1971 and at the end of 1972 Howard [Dreyfus chairman Howard Stein] asked me to take over the trading desk, I was very apprehensive. I was 29 years old then, I was president of the mutual fund that I managed, I felt comfortable, and I was afraid, really, that when I took over trading, people would look at me and say, "What did he do wrong?" You know, "They put him on the trading desk with green eyeshades and garters on his sleeves." I was a little concerned about that.

Then I had a chat with a fellow who was a vice president at Dreyfus at the time, David Burke, who subsequently left us to become [New York] Governor [Hugh] Carey's secretary. David said, "Joe, what do you think of Gus Levy, Cy Lewis, Jay Perry, Will Weinstein?" And I said, "Jeez, these people are incredible, they're outstanding, they're legends in the business." And he said: "It's funny, but you know where they spend their time? On the trading desk. They're not in the corporate finance department. They're not in the research department. They're on the desk." And I said to myself, "Well, he's got a point there."

So I went on the desk, never having traded a hundred shares of common stock in my life. I went in, and the people I read about, the legends of the business, all of a sudden were all over me like a cheap suit. I never got more attention in my life. Danny Murphy [head trader of Shields & Co.] camped on my doorstep. Maybe it was because they all wanted to rake the rookie over the coals. But that's how we started.

The nice thing about that time was the abundance of talent; I was covered by an incredible array of people. Mickey Tarnopol covered us at Lehman. Johnny Rosenwald and Dickie Fay covered us at Bear Stearns. Mnuchin and Bob Menschel covered us at Goldman. Carl Tiedemann covered us at DLJ, and Jay Perry and Mike Bloomberg covered us at Salomon Brothers. It was just incredible. The only thing was, during that period at some institutions the level of ability of the trader wasn't what it is today. The best guys in those days were running money. So you had guys like Perry and Mnuchin shooting against the weakest links at the institutions. It's almost like taking the strongest team that you have and pitting it against the weakest part of the system.

All most institutions knew about their trading desks was that they were the second door past the men's room. It was never like that at Dreyfus; Howard, here, has always had an appreciation of that function. He would call and say, "Listen, I'd like to buy about $200 or $300 million of utilities. Why don't you go through them and see which ones you want to buy?" Or he'd say, "Look, if the market starts to move up, I'd like to raise $200 or $300 million in cash. Here's the list; do whatever you think ought to be done." So you're calling analysts; you're getting the numbers. You felt like you were a portfolio manager.

When the market was really on its ass—I guess it was in 1972— Howard and I were talking and we said, "Everybody's kind of down, the market's getting killed, so why don't we host a cocktail party for all the traders and the people who cover Dreyfus?" It was really for the people who covered the trading desk, not necessarily for the managing partner of the firm. So the guy who handled the Dreyfus wire at C.J. Lawrence was there, people like that. We had it in our office and we had three or four bars around the office, and the bartenders that night were all the portfolio guys. Even Howard was a bartender. I remember guys going up to him and he'd say, "What can I get for you?" and the guy says, "How about your research list?"

The perception of traders changed a lot with Mayday and negotiated rates. For the institution there was the fiduciary strawman business: "Am I negotiating right? Am I paying too much for this?" People became paranoid about best execution. They would tell the broker, "I bought the stock at 27, so you better not let that stock trade below 27." A sell program would come in, knock the market down to 30, and make the trader look like an absolute bum. He'd say to himself, "Wait till the portfolio guy sees this execution. Jeez, is he gonna tear into me." That never bothered me when I traded. If I sold a stock and twenty minutes later a buyer comes into the marketplace and takes the stock up a dollar, what are you gonna do? The next tick is an accident. To me, the most egregious missed executions are when someone quibbles over pennies—when the last sale is a half and the brokerage firm makes a quarter bid to the institutional trader and he says, "No, the last is a half and I'm at three eighths." The stock trades down a point and a half or two points, and the portfolio guy looks at it and says, "Well, what more could you do?" What you could do is shoot the guy because he should have hit the quarter bid.

I think we at Dreyfus got misunderstood after Mayday because we paid two different rates: one on business initiated by us and the other on business in response to a broker inquiry. People focused on the initiated rate and said, "Well, they want to do everything at a certain price." Everybody was saying, "Dreyfus is 10 cents a dance." But to me, the basic tenet was to match the commissions on that order with what it takes to get that order done that particular day. There are times when it's hard to do it, and there are times when it's easy to do it. There are times when people put up capital to do it, and there are times when you can sell it like you can sell Telephone on the floor. And the fact is, on commissions we turned out to be mild by comparison to some other people.

In the middle of all this, in the 1970s, you had the institutional payola scandals. There was the Langfield investigation [William (Junior) Langfield, then head over-the-counter trader at Investors Diversified Services, was accused by the SEC of obtaining special treatment for his personal trades from a number of brokerage firms; as a result of the probe, the SEC barred Langfield from the securities business and censured a number of leading traders and firms]. A lot of people perspired an awful lot about that one. On the other hand, a lot of people felt good about it because it's something like the Boesky scandal, where you finally get a chance to clear the air and cut the nonsense. It really was a cleansing thing. But it also, frankly, scared the hell out of a lot of guys, because, let's face it, the image of the high-living buy-side trader was pretty close to reality. You know, the old hockey game, football game, basketball game routine. You'd kid around that there were some guys who would go to the opening of a door if you asked them.

A lot of people—second, third, fourth people on the desk— were going out to dinner six or seven nights a week. They went to shows, there were limos. A lot of that went on. I think probably a lot of it had to do with the recognition that the institution gave the person on the desk and what they paid him. The traders would see all these rich people they're dealing with, guys who have great cars and great homes and live high on the hog, and here's this buy-side trader making $20,000 a year who has difficulty taking his wife out to dinner. Somebody like that's probably more susceptible. Not that there was anything wrong with entertaining per se, but it was wrong if it affected your judgment.

Here at Dreyfus, Howard always had a thing about this. He would always pick up every check. I tell our staff now that if you're seeing people from firms that we don't do business with, you always pay the check; don't ever put yourself in a position where you're gonna feel obligated. If you're going out with a bunch of guys from Salomon, it's different; you have an established relationship there, so it doesn't mean anything.

But in many ways it's a different world today. It's different for me. Here I am, president and chief operating officer of a public company, a New York Stock Exchange–listed company—when I think about it, I say, "Jeez, I don't know how the hell you did it, but you really got lucky." I get gratification in other ways now: in building things, in helping people with their careers and in hiring the right people to do something. It's a different kind of strain, a different kind of aggravation. It's not instant gratification anymore; it's more like instant aggravation before you get gratification.

I still see the people I met when I was on the desk. They're probably the closest, the most enjoyable, the best friends I have in the business. Some of them are running firms now, some of them are still doing the same thing, some of them are out of the business. But no matter what, you can still pick up the phone and call any of them just like it was yesterday. People have kept in touch; it's almost like a fraternity, like you went through something together. It's kind of like listening to 1950s music—like all of a sudden you can almost breathe the fresh air on a summer night.

Sure, it was trench warfare back then. The problems I had with guys who threatened to take out the wires, or who went to Howard over my head to complain about me because I was drawing the line on what I thought was the right thing to do—still, I always found there was a lot of mutual respect there. It's a hard thing to put your finger on, but to me it was just a fun time. You worked, you rolled up your sleeves, you fought, you yelled, you screamed, you took out wires, you tore up tickets, you got upset. But that was the business.

I traded with Gus Levy. I traded with Cy Lewis. I remember Cy

281

used to get up in the trading room, unhitch his trousers, unzip his fly and tuck his shirt into his pants. He never thought for a minute that there were girls in the trading room, because when he was coming up in the business they never were allowed on a trading desk. As tough as he was, one of the hardest things you had to do was say no to him. He'd make this growling sound. But you had to do that, and I think Cy respected you for it.

Today, to me, when you look at the trading business, it's like you're looking at scrambled eggs. It just doesn't have a body; it's all over the place. "I trade the A's to D's in this one," "I trade the A's to C's," "I only do the month of August"—you know, that kind of business. The leverage is enormous; the positions are enormous. I venture to say if you brought back Cy Lewis or Gus Levy today to look at the positions their firms run, they'd have coronaries.

Thinking back on the old days, it really did seem simple, clean and light. It really is like listening to music of the 1950s.

Editor: Cary Reich

282

Robert Haack

Former President NEW YORK STOCK EXCHANGE

Robert Haack was president of the New York Stock Exchange during what were probably its most difficult and dramatic days since the 1929 bust. Among the crises he had to deal with during his term (1967–1972) were the brutal paperwork crunch, the failure of dozens of undercapitalized firms and the beginning of negotiated rates.

My tenure at the exchange was pretty much one continuous crisis. Shortly after I got to the exchange, we got into the horrible back-office crunch, which lasted too long. It was not a pleasant time, because we were always picking up after somebody, trying to straighten somebody out, monitor them, rehabilitate them, consolidate them, merge them or put them out of business. It was not a happy, constructive period. We were always playing catch-up.

I think probably one of the reasons the crunch lasted so long was the fact that the Street up until that time had never put much emphasis on operational problems, had never dedicated much leadership or talent to that phase of the activity. The back office, by its very name, showed that it was regarded as secondary. And as a result, when the crunch came, they had neither the equipment nor the people nor the talent nor, in some cases, the know-how to handle it.

A lot of the people didn't like the shorter hours, advertising restrictions and other measures we took to cope with the crisis, and I didn't like the procedure myself. Anyone hates to curtail their business or to reduce the scope or activity. But it was almost mandated by the fact that the Street was getting farther and farther behind, and with that being the case, it was stupid to make the problem worse by maintaining normal business hours. A lot of people were affronted by the restriction, particularly those that were in pretty good shape. But it was, I think, significantly helpful.

After the paperwork crunch, the market slumped and volume dried up, seriously straining the capital resources of many firms. Our big problem in this regard was the fact that we were dealing with soft numbers. Many of these firms were literally out of control. We would take their numbers and find out on examination that they were not accurate. I'm not suggesting that they were deliberately distorted, but they were literally out of control as far as differences, fails and the like, and it was just impossible for them to come up with meaningful, valid, hard numbers. As you got into it, you found out that there were capital violations and that it would get worse and worse, and that's what precipitated the need for consolidations, takeovers and so forth.

Goodbody was one of the major players that were having grave trouble. They were on the brink, and had they toppled it would have been a disaster. They had something like 300,000 or 400,000 accounts and a branch-office network that covered the country. I think that if they failed, it would have created a crisis of confidence that would have spilled over and maybe caused a run on a lot of other firms that couldn't have handled it.

We had a special committee—Felix Rohatyn and Ralph DeNunzio, Steve Peck, Bunny Lasker—and then a number of staff people who worked in conjunction with the committee. We had a meeting of a number of firms to see whether, individually or collectively, they would step up to the plate and take over Goodbody, and to a man they said, "Count me out." There were great risks, great unknown exposures, so forth and so on. Then I saw Don Regan, who was then chairman of Merrill Lynch, and I think he had enough public interest to realize that Goodbody could not afford to be lost. I will admit, I'm sure that he saw some economic opportunities for himself, for which I don't blame him. But he made up his mind in reasonably short order that, subject to certain conditions and indemnifications and whatnot, yes, they would take over Goodbody. And I remember he and I saw the—I think it was the U.S. attorney in New York—and on the basis of the "failing-firm doctrine," we got a very quick approval and Goodbody was saved. I think that was a strong indication of Don's vision and willingness to bite the bullet.

The Hayden Stone problem was also a particularly hairy one because there were a lot of loose ends to put together. There were a lot of subordinated lenders, some of whom didn't want to go along with a merger into Cogan, Berlind, Weill & Levitt, some of whom wanted a better deal for themselves than we were offering generally. There had been a significant change of ownership at Hayden Stone, with a group from the Midwest having assumed a control position, and it was very, very difficult in that last hour trying to corral these various interests and get them in line. In the last two days before we would have had to put the firm out of business, the special committee dealing with the problem worked incessantly around the clock.

As I remember, Donald Eldridge—a founder of Memorex, who was then in London—was one of the two or three remaining holdouts, and we needed his approval, along with a couple down in Oklahoma. And so I went over to London one evening, met with him the next morning for about two or two-and-a-half hours and explained it to him. It was a hard visit. We didn't like to give people ultimatums, but in this case we simply told him that if he didn't acquiesce, we would put the firm out of business and he'd lose everything. I was scheduled to come back at, I think, around 2:00 the next afternoon, and we agreed that I would call him from the airport and get his response. So I called him from the airport and he gave an affirmative answer, he would go along. It was not a scenic tour, by any means. It was a round trip in 24 hours.

It was a very hectic, frustrating kind of activity. I mean, you are always trying to salvage something or rescue something. And you're doing it amid strong feelings. I remember talking to partners of member firms at 2:00 in the morning in the exchange board room and telling them, "Gentlemen, you've got all my sympathy, but the fact is you've got to go along or we're going to wipe you out tomorrow." Those are hard things to do, particularly when they are people you've known for many, many years, who you like personally even if you didn't admire the way they

285

managed their business. See, because I'd been in the business twenty years and many of these people were my friends, it made it a little more difficult.

It was unbelievable. The hours were long. There were times I didn't get home. I remember vividly one weekend I went down to Pine Valley to play golf. This was one of the Goodbody weekends. I was supposed to be down there for dinner. I got there at midnight. The next day I was called off the golf course three times, and finally I said the hell with it, I'll come back to New York. Which I did.

There were times I got criticized for not enforcing the exchange's rules literally, such as Rule 325, covering net capital requirements. Well, I admit that we didn't enforce those rules to the nth degree, because if we had, there would be no New York Stock Exchange. I dare say we could have put, at one time or another, 50 or 100 firms out of business by literal enforcement of the rules, and some of these firms would have been the major firms on Wall Street. It was my judgment then and now that had we done so, there would have been such turmoil, such lack of confidence in the viability of the financial community, that there would have been no securities industry. Now, I don't think that's hyperbole by any stretch of the imagination.

The alternative was to bend and give and tolerate and hope to correct some situations and bring these people back into line so that the business could be conducted as always and so that the public would maintain its confidence in the exchange community. In retrospect and with the benefit of hindsight, I still think that was the best path to follow. The SEC was concerned that we were a little lax in our rule enforcement, but we told them our point of view and they never crowded us to the point of literal enforcement. I think they knew the problem.

Toward the end of my tenure at the exchange, we began grappling with the issue of negotiated commission rates. In November 1970 I delivered a speech expressing my personal view that negotiated rates deserved a tryout. My basic thinking, which originally favored fixed commissions, was altered by the fact that the fixed commission schedule, in my judgment, was the root of many of our problems. First of all, there was no fixed commission schedule; it was fixed nominally. But, you remember, this was the day of the give-up, the rebate. The commission dollar was being used for a lot of things other than compensating the executing firm. The firm that was giving away 40 or 50 or 60 percent of the commission was in effect negotiating a commission right there, because it was keeping only 40 or 50 percent. So the fixed commission schedule was a myth.

I felt, too, that as institutionalization of the market was increasing and the orders were getting bigger, there was no real recognition of the economies of scale. You know a 100,000-share order shouldn't cost as much per 100 as a 200-share order. It was unusually lucrative. Some firms were getting very, very rich. But in the process, it was laying the groundwork for some other major problems, one of which was institutional membership, which I felt would be detrimental to the membership of the exchange.

Third, the fixed commission rate structure was enhancing the growth of the third market. So all of those things tended to make me feel that—this was a personal feeling—the exchange was not being competitive, I guess maybe in retrospect I was one of the early deregulators, rightly or wrongly. And so I made that speech.

Some of my harshest critics, I'm sure, never read the speech in its entirety. I've read it once or twice in the last ten years, and it still reads pretty good, if I may make a conceited statement. But I did not, as some of my critics suggest, propose an immediate step over into negotiated commissions. I was not for abolishing the thing overnight. The wording of that speech suggested that the exchange examine, analyze and experiment with negotiated commission rates on large orders.

Still, all hell broke loose. My friend Bunny Lasker was aghast. Jim Davant [former Paine Webber chairman] was shocked. Ralph DeNunzio was surprised. My good friend Bob Baldwin [former Morgan Stanley chairman] was mortified. On the other hand, there were a number of people who supported it. Don Regan supported it, Billy Salomon, some of the people at White Weld. So there was no 90 percent majority on either side. The Street was reasonably split.

I said in the introduction to the speech that it was purely my point of view and I was not reflecting the position of the board of governors. But there were some people who said I had no right to express a personal point of view. Well, I think that's hogwash. When they hired me as president of the exchange, I don't think they, in the process, bought my silence for five years, my freedom of speech. I am conceited enough to feel that even though there were those who disagreed, they didn't take it as a personal matter.

Each of the chairmen I worked with was a different type of person. I was a great fan of Gus Levy. I had known Gus for many years, going back to my trading days, and Gus was chairman when I got to the exchange. Gus was a broad-gauge individual, a tireless worker, very bright. Sure, he could be tough. But he recognized that the president of the exchange was the chief executive. He made his presence known, but never tried to run the exchange.

Bunny Lasker—and I don't say this disparagingly—had a somewhat different point of view and perhaps felt that it was his province to inject himself into the day-to-day operations of the exchange to a greater degree, which I didn't agree with. Bunny and I had different points of view on a lot of subjects. I think we got along on a friendly basis, but he did not share my points of view, nor I his.

And then there was Ralph DeNunzio, who was knowledgeable about the business and who was attentive to many of the projects that we were undertaking. We got along very well. No problem.

I think the exchange staff worked very well and had great experience and competence. There will be some who will dispute that. But keep in mind that the member firm department was deluged by the so-called back-office problem. It had oversight responsibilities, some of which were very unpopular and unpalatable. And the first thing that people would do would be to criticize the staff. I don't share that. I think people like John Cunningham, Lee Arning, Bob Bishop, to name a few, were totally dedicated and competent people who did a whale of a job.

One of the things that I'm pleased with in retrospect was the fact that during those years we started the central stock depository. I remember there were people who were suggesting we abolish the stock certificate, making a lot of suggestions that weren't all that attainable or achievable. We took the viewpoint that instead of abolishing it, we would immobilize it with the central depository, and we brought about bookkeeping entry. That grew from a relatively small number of companies and shares being deposited there to now, I don't know, but I suspect they're in the billions of shares. And I rather feel that were it not for the depository, the Street would not be handling the volume today, because that's so much paperwork that's eliminated.

I look back at it all with mixed feelings. I had a lot of fun, made a lot of friends, created a few nonfans. But I am immodest enough to think I didn't lose any respect in the process.

Editor: Clem Morgello

James Needham

Former Chairman NEW YORK STOCK EXCHANGE

James Needham was an SEC commissioner when he was recruited
in 1972 to be the New York Stock Exchange's first full-time chairman. His familiarity with the Washington political scene was a big
plus in dealing with legislative issues such as competitive rates and
off-board trading that were important to the exchange. But he had
problems with his own board—exacerbated by his pugnacious
manner—and ultimately was forced to resign. Today he is a consultant and corporate director.

Back in 1972, there was a selection committee that set about
to find a new chairman of the New York Stock Exchange,
someone who they felt obviously could do the job but in
addition would bring certain characteristics, principally credibility
and integrity—someone who would probably be accepted in
Washington. So what happened was, they went through the list of
who's who and cabinet officers. Someone reported that there were
ten candidates, and as everybody said no, I was then asked. How
could I turn down such a challenge?

The actual approach was made very directly by Ralph DeNunzio, chairman of the exchange, who called me up at the SEC. He
said, "Jim, would you be interested in being the chairman of the
New York Stock Exchange?" And I said to him, "Sure, why not."
You know, just like that. He then said: "Well, if that's the case,
then why don't we get together tonight. Can you do that?" And I
said, "Sure." That meant coming up to New York, which I did.

Right after I received that telephone call, I went out to my legal assistant and said to her, "I don't want any more correspondence for the SEC that a commissioner would receive." I said, "And I will not attend meetings." I told her exactly what I was up to. I also told Bill Casey, who was chairman. My resignation came soon afterward. Once I found out what DeNunzio was talking about in terms of contract and amounts, I handed in my resignation to President Nixon.

It was done very swiftly, which is the way I made decisions. I have good instincts. I have a lot of confidence in my decisions about what I do personally.

I really was in the ballpark for the exchange job for a lot of personal reasons. I did not anticipate, though, in leaving the commission that I would have to leave Washington, and that was a very difficult personal decision for my wife and myself. I must say, the exchange was absolutely incorrect in forcing me to leave Washington, because I ended up spending most of my time down there. I could have been even more effective in Washington had I lived there. There's a camaraderie and a social life in which you can accomplish things more easily. Even though the chairman of the exchange has to do his job in New York, he doesn't have to live there. But when he sets up shop in New York, whenever he goes to Washington it's a cause célèbre—the limousine, hotel rooms, receptions, the whole bit—it was just too high profile.

Now, when I arrived at the exchange, needless to say, the floor members were very concerned that they were going to go out of existence. There were lawsuits threatening Rule 390 [formerly 394], which is the rule that required that all trading by member firms of listed stocks be done on the exchange. So the floor members were very, very upset about that. Upstairs firms were burning, and the floor was angry with the upstairs firms over other matters. And there were, of course, a lot of failures to dispose of. In the end, I walked into a situation of hysteria.

The real problems were at the board of directors level. The board of directors was thrown together with very fine people with outstanding records. But I had several handicaps with that board. First of all, there were three former chairman of the exchange on that board, and that shouldn't have been. Bunny Lasker, Walter Frank and Gus Levy were three dynamite people, very powerful people. They knew what they wanted, and I knew what had to be done; that was the difference. But they had chips to play with and I didn't. I was the first chairman from outside the industry.

One chip was just the prestige of being a big friend of President Nixon's. I mean, that had a lot of clout. That was like having your own private Marine Corps. Bunny had that. Walter Frank had the support of the floor. Gus Levy had Goldman Sachs, which was a major player. Gus Levy had a reputation as being a powerful, forceful, aggressive individual. So he was accustomed to getting what he wanted.

Please understand that the board was made up of very intelligent people, fully capable of making decisions, but they had walked into an environment they were totally unfamiliar with. The ten public directors didn't know anything about the Securities and Exchange Acts. I mean, ten of them had never had any contact with the exchange, except as issuers or maybe readers of what went on there. And with possibly one or two exceptions, the directors didn't understand Washington at all, didn't have the vaguest notion how to get anything done down there. And yet, they would advise me on how to do it. While their advice tended to be objective and good, lots of times it was just, "Well, Jimmy ole boy, you know, you're 40, whatever, and I'm 65, and I've been chairman of one of the largest companies in the United States, and let me tell ya how you do things down there." That was the patronizing attitude of some people.

As for the exchange's floor committee, by the time I left the exchange I put a complete end to it. It was one of my "hidden agenda items." It was to eliminate the way that stocks were allocated to specialists. They had real power. A handful of people would decide before they ever got to a meeting as to who was going to get the new listing of AT&T, for example. You can imagine what that meant to the floor members: to be able to know that they were going to be the specialists in an active stock.

Now, at that time they were working with an eighth as a spread, which may not seem like much, but you know as well as I do that if you have a high-volume stock like an AT&T doing more than a million shares a day at an eighth and you do that 200 days a year, that's not a bad living. Whether the market was up or down, you'd get an eighth times the volume.

As for the floor members, my impression was they were very isolated. I mean, they're down there in a community within a

293

community. They were accustomed to having someone from the Street as chairman. They were accustomed to that person being someone who understood the floor thoroughly. I think they were hostile toward Ralph DeNunzio simply because he wasn't from the floor. They preferred a Bunny Lasker or a Gus Levy, who is known to be a trader, or a Walter Frank or a John Coleman. They liked and identified with them.

Now, as for my hidden agenda, it consisted of certain things I wanted accomplished down there. I wanted to put an end to the stock allocation system, and I did that. You don't hear anyone talk about specialists' performance anymore. You don't hear anyone talk about the way stocks are allocated, except the members of the floor. I introduced a whole level of credibility into the selection process and into the performance evaluation. That was a major accomplishment.

Another agenda item concerned Rule 390. The strategy was to work very hard in Washington to preserve Rule 390. That was the strategic goal. Everything else was tactics. Third-market broker Morris Schapiro had sued the SEC over some matter related to Rule 390, and he was saying, in effect, abolish Rule 390. So along comes Jim Needham, his first major public address, in February of 1973, I think. We wanted the whole world to know what our position was on Rule 390 and the third-market firms. We had to get everyone's attention. We wanted them to know. We didn't do it through any subterfuge. We came right out and said honestly, candidly, forthrightly, "We are opposed to this type of arrangement." Did that mean we were opposed to a national market system or a central market system? No. We just felt that if you wanted to trade listed stocks, do it under exchange rules: no dealer markets, but auction markets.

As I was working with the various members of the exchange, including floor brokers and specialists, firms were continuing to lose money, the value of seats was dropping, and the prevailing feeling was that Needham doesn't care 'cause he doesn't have an investment in the seat. If I could have, I would have bought a seat the day I went to the exchange. But the Martin report said the chairman shall have no identification with the securities industry. Meantime, here's a floor broker watching the price of a seat go from $500,000 down to $150,000 and ultimately to $35,000. And he has borrowed the money from someone to buy that seat. And he says to himself, "Well, what does Jim Needham know about my problem?"

Well, I did, and I empathized with him. And to show my concern, I would try to have breakfast at the exchange every morning. I sat at a table so that everyone who came in had to go past me. That gave everyone an opportunity to say what they wanted to. They could have stopped, talked, and many did. I had lunch there as often as I could. And then, of course, my door was always open. If I was in town, no member of the exchange had to wait more than 24 hours to see me. And most of them, those who really wanted to, did. Now, there are some who said that you couldn't get near me. Not so. That just isn't true. If they didn't see me, it's because they didn't try.

In the end, despite the membership meetings I held, there were some people who just didn't like me. And they wouldn't hesitate to express themselves. Like the time I created the institutional trading committee because it was important that the Fidelitys and Dreyfuses of our industry that supported the exchange be represented. Still, the floor members were angry about that. They said: "You're letting our competitors into the building. That guy Needham is a Trojan horse." Sure, there were some people who liked me and some people who were neutral. But the closer we got to resolving issues, the wider the schism, because they could see they couldn't influence the decision making.

One of the problems of the job was, I wasn't around a lot to do it. I had to be in Washington a lot. I had to be at political affairs, dinners and seminars explaining and defending the New York Stock Exchange. There was a lot of speech writing and making all over the world. Long-range planning required me to go abroad. I was the first exchange official, really, to put the imprimatur on the International Federation of Stock Exchanges. I saw that international markets were going to become more important because of the advancements in telecommunications and computers.

It was a very difficult job in the best of times, and I had it in the worst of times. I had the worst recession to deal with since the Depression. I had firms failing. I had the commission rate controversy.

Adding to my difficulties was the fact that exchange directors are selected by an independent nominating committee. And the nominating committee was elected by the members. I felt that was somewhat of an incestuous arrangement. At one point, the nominating committee reached certain conclusions about directors and just announced a new slate. I was furious with them. And I let them know it. And Don Regan let them know it, too. We damn near sued members of that nominating committee. That's how upset we were with them. I mean, who are they to come walking into an institution and decide that a member of the board should be thrown off? Who are they? From that point forward, the nominating committee consulted at least once with the chairman.

The nominating committee members, of course, were upset that we would dare to have anything to say about what they had done. Well, that's fine—except then they go away and leave *me* with a public relations problem. You know, I didn't need that kind of help.

I didn't like the way the board meetings were run, either. At that time, the exchange meeting room had steps in it. It was like the House of Burgesses. And I sat at a huge magistrate's desk, looking down at the board. And I said to myself, this whole atmosphere is conducive to some type of monarchy. Maybe it was appropriate for the House of Burgesses, back when, you know, Patrick Henry said, "Give me liberty or give me death," but it doesn't suit the twentieth century. So again I did something that steamed up a lot of the members of the exchange: I leveled the board playing field. I literally leveled it. No one sat at the top. No one sat at the bottom. I had them build a horseshoe-type table so every director could see every other director.

I also refused to follow Robert's Rules of Order. After all, I was dealing with ladies and gentlemen. I never had to worry about order. Actually, I had had one director resign because he started to say something at a board meeting and one of the other board members invoked one of Robert's Rules of Order. Fortunately, the director who resigned was a gentleman. He did not make a public issue of it. But I was very upset.

On the matter of competitive rates—which I knew well in advance we were going to have—the decision had actually been made while I was at the SEC. It just hadn't been implemented. But what I wanted to do was to be sure that the commission rate was high enough so that when all of these member firms started to compete with one another, they didn't take rates from X down to zero but from X-prime down to some lower level. So I was successful in obtaining from the commission two commission rate hearings within a period of a year, which added $500 million to the gross income of the industry. That was a big achievement. It took them over three or four years to obtain the previous rate increase. But the granting of that $500 million was really with the tacit understanding that the SEC expected the exchange's support to make competitive rates work. And they had it from me.

But I still wanted to keep the public confused about where Jim Needham stood on this issue of fixed rates. This dovetailed with my hidden agenda of preserving Rule 390. Everything else was a diversion. Commission rates were a diversion. I knew they were coming. What I had to do was force the board of directors to make the decision.

It was around this time that I was having breakfast with John Coleman, a former exchange chairman, who was getting on in years and could be a little cranky at times. But I liked the guy. What I liked most about him was that if he didn't like what you did, you heard about it from him. That morning Coleman said to me, "You know, Mr. Chairman"—he always called me Mr. Chairman. He said, "Mr. Chairman, what you should do is get up and tell the SEC you'll meet them on the courthouse steps at Foley Square." I said to him, "John, that's great advice." And that was the end of the breakfast. And I went downstairs to my office, and a reporter from *The New York Times* called me. And he said to me, "Well, what are you going to do about the commission?" And so, jokingly, I said to him just what the quote said. And the reporter said to me, "Can I print that?" And I said, thinking quickly, "Yeah, print it." Why? Because it would confuse people. They wouldn't know what I was really working on. So it got printed, and you know how you sometimes wish that people would remember something else? They often don't. I gave some great speeches. I made some wonderful statements. I opened the exchange to the press. All those things get overlooked. My statements on the internationalization of the securities markets, the call for 24-hour trading fifteen years ago. No one remembers that. All they remember is that one, isolated quote. But it was all part of my scheme to force the board.

Now, when we had to make the decision about the exchange's position to accept the commission's edict that on May 1, 1975, there would be competitive rates, the board vote was tied, 10 to 10. I remember it was Gus Levy—God bless former chairmen—saying to me, "Well, Jim, you'll have to decide it." And I smiled at him and I said to him, "Gus, if I decide this issue, I don't need a board of directors. Because what you're saying is that I, Jim Needham, will decide the issue. The board isn't deciding." I said: "You've always wanted to participate. This is your moment to set the course of history." I suggested we recess for a few minutes. The board came back. They understood the wisdom of what I had said to them. They came back, and they all voted to accept the SEC's decision.

Keep in mind that I just wanted 390 left alone in terms of legislation. The Senate and House committees were going into conference, and we had a commitment from members of the Senate committee that they would work to retain Rule 390 by striking [Representative] John Moss's language from H.R. 5050. I had developed a rapport with John, and the understanding was that the exchange would support the legislation and, although it was never said, John Moss would not object in conference to the dropping from H.R. 5050 of the repeal of Rule 390. That was the basic deal, and H.R. 5050, combined with the Senate version, passed the conference committee and was going to the floor for a vote.

And then the board did something very foolish. I walked into a board meeting, and, to my total shock and surprise, one of the members of the board said, "Why do we need this legislation?" I just couldn't believe what I was hearing. My Washington staff and I just sat there. We had worked for three years to get the legislation fine-tuned. It worked to the advantage of investors, to the exchange, the SEC. It served the public interests. I mean, at that point, there was nothing to object to. Finally, I remembered Gus Levy turning to me and saying, "Look, Jim, everyone on this board wants to stop the passage of this bill except you. Why are you in favor of this legislation?" Well, when someone asks you a goddamn stupid question, how do you answer them civilly? And that, I think, ultimately led to my leaving the exchange.

What I realized was that this wasn't my board. This was the board someone else gave me. The selection committee said Jim Needham will be the chairman. The board didn't decide it. This was a very bad arrangement where a selection committee selected me and another committee, a nominating committee, selected them. And we were put together.

I was confused because I had *tried* to keep a good relationship with the board. In fact, that year, in mid-'75, I started to institute dinner meetings the night before the board meetings. But there was still a huge level of distrust when these people were brought together. The public directors were so concerned, and probably correctly so, that they not be used to advance the interest of a very parochial institution like the New York Stock Exchange. There had to be some public service aspect of it.

When Don Regan went off the board, I lost a lot of support. I mean, he was really my Marine Corps, my Special Forces guy. They had to be careful with Don for obvious reasons: He ran the biggest firm, he was a man of integrity, he had a vision. He and I saw the world the same way.

Some of the directors were concerned about me becoming bigger than the exchange itself. But to do what I had to do, I *had* to step out in the public a lot: TV, seminars, press interviews. I took the exchange board around the country to different cities. We took full-page ads announcing we were coming to try to get across the idea that, "look, we're not just a New York operation. We're part of the investment community throughout the country."

I had press conferences after each board meeting. Sure, I wanted to invite the press in. I had nothing to hide. I think that was one way of establishing credibility worldwide, to have the press as a partner to the extent you can have the press as a partner. But there was another reason. That was to prevent members of my board of directors from calling up the press after a board meeting and leaking confidential information. That used to go on all the time. But press conferences put an end to third-party conversations. We established the focal point of interest as the chairman of the New York Stock Exchange, which was very risky stuff for me personally.

All of this work, public relations and otherwise, tired me mentally, physically. I had had it. Gus Levy had said to me when the legislation finally went through, "Jim, no one else could have done this." He said that at a board meeting. And I believe the board really felt that way. I felt that I had done what I had to do. Mission accomplished. At that point, I just wanted to coast. And I spoke with Don Regan and several other people about leaving. This was at the end of the third year. And the response was: "Look, you did the job. Why don't you just stay in office and hope for a bull market?"

And it was just at that moment I heard I was having a palace revolt. Things had been brewing, and I heard there was a candidate who wanted my job. I knew who it was long before it all finally happened—I knew it the first day I had met him that he wanted the job. I called that candidate in. And I asked him. I said, "Do you want the job?" Because all I was concerned about was the way I would go. I thought I was with gentlemen. Obviously, I was wrong. Breaks at that level are never clean. Parties on both sides are always bruised.

I was very philosophical about the whole thing, frankly. I was in Germany when I learned about what was going to happen. I had a whole schedule of speeches to give throughout Europe. I was then president of the International Federation of Stock Exchanges. I mean, the behavior of some of the individuals was quite ludicrous. When I received a call to come back, I said: "Look, can't it wait a week? Let me finish my speech tour." "No, you have to come back now," they said. I said, "Why?" No good answer ever came. They bought tickets for me under another name. I mean, this was absolutely insane. They had bought—"they" shall remain nameless because I don't know who "they" are—a Lufthansa ticket for me under the name of Fritz something-or-other from Darien, Connecticut. As if I needed someone to buy me an airline ticket. But it was all so clumsy, so unnecessary. Would you do that to someone who had been loyal to you for four years? But it was the mood of the time. What the hell, we had just thrown a president out of office.

I guess they thought my profile was too high. But I was just trying to do a job. That's all. If there were jealousies, I would understand that. Although the board encouraged me in certain areas, their support was never full. I remember Senator Williams [Harrison Williams of New Jersey] making a public statement to the effect that Jim Needham doesn't speak for the exchange anymore. And that was a headline in *The New York Times.* I called Williams up and said, "Hey, Pete, what the hell is this all about?" And he said, "Well, some of the members of your board have been down to see me and some of the members on my committee and said, 'Don't pay any attention to Jim Needham.' "

But they knew what they were getting when they brought me in. Did they think that by paying me a salary they were going to change my mind? No way. I think there are some people who think that if you pay someone a large salary, you can alter their integrity and their value system. I am one of those people you can't touch. Win or lose, I have my convictions.

In retrospect, I should have spent more time planning for my future. In my judgment, I was selflessly dedicated to the New York Stock Exchange. I have no regrets about that. In retrospect, I think long term I might have ended up doing some things differently.

As for what happened, I'm not bitter, because I understand human nature only too well. It isn't always possible to control the movement of a group. I personally could never do things the way those people did. Does that mean I am not tough? I don't think you'll find anyone saying that. I feel you deal with human beings the way they should be dealt with. Demanding, yes. Tough, yes. I had to work like that because those years—I'm told they were the worst years at the exchange since the 1930s—drew every ounce of skill and talent I possessed.

Editor: Andrew Marton

301

William Batten

Former Chairman NEW YORK STOCK EXCHANGE

> The New York Stock Exchange had just fired chairman James
> Needham and morale was at rock-bottom when William Batten
> took over the top spot. During his tenure (1976–1984), Batten
> tightened up exchange management as it wrestled with reforms
> dictated by Congress and with the changing securities business.

M y perceptions of the exchange were clearly affected by
the fact that I was chief executive officer of the J.C.
Penney Co. for almost seventeen years. We only occasionally had contact with the exchange, and that was usually when
our stock acted, shall we say, "funny" in terms of volume or price.
But my overall feeling was that the exchange, and the industry as
a whole, was not that well managed. I saw through the '60s and
the early '70s that member firms had to reduce hours and couldn't
handle volume. Now, as a listed company executive, I couldn't
imagine having to close the store because you had too much
business. That seemed rather preposterous to me. The message I
got was that somebody wasn't managing the business very well.
The other view I shared, though perhaps not as extreme as some,
was that the New York Stock Exchange was a private club. So I
went to the exchange with those two perceptions.

I first arrived on the board of the exchange in 1972, when its
governance was changed to establish a more corporate type of
board with ten so-called public directors and ten industry directors. In our initial meeting, Ralph DeNunzio, the outgoing chairman, briefed us on some of the problems the exchange faced and

303

that we were going to face as directors. He did an excellent job. But as a public director, I'm sure I didn't understand the implications. And when I became chairman in 1976, I began to appreciate better the kind of difficult period the exchange had lived through. What I did not realize was the low morale among the members and the employees, with some of them thinking that the SEC was out to get them. Others thought the Securities Acts Amendments of '75 would eventually cause the demise of the New York Stock Exchange.

Now, the idea of survival never had even been in my mind. I'd always taken that for granted. And to have people ask that question shook me up. Of course, you must remember that was during the period when there were a lot of people who thought the black box would replace the exchange. Everything would go to automatic trading. That thinking was very prevalent then. And that, of course, was the reason why they were asking the question, "Will the exchange survive?"

Before becoming chairman I was, as a member of the board, chairman of the stock allocation committee. We were to study the way stocks were allocated on the floor. And after doing some preliminary analysis, it seemed to me that the mission we had been given was too narrow. There were things that needed to be looked at beyond just the mechanism for allocating stock. So I went back to the board and asked for an enlarged mission, which they gave us. And over a period of about fifteen to eighteen months, we made a very comprehensive study of the infrastructure of the New York Stock Exchange and made some recommendations, which were accepted.

We eliminated completely the floor committee, which was the power center of the exchange. And we established a quality-of-markets committee at the board level. Previously, we had had a committee for a lot of things but not for the most important thing, the quality of our markets. So that committee then oversaw two new committees: the market performance committee and the stock allocation committee.

Working on the committee gave me the opportunity to get to know the operation of the exchange in a far better way than I would have had I remained just a board member. As I was working on the committee, there was a load of legislative activity going on prior to the enactment of the 1975 Securities Acts Amendments. It was a time that built up a lot of anxiety and concern among everyone. Jim Needham, who came from the SEC, was there at a very difficult time. And there were, as in any organization, different ideas about how you should approach something. Controversies developed, and then, when a decision was made by the Congress, there were members who felt maybe the New York Stock Exchange staff, and Jim in particular, had not done as good a job as they might have. There was always some amount of second-guessing that went on. Finally, and this is conjecture on my part, I had the feeling some of the board members felt that Jim didn't have a good rapport with them, that he wasn't close to the corporate community. That's understandable, because he didn't come out of the corporate world.

Now, I happen to like Jim personally. But in order to understand him better, you have to go into his background. Jim had been in individualistic types of jobs. He was an accountant. He was an SEC commissioner. And certainly, as an SEC commissioner, you are not exposed to management. There are some jobs that are highly individualistic, and therefore the person doesn't develop management skill. And management is a skill. It's just like if you said to me, "We'll set you up in Carnegie Hall to play a piano concert." I'd still have to confess that I've never played the piano, no matter where you might put me. First I'd need to learn how to play, as one must learn how to manage. Jim's background rarely put him in a position to manage anything.

Now, the exchange was operating under some pretty trying circumstances, so there wasn't time to let somebody learn how to manage. Something had to be done right away. Interestingly, I don't ever recall anything about Jim being brought out into the open at a board meeting. Any dissent I heard was more like "corridor conversation." I think there were two or three meetings held in other places that might be thought of as unofficial meetings, where the people who felt there needed to be a change expressed themselves rather strongly.

I felt that perhaps not enough had been done by the board to support the chief executive officer. I thought maybe we were a part of the problem. If we were dissatisfied, then a small group of two or three people should sit down with Jim and point out the reasons for the dissatisfaction and work it out. I didn't feel entirely comfortable putting the blame completely on one person. I expressed all that, but, obviously, it did not prevail.

Now, you can't do something like replacing someone without saying, "Who's going to take Jim Needham's place?" So when they asked me would I take his place if he did leave, my initial reaction was, "No way, I'm not looking for a job." I was already on the AT&T board, the Citibank board and the boards of Boeing, Texas Instruments and J.C. Penney. So I had a full and interesting life. And I did not want to do it. And certainly, my wife didn't want me to do it, because I had promised her I was going to retire. And she remembered that promise. My mother didn't want me to do it. She was in Florida, and I called her to talk about it. And she said, "Oh, I don't want you to do that at all." And I said, "Why?" "Because I don't want you to get in with that Wall Street crowd," she answered. But later when we talked, she was watching [Reynolds & Co. chairman Robert] Stretch Gardiner being interviewed on television. And my mother said, "You know, I saw Mr. Gardiner on television, and he's from Wall Street." And I said, "Yes, he certainly is." She said, "You know, after seeing him, I thought that maybe those Wall Street people can't be that bad."

So there I was: I had taken the job and people would then ask me, "Why in the world did you take this crazy, impossible job?" When I think about how I answered that question, I also remember believing quite unequivocally that the exchange would survive if it deserved to, because it's too important in our capital markets and our economic system. If we get out of business, we will be put out because of ourselves.

It was a difficult time, but, as I said in many of our meetings, I didn't come there to be the purser on the *Titanic*. To improve the mood, we held a series of member meetings, usually two a day, in groups of, oh, 50 to 75. I called the members into the exchange and talked to them about the exchange's survival. "Let's try to develop a positive attitude," I told them, because that's so necessary to survival.

I think the members' natural reaction to me was: "What can he contribute? What in the world does a rag merchant know about our business—about trading? What does he know about capital markets? What's he know about regulation?" I think those were all very natural questions, and I did not resent them. In fact, if they weren't asked, I would have wondered why. Obviously, I didn't go in there to teach specialists how to make a market. If they didn't know how to make markets, I wasn't going to help.

To win the members over, the best I could do was go to work and do a lot of listening. It was important to set up structures and decision-making processes where the pros in the business had ways of inputting their views. It was also important that corporations keep providing the exchange with product ideas. I had felt that the exchange had not really, through the years, properly communicated with the corporations. So we amassed a rather strenuous communication program with the CEOs of listed companies. We held meetings around the country. We sent out lots of communications. We tried to have them feel it was their exchange, not ours, and that they had a tremendous stake in the continued existence of a healthy, viable marketplace.

We faced a congressionally mandated decision to create a national market system. Although there was talk about the electronic linkage of markets, there were no specifications of the components of the new market. Nobody knew, not in Washington or in New York, what that market would look like. So we were all starting from scratch. The SEC wisely did not mandate a specific system but put the responsibility on the industry to come up with one.

We proposed what later became known as ITS, or the Intermarket Trading System. We requested a meeting in Chicago of the other exchanges to explain it to them as we visualized it, and we got their input as to how it might look. There was very great resistance in that meeting. There were fears—which, again, were understandable—of electronic linkage leading to the New York Stock Exchange draining business from their exchanges. That was a natural fear because of the difference in size and resources of the New York Stock Exchange vis-à-vis the other exchanges. So that Chicago meeting did not end up with any kind of agreement. In fact, we couldn't even get an agreement on a date to have another meeting. Now *that's* major disagreement!

So we scaled our thinking down to linking with one exchange, which would be more digestible. And also, if it worked, it might convince the other exchanges we were not out to grab their business. So we started with an experimental linkage with the Philadelphia exchange. And after that was in existence for a while and the other exchanges saw that nothing really bad was happening to the Philadelphia exchange, we could start linking all the exchanges together.

At the same time, the exchange was under great stress to meet with an SEC requirement to establish a national market system free of any anticompetitive practices. Anything that wasn't absolutely necessary for the continued existence of the exchange had to be eliminated. That meant that every one of our rules had to be analyzed, just for anticompetitiveness. And, of course, the one rule that was very important was 390—originally 394—requiring trades to be brought to the exchange.

In the exchange's attempt to implement the legislation, we were on the defensive. It seemed to me we were spending half of our time just replying to SEC initiatives. It took an awful lot of our resources, because we were being examined very, very carefully.

One of my most important personal areas of concern from an operating standpoint was capacity—how much business could we handle. So we started then working closely with the member firms to expand our systems to handle 100 million shares a day. Now, at that time I think our average daily volume was 16 million shares. Occasionally, we'd get up to between 20 and 25 million. So when you started talking about 100 million shares a day, that seemed like an absolute impossibility.

Some of the members were very much opposed to building a system that would handle 100 million shares. My answer to them was that I had taken risks most of my life and I wasn't adverse to taking a reasonable risk—but I wasn't willing to risk the continued existence of the New York Stock Exchange. If the volume came and the industry and the exchange were not prepared, we could count on very serious intervention by the government. Then one day we traded 82 million shares. Well, that eliminated most of the skeptics.

But more controversial than the capacity question was the access debate. There were some bitter words and bitter meetings over access. And we had a special committee established to work on opening up the access to the New York Stock Exchange. The limited access, of course, was a target of outsiders and Washington people because that contributed to the idea

308

that the exchange was a private club. Although I could understand the sensitivity of the members who had their equity position, and their livelihood, I still felt strongly that we had to
open up access.

Another area that I felt a need to expand on was the product
line of the exchange. I remember once bringing up option trading at a board meeting, and the reaction was, "That's a business
the exchange has no business getting into." Now, back in 1972 or
so, I had had experience using options with the Penney Co. I just
felt the exchange should be into them as well. I didn't view it as
something beneath the dignity of the exchange to be in. Opposition to options reflected the exchange's big market share and not
being hungry. Let's face it, when GM had 56 percent of the
market, they weren't as hungry. Now their market share is down
to 40 percent. They're hungrier.

Talking about product expansion eventually got me around to
examining the exchange's budget. Well, I saw one, and the numbers just came out even, expenses and revenues. And I thought,
well, that's an odd coincidence. So I asked to see the other budgets. And every budget, the expenses and revenues came out
even. Well, when I realized that couldn't be a happy coincidence,
I asked why the revenues and the expenses always came out even.
And I was told that it was done that way because that was how the
governors tried to control the expenses. Well, my view of a budget
was entirely different from that. I saw it as a tool to manage the
business. Why have it otherwise? So we changed our whole budgeting procedure and put in a more corporate type of budgeting
system. Many times people would ask me, "Do you think the New
York Stock Exchange can be run like a business?" My answer to
that was, "Well, somebody better run it like a business, because
that's what it is."

The contract I had signed with the exchange was one where
at any time they wanted to fire me, they could; or if I wanted to
leave, I could. In reality, I felt I was just at the exchange on an
interim basis. And I thought my main job was to try to find my
successor as soon as I could, because I had a very nice life doing
a lot of other things. I didn't want to be another prisoner of a
full-time job. I'd done that for 40 years. I soon realized, how-

ever, that the kind of ball game I had gotten into wore away at thoughts of just being a temporary person. Somehow it just got lost. So I ended up at the exchange for eight years. I probably wouldn't have taken the job if I thought it was going to be eight years. But I must say it was one of the most interesting chapters in my life.

Editor: Andrew Marton

John Phelan Jr.

Chairman and Chief Executive Officer
NEW YORK STOCK EXCHANGE

John Phelan Jr. inherited more than a specialist's post on the floor
of the NYSE from his family firm. He was also imbued with a tradition of activism that has placed him in the middle of the Big
Board's turmoil—as a specialist, board member and now chief
executive—for more than twenty years.

My involvement in the exchange was an outgrowth of my
background and history. My father was on the board of
governors and was a real guru on rules and things like
that. He not only knew the rules, but he knew the background to
the rules—why they'd been put in place, what they were trying to
solve.

There was a natural evolution from what my father was doing
at the exchange to my own activities. We were specialists in about
twenty stocks in 1967, the year that I became a floor official—one
of those people who adjudicate differences and give rulings on
stock trades and so forth. And as you became proficient and
people gained confidence in your judgment, they'd come back
more and more.

The driving force behind my efforts at the exchange was a
desire to make our business more efficient. To do that, you have
to make the exchange more efficient. The locking of the two led
me to realize that there's no sense sitting here and complaining all
the time. Even if you think you don't have all the answers, maybe
you ought to get in and put your oar in the water.

So in 1971 I went on the board for the first time. We were reorganized in 1972 and I was dropped from the board, but I was re-elected to the board in1974. When Don Regan retired from the board in 1975, I was elected vice chairman. The next thing I knew, I was spending more time in the exchange's offices than down on the floor.

The industry was really tearing itself apart after the trauma of the '67–'71 period, when business was good and then it was bad. During that period we came close to losing one third of the member firms. We asked William McChesney Martin, who had been president of the exchange in the 1930s, to review the exchange. He suggested that we have a permanent professional staff, to stop running the exchange on our shirtcuffs. He also said we ought to reorganize the board, cutting it down from 33 to twenty members, and balance it between industry representatives and public members. He said that we should balance the industry representation between the different segments, so that the floor didn't have a majority but neither did a lot of other people. Then he said to get a paid chairman, who would be a full-time employee of the exchange.

It wasn't the best time to change things. By 1974 we were in one of the real granddaddies of bear markets. Trading volumes were very bad, and the businesses were very bad. There was really a feeling that the exchange probably only had a couple of years to go.

The changes were coming along with all of our other problems. Factions within the industry were continually at war with each other, while we were trying to put a new regulatory scheme together, including a new board. Once the exchange had gotten all of that approved, Jimmy Needham, an accountant and formerly an SEC commissioner, came in as the chairman. I and any number of other people were concerned about bringing somebody in from the outside who knew nothing about the industry to run the exchange at a time like this. It was a very difficult job, and it wasn't clear whether it should be done that way.

But the public board was the best thing that happened to the exchange. It added balance. It stopped all the internecine warfare within the industry. When I was first on the board, all the discussions were very parochial, having to do with turf matters between

312

different people—two-dollar brokers, underwriters, specialists, retail firms, large firms, small firms, regionals. When I began to serve on the new board, I was amazed at the changes that had taken place, not so much in the things that were done but in the attitude of the board. Some of the parochial talk was still there, but discussions were on a much broader level. A lot of the things you would get into fights and quibbles about before were now being done by a professional staff and not by a board. You went from an operating board to a policy-making board, and that's an enormous difference.

Somewhere around 1972 or 1973, I became an advocate of unfixing commission rates. It seemed to me that we were binding ourselves into a public utility ratemaking, where income depended on how much capital you had and how much return on capital you could get. I'd become convinced that that was an insane way to run a business. We were better off taking our chances with losing the business rather than getting into utility-type rate setting of commissions.

I became interested in automation when I first came to work as a broker in 1957. That summer I didn't get home before midnight. We had a couple of stocks that were extremely busy, and I was sorting papers and doing this and that and the other thing. It seemed to me that there was a better way to improve your bottom line and your quality of life, so I asked my father, if I could find somebody who would automate part of our back office and commission business, would he give me a chance of doing that. He said yeah. So that's how I got into the automation business, to make our business more efficient, so that we could handle three times as much volume without hiring twenty or 30 more people.

So when I got on the board, I was absolutely convinced that for the exchange to avoid going into the same tank as '68 we had to use automation as a support system. Needham had formed SIAC [the Securities Industry Automation Corp.], but we made such a complaint about a system that nobody asked for and nobody had any use for that, to keep me quiet, he put me on an advisory committee. The upstairs firms were saying that they wanted automatic execution. I asked them if they cared whether it was automated or not, or whether it could just look like it was automated. Did they care whether we took the order out of the system and exposed it to the floor? And they said they didn't care if the order went out of the system, as long as they got it back on a timely basis.

The advisory committee members then said to SIAC that we wanted a thing where you can input an order in Juneau, Alaska, and send it to the floor. The specialists will take it out and interface it with the crowd so that all the participants would be involved, execute it and then put the order back in. But to the guy in Juneau, the order looks like it stayed in the computer.

I wanted $1 million to develop the initial designated order turnaround system. At the end of the year, I raised such a fuss about authorizing the money for DOT that the budget didn't get passed for '74 or '75. Gus Levy was chairman of the finance committee in those days. And one day he called me. He was a nice fellow, and he called me "kid." We sat in the office, and he said, "Listen, kid, what is it you want?" And I told him about Juneau, Alaska.

"Yeah," he said, "but what's your problem with the budget?"

I said: "There's no funding for the system. And we need to do this right away. Otherwise, we're going to be at a competitive disadvantage" because the Pacific Stock Exchange then had ComEx up, which they later changed to SCOREX. And the Philadelphia Stock Exchange was coming up with its version of a system. And others were beginning to appear on the horizon.

So he said, "Well, how much money do you want?"

And I said, "$1 million."

"What else do you want?"

"That's all."

"All you want is $1 million?"

"Yes."

"Well, you got it."

And that was the end of that, how we got the funding for the original DOT. SIAC put it on an experimental basis to begin with. Eventually, we went floorwide with it. That's how we rolled into floor automation.

Along with the end of fixed commissions, the 1975 act and amendments said that you had to develop a national market system including quotes from competing markets. So we had to go and see how the heck we could do it. Like we did with DOT, we went out and talked to them. And what the traders on the re-

314

gional exchanges really wanted was to be able to stand on the floor of the Midwest or the Boston exchange and execute an order on IBM just like they were in the IBM crowd on the floor of the NYSE. That way they would get credit for one side of the trade, and we'd take credit for the other side.

We eventually came up with an agreement with the regionals, but it was not easy. God almighty, there were several years of acrimonious meetings. It was a big bullet for the exchange to bite—we had to agree to lose some market share by giving them electronic access. Finally, everybody came to an agreement to create the Intermarket Trading System. We called it the national market system.

We got ITS up in 1978, amid a lot of skepticism. We put 50 stocks and 70,000 shares on ITS that year, I think. It took two-and-a-half minutes to get one of these executions done. But by 1983 or '84 we were doing a heck of a lot more, millions of shares per day. It was taking 29 to 30 seconds for an execution, and we had 1,200 stocks on it.

⁂

Once we got over this national market issue business, we were on the same team with the SEC and Congress on about 90 percent of things. We had had a terrible relationship with the SEC, and we had a worse relationship with Congress. After Mil Batten came in 1976, one of the things that he and I talked about was to stop fighting with the SEC. First we had to turn around our own internal attitude toward them. We had to convince our people that the SEC and the Congress weren't the enemy, that they had an obligation and a responsibility, and we had obligations and responsibilities as well. At the same time, the SEC began to change its attitude as well because of what we were doing.

The other thing is that we began to treat the congressmen like human beings, people we had an obligation to, because they had oversight over us. We spent a lot of time trying to get them to understand what we were trying to do. Also, we spent a lot of time trying to understand their concerns and needs and to begin to work with them.

It was fortunate that we had that slow period in 1980 and 1981, because we had to adjust to the changes on the floor. That period was really a period of adjustment as we began the next phase of automation, which really had to do with the [trader's order] books and some more systems in the back office and updating DOT and working on the next generation of systems. That's when I tried to get people to talk about volume. We talked about doing 100-million-share days and then 150-million-share days and then 200-million-share days, when we were only doing 20 million shares a day. I would get people telling me, "You're ruining your credibility by talking about this."

People had a hard time figuring out how you were going to handle those larger volumes. We did set up a plan to work with the member firms and their operations in the back office, because we learned a good lesson from the late 1960s: The front end can't do it if the back end can't do it. If you can't service the customer right, then neither the front end nor the back end is going to work. And when the 100-million-share days and 150-million-share days came in the latter part of 1982 and continued through 1983, for the first time people really understood that they couldn't do the volume without the automation.

From 1975 to 1980, I looked at the impact of negotiated rates, and I saw economic concentration and the bigger firms going overseas. The wholesale firms, like Salomon and Goldman, were developing government bond products that they were selling overseas. They also were becoming big investors in the Eurobond market. You could see globalization coming.

Europe was just beginning to stir then, and the Japanese were doing more than stirring, so you could see three financial centers coming. The international money flows were increasing, particularly in the Euromarkets.

We talked about how to penetrate those markets. You could see that they would begin to issue stocks and trade them in different areas, for political reasons, for business reasons, for practical reasons. The Toronto exchange had approached us about a link to begin with, but there was just no business in the Toronto connection.

As to whether there will be any trading link in the future or what other kinds of relationships will exist between market centers or exchanges, I'm not really sure. If you look at Paris and the consolidations of all the Italian exchanges, of all the German exchanges and of all the Hongkong exchanges, there's an evolutionary process going on as exchanges—including the one in London—try to find their way to do the other things. Until that all becomes a little bit more mature, it's almost impossible to do anything meaningful other than try to put up something just for a learning experience.

Meanwhile, the banks were doing things overseas. Subsidiaries of banks formed broker-dealers to join the exchange. They couldn't do underwriting, but they could be in the discount business. We decided to stay out of the Glass-Steagall debate because we couldn't get any reasonable consensus among our member firms. Some of them wanted to become nonbank banks, and we have listed practically every major bank in the United States so they're a part of our constituent group; those banks also lend money to the member firms, have enormous trust and custodian business and are the processors for much of the mutual fund business. Looking at these constituencies, we don't have an official position except that everybody should be allowed to compete.

The only concern that I have as an individual is in the securities underwriting business. You certainly don't want to get to the German system, where banks control underwriting. But with functional regulation and other things like that, it's going to be very hard over a period of time, I think, to hold back the banks.

In 1982 we figured the world had changed. The silver scandal signaled that something was entirely different in the universe. When the growth in mergers and acquisitions began right afterward, we reorganized surveillance and brought in people from member firms, the SEC and elsewhere. The problem with the surveillance systems is they can highlight potential areas of illegality but they can't tell whether something is actually wrong.

The other thing we decided was that we couldn't do it alone. We decided to link the surveillance apparatus of all the exchanges and the NASD into one group, called the Intermarket Surveillance Group. And then we began to put pressure on the member firms. We said: "Hey, listen, you too must improve. I know you've got something there, but we all must have more in the future."

Nobody likes to talk about surveillance. Everybody hates it. It causes you a lot of problems when things do happen. But it's an area that's extremely important, and it's undergoing as significant a change as trading.

The problems in regulation now have to do with a bunch of bad

317

guys doing things. People are tempted by money, and there's an incredible amount of money in the system. And there's a general attitude among the firms: "Get the deal done now and we'll worry about the repercussions later." As people get really burned, regulatory-wise firms will really understand that it's in their best interest not to have these things happen to them.

We live in a time where things will not calm down. You're going to see enormous swings in the marketplace. You're going to see volumes of at least twice the size that we have today. You're going to see enormous fluctuations in price. Out there somewhere, because you've had inflation and an enormous growth in debt, is another granddaddy of a correction. That doesn't mean a repeat of 1929, but it means some kind of adjustment, whether rolling or sharp or a combination of both.

Editor: Larry Marion

318

Albert Gordon

Honorary Chairman KIDDER, PEABODY & CO.

> Truly one of the grand old men of Wall Street, Albert Gordon was
> the dominant force at Kidder Peabody from his arrival there as a
> partner in 1931 (he had previously been with Goldman Sachs) until
> 1968, when Ralph DeNunzio was named president and chief exec-
> utive officer. His influence as the firm's éminence grise remained a
> palpable one over the last two decades, and he kept the Kidder
> Peabody chairmanship until October 1986, when he was elected
> honorary chairman. Long one of the Street's most remarkable
> physical specimens, Gordon ran the London Marathon at age 81
> and still maintains a pace that belies his 85 years.

I've tried to keep a low profile. I never liked giving interviews,
and I tried not to join boards, though I only would agree to
become a director if it looked as though if I didn't become a
director, we'd lose the business. For 30 years I've been on the
board of Memorial Sloan-Kettering Cancer Center. I accepted
that position because my mother died painfully of cancer and I
wanted to do something to memorialize her. I began giving money
to Sloan-Kettering without any thought of becoming further involved. Then one day I was asked to be a director. They still put
up with me, maybe because I give money.

Even though I had no desire to get involved myself, I used my
best efforts to persuade Ralph [DeNunzio] to accept the chairmanship of the New York Stock Exchange. I was certain that he
would do a good job and that his enlarged experience would be
good for us.

I never found speaking out on the issues in public to be that effective. I'd rather be a worm than an eagle. We can get along without the eagle, but we can't get along without the worm. Of course, there are times when one has to take a stand. For instance, we stopped advertising in *The New York Times* because of its attitude toward Cuba and Castro. I knew about Castro inside and out, and I didn't like the way the *Times* idolized him, so we stopped advertising. I wouldn't allow the paper in the house. I remember my daughter coming home after working in Buenos Aires for a couple of years and asking for the *Times*. I told her, "We don't take it anymore." And she said, "But I've been longing for a good newspaper." So I said: "Well, I'll make a deal with you. You can go out and buy it yourself if you only read it in your room." All this lasted a couple of years, until the *Herald Tribune* folded.

I never believed in telling people what they should do. In talking to our clients, Kidder tells them what they *can* do. We give them a list of ideas and tell them, for example, "We'll give you the pros and cons, and you make up your mind." This doesn't mean, however, that we don't try to steer our clients in original directions. For example, years ago we suggested to a client that he have us go directly to the institutions for the sale of securities rather than have his company go through the laborious preparation of a registration statement. The result was what we believe to have been the first private placement. As a result of this learning experience, we did more private placements than anyone else for a number of years. One must try to do something for clients ahead of the competition. That's why I bridle when people talk about our "chasing business." If you "chase" business, you're not going to get it.

I remember the first week that jets flew to Tokyo, my wife and I went over there. Without a reservation, without an introduction. We went to the tourist agency to get a hotel room. And it was obvious at the end of ten days that the Japanese people were very, very friendly to the Americans. So then we made a real play for Japan.

I see clients whenever anybody wants me to do so. If I see an opportunity, I'll go after it. But obviously, most potential clients relate to people their own age. I recognize the fact that some people might say, "What's this old duck doing around here?"

320

I'm very happy I gave up administrative responsibilities when I did—in 1968 or so, when DeNunzio succeeded me as chief executive officer. I was approaching 70 years of age. The approach of that anniversary encouraged me to accelerate that decision. I felt that if my advice were worth anything, I'd be asked for it, and that I could, perhaps, have a more meaningful role than if I took myself too seriously.

Ralph was only 40 or 42 when he took over; he succeeded on his merits—it was a consensus decision. And I think we were lucky to have him. He has been great on details and very good in investments and hasn't tried to hit home runs. Ralph never went in for ego trips; he wasn't diverted by social ambitions.

In my opinion, the greatest threat to the securities business is not federal regulation but the possibility of economic stagnation in the U.S.A. We didn't get too worked up when negotiated rates started, though there are very few businesses that have to readjust almost immediately to a 25 percent decline in gross revenues. But it was apparent that the industry couldn't go on making the profits it was making. Life isn't that easy. When we realized negotiated rates would become a reality, we beefed up our research department and added more offices and more salespeople in order to increase our clientele, in the belief that clientele would be willing to pay for tailor-made services.

Our reaction to Rule 415 [the SEC rule permitting shelf registrations] was somewhat the same. The old registration system with its twenty-day waiting period had become archaic. To a degree, Congress had recognized that, because it never gave the SEC the money to oversee the monstrous registration statements that the SEC felt it required. It was finally proven that to spend all that money on registration statements and delays and all the rest of it was unworkable. Some people predicted Rule 415 would destroy the distribution system. If it had, the distribution system deserved to be destroyed. If you don't render a service, you ought to quit.

The changes brought about in 1975 by mandatory negotiated stock exchange rates increased the need for much more capital. There were all these commitments that one had to make—one couldn't risk taking them if one didn't have a lot more capital, or access to it. It's like filling up a glass of water: When it gets half full, you don't pay much attention to it. When it gets three-quarters full, you wonder whether the water's going to stay in.

We sensed the capital situation was getting out of hand a couple of years ago. It seemed to us that it was no longer possible to remain independent and be competitive in the industry. We had to have access to much more capital.

We didn't think going public would solve our problem. Number one, later there might be a need for more capital. Number two, as it would freeze the stock in the hands of the then-holders, there would be no chance for our younger people to come in, except at the market price. Kidder has always thought it was important for young people to own a piece of the business. Over the years we set up a system in which there were two classes of stock, both with equal claim on earnings but with one for sale to our younger people at a price that started out at one tenth the price of the regular stock. In effect, we older people in Kidder gave millions to the younger people to encourage their ownership. In the GE merger, both classes received the same price.

I was very enthusiastic about the sale of 80 percent of our stock to General Electric. I had a good deal of influence in getting other people enthusiastic about it. One has to face the facts of life: We had to have more capital if we were to have an exciting and constructive business life.

Greed had nothing to do with our decision to merge with GE. Over the years I could have had more stock in Kidder Peabody if I'd been greedy. I've had enough to satisfy me. I never took a bonus. I didn't want people coming into my office, smiling in my face and saying to themselves, "What's this greedy son of a bitch doing here?"

I didn't need the money. Not for the way I've lived. I have one Chevette automobile. And my wife never had a fur coat, and didn't want one. I'd much rather have an austere lifestyle: traveling in a truck for example, from the Strait of Magellan to the Bolivian border. You can't spend a hell of a lot of money doing that.

—⁂—

People sometimes ask me what my investment philosophy is. Well, to me it is obvious that before one is able to invest, he or she has to have saved money. In selecting stocks, you should use common sense. And if you're managing your own money, you should not let it interfere with your main occupation. I know that in the '20s, when speculation was rampant, the thing to do was not think about the market between 9:00 and 5:00. You could think about it after that, or before 9:00.

I've always had enough self-confidence so that monetary considerations never meant much. In my opinion, physical freedom means more than monetary freedom. I didn't believe in leaning on crutches. Like aspirin—I haven't had five aspirin pills in my life. Heaven knows, one never needs an aspirin. I can see using penicillin, but I don't see needing an aspirin pill. What happens if you get a headache? You go out and exercise, and then you forget you've got a headache.

Editors: Gilbert E. Kaplan
and Cary Reich

Robert Genillard

Former Chairman CREDIT SUISSE WHITE WELD

In one sense, the origins of the Eurobond market can be traced to Caracas, Venezuela. For it was there, in the merchant banking subsidiary of the old Wall Street firm of White Weld, that Robert Genillard and his fellow partners, John Cattier and John Stancliffe, cut their teeth in investment banking. Dubbed the "Caracas mafia" when they moved to London and Zurich in the mid-1960s, the trio made White Weld the fledgling market's most creative force. Genillard went on to preside over the firm's successful link-up with Crédit Suisse (in what became the present Credit Suisse First Boston), then left in 1976 to become chief executive of Thyssen-Bornemisza.

We all had a dream of the Eurobond market becoming *the* supranational capital market. This has happened to such an extent that the market is no longer a Eurobond market, but the world capital market. The exciting aspect of this adventure which we all lived together was that we were convinced the world had changed. We really felt that the internationalization of trade and industry was going to be followed by the internationalization of finance—that as the world became more open, with freer exchange and greater mobility of people, data and telecommunications, financial functions quite logically had to follow. No *single* national capital market was going to be able to really provide the requirements.

I gave dozens and dozens of speeches on three continents, saying "Gentlemen, something is going to have to happen. The world is changing, but finance is remaining archaic." Early on, people were not particularly interested; they thought that all this talk might just be propaganda to float a few issues—visionary talk perhaps—but probably just merchandising or something.

But little by little the idea grew and some issues got floated. Some people claim that the Eurobond market actually got started with the Autostrade issue of Warburgs in 1963. But that issue was only one of several occurring around that time. Philips floated a dollar issue out of Holland. There were the unit of account issues of the Kredietbank, such as for Sacor, the Portugese company. The Autostrade issue, though, was a key factor because it was a more structured effort and syndicated in more of a Eurobond fashion.

It became very important for the market at this point that some prestigious personalities got behind it. People were clearly intrigued by the concept. They could see the beginning of an entirely new market that would let them rise out of their often hemmed-in positions in their smaller home economies, with all the regulations. They could see climbing on board of a development that would help their internationalization.

For instance, [former Deutsche Bank chairman] Hermann Abs, whom I got to know quite well, espoused the idea of a Eurobond market. He saw a chance for Germany to become a center of issuing activity and for Deutsche Bank to play a world role in it— and rightly so. He started speaking out on the subject and gave it a lot of weight. And Abs was a most eloquent and gifted speaker with—uncharacteristically for a German—a subtle sense of humor. Then his successor, Wilfried Guth, really took the torch from him in supporting and promoting the market. Guth was really one of the great banker-diplomats. He brought a lot of borrowers to the market.

John Young of Morgan Stanley was another towering figure, this time from Wall Street, who was very interested in the market's future. He knew all the central bankers and finance ministers who mattered in those days. Banca Commerciale Italiana's Carlo Bombieri was another great international banker who took an early interest. Jean Reyre, who was then chairman of Banque de Paris et des Pays-Bas, was also quite keen. Nat Samuels, who was the senior partner of Kuhn Loeb in those days and a man of considerable intellect and vision, very much espoused the whole concept. Then, too, the London Rothschilds were also very interested—Leo and Jacob being the two who really took hold of it. André Meyer once mentioned to me that Lazard Frères had really missed the boat on that one, and they did. In 1966 they were No. 4, and five years later they were nowhere.

Siegmund Warburg obviously was a key figure. Although he was much older than me, he was very good to me in my career, very helpful, and we became good friends. We worked very closely with Warburgs from the very early days, with Siegmund and his partner Gert Whitman, an American. Gert really knew the international markets—better probably than any of the native European bankers—and Siegmund very much relied on him for Eurobond business. He worked very closely with us on pricing new issues. Warburgs had the standing and the prestige to buy issues, but they didn't at that point know how to price them or how to place them. So we placed a lot of the issues they floated early in the game.

At White Weld we had a large group of international investors who bought foreign dollar bonds and, subsequently, Eurobonds. We also had the largest trading operation in such bonds in the secondary market plus substantial international asset management. So putting those [strengths] together, we had what London houses that had just started going into issues, like Hambros or Warburgs, didn't: placement power and after-market care. We had the clients; we knew how to place bonds.

Once, Warburgs floated a multicurrency issue for Mobil that was difficult to move, and Siegmund was on the phone with me night and day because it was a terrific flop. We moved heaven and earth and managed to place 60 percent of the total. When it was all done, Siegmund called and said, "This was such a difficult experience, and we worked so well together, can I send you a book or something just to show you my appreciation?" I said, "You don't really have to," but he pressed and asked whether I liked old coins. "Well yes, it so happens I like old coins." He replied, "Good, I'll send you a silver taler." But somehow I never received it. He must have thought I was the greatest boor on earth for not having written him a letter of thanks. I never mentioned it to him, and he never mentioned it to me. After he died I had some regrets, because I started wondering whether he had sent it and it had not arrived.

Siegmund *was* a very charismatic figure. He was a smart and wise financier. He was very pleasant, I must say, to work with. He struck you at first as aloof, but once you got to know him, he was extremely accessible, very friendly and a fascinating man. He was simply intelligent.

In those days there was a lot more protocol and a lot more formality than there is today, especially when you dealt with older persons or greater banking figures. It was a matter of tradition and courtesy to make personal calls. I will always remember when Abs just called me one day and said, "I'd like to come and talk," so we went to lunch. To me it was a great honor, because I was just a young partner in a Wall Street firm, whereas he was, of course, a renowned international banker.

The early days were the greatest period. It was really fun, because you felt you were creating something, building up an entirely new structure, an entirely new market. It wasn't just dealing in abstract financial paper—it wasn't just a financier's job. It was really an architect's job. It was building a house, building a structure. I enjoyed myself tremendously, I must say, because it wasn't just doing the deals, which I always liked, but it was really writing about the market and speaking about it. You have to bear in mind that Cattier, Stani Yassukovich, Stancliffe and Michael von Clemm, who played a very important role, too, after he joined White Weld a bit later, as did John Craven, were quite young by the standards of that period—all of us were in our early 30s. Obviously, anybody who is in his 30s today makes a half-million dollars if he is highly creative, but in those days being 30 was a tremendous liability. And we were dealing with the chairmen of banks and being the subject of articles and interviews, which normally occurred only if there was a scandal or you were over 50. So that was great fun.

There were terribly long hours and intense worldwide travel, but, you know, you didn't notice. First of all, we all got along with one another extremely well. I have very fond memories of this group of people. We worked very well together. And all of us were fired up by the feeling that we were breaking new ground, we were innovating, we were doing something momentous.

I remember, for instance, the syndication of the first-ever corporate issue in the Eurobond market. It was for, of all things, a Finnish company—Kesko—because that was the only company we found we could interest in doing such a thing at that point. Though large by Finnish standards, it was certainly not a world company of any kind.

At this stage, in the 1960s really, there were two phases to the growth of the market. At first, it was very difficult to convince anybody to float an issue: The market wasn't respectable, it was unproven, the concept was esoteric, it was legally complicated. Then in the second stage, the interest equalization tax passed by the U.S. gave a new dimension to the market by bringing in top-grade U.S. corporate borrowers for both straight and convertible bonds. And I must say, we at White Weld, which soon thereafter became Credit Suisse White Weld, had a great run. We were not bankers to a lot of these top companies in the United States, but we got a jump on our American competition because we had the position over here.

By the latter '60s, we felt the market was here to stay. By then, the entry of top-class American corporate names had given it a whole new respectability and dimension—to the extent that we'd begun worrying what might happen when the interest equalization tax went off. We asked ourselves, are we going to revert to a more provincial market or one in which just a few sovereign governments and some multinational corporations outside the U.S. will be issuers? When the market reopens in America, will a lot of this business go back to America? But for the same reasons that America could no longer finance all the requirements of a world economy—no other single market could, either—that didn't happen.

It is fair to say, none of us guessed how huge the market would become. I remember in 1966 when we floated the first issue of bank Eurodollar certificates of deposit for Citibank—I think it was $10 million or some such number, which was big money in those days. We gave a press conference, and the questions reporters kept asking were: "Does this new instrument really have much of a future? Does it make sense? Why would people bother? How large do you think the market might become in a few years?" I said, "Well, I can't tell you five or ten years out, but it could be a

329

billion-dollar market in a few years." But two or three years later the market was only a few hundred million dollars, and I looked like an idiot for a while.

Convertibles created a whole new stratum of interest in the market, because they attracted buyers who were not traditional buyers of fixed-income securities but were interested in equity-linked investment. We were very proud of having floated the first convertible, for Monsanto, in 1965, and that was followed the next year by the first European convertible, for Beecham, which we also did. We also did the first straight Eurodollar bond for a Japanese corporation—Sumitomo Chemical—in 1964. In 1965 we floated the first investment trust to specialize in Eurobonds. We floated the first Eurocommercial paper in 1970, for Hoechst. The first floating-rate note issue altogether was for ENEL, and though we were not the lead manager—Bankers Trust was—we really did develop the idea with them jointly. But we did do the first floating-rate note issue for a bank—Banco Popular—in 1976.

Maintaining creativity in a firm is paramount, and the key was of course our people. They were the creators. They were the doers. People always wonder why you pay people as well as you do in this business, and some even think it's a scandal—but you need self-starters who create opportunities themselves. If they are really good they can go and do it somewhere else or for themselves. Take a John Craven, who, like many of us, had gone out and done his own thing. So if you don't give them freedom to innovate, and if you don't pay them highly, why the hell would they stay with you? It's not a structured functionary type of job. I try to always be sensitive to that.

On the other hand, you cannot manage without discipline. If the people are sloppy and make loose and dangerous commitments, you have to be unpleasant and tough. It is a high-risk business, but you are disciplining, basically, prima donnas. It's the old Catch-22. In this business it's like running an opera house. You've got to have the best prima donnas in it, and if you have them, they are temperamental, they don't like to be managed, and yet if you want the business to succeed, you have to manage them. You have to have a creative tension. You have to have a combination of freedom, creativity and discipline.

In 1970 I negotiated the deal that was to wed Crédit Suisse to White Weld. I became convinced that we had to have a firm in Europe with substantially more capital than White Weld, which was still a partnership, could provide. And also we had to get out from under U.S. regulations and could not operate just as a U.S. securities firm. I thought, therefore, that we had to find another structure. So the partners of White Weld who were over here—myself, John Cattier and John Stancliffe—changed our ownership in White Weld in the United States into the new firm. We ceased to be partners and became only limited partners. And we created W.W. Trust [today Financière Credit Suisse First Boston] and became shareholders. Then we began looking for 51 percent foreign capital. Eventually, we got Crédit Suisse to take a participation.

We'd had a long historical relationship with Crédit Suisse and felt that, of the three big Swiss banks, they were the most investment-banking minded; they knew all facets of the business, and we knew them very well and had an excellent relationship with them. I negotiated the original deal with president Reinhardt and Messrs. Lutz and Kurz, the two general managers responsible for the areas of business we were in. But this was a small, passive participation. Then Rainer Gut came on the scene. He was a real international investment banker and a top strategist. He immediately realized he had a problem and an opportunity. The small participation was both too much and too little. That is when he and I negotiated the full association and Crédit Suisse added its name to the venture, taking a large interest and making it its chosen instrument for supranational investment banking. He correctly said that if I was the father of the deal, he was the mother; and that is because the conceptual and structural basis of the firm was really conceived at that point and has endured and prospered immensely, thanks to Gut and my successors.

I had some trouble selling the original Credit Suisse White Weld concept to my colleagues. They clearly agreed there was a need to have more capital, to become independent of the United States and of White Weld and to have an association with a first-class, large, very international and compatible European firm. What they were afraid of was the idea of association with a commercial bank, because they had visions of commercial banks being stodgy and stuffy and bureaucratic, all of which was fast changing and never proved a problem with Crédit Suisse.

331

White Weld was later absorbed by Merrill Lynch in 1978. If CSWW had chosen to just remain within the existing association, our holding company, Financière Credit Suisse White Weld, would have owned 9 percent of Merrill Lynch, which was contrary to the operating principles in the initial charter. Gut immediately saw the problem and said: "That is not a position we should ever find ourselves in. Better disconnect altogether and look for another association." That's when he found First Boston and reproduced with them the arrangement and cross participations of Credit Suisse White Weld. Gut felt, quite rightly, that the firm needed to find another American anchor of very, very top quality and put together a masterful partnership.

At the time of the switch from White Weld to First Boston, John Craven had his qualms about size and felt that a smaller firm rather than a bigger one might be more to his personal liking. John has always been uncomfortable with very large organizations. That's the history of his life. And while I have managed large organizations, including a company with 20,000 people, and enjoyed it, I have sympathy for such a view. So with the prospect of First Boston coming in, he saw a very large, structured organization with Crédit Suisse on one side, First Boston on the other. He worried, therefore, that he couldn't work things out as he had before.

I was already out of the business, but I was still a director, and some of my fellow directors asked me to talk to him. I went up to Verbier, the ski resort, to have a chat with him, but there was no way to talk him out of this idea that the thing was going to become too big to be successful. He was wrong. But then, he was right about what he did for himself. He was eminently successful.

I always thought highly of John Craven. He was a very high-strung individual—as I think all of us were—but a very gifted one. An extremely hard worker with a great sense for deals. He could smell a deal miles away, and not only could he smell it, but he could bring it home and bring it home profitably. Now, he was accused of being insensitive, and he was such a hard-driven kind of person that maybe he was at times—he didn't have enough patience for people who were maybe not as good as he was.

Firms, like countries and economies, have cycles. In the United

States, White Weld, unfortunately, didn't grow with Wall Street and found it more advantageous to be absorbed by Merrill Lynch. Its international end became bigger and more successful than its domestic one. Credit Suisse First Boston has remained at the leading edge of innovation—it didn't have any kind of down cycle in this respect. To me, having had something to do with the origins is very, very gratifying. You are always afraid that when firms grow, they become institutionalized and bureaucratic—they lose their drive.

That hasn't happened at Credit Suisse First Boston. One reason is that they are totally committed to international investment banking. Credit Suisse First Boston remains totally dedicated to the international market. This isn't a side activity for them; it is their primary task. And therefore the necessity to innovate and create is greater there than it is anywhere else. And the firm's leadership, including Rainer Gut—who is probably the Abs of today—has always been among the very best. He is certainly one of the very top international bankers in the world.

When we set up our association with Crédit Suisse, we agreed on a principle that is still in force today: that Credit Suisse White Weld would be the chosen instrument for international investment banking by the two institutional shareholders. They would refer all such business to it and therefore never find themselves in conflict with their own subsidiary, such as occurred with consortium banks. Of course, it would never have developed as it did if Credit Suisse White Weld had not been successful in generating most of the business itself. The shareholders, like any shareholders, would have eventually said: "Well, you know this thing doesn't work. What do we do about it?" But so long as the sum of the activities of the three produces much more than the pieces, there is no problem. And this is what has kept this thing going—and so successfully. The sum of the three entities is more than three; it's a case of one and one makes five.

Another thing which has helped to make Credit Suisse First Boston so successful is that we tried to create an entity where you could have a profitable and distinguished career without ever having to work in the parents. All the other joint ventures, we always felt, had this problem. If you wanted to make it to the top at Salomon, you had to go back to New York at some point. If you wanted to make it big at Deutsche Bank, you had to go back to Frankfurt. This has never been true at Credit Suisse First Boston.

I am sure that Jack Hennessy, who is an extraordinarily able and successful leader and holds that thing together beautifully, feels that way. Besides him, there is an impressive array of talent who feel that CSFB is a top career place—people such as [Hans-Joerg] Rudloff or [Oswald] Grübel who have sheer market genius besides being top managers.

I left Credit Suisse White Weld at the end of 1976 when I felt the child had come of age, that the frontier days were over. The new team has taken it to heights that maybe I never could have. I loved the pioneering, the opportunity to be in on the ground floor, to really be directly involved in the process of innovation. Maybe, in a sense, I had a "Craven bias"—although I really believed in the future of the business, I saw it becoming institutionalized.

Also, I have always been very much attracted by industry. I've been interested in venture capital, in industrial investment. Back in my Venezuelan days, when we promoted new industries, I was a director of a dozen companies down there at the tender age of 30. I had always wanted to have a more direct hand, rather than just looking at it from an investment viewpoint. So when I got the chance to manage a very large international, very diversified, industrial group [Thyssen-Bornemisza] that was open to going into all sorts of different activities, I decided the time had come to do something else.

I think, importantly, people shouldn't be chief executive of anything for more than ten years. I've personally experienced being on boards. I've had unpleasant experiences. I've seen people who stayed too long in a leading position. If they are creative people, they invent a new religion, and then sooner or later they believe their religion is infallible. They start believing in their own myths, and they are not able to rejuvenate themselves. I think that in any activity—industrial, financial or anything else—ten years is a good number, in that it takes one to three years to map out a strategy, to understand the guts of the business and to have a vision of the future. And it takes at least five years to build up the organization, to have a place in the sun in the business you are in. Then it takes another year or two to be sure you have arranged for a succession, and that you can walk out of the business honorably. Beyond ten years, nobody is capable of being objective about himself and his own achievements. Meanwhile, the world has changed, you need a new vision. People who are pioneers are not necessarily good administrators or managers of the next phase.

I am by now the grandfather, not the father, and therefore can take even more pride in the fantastic achievements of CSFB. You always have aggravation as well as satisfaction with your own children, but with grandchildren you usually only see the good side. You only have the immense pride I have for what my successors have done.

Editor: Kevin Muehring

Evan Galbraith

Director MORGAN STANLEY INTERNATIONAL

Evan Galbraith began his career as a Eurobanker in the early
1960s at Morgan et Cie., Morgan Guaranty's Paris investment
banking arm. Galbraith quickly earned a reputation as one of the
most creative minds in the burgeoning market and claims credit
for inventing at least one of its most popular instruments: the
floating-rate note. In 1981 the Reagan administration appointed
him ambassador to France, and today Galbraith is based in New
York as a senior adviser on the development of Morgan Stanley's
international business.

The so-called Eurobond issue, unbeknown to most people,
developed as a Euroequity. Near the end of 1962, we had
a lead through Morgan Guaranty to see Neckermann, a
German mail-order house, and were put in touch with the then
majority owner of Neckermann, Frederick Flick. The Flicks said
they would be willing to sell their interest in the company and
were anxious that the German banks not get control of it. Particularly, they were worried, as they used to be in those days, about
Deutsche Bank. They were very clear that they wanted it syndicated worldwide, and only a portion of it was to be placed in
Germany.

That deal—which came in February 1963—was, in fact, syndicated widely around the world, including private placements in
the United States. Four or five major funds took some of the
stock, and we placed it with insurance companies and bank trust
departments. This was in February 1963, before the famous Autostrade issue, which was given all the credit for being the first

337

Euroissue. Of course, ours was an equity issue. The Eurobond market didn't really start until the Autostrade, although prior to that there'd been indications of notes being placed here and there, nothing really syndicated. But that led to the Council of Europe issue, which was done in a fairly limited way and was the inspiration to Warburg to do the Autostrade.

We stepped up and bought the stock from the Flicks against orders that we had, and so it was done very swiftly and without a lot of hoopla, since we bought it ourselves and syndicated the entire thing ourselves. "Syndicated" is not really the right word. We had buyers. All the usual suspects were invited outside of Germany, banks that we thought had investment clients. We invited the Belgian, Swiss and Dutch banks and the British merchant banks. It was a fairly quick maneuver with a certain amount of verve. It was a big deal. We sold something like [the deutsche mark equivalent of] $30 million of stock, which was a lot in those days.

The stock went to a premium immediately. People made a lot of money in it. The German banks were very irritated and raised a stink about the fact that it was sold outside of Germany. They were to get revenge about two years later when we did a similar enterprise for Schwab, another German mail-order house. The Germans told banks around the world that they should not participate, and we got stuck with a big wad of Schwab stock. We took a bath and should probably have quit while we were still ahead.

But anyway, the widespread placement of Neckermann, the anger of the German banks and the stock going to a premium instantly after we closed the deal caused a lot of publicity, and people could see that there was sort of a worldwide market out there. People said, "Jesus, Morgan made a ton of money on this, why don't we get in there?" I don't think that phenomenon is adequately understood—the impact it made on people's thinking, which ultimately led to the Eurobond market.

Our thinking was always to do equity; we were convinced that this was where the real juice in the business was. First of all, you made more money on the equity business. Second, there were more buyers out there, because it was a more institutional market.

The whole problem for years in the Eurobond markets was that the issues had to be small, because there were no traditional institutional bond buyers in the market. We decided that a good way to go after the market was through convertibles; that was an easy step. So we went to work on a deal for Takeda, a Japanese pharmaceutical company. But that deal encountered some accounting delays, and in the meantime Warburg brought the Autostrade issue. We went to work on that and sold some of the bonds, and we were quite anxious to see how it would go. We wanted to participate in that sort of business, but we were also doing it to see how realistic it was to sell bonds.

Somewhere along the line that summer, about the time of that deal, we were called by the city of Copenhagen and asked if we could do a Swiss franc bond deal for them. That was September of 1963, and I think it was the first and last Swiss franc issue done outside of Switzerland. The Swiss banks went bananas. They called up Henry Alexander, the chairman of Morgan Guaranty, and said: "You can't do this. Swiss francs are *not* an international currency. They should be controlled by the Swiss, and franc bond issues should be controlled by the Swiss banks." They threatened and pleaded and pushed and shoved, and people were afraid of what might happen, with all the power the Swiss banks had together. So while the deal was a big success and we got money at a cheap rate for Copenhagen, nobody ever did another Swiss franc issue in the Eurobond market.

In the meantime, toward the middle of '63, the interest equalization tax closed down the U.S. capital markets and brought American borrowers into the Eurobond market. So the bond business went ahead and took everybody's energies at the same time that we found it difficult to line up issuers to do equities on a worldwide basis. The equity market was active in the U.S., and there was a withholding tax on dividends, so there were a lot of obstacles to getting U.S. issuers; and potential issuers from other countries were usually inclined to do equity in their own markets. So the equity market, such as it was, developed largely through convertibles. After our deal for the Japanese pharmaceutical company, there were a lot of big ones. Texaco did one early on for $400 million. I remember that was a shattering amount at the time.

In about 1966 or '67 the Eurobond market just closed. Interest rates were starting to go up, and it dawned on people that to buy a long-term bond or a fifteen-year bond was dubious. So we tried to develop another piece of paper. It was clear that individuals wanted shorter-term paper, but we had to make it long enough to get a satisfactory commission out of it. So we settled on five years as a piece of paper that would be liquid enough so that individuals would buy it and long enough to support a spread that would get the banks to go to work selling it. I went back to Morgan Guaranty in New York and discussed the concept, and they all laughed. People today don't remember this, but back then buyers either wanted Treasury bills or long-term bonds; there was nothing between one and ten years.

Oh god, I worked like a dog to find an issuer, and finally Continental Oil came along to do a five-year note deal. The idea took off and there were hundreds of millions of dollars of this stuff sold, and it attracted people to the idea of buying internationally syndicated fixed-rate bonds. It seems to me in looking back through the history of these things, this is the one area that is not adequately understood. Five-year notes sort of saved a sick child; the market had grown up a little bit, but it wasn't there and it was fading. Five-year notes revived it. In fact, I think that was probably the biggest contribution I ever made personally to getting the bond market going, in many ways more important than floating-rate notes.

In November of 1968 I moved back to New York from Paris to do the most complicated thing I ever did in my life. In early '68 Morgan Guaranty had announced that they were going to start Euroclear, a clearance system for Eurobonds. They had announced this thing with great fanfare and set it up in Brussels, but nobody there really had a clue of what to do, and the thing was terrible, snarled mess. So I and John McDaniels, a lawyer from Davis Polk—who is now an investment banker with Kidder Peabody—went to work to try to create Euroclear, after it had been theoretically created and announced. There were legal problems that were unbelievably difficult because of the cross-border nature of these transactions, and there were trading practice and competition problems. People were reluctant to come into this thing and give Morgan the advantages they thought might accrue to them as a result.

340

There was the feeling Morgan would know too much about what they were buying and selling. And we had to transfer real trading practices into a mechanism that would accept these practices. A guy sitting at a desk buys something and sells it in two minutes. In a matter of an hour, ownership of that paper can move ten, fifteen times, and to have it chased through all those ownerships before it clears is very difficult. I set out to go up there for a couple of weeks and help them get it going. It took a year. I didn't know anything about the use of computers, which were all quite crude in those days. You had these big machines up there with punch cards flapping through, and the cards would fall all over the floor. It was like a Keystone Kops movie.

Both McDaniels and I were all over the world trying to get people to participate in this thing. It was a big sales job. The traders all wanted something; they knew the system was breaking down. But it was sort of a Catch-22: They wouldn't come in unless they knew that it was going to work—but it wasn't going to work unless they came in! So we had to create a lot of chickens before there were even any eggs to give rise to them. It was a landmark thing; only after that clearing system was up could people actually trade in bonds in any numbers or in any size.

In September of 1969 I went to Bankers Trust International in London, and soon after I got there the bond market broke down again. Interest rates were starting to rise rapidly and the markets were in very difficult shape. I was trying to figure out how to get the major holders of money—the banks—into the Eurobond market.

Through the syndicated loan—we'd done one way back in '64 for British Petroleum—the banks had shown their willingness to lend a great deal of money, but on a floating-rate basis. So I reached the obvious conclusion: Let's take their willingness to lend on a floating-rate basis, and instead of doing a loan, let's securitize the loan into bearer paper. And it will be much more interesting to the banks to buy negotiable paper than to sit down and write a loan that they're stuck with. One reason the idea came to me was that I was involved in the early days of the syndicated loan, first with Morgan Guaranty and later with

341

Bankers Trust, so I knew that market, and very few of the bond guys did.

The story that the idea came to me in the bathtub was a theatrical wisecrack. When somebody asked me where I'd thought of it, I made an analogy to Napoleon, who would sit in a bathtub and plan his battles. He carried around this great big copper bathtub and had his minions pour hot water into it so he could lie there in the tub and think about how he was going to destroy the enemy the next day. So some reporter picked that up and said I'd thought about the floating-rate note in the bathtub; I think the Napoleonic thing got dropped somewhere along the way.

From February of 1970 we started trying to sell the idea, and we couldn't get anybody to do it. We went to sovereign risks, trying to get good credits that the banks would buy. The Italians were borrowing quite a bit in those days on a floating-rate bank credit, so we tried a couple of Italians, and it didn't work. I knew, however, that Siegmund [Warburg] knew Guido Carli, the governor of the Bank of Italy, quite well, and I thought: "Well, I bet we'd do better if Warburg goes there. So I think I'll take the idea to Warburg."

By this time I was a little desperate—we'd been working for three months to get a borrower and we couldn't find one—or I ordinarily wouldn't have done that. But Siegmund had enough sense to see that it was the right instrument at the right time, and he sold the deal to Carli, who called up ENEL, the Italian electrical monopoly, and told them to do it. It was set up as a bond issue for $125 million, which was enormous—there'd been no straight debt issue anything near that. So in that sense, Siegmund was one of the creators of it. He sold a customer on a piece of paper that we at BTI had laid out for him. But Siegmund took the view that BTI, which had just been formed about six months earlier, was not of the character that should be in the international markets, and he tried like mad to shove us out of the leadership of the issue.

Siegmund and I eventually became very good friends—I saw him until the time he died—but he certainly demonstrated how he was the aggressive developer of Warburg & Co. He had started out as sort of an outsider in England and bucked the

342

establishment, and finally made it. So you always had this sense of him wanting to enhance the position of his bank. It was so strong that he would overcome certain scruples about who was to get credit for what. And this was the case in the floating-rate note issue. He saw this was going to be a big thing, and he wanted to be regarded as the innovator. He was very aggressive about it, very smooth, very courtly and always very diplomatic. I never had any heated words with him. He would usually get somebody else to do it.

I remember David Scholey [now chairman of Mercury International Group] was given the mission of trying to talk me out of running the books on the issue, and I said, "There's no way that this is going to happen." They had a good argument, in that they had gotten the buyer, the customer. But it was our product, so there was something to argue about. We had some heated negotiations, and the Warburg people finally came in and said: "Well, we'll do it without you. We've got the issuer." And I quietly said: "Well, I'll denounce you in the press. I'll hold a press conference and tell them exactly what you did." They said, "You couldn't do that—it would ruin your career," and I replied, "I'll ruin yours!" I mean, it escalated. I also threatened to go down and talk to the issuer. We had a bird in the hand and I didn't think we were going to lose the argument. We had documents to show when we created this and a record to show we'd brought it to them, and there was no question that we would have been able to make them look bad. Ultimately, it was diplomatically settled. We worked out an elaborate compromise that only investment bankers would come up with. We indeed ran the books—the telexes came in and out of our offices—but Warburg appeared first on the prospectus and in advertising outside the United States, and we appeared first on advertising inside the United States.

Siegmund and I had both decided to bring White Weld into the operation, because they had a trading function that neither of us had. So Bob Genillard, who was a big wheel in the bond market, got himself involved, and so did Stani Yassukovich. It started out as a tough sell, because people didn't understand. But once they got the idea of what we were doing, we started getting some big orders, like $5 million and $6 million at a crack. And then Barclays came in for *$10 million,* and we suddenly figured, "We're right! The banks will buy this stuff!" So we went to work right away and went back to the United States and got Pepsico to do one. It followed within a matter of weeks. And Warburg got General Cable and we did Argentina, and those were the ones we banged off in the beginning. But it wasn't until the banks started issuing floating-rate notes that the market really exploded.

Editor: Nancy Belliveau

Michael Sandberg

Former Chairman HONGKONG AND SHANGHAI
BANKING CORP.

By virtue of his position, the chairman of Hongkong and Shanghai
Banking Corp. must be part commercial banker, part central
banker and part local politician. As the consummate colonial
banker, Sir Michael Sandberg excelled at all three functions. During his decade as chairman, he presided over unprecedented
growth, both domestically and internationally, for the Hongkong
Bank and also succeeded in steering it through a major financial
scandal relatively unscathed. But his most enduring legacy may be
that he helped negotiate the eventual return of Hongkong to
China on terms acceptable to his entrepreneurially minded coun-
trymen.

Hongkong is rather different from, say, Singapore, where
they make a cabinet decision and say, "Well, I think next
Monday we'll have a financial center." It may work if you
say, "Next week we're going to start making teacups." But it
doesn't really work that way with a financial center.

So Hongkong grew rather naturally. Sir Phillip Haddon Cave,
the financial secretary [from 1971 to 1981], had a very agile and
active mind and could see the benefits that a service industry like
finance could bring to Hongkong. And it has put Hongkong on
the map.

Of course, during the development period, there were no new
banks coming in; there had been some banking crises in the
mid-'60s. So the Hongkong Bank—certainly I, myself—was very
keen to see barriers to foreign banks removed, because although

one doesn't invite competition, in fact, it's good for you. You need somebody sticking pins in your backside, whether it's your boss or competitors or shareholders. If we hadn't had competition, we would be fatter, very much more complacent.

The Hongkong Bank was viewed as *anticompetitive*. But that was because we just happened to be damn successful, and people refused to give credit where credit was due. They'd say, "Oh well, of course, you got this way because you've got a monopoly." Nothing could be further from the truth! There are something like 250 international banks, in one guise or another, in Hongkong. So, to the people who have talked about the Hongkong Bank's monopoly, I'm afraid my answer is: "I'll lend you a handkerchief. But get off your backside. You can do the same thing yourself, if you've got the energy to do it."

Some people, of course, have criticized Hongkong for being too laissez-faire in its development policies. Of course, regulations are never absolutely right. There's always some clever sod who's about to find a way to either legally or perhaps illegally go through them. It's what corporations hire lawyers for, sadly. Perhaps there should have been some stronger banking regulations. But much more important than the structure of the regulations were the regulators—I'm talking about the people who were not really regulating as they should have done. It's generally the policemen—whether the commissioner of the SEC or the commissioner of banking or, indeed, the chief superintendent at Precinct 234—who are not monitoring the laws as well as they should who are at fault. But about two years ago—or was it three?—there was a fair switch-around in personnel in the banking commissioner's office, and things are much tighter.

I'm sure stricter regulations might have made the Hongkong property boom and bust less traumatic. But I'm not sure that doesn't come down in the end to a question of a fool and his money being easily parted. People are greedy. You know, Hongkong is a fairly frenetic place, and property booms and busts are, I'm afraid, slightly endemic to our part of the world.

I suppose, on reflection, we shouldn't have done banking with Carrian [the Hongkong property and financial group whose 1983 collapse was a major Asian financial scandal]. But [Carrian chair-

346

man George Tan Soon Gin] is not the only person I guess we wouldn't have banked if we'd been clever enough to see the future. Of course, there are also people whom we wished we had banked for, whom we must have turned down. But that was always so and will ever be so.

Some aspects of banking you have more control over. When I took over the Hongkong Bank in 1977, I thought we needed to break out of our regional role—not that I had any lack of confidence in the role we had. But we'd really just become a little too big. There was no way we were going to be able to increase our market share. Banks were coming into Hongkong and other parts of the region, and while the pond was going to get a bit bigger, since we were the biggest fish in the pond, we weren't going to get bigger in proportion to the pond. Anyhow, I felt we needed badly to have a proper presence in America and in Europe.

I think we did pretty well with acquiring Marine Midland.

Of course, acquiring the bank was no easy chore. The comptroller of the currency seemed absolutely happy with the deal. So did the Fed; so did the SEC, to which we had to submit our proxy statements. But the [then] New York State Superintendent of Banking [Muriel Siebert] objected. I really don't know why. I've asked myself that question and been asked it so many times. God knows, we explained ourselves and undressed enough.

I mean, there was a suggestion that people thought that somehow there was something immoral about our being able to get a bank at what was a discount from book, where others were paying X times book. But you know, special circumstances [Marine Midland was having financial difficulties] warranted that.

But we knew what our objective was, and I had a pretty good chemistry with [former Marine Midland chairman] Ed Duffy. We owe credit to him for keeping his word and his side of the bargain. And he didn't weaken.

Basically, in the end it was [former New York governor] Hugh Carey who made the decision. I didn't know Hugh in those days, and I went and saw him. I suppose I was getting a bit impatient and frustrated, and I rather tended to thump the desk a bit and say: "For God's sake, do you want us? Or do you not want us? We've been hanging on the end of a screen for months now. Say something, even if it's only goodbye. But for God's sake, let us know, because we've got better fish to fry."

So then he took an interest—vetoed a bill [to block the acquisition] which was going through Albany, and that gave Marine Midland a window to apply for national bank status. Then once that was done, things moved pretty quickly. That cut the Gordian knot, because we were starting afresh with a set of controllers who had not put themselves in a corner. So any mistakes we made vis-à-vis the New York superintendent's office—and I'm sure we made some—were put aside and we started afresh. I think one got frightfully impatient and frustrated, but I didn't think it was up to us to pull the plug on the deal.

In Europe, meanwhile, we failed in our commercial bank hunt. But I think in hindsight everybody lost in the Hongkong Bank's [unsuccessful] bid for Royal Bank of Scotland. We lost, obviously. The competition—Standard Chartered—lost. Royal Bank of Scotland's shareholders certainly lost. Royal Bank of Scotland itself lost, I think, because with us they would have been part of a bigger group and yet autonomous. I suppose the Bank of England also lost because they had backed one party [Standard Chartered], and that party didn't succeed. So, really, in the end everybody lost.

But my wife cheered me up—she's always been a great shoulder on which to cry. She said, "You win a few and you lose a few."

It's absolutely untrue, by the way, that [then Bank of England governor] Gordon Richardson had a personal score to settle with me. But I think what did happen is that he felt he had put this deal together, been very much the marriage broker, the midwife—call it what you like—of Standard Chartered and Royal Bank. And as governor of the Bank of England—well, *the marriage that the Lord has put together, let no man set asunder.* So, yes, we weren't popular.

But I've known him for many years. He'd been extremely helpful to us when we took the headquarters of the British Bank of the Middle East from London to Hongkong. Gordon saw our side of things perfectly well and was extremely helpful. And I now sit with him on an organization called the Malaysian-British something-or-other, and we're perfectly friendly. It isn't as if we pass each other on opposite sides of the street. I mean, I know him as Gord, and he knows me as Mike, and if I was here in New York and he was too, we'd have a drink together.

But he had his point of view, I had mine. I paid him a few visits and got beaten up a few times, but I guess that's what I got paid for. Oh, it got pretty heated at the time. But, you know, you get that in the cut and thrust of business, and you expect it. When you get decisions, that's the testing time: Do people carry their vendettas on beyond the decision? I'd have to say he has not carried on any vendetta, and for my part, I certainly haven't. I see him frequently, and as far as I can see, we get on well together.

At the time of the Royal Bank battle, I took some soundings among my peer chairmen of British joint-stock banks in London. I saw two out of the four and asked, "You know, am I really making a bit of a fool of myself?" These were men whom I admire and who really did have their fingers on the public pulse, and they said: "No, go for your life. You press on. You think you're doing the right thing, you press on."

As the battle progressed, we got caught up in a propaganda war. You know, everyone in a battle always puts forth his own point of view, and our opponents accused us of not being a British bank. But in fact, the privy seal in the British government—don't ask me to explain what the privy seal's job is, though he's a member of the cabinet—got up in the House of Commons in answer to a question and said, with the full authority of government, "If anyone says the Hongkong Banking Corp. is not a British bank, they're incorrect," and sat down. So I mean, that was fairly cut and dry.

The real point of the propaganda, though, was not that we were not a British bank but that we were not *incorporated* in Britain— which is absolutely true—and therefore we were not subject to British banking laws. We were subject to our own masters and authority in Hongkong—in this case the financial secretary and the Banking Commission, etc.

Of course, our side of the propaganda was: "Well, obviously, if we come into Britain, those operations we have in Britain would be subject, just as our branch there is at the moment, to British regulation." You put your best face forward, and the opposition put theirs forward. And one understands that.

After the Royal Bank acquisition fell through, well, we looked at *everything* in Europe, okay? The problem was that in Britain—

unlike in America, where you've got 15,000 banks or something like that at last count—there are only about half a dozen banks one can really go for. And after the ruling we'd had from the Monopolies and Mergers Commission [blocking the Royal Bank takeover], it would obviously have been foolish to look at the time at another large bank in Britain.

Europe we also looked at. In fact, people brought us—and I have no doubt continue to bring us—banks in continental Europe that are available either for de facto or de jure control. But you know, if you've been left at the church door, as it were, one of the biggest problems on the rebound is not to marry somebody else in haste and repent in leisure. I was very determined not to do that.

Now, we didn't find anything which we felt really fitted in, as Royal Bank would have done. And so, although my successor may well, and I hope does, find a fit sometime or other with a commercial organization, we went the other way around when the opportunity presented itself of expanding into the capital markets instead. With the coming of Big Bang, we took control of [British stockbroker] James Capel.

That was a pretty big step for us, really. One could either stand back and say, "Well, we'll wait till the plums fall off the tree," as some banks did. Or one could go in and buy a broken company, as some other banks did. So I agonized about this for a bit, and I finally said, "You know, if we're going to go in, we either go for the top of the pops or we don't go in at all."

It was a good sort of marriage, because my philosophy has always been to let your subsidiaries get on with their job. Otherwise—if you dictate to them—they lose their cutting edge. And they know their markets better than we do. So that fitted in with James Capel, which wanted autonomy. Obviously, the strategy remains with the proprietor. And they've been an outstanding success. They continue to get higher and higher ratings in these analyst polls.

Then last December, just when I left, we acquired the Bank of British Columbia. You know, when you find a country like Canada, which is very stable and has laws and a language you understand, it's great to have an opportunity to expand. You can't always do so. Here was an outstanding opportunity to have, as it were, instant growth.

Japan is a rather different matter. We do make a profit in Japan, which is probably more than quite a number of foreign banks there do. But I don't think banking is any easier in Japan than selling Cadillacs or Californian orange juice. It's a damn difficult market. As it opens and liberalizes—as the Japanese keep on saying it's about to do—I think we've got a pretty good platform from which to expand.

But it's not a problem you can throw money at. If you go down to Wall Street and talk to American bankers, I don't think you'll find they've exactly got something to be excited about there. Yes, it's a disappointing thing to have this economic giant—and by God, it is a giant—and none of us really playing a part that makes even a dent in it. It's disappointing. Hopefully, it will change.

Change, of course, is coming for Hongkong. I served on the Executive Council, which consists of about half a dozen ex officio members of the government, like the financial secretary, and about nine or ten of us from the private sector. It's the cabinet of Hongkong, if you like, and advises the governor. We were absolutely in the know concerning the negotiations [to return the colony to China]. And it was a very—to use that overworked word—traumatic period, and an enormously busy one. In normal times we would meet every Tuesday morning, from 9:30 to about noon. But in those days we were meeting perhaps three, four times a week, and traveling to 10 Downing Street from time to time. We weren't directly negotiating, but we were directly in touch with the British government and the British negotiators, saying, "We agree with this, but we don't agree with that."

It was a long, long drawn-out affair. It took two years, but it felt more like twenty. But I think at the end of the day it was the best agreement one could hope for. If you look at it in absolutely the simplest terms, nothing changes in Hongkong except that the Chinese flag is flying on the flagpole instead of the Union Jack. Of course, it's not as simple as that. But because it's not, the broad outlines are very carefully specified in the agreement. In effect, it says that for 50 years after 1997—in other words, another 60 years to go—Hongkong's free-enterprise system with capitalism as its core—will remain in being. As a West German friend said, "I certainly can't guarantee that the Bonn government will still be capitalist in 60 years' time." I mean, the agreement is a blueprint for the enterprise system for 60 years—a guarantee. I don't think you get that anywhere else in the world.

Of course, there's already been a tremendous transfer of power within Hongkong to local Chinese, mainly because Chinese entrepreneurs have gone upward, and less so because one or two of the old hongs have gone downward. It didn't take too much divine wisdom for us to see that the local Chinese like power—such as Li Ka Shing [a Hongkong property developer and industrialist who's close to the Hongkong bank]—and that they were obviously going to increase very much in importance.

A very large proportion of our business is Chinese business—perhaps that's the secret of why we've done so well. They're easy people to deal with. Generalization is, of course, stupid, but in very broad terms, they're very honorable people to do business with. They happen to have grown terrifically in the last few years as they have got their acts together.

Of course, we've been criticized for seeming to turn our back on our old [non-Chinese] clients. I remember in one week being soundly criticized because we had helped the consummation of an old British company's takeover by a Chinese company, and in that same week, helping to engineer the takeover of a fairly long-established Chinese garment manufacturer by an American company.

So I was accused of selling the Brits down the river on the one hand, and the following morning, it was suggested I was selling Chinese industry down the river to foreigners. You can't win. I suppose you can only do what Liberace did and cry all the way to the bank.

We were probably slow, I suppose, in taking on local, top-flight Chinese people to become executives. We would hire our clerical staff locally, naturally, but our executive staff would come from overseas, and there would be this sort of great divide. I don't think we were particularly slower or more or less arrogant than anybody else. I think you'll find that ABC Bank and XYZ Bank were doing the same thing. I don't think there was any reluctance on our part to hire Chinese; racism, thank God, has never been our problem. It's just that the old system worked, and it's nice and cozy with a system that's worked.

But what eventually happened was that we got hoist on our own petard, because when we tried to recruit Chinese, they would say, "But there isn't a career path for us in the Hongkong Bank!" Of course, you've got to have the guys there first before you can promote them. So it was a rather chicken-and-egg situation.

When we built our new headquarters, I'll tell you what we wanted to do, apart from wanting it to be the best. We took the point of view that every building you build is obsolete by the time you finish building it; you know, technology is moving so fast. So we tried as far as we could—and of course we won't succeed 100 percent—to build a building that would be able to keep pace with technology.

It also happens to be fairly cheap to maintain and to administer. We think—I think—that the savings will come through over the years and that in maybe 40 years it will prove itself a rather cheap building. If that doesn't sound Irish.

Of course, it did cost more than it should have done. Somebody coined the phrase "world's most expensive building" to describe it. We had a horrifying overrun on the steel, but everything else was more or less within budget. But certainly it's the best bank building in the world. And it works—it works like a dream. And the staff love it. That's important. People travel by escalator, for instance, rather than by elevator, so that instead of waiting for five minutes for a lift and then being huddled in, you go up and down escalators and say, "Hi, morning. How are you?" Thus the open plan is good.

I personally took a tremendous interest in the plans. But I'm no architect or engineer. I got involved only as much as one sensibly can when one doesn't actually know very much about the properties of aluminum or glass or concrete or steel. For instance, there were supposed to be three escalators going up from the ground floor, which is dedicated to public use, to where the banking hall is. I thought two were enough. But these are details. Someone else might well have thought of that anyhow. The building, by the way, is no monument to me, as some critics have contended. Oh God, no, no, no. I'm afraid we're not a one-man bank.

During my tenure at the bank, I got a reputation that I personally think rather overemphasizes that somehow I was a great entrepreneur. I was really trying to lead the bank first and foremost, and a lot of that's very mundane. We happened to do two or three deals which caught the headlines for one reason or another—Marine Midland, Royal Bank, though that one didn't succeed. But I think, really, that you catch the reputation of an age in which you happen to live. We needed to get a new suit of clothes because we'd grown out of our own. But the old suit had been pretty successful and quite satisfactory for many years. Therefore, when you change a suit after many years, perhaps it gets rather more publicity than it warrants.

I'd been chairman myself ten years when I decided to go. Contrary to some speculation [that he was pushed out], we have a kind of organization, and within reason, obviously, you [as chairman] can choose your time to go and your successor. Of course, if I'd wanted to make my wife chairman, I expect there would have been some opposition.

Five years is too short to be chairman; you can't put your imprimatur on an organization. You can't really start things going and see them finished. If you stay twelve years, you're going to get out of touch, because a chairman is, whether he likes it or not, a bit isolated. And certainly you get more isolated as you go along. When you first become chairman you've got some contemporaries and colleagues who know you well enough to say, "Aren't you making a bit of a fool of yourself?" And you don't have to take any notice, but it gives you pause for thought. You know, if you've been there too long, people are inclined to salute and say, "Yes sir, no sir." I don't think that had happened with me, but I think if I had stayed another few years it might have done.

I must say, though, that before I left I felt rather like what I suppose a drug addict feels—that you want to get off the treadmill but you fear withdrawal symptoms. In fact, I've got off the treadmill and happily so, because my successor—Willie Purves—is a really first-class chap. As I said at a farewell speech, I've had a love affair with the bank for 40 years, and therefore I was very conscious of wanting to hand my love over to someone in whom I have confidence. And I've got 101 percent confidence in Willie. He's a really good guy and a personal friend. So that made leaving easier. To put it more bluntly, if I hadn't had someone as good as that, I *wouldn't* have left.

You know, the Hongkong Bank is a funny old institution. We come in and we make careers. We don't bring in outsiders. It'll be a sad day if we have to go outside to recruit chief executives. Basically, we grow our own wood. Perhaps we're a rather cliquey lot because of it.

I've no doubt in some ways we are [Colonel] Blimpish. I remember being told I was living in Victorian times because I rebuilt the bachelors' mess—dormitory-like quarters in which new male recruits live for their first couple of years at the bank. But I happen to believe that people who spend their early banking life living together and mucking in together look back later with rather larger paunches and say, "Yes, that was valuable."

Perhaps I'm not the right person to judge, but the esprit de corps at the Hongkong Bank is second to none of any corporation in the world. You know, there really is a great desire to pull on the rope in the same direction, whether you're fairly junior or fairly senior. Even though we've grown enormously, we've managed to keep that sort of family feeling. I myself would feel morally unable to take a job at another financial institution, even though there are no legal inhibitions to doing so, because my love affair with the Hongkong Bank carries on.

**Editors: Cary Reich
and Firth Calhoun**

John Heimann

Former UNITED STATES Comptroller of the Currency

> John Heimann has been in and out of government service often
> during his long career in the financial world. A pioneer in pension
> fund investing, he branched out into real estate finance early on
> and then served in a number of housing posts on both the federal
> and state levels. Heimann was New York State superintendent of
> banks in 1975 and 1976 and comptroller of the currency from
> 1977 to 1981. He is now vice chairman of Merrill Lynch Capital
> Markets.

When I was very young and working as a registered representative at Smith Barney, I came across a whole area that nobody was paying very much attention to called pension funds. It was a business waiting to be discovered. In those days most pension funds were being managed either by life insurance companies or by the trust departments of banks. And it seemed to me, as others probably realized, that this could be an extraordinary market for securities firms.

Even though the idea seemed to be a good one, there was a reluctance on the part of the investment bankers at that time to jeopardize relationships with corporate clients. I had a background in the trade union movement; when I was younger, I had acted as an organizer for the International Association of Machinists, and I had been brought up in and around the International Ladies' Garment Workers' Union. So I figured, if I can't do it with corporations, I'll start with the labor unions.

It took me two solid years of plugging away before I got my

first account, the American Federation of Television and Radio Artists, and then the floodgates opened up. The primary job was translation, and for somebody in Wall Street, you were basically living in a bifurcated world—living with stock and bond markets and simultaneously with the trade union leadership. They may not have been too well educated, but they were smart as hell.

I remember trying to explain what Smith Barney did to one union member, I forget which union it was. This guy was dressed in a double-breasted suit with a T-shirt underneath, and his stomach bulged out from under the T-shirt. Anyway, this guy swung around in his chair and said: "I understand, kid. You're different from Bash [Bache] & Co., right? They're for the two-dollar bettors and you're for the big-time guys." As I said, it was a matter of translation.

After a while, it did so well that the corporate banking types at Smith Barney looked around and said: "Holy cats! These people in the pension funds investment department [where I was by then] are doing a really good job." And then it got expanded to the corporate world.

By this time we had six or seven people managing pension money. And I remember that a 3½ percent General Electric bond came to market and you could not buy that bond, which was exactly, of course, the quality that pension funds would want. Almost that very day, a fellow came in and told me about something called the VA and FHA mortgage that I could own for pension funds, insured by the government—at 5¼ percent.

It took about two years of my life trying to figure out how to get this done. And finally the first mortgage-backed security—it was really a participation certificate—of a package of FHA mortgages was created by Smith Barney for pension funds. This was a great field, brand new, and nobody in the securities industry had thought much about it. That's what got me started in the whole field of housing- and mortgage-related activities.

I was fascinated by real estate and by the concept of venture capital. So when I returned to Wall Street after a leave of absence around 1965 to advise the secretary of Housing and Urban Development, I became one of the founders of what is now E.M.

Warburg Pincus. We were active in venture capital, real estate, financial consulting and investment counseling. I took a leave again in 1969, to serve in the transition period for George Romney [then secretary of HUD]; I was a Democrat in the Nixon administration. Then I was called back later for a period in which I worked directly in the creation of Ginnie Mae and the going private of Fannie Mae. I remained with E.M. Warburg Pincus, however, until I became superintendent of banks for New York State.

I was brought up to believe that you really owe something of your life to your own country. I know that sounds a little bit fancy, but I always had a hankering to do something that I felt proud of outside of having a nice family, wonderful children and doing your business well. This had the effect on me of deciding to tithe my time to my country.

In the mid-1970s I was a supporter of New York governor-to-be Hugh Carey. And after he got elected, he asked me to look at the New York Urban Development Corp. I had the unbelievable task of telling him it would be broke within five or six days. As some of the people around the Street remember, I went out and negotiated a short-term loan—$30 million for 30 days, led by Morgan—just to tide the UDC over until we could get at the problem.

The governor also asked me to find him a superintendent of banks, among other things. I went out and looked and couldn't find the kind of person that the governor wanted. Then one day he said, "Why don't you do it?" and I realized I ought to put my money where my mouth was.

I became superintendent of banks in 1975. It was not an overly turbulent period except for American Bank & Trust, which was front page forever. When I closed the bank down, the chairman sued me for $100 million. The governor called me up and said, "My only suggestion is that you transfer $98 million into your wife's name." Of course, the suit never got anywhere. Next the governor asked me to take over Housing and Community Renewal. And I was there for approximately six months; then I ended up in Washington as comptroller of the currency.

It's always difficult to tell just how these things come about. The best way I can reconstruct it is that Pat Harris, the secretary of Housing and Urban Development, asked me to become chairman of the Federal Home Loan Bank Board. Jimmy Carter had been elected president, but I had never met the president nor did I know him and his people. The reason I was selected, I suspect, is that I came from the financial world, had been involved with HUD before and was fairly well known for having done all of this mortgage-financing work.

Then Mike Blumenthal became secretary of the Treasury, and he asked me if I would like to become comptroller. I asked what about the HLBB, and he said not to worry about it. So I was nominated, went to the Senate hearing process and became comptroller in July.

In a way, I was in a better position than most people who go to Washington because I had already been in government for two years. And all the disclosure and that kind of stuff you have to do was fairly easy for me because Governor Carey had such strict disclosure forms for the state of New York. I didn't have the great trauma of saying, "Gosh, I've got to disclose everything," because I'd been through the process before.

I was confirmed by the Senate and signed the oath of office, as I recall, on July 12. Two days later I received a call from the Senate Operations Committee, Senators [Charles] Percy and [Abraham] Ribicoff, saying that Bert Lance was asking for certain exemptions from what he had agreed to regarding the sale of certain stocks. The papers were beginning to be flooded with stories about Lance and what he allegedly did and didn't do. And I was told that as comptroller, it was my job to find out if all of this was correct or not.

He was the president's best friend. I was with an agency where I did not know the people. And I had to conduct an inquiry that took the rest of the summer. We worked I don't know how many hours a day, including all the staff in the comptroller's office, trying to present a report that was complete and fair.

It was complicated, but what we did was relatively simple. There were a series of allegations. They were either true or not true. And I believe that the success of the inquiry was that it was totally objective. Number one, every allegation was studied, but they were presented in chronological order so there was never a matter of the worst thing coming first. Secondly, there wasn't a single adjective or adverb in the report. It was the dullest, driest reading anybody has ever seen. It was simply a recitation of the facts and then a conclusion drawn from those facts.

I must say, it was a heck of an introduction to Washington, D.C., with all the television cameras and the klieg lights. I would rather have been anywhere else in the world. Of course, Lance had a chance to answer all of it, and finally he resigned. Actually, I spent my first couple of months in Washington as an investigator and didn't become comptroller until the Lance thing was over.

This period of time was really the beginning of active deregulation of the commercial banking industry. There had been deregulation before, but these years were the ones in which a lot of the advances in thinking about the liberalization of the banking system were put in motion.

For the period of time I was there, we went through some economic crises. The big blow-off occurred in 1980 with price controls, the prime rate of almost 20 percent, the silver crisis, the near-failure of the First Pennsylvania Bank and the problems of other banks. First Pennsylvania was the big bank crisis. It was the 23rd-largest bank in the United States.

This was the first time we had the combination of the FDIC stepping in with the private sector to save a bank with the FDIC winding up with partial ownership—which then got repaid, in the case of First Pennsylvania, very successfully. The idea was that if the government bails an institution out, there ought to be a reward. The taxpayers ought to get something back. The shareholders, directors and management should all be punished, but there should be some return to the government for putting up all this money.

In the case of First Pennsylvania, management had bet the bank. They had put about a third of their portfolio in long-term U.S. government bonds at a rate of interest of 8 percent, or something like that, at a time when current rates of interest for short-term deposits were 11 percent. Every day they opened the door, they lost money. It wasn't a bet on assets. The quality of the assets was government bonds. It wasn't like they had lent money to a bunch of bums. But the management had done that before.

This was the second time they had bet the bank. Once might have been a mistake, but twice is inexcusable.

Banks usually get in trouble incrementally. They hardly ever get in trouble overnight, though that can happen, particularly in the case of smaller institutions. And the examiners had been concerned about the practices of First Pennsylvania for some time. But it wasn't until interest rates started to skyrocket that they were caught in this mismatch. All of this was an inheritance of the inflation caused by OPEC and then the policies of the central bank to halt that inflation through tight money.

This came to fruition, as it always does, on the backs of debtors. Debtors are the ones who pay the burden, and, of course, banks have as their primary assets the debts of others. So it always falls back into the banking system. Some banks manage it very well, are prepared for it and have not exposed themselves; so if a debtor gets into trouble, it's not terminal for the bank. Other banks concentrate their assets, which they are not supposed to do, and then if those debtors get into trouble, the bank has big troubles.

As comptroller of the currency, you're also deeply involved in international matters, with the banking supervisors and central banks of other nations. As superintendent of banks in New York, I had dealt with the foreign banking community, because New York was the primary location of foreign banking in the United States. The 1978 law changes then opened the national banking system to foreign banks.

I think a great number of what I would call obvious advances were made in opening up the financial system in this country and the world. During that time we approved the Hongkong and Shanghai Bank's purchase of Marine Midland. There was a question because that was a state-chartered bank and the then-superintendent of banks in New York wouldn't approve. There were all sorts of concerns that Red Chinese hordes were going to subsume upstate New York.

I thought that was wrong, since Hongkong and Shanghai was willing to abide by our laws. This is an open, free country. Our financial system is based upon open entry and freedom of operations as long as you meet the regulations and the requirements that an American bank does. So I approved it because they changed their charter to a national bank. This was especially interesting because I entered for the first time into an agreement

362

with the Hongkong authorities that we were able to go and examine the Hongkong and Shanghai Bank—learning what really
was inside it—to make sure it was a well-run institution. Which in
deed and in fact it is.

Leaving out the crises, I would say the biggest happening while
I was in Washington was the really constant drive toward deregulation of the banking system. I am strongly in favor of interstate
banking. I believe in much more competition. My theory is that
you have to have a dynamic system to convince people to come in
and let people go out if they cannot keep up and operate successfully, profitably and prudently.

I had been six years in government and felt frankly that it was
long enough. It's amazing the effect it has. It's like drawing down
your bank account. Not in the pure monetary sense, but government is unlike almost anything else. The demand it makes on a
person is extraordinarily high. I mean, you have a board of directors of 535 members of Congress. Each of them has exactly the
same vote, and they all feel they have an equal right to ask anything they want.

I stayed on until the middle of the first year of the Reagan
administration. I had made up my mind to leave and went to
Secretary of the Treasury Don Regan and said that since he had
so many jobs to fill, I'd stay around for five, six or seven months
until he got himself organized.

Anyway, I came back to Wall Street to join Warburg Paribas
Becker, which was a consortium firm. The firm was a wonderful
idea but the concept could not be carried out, simply because the
principals could not come to a true accommodation and understanding of what the firm was supposed to do. There were a lot of
problems and personalities, but if you cut away all of that nonsense, it's a clear indication that consortiums don't work unless
they are very small and all of the participants have exactly the
same goal. I waited until all the Becker people were placed, and
then I came to Merrill Lynch.

Finally, I should point out that one of the wonderful things
about the comptroller's job is that Congress in its wisdom back in
1863 [decided] that the comptroller is appointed for a term and is
therefore free of direct influence on the part of the executives

that appointed him. It's an interesting question. What would somebody whose job was dependent on the president have done with Bert Lance? I choose to believe that anyone in that job would have done exactly what I did. But by the same token, knowing that I was protected by law, that I couldn't be fired unless I did a lousy job, that's a little extra something that gives one the courage to do the right thing.

Editor: Peter Landau

Sanford Weill

Chairman COMMERCIAL CREDIT CO.

Sandy Weill and three partners started Carter Berlind Weill & Levitt in 1960. And when he left its successor, Shearson Lehman Brothers, 25 years later, the firm whose growth he had spearheaded had acquired more than twenty others—effectively more than 40 others, since most were the products of mergers of their own. In the process, Shearson became the second-largest New York Stock Exchange firm in capital and had itself been acquired by American Express. In late 1986 Weill took over as chairman and CEO of Commercial Credit Co., newly spun off from Control Data Corp.

Twenty years ago we made our first acquisition—the money management concern Bernstein-Macaulay. We felt it was important to have a recurring source of income, and not just income related to the exchange volume or the direction of the markets, but the kind of income you can earn at night and Saturday and Sunday. That acquisition started a thrust for our company into the area of money management. Today I would guess that Shearson is among the top three or four money managers, including banks.

But most of our acquisitions were within the brokerage business, because that gave us the outside reach to consumers, and through those consumers we were able to bring in additional accounts for money management. They all really fed off each other. Plus, in the brokerage industry you can make money on Saturdays and Sundays also, through margin accounts and, with enough accounts, by lending out securities. And you also needed enough business to be able to pay for back-office costs in bad times, always being able to just expand that back office, through overtime, without big fixed costs. We really didn't have layoffs. We ran lean in good times.

Many of the mergers that built Shearson doubled our size—or more. A major reason they went pretty smoothly, when some other people's didn't, was that we believed in the importance of operations and gave recognition to the back-office people. When we started out in the '60s, we cleared through Burnham. "Tubby" Burnham is one of my heroes. I worked at his firm before we started ours, and I watched the excitement and love of somebody building a company. But in the latter half of the '60s we were growing faster than they were, so they asked us to take our business out of their shop. So we hired Frank Zarb [now a partner at Lazard Frères], who was then No. 2 in the back office at Goodbody, to build our own operations. All of the key people that worked with me got to know the back office, which was where I had had my first job many years earlier. We had a meeting with our key operations people every week where they were encouraged to say, "That guy is full of baloney," or, "That's not what happened; this is." So the back office was a key part of the company.

In 1969 we set up our own system and ran it, practicing, for a whole year. We pulled the switch at the beginning of 1970, so that in the fall of 1970 we were able to make our first big acquisition—Hayden Stone—even though we were a little company with two offices and maybe 5,000 accounts acquiring what had been shrunk down to 28 offices and 50,000 accounts. Frank and the rest of us came up with a system to bring those accounts in, process substantial added volume and keep it under control. We couldn't afford to lose, and I guess that first one really taught us how to do it right and created a lot of enthusiasm and tremendous pride among our people. And their dedication made more of a difference than our systems did.

People worked really hard through that summer—nights, weekends—and I would be down there with them. All of our deals were done through the summer. We killed everybody's vacation every single year, but then, once the deals were done, we'd go away on a trip together.

Most of the companies that we bought in the early '70s were not doing poorly in the business; they were just not capitalized properly. Much of Hayden Stone's capital was in short-term subordinated loans from retired or retiring partners, and not in cash but in securities from their portfolios. So when you hit a bad market, the stocks would go down at precisely the time the firm needed capital. The stocks had haircuts for capital-stating purposes, but they were never enough. Many were little companies; one of them was National Student Marketing, which went down to *zero* in a couple of weeks from whatever number it was at. These old partnerships really didn't have permanent capital: When a partner retired, that money went out. Not many young people came into this industry from the 1929 crash until after the Korean War, so firms didn't have enough money to replace what left. So the capital structures were really crazy; they created capital with mirrors, not with cash.

Because we were looking to grow our capital through retained earnings, we incorporated CBWL in 1965. We were one of the first brokerage firms to do so. We also raised capital in a private placement of convertible debentures in 1969. And a lot of our suppliers, like ADP and our landlord, invested in us. So we only had to raise another $2 to $2.5 million out of the $5 to $6 million it took to buy Hayden Stone.

Obviously, the markets are much bigger today, but $5 to $6 million was a lot of money then. It was more money than Goodbody could come up with, so they were sold to Merrill Lynch. The New York Stock Exchange trustee funds stood behind that merger, and I think they charged the industry something like $20 million for the problems in integrating those two companies' back offices. And certainly, Merrill should have been a heck of a lot better prepared to take over Goodbody than we were to take over Hayden Stone—nobody had heard of us—but we didn't cost the stock exchange or the industry anything.

We had already had a little experience with what it would be like to deal with a branch that was far from the home office, in that the year before we had bought an office in Beverly Hills from McDonald & Co., which was going out of business. We made a ton of mistakes with that one branch that we wouldn't repeat with 30. We'd left them too much on their own as to how they ran their business. We learned about the need for controls, for audit, for discipline, for communicating your philosophy as well as your

367

research and other products and yet how to still keep people motivated. It was a difficult thing to manage, but it was a good excuse to go to the Beverly Hills Hotel once in a while.

CBWL, or "Corned Beef With Lettuce," as we were sometimes called, at the time we took over Hayden Stone, an old WASPy firm, obviously wasn't their company of first choice. Their alternative was to merge with Walston, and that deal was going to be done in the same old stupid way, whereby Walston was going to pledge its employees' pension fund as capital. And that sort of thing is why all these companies got into trouble in the first place. We really made our pitch not so much to the Hayden Stone people as to some lenders from Oklahoma who had put their securities into a proud old investment banking firm and in a few months found out that they were in a bottomless pit and might even lose all their money. And I think they felt that they had a better chance of getting some of their money back with us than with Walston.

The merger worked out fine, from a human standpoint. For instance, someone who is in top Shearson management today, Wick Simmons, was the grandson of one of the founders of Hayden Stone and one of the top people in HS at the time of the merger, even though he was very young. We sent him on a backwards journey to become a branch manager in Boston, and he worked all the way back to running the whole retail operation at Shearson. Hayden Stone president George Murray is still with Shearson, and that's a lot of years later. Top Shearson management today includes people who came also from Hentz, Shearson, Lehman—many of the companies with which we merged.

In the first quarter of 1971, Merrill Lynch filed to do a public offering, and we filed two weeks later. We could do that because, since 1965, we had kept all of our numbers in a form where we could file. We thought that going public might be a possibility, and we wanted to cut off each accounting year at the same time rather than the way the industry used to do it—based on whenever the stock exchange did its surprise audit. We did what we had to do for the stock exchange, but also did what we felt we had to do to run our business.

So we could react fast when Merrill filed. But it took six months to get through the SEC, and part of the process was a taxi ride with [then–SEC chairman] Bill Casey, who was going to make a speech out on Long Island. We rode out with him, explaining that if they let Merrill go public, we should have the same rights. After we dropped him off, we came back in the same cab, and I asked the driver, "How do you think we did?" And he said, "You guys are some salesmen."

The next day the commissioners met and approved our offering. We were cleared by 4:00 p.m. on Friday, October 1, 1971. So we stayed working till about midnight, selling the stock. We thought, "So what if it's Friday afternoon?"—which was unheard of then.

We went public at 12½, and our stock rallied to 12⅝. Three years later it was 1⅜. That was the bear market of '73–'74. It was tough times, but we never really did that badly. I think in 1973 we lost about $1.1 million, but it was basically just depreciation; in cash, we made money.

That year Hentz was going under. All of their money was a short-term subordinated loan from one person that was due in six months. They were selling the company to Equity Funding, and one day before the deal was going to close, the Equity Funding scandal was exposed and Hentz was out of money. That purchase gave us entrée into the commodities business and Europe.

Then in 1974 Shearson Hammill thought it had a deal with Carl Lindner, but his stock reacted unfavorably when it was learned that he might go into the brokerage business. Again, as with Hayden Stone, there were a lot of good people in a good business, but with terrible capitalization. We'd just gotten excess SIPC [Securities Investor Protection Corp.] insurance from Aetna, which at that point was really deciding who the survivors in the industry would be. So we bought it. We doubled our business with Hentz and then doubled it again with Shearson. We could do it because we had people who were dedicated to making it happen and making it all work.

There were really two difficult parts to it. One was the back office, which I talked about already. The other problem in each merger was the sales force. A lot of the people at Hentz or Shearson or whatever had had a dream that was sold down the river. So when we made an acquisition, our competitors would come up with all kinds of statements to try to lure away our incoming salespeople—you know: "This is not going to work," and "Your accounts will be all screwed up," and "They're really lousy people" and so on. So we really had to sell ourselves and show how we were going to build a great company and that it was going to be very good for them. But a lot of the good ones were offered the best opportunities elsewhere and left. However, we would always catch them again. They'd leave Hayden Stone, say, and go to Shearson Hammill, or they might have left Hentz to go to Hornblower. By the time we acquired Loeb Rhoades, we did very well, because it was the third time that we had captured some of those people, and they surrendered.

We would give stock options to those who stayed, or the chance to buy our stock at a discount. Those who did stay wound up making a heck of a lot of money. The low was 1⅜ in 1974. When I left American Express, it was at about 240. And you can add a third since then.

In 1975 we had a summer off, and then in 1976 we acquired Lamson Brothers, a 100-year-old midwestern, twenty-office firm that was really well regarded in their small communities. We paid top dollar for it, but it got us into places that we probably never could have gotten into on our own. And we felt that by eliminating the back office, and with the cash flow we could generate from their quite-large commodities and stock loan business, it wouldn't end up being a high price. And that turned out to be true. Then in 1977, thinking that institutional rates had hit bottom, we acquired Faulkner, Dawkins & Sullivan. But a lot of their people had gone there to be with an institutional boutique and to get away from those big, faceless, boring, dumb firms, so a large percentage of them bolted over the next year. One of the mistakes that we made was in dropping the Faulkner identity. People in the securities business are pretty funny ducks; we might have been able to keep the thing together had we kept the name. It was a lesson we learned, so that when we bought Robinson-Humphrey in 1981 we kept their identity. And I think they still sell themselves as a regional firm that has all the advantages of a big parent but still can relate to the local areas.

When Ross Perot took over DuPont and applied a concept a little like the Marines to the sales force, it didn't work. He lost a lot of money. They couldn't even sell the firm; they had to liquidate it branch by branch. It showed how hard it was for someone outside the industry to come in, and that cooled a lot of people on the business. So then came the realization that the industry had to rely on itself to raise money.

And soon Bob Baldwin was chairman of the SIA, and he was making all those speeches about how the industry had to raise a lot of money. So I went to see him, and I said, "Well, we would like to raise some long-term debt, and we would like your company to be one of the underwriters." Morgan Stanley was a pretty snooty place in those years, but they came into the deal, which I think gave it a lot of credibility and helped it to happen. It was one of the beginning signs of the industry's recognition that, while we compete with each other, we'd better all help the capital-raising process along rather than go by all the old club rules. That was in the middle '70s, and I think that was an important event.

In 1977 we diversified further to get more recurring income by buying a mortgage banking company, Western Pacific. To date, that hasn't worked out too well because we had operational problems. On the other hand, we paid $15 million and it's probably worth a hundred.

Then came Kuhn Loeb. Frank Zarb, who was by then running investment banking at Shearson, felt that we had to do something like what we did in retail to *really* get into the banking business, and Kuhn Loeb had the kind of name that really could help. It gave us such a thrust into something we thought could be very important that I told Harvey Krueger we would be co-CEOs, which I wouldn't have said to many people.

But there were a couple of partners at KL who didn't like the idea, and one of them leaked the story to the *New York Post* and then used the story as proof that his customers were calling and saying that they would take their accounts away. This scared some of the other partners. And at about that point Pete Peterson made a run at KL, and the partners voted that way rather than our way. I think this was the first deal that we'd gone public with and then not closed.

But like all things in life, it turned out to be a blessing. Because had we bought KL, we would not have been in a position to say yes a year later when Tommy Kempner called to ask if we'd be

371

interested in Loeb Rhoades Hornblower. But as it was, since we were not strong in investment banking, it was very easy to let the senior people from LR be the top people in banking and important people in the company.

When we took over Loeb Rhoades, its merger with Hornblower was in name only. Whatever city you went to, there were the Hornblower people and then there were the Loeb Rhoades people, and they didn't talk to each other. As a matter of fact, in one Los Angeles office they had two managers—one from each firm. We absolutely didn't let that continue. Our philosophy has always been that you've got to make a choice as to who's running what, and make it fast. If you don't, you'll find out after the fact what your choice should have been, because the good person will leave.

By 1980 internationalization and securitization were beginning to make it clear that companies had to have access to a lot of capital and that technology was really going to be key. So I was wondering, How do you get both? And I was not averse to doing something with another company where personally I might have an opportunity to try something different. I had been running Shearson for eight or nine years, and we had the best numbers in the industry. When one looked for where the potential interest in our industry might come from, the German banks didn't interest me. The Japanese were pretty complicated. I felt we would have a hard time relating to the insurance industry in those years. A conglomerate would divert what we might be doing. With a retailer like Sears, it's a whole other thing. And it's in Chicago.

And then you had American Express sitting across the street, with a small corporate staff and an unbelievable reputation for quality and great technology. And they had gone into the brokerage industry before, but with the wrong vehicle: Donaldson, which they spun off to their shareholders so as not to take the loss. Would they be willing to do it again? We had approached them in 1977 about selling them 25 percent of the company to raise additional capital, but that was too close to the Donaldson thing for them to be interested. Sandy Lewis was very friendly with Robinson and he approached me, and I said: "Geez, I don't see how that's possible. I don't think that Jim is ready to retire, and if he's not, I don't see how we can do anything. But I'll meet with him."

And we met and we talked about the future, and we decided to see if together we could create a product competitive with Merrill's Cash Management Account, using the American Express card. We courted each other a little.

I was out in the Far East on a trip with President Ford when I read about Prudential taking over Bache. And I thought, "When I come back, I'm going to be very busy, because this is the kind of thing that's going to give the impetus to our conversations, because it's going to be something that can be more readily understood by the board of American Express." We met when I came back at the end of February, and we worked out a deal Easter weekend. We did the financial part of it in two minutes. Who did what to whom personally took a lot more time.

As for Lehman, it first came to our attention in 1983. But they had big ideas of what they were worth, and we turned it down. Most of this has been in the paper, and most of what's been in the paper is true. And there's been an entire book on it. I'm glad I wasn't in that book, except briefly.

I wasn't even No. 2 going into Amex. I was No. 3 [after president Al Way]. The biggest lesson of these twenty years is that I'm happier running my own show. This doesn't mean I shouldn't have gone to American Express; the experience was valuable. For one thing, I learned that my skills are transferable. But I forgot how much I enjoy being the top person. I also believe that eventually you have to move on and leave room, leaving a good team behind. So I left Amex.

One of my later assignments at American Express was to try to make Fireman's Fund profitable, and so I've taken an interest, of course, in the stories about the sale by American Express of the stock and the alleged manipulation. It certainly had nothing to do with Fireman's Fund, because the fund wasn't selling any stock, and they couldn't care less what the price was. Basically the players were American Express, selling the stock, and the public, buying the stock, and allegedly Sandy Lewis, asking somebody to mark the price up. It would surprise me if anybody from American Express had directed him to do that. But I have no idea what happened. And I don't want anybody to tell me.

It was not unnerving being on the beach for a while; on the contrary, it was rewarding. I found out that I had relationships with people because of *me*. Relationships improved; maybe I was less intimidating. When I started fundraising for Carnegie Hall, I wondered if people would see me. I got in to everybody. I wasn't asking anyone for less than $100,000, and I couldn't pay them back. We raised about $54 million; when I went in to take on the fundraising, we had about $16 million.

During that year's sabbatical, Bank of America appeared to be the largest troubled financial thing around. It was a shame what was happening to a great old institution. I tried to develop a plan that might have been useful in giving it some direction. I called some of the directors; I spoke with all the regulators. I never had any intention of doing anything on an unfriendly basis. And when they weren't interested, so be it.

Besides, Baltimore is much closer than San Francisco Bay. And BofA would have been fix-fix-fix, problem-problem-problem, whereas here at Commercial Credit it's been a little fix, and if there are any insurmountable problems, we haven't found them yet.

We're able to start building something where you have $1 billion of net worth, or just shy of that, with no goodwill on the balance sheet. That's a pretty big, solid institution. Shearson has a book value of $1.3 billion. What are we planning to do? Well, I am not planning to go into the brokerage business in the immediate future. Prices are too high, and you don't know what legislation will arise. Besides, we still have a lot to do in getting our own business to work better.

Here's an opportunity to see if we can bring people together in a big company who will not get involved in intramural fights but will realize that our competition is external. I have always tried to build a family kind of environment. Part of my philosophy as CEO is to be responsive to the people—not just about what's happening in the company but about any other problems they have. Anybody could call me; we had an open-door policy. I just got a box of cigars from a guy last week who said, "I'm sure you remember back in 1979 that, when you hired me from XYZ to work in the Coral Gables office and I called you about this big customer problem, you took time out from some big merger you were working on to help me to resolve that problem. And I just want you to know that I own some stock in your new company. And there's this Cuban guy here who has these cigars, and I hope that you enjoy them." And, you know, that's eight years later.

When we had our public offering for Commercial Credit and were looking to raise $850 million, we arranged to have meetings with Shearson brokers all around the country, and it was like a tremendous homecoming. It's not that they *were* our friends; they *are* friends, to me and my wife. It's really a good feeling. You know, whenever I go to these towns, they say, "Hi, boss." Well, I'm not their boss, but it's fantastic. And just now Shearson has in street name 15,961 shareholders in Commercial Credit.

In my career, the things of which I'm proudest are the family environment at Shearson and that a lot of people are owners. And raising the money for Carnegie Hall.

Editor: Heidi S. Fiske

Babette Guthrie

Vice President PANDICK, INC.

Babette Guthrie, who started out her working life as a biochemist, joined Pandick, one of Wall Street's leading financial printing firms, twelve years ago. Since then, she has, as she puts it, "held the hands" of hundreds of lawyers and investment bankers, as they perform one of the Street's most grueling rituals: the all-night marathon at the printer's, grinding out the documents for a deal. Here she gives an inside glimpse of what it's been like—and how it has changed.

I remember one of the very first jobs I worked on—the first time I ever stayed overnight. I'd never done this before, and I couldn't believe I was doing it then. I remember running backward and forward and getting the proofs ready and doing all of this. Suddenly, it was 7:00 in the morning and they still had another whole day. They didn't think they'd be finished until the end of the day, and, of course, they didn't realize that in the beginning. So I remember that I had to send out for socks and shirts and other things. I couldn't believe it.

The business used to be a lot more polished, a lot more classy than it is now. Our clients are much more interested in the service now than in the limos, the theater tickets. It was fun in the old days. I had a good time when I took them to the best restaurants, and we had limos and went to Studio 54.

It's a different group of people; it's a different business world now, too. Everything is rush, rush, rush; do it now. There are different documents now than there were then, but everything was done much more slowly.

377

Your people come in now and they do the work the night of the filing, whereas before they used to have ten days and then go and file. Nothing was in such a hurry. Now everything's got to be done quick as a bunny.

The younger crowd is much more ambitious, much more into the work than going out to dinner and having a good time. You still have a few old people who still do that, but rarely. And that makes it hard for some of the older salesmen, who are used to dealing with this kind of slower method of doing things—dinners, lunches. There are two things that are important in financial printing: service and the bill. If the service is good, if the pages come back quickly, if the job looks nice and if the bill is satisfactory, that's really all there is to it. And I don't blame them. You take your car in to get it fixed and you don't care how they do it, just as long as they get it fixed and it's not an enormous amount of money. It's the same thing with financial printing.

Another reason for the changes in the attitudes is changes in technology. Things are going much faster than they used to with the hot type. I mean, it used to be you waited three-and-a-half, four hours, and so you'd troop out to a four-hour dinner and come back drunk and look at the file package and go home. But now the file package is done in an hour and a half, and God forbid they're not done in an hour and a half. Woe is me. They'll ask, "How come we have to wait so long?" I say, "Hey, you used to wait three hours. An hour and a half's pretty good."

Today they're doing a lot more work on their own word processors and then getting it down to us after the job is almost okay to print. That minimizes the job because where the money comes in for the printer, of course, is when they make changes. And if they do it all on their word processors, there are no changes.

I started off in customer service about twenty years ago more to learn the business. These are the people who do all the paperwork, stay in the office and man the phones and track all the deliveries. They do a lot of things, except that they work for eight hours and then they go bye-bye. After I worked in customer service for a while, we thought it would be a good idea if a customer had somebody to work with 24 hours a day as opposed to just eight and then have their job turned over to another shift.

This way they don't worry, they talk to me, and what they do is lay the whole thing on me, which is fine. I like that. I think it's better for them. As I got more proficient, they decided it would be good for me to work with salesmen, sort of be an inside salesperson. So the salesmen would go out and sell and they would bring a job in, and then I would make it so good for them that they would come back and give us more work.

I do the things that sort of fall between the cracks, because the clients are too busy thinking of the document or how they're going to word something. I tell them, "Hey, you've got to clear this thing; otherwise you're never going to get it printed in time to mail it out." Or, "What kind of envelopes do you need?" Actually, I hold their hands, I suppose. I'm one of the few people here who can go talk to the union composing shop, so I sort of help the customer and help our composing room—keep peace between the two. Of course, all the lawyers and investment bankers think they're a bit of a printer, and all printers think they're a bit of a lawyer and investment banker, so you've got a bit of a clash.

On the client side, you have four basic groups. You have the company and their attorneys, you have the investment banker and their attorneys. And they all have to be happy in order for a deal to go. Of course, all the attorneys are looking out for their respective clients, and it can get pretty icky sometimes. They don't agree about things, and then the deal lasts forever and ever and ever. I mean, it just goes on and on and on. There are going to be differences of opinion, but I think most of the time they fight it out in their own offices and then come down here. That's why it's such an unsteady business. They say, "Oh, we're definitely going to file tomorrow." Then they come up with something and they'll call me up—hopefully they'll call me up—and say, "We're not coming tonight. We're coming in tomorrow night instead."

The best deals are the ones that leave here at 6:00 in the evening. But they're rare. I think they think printers only open at 6:00 in the evening. And contrary to everybody's belief, we're not open seven days a week, 24 hours a day. We're supposed to be closed over the weekend, but we're not. I mean, obviously, if somebody wants to hire us and they're willing to pay for it, we're open. I was just talking to somebody, a woman lawyer I've known for quite a while, and she said to me, "It's very hard for me to explain to my husband that I'm wiped out, that I was at the printer's 'til 5:00 this morning." I know the problem, because nobody outside of this business can possibly understand what you can do at the printer's all night long.

The worst time of all is when we have an awful lot of business, really, because, of course, we get all this copy in at night and everybody wants it at 9:00 in the morning. And it's not possible. It's not possible, but everybody thinks they're No. 1. And so everybody says, "Just because you've got six other people in there filing and you've got 40 to 50 other jobs, that's too bad. It's not our problem; it's yours." And when I come in in the morning and I see that everything is late, it really freaks me out. I prefer people to scream at me the night before and I tell them: "Look, I'm not going to get this for you at 9:00. I'll do my best, but I'm not going to get it for you." So at least they know right away so they don't set up any meetings and stuff. That's my worst problem.

I have my own priorities. I know who is important. I know, after being in the business this long, when they really need it at 9:00 and when they don't. A tender offer's always top priority—always—because it's usually a hurry-up, hurry-up deal. If we messed up a job badly—we've done something wrong, we've dropped some lines maybe, God forbid, or we've messed up the pages and the proofs or something like that—then the next time around and from then on we try to make it up to them, because you're only as good as your last job.

We can do fantastically throughout three months, and the last day something can happen, something maybe minor, but it can happen and that's all they'll remember. They won't remember how terrific we were—this is not a job where you get a lot of kudos.

Editor: Beth Selby

James Balog

Vice Chairman DREXEL BURNHAM LAMBERT

James Balog, vice chairman of Drexel Burnham Lambert, has seen
as much of the institutional side of the brokerage business as anyone on Wall Street. After ten years with Merck & Co., he went to
work as a securities analyst and portfolio manager at Auerbach,
Pollak & Richardson in 1961, joining William D. Witter in 1969.
He was a top-ranked analyst in drugs on *Institutional Investor* magazine's first All-America Research Team in 1972, and he rose to the
chairmanship of Witter before it merged with Drexel in 1976.

When the boutique business began in the early '60s, all you
had were analysts and slide rules. You didn't even have
a trading department. It was a Camelot period in the
research business. We had fixed commission rates; recalling that
memory brings tears to my eyes.

Those were the days when we kept separate departments for
institutional and retail research. The institutional analysts were
the elite of the research business—no question. I happened to be
a drug analyst. I really did basic research. I could go anywhere in
the world to analyze a situation and prepare studies that were
contributions to the literature of the industry as well as investment
literature. I didn't have my own white rats, but at least I went to
the guys with the white rats, and I learned a hell of a lot. You only
covered ten stocks—fifteen at the most.

In the early part of the research boutique business, there were
no salesmen. When we finished our research, we would go out on
the road and sell it. We moved the information from New York to

the client by ourselves. We were it. It was very clear, even before fixed rates went, that it was not possible for the analyst to do all the selling himself and all the research. So then we started to get institutional salesmen. Our client base became much broader. The analysts couldn't run around the country and see 200 accounts or even 100 accounts.

But by 1967 you could see your overhead building very rapidly. The economics were changing. You had to start making capital commitments, so you had to have more money. Block bids were getting bigger, so you had to have a block desk. Once you have a block desk, what happens? You've gotta be able to lay off the blocks. Which means what? You've gotta hit a lot of buttons real fast. You've gotta have more salesmen. So it was all changing from a boutique to a department store. It was still a lovely, lovely business, but it was getting tougher all the time.

I left Auerbach in 1969 and went with William D. Witter. By then the changing structure was becoming more apparent. I was afraid that the basis on which we had competed so effectively—elegant service and research—would no longer be economically possible. In 1973 fixed rates were beginning to be eliminated. As commissions came down, the margin between costs and revenues was squashed, and out of the middle we had to eliminate services we could no longer effectively provide. We no longer had the umbrella of a fixed-rate system to finance elegant research.

Then the big firms started to build up research staffs. They realized the necessity of having strong research to go with their investment banking. The research boutiques were like little mice. We could run among the legs of the big elephants if those elephants stood still, but when the elephants started dancing, they could squash us mice.

So now the elephants began to dance. Before, they'd had the standard research department, with salesmen all over the country, but their salesmen didn't know a hell of a lot and we'd always been able to beat them. There were enough people on the institutional side who wanted the real basic stuff, and we'd go out and give it to them. With fixed rates, we could afford to fly to Topeka. But suddenly, you couldn't afford to fly anywhere anymore. The rates just wouldn't permit it. Size became valuable instead of disadvantageous. The big firms had more capital than we did, and they had the ability to distribute merchandise. There's no way we could take on a block of stock with twenty salesmen and hope to find the other side when Goldman Sachs, Salomon—Bob Mnuchin and those guys—were out there. Those guys hit the wires and—Boom!—they lit up lights all over America, offering to sell 100,000 shares of something. Within three minutes they could get rid of it.

Analysts ceased to be information generators and purveyors; they became a means to other ends. They became a way to get the first call on the block. Because you had an analyst, you got on the trading list. If you were high on the trading list, you got the first call on the block. And then you could distribute the block. But those who had other derivative uses for an analyst could outbid you, and that's exactly what happened. When Merrill Lynch announced they were going to be No. 1 in research, they could recruit with their checkbook. And they went right straight to the top.

At Witter we were the first to sell out, and we were very fortunate that we made our move early. If you didn't make your deal early, there was no deal left to make. Baker Weeks did a deal with Reynolds, we did a deal with Burnham. Mitchell Hutchins did a deal with Paine Webber—all within a matter of twelve months. I remember one of my partners asking me, "Jim, whatever made you decide to do it so quickly?" I said, "Joe, when you see the flood coming, the smartest thing to do is go to higher ground."

We got out at the top. Had we waited another quarter, our earnings would have been negative and our book would have been going south instead of north. It was exquisite—no, it was excruciating—how fast it all deteriorated. Once the elephants made their deals, all the rest of the mice got crunched. But I came over here, to Drexel Burnham, with my team of people, and we found a safe home.

It was a sad, sad thing to see the boutiques and the kind of research they did disappear. The most difficult part was telling the analysts who wanted to keep living in Camelot, "There ain't no more Camelot, guys." Now, a psychotic is someone who believes that 2 plus 2 equals 5 and that somehow they are going to make it. A neurotic, on the other hand, is a person who knows that 2 plus 2 equals 4, but he doesn't like it. And there were a lot of neurotics then who didn't want to believe the realities. I didn't like them either, but 2 plus 2 equals 4, not 5 or 6.

I think Camelot was lovely. Would I love Camelot to come back again? You bet your sweet ass I would. But it's gone. It's like your first love; somehow, you only get one in life.

Editor: Joe Kolman

Barry Good

Oil Analyst MORGAN STANLEY & CO.

During his 34 years as an energy analyst, Barry Good has
witnessed some of the most important developments in his profession, from the growth and demise of boutiques to the research
buildup of a major investment bank to the roller-coaster ride of
the oil crisis. He has been a member of *Institutional Investor* magazine's All-America Research Team since its inception in 1972.

When I left college [in 1953] my father said, "Why don't
you go to Wall Street? Nobody's been there since the
1930s." Dad was right. Everybody I was associated with
in the first few years in the business was a veteran of the '29 crash
and the '31 crash. The Dow was still trying to climb back toward
its 1929 high of 381, and every time the market would go up five
points, some elderly guy would come by my desk and say: "You
don't remember 1929. This is going to be it all over again." The
Dow finally topped 381 in 1954, as I recall, and there was a period
of great rejoicing.

Research was a completely different business in those days.
There were five or six of us in the [Dean Witter] "stat" department. Some guy wired in from a branch office and said, "Should
I buy Home Oil?" You would go to the wire file to see what answer
had been given to that question before. If you didn't like the
answers, you would dig out the *Financial Post* survey of oil and
mineral companies. And you'd look at the financial statement,
and you'd look at the balance sheet. You would read the description of the company. You'd write a wire back to the guy and say,

you should buy Home Oil or you shouldn't buy Home Oil, or whatever.

My first company visit was probably about 1957. I remember in particular going one day to Pittsburgh and seeing within two days Flintcote, Gulf Oil, Alcoa, U.S. Steel, Pittsburgh Plate Glass. You'd prepare by reading the guy's four- or five-page annual report, and you'd try to ask him whatever intelligent questions you could think of. The level of cleverness of the questions left a great deal to be desired. Like the "How do you think you're going to do this year?" type of thing.

The institution in the 1950s was a bank trust department, and the so-called portfolio manager was some very nice, kindly guy, always immaculately dressed, who put you into General Motors, Eastman Kodak or Du Pont. And maybe, if he was really imaginative, really creative, he might put you into a few shares of IBM. So there you were in this great bull market, where even IBM was considered a risky stock, and the key word was preservation of capital.

In 1965 an opportunity came up at Laird. It was one of the boutiques that had a good track record—excellent—a wonderful bunch of people. The first day I was at Laird, I went to a sales meeting and talked about a few things that we'd been recommending. And I think one of them was Standard Oil of New Jersey, basically high-quality, don't-have-to-apologize-for type of names. And I got through and about five guys immediately came asking questions about this, that and the other off-the-wall type of oil companies, really highly speculative, highly volatile. So I think I recognized pretty quickly that I'd walked into a very different environment.

It was a standardized research department. I was doing oils and electronics, and we had a drug guy, a chemical guy, a steel guy. There were only thirteen of us. We were considered to be among the top five research firms on the Street. Everybody was playing the 60-minute game. When I was playing football, we used to play both offense and defense. Today you have one guy doing domestic oil, another guy doing international oil, a third guy doing exploration companies, a fourth guy doing oil service. I used to do all of that.

When I went to Laird in 1965, I'd been in the business for twelve years and almost broke the research director's heart at Laird by getting paid $18,000. But during those days you had institutional marketing guys who were still getting a standard one-third payout on gross commissions. In 1968 you had guys making $500,000, $600,000, $700,000. So in a sense, you can say that the scale was completely out of line. Analysts were way undercompensated relative to salesmen—or you could say that the marketing guys were way overcompensated.

In the spring of 1973 Laird was in real trouble, and I got together with Barton Biggs. Morgan Stanley was hiring people from the outside, and we all asked the same questions. "Was the firm really trying to create a research product, or was it getting a bunch of hired flacks to follow the company clients? Is this another Lehman?" Lehman went through research departments like Tommy Manville went through wives.

Barton told us he had gotten the complete assurance of the senior management of this firm that our intellectual integrity would be completely respected—that we would never be required to recommend a stock because it was a banking client. We might want to be a little bit careful about sell recommendations—particularly, don't say that you don't like the chairman as you're recommending the sale of the stock.

I joined Morgan Stanley on October 1, 1973. I had a prearranged commitment to speak to the North Carolina Analyst Society in Winston-Salem on October 3. In the speech I warned them of the impending oil crisis. The Yom Kippur War started on October 6. So I'd been here one week and the Yom Kippur War started, and the embargo started two weeks later.

Oil analysts are perhaps a little bit different from other analysts because we constantly have to be very much aware of political developments, which have much more of an impact on business. In 1965 I had gone and visited OPEC. They were in a third-story walk-up in Vienna with five rooms. The so-called economics group was one person, an Iranian, a very lovely guy. I spent a day with him and wrote a report, and I called it OPEC—I had to spell out what OPEC meant. Nineteen seventy was the year in which we finally got up to peak production in the United States. Nobody foresaw a $10 price. The biggest movement we'd ever seen in crude-oil prices was back in 1957, when it went up 35 cents a barrel. So you didn't sit around and say the price was going to go up from $3 to $10 [which it did] in about two weeks in October 1973. Right through the roof. I'll always remember '73 with great fondness, not only because I joined this firm, but because I had five recommendations at the beginning of the year that turned out to be the top-five-performing stocks for the year as a whole. That's never happened to me since.

The absolute peak in the oils was in November '80. It was a crisis period. You're always trying to look at what's real and what's unreal in this thing, and there was something unreal about $40 barrels. Barton and I got to talking about it in late November. I said: "You know, Barton, I've got a problem with these stocks because they've been the only game in town for the last couple of years, and some people might argue that they've been the only game in town since 1973. And to justify these prices going any higher, you're going to have to see $50 oil and I don't think the world can support $50 oil."

Barton came out in the first week of December and said, "Over the next six months we're going to be selling oils." Well, of course, we should have sold them all between then and the end of December; they started collapsing right after Thanksgiving 1980. The only account in the country that I think will be willing to remember that I had made that particular call is Fayez Sarofim. I happened to be down [in Houston] at Christmas 1980, and Fayez came in and said, "What is it that Barton is trying to tell us?" And I said, "Well, Fayez, here are some numbers that I put together to show you what I think you're going to need to justify those stocks." I'm pretty good at inflection points. My problem is in between inflection points. The big entry points and exit points don't occur that often. Mostly, you are in a trading type of market.

One of the things that's happened in the oil business was the so-called restructuring. It was a very dominant theme, the question of who is going to buy out whom. Morgan Stanley has a very tough legal department, and we've perhaps handicapped our analysts by having been involved in most of the large mergers. There's been a lot of things I haven't been able to say in the last two or three years that have been important.

I was intimately involved in the Phillips restructuring every step of the way and I knew everything that had been considered, and people knew that. That did not deter them from calling me up and trying to find out what they could find out. They'd call up and say, "What do you think Phillips is going to do next?" You'd always start out and say: "Look, as you know, we are advising the Phillips Petroleum Co. I can't tell you what Phillips is going to do next. But what do *you* think they're going to do next? What does your work lead you to believe?" And the guy really goes off on a tangent and you just say: "Now look, why don't you think about that again? Because if you really think about it, I don't think you're going to come up with that conclusion."

We have Texaco on our restricted list. It's been on the restricted list for a year. I mean, personally, I regard that as an abridgement of my right as an analyst. I can't say anything about it? I say things about Texaco. I don't know what's going on from a corporate finance standpoint.

Originally, the bankers were very understandably a little suspicious of us. They were afraid we were going to say something nasty about some wonderful old client, and they were afraid to tell us anything that could be remotely regarded as a piece of information that wasn't totally on the public record. Over time the bankers have gotten to realize that we are a formidable asset.

I keep going back over this whole takeover thing and thinking there must have been some way I could have handled that one better, because I didn't recognize it as well as some people did.

Boone Pickens started giving the basic restructuring speech in early 1979. I had him on a panel in Boston at the Financial Analysts Federation meeting in June of '82. As we were flying back to New York, we got on his plane and I sat down opposite him, and he looked across at me and said, "Barry, you think the major oil companies are going to do all the things that I think they ought to do?"

And I said: "Oh, my God, Boone, you're asking me? You've been giving this speech now for three years, and I thought you knew." He said, "No, I don't know whether they're going to do them or not." And I gave a very faithful answer: "Boone, I don't think they're going to do it unless somebody makes them do it." So I guess I just never really understood how personal it was all going to be. Financing a company with no assets through junk bonds? No, I did not see at the beginning that he could so corral Gulf that Gulf would have to find a white knight.

There probably were ways, despite the constraints of working for this firm, that we might have been more responsive to what was going on. I sort of regret that. This was where you made real money.

I told Barton once, "When I come back in my next life, I'm going to be one hell of an analyst." I can remember every mistake I've made.

Editor: Joe Kolman

Robert Baldwin

Former Chairman MORGAN STANLEY & CO.

> Whether because of its enviable roster of corporate clients, its carriage-trade mystique or its storied "arrogance," Morgan Stanley has long been the firm Wall Street has most loved to hate. But it is also one of the best-run houses in the industry, due in no small part to its former chairman, Robert Baldwin, who, in the late 1960s and early 1970s, imposed on the small, reluctant partnership modern management and planning systems he brought with him from the Navy Department when he rejoined Morgan Stanley in 1967. Under Baldwin's leadership, the firm grew nearly tenfold, broadened its product-and-services mix and planted Morgan Stanley's flag prominently overseas.

When I came back from the Navy in 1967, we had just moved to 140 Broadway, which in and of itself was a traumatic move. That was a stage where people still wondered whether they could move their firm's address off Wall Street and still be considered a Wall Street firm. But the real moves hadn't really started at that stage. In those days, both for syndicate and other work, you used to remember the address where everybody was. And it was a very, very small world. When I first came to work at Morgan Stanley, every senior person left their office a little before 12:00 and came back a little after 2:00, and they all went to the Bond Club luncheons. Everybody in Wall Street did the same thing. It was a different time schedule than you have today.

The new-issue business was such an important part of what we did; everybody focused on it, and you worked up to a peak when the new issue came—new issues and positions, back and forth, going on 24 hours a day, almost seven days a week. And then you'd slow down some and maybe do some new business.

I'd seen some management ideas in the Navy about how we ought to budget better, how we ought to do more planning, to differentiate between policy and operations. These were not things that the Wall Street firms did, and certainly Morgan Stanley didn't. We were still a partnership, and most of the important—and some of the unimportant—things were solved at partners' meetings. We had, I would guess, at that stage not much more than maybe 200, 225 people. So it was possible to do. But it wasn't a very fruitful or economic way of going at things. In 1967 we would still sit down and take a first cut at what the bonuses and salary increases for the entire staff were going to be. And then every partner had the right to go over all the bonuses and all the salary increases. It was at that stage that I got together with our then so-called office manager, John Church. We set up a job classification schedule and got a compensation committee formed to try and come up with recommendations from each department and then present them to what was then the first policy committee we'd ever set up.

I think the funniest thing was that the first year, people continued to look over every compensation thing. The second year they looked over things they were intimately associated with, particularly their secretaries. And the third year they pretty well left it to the people down below who were running various areas. We operated by committee then, pretty much in each area. It was again a very uneconomic, inefficient way of operating. But it was much more by consensus than it is today. And this was true all over the Street.

A second thing that I noticed shortly after I came back was that certain firms I had thought were sort of dead in the water were all of a sudden rising up into our syndicate bracket. And I wanted to know why. Well, it turned out that you were starting to see much more trading by institutional people than you had before. And this picked up as we got toward 1970. In other words, institutions, for the first time, began to decide that they could add an incremental return, particularly on fixed-income securities, if they traded. Whereas up till then an institution would buy and give a certain allocation to the managing underwriter and a certain amount to the majors or the bulge group, they were then starting to give more orders to the people who had helped them do their trading. It became quite apparent to me that we had to do more trading and marketing.

Nineteen sixty-nine saw the big telephone issues; they had to raise a heck of a lot of money. We were asked by AT&T if we could do a billion-six issue or did we think we had to limit it to a billion-one, which were both huge. If you take the inflation rate, you were probably talking about $2.75 billion in the case of $1.1 billion, or in the case of $1.6 billion, you were talking $3.2, maybe $4 billion in today's terms. We talked about it and hit upon the warrant idea. And after thinking about it a long while—this was really a firm decision; we had a whole partner's room full—we said, "We think we can do the $1.6 billion."

Pricing that AT&T debenture-with-warrants issue was traumatic. Because of an IRS ruling, we had to guarantee to AT&T that for the first week the bond itself as a separate unit would not sell below par and not sell above par and a half. That was an absolutely terrifying thought to us, because the markets had started to deteriorate. We didn't know how the two units would trade on a detached basis. And I remember full well the day we went to John De Butts, who was then the vice chairman in charge of financing, and recommended a coupon of 8.75 percent at par. Just prior to that, Pacific Telephone had done an issue of debentures at 8.65. John looked at me and said, "'Bob, why should we, the parent company with a triple-A rating, have to sell a debenture issue with an 8.75 percent coupon when we've just done one for Pacific Tel for 8.65?" I said: "Well, John, the issue was for a much smaller sum"—I think it was in the $150 to $200 million range. "We're talking about $1.6 billion. And we're talking about having an issue that, with the warrants, will give value to your stockholders over a good long-range period. And we think this is the price that will hold for that period—most importantly, stay between par and par and a half during the first week." He looked me straight in the eye and said, "Okay, we accept it." And that was probably the easiest part of it, because then I went home and spent all night worrying about whether it was going to stay in that range. Fortunately, it did, and we got the IRS ruling.

I had attached several provisos. One, I wanted to invite every member of the NASD to participate in the issue; and two, we said we wanted to go to more cities than ever before on a dog-and-pony show to explain what we were trying to do, mainly because we wanted people around the country to understand just what a warrant was and how it was valued. In today's market, with options and futures and so forth, people would laugh at it a little, but we literally had to go around. We had to do some more work on theory ourselves.

It wasn't easy. We used some of the techniques that TV stations use, various montages and overlays, and came up with what I thought was an absolutely marvelous presentation that we did in about fifteen minutes that really caught the essence of how you valued warrants. But when we went to Miami, it didn't look like we were going to get very good attendance at the brokers' meeting. So Morgan Stanley people there fanned out, up and down the main streets of the financial area of Miami, and knocked on doors and went in and saw branch managers, most of whom had vaguely heard of this offering, but nothing much more. And we finally got a whole bunch of them to come to the meeting. One man, at the end of the meeting, said: "Well, Mr. Baldwin, I've heard all about the telephone company, and I've heard all about warrants. But I have one question for you: What's in it for me?" That epitomizes what you had to do to get their attention and then to put enough selling concession in it to get people to go out and sell the issue.

Another issue that got a lot of attention was Exxon's Dutch auction in 1976. [Exxon CFO] Jack Bennett and I are old friends, and when he was bound and determined he'd do a Dutch auction, we urged him not to do it. We didn't think it would work out well. Jack was adamant. Well, we went in and bid; we were trying to make an offering at a set price. And it turned out that you couldn't hold the price at all the way you do in an ordinary syndicate, because every time you thought you had a price, somebody was offering it away from you with some lesser price, trying to get rid of their participation. We and the rest of the people that were syndicate members with us took a good licking on it. It clearly put into our minds that if we ever did another Dutch auction, we would bid a considerably lower price, because we didn't think you could have a controlled syndicate that would get everybody to go along and accept a price.

A lot else was changing besides the new-issue business. There was the clearing and operations area. Just to give you a feeling of how small we were at that time, up until 1972, '73 we didn't have anybody on the stock exchange floor. We would deal through correspondents, and Morgan Guaranty would clear all our underwriting syndicates. The idea went back to the Depression, when our partners, when they started up, said: "We want to keep a very small staff. And if business is good, we're willing to pay Morgan Guaranty and our correspondents to do the clearance work. And if business is bad and we don't have the demand, well, we don't have that back-office force." We had just a handful of people working at what we called our syndicate accounting department. In fact, through 1971 we didn't close our own books; Arthur Young did. In the summer of '72, one man balanced our checkbook every month. He could do it because it was so simple.

What caused this to change was a planning meeting in '71 where we made the major decision to go into bond trading and marketing and to pay production-oriented compensation, which was a big break for Morgan Stanley. We said we'd do that first, since we felt we knew the bond business better, and the next year go into research, trading and marketing of stocks. So we saw the need to put in our own back office and to put people on the floor of the stock exchange. We went ahead and hired people to establish an operations department. And in the first year they were aboard, they saved enough money in interest to pay for their whole department.

We also finally decided to go into research. I can tell you that some of the more senior partners, or the retired partners, gave Frank Petito and myself a bad time in '73, when we started into research. That was the time I took over as president and Frank took over as chairman, and that's when we brought Barton Biggs aboard and started to hire research people and go into trading. What did they think was wrong with research? One, as [former senior partner] Perry Hall said, it could only be wrong; and, two, you would run into conflicts of interest with your clients. What I had to say to Perry was, "Look, we must do this if we're going to do a job for our clients." With the institutional volume being so much more important, we had to establish credibility. And it wasn't like the old days, when you just went and asked for business. You had to earn your stripes. And, in fact, when Barton first came aboard and started to hire research people, he had to bring each one of them in to see me, and I had to convince them that we were in the research business to stay.

I think a watershed was that planning meeting in '71. We'd had a planning meeting in '69, which really was to humor me, back from the Navy with my ideas about planning and management; that had been, in my opinion, a disaster. But the '71 meeting really took off, made us look and say, "What kind of a structure are we going to have to respond to this growing size?" And the big thing was the recognition that we had to get an equity organization in place before Mayday came in 1975.

Now, was it easy? No. We went through several processes of getting the kind of people to run the departments that fit in with our culture. And there was a turnover to get there. And a couple of times people said, "Morgan Stanley's been a failure at this or that or the other thing." But we persevered. But it wasn't easy, I guarantee you.

As we went forward, one of the things we also had to deal with was how we would do business abroad. We had set up in Paris and bought two thirds of Morgan et Cie. from Morgan Guaranty. And we did a tremendous volume from 1967 till about '72 or '73. Then the question was, What were we going to do? Was the Eurobond market going to succeed? A lot of people pulled out of Europe at that stage. We stayed and stayed in Paris—much too long for my liking, because I was trying to get us to move to London early on. I thought that was going to be where the center of financial activity was going to be; that's where the trained people were. But there were a number of people in the late '70s in the firm who thought we were spending too much money on international and we should pull back, that there wasn't going to be the return on it. Well, you've seen what's happened.

As it was, I think we made the move to London all right, but we should have done it sooner. When we did move, one of the things we did have trouble with was getting the right team aboard. There was talk, maybe even in the international edition of *Institutional Investor* magazine, about the fact that our bond team over there was failing. Well, we weren't failing; we were having trouble getting the people who were doing our bond business to do it the way we wanted it done. So finally, we took a team from the U.S. and put them over there to work for [Morgan Stanley International managing director] Archie Cox. It's just that many times you work with one group, and it doesn't work. Then you have to change a little and try and get things done. It's human chemistry.

Another thing would be the merger and acquisition business, which Bob Greenhill set up in the early '70s. I never dreamed it would be as big as it was and that it would continue that way. We set it up sort of as a separate unit. And there was a question whether *that* was the right thing to do. In fact, in '79 we had another planning meeting to try and look out and see where we were going to be ten years from now and where our revenues were going to come from. Well, the figures were all wrong, because we were much more into principal business as we went along in various things. But we were worried about the fact that the M&A business would be too big a percentage of our overall business. It's been very, very good but much less a part of the business than we thought.

Some people said in the mid-'80s that Morgan Stanley hadn't expanded fast enough and that we hadn't gone into commercial paper and municipal bonds. Well, in June 1970, when we incorporated, we had $7.5 million worth of capital, and we had 265 people. I think we had close to 3,000 people when I stepped down at the end of '83. Our revenues in 1970 were $18 million overall; you know what our revenues are today. So we grew tremendously fast. Our theory was to stay with those businesses that we needed to protect our various positions. And at that stage, commercial paper wasn't as important to a firm as it is today. Remember, it wasn't until about the '79 period and thereafter that we really went to so much short-term paper; the interest rate on it was so high, and you didn't have the money market funds. So we stayed out of that at that stage. I think it was a wise decision.

We try, as part of our culture, to make people be part of the overall team. We say: "Hey, look, sure you contributed this. But again, many of the clients are people that investment banking, that Morgan Stanley has gotten over a period of years. And don't think that just because you happen to do one deal at a particular

397

time for a client you can say, "Look at our profit margin. What are the rest of the people in the organization contributing?" You have to go back and say, 'Look, here's how much business we've done with this firm. Here's the kind of relationships we've had. They have confidence in us, and that's why we're getting the business.' "

It was never perfect, but we certainly worked very, very hard at trying to keep people looking at the overall picture. My best example was, suppose we sent somebody to try and do business in the Middle East, which we did. Now, you made lots of long, hard trips out there. Maybe all of a sudden you'd have a big piece of business; but in between, those people could be working just as hard as people in M&A or some other part of the business. Do you say to them, "Hey, you didn't do much for us. We're not going to pay you very well"? You were building a business, same way as I mentioned about international. A lot of people didn't think much of our international people. And, in fact, a number of people didn't want to get into the international business, because they thought there was no future there. Time has changed that, as you well know.

We'd try to work the best we could. In some cases, where we felt that there were tremendous hours put in [by one group], we would have a differential, but not as large as they would have liked. I've had people come to me and say, "Bob, I cannot see other people in this firm make more than I make." And this one person we had treated very well, given him a very big bonus, a very big stock increase, and he was fairly new to the firm. And we said, "Look, your future is good." He said, "I won't stand for it." So I wished him well. And he went elsewhere.

I was asked to speak to the financial writers in New York in the summer of '74 about what I saw coming, particularly with going to negotiated commissions in May of '75. It was at that time that I coined the phrase "Mayday" out of my Navy days' experience. And I said that if certain things held, plus the going to negotiated rates, I thought 150 to 200 firms would go out of business. The next day in the newspaper, they put in all sorts of things about "Cassandra" Baldwin predicts this and that and the other. And somebody sent me a story about the myth of Cassandra, which I didn't know at that time. But it was exactly right. She would predict correctly, but nobody would believe her. And I predicted—and predicted correctly—but nobody believed it was going to be the case. In fact, if anything, I was on the low side. It's like trying to turn the ocean tides back; you can't. I think that going to negotiated rates worked a lot better here than it worked in, say, Canada or is working now in London. Neither of those markets was deep enough to withstand the assault of negotiated rates. In London most of the business has gone upstairs. In Canada the firms have been undercapitalized, so they're having to let other people come into the business.

We also had to deal with the shelf registration phenomenon. At the stage the SEC was putting in Rule 415, we went down to Washington and talked to them and said: "This will change completely the nature of the securities industry. If you're going to do it, this should be a subject of hearings before Congress. Then come to a decision, if you want, rather than do it by regulation of the SEC. We'll still be around, but things are going to change as they've never changed before. And nobody knows how it might come out." People said, "Morgan Stanley's scared that all the business is going to be taken away from them." Well, it ended up much as we predicted. The big investment banking firms got most of the business in this area. Dean Witter, for example, was one of the ones favoring 415 because they thought they were going to come into a lot more business. But the old so-called wire houses really haven't done that much. It's not been that profitable a business for anybody.

Our market share has dropped since 415, but the point is that it dropped down and then came back to a certain level. And if you take a look at mortgage-backed securities, that's where a lot of the volume has been built up. If you look at the rest of it, it's not been that profitable a business. And so we had to change to respond to it. And we're doing much more principal business and working esoteric types of issues; that's where our money's being made today. We still stay in the other business, but if we had gone and continued to rely on that as a source of revenues for the future of the firm, we'd have been in deep trouble. We just had to change.

When I joined the firm, the question was: Could Morgan Stanley, Dillon Read and Kuhn Loeb stand up to the onslaughts of Halsey Stuart? Well, Halsey Stuart's gone the way of all flesh. Kuhn Loeb is now a part of a much bigger organization. Dillon

Read's owned by the Travelers. And Morgan Stanley is still operating on its own.

There have also been some wrenching changes in the way decisions are made. I always use one example to point this out. Sometime around '75 or '76 I was on the stock exchange board, and we had a committee that gave people the right to lease seats. Well, the members on the floor were just absolutely outraged; they told us that we were trying to ruin the floor, etc., etc. And somebody threw a seat on the floor for sale at $55,000; I think that was the price. I came back to our management committee and said, "Look, let's buy that seat, just to show we still have faith in it."

We went and bought it, and then the people on the exchange said, "Oh, Bob Baldwin forced the price down so he could get in cheap." But the more important thing was that up here one of our partners complained bitterly that we hadn't brought that purchase to the whole partnership before we did it. You get my point on the mental approach? Today people take tens of millions of risks—and just check with the risk committee; it's a completely different world. Remember, we incorporated in '70. And when we incorporated, we looked to see if we could incorporate without naming a president. We found we had to, so we named a president. But I believe that in the next annual report we didn't even mention who that president was. And in '70 we partially incorporated and stayed a partnership, so we were both. In '75 we finally incorporated fully. That was a wrenching experience for people, because the idea of not being a so-called partner went down hard. And we always used the title "partner" with other people for a good many years. Now I don't know how many managing directors there are—120, 130. Obviously, you've got to work in a different way.

Not all these changes have been for the better. I am crushed by the revelations of insider trading and some of the things that have gone on in Wall Street. As you well know, we had that one incident ourselves [in the mid-1970s], where we had two people who were found passing inside information. That was one of the great sorrows of my tenure as the head of the firm.

I made a speech just about a year ago down at Wharton. And at the end of it, more or less as a throw-away line, I said, "And be sure to spend enough time with your spouse and children, because success without them is a rather hollow victory." And I got a standing ovation. And I couldn't figure out what it was about. I went up to one person there who was my former secretary, who was in her first year at Wharton, and said, "Roberta, what's this all about?" "Well, Mr. Baldwin," she said, "everybody else from Wall Street is coming down and telling people not to get married or to expect to get divorced every five years if they come to Wall Street." I think that's a terrible attitude. And it wouldn't be worth it to me, no matter how much money I made. I hope that as a result of what's coming out in these trials, people will come to their senses.

Editor: Tom Lamont

Travers Bell

Chairman DANIELS & BELL

Travers Bell is chairman of Daniels & Bell, the first and still the only black-owned investment banking firm belonging to the New York Stock Exchange. In 1986 Daniels & Bell participated in $9 billion worth of municipal finance underwritings and ranked twentieth among all muni finance houses.

M y father was in the business, with the operations department of Dempsey Tegeler in Chicago, and he always tried to encourage me to see what the stock market was all about. One summer I needed some money, and he said, "Good, I've got a messenger's job for you." So I went down to Dempsey Tegeler in the Rookery Building on South Street the first day, and they gave me a briefcase and told me to make a delivery to a company called H.N. Billesby, which was in the Field Building right across the street. I unzipped the briefcase, looked at the raggedy papers in it, and I gave them to a guy, and he gave me a certified check for $175,000. My eyes went *boiiing!* The first thought that hit me was that this guy was paying me for paper!

I left Teachers College to stay on as a messenger. Then I got a job as a wire operator, then as an operations clerk. And in 1963, when I was 23 or 24, I got a break. Dempsey Tegeler acquired a firm called Straus, Blosser and McDowell in Chicago, with about fifteen offices. Out of the blue, they made me operations manager of the entire thing. I took courses in economics and business at Washington University in St. Louis, where Dempsey's home office was.

You see, I had made a decision before I moved to St. Louis that I would wind up in New York because that was where the securities industry was. Essentially, what made the decision for me was that Jerry Tegeler, who my dad had worked for for fifteen years and who really liked my dad a great deal, came to me one day and said: "Travers, you know there was no way for me to help your dad. I really couldn't move him, because nobody's mind was ready for that."

But, he said: "I'm past that point now. I think our people can react to the fact that you can deliver. And you're obviously good at what you do and you learn real fast. But I'm going to do something a lot of people aren't going to like—I really am. I'm going to teach you this business."

And he did. He taught it to me.

I learned it in the days when there were no computers. And at the end of the day you had to tie everything together. So while I was not buying or trading, I actually had to balance to the penny every day.

That was what made me make my decision. The one point that outweighed everything else was that as a black man I had had this unusual opportunity to learn the securities business and that knowledge just was not with anybody else black. I had an *obligation* to exercise that knowledge. That was really the triggering point. I felt it was more than me.

I graduated in 1967 and got a job at Fusz Schmelzle. I became an officer and director in charge of operations and new computer facilities. I knew that someday I would open my own firm, but I needed more trading and sales experience. I was at Fusz Schmelzle as chief operations officer for three-and-a-half years, until 1970, when I started Daniels & Bell.

There were other blacks in the securities industry at that time, and I'd been talking to them about organizing a black-owned securities firm. I had liaisons with a fellow in Los Angeles, one in Chicago and one in New York. And finally in 1970, when I decided that it was time to do it, the people literally could not make the decision.

The fellow in New York—he had been in the securities industry for thirteen years himself—he said, "Listen, this is too much of a risk for me at this time. I've got a good history and family and children, and I just don't want to take the risk." But, he said, "I know someone in New York who is trying to do the same thing. I'd like to introduce you to him. Willie Daniels." And he did. And that's how I met Mr. Daniels. Within about five or six months, we had organized Daniels & Bell.

It was Danny Lufkin of Donaldson, Lufkin & Jenrette who got Willie Daniels and me into business. Willie and I had cut a deal with the Small Business Investment Co. of New York for a million-and-a-half dollars. But two or three days before the trigger date, the Small Business Administration ruled that investing in our firm could be construed as relending money and that, therefore, they couldn't do it. Myron Kandel, who used to write *Wall Street Letter,* wrote a story about it, and Danny Lufkin read it. He ran into Daniels walking across Chase Manhattan Plaza and said, "Come on up to the office." And they went upstairs, and I came over, and he said, "Okay, I'll help you." And he did. He put up some cash, and then the Myron Kandel letter filtered back to the SEC, and they gave us an exemption, reasoning that the intent of the law had been to encourage business that could create capital for other minority businesses.

In the summer of the following year, we bought a seat on the New York Stock Exchange. It was an industry event. We had just a fantastic party, up at 120 Broadway in the Bankers Club. That's how we started our first day of business, after being up all night. And there we were, the first black member firm of the New York Stock Exchange.

The stock exchange is a buy and sell institution. Some members may be prejudiced; some may not be. But it makes no difference to them when you come down there. It's what have you got to buy, what have you got to sell, and what's the market? But I think there was prejudice from municipal administrations, which were all white at the time. As a municipal firm, we would go to people who did business in the city of New York or the city of Chicago, and they would say, "You've got to be kidding. This is not an arena you can play in." But the fact was, there

405

were small, regional firms doing business with various cities across the country.

We thought our best hope would be to try to find some black mayors. The only place we could find them was down in rural towns in the South. Mount Bayou, Mississippi, was a classic because it was the oldest black municipality in the U.S. It had never had a financing, and here we came, knocking on doors and saying, "We want to do a bond issue." And this guy says, "What's a bond issue?" So we did a housing issue there. As a result, Mount Bayou is a very progressive town today. Maynard Jackson was a lawyer in his own Atlanta law firm at that time, just a lawyer. We made him co–bond counsel in the Mount Bayou deal. It was the first time a black firm had ever been a bond counsel in a bond issue. And we made the Citizens Trust Co. of Atlanta co-trustee, which was the first time a black bank had ever been a trustee of a bond issue.

It wasn't until 1982–83 that there was a real turn on the municipal side. Prior to that, many black mayors had said: "Yes, we're going to put you in our deals. But we're getting feedback from the members of the financial community that it's okay if we give you a deal for, say, 15 or 20 million bucks, Travers, but when you're talking about $300 million or $400 million, it's hard for us." But Connecticut's treasurer, Henry Parker, eliminated the whole argument. After a lot of deliberation, he appointed us to a $5.5 billion transaction. Then anybody saying they couldn't put us on a $300 million deal had no argument. There was no longer any reason to say that we couldn't do it, because it had been done.

In bringing unknown black credits to the market, I've tried to convince people to forget whether this is a black municipality. We say, "This is the credit, this is the deterrent, and this is how we think it can be done." But I've run into literally hundreds of deals where people come to me and tell me, "Listen, don't you know that this deal will make history?" *All* the deals we've done have made history. But if the numbers weren't there, I'd put them on the shelf and say, "Not at that expense. I don't want to pay to make history."

Our interest is real clear and real simple: There must be independent financial investment banks in order to generate capital for minority financial institutions and minority businesses and to provide investment opportunities for the minority general public. But they have to compete in the overall marketplace. That's the key. I don't mind involving myself in issues that are charity, but I have to earn money to do that. My business is a profit-and-loss business. I've never lost sight of that.

Editor: Amy C. Pershing

[Editor's note: Mr. Bell died on January 25, 1988.]

John Neff

Managing Partner WELLINGTON MANAGEMENT CO./
THORNDIKE, DORAN, PAINE & LEWIS

When John Neff took over management of the Windsor Fund in
1964, its assets were $75 million. Today, though it was closed to
new money in 1985, Windsor is almost a $6 billion fund, with one
of the best long-term records in the mutual fund industry. Neff,
one of the best-known practitioners of value investing, runs several
other funds for his firm, Wellington Management Co./Thorndike,
Doran, Paine & Lewis.

When I first got into this business in the early '60s, it was
awfully easy to make money. It was a story period, story
stocks. Everybody made money. The only difference
was how much. And, of course, it was the era of gunslingers, of
guys like Jerry Tsai. Tsai would come whipping into things, and
whispers of "Tsai is selling such-and-such" would go across the
Street, and then he'd dump.

It was a time, too, when portfolio managers were appointed in
the battlefield, kind of like in the Civil War, when they made
generals in the battlefields. There were a lot of portfolio managers in their 20s. Now, I don't mean to say that it was a total piece
of cake. Stocks did go awry and exhaust their potential or even fail
fundamentally. And you had some pretty good black holes in
stocks that went wrong. But overall, it was a period pretty much
without penalty.

We were very much right of center back then. The prevailing
philosophy was one of high risk tolerance. Be in small compa-

409

nies and be agile. If things aren't working, why, get out one day and go back in the next. But our approach at Windsor has always led us to wear our contrarianness on our sleeves and buy and hold down-and-out stocks. We used to say, and still sometimes do, that if our portfolio looks good to you, we aren't doing a very good job.

I didn't get a lot of heat because of this, but occasionally I did. I can remember a conversation with a good friend of mine who was a partner at a Wall Street firm. We were going to the horse races and he said to me: "John, how can you own stocks like that? How can you buy that stuff when everybody knows this other merchandise is the way to go? You're going to get left behind."

He wasn't tongue-lashing me. He was just giving me a little bit of Dutch uncle insight into the world as best he could appraise it. And he couldn't understand how I could be so complacent with a bevy of stocks that were obviously out of favor. Well, you know, I was raised in a prudent-man climate of a bank trust department, and I've never forgotten that people have an appetite for the upside but not much of a stomach for the downside. Shareholders want to make some money, but they don't want to lose their butts, either. Our approach always seemed like the best way to protect their interests.

Although we beat the averages in each of the years of the late '60s, there were lots of records better than ours. We were a bit behind the parade. But then came comeuppance time with the market downdraft of 1969. I remember it well. Windsor really hung in through that period. We were selling it as a stick-to-your-ribs fund that offered downside protection, and along came a test and, by golly, it lived up to its intent.

I remember right around then going to one of the big mutual fund conventions. Mutual fund salesmen came from all over to those things as part of their reward, I guess. And mutual fund managers gave their pitches. Anyway, I remember I was cheered kind of spontaneously when I was introduced. Other mutual funds had let them down and we hadn't. It gave me quite a tingle because I knew these salesmen represented, to a greater or lesser degree, mutual fund clients.

The period after that was the worst we've ever gone through. Nineteen seventy-one, '72 and '73 were the years of the growth stock craze. We did poorer than the S&P and relative to a lot of managers, too. It was an even more concentrated, more irrational, more unfair period than the '60s. Seemingly deserving merchandise was just wiped out. And then, of course, 1973–74 followed on top of that. We didn't do too badly in that market in a relative sense, but in an absolute sense we were still going south. I don't think this period took a massive toll on me overall. I never cracked or changed or caved or whatever. But it was difficult because it was so sustained.

We made up for all that in the next two years. Coming out of the ashes of 1973–74, we moved from right of center on the risk pole more toward center. We sold off a lot of our solid citizenry—utilities, banks, telephones and that kind of thing—and bought some lesser recognized growth stocks that had just gotten killed in the previous few years. I mean, you could pick up 15 and 20 percent growers for just six, seven or eight times earnings. Because we did this, we were the best-performing mutual fund in the recovery years of 1975 and 1976.

I think modern portfolio theory grew out of the excesses of the late '60s and early '70s, when people had gone off the deep end and lost their link with reality. They hungered for some kind of systematic approach. Well, I, for one, have never been against a systematic approach. We've always used one. But I felt MPT was backward-looking and presupposed that markets and companies don't change—neither of which is true. Companies, especially, do change, and to discern a change in terms of a lower or heightened growth rate for a company is, if you will, where the sizzle lies.

When I look back over the past twenty years at all the stocks I've picked, Tandy would probably stand out as the best winner. It wasn't a John Neff stock in the sense of yield. In fact, it didn't even start paying a dividend until very recently.

But it had a lot of other things going for it. It was cheap. The company had a distribution system in terms of retail stores that was without parallel. Charles Tandy was the ultimate Texas entrepreneur and a master merchant. And while we never visualized PCs or anything, we did feel that all kinds of gadgetry would have a place in the sun. Later came the CB radio, and they just made a bonanza on it. Just a bonanza.

411

We started buying the stock around, oh, '73 or '74. And we bought it and bought it and bought it. Not too many others were paying attention to it back then. Ourselves and Charles Tandy, we were the only ones buying it. We eventually built up a pretty big position, maybe 3 percent. By the time we sold the last of it in the late 1970s, we had made about thirteen to fourteen times our money and that's pretty good buckaroonies. It was a winner like we never had before or since.

On the other end of the spectrum, the most disappointing stock was U.S. Industries, which was a conglomerate. We started buying it in the early 1970s and at some point had a 5 percent position—which, of course, is the maximum for a mutual fund. It had a good dividend and track record and was involved in a lot of fields we thought we knew something about: apparel, construction, machinery, cement, aluminum. Best of all, it was cheap.

It was run by a man named I. John Billera. His name always made it sound like he was testifying. Anyway, he was an impressive guy, self-made, out of Hell's Kitchen in New York. But he just couldn't bring it around. It was of such size and complication that it was unmanageable, and it didn't have a sizable position in any of its markets. We sold most of it by the late 1970s and only got something like 45 or 50 percent of our money back.

⁂

One thing about the money management business has changed. Back in the olden days, you could pretty much buy an industry. Now you can get some very dramatic differences between the performance of various companies within an industry group. Ford has almost tripled since we bought it in '85. Then we bought General Motors, and that's almost done nothing. The only reason for this change that I can think of is that competition is more important, probably a lot more important, than before.

I think that means there's a greater burden of proof, a greater burden of excellence, for want of a better word, on managers today than there was then. You as a money manager have to pick the right horses. So the person who's willing to stick his neck out and not buy the group, providing his selections are right, will be better served.

412

Beyond that, though, I don't think the market has changed that much over the past twenty years, despite all the economic and political changes, the rise of MPT and supposed advances on the educational and computer front. It gets just as depressed and devastated as it always did. Then it bottoms and gets just as happy or overzealous or overdriven or whatever as ever. The ebb and flow never stops.

Editor: Diane Hal Gropper

Robert Rubin

Partner GOLDMAN, SACHS & CO.

Robert Rubin was made a partner in Goldman, Sachs & Co. after only four years in recognition of the contributions the arbitrage department, in which he was senior associate, made to the profits of the firm. Here Rubin recalls Goldman's approach to risk arbitrage and some of his more and less memorable moments.

I came to Goldman in October 1966 from the law firm of Cleary Gottlieb as a research analyst and arbitrageur. I didn't know much about Wall Street, but I knew I wanted to go into either the research side or the deal, what they call the merchant banking side of it. L. Jay Tenenbaum was the head of the arbitrage department; it was he who eventually offered me the job.

Gus Levy [Goldman senior partner] founded the department, then L. Jay came along and took it over. I think people have forgotten L. Jay. And it is a shame because L. Jay was really very close to Gus. L. Jay was an important part of Goldman Sachs in those days; he was part of the arbitrage business at a time when the business itself had a low profile.

The good thing about risk arbitrage is that you're involved in a field that just by its nature enables you to learn a great deal about lots of parts of the business. You learn about companies. You learn about research. You learn about mergers and acquisitions. You learn about trading.

People do the business in very different ways. We were always very research-oriented and had what you might want to call a

415

very analytical approach. There are other people with a very trading-oriented approach. We always studied deals and did a great deal of analytic work. There are other people who rely a good deal on what I would call a relatively cursory kind of research job and then trading on a sort of market feel. Some people like to speak to a lot of other arbitrage people, and some like to run their business themselves. We were very much in the latter category. We tended not to be terribly aware of what other arbs were doing, except when stocks started doing unusual things.

We always tried to think of all the things that could possibly go wrong with a deal and then tried to be very unemotional in weighing the risks to rewards and probabilities in making our judgments. We weren't plungers. We tried to be cool and hardheaded—not scared, though, because if you were scared, you couldn't function effectively.

A "mistake" in the arbitrage business is a complicated notion because obviously some percentage of your deals goes bad. I used to study every deal that went bad to try and learn something from it. Every time a deal broke up, I would take my yellow pad and write down the name of the deal. We kept all the details of the deals in our heads. And then I'd go back over it. And there were times when we made judgments that either we shouldn't have positions or, more likely, that the positions should be relatively small—and then it turned out to be a bonanza.

I was there at very good times. I think it would have been hard not to do at least reasonably well. I became a partner on January 1, 1971. It happened relatively quickly. It may have been a function of the times. The arbitrage business had done extremely well, and I was then the senior associate in the department. I'd better not discuss profitability. But some years it was good, some years it was okay, and some years it was better than good. It varied.

I don't think there was ever a time when we had the business to ourselves. In the late '60s it was very competitive. Then in the early '70s, the business became quite bad. There were far fewer deals. You had a vigorous antitrust enforcement based on very broad-ranging theories that have since withered away.

You can't measure the scale then versus the scale today. But there have been outstanding deals over the course of time. There was something called certificates of participation in the Penn Central bankruptcy. And we were able to buy them at some point in the teens and we wound up getting 100 cents on the dollar for them. Then there was something called Roan Selection Trust. It was a stock that was listed on the New York Stock Exchange and it was liquidating. You got about five or six different securities. You got cash. You got an American Metals warrant. You got a Zambian 6 percent bond and something called Botswana common stock. We didn't even know where Zambia was, so one of the fellows called the consulate and said, "Where are you?" And they said, "Fifty-seventh and Madison." And he said, "No, I mean where is the country?"

There were also some nice oil and real estate liquidations in the early days. It was a highly inflationary environment, and what would happen is that a company would announce that it was going to liquidate and you would take a position. And in between the time of the announcement of the deal and the time the liquidation was actually completed, since prices were generally going up, the values were greater than you originally anticipated. We made a lot of money. But then people began to anticipate lower values rather than higher values, and we just didn't sense it until it had been going on for quite a while. And over a broad number of positions, that cost us a lot of money. We had some big losses.

[Ivan] Boesky had a substantial impact because he raised the profile of the business and then trained a lot of people who went out and set up their own boutiques. He contributed to the enormous influx of money into the business. But I wouldn't say he was responsible for it, because the business was so profitable for a while that I think it would have attracted a lot of money no matter what.

Down cycles are not fun. Because when you're in a down cycle, you never know whether this is a down cycle or the beginning of the end. Anyway, 1973 and 1974 were two years of it. And that was a period when people wondered whether the Street was going to come back. But then we started the options business, and it was a good business.

The beginning of the options business was the beginning of the CBOE and the success of the options on equity securities in April

1973. It was the first time you ever had an option on the kinds of securities Wall Street traded. When that started to work, the various firms got these quantitative people because this really lent itself to quantitative analysis. The whole way the trading rooms on Wall Street are run has been enormously affected by the availability of options. I really think that if the CBOE had not been successful, there is a real chance that none of the rest of this would have happened.

I remember back before the CBOE opened, I went to Gus Levy to talk to him about options, and Gus said: "Well, you know, I don't know if this thing's ever going to work or not. All you've done is develop a new way to lose money." And I said, "No, it's going to be real." And we were very active in the early days in spreading the word.

The day before the CBOE started trading, Joe Sullivan [then head of the CBOE] called me and said: "Everything's all set. The only thing that bothers me is that I have a feeling we will be all ready to go with the gun and the pit and nobody will show up to trade." But the first day there was real trading, real activity, and it was the beginning of a bonanza because it happened at a time when the Street was doing very badly. So having that new product that really worked and generated a lot of activity was very important. It started at eight stocks and we tried to put the first trade on, but I don't think we did. I think somebody else did theirs. But I think the volume the first day was 900 contracts, which was super.

We really thought it added value. It created a new way of dealing with risks and rewards and a new and much more flexible way of adjusting the risk-reward parameters in your portfolio. It became central to managing risk on Wall Street. There had been options before, but no liquidity.

By the time the rest of it came along, Wall Street was tremendously receptive and had a lot of quantitative people who were oriented to this kind of thing, especially in the fixed-income area. It used to be that fixed income was a question of being long or short. Now a tremendous amount is basis risk, relationship risk. And I think that one of the problems on Wall Street today is that people in management positions don't have the quantitative framework to evaluate the work that underlies the conclusions they're being presented with. I can't ask a quantitative person how he got this conclusion, because when you start talking about his equations, they don't mean anything.

I think as long as there are risks, there will be losses. If the day ever comes when there are no risks, there will also be no profits.

Editor: Henny Sender

Dean LeBaron

Trustee BATTERYMARCH FINANCIAL MANAGEMENT

Batterymarch Financial Management is one of the investment industry's major success stories of the past twenty years. Dean Le-Baron, its founder and sole owner, is also among the industry's most outspoken and—as a leading contrarian—provocative figures. Before starting Batterymarch, LeBaron was an analyst at F.S. Moseley & Co., then research director and fund manager at Keystone Custodian Funds. Batterymarch has specialized in computer-driven portfolios structured around themes chosen by LeBaron and his staff; the firm was also a pioneer in indexing, which it has since dropped.

The period of the beginning of *Institutional Investor* magazine roughly marked the end of the individual investor and the rise of what your magazine is called. Institutions began to change the way in which investments are made. They became more quantitative. There was the whole notion of operating more efficiently in the investment process and the stress on asset allocation. As institutions became more quantitative, they got more academic help, more machines and a whole flock of stuff. Batterymarch was the beneficiary of that trend. We started at just that time, in 1969.

I think Batterymarch was the first to use a sort of artificial-intelligence system to mimic the way an institutional investor behaves. Our trading system, for example, is essentially the way a trader would operate, or at least the way I would instruct a trader to operate, and the system does so in a disciplined fashion. Our way of screening for stocks, our way of measuring values, is nothing more or less than the way we would do it if we were making each individual decision on our own. I'm saying I'm indifferent to one stock versus another as long as the value parameters, however you define them, meet our test. You use machines to identify the things that you want to own. You don't have to go out to visit the company as you were previously taught to do. With this system, this firm could run a lot more assets than it is currently running. This is a factory floor that is very unloaded.

I remember David Babson sitting at this desk and putting some screening parameters on the terminal behind him—quality, growth rates and so on—and pushing a button, and it took about fifteen seconds for the names to come up. He said, "My God, it looks like a Babson portfolio." I've done that with other friends who run portfolios with a highly disciplined approach.

And interestingly enough, it's about twenty years later, and I think institutional investors are now trying to make up for lost time. Institutions could have been more conscious of quantitative techniques. They could have operated more efficiently, moved larger amounts of money around with, maybe, fewer people, and faster and more flexibly. I mean, the things they are doing now in a fury they could have done ten years ago in a far more reasoned fashion.

Of course, Batterymarch had the advantage of starting out fresh at just the right time. Our first conception was to utilize academic research. It was there as a free resource that no one was using. Myron Scholes, Fischer Black, Bill Sharpe . . . the whole field of research was open to us. Practitioners wouldn't talk to them, and they were eager to talk to people in the so-called real world. You could have an R&D facility for the price of a subscription to the *Journal of Financial Economics*, and I like reading that stuff.

Academic research has become much more empirical now. It's not terribly surprising that in these last ten years academics are discovering anomalies. Ten years ago they were discovering efficiencies. And they haven't started explaining the anomalies yet; they are just saying they are there, so let's design a strategy to exploit them. The academics have gone to the brokerage houses.

We didn't know anything about computers, because when we started, in 1969, computers were too expensive to contemplate. I gave my first computer demonstration at an Institutional Investor conference in 1976 or '77. I took a computer, and I put it on the stage and turned it on while I talked. I let it clack, sort of like an old teletype, in the background. It added to the drama. I said that basically there's a fully functioning investment firm operating unattended. And people would look at me and look over there, because that was much more interesting than anything I was doing. And I let some people go up and play games with it and do some stock screening and so on. These are simple things now, but they weren't then.

We got into passive investing, indexing, because of Roger Murray. I think he was at Columbia or CREF at the time, but he visited Batterymarch in its earliest days, 1970 or '71, and we described our investment strategy of buying value stocks, and he said, "That's all very well and good, but what would you do with mega-billions of dollars?" I said I would buy a couple of thousand of each of these stocks. And he said, "You can't do that, because no committee is ever going to let you buy a couple of thousand of a value stock." So I said that, well, I'd just buy a scattershot of the market, a little bit of everything. I would index to whatever index I wanted. He thought that was a terrible idea, because he was a growth stock investor and he thought you should buy a collection of growth stocks.

Roger and I met in New York shortly after that and discussed it all. He was unable to convince me that it was a bad idea, and I checked with a few academics who thought it was a good idea, so we went ahead and did it. We did the first stuff by hand. We had rolls of calculator tape to calculate the number of shares in each of the little segments strung on a clothesline through the office—literally a clothesline; this was steel and that was computers, with a little tape wrapped around the papers as to what each was.

Roger and I became the debating team for active versus passive investment, and it was reasonably popular on the meeting circuit. But we got quite bored with the arguments. I think the last time we did it we even switched roles just to make it more interesting. You know, I'd heard his speech so often, I gave his and he gave mine.

Indexing shouldn't have been a jarring idea, because the investment strategy wasn't new. We just introduced S&P strategies to people who were already doing S&P strategies but not calling it that. Most large portfolios were closet indexing anyway. But it was clear at the first presentations that this was a jarring, radical new investment approach. There were three indexers then—Bill Fouse at Wells Fargo, Rex Sinquefield at American National Bank and ourselves, and we used to meet at conferences and talk things over—whether it was wise to index to the full index or to a sample and how to measure trading costs. We had constant arguments over whether you should index to the S&P 500, which all of us decided was not the thing to index to, because it was not, in the academic sense, an efficient portfolio. But it was the one that was the most popular.

I think we were the first firm that ever had a positive commission. We'd put out for bids on large baskets of securities, without describing the names of what we were buying or selling—just so many stocks, average daily trading volume and so forth. They were probably the first program trades, although we didn't know that that's what they were. And the bids would be pretty good because it was providing the brokers with merchandise, which, on the other side of the trade, would be more than paying for the trade. So we got down, pretty consistently, to bids of zero. Finally somebody said, "Well, how do I bid a strong zero?" And that was a positive commission. That was in the mid-'70s. Our clients got checks, some for very sizable amounts.

Early adherents of indexing were probably philosophical believers in the idea, and they are likely to stay there for a long time. Indexing is, I think, a very sensible strategy over a long sweep of time. But when people are doing it because they think it's going to perform better in any given year, it is something else. They are setting themselves up for a disappointment. Or when indexing in order to prove its quality has to track the index within one basis point month by month, you pay a high cost to do that. So I think some of the things that we started with—I won't say they've been twisted, but they are being exploited and are offering promises that are not capable of being kept.

The notion of contrarianness has been important to me since the earliest days of my career, some 25 years ago. I read some stuff by Humphrey Neal, who was a sort of Vermont ruminating contrarian who held meetings in the fall in Manchester. Mr. Johnson of Fidelity occasionally attended. The idea, primarily, was to avoid the crowd, that that's where the danger is. After 1969, for example, we didn't buy the growth stocks at 70 times earnings—and the arguments for growth stocks were exceedingly compelling.

In the summer of 1974, I went off to write a book. The market had gone down a lot. We were at a very slim level of business, and the question was the survival of the firm. I needed to address the question of whether our investment approach, of identifying value through quantitative techniques, was sound, and writing forces you to think in a little more disciplined way. I decided the approach made sense. So we might as well run it out. Run it right to the ground, if that's what it took.

Well, small stocks had a pretty dramatic turnaround. They started to outperform large stocks just about the time this introspection was taking place. And that caused a number of pension funds to think that they might be underdiversified in small stocks, and, through our activities in indexing, it was reasonably clear that we had the skills to handle large sums of money fairly efficiently, so we became a logical place to put that money.

We don't have a marketing department here, and the reason I haven't wanted one is that it would be too successful. I would become the victim of the marketing department. The department would come in and say, "We can sell a $500 million LBO fund," which they probably could, and I would say, "Oh, it's too late in the game," or "It would damage our reputation," or something. But the marketing department would be very effective at selling me to do something like that. If I hired the right people, they would succeed. They would drive the products, and they would drive me. And so my protection is to not have them.

We've been on a ten-year kick to drive down transaction costs, which in most cases clients haven't particularly cared too much about. In most institutions the portfolio manager has a degree of influence over trading. And clients like to use soft dollars to pay for services, and we make soft-dollar payments very difficult. We make a couple of things difficult. I knew our position on corporate governance issues would not make us very popular. You know, voting against your clients on key issues that are important to the survival of their jobs does not ensure client goodwill. And, certainly, telling some of our clients not to buy bonds hasn't made us very popular either.

We've always run a fully invested equity portfolio, and it seems strange to me—one of the great anomalies—that pension funds, which are a tax shelter for corporations, are run with less risk than

425

the corporate stream of earnings. Look at the typical fund's mix of 60 percent equities and 40 percent bonds. I don't think bonds are terribly useful. You wouldn't find bonds being bought by the company. If I offered you two pots of money that you could make money in, and one is going to be taxed and the other is not, I would think you would put the high-risk, high-return investments in the tax-free pot.

But eventually, the pension fund will be seen as a part of total corporate activities that should be run very aggressively—probably when things go bad. That's when changes happen. Management will say: "My God, were we really doing that? You mean to say we have portfolio insurance that means we bought stocks when they were up and sold them when they went down? Are you really telling me, Mr. Pension Officer, that that's what we were doing?"

I've worked in a couple of organizations, and I knew the kind of environment I liked. I've always wanted it more informal—the open office environment. So before we moved into this office and went to an office design place, I sketched out on the back of an envelope how the office should be designed. The design fellow put me in my place. He said, "Mr. LeBaron, you've never built an office before?" And I said no. He said what you do is, you start out by making a survey of your employees and then incorporate what they want into an environmental plan. It was such a put-down. And they came and talked to everybody and somebody wanted French provincial furniture with a southwest view, and somebody else wanted two windows and somebody else wanted three and so on. And they came back with a design that incorporated all of these things, with a massive office for me in the corner and all the systems managers squeezed into a tiny cubbyhole in the back with no light and no view. I thought it was awful. I pulled out my grubby little envelope again and said this is what I want. Well, they said, maybe we can do that. So we did.

I am sometimes criticized for concentrating the ownership in a single person, but that's the only way you keep it simple. Otherwise, you have people all over the place wanting to have an input into policy, complicating it. I've been approached 30 or 50 times or whatever to sell the firm, but I've never been tempted. Now, in firms where there's broad ownership, it's a very, very compelling thing, and it's very hard for somebody who doesn't want to sell to say to somebody else who has ownership, I'm going to keep you from selling. Here it's easier, because there is nobody else to say that I am keeping them from doing that. If they want to do it, they go someplace else.

All of us complicate things. I remember, five years or so ago, a fairly major company had been running its pension fund for years with almost all equities—80 or 90 percent—at a few large banks. And we all know that they were out of step. So they were visited by a consultant, who was looking for some business, and the consultant asked the pension officer if the chairman of the board knew that the officer was responsible for more assets than the chairman was. To which the pension officer replied, "The chairman doesn't even know my name." The consultant then asked a few people to come in and talk to the chairman about how important the pension fund was and about the new things going on in the field of investments, and I was one of those people. And so it was designed that the pension officer should have some venture capital, some oil and gas, and some overseas and derivative securities, and bonds, of course, and equities of defined types—all in a very complex structure. I was apparently there by mistake, because I said, "Leave things alone; you're doing fine." But they didn't do that. They ended up hiring six people for the pension department, promoting the pension officer to vice president and hiring the consultant, of course. And results went down. The last I heard, the pension officer was promoted again, moved up to a higher position because he needed more people to fix the problem.

I did fairly well compared to the group of people around me at the Harvard Business School, and presumably they were a select group, so I thought I'd probably earn a reasonably good living. I had no particular desire then, nor do I now, to leave a large memorial estate. I thought I'd make more rather than less, but it's not of a terribly high order, and there was no particular target; nor is there now. I mean, there's no target that I must make more money this year than last or that it's got to go up by X amount. I'm assuming that something of what I earn is the equivalent of a return on capital for the early days, for having done an entrepreneurial thing that worked out reasonably well.

**Editors: Everett Mattlin
and Cary Reich**

Howard Stein

Chairman DREYFUS CORP.

Howard Stein's career at Dreyfus Corp. spans some 30 years, many of them spent as manager of its flagship mutual fund. In 1965 he became president and CEO of the company and chairman a few years later, upon the retirement of its pioneering founder, Jack Dreyfus. The company, which went public in 1965, currently has assets under management of some $40 billion.

I was born lucky, but I guess I knew what to do with it. Luck doesn't mean that you don't have bad times, but even in the worst of times, something good comes out.

The worst of times for me personally, I guess, was a little more than a year ago, when I had open-heart surgery. But for the business, that wasn't a tough time; on the contrary, we raised equity in the corporation. People were on the street corner giving money away, so we took some.

The worst period for me in the business was the early '70s. At the end of 1967 I took a leave of absence to be finance chairman of Eugene McCarthy's presidential campaign because during the preceding years I began to feel rather concerned about various issues outside the world of stocks—the Vietnam War and the guns-and-butter issue that led to so much turmoil and, ultimately, the inflation that developed during the '70s.

I was away until 1969, but even when I came back, though I remained as chairman, I really delegated management of the business until late 1973. It just wasn't a period I felt comfortable with. I didn't want to get involved with letter stock and the other go-go investments of the day and later the Nifty Fifty. But it was difficult because people would say, "You should have this fund and you should have that fund, and why don't you come back to work?" You'd constantly be hearing about all the money that was flowing through these various funds and how we were falling behind and losing market share and all the other phrases that go with it. But I just felt that it was not the appropriate posture for us. Things did develop somewhat: the Leverage Fund was a little tiny step we took in the direction of the mood of that time. But it was another bit of luck that we weren't dragged into it more.

Being off with the campaign in 1967–68 taught me a lot. You're on a different stage, with power and trappings. Even though it was a lost effort, that can change a person pretty drastically. I can imagine what happens when you win. In the office we lead a very sheltered, insular life. You know, you're used to being with your Standard & Poor's and Moody's reports, and you talk to a few people here and there and watch the tape all day. You never wander out into the world.

And then suddenly you're out in Indiana and you've never been to Indiana before. You get to know what people are. They're not very knowledgeable about investing. They're caught up with what's on the front page of their newspaper, and for something to be there, it has to be pretty far advanced along the greed curve. I became more value-oriented and felt that we had to protect investors, that you cannot always provide the most popular vehicle at the time that they want it.

I came back in late 1973 because the go-go era was over, and then with Watergate and the market decline, things became more difficult. Our stock hit a low of 3¾. My own holdings in the company were underwater, so I had to put up other assets. But I didn't sell any of our stock then. It's down and you don't know whether it will resurrect itself. But you're an insider and a principal, and if things are not going well, you just really shouldn't be selling the stock.

I didn't notice any very aggressive runs on the company when the stock was at that level, when it was 3¾. Nobody wanted it. The only one that showed up as an interested buyer was when the stock was around 16—after splits, that's equivalent to about 75 cents today. The Scottish Edinburgh Trust bought shares and finally went up to a 7 percent position. They said they bought it really off the Standard & Poor's manual; they looked at the earnings and looked at the book value, and they just thought it looked like a very interesting investment. It's been one of the greatest investments they ever made. They sold some, down until they're a touch under 5 percent.

From time to time, people have shown up to try to acquire us. I talk to them for a while, and then basically I tell them to forget it. To work well in this business, I don't think that it's good to be part of some structure, because it inhibits managers' freedom. I don't know of any that have been part of structures that have done particularly well. It's not the kind of business that lends itself to that.

And it's very hard to take over a fund management company without the cooperation of its present management, because the buyer has to get approval of the shareholders of all the funds for a change of contract. And there's always the temptation, since we all enjoy our freedom in this business, to go to the shareholders and say, "Well, either you like the old management or whoever this new person might be, so here's the choice." And if you haven't mistreated them, why should the shareholders vote you out?

What brought people to the office was the cash on the books. We operate very lean here; we have no debt and few obligations beyond our lease. For many years the fund sold around its book value, which was its cash value. So it represented a pretty good vehicle. It's also always made sense to insurance companies or others that might have losses, because we pay full tax, so they'd be buying us for half price, in effect.

So there were many times when Dreyfus was appealing to different groups of people. But if someone buys the company, and the managers walk, and the shareholders decide to keep the old managers and the new people don't have the contracts, then *all* they buy is the cash, and they may have paid three or four times cash. So it really doesn't make much sense for a raider type.

The first effort I made when I came back was to develop Dreyfus Liquid Assets [the second money market fund and the first to be advertised to the general public], which was the height of a conservative approach and gave investors a better yield than the banks. We brought out the fund no-load in 1974, and that was a tough decision for us, because everything had been load up to

431

then. We started to run some ads and found that people were answering. And we sent out a few letters. We found that people were responding. So we sent out a few more and a few more. We knew the time was right. The program was right for people. And it just goes from there.

If we had stayed with a load for that fund, there would not be a money market industry, because it would not have brought people out of the banks, where they're used to putting in a dollar and getting a dollar back. We went a step further in bringing the first tax-exempt income fund to investors in 1976. That was sort of an outgrowth of my experience in the presidential campaign in that we had to lobby in order to get legislation allowing the pass-through of tax benefits. We hired a single-issue lobbyist, and I knew it would benefit the cities and states, so we gathered the support of mayors and governors. All that wouldn't have occurred before my involvement in the campaign, because we wouldn't have known how to proceed.

Nineteen seventy-six to 1982 were good years; we just rolled along. The business was a normal, growing business. Liquid Assets was building up to the crescendo of '82, '83, when the banks got the power to have money market accounts. At that point, I became curious about the other side of the ledger, whether we could charge people less for their borrowings than other banks. So we acquired a small bank in New Jersey and renamed it the Dreyfus Consumer Bank in early 1983.

It's always easier for me when I'm doing something with no competition around—for instance, buying a bank in East Orange, New Jersey, for a couple of hundred thousand dollars over and above the capital. If it turned out to be a failure, no one would care, no one would see it. By contrast, when you're in a crowded arena, everybody is taking a piece of whatever you have. The best you can do then is just hold your own and wait for the competition to expire and be in a sound position to pick up the pieces.

Our bank came out with a gold credit card charging 16.9 percent interest, and there were very few if any others in the country at 16.9, I think. It's now 15.9 percent. And we offered mortgages with less up-front cost: 175 basis points versus the industry average, which is about 300. And the other costs, like legal fees, are

432

scaled down so that there is an initial saving. With credit cards and mortgages, you've got most of the lending people could want. It worked out; earnings went from $247,000 to $6.8 million in three years. So we're doing something that is not in the mainstream of the mutual fund industry at the moment. With consumer lending powers, this may become a very, very interesting area for us.

We're also working with other banks, but in our traditional business, offering funds. Here we're using a 12(b)1 charge, which makes possible our introduction to the mass market that's available through the banking community—the nonreaders of *The Wall Street Journal* and the Sunday *Times*. Everybody watches television, but it's too expensive to advertise in that medium. The theory was that since most people do go into a bank, let's make things available there. We have investor centers developing in, or funds available through, Manufacturers, Chase, the Bank of New York, First Chicago, Security Pacific and hundreds of other banks. We're really working together in the development of the business. This is still at an early stage. And we are selling some new funds with a 3 to 4½ percent load through the broker-dealer community.

We also own two insurance companies, but we're not doing anything. We sold a product called Rainbow [an annuity wrapped around a money fund], but the regulations governing wraparounds changed, so we stopped what was a very good program for people. We also tried to sell a universal policy, but we found that it was very difficult to sell insurance by the no-load route—on the phone or through the mail.

To sell no-load, you have to have something that the customer recognizes by comparison is a better product, so that they come to *you*. However, we have found that it's very difficult for people to recognize a better insurance product. It's also very difficult for them to undo the insurance they already have. They take your product idea to their cousin who sold them their existing policy and say, "Look what we have here," and he comes back with every excuse possible, or he'll give them something else. All of which means that in order to make that product go, you have to put a sales load and other expenses on top of it, and we see no reason to go into that very expensive arena. We will do so only if we can bring out a product with a discernible difference.

I think there are lessons for today in that difficult, early-'70s period—namely, if there's a problem arising in the markets but there is money available that wants to go to work, it will override the problem and prolong the condition. Going back to the Nifty Fifty, the pension funds had a flow of money and were going into common stock with a larger percentage of it than ever before, so they just went ahead—on the belief that the earnings would always bail them out, no matter what they paid for a stock.

And I think you have a very similar situation today, where the money is available, so that 80 times earnings for the average stock in Japan is just fine. It's not fine for me, but it is for them. Excess money was created during the guns-and-butter inflation of the '60s and '70s. A lot of money was printed in that period that has not been totally destroyed. Some of it was loaned to South America, which is not coming back, so that's part of the destruction, but there is still a lot left over. It's being spread around the world and not used for manufacturing purposes, so it's taking stock markets to new heights. If it *did* go into manufacturing, that would be good for the economies but might be bad for the markets. I don't know quite what's happening now, except the money that was printed is probably building excesses, and there may be a day when those excesses will be washed out.

In the meantime, it can be very frustrating, because the trend that you think shouldn't continue goes on because of the availability of money to fuel it. Meanwhile, people like Warren Buffett and Larry Tisch, I believe, have abdicated the market because they feel it is not an attractive place. But it keeps going up nevertheless, and I'm sure they are climbing the same wall as I am. On the other hand, all during this period they're making money because they have things they won't or can't sell, like Larry Tisch has Loews. And that's again a person who has luck and who knows what to do with it.

During such periods of frustration, we may be starting something quietly in the basement while others are off in the wild blue. We've got something just out of the basement now: the consumer bank.

Another thing that worries me is that there are fewer standards than before. The mood piece of this era, created by the Reagan administration, is deregulation, which in the financial community

434

brings with it a sense of greatly lessened surveillance. We need more regulation, not less. If you had old-time surveillance, the conditions about which we are all reading in the papers would not come up in our industry. When you see there's a red light and you know there's a police car standing around the corner, you stop. But if you know there's no police car and you don't want to stop, you just go through. And that's, I think, what has happened.

I think we're getting out of this administration the same things that went into it. Early in Reagan's tenure I read an article about something called Citizens for Reagan. From the article it seemed a reasonably good idea to participate. So I went down to Washington to see the people who were heading it up, and I was struck by the lack of morality in their ethics and purposes. And now you see the results. If the administration can't tell the difference between right and wrong in Iran, how do you expect them to give the SEC enough funds, for instance, to quickly study and resolve the issue of how a fund yield should be stated? This is a current problem in our industry, where yields on bond funds are reported many different ways. The SEC is just beginning to grapple with this problem. They *are* trying, but the point is that this trying has been going on a long time—maybe a year—and all during this period people have been buying primarily yield securities. If you had the old surveillance standards, an issue like this would have been resolved much more quickly.

One of my good friends until he died in 1976 was [Goldman Sachs senior partner] Gus Levy. You sort of kind of miss talking to Gus. God, what would Gus make of all this *mishegas?* Obviously, he would be deeply hurt to think that it might have happened in his place. Of course, we don't know yet whether it did. But I don't think that it *could* have happened in Gus's day. It's not so much what Gus would have done to make a difference, though he set a standard that was in keeping with the time. But right above Gus's halo there was a regulatory environment under which people operated. People in this business are the brightest and most imaginative—they have to be in order to gather capital around the world and invest it in areas that are productive. They're always pressing against the wall, trying to move it. It shouldn't move.

Recently, our stock hit a high of 45. It's split so many times that the 1974 low of 3¾ is equal to 20 cents based on the current price. As a large shareholder, obviously I'm doing okay. But you ask me how much money I think is enough and the answer is "$12.16." I never really paid much attention to money for the sake of it. Things always work out somehow. I told you I was born lucky and I guess I know what to do with it.

Editor: Heidi S. Fiske

Dan Dorfman

Wall Street Columnist

For more than two decades, columnist Dan Dorfman has been the journalist many Wall Streeters and corporate leaders have loved to hate. Starting with the "Heard on the Street" stock market column in *The Wall Street Journal* (1967–1973), where his often controversial disclosures began to have a market impact, he has wielded his pen for *Wall Street Letter, New York* magazine and *Esquire,* and now is a columnist for *USA Today* as well as a frequent television commentator.

When I started to write in 1967, it was the era of dart throwing, when you could do no wrong. All these go-go players had come out of the woods. And you had Charlie Bluhdorn [then CEO of Gulf & Western] and Jimmy Ling of LTV fame. It was the era of the conglomerate. You know, buy whatever you have to buy to get the price of the stock up. That was the name of the game. Just buy anything, whether it fit or not. It was an era of the development of worthless paper.

In terms of reporting, though, it was a great time. You'd meet some guy who was struggling, and then you'd meet him six months later and suddenly he's worth $80 million, $100 million, $200 million. It was almost unbelievable.

And I liked some of these guys. I remember Meshulam Riklis of Rapid-American Corp. We had a good relationship—until I began to write about him. I liked Charlie Bluhdorn, too, the guy who built Gulf & Western. I had a real feeling for him. But I remember once I went up to lunch with him and Clay Felker

437

[former editor of *New York* magazine], and Bluhdorn was furious about something I'd written. He had this great grin on his face and this tough accent. We were standing by a window on the 40th floor of the building, looking down at Madison Square Garden, and Bluhdorn says, "I feel like cutting your goddamn throat. I'd like to throw you out of this——ing place!" I'll never forget it.

Anyone who wrote "Heard on the Street" automatically had access to great power. You wrote a negative story, and by and large the stock would go down. You wrote favorably, it went up. Not all the time, but more often than not. Of course, the market environment had a fair amount to do with it. But the significance of your revelation was important. Were you saying something that everybody knew? Or were you finding out something that only a relatively small number knew? If you did that, you had a pretty powerful impact on the stock.

People would come to you with stories—institutional investors, private investors, real estate people who played the stock market. More often than not, they'd come with favorable stories. But if you have a reputation for calling a rat a rat—not a rodent— people have a tendency to come to you with negative stories. I welcome both sides. Probably the best thing I did when I was at the *Journal* was exposing a lot of the bullshit in stocks.

I also gave access to the column to the minds of people who had never before been quoted in their lives. All they did was make money. They were very smart, sophisticated. I think of people like Robert Wilson, Michael Steinhardt, Jimmy Rogers, George Soros. I'm not saying they were unknown, but they were known only in the Wall Street community and there is a limited number of people. New York is not the United States.

When someone did approach me, I felt that if they owned a stock or were short it, that took on more significance, because it meant that they were putting their money where their mouth was. I didn't differentiate if somebody had an ax to grind. I assumed they *all* had axes to grind. I'd always check and double-check. And sometimes the reactions I'd get would be very chilly. Some companies got irate. Meshulam Riklis got irate.

I remember I questioned his salary. He was making some out-landish sum—$700,000 or so in 1960s dollars. I felt his stockholders were going from riches to rags while he went the other way. I thought his house was bugged, so I insisted we meet in a coffee shop. It was wild. I said, "So what makes you worth so much money?"—remember, I knew the guy well—and he started to bang his fist on the table. He's banging his fist and screaming out, "I'm worth $700,000. I'm worth it. Who built this company? Me!" He's screaming.

We get up to leave—and he has no money. To pay the check, he has no money. We're in some hotel at 55th Street and Seventh Avenue and he says to the waitress, "Do you know who Larry Tisch is?" The woman doesn't know Larry Tisch from Adam. So he's ready to give a credit card and she says, "It's a coffee shop, sir. We don't take credit cards." So he says, "Danny boy, could you lend me $10?" So I lent him $10 and I had to wait like two winters to get it back. I had to write him twice. And I wrote a very negative story, and he never talked to me again.

I frequently get hostile reactions. If I serve any purpose whatsoever, it's that I don't accept at face value the views of corporate management. They're always trying to promote. What else is corporate America there for except to paint a sunny picture? You know, it never rains. That wasn't my thinking. And I got a lot of flak. One reason was that the general run of financial reporters at the time were writing essentially bullish stories. There were exceptions. Alan Abelson [of *Barron's*] was an exception. But most reporters were writing stories about companies that went up dramatically and had no earnings, no substance to support their stock prices. These reporters brought sunshine. They were hot air. And investors were being enticed in, and when someone began to sell, the stocks would collapse.

There was just something about the atmosphere of those years [the late 1960s]. A hunger to believe. Greed on greed. Greed is what Wall Street is always about and people *wanted* to believe, and the operators fed out this stuff and the public got sucked in and got butchered. There are people today who will never be in the market because of what happened in '69 and '70 through '73 or '74. Once the confidence began to diminish, people began to dump stocks and found out that they were hitting air pockets.

Reporters were less skeptical then. I remember I used to call *Business Week* "Bull Week." It's much better now, but I remember one time when Polaroid had run up into the hundreds, then tanked out to $27 or $28, and *Business Week*, in its infinite wisdom, had discovered that there was something wrong. Where were they at $100?

When people were bearish, I wanted to look for the sunshine. I would take a look at the stocks that had hit new lows. Maybe there were legitimate reasons. But maybe, just maybe, there was among the new lows a Chrysler, a reason to believe, a reason for hope. I looked at that. I didn't want to be like everybody else, but I didn't buck the crowd just for its own sake. I just didn't want to be a carbon copy. That's the point in journalism.

Financial journalism is better now, but I still see a lack of digging in many publications, a lack of going beyond a yes or a no, an inability by reporters to get off their duffs.

There was a lot of crap around in the 1960s, a lot of touting—and it's back right now. I just think you're doing a great service if you save one investor from buying one bad share. Then it's worth getting up in the morning and going to work. You've achieved something. You write for someone who buys and sells stocks. And you've got a goddamn obligation not to write a puff piece. But I don't want you to think I do only negative stories. I do a lot of positive stories. No one ever remembers the Dan Dorfman who writes positive stories. There's always the Dan Dorfman with the knife, the ax. No one ever looks at the reporting I do. I'm really not the devil. I don't lead a wild life. I just believe a financial reporter has an obligation, and the problem is a lot of them don't understand it. I mean, they call analysts time and again—some of whom have been absolute disasters.

In my view, financial journalism means working at it. Working at it. You can't do that 9:00 to 5:00. I guess if you're a banker, you work 9:00 to 5:00. I'm 55 now. Maybe I don't run as fast as I used to, but my mind is attuned to hearing. I listen better. And when I do a story from a guy who's short a stock, I say so.

That's important because the public is becoming more sophisticated. You go to a party now, and people are talking about interest rates. People are aware of money. I mean, they've always been aware, but now they're aware that you can make it, that there are ways of keeping ahead of your neighbor by being a little smarter.

But there are tremendous risks for the small investor. Nobody cares about him. He's a misfit. I'm a broker, you come to me and I ask, "How much money do you want to invest?" If you say "$1,600," you become almost a nonentity. The average investor—unless he's someone who can spend the time, do the homework, look up the Standard & Poor's reports and the Value Line reports, talk to a broker, get research—how is he going to compete against the likes of Morgan Guaranty? Who has access to management? Who gets the best information first? The real answer is, the small investor can't compete. That's why he should probably go with a mutual fund.

Then there's the matter of sharp practices by market insiders. Wall Street isn't a street of ethics, but that doesn't mean everybody is a crook. That means everybody's trying to get an edge on everybody else. Those pressures never end, they only intensify. What about when five or six people get together and push up the price of a stock? Is that ethical? To me, that's just as bad as trading on inside information.

There are stocks in the 20s and 30s over the counter that have no earnings, mundane businesses and a couple of investors keeping their price up and squeezing the shorts. It's treacherous to be short in this kind of environment. I remember the way the shorts used to come running to me years ago, saying, "We're getting killed." What could I do? I'm not their psychiatrist.

One time when I was writing the column, two fellows from a bank suggested to me going into something they called "new business." They approached me and said, "Look, why don't we set up a separate account for you?" They were going to put in $25,000. I think I was earning $22,000 a year at the time. They asked me to advise them in advance what I was going to do in the column. And I said, "You don't have to pay for it, it's free." I said, "If it's okay with the *Journal*, it's okay with me." That was the end of that.

As a financial journalist, you've got to divorce yourself from these temptations. How can you be a financial journalist commenting about other people and companies when you have an ax to grind in the situation? This may sound corny, but money never motivated me. I only want to be a reporter. I'll be pleased if, when I die, they put on my tombstone, "Here lies Dan Dorfman, a reporter who cared." Because I do care. I could be just like a lot

441

of other reporters: go interview someone, don't think, don't do the analysis. The time I spend, I dig and dig and dig and ask and ask and ask.

Still, as I look back over the years, I look at my lack of sophistication. Times when I courted analysts who weren't the best. Times when I gave access to the column to people whom I shouldn't have. And I've learned that you have to be very careful with SEC investigations. I remember stories I wrote when I was young about the SEC looking into this or that. I mean, the stories were accurate, mind you, but I have some remorse and anger at myself that I didn't know better.

On the other hand, I'm a reporter, not a market expert. I'm sorry to admit that I finally became bullish about this market at about 1,500. I recognized that the Federal Reserve is now committed to a policy of bailing out the world. Print and print and bail out the world. That policy hasn't changed. Brazil is the latest example of why it continues. You have to have an overall point of view. And my point of view is that the market can go still higher if people can still believe. Maybe it's time to be concerned when the foreigners come in. Foreigners are coming into this market like crazy. Foreign buying is hitting records.

But I'm not a big stock market player myself. I wish I were better. My problem is that my best information is information I hear and then report. I get super information, but I never buy those stocks. If I buy a stock, I rarely, if ever, talk to management, but if I do buy, it's at least six months since I talked to the company. And I never sell short.

Why do stocks go down $10, $15 in a day? Because expectations were too rosy. And how did they get so rosy without some members of the press noticing on the way up, "Hey, what's going on here?" That's one of the things I like to do. I know it helps the average guy on the street to get a better shake. You've got to raise questions in this business. A lot of people still write like they are working for public relations agencies. That's also why stocks can go to 40 and 50 and 60 with nothing behind them but hot air. You need a very sharp, objective pencil.

If you're going to give someone access to the world in print or on TV, and let him tell what stocks he thinks everyone should be buying or selling, you have an obligation to give his track record. People are gullible and, when they hear someone talking about buying stock, they want to make a fast buck. I get lots of letters

442

from people who say they watch me, and I tell them to go out and do their homework about whether something does or does not make sense. At the same time, I think that over the years a lot of journalists have not taken the time to do the homework *they* should have done for their readers.

As for the regulators, where was the SEC and the Big Board when all these takeover stocks were running up and people were profiting like crazy? I could show you long lists of stocks that ran up dramatically before bids. Where were the regulators then? They were nowhere to be seen. Suddenly, a letter comes in [implicating Dennis Levine on insider trading] and they're heroes. I was incensed. I mean, I broke the story that the SEC was investigating Boesky. I was incensed that they allowed him to sell his stock. That was outrageous. And anyone who thinks the Boesky scandal is really going to change things must believe in the tooth fairy.

I make it my business to know as many new people with access to information, whether they can be quoted or not, as I can. If a reader gets one idea a year from me, I've succeeded. That makes it worthwhile getting up at 6:00 or 6:30 and going to bed at 1:00 A.M. I go to places to meet sources who never want to be seen with me. I mean, some people will go out in midtown. Others want to go to Little Italy. I have one guy I see two or three times a year that I wind up going to Brooklyn with because he doesn't want to run into anybody on Wall Street.

I've had problems with newspapers, too. One of them, for example, dropped my column because I wrote a negative article about Digital Equipment when there was a flood of insider selling. There were like 23 sellers and no buyers, and guess what? The earnings collapsed, and these people saved themselves millions of dollars. It cost me a column, and it soured me on that paper. I called a reporter there, and he told me they dropped the column because they weren't happy with the Digital story. That's for the birds. If they dropped the column because it was dull or wrong, that's legitimate. But to drop a column for breaking news—that's disgraceful.

I love breaking news stories. You're talking orgasm. I feel terrific. I love it. I love being first, love it. I relish it. I can't do it all the time, but I do it often enough. And when I do, I'm as excited about my job as I was when I started.

I don't want to be predictable. I just want to have a reason for being. And I *have* a reason for being. I believe I understand what people want to read. I gear my writing to my audience. I want to give them a chance for an even shake, to level the playing field. That's my intent in journalism. That's what it's always been, and it's never going to change. I'm going to have lots of problems along the way because I'm going to write stories that will infuriate people, will get people to complain to my paper. That's never going to stop. When that stops, then I've stopped writing.

Editor: Lenny Glynn

Jesús Silva Herzog

Former Finance Minister MEXICO

Jesús Silva Herzog, Mexico's former finance minister, was at the center of some of the most tumultuous events in finance in the last twenty years. While he was finance minister for two Mexican presidents, his country took a nose dive from the high-rolling oil boom days to the red ink that ushered in Mexico's debt crisis and economic austerity. Silva Herzog himself took a roller-coaster ride, gaining renown in financial circles for his leadership in negotiations with international bankers and then abruptly resigning in mid-1986, a victim of the political turmoil unleashed by Mexico's latest—and worst—debt crisis.

I became minister of finance in the first months of 1982, just when perhaps the most serious crisis experienced by Mexico since 1920 began. One of the most outstanding aspects of this Mexican crisis, which is a Latin American crisis, was the problem of debt. It doesn't cease being ironic that it was up to me to handle the debt crisis, since in my personal life I have never liked owing one centavo; I don't like having personal debts, and I hardly use a credit card. I prefer paying cash.

What became known as the beginning of the debt crisis took place Friday, the twentieth of August of 1982, when we called a meeting of the most prominent representatives of international banking in the building of the Federal Reserve Bank of New York. That morning there were about 180 people, representatives of the world's banks, to whom we said Mexico did not have sufficient resources to continue paying the service on its foreign debt. That day Mexico had a little more than $180 million in liquid

445

reserves, and the following Monday, August 23, we had to make payments of almost $300 million to international banks.

We had faced very serious problems for several months. In February 1982 we had devalued the peso after suffering, in the second half of 1981, an increase in interest rates, a fall in prices of our exports and an enormous and dramatic flight of capital—the product of uncertainty in Mexico, an overvalued exchange rate and a lack of confidence. Several weeks later we made an adjustment of salaries throughout the country that sent the signal that the adjustment needed after a devaluation was not going to be sufficiently strong. And capital flight continued and accelerated, probably worsening during June and July of 1982. Those were truly dramatic moments, in which the financial authorities felt a great impotence to prevent or detain capital flight. We took some compensatory measures to restore confidence, but the crisis was such that we could not detain capital flight. There were times when Mexico lost $200 and $300 million in a single day.

We carried out various emergency measures, among them a support of $700 million from the Federal Reserve Bank of New York, which was nearly used up in a week. We signed the last "jumbo" credit, headed by Bank of America, in June of 1982 for $2.5 billion. That was also used up after a few days.

So there was no alternative, and it was one of those decisions that are relatively easy, since there was no other way to resolve the problem. It was up to me to tell the bankers that we lacked resources to continue servicing the debt. It was a rare privilege, a moment that I will probably not forget the rest of my life, because at that moment we were, I think, determining an important phase in the life of the world.

We spoke, of course, first with the authorities of the U.S. government, and with the authorities of the international financial organizations. I had to call personally the principal directors of the major banks of the world. The problem was that it was August, and the Europeans especially are hard to find during the month of August. I found one playing at his recreation spot, another returning from a trip on a yacht. I was trying to talk with them and reach a consensus about what would be the best way out of a situation that had no alternative.

We felt we needed new conditions of repayment periods to be able to continue meeting our financial obligations. The impact brought about by our meeting with the bankers was very perceptible. That first day, the stocks of the principal banks of New York fell on the New York Stock Exchange. Here in Mexico people talked of a possible collapse of the international financial system, of a run on the principal banks of the U.S. and a domino effect throughout Latin America.

The problem that arose on the twentieth of August was a surprise for the great majority of participants in the international financial market. Neither the high officials of the governments of the industrial countries, nor the most prominent bankers nor the less sophisticated bankers, and least of all the financial academics, foresaw the debt crisis. I don't think any one of us attending the August 20 meeting realized the consequences of what was happening in those moments. We knew, of course, that it was a delicate, important, far-reaching moment, but we never thought—at least I did not think—that it would begin the so-called debt crisis in the developing world.

A difficult moment occurred when we negotiated with the U.S. government [August 12, 1982] a series of support mechanisms for getting out of the crisis. We negotiated for three days. One Saturday, for example, at 4:00 in the morning, and on the following day, Sunday, when we were in the final parts of the negotiation, I had to decide to reject the offer the U.S. government made us. I consulted with the [Mexican] president, and he ordered me to return at once to Mexico. Those were moments, or hours, in which I felt deep emotions and a great responsibility; on the following day the history of the world would probably change, since Mexico was probably going to declare a global moratorium on all its external payments. When I was on the verge of getting on the government plane to return to Mexico, the U.S. Treasury secretary got in touch with me to say that they accepted the Mexican proposal. That allowed us to renew the talks. Those were especially dramatic moments, which, fortunately, I could handle well because I like to practice sports early in the morning.

In that week of August 1982, we saw an effort of international cooperation without precedent. In the case of Mexico and in the cases of Brazil and Argentina, it was possible to mobilize in relatively short periods of time the treasuries, the finance ministries and the central banks of the principal countries of the world, the

447

international organizations and the debtor countries. And I think everyone played a very outstanding role and that it has been extraordinarily positive. If any one of the members of this troupe of actors had performed in a nonresponsible way and had not played his role, we would at this time be talking of other things and living in a very different world.

We erred—the debtors as much as the creditors—in interpreting the essence of the debt problem. At that moment, August 20, 1982, we in the debtor nations and equally the creditor nations and the international organizations thought it was a liquidity problem. In other words, we believed that it was a short-term problem that would be resolved through restructuring the existing debt, obtaining new resources and adopting internal austerity measures in each of the debtor countries. As finance minister, I myself made a public statement upon my return to Mexico—which was often repeated—pointing out that we were facing a cash-flow problem. I was wrong; five years later, no one speaks of the debt as a liquidity problem. Rather, it is a deeper problem of a more structural nature and tied more to the basic economic problems of debtor countries and to international economic relations in general.

Shortly thereafter, the World Bank and International Monetary Fund met in Toronto in September 1982. Mexico had just nationalized the banks, imposed exchange controls and, a few days before, declared the moratorium on principal payments of the debt. As Mexico's finance minister, I was one of the most sought-after people at Toronto. I had more than 100 requests for press interviews, and I did not give a single one. One of the finance ministers of one of the important European countries, upon learning that I was in Toronto, that we had just declared the moratorium, that we had nationalized the banks and imposed exchange controls, that the director of the Banco de México [the central bank] had been changed, asked me, when we began an interview, "Are you the right man to talk to?" I responded that I understood his question, but that if I were not there, imagine with whom he would be talking. So he understood the sense of my reply, and we were able to have a constructive, amiable dialogue.

In the first exercises of restructuring and obtaining new money within what is now called forced lending or involuntary lending, it also fell to Mexico to be a pioneer. At that stage, nobody knew what path to take. The banks, at first, behaved with a high degree of myopia, thinking that the risk of a restructuring was greater than that of a normal operation and that, consequently, they had to increase the spreads and commissions—that is to say, to make more expensive, more onerous the servicing of the previously contracted debt. We debtors understood this reasoning, although we considered it unjust. As the years have gone by, that attitude of myopia has changed gradually, and we now have interest rates, commissions and spreads lower than they were before the beginning of the debt crisis.

It was necessary to break many clichés. The first restructurings were for only two years in the case of Mexico. Brazil committed the error of going to a restructuring of only one year, and before finishing the exercise, the year was ending. Mexico was a little more advanced, and we went to a first restructuring that covered all the maturities of our debt from August of 1982 to December of 1984.

As time passed, we have increasingly realized that the basic problem is not the debt principal; it makes little difference if the period for paying the principal is ten years, twelve, fifteen or twenty. The current debt problem is servicing the interest of the foreign debt, and rates have remained high.

The subsequent restructurings—the famous "multiyear restructuring arrangements," the "MYRAs"—were a bit more audacious. We signed MYRAs that six months prior to the signing had been completely rejected by the financial community as utopian schemes. If something is considered utopian in December, and it is signed in June or July, that means we are confronting a very dynamic environment with a remarkable velocity of change.

There has been speculation that I was favoring a moratorium last year. A few days before my resignation in June last year, I did tell correspondents of the Associated Press that we had not discarded the possibility of a moratorium. There are occasions when one needs to use distinct instruments for negotiation. When I was finance minister in the middle of last year, I felt the need to adopt a harder position regarding the debt. The country had suffered a loss of $8 billion, and we could not continue paying what we had to pay, and it was necessary to find other routes. We were heading toward a situation in which we were going to be left without reserves. And before getting to that extreme, it was necessary to seek, in the best negotiating environment, the temporary suspension of interest payments on the debt.

I had not recommended the moratorium except as a negotiating tool, a card of last resort. However, that was a personal expression of mine, and I think it has never been thought that a moratorium was a solution. A moratorium solves the problem for one, two, three months, but unfortunately, there is no moratorium that makes the debt disappear.

The case-by-case approach that was adopted in August of 1982 has not really been case by case, but rather the solution has been pretty homogenous. The same solution has been given to Brazil, which imports oil, as to Mexico, which exports oil. The same solution has been prescribed for Venezuela, which exports oil, as for Ecuador and Colombia, which are in different situations. And I think that what is needed now is to move toward a focus that is truly case by case, in which you look at the possibilities of growth for each country, its exports, its debt structure, and you fashion a tailor-made suit cut to the measurements of each debtor.

At the Cartagena meetings the theme of a debtors' club came up, and there were some discussions about it. But in reality, no delegation ever thought of using this new club to act in a unilateral, immature and irresponsible way. On the contrary, I think Cartagena has been a mechanism that has countersigned the responsibility with which Latin America is responding to the debt problem. Also, Cartagena has been an extraordinarily useful vehicle for the exchange of experiences regarding the debt.

One must recognize that the creditors have their creditors' club. And yes, they behave as a group and in a coordinated fashion since there are permanent meetings in which they reach agreements about the position they will take relative to the debtors.

In the years before the debt crisis, there was as much irresponsibility in seeking loans as in granting loans. For that reason, I am convinced that the responsibility for the debt problem must be shared between debtors and creditors. The debtors had the chance to accelerate their growth rate with resources from the outside. That they did, and the rhythm of development in Latin America in the years to 1982 was the most accelerated of any

450

region of the world. The banks were full of petrodollars and were facing a recession in industrial countries—they did not have anyone to loan their money to—and the developing countries, especially those that had petroleum, became very attractive clients. In our case, we were pursued by the international bankers offering us financial deals, one always better than the other.

For Mexico, I think the temptation of being able to grow more rapidly and take advantage of this unique circumstance could not be resisted. To the oil revenues of just under $50 billion from 1976 to 1982, we added a debt of almost $50 billion. We spent $100 billion in five years. Of course, we grew more—at 8.4 percent a year from 1978 to '81. If we had grown at 6.5 percent, our indebtedness probably would have been half of what it was and we would not be in these problems today. But to be *nouveau riche* is a very difficult situation that almost nobody can resist, and we were *nouveau riche*. The country was growing too rapidly. However, the voices of caution in '80, '81 and '82 were very few, and those few were not heard.

I think the crisis of Latin America will be with us for some years. And if we are in a boom, we have to be much more prudent and much more convinced of simple things. There is nothing that goes up that does not come down. And it was more valuable to walk hurriedly over a long stretch than to spring and then fall.

I don't think that more debt to resolve the debt problem is the solution. We must enter into a new stage in which growth is one of the fundamental variables. We have to resolve the debt problem by growing, not by stagnating. We could establish jointly, by common agreement between debtors and creditors, a minimum rate of economic growth that the developing countries should obtain, and guarantee the volume of necessary foreign exchange to secure that rate of growth, and the rest would be dedicated to servicing the debt. If things turn out better, we can amortize or service more of the debt burden. There is an infinity of proposals, with a common denominator that the debt service must decrease during X number of years. In some form, we have to seek to make debt payments more closely linked to the real capacity of each country to pay.

I don't see the way to resolve this problem unless it is with an adequate dose of debt relief. What is required essentially is a change in the political will on the part of the industrial nations. If not, we will continue facing recurrent foreign debt crises, like those we currently have with Brazil and Ecuador. As time goes by and a more definitive solution is postponed, the danger of chain reactions increases.

Up to now we have managed to avoid a crisis in the international financial system; we have gained time—we have gotten a breathing space for the debtor nations—but at a very high cost in terms of growth and standard of living for the populations of our countries. We must not forget that 94 percent of the population of Latin America now lives in democratic regimes. And we must not forget either that democracy and austerity do not co-habitate for a very long time.

Editor: Lucy Conger

Mario Henrique Simonsen

Former Finance Minister BRAZIL

Faced with the fallout from the first oil shock, Mario Simonsen, who was General Ernesto Geisel's finance minister from 1974 through 1978, set Brazil on a course of import substitution involving huge investments financed largely through foreign borrowing. Under the government of General João Baptista Figueiredo, Simonsen, who had become minister of planning, was outflanked in his structural adjustment efforts by Antonio Delfim Netto, the "czar of growth," and resigned in July 1979.

The central concept of the Geisel government was, let's invest so we can have import substitution and increase the export capacity at the same time. That was in essence the whole concept. Of course, the strategy that was designed took into account the first oil shock. But in 1974 nobody was predicting a second oil shock. On the contrary, most economists were asking whether OPEC's cartel could be maintained or not. We tried to act on the safe side, although without predicting either the second oil shock or the interest rate escalation of '79 and '80. We had a planned policy to increase the debt and at the same time to have investments that would create additional exports and reduce the demands for imports; so as a result, we would be able to service the debt.

Well, I don't think the strategy worked badly in spite of all the shocks we had afterward. Of course, once the second oil shock

453

became visible and interest rates went to 15 or 20 percent, it was obvious that we needed more short-term adjustments, which were only adopted in 1981. If you look at what's been the change in the balance of payments of Brazil from 1974 to 1984, this was consistent with growth. After 1984 we come to a very clear conclusion that what you find in additional exports and reduced imports is substantial enough to justify the amount of the debt. Let's make some extrapolations: Imagine that Brazil kept the same coefficient as in 1974—the same imports–gross national product ratio—and that exports grow 6 to 8 percent a year. In accordance with that calculation, you find that by 1984 trade deficits would be something in the region of $20 to $25 billion a year, if the economy had continued in its old-fashioned mode. Of course, nobody would finance such huge trade deficits. This indicates the debt was well used in the sense of reducing imports and expanding exports. That leaves me in a somewhat comfortable position as an administrator.

Looking back—which I don't think is a pleasant exercise—you never do 100 percent of what you want to do; and second, if you could foresee the future, everything would be different. Well, as a basic strategy, I think fundamentally what the Geisel government did was the only viable alternative. If you had chosen to adjust the balance of payments without investing or making structural adjustment, you'd simply have prolonged the stagnation. And Brazil would still have the same GNP as in 1973—with a much larger population and perhaps with a $20 billion-plus import bill that could not be financed. Basically, the strategy had to be what we did. Of course, if you could move back and foresee in 1977 the second oil shock, it would have been a period of quicker adjustment in the balance of payments. We had improvement in the balance of trade from a $4.7 billion deficit in 1974 to a slight surplus in 1977, a few hundred million dollars. It should have been $1 billion or $2 billion in trade surplus. But nobody had a crystal ball.

In 1975, when I was minister, I made a study that predicted the debt would peak at $35 billion. The projections were very realistic until early 1978. Then we had some deviations which escalated the debt to a peak of around $40 billion because of bad crops that reduced our 1978 export capacity. But that wouldn't have changed very much the substance of the idea. The substantial changes came from two facts—the second oil shock and interest rates—while at the same time there was not an immediate reaction from the government. I had a number of conferences with bankers in the U.S. and Europe to discuss the way debt dynamics work and things like that, and one concern I always had as finance minister was to explain all the debt projections. Obviously, I told bankers they weren't financing projects but the balance of payments; I felt this was a point they should have recognized. I think some did, but others didn't. Even the ones who did probably didn't anticipate that we might have the troubles of the second oil shock and interest rate escalation; all that was very hard to detect.

In the '60s and '70s you had a role played by dynamics that was very favorable to international lending in the sense that both GNP and exports grew at rates above international interest rates. When things changed from what I call pleasant to unpleasant debt arithmetic, I was no longer in office; the change occurred in 1981, and I left in 1979. But in any case, I always explained to bankers that there *was* a possibility of a change from pleasant to unpleasant arithmetic. I think this has been the case with Brazil. And our equation still appears to be solvable even with unpleasant arithmetic.

Going back to the period when I was minister, of course we had a plan for structural adjustment. We knew it would take some time to operate; import substitution does not immediately produce export promotion as a result of investment. First we tried to speed up the exchange rate devaluations. That was only part of the problem, for very abrupt change in exchange rates in an indexed economy tends to give you much higher inflation rates. But it's curious to note that at that time the IMF did not recommend exchange rate devaluations for deficit countries, because it was believed that the deficit was an inevitable counterpart of the OPEC surplus. It was believed that if every country tried to correct its trade deficit by devaluation, you'd have a repetition of the competitive devaluations of the '30s. What we did was introduce import controls, encourage export incentives or subsidies and reduce the level of aggregate demand, which was overheated by the beginning of 1974.

We had a lot of discussions at the beginning of the Geisel government. From 1968 to '73, Brazil had been growing at rates

455

above 10 percent a year, and there was an idea that we should continue this. But that would be impossible under the new balance-of-payments constraints, because the growth of this "miracle period" was partly based on low capital-output-ratio investments. But the consensus at that time was that any rate of growth below 7 percent a year would mean a deep recession! I was always labeled a recessionist at that time because I said the economy couldn't grow at more than 6 or 7 percent. But the planning minister had more ambitious plans in terms of keeping the old growth rates. At the same time, there was the idea that the supply of credit to Brazil was infinitely elastic, that we could go on borrowing indefinitely with no counterpart in terms of projections of future imports and exports. The final decision was, let's keep the country growing at a rate close to 7 percent a year. But let's also make structural adjustments.

In a sense, you could say the key LDC policy decision is always the same crunch between domestic growth or external adjustment. Which comes first? The movie is the same, and it always has been. It's true; this movie appears throughout the world. But look, to make external adjustment at the expense of growth means bad policy. For one reason, if you want to reduce the rate of growth because of external adjustment, you need to do that indefinitely. In the case of inflation it's different. A recession to fight inflation, that is only temporary; but to adjust the balance of payments, that's eternal. That's bad economic policy. Sometimes you need to do that to recover reserves, you have no other way out. If you can make a smoother adjustment based on structural changes—import substitution plus investment in the export sector—then, of course, it's much better. But you can only do that if you have a bridge of external capital. I think what's needed is a mixed solution.

Whenever you're in government you have two types of appreciation of your behavior. Those who like you say you're a "fine-tuner." Those who don't like you say you're a "stop-go minister." The difference is a very grave one; it depends very much on the perspectives of who's criticizing you. When I was in office I wasn't completely able to teach Brazilians to live within their means; but still I was able to teach them to borrow to invest, not to borrow to consume. The idea of my being a stop-go minister applies to every minister; you can even say Paul Volcker's monetary policy shows he's a stop-go central banker because of his policy changes.

One of the problems of being in government is that you can design a strategy but you must act on a day-by-day basis depending on what happens. An example is how we reacted to the increase in energy prices. Before the second oil shock there was this idea of introducing fuel-rationing coupons—a good instance of the Brazilian tendency for complicated economic solutions. Actually, the idea was not mine. The coupons just acquired the popular name "Simonettas" in my honor. The idea came from a Brazilian engineer who sent a letter to President Geisel, and the government decided to adopt it. I was never sympathetic to the Simonettas. Perhaps we should have made some increase in gasoline prices. It was discussed in 1977, but what would have been saved in terms of foreign exchange was very small. Don't forget that gas is only 30 percent of all oil consumption, so we would be saving $270 million, which is peanuts. Actually, the Simonetta was never implemented, and I had a strong responsibility for its abortion. But it still bears my name; I've still got two of these coupons at home as souvenirs.

Some people now ask me what it was like working for a general. I reply that it all depends on who's the general. Generals are not a uniform product. In the case of Geisel, I liked working with him because he had an extreme interest in everything, he wanted to know every detail. He was very informal in his talks—we could ring him up at midnight to work. He was involved in decisions. As a result of that, once you took a political measure that could be tough, you would be backed absolutely by Geisel, because he knew the reasons and he was convinced they were right. In the case of Figueiredo the situation was different. He was a very liberal man and so on, but he didn't have too much interest in economic affairs. So his initial cabinet was obviously split between those who believed that in 1979 Brazil should make quick adjustment to the second oil crisis plus interest rate escalation and those who wanted to continue expansion at 8 or 10 percent a year. This group said, "Let's solve all our problems and inflation by growth." At that time I resigned, simply because I perceived my ideas were not being accepted by the government.

The president was accepting the ideas of my opponent, Delfim Netto [who succeeded Simonsen as planning minister], and he had a clearly different view than mine. Delfim believed the country could continue to grow fast without making adjustment to the external situation. It's important to say that I think the late 1979 and 1980 policies were actually wrong compared to the needs of the country. But Delfim made a very important change in 1981 when he turned from unorthodox to orthodox economic policies. As a result of domestic expansion, reserves started declining, and with escalation of the debt and the beginning of the international economic recession, the process went further in 1981. The way Brazil found to keep reserves was to increase short-term borrowing from commercial credit lines and by using the overseas branches of Brazilian banks to borrow on the money markets and to re-lend to Brazil.

This is the point where you can start to attribute blame. But I won't say the basic fault was of the debtor or the lender. It was of the regulators. I think there was a basic mistake, and the U.S. has some responsibility because there was the idea that competitive markets are efficient in every circumstance to solve everything. In the case of balance-of-payments problems, it's more subtle, but the banks at that time were trapped by a fallacy of composition. They believed, "If I have a short-term credit I'm on the safe side of the fence, because I can get out immediately," which is true for each one individually but which is collectively wrong. When you have these problems the regulators should intervene. They had never done so until the debt shock. So conventional wisdom about LDC finances changed drastically from 1980 through 1982. In 1980 everyone said the banks would perform a valuable social role by extending credit to nations that needed to import and to finance development, and that helped U.S. exports and so on. After 1982 everyone asked, "Who's responsible for the debt crisis? Those who lent imprudently or borrowers who wasted money?" Actually, both lenders and borrowers made mistakes, but you cannot have a crisis unless you have some systemic flaw.

A very important point that I had the chance of speaking about at the IMF interim committee is that pure commercial bank lending in the international field without the support of strong international financial institutions is a weak system. What one bank

458

likes to supply each country depends on what they think other banks will supply, so you come to the roll-over assumption. The result is, if you don't have a buffer provided by strong international organizations—basically the IMF and World Bank—you tend either to overfinance countries or to produce credit shortages. Just after the first oil shock, debt recycling was almost wholly conducted by commercial banks; it was a good temporary solution. There was no other way; recycling had to come one way or the other, and commercial banks played this role. Now at that time, what naturally should have been suggested was that there was an obvious need for strengthening both the IMF and the World Bank, so they'd both play a major role in the following years, when recycling would continue to be a problem. Given the fact that commercial banks were providing credit to all the world, there was the wrong perception by the regulators that nothing needed to be done.

What I'm also very critical about is IMF conditionality as applied to debtor countries after the debt shock in 1982. Basically, it's a naive model in terms of economics. It needs a lot of improvements and often leads to bad adjustment policies. Most IMF-supported programs since the debt shock were not able to meet either growth or balance-of-payments adjustment targets, so they're not efficient from this point of view. It's true that the IMF has recently changed; it's softened very substantially its criteria. The Mexican agreement, for example, accepts the operational deficit instead of the nominal deficit as a target variable. I'm not discounting IMF conditionality; I think the IMF has to *change* its conditionality.

A number of things are needed to have a vision of this problem. First you need to have trade–debt links. The issue of the debt cannot be discussed without a resolution of trade, and from this point of view you need much closer cooperation between the IMF and World Bank on one side and GATT on the other. The fact that GATT has its headquarters in Geneva should not be an obstacle to having more discussion about debt and trade. For the debt problem to come to a happy end we should allow debtor nations to increase their exports. In a number of cases you need additional money for these countries to allow them to invest to increase exports and substitute imports, and so improve their trade balances. This is the spirit of Bretton Woods, and you need to have economic policy coordination to have that. Also, you need to require debtor countries to make a number of adjustments. Nobody is going to lend money to these countries to allow them to increase consumption without investment. Actually, you need a coordinated approach in which you allow debtors to invest and grow according to consistent economic plans, and on the other hand, you need trade negotiations that would allow them to export more.

But there's another more basic critique that needs to be made of the IMF: bad economics. It's systemic bad economics, because when you speak individually to economists in the fund they all realize that. But if you work for an institution, you have to work according to its rules, and the rules still stick to a model which was inspired by the Bretton Woods tradition. That meant small adjustments in individual countries that had a current account deficit or became illiquid because of excess aggregate demand. That's not necessarily the case of most debtors today.

What I'm saying is pure arithmetic. There are two ways out of the debt. One is to have growth of both GNP and exports in debtor countries. That problem tends to be solved by itself, because once you expand both these two you can borrow additional money, because your basis has been broadened and the need to transfer abroad is not the same. And transfers abroad decline in relation to exports and GNP because of the increase in the denominator. This is the favorable case. The second case is what has happened since 1982—a world with stagnant trade. Assume exports of debtor countries do not increase. If so, new lending to these countries is nothing but disguised interest capitalization, and the debt–export ratios just escalate. This means that you're going to come to an impasse. In practice, it's happening throughout the world. Of course, the great difference you should establish is not whether the form is new loans or simply capitalization. The difference is whether the country's exports are growing or not.

I won't say Brazil's the best of the bunch, the only viable debtor. You have a number. Colombia is one; it's not a large debtor. Venezuela is another; in fact, it's never really been a debtor. It's a net creditor country—except they don't know where the credits are. In Brazil's case, you have clear signs that the debt weighs heavily on one side of the equation. But on the other side you have import substitution and export promotion, so the problem appears to be solvable.

Look at what's happened between 1984 and 1986. Brazil had a unique experience; it was the only large debtor country that was fully servicing the debt without borrowing new money and having very high rates of growth. That came to a sudden end because, simply, last year was dominated by a carnival party of spending with the Cruzado Plan. The beginning of the plan was very promising—it was exactly to eliminate the complications of the Brazilian economy, to have de-indexation, and as such it was very well conceived in its details. And at the same time, the government was expected to have adequate monetary and fiscal policies. The government announced the fiscal deficit had been reduced virtually to zero. So the Cruzado Plan came with great hopes and great popular support.

The distortions started one month later when it became evident that remonetization of the economy was too quick and the economy was overheating due to excess demand. Then there were lots of shortages and development of black markets and the evaporation of both exports and reserves. Inflation was duly repressed, and then out it came again with all its force. The lesson of experience is that you should have a blend of both orthodox policies and income policies, that they should be well coupled and well designed to defeat inflation.

If you take a long perspective, the main cause of inflation is the fact that we have a budget deficit that has been financed by expansion of the money supply. And the fact that we have no independent central bank helps to create money supply to finance budgetary deficits. That's an orthodox but a correct long-term perspective on the problem. Now of course, once you try to live with inflation by using widespread indexation—as we did and still do—what you create is self-propelled inflation. That is the reason we have had endemic inflation since the '30s and high rates since the '70s. When I was in office what we tried to do was prevent inflation from escalating, given the fact we were an indexed economy with a number of supply shocks coming from abroad. My successor, Delfim, went through a number of phases in his period. In 1979–80 there was no attempt to reduce inflation, but later he returned to classic instruments. Then in 1983 we needed to make the maxi-devaluation because of the external adjustment at the time of the debt shock. We had to move from virtually no trade surplus to $6 billion. When you have a devaluation in a fully indexed economy, you lift the inflation rate—so it moved up from 100 percent to 200 percent-plus. This was perfectly consistent with the IMF program, which shows the IMF does not understand very much about how indexing works.

If you take the debt problem as a whole, not only Brazil but other nations that did not invest but used debt to increase consumption or to finance exchange rate overvaluation—Argentina and Mexico are examples—what you can say is that transferring 4 or 5 percent of GNP is not a very stable solution. Now, if you ask how you solve the transfer problem, I'd agree that sending abroad 4 percent of GNP is too much. But why is Brazil doing this? Simply because you no longer have direct investment and because you're not exploiting the potential access to both official loans and perhaps additional commercial bank loans.

Since I left government I've been getting a bird's eye view of the economy at the Getulio Vargas Foundation, a semi-official institution where I'm in charge of the graduate school. I'm also an outside member of the board of Citicorp in New York. But Citicorp has never asked me to teach Brazilians; I'm expected to give advice to the bank's top management and to take all the responsibilities of directors, not to tell Brazilians or other people what happens. I have written about the debt situation since the mid-'70s and have always discussed issues with Citicorp.

Both Walter Wriston—with whom I dealt when I was in government—and John Reed have been very favorable to Brazil. Reed never took this position as a tough-liner now being portrayed in the American press. I've been discussing these issues with him, and he appears to share my views that the debt problem has to be solved by growth; that's the spirit of the Baker plan. I think it still has to be implemented, but the central idea has been a breakthrough. What Reed insists is that this should be done in terms that are accepted by the markets and not in terms that the markets wouldn't normally accept. I think he's probably right. The top management of Citicorp surely understood right from the start they were financing balance-of-payments problems, not just projects. Did Walt Wriston or John Reed have an idea there was something called sovereign risk separate from commercial risk? I'd say they surely did. The problem, of course, is that in the '70s or early '80s they couldn't realize the debt crisis was coming. Nobody did.

When you assess country risk, you must have an idea of what the country does with its money, and you must be more involved in long-term considerations than in the short term. Over the short term the country can be in a bad state—as Brazil appears to be now. But if you look ahead, the Brazilian case doesn't seem that hard to resolve.

Editor: Richard House

Guido Carli

Former Governor BANCA D'ITALIA

Guido Carli, one of the towering figures in international monetary affairs, was governor of the Banca d'Italia between 1960 and 1975. Those were critical times for Italy. Violent student and labor unrest rocked the country in 1968 and 1969, leading in turn to inflationary wage settlements throughout the 1970s. Almost exclusively dependent on imported energy, Italy saw its creditworthiness on world markets plunge, not recovering until the late 1970s. Nevertheless, by his last year in office, Carli was given credit for having engineered the onset of recovery.

The generation that came out of the war was dominated by two fundamental ideas: One was to resist at all costs the establishment again in this country of an authoritarian regime; the other was to expand production in an open economy. If you combine these elements, the conclusion is that in the absence of a well-organized fiscal policy, the only instrument is as much monetary stability as possible at the expense of a more balanced growth. Certainly we had no balanced growth at that time; on the contrary, it was all export-led. But the preponderant consideration in the '50s through the '70s was to maintain an export-led economy so as to avoid collectivism.

One way to resist the strong pressure of the Communist Party was to make the structure of the economy ever more dependent on being competitive in international markets. The experience today of the communist countries confirms how difficult it is to reenter the world market after establishing a centrally planned economy. Sooner or later they will discover that there is a limit beyond which they can't go without changing their political system.

In writing economic history one should never forget the social and political circumstances in which events took place. We had the strongest Communist Party outside the Soviet Union and, I must add, a party at the time—I underline at the time—with the cleverest leaders. All those people had the experience of a fascist regime, of the resistance. You couldn't agree with them, but they were highly respected; I knew them all.

These considerations played a major role in our monetary policy. Nineteen sixty-seven to '68 was an important time. In 1967 sterling was devalued; the world moved from a sterling to a dollar standard, and then things deteriorated. The American government constantly rejected all proposals to increase the official price of gold, so that the dollar tended to become the only component of international liquidity. In order to adjust liquidity to the needs of expanding trade, therefore, the only possibility was to create an artificial financial instrument. Since the French were adamantly opposed to creation of an artificial currency, the compromise was to call it not a "currency unit" but rather a sort of credit—the special drawing right created at the IMF meeting in Rio. I had a part in that compromise and also in the decision to create the so-called two-tier system, which limited the convertibility of the dollar into gold to transactions among central banks.

What were the alternatives? To increase the price of gold or sell gold on the market? This was impossible; we couldn't explain to our public that we were selling gold at a price at which we could have lost the totality of our reserves. So I was in favor of the two-tier system. One could ask, was this the behavior of a personality who pretends to be a good economist? My answer is no, certainly not. But we thought that the fundamental objective was not to be disruptive but to keep an imperfect system working— probably less imperfect than the present one but certainly imperfect, no doubt of that.

As to our actions as a monetary authority in 1967–68, we, and to a certain extent also the Germans, were considered somewhat subservient to the Americans because, more than other countries, we were prepared to take dollars into our foreign exchange reserves. We did this because we considered the No. 1 priority was to maintain the functioning of the system based on liberalization of trade and liberalization of payments linked to trade. I believe that international cooperation in managing monetary systems, whatever they be—fixed exchange, floating exchange—is part of political cooperation. I am prepared to admit that this was more a decision of a monetary authority exercising, rightly or wrongly, part of the political power than it was a monetary policy decision.

But we ignored the need to have the social infrastructure develop at the same time. To speak for myself, I think this was a great mistake. In 1968, almost every day, young students, very young, marched in front of the Bank of Italy crying slogans against me, considered as an intellectual at the service of the capitalists. (Now these people are probably bank clerks. They have forgotten everything.) I think that I—and we—made the mistake of profoundly underestimating this phenomenon. The explanation once again is that we thought that to stabilize our society, what was essential was to create an institutional framework not allowing room for collectivism, for communism, while at the same time to concentrate all our efforts on the transformation of the economy—from agriculture into manufacturing and into an open, competitive market economy.

In any case, we had an explosion. In 1969 came the *autunno caldo,* the "hot autumn," in which labor unrest led to the three big unions banding together. In the early '70s we had to counteract the consequences of three major events: first, the inflationary wage settlements that resulted from the *autunno caldo;* second, the suspension of the gold convertibility of the dollar in 1971, followed by floating exchange rates in 1973; and third, the oil price increase. The adjustment process here was more difficult because 4 percent of GDP had to be exported to pay for oil imports. At the same time, wages increased in real terms, beyond increases in productivity, which meant a shift of income from firms to workers.

I think that from the point of view of pure economics, Italy offers a textbook case of how an oligopoly—in this case the oligopoly of labor—destroys itself. Because what was the reaction of the Italian economy to these wage settlements? In order to survive, corporations had to concentrate on labor-saving investments, and this had the effect, on one side, of keeping the system alive,

467

and on the other, of showing clearly that the unions were working against employment. As a result, at the end of the '70s and the beginning of the '80s the unions lost influence. I think they themselves recognized that they had destroyed their own power.

In those days we used some administrative measures to limit the expansionary effect of a monetary base that was growing beyond the amounts that the central bank thought to be appropriate. As soon as a central bank loses control of the creation of the monetary base, because a part of the public debt is monetized, the recourse to administrative measures is unavoidable—not desirable but unavoidable. We tried to keep these measures of short duration. We did not want to introduce a policy of *dirigisme* such as France had, where, by controlling the distribution of credit, they oriented the development of the economy. We never oriented credit sector by sector, never. If I am proud, I am proud of having resisted all the temptations to move toward a *dirigiste* economy, which opens the door to one form or another of political authoritarianism.

My idea was to control total domestic credit, but with priority given to the government at the expense of production in this emergency period in the early '70s. One could complain that we should never have allowed money creation to finance the needs of the Treasury. My answer during this emergency was that we first had to pay salaries to the civil servants, the military, the police. And if somebody had to suffer, it was the economy. I know again that from the point of view of an economist, this is absurd. But in this condition, was it possible not to pay policemen, to be without them? This was the problem. As a result, we had a very, very sharp credit squeeze starting in 1973–75, the worst period we had, culminating with the assassination of Aldo Moro in 1978.

As a consequence of these adjustments, we had great difficulty in borrowing abroad in 1974–78 to finance the balance-of-payments deficit generated by the deterioration in the terms of trade caused by the oil price increase. I thought that we could consider this situation as a transition to a new equilibrium, which in fact happened. My idea was that in general the oil exporters were unable to spend the totality of their surpluses, and therefore there was need to use these surpluses to finance countries in deficit.

And that is what the American banking system preponderantly did; they even went too far at the end of the '70s. In 1974 the U.S. government discovered the idea of country risk, but the parameters on which they based the creditworthiness of various countries proved later not to be very effective. At the time I expressed some views on how to manage the surpluses and the great danger of the banking system taking over the function of financing countries in balance-of-payments difficulties. The idea was that some mechanism had to be established in order to prevent commercial banks from doing what they should not do. I think that this is a problem which is still before us.

In 1974 Italy was in a major balance-of-payments crisis; by the time I left the bank in 1975 an improvement was visible. The action of the bank that contributed most to the change was the credit squeeze. This country reacts to a credit squeeze, and I think this proves the country's vitality. Italians want to be elegant, to have good food, to travel abroad; but what they want to do first of all is to survive, and to survive they are prepared to accept restrictions in their standard of living that others are not willing to accept. They are wise people.

A painful incident in the latter part of my time at the bank was of course the Sindona affair. First of all, I considered Michele Sindona extremely intelligent. At the same time, I think that, having had the experience of the Euromarket, he had the feeling of a market without rules. When you combine intelligence and no rules I think you get the kind of product he generated. He invented a lot of the new financial dealings: greenmail, for instance. The first case of greenmail—and we opposed it—was in 1969 when he purchased a large interest in Italcementi, which at the time had full control of Italmobiliare, which in turn had controlling interests in a number of banks and in Riunione Adriatica di Sicurta, the second-largest insurance company in Italy. He bought enough shares to threaten to control the company, which meant cement on one side but, much more important, insurance and banking. And he came to Carlo Pesenti, the largest single shareholder, offering to buy the insurance company and banks. Pesenti's reaction was to buy back Sindona's shares at prices much higher than Sindona had paid.

Some have criticized the Bank of Italy for not having seen the problems with Sindona soon enough. But that was difficult because the crisis exploded preponderantly because of the size of the so-called fiduciary accounts hidden overseas—a technique used to a larger extent by Banco Ambrosiano. The technique was to make deposits with respectable banks abroad but on the condition that they lend to so-and-so. On the books you find these accounts in the name of respected banks, but behind there is the commitment to lend to certain entities and to repay only if the borrowers can repay. What could we have done to stop this? We needed to have more control outside of Italy. After the Ambrosiano crisis the principle of the consolidated balance sheet was introduced.

Now, I think it certainly was a mistake not to have identified in time the conditions of the Sindona banks. But even though it cost the Treasury a lot of money, what I thought was important once the troubles became clear was to organize a system of interventions to make sure that deposits with these banks were repaid. So we established an extremely complicated system, quite different from the U.S. [Federal Deposit Insurance Corp.], which still exists today. I see the same principles repeated constantly by Paul Volcker: "Banks are different," he says, "and therefore you can't allow banks to go bankrupt. The depositors have to be paid." That was and still is my idea as well. Look at what happened in the United States in these years. In theory, deposits are guaranteed up to an amount of $100,000, but in fact *all* deposits have been in one form or another repaid.

Sindona's reaction and his lawyers' position was an extremely subtle one, and it was this: If the depositors are totally paid, then in fact there is no bankruptcy, and you can't apply the law of bankruptcy. But our position was even more subtle; it was that the credits toward his banks were taken over by other banks that substituted themselves for the bankrupt institution. The depositors thus became creditors of the intervening banks. Both the civil and criminal tribunals accepted our position.

Today our economy is still export-led, like those of Germany and Japan. It is very difficult to convince these countries to change their way of life and become less outward-looking, more inward-looking. Our experience in my time at the bank shows how difficult it is—and how important it is, for domestic reasons.

To correct the present imbalances among Japan, Germany

470

and the U.S., more expansionary policies by Japan and Germany could help, but not, in my view, to the extent that the Americans seem to expect. My analysis is different from theirs. When the price of oil sank and the exchange rate of the dollar sank, everybody thought the consequences would be expansionary for all industrial economies. But that was a mistake because, one, the purchasing power of oil-exporting countries declined; two, the indebted countries were and are forced to attain balance-of-trade surpluses to service their external debt; and three, the U.S. is slowly moving to improve its balance of trade. I believe that in the period of a few years it is impossible for Japan and Germany to have an expansion of the size needed to compensate for the negative effect of the three factors I just mentioned.

Going on in this analysis, I believe that a great change has occurred in the world, and it is the growing lack of authority and leadership. The United States no longer enjoys hegemony, and no other country is strong enough to take over its position. People have advocated a Marshall Plan for Latin America and the Middle East, but we do not have the conditions for it. That plan was announced 40 years ago by a general who was on the side of the victors and, at the same time, by a country with both prestige and resources—a country that is now a debtor nation. The dollar will be weak. The Five, the Six or the Seven will meet; they will decide to intervene or not; they will reduce the uncertainties for a while. But uncertainties will reappear; indebted countries will not solve their problems. See the case of Brazil: They made an experiment that was bound to fail.

I do not think all this will end in an explosion. It will just drag, drag, drag, as it does now. I don't see the temperaments for an explosion. I don't see the great leaders at the moment. I think that we are fortunate enough in this respect—to have no great leaders who might succumb to the temptation to create more authoritarian regimes.

Looking at another aspect of the present day, I wish we had done more during my time at the bank to create a money market. The present Bank of Italy governor, Carlo Ciampi, has made immense progress in modernizing the system and making it more

471

elegant. We did not take the steps that we could have, because we indulged, a little bit, a paternalistic system based on the principle that everything goes into banks, everything comes from banks, and everything stays with banks, banks being the center of the system. This has changed profoundly.

Editor: Heidi S. Fiske

John Loeb

Former Senior Partner LOEB, RHOADES & CO.

Long one of Wall Street's great mandarins, John Loeb founded
Loeb, Rhoades & Co. with his father in 1930 and steered the firm
(which was later absorbed by Shearson Hayden Stone) until his retirement in 1972. A self-described "jack-of-all-trades and master of
none," Loeb was one of the last of the old-line patrician leaders
presiding over a family-owned firm.

It seems to me that the securities business used to be, with a few
exceptions, a gentleman's game. People had pretty good man-
ners and followed standard rules of behavior. That seems to be
out the window today. Certainly, we were always anxious to make
money, but today all sorts of things are happening that I think are
inexcusable, like greenmail, poison pills, golden parachutes—not
to mention insider trading. People who controlled companies in
the old days would not make a deal unless it was offered to every
stockholder. And the personal equation seems to be gone from
relationships today. Everything is so large and computerized. I
have some friends who tell me their branches are like factories
now. They get new products to sell all the time and a lot of their
salesmen don't know what they're doing, but they sell whatever
they're told to by the central control: tax shelters, real estate
syndicates, all this sort of thing.

I regret that Loeb Rhoades isn't in existence anymore in many
ways, but on the other hand, I don't think I could be very happy
functioning in the present atmosphere. In the old days certain
investment bankers had long and friendly relationships with cer-

tain companies, and these companies had confidence in the bankers. Today it's open season. I don't think there's any real loyalty, with a few exceptions, between investment bankers and corporations. And to me, the fees that are being paid now for so-called investment banking advice—well, I would call them obscene.

We were a family firm, and I don't think a family could really run the sort of firm you have today. In the old days family really controlled the firm: It had the largest interest, and the other people were lesser partners. We didn't really have a particularly democratic sort of setup. But we had a very talented group of people at Loeb Rhoades in almost every aspect. People like Armand Erpf, Mark Millard, Sidney Knafel, Mario Gabelli, Sherman Lewis and John Levin, to mention a few. I think we were more good brokers than outstanding investment bankers; however, we were pretty good at certain kinds of deal making. We weren't one of the leading investment banking firms; we were majors and we were moving in the right direction, but we were pretty relaxed, relatively speaking.

Maybe we should have worked harder. But that wasn't the real reason we ran into trouble at Loeb Rhoades; the real reason was that our back office, which at one time was tops, didn't keep up with developments. That was the major problem.

There were a couple of firms we talked about merging with in the '70s. One was Kuhn Loeb. I remember a dinner meeting at Freddie Warburg's house on the East River; Freddie was a close friend of mine and one of the senior partners at Kuhn Loeb. The meeting consisted of Johnny Schiff, Freddie and me. I remember as I walked in—this I'll never forget—I stepped in a big mound of dog shit. That's one thing I remember about the meeting; the other thing was that Freddie was for the merger but Johnny was quite reluctant. And then we were reluctant because we were making a lot of money and they weren't. So that blew that.

We also had talks with Drexel. There the problem was that Tubby [Drexel chairman I.W. Burnham], whom I knew and liked, wasn't going to continue, and Léon Lambert [chairman of Groupe Bruxelles Lambert, a major Drexel stockholder] wanted control. That, I think, was the main reason that caused us not to do it. I certainly didn't want to turn over control to him. We also

474

considered—although it wasn't decisive—that so much of their profit, even then, was in Milken's activity in so-called junk bonds. I felt it was good business, but it made the firm very one-sided.

The merger we did end up doing, with Hornblower, turned out to be a big mistake. They had a different back-office system than we did, and that created real problems when business picked up suddenly. That was a basic error: to merge with a firm that had a different back-office system. The logic of that merger obviously wasn't studied enough. What we should have done at the time was *shrink*. It might have cost us $10 million to shake down, but it would have given us staying power.

Looking back, I really gave up running the firm at 70; I'm 84 now. In retrospect, I believe that was a mistake.

What I am happy about is that so many of my former partners have done so well in their new associations.

Editors: Gilbert E. Kaplan
and Cary Reich

Richard Cheney

Chairman HILL AND KNOWLTON

Richard Cheney, chairman of Hill and Knowlton, has been a pioneering figure in financial public relations, particularly as it pertains to proxy fights and hostile takeovers. Probably no one in his field has been involved in more bloody M&A battles. Cheney helped Unocal stave off T. Boone Pickens Jr., Walt Disney Productions fight Saul Steinberg, and Carter Hawley Hale Stores defend itself against an attempted takeover by The Limited. . . . The list goes on and on.

I first got involved in hostile takeovers because of a proxy fight in 1960, just after I'd come to work at Hill and Knowlton. I helped Alleghany Corp. fend off a takeover from Allan Kirby. Interestingly, in the middle of that fight, Kirby went into the market and bought $20 million worth of stock in three days, which was a big deal back then.

One of his candidates for director was Gene Tunney, the old heavyweight boxing champ. At the time, it was common to get an athlete as a director candidate in a proxy fight—the ex-coach from Notre Dame, somebody like that. Anyway, he got Tunney. The night before the fight, the two of them went out on the town, had a few, and Kirby's nerve was all steeled up. The next day, he walked down to Kuhn Loeb and said, "Buy!" They bought for three days, which is how I first learned about arbitrage.

The head of Goldman Sachs then was Gus Levy, a true arbitrageur. Alleghany had warrants and preferred stock, just like many of the closed-end companies of the late 1920s. So while

Kirby was buying up Alleghany common—because he needed voting stock—Levy was selling it to him short. At the same time, Levy had his people over at the American Stock Exchange buying up warrants to cover his shorts, and he had his people on the floor of the New York exchange buying up convertible stock. Levy converted the preferred and exercised his warrants at the right time, at the time of the vote. As a result, Kirby didn't buy stock from the people who were going to vote against him; he bought all new stock.

In the old days the proxy fight often tended to settle matters. You finished it, you won, and the other guy went away. But today the proxy fight is like a theater stub after the show. When the fight is over, it hasn't changed the positions of the stockholders at all. In Alleghany, for instance, we won the proxy fight by 800,000 shares, but Allan Kirby was still by far the largest shareholder, and two years later he came back and took over the company.

I worked with [takeover lawyer] George Demas in the Alleghany fight. He was the guy you always wanted in a takeover fight; if you couldn't get him, you got Joe Flom. George had been in proxy fights throughout the 1950s, all sorts of wild battles. He had a tremendous record at a time when you could really be flamboyant, and he always said, "Look, we need PR." So I teamed up with him.

Takeovers really supplanted proxy fights in the mid-'60s: George and I were in the first, a Pennzoil tender for United Gas. The big difference in the takeover game back then was that people used a lot more funny money in the process. When a conglomerate used paper to acquire a company, it was subject to attack. You could go through the prospectus and look for flaws, and you could go to the SEC and claim that things weren't all they were cracked up to be. For example, when I worked for McKesson against Victor Posner, we ran a full-page newspaper ad listing all the problems with the offer. It all boiled down to, Why would you want to do business with Victor Posner? That used to be a deterrent.

But now all the financing is done off-premises. You just put your junk bonds out there, and you get the money. Or you make the offer and you say, "I'm sure I can get the money through junk bonds." The takeover becomes easier because the raider's finances

478

aren't scrutinized. He's saying to the shareholders, "You want the money or not? What does it matter if I'm a thief? It's money, right?"

Still, even though money may always prevail in the end, a real vocal attack on an offer—if it's not subject to attack in court—can do an awful lot to make the offerer more interested in raising his price. I think boards are often afraid to do that. They don't feel that it's gentlemanly, or else they fear legal liability.

In the Sun Oil–Becton, Dickinson fight a few years ago, Sun decided it would try to save wear and tear by accumulating a huge block of Becton, Dickinson stock in just three days. The problem was that the purchases were selective. They made selected calls to institutions, and even the institution itself couldn't take advantage of the offer for all of its stockholders. It could only take advantage for those over whose accounts it had discretion. So it was a very selective tender offer.

The guts of the defense was that it hadn't been fair to the Becton stockholders, because it hadn't been offered on an equal basis. We gave reporters for local newspapers the list of institutions that had been called and suggested that they ask their hometown institutions why they had either taken the offer or not taken it. We also suggested that they ask about the reaction of stockholders who had had their money in trust, but without the trustee's having discretion. We created a lot of embarrassment for the trust companies that had participated. The discrimination turned out to be particularly unpleasant because the chairman, Fairleigh Dickinson, who had allied himself with Sun and helped to instigate the offer, had sold his block of stock at the first opportunity, so he had gotten his!

It's been my experience that the average board is very diligent, but very few want to do anything flamboyant or wild, and sometimes you have to do those things to get the guy to pay more. For instance, when Ben Heineman of Northwestern Railway went after B.F. Goodrich, he made his offer in December, just after he'd split his stock and made it sound like he was going to have a great year. In reality, he knew that the probable outlook was for declining earnings. But he was using stock to go for Goodrich, so he wanted to get the offer launched before the earnings report

479

came out. We put up such a stormy fight that he eventually had to come out with his earnings, and they were down. He blamed the poor results of Northwestern Railway on bad weather, too much ice and snow. So I went through all of his old releases and found that every year he'd blamed bad weather for *something*. And so we ran an ad quoting all of his old releases about bad weather and asking, "Does it only snow on the Northwestern?"

Until recently, there was no way you could take over a company in a proxy fight unless it was at death's door. Then you might have a chance of winning, but still it would be tough sledding. But in the last few years, the huge arbitrage pool and the junk bond business have made every company vulnerable, and the quality of the management doesn't really make any difference. In fact, I think most raiders would prefer to find a pretty good management in a target company because that way the company's going to be in good shape—and the pension fund may be overfunded, so you can raid it. The kind of company that's vulnerable now has changed dramatically.

Back then people really *cared* about who would run the company. Nowadays, when a proxy fight is only part of a siege to determine what kind of deal the shareholders will get, the only thing you really care about is whether people are going to get paid. I don't know quite when the tide turned. In fact, we were in an old-style proxy fight very recently, representing Chock Full O'Nuts. It was one of those old-fashioned battles in which you can do wonderful things. You ask shareholders, "Who are these men who are trying to take over your company?" It makes a great headline. In this instance, it happened to be Jerry Finklestein. The dissident stockholder always has trouble putting together a board because he's doing everything on spec. He's telling people, "Join me and we'll take over the company." But there aren't too many responsible people willing to join that slate. Who wants to get into a fight with so little at stake? Who needs it? So you almost always find easy pickings on the dissident slate. You say: "Who's *this* guy? . . . His brother-in-law. Who's *that* guy? . . . His lawyer." Then, at the end you say, "Who do you think will *really* run the company? Is this a board?" By the time you finish, you kill 'em with a word.

Editor: Edward E. Scharff

Donald Howard

Chief Financial Officer CITICORP

Since banks know a thing or two about raising money, being the chief financial officer of one is a special test of a CFO's mettle. As CFO of Citicorp, executive vice president Donald Howard has proved to be every bit as innovative and sophisticated as the bank itself. More than one new financing technique—including shelf registration—bear this 30-year Citicorp veteran's imprimatur.

I n 1969 I'd gone to senior management and said I'd like a job change of some kind, and so Mr. Wriston called me on the phone and said, "How would you like to go up and be deputy comptroller?" I was *not* excited. I thought it was dullsville. But Walt was the first boss I had when I walked in the bank in June of '57, and when he asked me to do something I never said no. We'd just created the holding company and were on the verge of becoming a widely held public security. This was the stage at which the combination of our corporate structure, the fact that the bank was doing exciting things and the fact that for the first time banks had to report to the SEC gave a whole new dimension to the accounting areas.

At the same time, funding was becoming more difficult because we had the Regulation Q ceilings. We had to limit our loans because we couldn't very well buy our money at 10 percent and loan it out at 6 percent. Then in 1974 we were faced with an incredible loan demand and no way to meet it. Walt Wriston came up with the idea of applying the floating-rate concept to a public issue of Citicorp securities in the U.S. Now, this had been a

481

standard way to do business in the Eurodollar market for fifteen years, but it never really had been done in this market. Walt went down to see several investment banking houses and asked them to think about the concept, and in due course two of them came back with ideas. We decided to add a third, and then we went public with the first FRN in the U.S.

Of course, it wasn't as simple as all that. We had to make adjustments to make the issue acceptable to the Fed. Before those, the formula was very attractive to investors, and at one point we had investment bankers prepared to underwrite in excess of $950 million. It eventually was done at $650 million with a formula that was somewhat less attractive to us and somewhat less attractive to investors—but much more acceptable to the Federal Reserve.

We were able to borrow money short term and reprice frequently in *excess* of Regulation Q because it applied only to bank deposits. Here was the break in the dike that permitted us to get the money to lend to our customers profitably. Essentially, what we did was to take the $650 million and repay very short-term commercial paper, so we added significantly to our liquidity at a time when it was very difficult to fund in the professional market.

Nineteen seventy-four was the last real liquidity crisis we've had in the U.S. It concerns me that there are very few people concerned with financing the liquidity of banks today who actually lived through that period. The biggest risk in the banking industry today, in fact, is this lack of people who've been through a liquidity crisis. When the next crisis comes, we just are not going to have the same battle-tested people. Citicorp, though, has *never* been as liquid as it is today.

Back in 1974, however, I worried about the liquidity crisis all night. I went to church regularly. How are we gonna do it? We tried everything we could think of. And we were successful. The pressure came off a little bit, a little bit, a little bit—until finally, instead of worrying about what was going to happen that day, you worried about what was going to happen tomorrow.

We started to innovate in the capital markets. Necessity is the mother of invention, and we were so large that we had to access different types of investors wanting different instruments. With investment bankers, we concocted a number of new securities. Other people did too, of course, and sometimes we followed them as well as led them. We weren't the sole innovators but we had to use every new idea, whether it was ours or somebody else's.

Anything that we think is a reasonable idea and has a chance of selling we will try. We've tried some things that are very much orphans out there. For example, we issued a preferred stock—par preferred—that has a unique formula for determining the rate. Nobody else has ever issued one. Yet they have not been a bad instrument from our standpoint.

Another example is perpetual debt. We're the only U.S. bank to have issued perpetual debt in the Eurobond market—$500 million worth. A very lonely issue. A number of our floating-rate issues are also one of a kind. By and large, though, they have been good issues for us. They appeal to a limited number of investors on one day. But they haven't really developed into a market, and that's to be expected. You can't be an innovator and expect to create new markets all the time.

You know when you *have* created a market when somebody else does the same kind of issue with a different underwriter within 24 hours—at a better price. That happens to us with some regularity. That happened with floating-rate notes, for one. Another example is mandatory convertible debt. Conditions change in the markets. Psychology changes dramatically. So I don't think there's too much innovation. There *are* an awful lot of issues out there that have not caught the public's fancy. But if you don't innovate at all, you won't find what the buyer wants, either.

As we became more frequent issuers—six, seven deals a year—it became apparent to us that the simple mechanics of registration could be simplified without in any way diminishing the protection afforded the investor by disclosure. All you were doing with each issue, after all, was repeating the disclosure. John Schmidt, a lawyer at our outside firm, Shearman & Sterling, talked frequently with the SEC, and he came to me and said: "I think we could get the SEC to approve of the concept of doing a registration but then not doing the issue immediately. But it would have to be basically under private placement rules."

So in June of 1980 we did register in this fashion, and almost immediately First Boston called us and offered a 30-year transaction as a "bought deal." We answered yes on the telephone. The firm then invited Salomon in because it found a big market for the deal. Then First Boston called us back and asked if we would take Salomon in on the same terms. We said, Yes! An hour later First Boston called back and asked if we would increase the total issue, so in the course of about two hours, we had issued $250 million of 30-year bonds under a pre-approved registration.

The SEC said that what we had done was clearly legal. From the standpoint of the words of the law, we had not violated anything, but the SEC had not conceived that we would use pre-approved registration that way. Technically, First Boston and Salomon had bought those bonds for their own account. But in turn they had distributed the bonds in a way that looked awfully like a traditional syndicate. The SEC said: "We hadn't really intended to give you that much flexibility. It's okay, but if we're going to do it for you, we've got to do it for a lot of other people. So please, don't do any more for a while."

The next obvious step was Rule 415, which came out in a matter of a few months. John Schmidt, then, was really the father of 415, though the SEC had been thinking along the same lines. And Citicorp was the first company to register under 415 and also the first to actually issue under shelf.

I have done my share of dumb things. The biggest one is that I've missed interest rate cycles badly. I built the bank's investment portfolio in September of 1981 and watched it go to a tremendous discount. Senior management approved, but it was my recommendation. That was right before Labor Day, and Volcker made his declaration [that the Fed would begin paying more attention to controlling the monetary aggregates than interest rates] on October 7. That cost the bank $100 million in 1982.

You can't be a hero when the world is running against you. But when the wind is at your back, you can run pretty fast. By and large the wind has been at our backs.

Editor: Beth Selby

Abdulla Saudi

President and Chief Executive ARAB BANKING CORP.

If the phenomenal accumulation of wealth in the Middle East in the 1970s produced dozens of Arab banks, it produced only a handful of Arab bankers of real international stature. And perhaps the most prominent—and successful—has been Abdulla Saudi, CEO of Arab Banking Corp. Beginning in 1972 at the unlikely power base of Libyan Arab Foreign Bank, Saudi was a leading participant in the planting of Arab banking flags in Europe, Latin America, the Far East and the United States. Saudi's efforts culminated in 1979 with the creation of ABC, his "bank of banks."

Before there was the liquidity derived from oil exports, even more than twenty years ago, there were some small branches of Arab banks in London and maybe one or two branches in Paris as a result of relations of the French with the North African countries. But those branches were very small and were directed toward very limited activities, more related to trade. These banks would never have had an international role to play—arranging loans, leading loans or even thinking about investment banking—without the oil boom, which really gave them a push. Because before this time, the Arab countries had always relied on the support of what we can call the most advanced or industrialized nations.

And to be honest, even when there were talented Arab bankers, if they didn't have a sponsor they would succeed only in getting a job. They would never be able to be leaders or to sit at the top of important institutions, because the owners were providing the money and were themselves controlling their own institutions.

Those talented Arab bankers didn't have the muscle. So, at least in that respect, oil did help bring some of the few Arab bankers into the arena. But I think the problem lies in the Arab system, the way that the Arab countries operate. The fortunes or money generated through oil were either in the hands of governments or, through the last decade, of private individuals. These private individuals succeeded in accumulating a lot of funds, but they have always lacked the experience.

European-Arab consortium banks were a good idea for the '70s, but they are no longer realistic in the '80s. They were good for the '70s because the Arabs were emerging in the international market and they needed someone to sponsor them. Banking is not something where you just step into the market and say you want to do banking. And I think the consortia played a very important role in this introduction. But as I stated several times at that time, we had a *presence* but never a real *participation*. We have to be realistic. Crédit Lyonnais sponsored UBAF, Société Générale sponsored FRAB, BNP sponsored BAII. All right? This is the way it started. And the French banks were right; they needed to be in contact with very important bankers from the Arab world for the sake of introduction, to attract Arab investors, Arab money, and I think this was good.

I'm not saying it wasn't good for the Arabs as well. It was very good, because through these consortia we were able to meet very long-established bankers, and we gained experience. And from there we have been able to tailor institutions that will enable us to get a share of the market rather than just being present in the market. But these consortia will never grow to the size of, say, Crédit Lyonnais. UBAF will never grow; Crédit Lyonnais will not let it. Because then there will be competition, especially when you are in the same market. The European shareholders wanted to see them stay small.

I started on the international side in '72. That was with the creation of Libyan Arab Foreign Bank, in which I was involved. Before that I used to be at the central bank, and I suggested to the authorities that we needed to have a unit to take care of foreign investments. Such an entity was not needed before the '70s, because the Libyans didn't have enough money for investment. So I established the bank, and this was for me a very good experience, something I'm proud of. Because I also succeeded in creating a truly commercial and international bank which, during my time there, achieved participations in UBAF, Banco Arabe Español, Arab Turkish Bank, Arab Hellenic Bank and so on. This was a very good expansion.

And then when Libya decided to make some investments, the question came, where to buy? And one of the deals was Fiat. The deal started in late '74 with negotiations with some of the people from Fiat, and it took us eighteen months to decide on that; the signing was in December of 1976. I remember at the time there was a lot of criticism; even some Libyans said it was a bad deal. And I also remember my press conference in Rome in 1976; a guy—I think he was from *The Wall Street Journal*—asked me two questions. One of them: "How come you're investing in a deteriorating economy?" And I told him that the Italian economy was not that bad, but what it lacked was management; Fiat was very well managed, and we were buying a company that had good management and good potential.

The other question was very delicate. He asked me, "What would be your stand if tomorrow Fiat decided to build a factory in Israel?" Well, I told him, "This is a good question, and it comes from a reputable newspaper. And you know, in business any board of directors, when they want to make any business decision, will take into account what is good and bad for the company. I will leave this until the time this question is presented to the board. If it is good business, they will decide for it; if it's not, they will not do it." So the following day, an Italian newspaper, *Unita,* put the headline, "Saudi says as long as we make money we invest in Israel." I mean it's sometimes the way journalists behave. But getting back to Fiat, we came to the company when it was facing difficulties; they needed $200 million in '76. In fact, it was $400 million—$200 million in capital and $200 million in loans, which were repaid. And now the investment has been sold for $3 billion, so that is not a bad investment after all.

As for ABC, well, put it this way: I've always had the dream or the desire to see that we have a good bank. But up to the late '60s, we didn't have the means. When I came to London in '61, working at Midland Bank at that time, I saw all those big banks. When I used to be in my own country, in my town, we always had these small branches of foreign banks, and I thought, "This is the size of a bank." But coming to their head offices, I found they had 2,000 branches, 30,000 in staff, and I said, "What am I talking about?" And, of course, we started to think we could put together a good, big bank. Then, during the '70s, we started to have money, and I was sitting on boards like UBAF's. Things started to build up. And *that* was the time to create a bank.

I was thinking of a "bank of banks," and it was in '76 that I had a big argument with the UBAF group, especially [chairman Mohamed] Abushadi. I came to him in '76, I remember, because at the time UBAF was one of the leaders in syndicated loans; they ranked about sixth that year. So one day I said, "Dr. Abushadi, you've done a fantastic job in the last six years." But, I told him, "You have to plan for the future. This is a consortium bank, and if you disappear I'm afraid the bank will disappear. You have to build a good network; bring up people who can take over." At first, he seemed receptive to the idea, but after some time he no longer welcomed it. So, in a further meeting with him, I voiced my disagreement with his approach and began thinking of an alternative. I said to him: "I'm not going to be part of this bank anymore. I don't think you plan for the future; you're just keeping things as they are. And if you move this way, this will not serve as a real international bank."

My concern with UBAF was not only with the chairman, whose technical abilities I hold in the highest respect, but also with its structure. Usually, when you have 29 shareholders and none of them has more than 5 percent, they have no incentive to step in and support you if the others will not. I also disagreed with the fact that UBAF's origins were political and that Abushadi insisted that all Arab League members must be shareholders.

As a result, I said that this wasn't the concept I was looking for and started seriously thinking of ABC. The first approach was in 1977 in Lima, when we created Arab Latin America Bank. Together with my friend, Abdul Wahab al-Tammar [then chairman of Kuwait Foreign Trading, Contracting and Investment Co.], we invited the ministers of finance, [Abdul Rahman al-] Atiqi of Kuwait and Muhammed Rajab of Libya. And we told them, "Listen, we have this idea, and we want you to support us." (I just want to confirm that ABC was not promoted by the politicians or

488

by the governments; it was promoted by the technicians and *sold* to the governments—because we needed big money.) And I remember Atiqi said, "I will support you on one condition: that you come and run it." He said he received a lot of ideas, but then they always disappeared.

And then we prepared memoranda for them and succeeded in getting the two ministers together again in March 1978. There was a sort of quietness, when you had to push these governments. It was only at the beginning of '79 that things started to move again; I was always running after it. Of course, they always said, "Yes, it takes time, we have to go back to our governments," and it wasn't until March of '79 that we had what I would say was a positive meeting when we signed the first agreement. And it was in December '79 that we established the bank and I made my first trip to Bahrain.

But I did not feel in those days that there was a sense of welcome. Even with some of the most important shareholders, there were one or two ministers who were not in favor of ABC in the beginning. And a lot of people said, well, ABC was only created because of Gulf International Bank and the differences among their shareholders—which was not the case. My answer at that time was that we needed in the Arab world more than two or three big banks. And it's still a problem we are facing today. I can give you an example, that out of all the money lent to Arab countries, two banks represent 40 percent of these loans—ABC and GIB, because of their size. So that means it was the right thing to establish a strong and well-capitalized bank, because in banking you cannot expand if you don't maintain the proper financial ratios. And we think that some of the Arab banks are still not capitalized enough, and I have been saying this. The Arab banks did not take advantage of the boom; they could have built much stronger banks, but nowadays they are no longer able to.

In '80 and '81, a billion-dollar bank was very easy, but after what has happened in the Arab world, they are a bit frightened of putting big money together. Where are they going to derive their deposits from? These banks were created simply to attract money from the interbank market, but the liquidity in the Eurodollar market has declined a lot. Five years ago the American banks were net lenders; now they are net borrowers. The oil countries used to have a lot of liquidity; now they have less. So Arab banks will not be able to grow, even if their capital base is good enough. You have to have permanent deposits, not deposits subject to the war in Iran and Iraq or to a private sector which isn't meeting its commitments. These banks will suffer, no doubt.

I think all of us would agree that no successful business can be achieved without someone to believe in it, in an *idea*. And you have to come up with some innovation to be able to sell it. You need a man of vision who can change with changes in the market, not just live on traditional things. If you are banking with, say, Manny Hanny or Citi or Chase, I will never be able to attract you to bank with me unless I come with something different—either in service or a better yield on your investment or just catching a trend. So I believed that if we were to take a share of the market, we had to be from day one what we call "born big." It's a good calling card; when we open doors they say, "Look at this billion-dollar bank."

But that's not enough. And I told some of my colleagues at Arab banks that they had to make a distinction between international banks and regional banks, and if you are an international bank you have to take your share of good things and bad things. You must accept some risk if you want to be international. You should not just sit and relax in your swivel chair and say, "Now here I have $1 billion; everyone should come and knock on my door." Such a bank will never be successful.

And if you are talking about risk, I think there are risks in the Arab region, as there are elsewhere in the world. ABC was established at the height of the *souk al-manakh* in Kuwait. Everybody was involved, but ABC did not give even one single dollar. Why? Because from day one, when I said I wanted to establish a bank, we said it would be an *international* bank, based on professionalism and prudent management. No one will get a loan from ABC before he submits his balance sheet, his cash flows, etc. At that time, when I was in Bahrain in '80, if I called on a very well-known name in the area and said, "Give me your balance sheet," he would say, "What the hell are you talking about?" It was more name-lending in those days. And I ran into a sort of embarrassment; they would ask me, "How come you are here and not lending even one dollar to this part of the world?" So my answer was, jokingly, that I wanted them to learn how to submit an application to borrow money.

Although I happen to be an Arab, I'm an international banker, so I have to staff ABC internationally. We don't hire people for the color of their eyes; I take them for their qualifications and professionalism, not their nationality. I was concerned to create a bank which, over time, would have its own culture; I wanted people to say "ABC" the way they say "Morgan" or "Citibank."

I was talking to the head of our ABC/Daus [in Frankfurt], and he said, "my chairman." I looked at him and I said, "Do you mean me or your old chairman"—because every time he said "my chairman" he meant [Hermann] Abs of Deutsche Bank, not me, because he was with him for 24 years; it always stuck with him. And he said, "No, I meant you." Well, I always have to be sure. This is one of the most difficult things with ABC at the moment. We are still a young bank; in banking, five or six years is really nothing. So this is what we are trying to do, to see that we have staff who, when they say "my bank," it's ABC; when they say "my chairman," they mean the chairman of the board of ABC. But no, this is not easy to accomplish.

Getting back to the Arab countries, today a lot of international banks, not necessarily American, have closed down in Bahrain or have scaled back their staff and activities. I say that is a fair decision from a commercial point of view; if you don't have the business, why should you maintain an office? But the thing I don't agree with is to cut your business with the region because of one bad country, or cut your business in a country because of one bad client. This is *not* fair. Or to decide on your relations with the Arab world based on liquidity and the changing price of oil; prices are changing, but what is more important is the *asset*. The asset is always there; 60 percent of the crude reserves is still in the Arab world. And whether oil is $2 in '71 or $35 in '81 or '82, it's still a valuable asset, even at $16 or $18.

Another factor relevant to foreign banks' departures or scaling down is the immaturity of some individual businessmen in the Arab world. They have money, but they use the *shariah* to avoid paying interest or, in some cases, the loan principal. They say they'll go to court. This is very bad, and I share the concern, especially of the foreign banks.

Editor: David Cudaback

491

David Scholey

Chairman MERCURY INTERNATIONAL GROUP

For much of his career at S.G. Warburg & Co., David Scholey was the heir apparent: a key behind-the-scenes player whose true influence was often obscured by the formidable presence of the merchant bank's founding father, Sir Siegmund Warburg. But since his ascension to the chairmanship, and Warburg's death in 1982, Scholey has truly come into his own as a force to be reckoned with on the global banking scene. His most impressive achievement—positioning his institution for Big Bang by merging it with two U.K. stockbrokers and a stockjobber to form Mercury International Group—led *Institutional Investor* magazine to name him 1986's Banker of the Year.

Even though, of late, I am sometimes described as a traditional City insider, I certainly don't think of myself as such. There is the traditional Eton-Oxford-Brigade of Guards mold. I went to Oxford, but I went there for one year. I did not take a degree and I behaved reasonably irresponsibly—or unreasonably irresponsibly—while I was there. I have never thought of myself as a natural member of what people here and elsewhere refer to as the establishment. Now, when you say things like, "Well, he is a member of the Court of the Bank of England," you must remember that my membership at the Court of the Bank of England derives entirely from what I've been able to do here at Warburg or how I'm recognized here. I'm not on the Court of the Bank of England because I'm David Scholey. I'm on the Court of the Bank of England because I'm the David Scholey who's had all these opportunities and chances here.

And certainly at no stage, including today, did I ever take my position at this firm for granted, either from the point of view of other people's expectations or my own expectations of my ability to fill that role. In the context of good fortune, everything that has happened to me, whether it was being offered a job in the firm, or being appointed a director of the firm, or being appointed a director of the holding company, or being appointed a vice chairman of the firm, has come as a surprise, if not from the point of view of my ambitions in my heart of hearts, certainly from the point of view of their timing. Everything that has happened to me as far as that is concerned has happened far earlier than I would have even secretly hoped, let alone expected.

I joined Warburg in January 1965, and by 1966 I was a general manager working in the corporate finance division. I was also the junior member of the firm's steering group, as it was called then. I was the secretary of that group. And that was a group which then consisted of, I suppose, Siegmund Warburg, Henry Grunfeld, Frank Smith, Geoffrey Seligman, Ian Fraser and Peter Spira. As a secretary, one tended to speak only when invited, unless one had a burning contribution to make. It was a very impressive group to be participating in. So I was certainly daunted by being part of that. On the other hand, such was the atmosphere created by Siegmund Warburg and Henry Grunfeld and the others that it was not daunting as such. It was very welcoming and encouraging.

I think the firm at that time was probably somewhere between 250 and 300 people. It was the period when the corporate finance activities were growing very fast, and we were beginning to act for an increasing number of significant companies—both U.K. and international. Also, alongside that, we were then about three years into the Eurobond market. And that was an area of quite clear development as far as we were concerned. That continuous involvement in the development of the international capital market was new and fresh and exciting for us.

The competition was tough on the issue side, because it was a new market and there wasn't that familiarity. On the other hand, there was a great deal of friendly cooperation among the managers: ourselves, White Weld, Kuhn Loeb, Deutsche Bank, the Belgians. And it wasn't ruthlessly competitive on the fee side.

Real distribution developed relatively slowly. Underwriting groups tended to be comprised of large numbers of people who were there for appearance's sake, without the necessary ability to distribute. There was one very major bank of whom it was said that the sun never set on its position.

I can remember very well more than one occasion when Siegmund himself sat at his desk all day and much of the night talking to his various friends around the world and placing an issue. In those days a deal would be placed very much by the senior people. It would go across the borders at that sort of level and then move down into the system, which would be very strange today.

I remember, for instance, the first floating-rate note deal, which we did with Van Galbraith when he was at Bankers Trust International. He was in touch with me one day and said: "I have a very interesting idea which would suit a very major international client. If you can think of the client, I'll tell you the idea." Siegmund had been talking with [Bank of Italy governor Guido] Carli about the Italian foreign borrowing requirements and, in particular, about ENEL, which was a vehicle we knew and which was one of the favorite borrowing vehicles of the Italian government. So I went back to Van and I said: "I think we have got the sort of client who sounds as if they would be both constitutionally and psychologically interested. I'll even tell you who it is before you tell me your idea—it's ENEL." And so he said, "I'll come right around." And he then put forward this idea, which was, in fact, the idea of floating-rate notes.

In a way it was the first securitization of a banking product. Because his idea was that the floating-rate approach could be attached to negotiable and traded instruments and that the big buyers would be the American banks. We talked about how that might work and what the size might be. We all got the idea that we were going to be talking about something that would be a billion-dollar transaction. And that is very exciting now, but it was even more exciting then. So we went to work on this, and Siegmund put the proposition to Carli and ENEL. But then we ran into all sorts of problems because of the U.S. Internal Revenue Service code: U.S. banks would not be permitted to invest in these instruments.

So, with Van I took my first flight on a 747, going over to New York to discuss this with a very clever lawyer named Stanley Rubenfeld. And Van had an old friendship with Paul Volcker, who was, I think, assistant secretary of monetary affairs at the time. Van said he would go down to Washington and try to fix it with Paul. It didn't quite work out that way. What happened in the end was that we concluded that it actually would not be feasible to create a note at that time which would be viable for American banks. So we constructed the transaction as a large syndicated credit and a simultaneous related issue of floating-rate notes for non-U.S. banks, which I think was $125 million. And the first FRN was born. It was born in Galbraith's bath [referring to stories that Galbraith came upon the idea while in the tub], but it was implemented in our office.

The development of the Eurobond market was fascinating because there were people in our firm, such as Siegmund and Gert Whitman and Eric Korner and Henry Grunfeld, who had been active participants in the international bond market of the '20s and '30s. So this was another time around the same tree for some of those people. And I think that was a major factor in our firm getting into this business; it was a business which many of our seniors had seen before.

We saw it as being an important means of distinguishing ourselves from other merchant banks. It seemed to us that the international divisions of London merchant banks were very much concerned with the finance of trade and hadn't really moved into either the corporate finance area or into the securities markets area. And one of the considerable frustrations we had was that the London Stock Exchange was supremely disinterested in this whole area of the market, with one exception, Julius Strauss at Strauss Turnbull. He was involved in just about every issue that we managed and everybody else managed. Otherwise, the stock exchange was supremely disinterested. They had their rules where X percent of any issue, if it was going to be listed in London, had to go to the jobbers. The jobbers and the brokers there didn't have the slightest idea where they were going to place or how they were going to trade in these strange things with strange currencies for strange borrowers. And yet they nevertheless said that had to be the case. So it was not only of no assistance but it was a positive disadvantage to list in London. And that was the reason for the Luxembourg listings for Eurobonds.

Of course, there was a feeling in some quarters that this whole market might be ephemeral; there were a lot of people in the marketplace who were all too ready to say that. But in our firm there was a conviction—and I use the word advisedly—that it wasn't. That it was a secular change. Nevertheless, there was always a fear that the business would go back to the U.S. and that the U.S. houses would pick it up internationally, as indeed they did.

I think we envisaged the possibility or likelihood relatively early on that big Continental banks would come to dominate this market. And it would have been all too easy, I suppose, to say, "Oh, well, if this is the good business we think it is, then everybody is going to be attracted to it and we are going to be overwhelmed by the big battalions." I think that some houses perhaps analyzed it that way and then allowed themselves to be convinced by their own argument. While we did think that others would come in, our feeling was that we should bring into our syndicates the ones who were likely to take the business seriously, and that that would be to our eventual advantage in the future. That always has been very much the approach of this firm: to work with other people.

The thinking here was never, "We shouldn't be in this business." The thinking was very much, "How do we stay in the business?" At one point we thought about whether we needed in one way or another to associate with the money in the bank: the old thing about their checkbook and our pen. It was the time when consortium banks were developing, and we had some discussions as to whether we should become part of one. But we concluded this would be slightly strange for us. Perhaps it's because of the classic upbringing or the sense of history which our founders had, but we felt it's one thing to have close working relationships with people, but that firms and people change. To institutionalize those relationships through a consortium setup was potentially constraining, potentially limiting.

Then there was the Arab boycott. In one sense it was an irritation, particularly to people on the syndicate desk and the trading desk, who felt it constantly as a handicap. In the upper reaches of the firm, it was felt very much to be a matter of principle. That sort of discrimination was seen by us as repugnant and something to be resisted and never accepted. And there were many occasions when people would say to us in arranging an issue for a borrower whom we knew or, indeed, a borrower we had been courting, "I'm sure you'll understand that we can't invite you into this because we have Middle Eastern bankers in the management group." And we always said: "We don't understand. We don't understand and we don't believe it's right and we don't think that you should accept that sort of limitation." There were some major firms, big firms, big banks, who always supported us, who declined to participate if we were excluded for that reason. And those are people whom we shall never forget. Actually, we shall not entirely forget the ones who had the opposite view, but it's much more important to remember the people who really supported us.

I remember someone came around from a bank one day to say that they were doing an issue for a U.K. public sector borrower which they had arranged and syndicated with a particular group of banks. And knowing our relationship with that issuer, they thought they should come around to tell us they were doing this, but they couldn't include us. There were one or two firms around the world who were excluded for boycott list reasons but who were prepared to take underwriting or selling group participations on an undisclosed basis. We always set our faces firmly against that; we thought that was a sort of venal condoning of it. So when this bank came around to say this and that they hoped we would understand, we said, absolutely, flatly, we did not understand. And we then went to the authorities here and expressed our view to them as to why this was particularly damaging, and not just to our firm.

So the issue was canceled. We did not make any friends among those who had the business in their hand and who were about to do it. But we just felt that it was important. And the cancellation of that issue was due to an act of very considerable courage and justice by the governor of the Bank of England at the time, Gordon Richardson.

I'll always remember the meeting in his room. There were four or five of us there explaining these circumstances to him. He'd come out of a business lunch early, especially to see us at very short notice; there was considerable urgency, because the issue was due to be launched that afternoon. And he heard what we had to say, in his customary way. And then one of the people in the room said: "It's a very pressing matter, Mr. Governor. We're

worried, you know, there isn't much time. There isn't much time."
And Gordon Richardson looked as really only he can and said, in
that penetrating quiet voice, "I think you'll find there is enough
time."

In the formation of our partnership with Paribas, the boycott
was a matter which was certainly of concern to them and therefore to both of us. Because Paribas had a branch network in the
Gulf and had very close and important relationships there. And it
was a network which was only at a relatively early stage. But to the
credit of [Paribas chairman] Jacques de Fouchier and his colleagues, they never at any stage indicated that it might be an
insurmountable obstacle in our partnership.

The basis of the partnership with Paribas was described by
somebody at the time in military terms: We would march separately, but campaign together. And one of the things that I think
was very effective, certainly in the earlier years, was this ability to
operate separately and then, if the conditions were propitious, to
cooperate very closely. As one of our competitors said, "It is
characteristically and wonderfully confusing." It was said that we
competed until it hurt—and when it hurt we cooperated. Well,
that was maybe a facile and trite way of putting it, but it had its
foundation in fact.

The United States was one of the areas where we felt that we
should cooperate, because of the size of the market and because
of the breadth of our combined expertise and contacts. Interestingly, although we were starting to look in that direction, in fact
the initiative for the A.G. Becker transaction came from Becker.
Paul Judy, who was head of Becker at the time, had noticed our
partnership and concluded that it would be a very interesting and
different way for his firm to go. The idea seemed to all of us to
have considerable attraction.

The reason we found increasingly that it didn't work out was
the size of the Becker firm by that time. It was already then about
2,500 people; it was then the size that we are now. So Judy became
more interested in the management aspect, and this meant that he
very largely withdrew from the practitioner side. Now in building
corporate finance business, you need to have your heavy hitters
hitting, and Judy definitely was a heavy hitter. He was responsible

499

for the relationships with some of Becker's oldest clients, companies like Cummins Engine, Parker Pen and First National Bank of Chicago. And the younger people then were not equipped to pick it up and follow through.

When Paul decided that running the firm for ten years was enough, he didn't have a designated successor. Ira Wender, an old friend of ours who had been a very successful lawyer at Baker & McKenzie for a long time and who had then started his own firm, was the chairman of the Judy successor selection committee. After they'd been sitting for a while, the rest of the committee members turned around and said: "Why are we looking any further when we've got the man to do it among us? If Ira Wender would switch from the law to investment banking he'd be terrific." The idea being that he was, and I'm sure still is, a superb and creative financial engineer, just the sort of person who could make the switch from being a lawyer to an investment banker. The problem was that once he joined the firm as chief executive, he became absolutely fascinated and enthralled by management and organizational questions. And he went in exactly the same direction as Judy. So the corporate finance activity never achieved the attention or the momentum at the top.

That was one of the problems. What happened also was that the market changed. The capital markets started to become very much more cross-border, very much more international. Now, to the extent that there is an international dimension, where did that business go? Did it go, in the first instance, from the U.S. to Warburg or from the U.S. to Paribas? Because although we were friends and partners, we weren't combined. And then we all considered in a very open-minded and friendly way whether the capital market business should all be rolled together: whether we should have an international capital market entity in which we'd all have a participation. But that would have involved a degree of separation from the other parts of otherwise unintegrated businesses, which was just too complicated. I mean, one would be creating four firms, really. And it would have meant establishing in London a second firm, and we couldn't make that fly.

Then, of course, came the nationalizations in France. Well, that was another rock in the pool, I suppose, and the pool was already rippling. That was a very ironic development, you know, because at the time we embarked on our original partnership with Paribas, the Labour government was in power here. And one of their

manifesto commitments for the subsequent election was to nationalize the clearing banks, major insurance companies and one merchant bank. They never named the merchant bank. But there was
a certain amount of speculation at that time that if they were
going to nationalize a merchant bank, a likely candidate was our
firm. And that didn't appeal to our prospective Paribas partners.
So they thought that it would be only right and proper that in that
event they would have the right to unwind the partnership. Well,
we could understand that. But we didn't believe in a call without
a put. So we concluded that if they wanted that, then however
ridiculous it might seem, however remote it might seem, just for
good form there should be a reciprocal.

So when it turned out that it was they, not we, who would be
nationalized, we could, and did, exercise our put. As for Becker,
I think probably the deciding factor there was that Becker had
become a management problem, which had become a capital
problem. And the organization better equipped to absorb that
problem was the very much larger one. So the ultimate decision
was difficult, it was agonizing, it was sad, but it was, in the final
analysis, reasonably clear. And we started in America on our
own—again!

It was around this time that Siegmund died. How would I char-
acterize the impact of his death on the firm? I suppose, in family
terms, it was like the death of a father, and in personal terms it
was the loss of a second father. On the other hand, although in
the last few years of his life, Siegmund made a very considerable
effort to see and talk to the younger people, there was obviously
a large number of people who'd never had a close working relationship with him. But among those—and they cover a wide range
of people—whom he did see a lot of in the organization, people
like foreign exchange dealers who'd been around a long time or
even some of the younger people on the international capital
market side, his precepts and his spirit are pretty far-reaching.
He's unforgettable.

What would Siegmund have made of the changes and the
growth of this firm since his death? Well, if there was one thing
one could say about Siegmund, it was that he was very much a
man of the moment and of the future. He was, if anything, up to

date and also ahead of the date. So he would be the last person in the world to say, "Things have got to stay as they were." It's a trait all the founders of this firm had. I can remember Eric Korner, aged over 80, inviting some company chairman to a meeting and saying afterwards, "Well, we may not do anything in the near future, but in five or ten years we'll do some important business with him." He didn't even say, "You'll do some important business with him." He said, "In five or ten years *we'll* be doing business with him."

The fact of the matter is, from 1979–80 onwards, we reckoned that we were moving into a new environment. And therefore we had to consider all the options to see which suited us best. You've got to look around the table and say: "What is our character, our personality, our talent? After all, all we've got to work with are the people. Are we a bunch of Rohatyns or are we something different?" So, we took the route which seemed to present us with the greatest possibility of development and continuity.

Nevertheless, there were still people who second-guessed us when we embarked on our four-way merger, people who said, "Wouldn't Siegmund be turning in his grave?" or "Wouldn't he have thought this was exactly the way not to go?" Well, my response to those two questions is that I think it would be too hypothetical and it would even be presumptuous of any of us to predict what Siegmund's view would be in any given situation, because he was one of the most unpredictable men, in many ways, that I'd ever met. So if the popular conception was that he would be against it, then the chances are that he would be in favor of it.

But the other aspect is that for as long as I can remember, which is over twenty years now, Siegmund firmly held the view that one of the great obstacles to the development of London as a truly leading financial center was the demarcation of functions among the traditional cartels and the sort of parochial and un-international outlook of the London Stock Exchange. I won't say only the London Stock Exchange; Siegmund had a deep-rooted dislike of all stock exchange bureaucracies. His views on the New York Stock Exchange, from his experience as a partner in Kuhn Loeb, produced invective of a style and force which could rival Swift. And so I believe that with the dismantling of exchange controls and then the breaking down of the stock exchange cartel, he would have said, "Now we can get into the

502

securities business in a way that a merchant bank should be in the securities business."

Of course, there's this whole question of size. Even if he would have never used the phrase "Small is beautiful," that's what he always thought. But then you say, "Look, you know, are there no good businesses or businesses of the right sort of quality of spirit of a larger size?" And you'd say, "Ah, well, there's Deutsche Bank." Now there's a firm. Then you'd say, "Well, what about Morgan Guaranty?" And I know that he had a very high regard for Morgan Stanley and Goldman Sachs. So our growth might have been a source of regret, but more because of the loss of personal contacts and relationships. He loved knowing everybody in the place and everybody knowing him and that sort of thing. Which is difficult to do with a few thousand people.

Had Siegmund been around at the time of our [Big Bang] mergers, I believe he would have said, "The key thing is the quality and the spirit of the people with whom we do it." And I have no doubt at all that as far as that is concerned, his shade is smiling on us—maybe with that look of his of "Ah, yes, but it's only a start."

Editor: Cary Reich

Robert Roosa

Partner BROWN BROTHERS HARRIMAN & CO.

For three decades, Robert Roosa has been an influential éminence grise in the world of international monetary policy: an adviser to U.S. presidents and a confidant of Federal Reserve chairmen. A New York Federal Reserve Bank veteran himself, Roosa served as under secretary of the Treasury for monetary affairs in the early 1960s, a period during which the U.S. balance-of-payments deficit was particularly worrisome. A partner at Brown Brothers Harriman & Co., Roosa, now 68, reflects on the evolution of current monetary policy.

Looking at the U.S. presidents of the past twenty years, I'd say they varied widely as to whether they took a delighted interest in monetary policy or thought, well, it's not exactly my thing but it's okay. Johnson took the second attitude but still got very involved in monetary policy. You see, Johnson had decided he was going to run a deficit and not increase taxes in order to keep the Vietnam War going. At one point, he thought he ought to try to run monetary policy out of the White House or the Treasury. Chairman William Martin, with his great skill, managed to make it clear to the president that it was possible for the Federal Reserve to remain independent yet be supportive of his policies.

I myself met with Johnson and told him that if he didn't increase taxes, we would experience serious inflation—which, of course, we later did. But he made the forthright answer that if he asked for higher taxes, people wouldn't support the war. "We have to remain strong there and win, whatever the price," he told me. So as commander-in-chief, he had great influence over both fiscal and monetary policy.

⁕⁕⁕

Then we had the whole Nixon era. Nixon, of course, was fiddling around to see what he could do about the Vietnam War and was also engaged in other kinds of external experiments. So he tended to only periodically dabble in monetary policy, although he was very fond of and had great confidence in Arthur Burns, whom he had brought in. Ford, by contrast, got very involved when he started his Whip Inflation Now campaign. He even called a national conference and had people submit prepared papers in advance, which he wanted his Treasury and Federal Reserve people to pay attention to. Carter was also active. In this and many other areas, he was very inclined to ask his advisers all kinds of questions to make sure they knew what they were doing.

As for Reagan, you'd have to say that the Federal Reserve has been more harassed during this administration than at any time during the whole twenty-year period we're talking about. It isn't the president. He has such a happy-go-lucky view of life and affairs, and his relations with Volcker, as far as I know, are pleasant. In the meetings they have, he makes no attempt to tell Volcker what to do. He's just trying to find out what Volcker is doing.

But as White House chief of staff, Donald Regan was very much at odds with the Federal Reserve, and then in the Treasury we had Beryl Sprinkel, always anxious to tell the Fed what to do. But things have quieted down with the disappearance of Regan and Sprinkel, who now sits on the Council of Economic Advisers and has less power than when he was at the Treasury.

I think we've been terribly fortunate with the whole group of Fed chairmen we've had over this period. William Miller was the only one who didn't have much impact because he was really a transitional chairman. Bill Martin was chairman for seventeen years and was strong. Burns was a good chairman and left a mark by inventing the idea of focusing on the federal funds rate. He also opened up relations between Congress and the Federal Reserve, encouraging Congress to get periodic reports from the chairman. Then he would go ahead and give explanations that had a certain professorial dignity that came with his manner. He certainly held the integrity of the Federal Reserve intact, as did Martin.

In the Volcker period, however, monetary policy has become much more problematic. And alongside all that, the debt problem of the LDCs had to be handled. Volcker has had more challenges from more directions than any previous chairman. He would have to go down as the greatest chairman the Fed has ever had.

I think monetary policy has evolved over the past twenty years from a one-dimensional into a three-dimensional exercise. The first dimension is the original concept for the Federal Reserve, which is to focus on money and credit. But today the Federal Reserve looks beyond just M and its influence on the price level and is concerned about the level of interest rates and the exchange rate as well. The events of the past twenty years have brought this about by demonstrating the close interrelationship between domestic interest rates, the exchange rate and the domestic and external deficits.

You can see this if you trace those events, starting with the very interesting transition we've gone through in the role interest rates play in monetary policy. When he was chairman of the Federal Reserve in the early 1970s, Arthur Burns invented the idea of targeting the federal funds rate as a means of giving Congress a clear way to judge whether or not the Federal Reserve was doing what it had promised. Over time, however, this unintentionally led to distortions in the money supply, producing inflationary or deflationary consequences.

By the time Paul Volcker became chairman in August of 1979, it was very clear that this fixation on the federal funds rate was diverting monetary policy from its stabilizing and growth-promoting role and, by adding to the money supply, feeding an inflation that was rapidly gaining strength. And so within two months of coming into office, Volcker persuaded the Federal Reserve Board to abandon this fixation and instead focus on the money supply, trying to impose enough restraint to bring it down.

Now, if you were going to get the money supply down, that meant interest rates were going to rise. Well, what happened was that at the same time that interest rates began rising, we had a change in government in 1981 that brought the introduction of the most extreme form of Keynesianism, unacknowledged, that the world has ever seen. We had a president saying he wanted to cut taxes and increase the defense budget by mammoth amounts, creating a federal deficit that has now reached phenomenal proportions that no one could have ever believed twenty years ago. This came at a time when inflation was already strong, and it contained the seeds of even more inflation.

The Federal Reserve, of course, had to be the counterweight. So we went on this continuing upward rise in rates. As interest rates went higher, the government deficit increased. And we found that foreigners were investing in dollars inside the U.S. or offshore, pushing the dollar higher and higher. That meant, from a trade point of view, the U.S. was buying more and more goods from abroad. We became the locomotive for stimulating the world economy. So the growth in our domestic deficit was paralleled by an increasing external deficit.

All this proved monetary policy couldn't be run in a vacuum. It became appropriate, and will forever remain so, that monetary policy be developed in concert with the Treasury, although the Federal Reserve must preserve its own independence within the government structure. Today the Treasury and Federal Reserve are working much more closely together in harmonizing policies on the fiscal, monetary and exchange rate sides. It has also become clear that the floating-exchange-rate system must be more actively managed, with central banks and Treasuries across countries coordinating policies—particularly the five countries whose currencies lie at the center of the SDR's value. This kind of cooperation was given dramatic initiation in the meeting at the Plaza Hotel in September of '85 and hopefully will grow.

Today, of course, everyone recognizes that the U.S. has to get its domestic and external deficits down. But this can't be done with a meat ax. It has to be done gradually because inside each economy and the world economy are many things that have gotten geared to the way the system stands now. Even then, we run the risk that we could revisit a great depression for the world. The comfort has to come from the fact that if countries and international organizations such as the IMF and World Bank recognize this danger, they'll be able to take action to head off a crisis.

Editor: Diane Hal Gropper

Richard Bliss

Chairman ASIAN OCEANIC SECURITIES

Richard Bliss was only in his mid-30s when, as president of Bankers Trust Co.'s international subsidiary, he invented the Eurodollar syndicated loan in 1966. Over the course of the 1970s, the syndicated loan came to be the dominant financing vehicle for governments and, to a lesser degree, corporations. Bliss went on to hold various top-ranking positions at American Express International Banking Corp. and is now chairman of Asian Oceanic Securities, the merchant banking firm he founded in 1981.

Around 1964 or '65, you were seeing in London a large pool of short-term money that was sloshing around for an eighth or a quarter or a sixteenth over the offered rate. It was an accumulating source of funds, this so-called Eurodollar market, and I concluded two things about it. One, that unlike the U.S. prime situation, it was going to be a market based on the actual cost of money. And two, that you could turn this short-term pool into a longer-term pool by adding something to the current short-term cost. So I decided, let's try to find an example, a borrower, and see if we can tap a large sum of money in this market.

We found our example when Frank Manheim's guys at Lehman Brothers brought us the opportunity to make a proposal to the Finance Ministry of Austria. Persuading the Austrians to do it was easy, because they were very keen on raising a large sum of money. But the question was, could we do it? There had been Eurodollar loans before, but each bank did its own deal. The concept of a syndication was a new one. So we really didn't know who to call and who would come in and who wouldn't.

Sure enough, it was hard to form the syndicate. A lot of banks said to us, why should we lend to Austria through Bankers Trust when we can just as well pick up the phone, shave an eighth off your rate and give it to them directly? And that kind of attitude lasted for quite some time. I remember the struggle we had later on in doing a $25 million Korean deal. It took months and months. When we got to $25 million, we closed the book. I don't think we had a dime over subscription.

Finally, though, we got the Austrian deal done, and out of all this in '66 came the first syndicated loan. I think it was for $110 million, had a five-year term and carried a rate of about three quarters. We added some commission, too, which was a daring thing in those days because management fees were not something that banks charged. But there we were, charging the customer a management fee to be paid to us as a lead bank, without sharing it with the other banks in the syndicate who were putting up the money. When we went around to the other banks and told them what we were doing, we got comments like, "How can you do this?" But we did it anyway and it set a precedent.

What happened with the tombstone is amusing in retrospect. We didn't run one because I was concerned that if we publicized our activities as the lead bank, the other banks would balk and say, "You're getting all the credit while we're putting up the money." But Frank Manheim said to me, "If you're not going to run a tombstone, I will." So it appeared with no mention of any of the banks but Lehman. That infuriated everyone because all Lehman had done was introduce us to the borrower. It was very naive of me to have let this happen.

There wasn't any signing ceremony for the deal. In fact, I'm not sure where the hell the thing was signed. It was in a lawyer's office someplace. The only memento that flowed out of it was a white porcelain thing, a man on a horse, that somebody gave me.

Right from the beginning, there was no question in my mind that this was going to become the way to do business. It was a natural. The money was there. The players were there. And the demand was there. It was just a question of who was going to play in the market and what share they were going to get.

The players showed up pretty fast. Manufacturers Hanover

Ltd., which was then a joint venture with [N.M.] Rothschild run by Minos Zombanakis, came in right after us. For a while, Bankers and Manufacturers pretty much had the market to themselves. I remember very vividly sitting down with Bill Moore, who was then the Bankers Trust chairman, and how great the excitement was at seeing Bankers Trust at the top of the list. Up to that point we had been watching Citi disappear over the horizon, and there was a desperation to do something international. And here we came up with something that was innovative and very much welcomed. It was very heady stuff.

And then Morgan Guaranty and Citibank—who later became the two largest players—got in around '71 or '72. There were some European banks as well, like Banca Commerciale Italiana and Deutsche Bank, and there were lots of deals done by investment banks, merchant banks and consortium banks. The Japanese didn't really become a factor until later in the 1970s. With them, the spigot used to go on and off. The MoF would push them into the market, and then the MoF would take them out of the market; you'd have a deal all lined up and then the spigot would shut and they'd disappear.

The investment banks were much stronger in those days, in terms of numbers of deals done. They used to make the argument, "If you go to church, you've got to have a priest marry you." It was an argument I got tired of listening to, because it had no basis in fact. But a lot of people continued to use investment banks, until it became evident that if you wanted to use them, you ended up paying more.

The borrowers loved these loans because they could get large sums of money by dealing with just one bank. How infinitely superior to going out and negotiating ten deals with ten banks! Most of the countries I dealt with over the years were perfectly reasonable in their negotiations, maybe because borrowers in those days weren't as sophisticated as they are today. I can remember only one really tough negotiator, a French lawyer in New York who represented the Ivory Coast. He was unreal. I mean, the Ivory Coast was not exactly General Motors but he fought and fought for every point, every nickel, every paragraph.

At first, international lending was an add-on in terms of income. It took about five years before it became a major profit center, and that was after I had left Bankers. Once the petrodollar days dawned, the whole international banking business became extremely profitable. Spreads had widened and there was a deal a day. Lots of fees and lots of action.

There was this frantic dash for the Middle East. Everyone got out their bags and tickets and headed over there. Many of these people were absolute carpetbaggers who were flogging everything they could think of, most of it junk. The Arab world was unequipped to handle this. So I think a lot of the early money just got frittered away by doing business with unscrupulous people.

The banks sent people over there, too. They hired people they wouldn't in their wildest dreams have sent to Chicago or anywhere else, but somehow these guys got the mandate to go fishing around the Middle East for this bank or that bank.

The international banking business has changed so much over the past twenty years. In the early days, there weren't nearly as many players as there are today. But it mushroomed. You had a few players, then a few more and all of a sudden there are a zillion players. At one point, you knew most of the people, and now, God knows how many people there are in this business.

Something else was different then, too. No matter how many things you did, there were 50 more for me to do and for him to do and for somebody else to do. So you had a feeling of being part of something that was exploding. Whereas today the market is constricting. It's still fun and there's still lots of opportunity, but it's endlessly cutthroat and much more mechanical than it was in the early days.

It was fun back then. We were all young guys. I don't think there was anyone over 40 in the business. And we got totally caught up in it. Each deal seemed more exciting than the last. It was a great period. In retrospect, the syndicated loan has proved to be a Frankenstein in some ways. But it was also a hell of an efficient way to raise money. If we hadn't done the first one, someone else would have. It was absolutely inevitable.

**Editors: Cary Reich and
Diane Hal Gropper**

José Angel Gurría

Director General of Public Credit MEXICO

José Angel Gurría's career in international finance began two decades ago when, at age seventeen, he joined Mexico's Federal Electricity Commission as a translator and messenger. For the past ten years, since he joined the country's Treasury Department, Gurría has been Mexico's chief debt negotiator, rising steadily through the ranks from deputy director of public credit to coordinator of foreign financing and now director general of public credit.

I joined the Comisión Federal de Electricidad in 1967 in the days when it was a pioneer in doing foreign debt. CFE was doing bonds in European units of account. It's not the kind of thing you do every day. It's like your graduation exercise, your Ph.D. You *finish* with that, whereas Mexico *started* with bond issues in the early '60s. The government was actually using the CFE as a vehicle to borrow money. The dollars would be deposited in an account in the central bank, and it helped the overall balance-of-payments situation. The men at CFE were dealing with the World Bank and with bond issues, and they didn't speak English. They had this intuition, but they also had bankers, mostly Europeans, who led them. People like me were looking on from the sidelines; I wasn't making any decisions at eighteen.

I would literally translate even the agreements with the World Bank. My technical Spanish was obviously not very good; I did not know the right words in Spanish for the things we were talking about. That's where I learned the jargon. We would show the translated agreements to the people in CFE, who would discuss them with the people in Treasury—Miguel de la Madrid was then deputy director of public credit—to ask authorization to do these bond issues.

In those days—it was probably '69—we did our first Euroloans, for $5 million; then, I think, for $15 million. It was a fortune. About that time, I was delivering promissory notes [to New York] and staying at the Taft Hotel for $12 a night on 42nd and Broadway. My mother was so obsessed with the security that she said I should buy one of those diplomatic attaché cases that you chain to your wrist. I said, "Listen, Mother, probably nobody gives a damn about an eighteen-year-old going down the street, but if I have an attaché case with one of those chains, then probably somebody will come steal it from me."

My first experience with a steering committee was for Nicaragua in 1979. We were there two weeks after the revolution, and some of us were dedicated exclusively to helping the Sandinista government deal with its foreign debt problems. That's where I met Bill Rhodes of Citibank, and we organized a meeting in Mexico with all the banks. We got in cahoots the night before to see who was going to be a member of the committee and then helped them to negotiate. Then, of course, we left them alone. But the Sandinistas would complain to us that the other guy was doing something they didn't like, and the banks would complain to us, and then the government would complain to us and we would tell the banks. Bill Rhodes is a man who will deal with any particular situation, in any particular context. He just goes in there and does the thing and does not get bothered very much by whether they were one or another type of government. He is an extremely pragmatic individual.

We have never done a restructuring as good as that since. There was an enormous outflow of sympathy for the Sandinistas, a revolutionary government sanctioned by everybody in the world, including the United States government. So, in a sense, there was absolutely no problem; we were all dealing with a government that had the full support, financial and otherwise, of the world at large. The atmosphere was completely different from the one prevailing today, politically.

The explosion of Mexico's debt problem was really created in six months, during the second half of 1981. The oil price dropped; we decided we would keep it up. We lost a lot of traditional clients who did not want to continue buying from us at $4 more than anybody else. In 1981 alone we borrowed, net, for the public sector alone, $19 billion. Our total public sector debt was $33 billion at the end of 1980, and by the end of 1981 we finished with $52 billion. I was director of foreign financing in the Finance Ministry, so I had the dubious privilege of organizing all that borrowing, half of which was short-term. If I had known in January [1981] that I was going to have to borrow $20 billion, I would have said it was impossible.

By that time, we had an institutional apparatus which was fully developed, with a lot of sophisticated borrowing expertise. We were kind of conducting an orchestra, saying: "Come on. You go there, and now you go there; you do a billion there, two-and-a-half billion here." And at the end, you had $20 billion more debt. That was the problem. In '82 the curtain came down.

The first instruction that Finance Minister Jesús Silva Herzog had given me was: "Tomorrow you are going [to New York] to start negotiating with the banks. Strike a deal as fast as you can." We were told this at night, and we had to leave the next morning. I didn't have any money—*we* didn't have any money, any dollars—and all those American Express cards that started with some code indicating Mexico were no longer being accepted. One of us on the team had 35 American cents in a box, just enough to make a phone call. Somebody else kept $30 or $40 at home; the chief clerk, I think, got $200. So we all assembled a little kitty. We got to the airport, and I think we actually paid for the tickets with a check—one-way tickets. We got there, and we had some people in Nafinsa in New York pay for the taxi, and then they gave us some money.

Before the August 20 [1982] meeting with the banks at the [New York] Fed, we had an idea of what we were going to say, what the problem was and how we had gotten there. But at that point, we really did not have a very clear blueprint of what was going to happen the next day and the next. That's why we created the advisory group of thirteen handpicked banks. We chose our largest creditors from each country as well as banks that had been particularly active supporters of Mexico. I didn't sleep the night before the meeting. You would think again and again what it was exactly that you would say and how you would put it, what was the right expression, the right tone to give to the presentation.

515

I personally was very nervous; Silva Herzog was very cool. He told me that he was just playing it as it went, because this had not been done before, there were no manuals to do this. We felt a combination of anguish and concern and a very deep-seated sense of responsibility vis-à-vis these people—the people of Mexico, the international financial community—who we had been telling only three months ago how everything would improve.

There were questions that we had not faced before. Silva Herzog, the director of Nafinsa and myself sitting there with some people from the Bank of Mexico were not improvising, but thinking for the first time what are we going to do about the twenty different categories of debt. We were giving out an intuitive reply that in the end was very accurate, in that it became the list of "excluded debt," which continued to be paid and has become almost a standard operating procedure in every country restructuring.

At the August 20 meeting with about 120 of our principal creditors, the banks stood up and said, "I pledge my support and my bank's support to Mexico; we trust Mexico, we have confidence in Mexico." It was very moving to me; I felt a lump in my throat. We knew almost everybody in that room on a first-name basis and had been doing business with them on a normal basis for three years. I remember Guido Hanselmann of Union Bank of Switzerland, and I remember Mont McMillen from Bank of America, who stood up and said, "We have so much money on the table that we are willing to lend to Mexico to overcome this problem." We had applause at the end of that meeting, we had laughter, there were jokes, and generally it was an extremely constructive "we" kind of atmosphere. *We* were all in it together; *we* were trying to solve the problem.

In '82 there was ignorance about what was going on and about the implications that this was the beginning of a very long problem. There was also a certain optimism that things could be solved fast—people like Jacques de Larosière saying, "No loan to Mexico from the IMF if [the banks] don't put $5 billion on the table—like in two weeks." And they would. Things like that were being done for the first time ever.

The system came up with people like Larosière, who came out

of the blue, somebody emerging and getting as tall and as big as you needed to be for the moment and saying, "Hey, guys, deliver the goods; we need a new kind of approach to this." And then people like Rhodes with his whip, moving the committee, and Paul Volcker with a statesman's role and attitude—a combination of the right people emerging at the right time.

That afternoon, with the advisory committee meeting for the first time, we sent out a long telex saying exactly what we were going to do next Monday, the whole blueprint of the strategy. Only 120 bankers went to the New York Fed meeting, but we had 500 creditors and 1,000 lending officers. We got a Citibank syndication computerized telex list of banks; we sent it to probably 2,000 banks, knowing that we were surely going to hit our 500 creditors. Then followed a telex from the advisory committee that had been formed that day, saying, "We are individually supporting the suggestion of the Mexicans, and we encourage you to do so, too."

In ten days around the clock, we did the deal, and then we had this twenty-foot-long telex ready with the first restructuring—eight years with four years' grace for maturities over the next two years. It shows you there was a certain perversity in the process, because the new money—$5 billion was negotiated as part of the package deal—was the most expensive loan we ever did. Here we were without any money, and we were being charged the highest spread ever over prime.

The money we restructured later was of twenty years with seven years' grace, and the new money was twelve years with seven years of grace, and the cost, instead of being almost 2 percent over prime, is now only 0.8 over LIBOR. The awareness of the size of the problem and the fact that the problem is going to be with us for some time has grown. We took all the right policy decisions, and in '84 new money was a piece of cake. We got important improvements in terms and conditions, and we got the money real fast, too. Everybody was on a roll.

The atmosphere soured from '84 to '85 because there was an objective deterioration of the economy. We overspent, but mostly due to very high interest rates. People tended to associate the overshooting of the fiscal targets with lack of fiscal discipline. We basically had an interest rate problem, but the perception was very bad, the timing too. Immediately after the September 1985 earthquake, the IMF announced we were out of eligibility for drawing.

517

There was a second thing. In 1984 we were doing everything by the book. Then we overshot the fiscal target, which was bad in itself, and then the disenchantment. We had failed them. We weren't a model anymore.

We went to the U.S. several times in '86, between February and July, and we came back empty-handed. In the higher levels of government, certainly in the Finance Ministry, we all started thinking very seriously about suspending payments. We started contingency planning; we had all the systems ready to, in effect, start a mechanism of peso deposits. Instead of paying out the dollars, you pay pesos into the central bank, and the central bank will put in favor of you [the creditor] a dollar amount. But it won't pay it to you. It is not particularly original, but it meant that you went to the mats, as you say in gangland wars; you actually were stopping payments.

Silva Herzog became increasingly radical in his approach to the whole thing, because there was no response. He had obviously been telling the bankers that the stopping of payments was in the cards if we didn't get a deal soon. We were always going to do it in a very serious, professional, well-thought-through manner that could help the banks continue to put it in their books as if they were accruing. And then Silva Herzog resigned in June, and that electrified the whole thing. It focused people's attention on the problem—in Washington, the IMF, the World Bank, everywhere. Because the first reaction to Silva Herzog's departure and the appointment of [Gustavo] Petricioli as the new minister was to say, "Tomorrow they are going to declare war on us." A month after the minister changed, we had a deal with the IMF.

The resignation changed the whole mood. I don't think [creditors] believed that we were in a very tight situation with oil at $8 instead of $30, and how politically impossible it was for a country—even if it had reserves—to continue to pay its debt service regularly without receiving a penny in support. We hadn't gotten any new money in eighteen months, not a penny. We had paid all the interest.

The signal we've gotten from many of the banks to the latest restructuring is that even if you have the support of the political

518

authorities, the multilateral institutions and the big commercial banks of the world, you still will not be able to get many small and medium-sized banks into the package. This time around we had more medium-sized banks than before that will not cooperate but that will still seek to get their interest paid on time. We are still pondering what our reaction is going to be.

The way to do it is to find much more efficient, more automatic ways of getting banks' contributions. But for automatic ways to function without too much pain, there ought to be important changes in the regulatory, accounting and legal environment, mostly in the United States. Or they should put in front of the banks—which is probably a more constructive way to do it—a menu of options, some of which have been discarded in the past, like capitalization, like taking a hit and saying, "I'll take 60 cents on the dollar, but please, never come back and knock on my door."

Mexico could not do a menu approach this last time around because the banks didn't want it and the regulations prevented it; also the deal had to be closed by September 29 because of the Baker plan, the IMF meeting; Larosière was leaving, and it had taken so long. The bankers knew capitalization was not in the package, and they proposed it anyway. It was so elegant, but it couldn't work, so they said, "Well, if you won't give me capitalization, I won't come in." Or they said, "We are big boys now; Manny Hanny and Citibank and Chase cannot take a hit, but we can take a hit." Some regional banks were making a lot of noise and acting like statesmen, sending telexes around saying, "This is the solution, let's take a hit." But the package had been designed in another way, so this was an excuse to be out.

In the whole history of the debt, there are lessons in many places. The constant lesson is to go back to Economics 1 all the time. There is nothing very new that has been discovered in the science of economics or in the science of the public sector or financial management that is very different from keeping your expenditures as close as you can to your income, and therefore do not overspend. And if you have to incur a deficit, be sure it is one that will not produce inflationary pressures that get out of hand. The lesson is: Always be prepared for something to go wrong.

The Catch-22 principle applies absolutely. And if you make mistakes, it's like that old adage in baseball: "After the error comes the hit." You screw up, and then something happens that compounds the problem, which is out of your control. So the rule is: Don't screw up.

Editor: Lucy Conger

Ellmore Patterson

Former Chairman MORGAN GUARANTY TRUST CO.

Ellmore Patterson started his banking career at J.P. Morgan & Co. in 1935, right out of the University of Chicago, and was a member of the bank's first training class. He served as chairman of J.P. Morgan and of its subsidiary Morgan Guaranty Trust Co. from 1971 to 1978, during a period when the bank began to expand rapidly beyond its traditional base of blue-chip corporate lending. During that period New York City also went through its worst fiscal crisis. Here Patterson recalls the key role he played as chairman of the committee of top New York financiers recruited to help the city.

In the fall of 1974, September or October, I had had a back injury and an operation on my disc and was obviously out of the bank for a while. When I came back—it must have been November or December—I remember reading in the paper that the New York City comptroller had been making comments about the city's finances. I got an invitation to go to Gracie Mansion for breakfast one morning, so I called up the chairman of one of the other banks and said: "I don't know anything about New York City finance. What's this all about?" And he told me that the mayor had asked the heads of all the big banks to come and that the fiscal situation was looking a little shaky. There had been trouble, a slowness in the underwriting of the city's notes, and the word was getting around that New York might not be in the best position. And Mayor [Abraham] Beame was concerned enough that he wanted to get some advice and help.

I attended that breakfast—as a matter of fact, I was sitting on a special seat because of my back. The mayor wanted us to aggressively do something as a group to help, and our response was simply: You just can't go out and sell bonds; you've got to have a good product. Someone said, "Well, let's form a group," and David Rockefeller said, "Well, why doesn't Pat chair the group?" because I happened to be chairman of the New York Clearing House—every two years we'd rotate the job among us. So I just happened to be there, and I said okay.

I was very naive—I'd never gotten myself involved in municipal financing, but I figured I had a job to do. And so I formed a group that we called the Financial Community Liaison Group. It had maybe four or five chairmen of banks: Don Regan, head of Merrill Lynch, and heads of two or three insurance companies and heads of two or three savings banks. And that group stuck together and worked with the mayor and the city government right through the creation of the Municipal Assistance Corp.

There were some tough times with the city's finances, and then, of course, it rubbed off on the state's finances. By that time, the governor had enlisted Felix Rohatyn and some other leading citizens to coordinate with our group. Felix was a very influential catalyst in getting people to work together. I can remember a lot of meetings between the labor unions and ourselves. Of course, when we started there was a question of what the labor unions and Mr. Gotbaum were going to do. We didn't get along very well for a while, and what finally got us together was the realization that it wasn't going to do us any good to be on different paths.

We looked carefully at the books and spent a good deal of time getting the financial picture in order so that it was understandable. Basically, one of the real problems was that it was mostly short-term debt—billions in short-term debt that had to keep rolling over. They were financing capital projects with 30-day notes, and about every month a new issue would come up, and the new issues got bigger and bigger and bigger. And then everybody started to worry, and the market dried up. That was the real problem: How can you get the budget balanced?

I remember that when we formed our group, we were warned by all the political people that the last thing you should do is give the impression that you financial people are running the city.

That is just out. You'll never get anywhere; they all will resist that and you'll get no cooperation. You've just got to persuade and come up with suggestions—and money. So we carefully stayed in the background. And our meetings were not publicized.

Later on, as the crisis deepened, we got more publicity and I was the point man. We would have many, many meetings at City Hall and at Gracie Mansion and in the offices of Morgan down on Broad Street. And the press was always there. [Labor leader] Victor Gotbaum and I would leave the meetings by the back door, but the press found it. And so Victor would be interviewed and I'd be interviewed on how we were coming. It was constant. At the peak of the crisis, I was on TV with Mayor Beame and Victor Gotbaum, being interviewed by Gabe Pressman. We got through the program, and I remember Gabe came up to me and said: "Well, Pat, I want to thank you for being on my program, and you were wonderful. You just really spoke from the bottom of your heart. But," he said, "I want to give you some advice. When you go on a program like this, you should make up your mind ahead of time what you want to say. Take the question, and quickly answer it—and *then* get your point over." I learned a lesson then.

The framework of MAC came out of a meeting of our group with Felix's group on Decoration Day at the home of Dick Shinn, the head of Metropolitan Life. There were people who thought the best course was bankruptcy, because it meant they could rewrite their labor contracts and just forget the debts for the time being and show that the government was no good anyway. That was their attitude. But we stuck by our guns. Our joint group was dedicated to not having bankruptcy, because of what it would do for the future of New York City finance as well as municipal finance all over the country and the world. We fought night and day to avoid that bankruptcy.

We were the core of the machinations to get the budget balanced, the figures certified and to work with the state. And we didn't get any help from Washington at the time. At one point I called the White House and said, "Can we come down and see you?" So we flew down—David Rockefeller, Walt Wriston and myself—and we had a meeting in the Oval Office with President Ford. We got no reaction other than just, "Thank you very much, and we've heard your story." And then there were some suggestions—maybe taxes ought to go up in the state and the city to help pay back all that debt. But the next day the *Daily News* had their famous headline: "Ford to City: Drop Dead."

After the meeting with Ford, a bunch of us, including Don Regan and Bill Salomon, went to Albany to talk to the legislators and Governor [Hugh] Carey, and I came up with a suggestion that one possible thing would be to raise taxes. And boy, that meeting was no sooner over than the governor said, "Will you come in this room, Pat?" And there were about 60 reporters, and Carey said, "Now tell them what you just told me." He was saying to the press, "Here the *bankers* want to raise taxes."

I practically lived with Abe [Beame] during that period. He'd call me in the middle of the night and he'd want to see me. And I'd be out on the golf course and I'd see a golf cart come out with a pro in it, and I knew exactly what it was—every time. Some crisis, one crisis after another. Something would always go wrong. For example, once we had a financing all organized and someone brought a suit. I was away on the weekend, and, I remember, I got the call and then told my family: "I've got to go back to New York. Someone has brought what they call a frivolous suit." And my son, who was in law school at the time, said, "There's no such thing as a frivolous suit, Daddy."

I remember the first issue of MAC bonds. It was the biggest public issue ever, and Morgan and Salomon were the lead. And we had a dinner together at the "21" Club to celebrate that, God, we'd got it done. But the bonds weren't going very well, so the dinner got rather cooled off. But the market finally recognized that it was a good bond, it was backed by the sales tax.

It's interesting that in the '30s Morgan had been involved in a similar rescue of the city, which had been pretty much forgotten. In my office, when I was chairman, there was a framed letter signed by all the chairmen of the clearinghouse banks, on Mr. Morgan's stationery. All those banks had pledged a total of something like $50 or $60 million, but that was all that was needed back then.

Editor: Nancy Belliveau

Irving Pollack

Former Commissioner SECURITIES
AND EXCHANGE COMMISSION

During his long career as an SEC staffer and then commissioner, Irving Pollack played a key role in many of the Street's major events—from the back-office crisis to the abolition of fixed commissions. Currently, he's a consultant to companies on SEC compliance issues. Many of Wall Street's reforms, he insists, would not have taken place without the SEC's prodding.

I n the late '60s we had the back-office crisis. The paperwork was overwhelming the industry. We used to run a very simple complaint-analysis file, and during this period I began to see an increase in complaints from customers saying they couldn't get delivery of their securities or firms weren't paying quickly enough. So I asked the fellow who was the chief of enforcement to send out a questionnaire to the big firms whose names I was seeing in the file for the first time. We might have sent out about a dozen letters and didn't get prompt responses. After some pressing, eleven out of the twelve said, "This is a private business problem, an industry problem, and you people in enforcement shouldn't be paying any attention to this." But one firm wrote back and said that yeah, it *is* a problem. The firms could not handle it anymore, the industry couldn't handle it. In those days they stopped trading for an afternoon or a day in order to try to catch up; they took all those ameliorative measures that really didn't meet the basic cause.

I remember sitting in a commission meeting where some big

consulting organization, whose name fortunately I don't remember, was presenting how they were going to clean up this industrywide problem of settlement by going and making studies in Europe. I remember saying to the commission, "Excuse me, Mr. Chairman, but I think I ought to take these people downstairs and talk to them." And I took them downstairs and I said: "You know, gentlemen, they're bleeding to death up there and you're going to go do some research product and all the blood's going to be on the floor. We don't need that; we need something very promptly."

The New York Stock Exchange was overwhelmed, and they couldn't undertake a new net-by-net clearing thing, but the Pacific Stock Exchange was able to start that. So while the New York Stock Exchange was doing whatever it could do to stem the tide, we started this new system and also got the NASD to start a clearing system because that was where a great number of the problems were. You didn't have any clearing organization for over-the-counter transactions at all.

The short and long of the whole thing is that it demonstrated that an agency like the SEC had to use its functions to correct business practices that you might not think normally an agency should be required to do. The NASDAQ system today was caused by the SEC's pushing the NASD to get this program going.

Commission rates were a big item then. The 1963 special study of the securities markets had shown that the SEC had no reasonable basis for approving a fixed-rate system. So what we did in implementing that, under tremendous opposition from the industry, was first take the easy one, which was the odd-lot rates. Once we knocked off the odd-lot rates, then, under the handling of Gene Rotberg—who was responsible really for conducting the hearings for the commission—we demonstrated that the fixed rate really didn't exist. It was just a method by which the members of the New York Stock Exchange were really able to control all those commissions and allocate them for other business opportunities that they had.

Once you get that kind of a thing, it leads to bad practices. You have a rule that says you have a fixed commission, and everybody has got holes running through it. It caused a disregard for the law, and one of the things that we were very, very insistent upon in the SEC—if we had a rule, it had to be complied with. We could have prosecuted many of these people for violations. But that was subsidiary. We were interested in the remedial side and getting the evidence that we needed to unfix the rates.

The whole thrust of the commission was you have got to come up and show us the basis of your rates. And that took years, by the time it all went through. The commission kept hitting and reducing the fixed rates by saying you've got to have a volume discount rate, you've got to have other things, and then Congress, meanwhile, was raising the same questions.

There were always adversarial statements made by the industry, and the exchange for a while tried to support it by bringing in experts to demonstrate why a rate that they were proposing to the commission was a proper rate. It wasn't until Bob Haack became president of the exchange that he in effect made a statement that if the industry recognized what was best for it, it would accept the unfixing of the rates. The SEC brought the industry along by uncovering all of the practices that were going on—it shows you how enforcement in the generic sense can do it.

I would expect that if you had talked to some individuals, they would have accused us of being Communists in doing what we did. Someone once accused me of that over the question of whether you can prosecute a broker-dealer for a federal offense if you can't prove the use of interstate facilities—such as the mail. There was a big commission meeting at which they had various representatives, including somebody from the Midwest Stock Exchange. The chairman said to me, "Do we have cases where we weren't able to prosecute because we didn't have the use of the mails?" And I said, "I'm sure we did." But, I said, "I don't understand why this question is being raised. Is there anybody in this room who thinks that a registered broker-dealer ought to be let go because he commits a fraud without using the mails?" And a gentleman from the Midwest Stock Exchange stood up and said, "Mr. Chairman, I didn't know you had Communists on your staff." At which point I just stood up and walked out of the meeting.

Editor: Suzanna Andrews

527

William Tuite

Senior Vice President for Data Processing
DREXEL BURNHAM LAMBERT

Bill Tuite is one of the financial services industry's computer pioneers, having installed Burnham & Co.'s first computer in 1962.
He then played a key role in most of the burgeoning firm's major
technological innovations. With degrees in meteorology, mathemat-
ics and business, Tuite is also remarkable for having spent the past
26 years with just one firm.

I installed the first computer here in February 1962. It was for
back-office accounting—bookkeeping, stock records, statements, confirmations, that sort of stuff. We received our first
modern-era IBM mainframe in 1966. We were fortunate enough
to get an early order in, No. 28. We really massaged the heck out
of that machine. I recall that during the crunch of 1968 we once
ran it 43 straight days without shutting it off. And it never bombed
out.

We were running the computer room in two shifts then. The
main shift came in during the day, then the night shift took over
about 6:00 P.M. They worked through until the work was done.
They probably worked till 4:00 or 5:00 A.M., a ten- or eleven-hour
day. And there was so much work to do that they were working six
and seven days a week. Those people really put their bodies into
the breach.

What helped us manage the turnover in the key operating areas
that I had any responsibility for was that we paid a bonus every
year. There's nothing like golden handcuffs, particularly for peo-

ple who work on the clock. I mean, the longer they work, the more they get paid. As these bonuses kept building up in those days, people were extrapolating what next year's bonus was going to be as soon as they got this year's. And that's not an exaggeration.

The surge of trading in the late 1960s caught a lot of firms by surprise. Look at the number of firms that went out of business because they couldn't handle it. Goodbody just blew up! At the peak of the boom, in the late '60s, there were about 700 firms in business. After the mergers, close to 200 firms were gone. We picked up outfits like Drexel Firestone and became Drexel Burnham in 1973. And we did a lot of other mergers, smaller ones, before that. We were able to do that because we had both the data processing and the operations expertise. It was a partnership. So we stayed in business, and the others went down the tubes.

Ross Perot, buying into DuPont Glore Forgan, got a lesson. There's no doubt about that. They tried to hire me, which I wasn't interested in. And they tried to pick my brain, which I wasn't interested in. They thought they were going to show the world how to automate a back office. P.S.—they didn't. DuPont went belly up. One reason I've been able to stay in the business so long is that I've always tried to be realistic in the estimates I've given. That way, people on the business side could make plans. Sometimes people make plans, and when it's time to go to data processing and say, "Hey, where is it?," too often the answer is, "Jeez, I'm only half there." A lot of people in my spot have lost their jobs because they gave unrealistic estimates about when they would have jobs done. When you're fresh on the job, you tend to tell people what they want to hear. And if you're new and don't know the business, it's difficult to give the correct estimate. It's always been my impression that systems and programming types are too prone to hearing what the user wants, holding their head and then coming up with an estimate that is always off by three or six months.

One high-water mark for us was when we put in our own in-house communications system to handle message switching and order-matching traffic. We started the process in 1977. Toward the end of 1978, I was getting very significant pressure, right from the top, to turn the thing loose. I kept saying: "It's not ready.

I'm not going to put the firm at risk." And my boss backed me up, which was very significant.

The initiative to design and build our own on-line trading system started about 1980. Our firm was originally an equity house, but by the late '70s, our bond trading department had grown. Once Mike Milken came in, you know, he was a man with a lot of ideas and ambitions. The guy in charge of trading was an ambitious, bright man. He wanted to grow, and Mike wanted to grow, and the firm wanted to grow. So the trading reached a point where we had a very large trading function in all of the equity areas, including options. We also had a high-grade corporate bond operation, and we were just starting to stick our nose into Treasuries and things of that nature. So Eddie Cantor came to me one day in 1979 and said, "Hey, Bill, I need an on-line trading system." My rejoinder was: "Fine. They're all over the place. Go buy one." So Eddie and I went and looked at an awful lot of on-line trading schemes. None of them fit the bill because we weren't just looking for a system that did on-line arithmetic. We wanted a system that allowed the traders to look at what they had and determine their exposure, their risk. It was also to be a tool that would help them determine how much capital they needed to finance this entire trading operation, and to tell them how much more capital they would need if they were going to do something over and above what they were doing now.

But we couldn't find any systems that made sense, so Eddie said, "Okay, Bill, would you tell me how long this is going to take?" Well, by this time I had a pretty good idea. I said, "Ed, it's going to take 24 months." Now, he had the typical trader's mentality and reaction: "I want it tomorrow." I said, "It can't be done." I said, "Why don't you hire a consulting firm that you have some confidence in, and let them come in and try to take a measurement and report back to you?" We asked Monchik-Weber to come in, and they said the first phase would take one year and cost a million dollars. Almost in the same breath, Eddie turns to me and says, "When can you get going?" Well, it took us two years and one month to do it.

But the trading room was just the beginning. People who had personal computers came to me and said, "Bill, you've got to see this." And I'd go to look at it, and it was very trivial. But I always told them it was very good, because you didn't want to crush them. In this early process I would describe PCs as a solution running

531

around looking for a problem. But technologically, I really was impressed. It was a more capable machine than the first computer I installed here many years ago for a hell of a lot more money. I think our first computer cost us something like $150,000 a year for the lease. And here, for maybe $2,000 to $3,000, you got something with the equivalent calculating capability. Maybe better.

This darn thing, data processing, doesn't just depend upon the data processing organization. It depends upon your partners, who you are feeding and providing help. And it depends upon a knowledgeable and understanding management. Without that, you've got all of the ingredients for a headache and a mess. I think that's one of the things that has been responsible for the firm's ability to grow and prosper.

In the last four to five years, we have had a compound growth rate of well over 50 percent. While we're spending like crazy, the firm has also been growing like crazy. If you had a firm that wasn't doubling every year, you'd see a decided change in the slope of the curve. But because of the rapid growth of our income side, the percent of revenues spent on data processing is pretty even. It's just that the dollars are significantly greater. I mean, I have more than 10 percent of the firm working for the data processing department. That is pretty typical across the board on Wall Street, though the central data processing department only spends half of the technology budget.

As the dollars involved got larger and larger, you had to learn or know what was the cheapest way to acquire equipment. That didn't mean buying a cheaper brand but finding alternative financial facilities—I was into leasing computers in 1970. You hear a lot of people say they want a manager rather than a technologist to run data processing, because so many of the crappy people who were managing this area and got into trouble had no business experience.

And that's why my job has changed from being a pure technician to being a businessman with a very strong technological background who still keeps his hand in decision making. And that's what I do.

Editor: Larry Marion

Joseph Sullivan

Former President CHICAGO BOARD OPTIONS EXCHANGE

Joseph (Mr. Options) Sullivan was responsible for the development
of the Chicago Board Options Exchange—first as vice president
for planning at the Chicago Board of Trade and later as the
CBOE's first president at its inception in 1972. From the CBOE,
Sullivan went on to the fixed-income division of Paine, Webber,
Jackson & Curtis and is today managing director of the Options
Group, a Manhattan-based advisory and consulting firm.

In 1967 the Chicago Board of Trade's markets were all agricultural. The agricultural futures markets had fallen on hard times by dint of the surpluses of the '60s that were pushing down prices while government supports were propping them up. And there was no price volatility. In the absence of that, there was very little activity in the futures, so the CBOT was looking for diversification. That was the *numero uno* institutional priority, and it meant pursuing nonagricultural futures. I worked on a couple developmentally—iced broilers, plywood—and investigated others—scrap steel, fish meal from Peru. Anyway, futures on anything and everything were being sorted out for their feasibility.

The great stock market fiascos of '69 and '70 resulted from the overloading of the operational circuitry more than anything else; the Street damn near gagged and choked on the business it couldn't handle. That whole environment was stimulating the board of trade—"Hey, if we could just get in on some of the stock market action, that would sure tide us over until the next big bean market." So we began looking at stocks.

After we determined that futures wouldn't fly, we turned to options because there was a precedent on stocks. There did exist a market in puts and calls, over the counter, and therefore it was harder for the regulators to disallow an exchange-traded option. So we turned to options with the thought that we could provide a bigger and better options market on an exchange-traded basis than existed over the counter.

The CBOE was formed as a vehicle for the members of the CBOT to make money. But over and above that, we finally managed to convince enough people that it had redeeming economic justification—a statutory requirement for new futures markets— to warrant at least a trial. And that's what the SEC authorized it to be, a pilot. We were put through incredible hoop-jumping exercises with the SEC to make the case that options served legitimate investment purposes.

Most people on Wall Street thought the CBOE was just some half-assed attempt on the part of the CBOT to pursue some nonsensical thing that never would be allowed to happen by the SEC and the Federal Reserve Board and, even if it did, wouldn't amount to anything. Irving Pollack and Stanley Sporkin [of the SEC's market regulation division] would have blocked this thing forever. They thought options were pernicious. Irv Pollack, at the first meeting we ever had with him in 1969, told us, "Don't waste a nickel on that hare-brained idea, because I can tell you there are absolutely insurmountable obstacles to it ever getting approved." [Commission chairman William] Casey, however, brought a freer mentality that said, "Well, hey, they've been banging away for three years at our doorstep and submitted all kinds of documentation and justification studies." He, more than anyone else, brought the commission around.

The doors opened on April 23, 1973. The governor of Illinois, Dan Walker, was there, and so was the SEC chairman, Brad Cook. The CBOE itself was a pretty jerry-rigged place. It was in the old CBOT smoking room, and the posts were on the periphery with the booths in the middle, a classic error of design. That was the day we traded 910 contracts, options on 90,000 shares of stock.

The 1976 SEC moratorium on the expansion of options products in hindsight seems like growing pains. We had these dual trading wars between CBOE and the Amex, where the name of the game was to generate as much volume as possible because the large wire houses were going to send their order flow to whichever of the two exchanges was doing the most business. And that was an unthwartable incentive to generate trade volume. CBOE was well nigh as guilty of that as the Amex. But, you know, the venality of it was relatively innocuous, and the competitive situation was such that I just think it was an imperative. The SEC was stuck with having to police all of this silly business about the impact of options trading on the capital formation process and its impact on the behavioral characteristics of stock prices. In my latter-day view, all that was angels dancing on the head of a pin. At the time, I must say, it did seem very serious, even life-threatening. We were viewed as highly suspect by not only the regulators but also the financial establishment and corporate America. And while it was bringing in a lot of revenue to the big wire houses, I think at the higher levels of Wall Street there was a lot of apprehension about what the hell perils existed in this phenomenon.

Bob Rubin at Goldman was a charter director of CBOE through those early years and one of the first believers in our concept at a time when most people on Wall Street didn't think the thing would work. Bob and I went to see John Whitehead together in 1975 or so; we asked him what we could do to build a better recognition for the positives of this market. His answer was, "Give it ten years."

A lot of the other heads of the big firms didn't have the time of day for me, though. I was just, you know, a brat. Some did. Don Regan. A very bright guy; he might not have understood all the intricacies of options, but he understood the big picture. I'm sure there were sides of Gus Levy that didn't think it was all just wonderful, but he was always totally supportive of me. I don't think I did a particularly good job of convincing anyone on Wall Street not to worry about a thing. But greed usually prevails over fear, and they all eventually got into the action.

During the period 1973–1979, the options markets grew like Topsy and became a very significant factor in the equity market. By 1979, though, I'd had it [at CBOE]. I just wasn't well equipped to be administrator of a large organization, and the politics of the place just stank. Don't ever work for a membership organization if you have other alternatives. When we started the thing, it felt like my own show, and I was treated so beautifully by the senior people at the Board of Trade. But when I got out in the real world of having a membership, then it was very different. CBOE was in its adolescence, at best, in those years, and the floor members had a lot of ideas of their own about how the place ought to be run. In the last analysis it really became their exchange, and it was no longer my thing. It was their thing, and it was time for me to go.

Look at the ways in which options are being employed today and the sophistication with which all of the Street has taken to them. The fascinating question to me is to what extent did the innovations that emanated from the CBOT and the Merc—financial futures and options—spur of all the gamut of derivative or synthetic securities available today? Interest rate swaps, caps and collars, heaven-and-hell bonds, securitization features. I think that financial futures probably caused interest swaps to come into being sooner than they otherwise would have.

The point of no return [for options] came symbolically in '81 or '82—Henry Kaufman's comment that without the futures market, the government securities market would be in a shambles. But, of course, a big, big factor in the way the world has turned certainly has been the regulatory environment of the '70s and '80s. When you go to the SEC today, you're going to people who are almost the antithesis of the Pollacks and the Sporkins of the late '60s, who believed the marketplace itself couldn't be trusted for nothing.

I was always a sucker for a cause, and options became my cause. I did believe in it, and I still do believe in it. What's so really edifying to me about the '80s is the way in which all of what we were asserting about the utility of options in the '70s—which was viewed with total skepticism by the regulators and most of Wall Street—has come to happen and then some. It's gone way beyond anything that I ever envisioned.

Editor: Beth McGoldrick

E. John Rosenwald Jr.

Managing Director BEAR, STEARNS & CO.

E. John Rosenwald Jr. was the first institutional salesman to sell equities instead of bonds for Bear, Stearns & Co. when he began his career in the mid-1950s. During the next twenty years, Rosenwald witnessed Bear Stearns' rise as a major power in block trading—which it had pioneered with his gunslinging Boston clients. One year after Mayday, Rosenwald took over the firm's corporate finance effort.

When I started as an institutional salesman for Bear Stearns in the mid-1950s, I traveled to Boston every Wednesday evening on a train called the Merchants Limited, which left Grand Central at 5:00 and pulled into Back Bay at 9:20. Boston institutions had never heard of me and some of 'em had never heard of the firm. At first, I was treated very politely but very coldly. I made up my mind that if I was going to get anywhere, I was going to have to dig into the organizations and find out who the comers were and start to build relationships with them. Shortly thereafter, I met a guy who was stored way, way back in the research department at Fidelity Fund as a steel and automobile analyst who said to me, "Don't stay at the Parker House. We'll have dinner and you can stay at my house." That fellow's name was Jerry Tsai. We became great pals. We did a ton of business together. I also got to know an oil analyst at Massachusetts Investment Trust named Roland Grimm, who ultimately moved to Fidelity.

One day in the late '50s I was having lunch with Cy Lewis, who was our boss here, and he said: "You know, we buy blocks of bonds from institutions all the time. And we have learned how to understand risk. Maybe what we should do is go into the business of buying blocks of stock." Now, of course, there is a very important difference, because all bonds of a given rating trade very close to one another, but equities have no comparable trading patterns. I said, "I think it is a great idea, because I know several portfolio managers who like to move quickly." I knew, for instance, that once Jerry Tsai decided to switch his Ford into Chrysler, he would like it done yesterday.

So I got on a plane, and Jerry and I had lunch at the Parker House Grill. I told him that we had decided to try this. We didn't know where we were going to go or how it would work, but that we would bid for blocks of stock. He said, "Let's go back to the office." When we got there he said, "Call your office and see if they'll make me a bid on 50,000 shares of Rexall." We made the bid and we traded the block.

Next, Jerry walked into the office next door, which was Roland Grimm's, and said, "Wait 'til you hear what Rosey will do." And Roland looks over his glasses and says, "Oh, *really?* Make me a bid on 50,000 shares of Food Fair." So we made Roland a bid on 50,000 shares of Food Fair and we traded that block. Those two trades, in my honest recollection, were the beginning of block trading. We had been getting 2,500- and 3,000-share orders for research, and here I'd written two 50,000-share tickets in one day. After that, other people jumped into the business very quickly.

In effect, this was a way for us to lift ourselves above the crowd. The institutional research business was starting to get quite crowded. I mean, people would hire some guys and say, "Okay, now we are going to write some big, thick institutional reports instead of the one-pagers." So here was a way, while we were knocking at the gates, to really differentiate ourselves. We were off and running.

All of us who were living in this world of institutional sales knew that it was just a matter of time before the negotiated commission hit, because we had, in effect, been negotiating commissions for years through the give-up arrangements [whereby the commissions on a trade had been split between a mutual fund's prime broker and smaller firms that had actively sold its shares]. The total amount of the commissions was not negotiated, but the portion that the executing broker kept was negotiated. In that way de facto negotiation had existed for a long time. Mayday, though, really went to extremes, as the issue quickly became market share.

Prior to Mayday, one of the major firms had gone off for a weekend retreat to plan a pricing strategy. They came back and announced to the world that at the opening on May 1, 1975, they would offer an 18 percent discount. I don't know where they came up with that figure, but I'll tell you, it lasted all of 60 seconds. Major institutional firms, full-service firms, in order to keep market share quickly became major discounters, and the discount from the old rate jumped dramatically.

On Mayday many institutions were so frightened of litigation they had lawyers sitting on the trading desk, watching the traders to make sure they were negotiating and getting the best possible price.

Mayday was a dramatic change. Very quickly one of the things we were able to do in this negotiated-rate environment was to develop a price schedule. I would call my accounts and say that if you want your teeth cleaned, that is one price, but if you want a gold inlay, you are going to pay a different price. Now, for example, a gold inlay would be somebody who wanted a bid or an offer on a block of stock, where we were going at risk. We clearly said that when we were at risk, the commission would be higher.

Not long after Mayday I executed an order that at that time was one of the biggest orders we had ever seen. It was for a million shares of Sony. When we were all through negotiating the commission, Ace [Greenberg] and I took a look at how much money we had made on that million-share order. What we saw was not a hell of a lot of money compared to what the order would have generated pre-Mayday. And that is when this whole idea of Rosenwald moving over to the corporate finance department was born.

Around the same time, three very talented and capable and creative partners in our corporate finance department decided to hang out their own shingle. Their names are Kohlberg, Kravis and Roberts. This left a big hole at the top of our corporate finance department. One night Cy Lewis, Ace and I were riding home together in Cy's car, and I started saying that we have got to do something about the corporate finance department now that KK&R are gone. And by the time we got uptown, a decision was made and my career took a dramatic new direction.

Editor: Erik Ipsen

Peter L. Bernstein

President PETER L. BERNSTEIN, INC.

Few individuals have bridged the worlds of academia and investment management as adroitly, and as successfully, as has Peter L.
Bernstein. As an influential teacher and thinker, he has written on
subjects ranging from money, banking and gold to the trends and
vagaries of the investment profession. He ran a successful investment counseling firm, Bernstein-Macaulay, taught at Williams College and the New School for Social Research and was founding
editor of *The Journal of Portfolio Management*. Today he is the president of Peter L. Bernstein, Inc., consultants to institutional investors and publishers of a semimonthly letter on economic and
financial developments.

I came into the late 1960s a man, and rather an old man at that.
I emerge from the late 1980s a boy. How did it happen that these
twenty years have made me feel younger, when most people say
that they have been through enough to age them prematurely?

In 1967 I was the chief executive and investment officer of
Bernstein-Macaulay, a family-oriented investment counsel firm
that had been started by my father in 1934. I had joined them in
1951, when my father died unexpectedly. We grossed $60,000 in
fees in 1951, out of which we paid salaries to three professional
men—I drew $7,500—and two women in support staff, paid a
dollar a square foot on a full floor at Madison Avenue and 44th
Street and booked a profit of $10,000.

Except for a few sports like John Hartwell, investment counseling in the mid-1960s still bore only a faint resemblance to what it is like today. It was almost totally a mature man's profession.

We insisted that our clients select their own brokers. We seldom saw any Wall Street research and laughed at most of what we did see. Value Line and our own common sense of the world were our only research sources. We owned only blue chips. Yet, we did fine for clients, even though we chronically and typically owned too many bonds—especially sticky municipals that we regularly churned to take losses at year-end. All of those features were standard operating procedure for well-established investment advisers. Our one big adventure was in identifying the puberty boom early on and taking big positions in Gillette and Tampax; the latter was barely mentionable in polite conversation at that time.

The clientele was typically widow-and-orphan types, although some business came in from people who had sold out their companies to others or who had taken them public. Most of these businessmen were so addicted to capital conservation that they put the widows and orphans to shame.

When my older partner died in 1967, my younger associates wanted to move into the big-time world of pension management. Screaming and kicking, I went along with their dreams. Bernstein-Macaulay ended up being acquired by a bunch of attractive, bright and aggressive men who looked very much like boys to me. Their names were Carter, Berlind, Weill, Levitt and Cogan. Bernstein-Macaulay had the distinction of being Sandy Weill's first deal.

To the world, and to myself, I was an old man on Wall Street in 1967, although I was only 48 years old at the time. The veterans of the Great Crash had mostly disappeared from the scene as a result of death or retirement, and almost no one else of my vintage had gone anywhere near Wall Street.

The tiny number of oldsters—which included titanic innovators like Gus Levy and Salim Lewis—was offset by a growing flood of whiz kids like our new partners, who made up Wall Street's first sizable contingent of business school graduates—risk-loving youngsters in their late 20s or early 30s. They knew about the Depression only from textbooks, and all of them seemed to know much more about everything else like trading and give-ups and the Charlie Bluhdorns of the world than I could possibly begin to understand or even imagine. I got 70 on my entrance test to New York Stock Exchange membership.

Our parent company principals enjoyed referring to me, with some pride, as the "dean" of this and that. They treated me with great respect and paid absolutely no attention to anything that I had to say. Nothing can make you feel older than that.

There was little respite from this sense of isolated old age when I turned to people in the academic world, once a comforting source of Keynesian dogma and confirming memories of the automatic relationship between risk and loss. The youngsters had taken over the academic world, too.

In 1969 an editor from Random House introduced me to a delightful young professor named Sharpe, who immediately beamed at me and asked whether I thought I could beat the market. Insulted by the question, although charmed by the smile, I replied that I thought the answer was obvious. The answer was obvious, all right, but his answer was the opposite of mine.

Bill Sharpe proposed a seminar to be held in some watering place in Mexico, to which my parent company would invite its major institutional customers, so that the customers could learn that neither they nor anyone else could beat the market, although there were some interesting things that investment managers could do to earn their keep nevertheless. The parent company, however, was in no mood to be a messenger of gloom to anybody, even in a watering place in Mexico.

Their enthusiasm was catching. The stodgy Bernstein-Macaulay portfolios began changing their character. The widows and orphans lingered on, but the pension funds started to receive more attention. Swinging customers from the brokerage side came expecting miracles. In the end, we produced fewer miracles than we had under our old system and ultimately had to try to find our way back toward more traditional approaches.

Anyway, not long after Bill Sharpe's visit, the stock market entered into a bear market that I had satisfactorily predicted but that lasted well beyond my comment in August 1969 that, thank God, it was over. Skies in the U.S. economy were much darker than I—or anyone else I knew—was willing to recognize at the time. The optimism of youth was beginning to grab on to me.

That bear market did have its pleasant consequences. Our original agreement with our parent company provided for us to receive additional shares of its stock under certain circumstances in which our earnings growth outpaced theirs. Nineteen seventy was just what the doctor ordered, as our business moved merrily along while theirs was going south rapidly. That was a deal in which the prisoners took Sandy Weill! I had by now turned 50 by the calendar, but I was feeling younger all the time.

My wife died in late 1971. The experience was a horror, but in time I realized that I was a single man again: another step back toward youth. Furthermore, those were the days of Vietnam upheavals, even on Wall Street, and the patriotic urge that had sent me glady into the Air Force in World War II began to look very old-fashioned indeed. At the same time, the imposition of price controls and the abandonment of gold did the same for the economics I had learned at Harvard in the 1930s and that had served me so well for so long.

Having made relatively little effort to learn anything new for some 25 years—not out of laziness but out of a sense that there was nothing new to learn that would be useful to me—I began to feel the need of an education. Bill Sharpe and the new interest in monetarism, plus a stint at the FAF Investment Management Workshop one summer at Harvard Business School, had done a job on me. They added to my sense of being a youth starting out.

By the middle of 1973, my intellectual curiosity had been stirred to a boiling point. In addition, I was remarried, which is a great way to feel young again. In fact, I was so full of the spirit of youth that I decided to go back into business for myself, taking my new wife along as a partner.

So I left the old stand and started the consulting firm that bears my name, giving me the chance I always wanted to pontificate on the linkages between what is happening in the economy and what is happening in the capital markets. Not many economists have had hands-on experience managing portfolios, and not many portfolio managers end up on the Visiting Committee of the Harvard department of economics.

There have been good calls and bad calls. You remember the good ones, of course, like pooh-poohing the shortage thesis in 1975 because of an unshakable faith in the laws of supply and demand. Or writing a screamingly bullish article called "HATE!" for *Institutional Investor* in November 1977, arguing that all the potential bad news was in the market. Or proclaiming the bottom of the bond market in September 1981, because all the potential bad news was in that market, too. Or in predicting a long, long period of high real interest rates as early as July 1980, because of the collective memories of pain that haunted the bond market.

There were plenty of fuzzy calls, too, which is one unpleasant reason why these years have made me feel younger and younger. I guess it is the sense of insufficient understanding, of all the cognitive dissonances. These disturbing sensations are not limited to those who are older. Everyone suffers from these same diseases. Young people had their own unique view of things in the 1960s and even in the 1970s, but today you can't tell the players by their ages or by their experiences. Uncertainty is a great leveler.

Part of the educational process that I began in the early 1970s involved reading the *Financial Analysts Journal,* which had previously struck me as a waste of time. I discovered that a whole lot was going on out there that I did not hear about at Institutional Investor conferences or in *Institutional Investor* magazine. I hounded Gil Kaplan mercilessly about this, refusing to shut up, although he insisted for a long time that the *FAJ* had only one reader—me—and that even I was too small an audience to justify changing the *Institutional Investor* style.

The squeaky wheel gets the oil. Gil finally broke down and proposed establishing *The Journal of Portfolio Management,* of which I would be the editor. It became a reality in the fall of 1974. I remember reading the galleys of the first issue when we were out at Montauk at the same moment that Richard Nixon was resigning.

The *Journal* has kept me younger than anything else, because the learning process has been so intense. When you have to read all that stuff—read it, not skim it, and the bad as well as the good—you just can't help learning from it. The process itself revives college days in the library, a mixture of watching the clock with one eye and trying to absorb unfamiliar ideas with the other.

The *Journal* has been one of those rare events when everything works out as you had hoped—or even better. The goal of the *Journal* has been to avoid the kind of confrontation that Bill

Sharpe and I had way back then. We have achieved that goal to such a degree that today the academics have so much respect for the practitioners that they are practicing and some of the practitioners have unashamedly gone into teaching.

The other sequence of events that runs your age in reverse is what happens when the computer enters your life. You have started out with a pad of paper, a pencil and slide rule. The hand-held calculator comes along and is a miracle, even though it can do only simple arithmetic. You go forward from there to the fancy HP calculators, which do regressions and calculate t-statistics and ANOVAs, steepening your learning curve, but you still have to write down each number on a pad of paper as the calculator produces it.

I was one of the first people to go from the HP to an Apple II+—not yet even a IIe. I was glad to have left the slide rule so far behind, but insisted that I would never let the computer draw a graph for me. That was a laugh. Today, without my PC, Lotus, and Microsoft Word, and all the nice embellishments, I would be lost. Life moves too fast for anyone to draw graphs by hand.

The one big loss for the investment management profession over these years has been the disappearance of the balanced manager. The stylish cafeteria of specialized managers that we see today leads to a mishmash of risks and covariances that most clients fail to understand. In a most profound sense, they simply do not know what they are doing—although I admit that they may have more fun this way than they would have with the old-fashioned approach.

One day, I'll have to figure out what I am going to do when I grow up.

Leon Levy

Partner ODYSSEY PARTNERS

While mutual funds have lately been an area of stunning growth for Wall Street, they are hardly a new phenomenon to Leon Levy. Now 61, Levy was one of the pioneers of the industry beginning in the late 1950s, when his firm launched the Oppenheimer Funds, as well as one of the guiding lights of the institutional brokerage business. A reflective, scholarly strategist, Levy helped shepherd Oppenheimer & Co. through more than two decades of growth before selling the firm and moving on to found Odyssey Partners, a privately held venture capital and investment group.

I used to work with my dad, who was an economist—helping him find investments. When it came time to earn a living, I was studying for my master's in psychology, but I thought I'd like to try my hand at being a securities analyst. So I got a job as a trainee at a firm called Hirsh and Co., which no longer exists. There I met Mr. Max Oppenheimer, who was a salesman. Max wanted Hirsh to begin trading blocked German marks—since a lot of Max's clients were receiving them as reparations and the marks couldn't be invested outside Germany.

Hirsh didn't choose to do so, and thereupon Mr. Oppenheimer decided to start his own firm in a glassed-off partitioned space in Hirsh and Co.'s boardroom. He asked me to join him as a partner. Since I was 25 and no one else was about to offer me a partnership, I thought I'd take advantage of it. In essence, for a short time I was the research department at Oppenheimer & Co., but it was a very small shop—there were only six or seven of us—so we all did a bit of everything. Actually, since the partnership eventually became Odyssey Partners, I've really only had one job since 1951.

We started the Oppenheimer Fund in 1958 and went public with it in 1959. It was one of the first funds with a performance fee. It was nondiversified. It had the right to influence managements and to sell short. I believe it was the first hedge fund that ever cleared the SEC. Its strength was partly due to the research department we had built up. There were many brilliant fellows—and I don't mean to slight any—but I remember Sandy Bernstein very well, who went on to found a very successful firm [Sanford C. Bernstein & Co.]. Another was Rodney White, who died very prematurely, in his late 30s. When that happened I recall *Institutional Investor* magazine running a memorial in *The New York Times* for him as "the man who founded modern money management." And he deserved it. Rodney very early on understood the concept of growth stocks. At that time Graham-Dodd analysis, balance sheet strength and other "fundamentals" were the dominant measures of stocks' worth. But Rodney understood the multiples that companies deserved if their earnings were very likely to improve dramatically. Our savings and loan analyst was Marion Sandler, who left with her husband, Herbert, to build up Golden West Financial—a superbly managed public company.

We had some unique criteria for picking research analysts that may not be applicable today. First of all, I thought that only young fellows would be good analysts, because anybody who was still an analyst and had lived through the 1930s would have a distorted and unduly pessimistic view of the world. Secondly, I have always believed that people worked best when they were doing their own thing, like entrepreneurs. So I looked for analysts who invested their own money. I wanted them to put a meaningful amount of money where their mouth was, you bet.

We knew at the beginning that there was only one way for the firm to establish a franchise for the fund—and that it would take ten years. That was to have the best performance record in the country over that time. We used every type of strategy to achieve that—and we had some shocks—but it finally settled down to a permanent portfolio managed by Archer Scherl. Nineteen fifty-eight, I recall, was the advent of the discount stores, and we had a very high representation in those stocks. We thought they would create a revolution similar to that when supermarkets replaced grocery stores. We also, in 1960 and 1961, had very large positions in the savings and loan stocks, which had just begun to go public. Those were very successful, but we were set back hard in 1962.

That was about when we evolved the ad program and the logo of four crossed hands gripping each other—the firemen's carry. We did a great deal of market research on the symbol—because a symbol was all you were allowed to advertise with by the SEC. Their regulations were so strict that one fund that wanted to use a rocket pointing upward was forbidden to do so because the SEC said it would give the wrong idea about performance. And the mutual funds were just then becoming performance-conscious. Arthur Lipper had started Lipper Analytical Services, and everybody knew how funds were performing. We could show charts—how much your dollar would have grown in ten years and so on—but you weren't allowed to advertise performance.

My role at the firm, then, as I think Sandy Bernstein pointed out, was to be the "partner in charge of outer space." I was thinking about what would happen several years hence. I should point out that Jack Nash was really running the firm by the early '60s and ran it until its sale to Mercantile House, the British investment firm.

I saw the necessity of Wall Street firms going public because the volume on the NYSE was growing so rapidly that block positioning came into being and the firms started requiring more and more capital. Also, inheritance taxes were high, and the older partners had most of the money. Wall Street firms were all partnerships, and I saw that there would be a need for other ways to finance them. I also saw that the institutions were beginning to call the shots and that even in the '60s you could project what would happen on Mayday.

In fact, there was a volume discount in the late '60s. Up until then "The Club" was able to hold commission rates high and keep anyone else from having access to the NYSE. They had a very good thing going. But in the late '60s, the institutions became larger and stronger than the brokerage firms and were eventually able to force discounts. We were very fortunately positioned, I should add, because our research was considered to be very good.

549

Our return on capital was extraordinarily high, much higher than one deserved, but it was the system at the time. We didn't want to become aggressive block traders, but the institutions started demanding not only research but also liquidity.

Going into the 1970s, we had achieved the goal of having the best fund performance of the decade and we established new funds. They were certainly by then in the hundreds of millions of dollars versus the $2 million we began with. I believe we had one of the largest fund complexes owned by a Wall Street firm. But there was some brilliant competition. Jack Dreyfus was certainly one of my heroes. His Dreyfus Fund was a top performer in his decade. He introduced advertising on television—with the lion coming out of the subway. And he retired. I always thought that somebody who had enough sense to retire and pursue other interests was remarkable. Jack did medical research, he was an excellent scratch golfer, a brilliant card player, and he raised one of the great horse-breeding farms of our time.

Aside from the funds, we also took positions in companies and ran an investment account from the very onset. In the late '60s we started a company called Dearborn Leasing, which went public. It was one of the first companies in the offshore drilling business. We also had a small oil company called Oppenheimer Oil and Gas. It was no shakes as an oil company, but it was very good as an investment banking vehicle because we merged it into another firm, American Quasar, and we showed them through our fund experience how partnership participations could be sold. They became the largest distributor of limited partnerships in the oil industry, and the stock we had in American Quasar did extremely well.

We were also doing arbitrage all through the conglomerate boom. It's a naughty word now, but it was only controversial at Oppenheimer & Co. when we lost money. There were conglomerateurs, as they were called, buying companies by issuing preferred stock, warrants, what have you. The more complex the merger, the greater the arbitrage opportunity. I should say, in light of the focus on inside information, that we had a code of ethics at Oppenheimer. We said that nobody should do anything that his mother would not be pleased to read about in *The New York Times*.

We were never immune to any decline that took place on Wall Street, and in the shakeout of the mid-'70s the mutual fund industry was more or less dead. Sales were less than redemptions for several years in the middle '70s. The mood was somber. But somehow we emerged as a stronger firm. In the '70s we acquired two or three mutual fund companies. The most sizable was the Hamilton Funds, which had been owned by ITT. They had to sell them because ITT management was about to be investigated on charges of having been involved in undermining the Chilean government. So they asked us if we could act in three days, and, being a partnership where we all spoke to each other easily, we said yes and owned the Hamilton Funds three days later—I think we purchased the management company at book value.

In some ways, the whole decade from the late '60s into the '70s can be seen as a breaking down of various "clubs" on Wall Street. If you look at 1967, when *Institutional Investor* magazine started, the leading investment banks had all been around since the 1920s or 1930s—Morgan Stanley came out of J.P. Morgan's bank, First Boston out of the First National Bank of Boston and so on. There were very few firms that had been started in the postwar period. Donaldson, Lufkin & Jenrette and Oppenheimer were two exceptions.

There were "Catholic" firms and "Jewish" firms and "WASP" firms. There was a sort of gentleman's agreement: You'd not have Catholics working for a WASP firm and certainly not Jews. It seemed to me in the '60s that all that was going to change. And it did.

The shift really goes back to the question of firms going public. Wall Street had had a certain cachet: It was the only aristocratic business in the United States. By that I mean the only business where a father, if he were a senior partner, could count on passing the business on to his son. That was because the firms required capital, the senior partners had the most, and that devolved naturally on the heir. Second, with fixed commissions, you didn't have to be a genius to earn a living. Finally, the loyalty of the corporations to their investment banks was a given. The industrial firms didn't have access to the broad public market. Therefore, investment bankers were passing on a franchise that was protected by "The Club." All the qualities for inheritance were there. Now they're gone.

The treasurers' departments at the corporations were growing in financial acumen and were able to do many things just as well as these mysterious Wall Street firms. And the abolition of fixed commissions at Mayday meant there was no more free lunch—you had to be out scratching for a living. I believe Prudential, among the institutions, was in the forefront of that change. There was an apocryphal story in those days that the president of the Pru was at a cocktail party and met an institutional salesman who made more money than he did, and he thought that if that was so, there must be something really rotten with the system.

And there were some wild goings-on. Bernie Cornfeld I never liked—even though he originally bought some Oppenheimer Fund shares. His scheme had a Ponzi-like quality to it. As I recall, all the stock was held by IOS employees, and it was supposed to go up 40 to 50 percent a year. It doesn't take much of a mathematician to tell you that that can't go on forever and that somebody is going to be very hurt. Bernie's mother wouldn't have liked to read everything he did on the front pages of the *Times*. But the remarkable thing was the blue-chip underwriting group he put together to sell IOS stock to the public—it would embarrass about three quarters of the top Wall Street firms of the day.

Toward the end of the 1970s, the Oppenheimer operation enlarged a great deal. We had well over 1,000 employees. Since we had started with eight, it seemed to be a great many. We had lost a great deal of our flexibility and charm, in a way. I mean, I enjoyed it less. There were too many constraints with a large firm. You had to watch your trading operation. You had to take large positions. The strain was really much greater. So we sold the financial businesses to Mercantile House in August '82. The key to the sale was the younger management, which then took over and continued to run the firm probably better than we did. Mercantile would never have bought Oppenheimer without Steve Roberts, now chairman, Nate Gantcher, now president, and Don Spiro, president of the Oppenheimer Funds.

The older generation, Jack Nash and I, kept the partnership. We changed the name to Odyssey because it had an "O," like Oppenheimer; it suggested what we were about; and the ancient history part of it appealed to me. Jack deserves credit for the structure and success of both the old and new partnerships. He has remarkable foresight for predicting possible trouble and keeping us out of it.

Several months later, when three partners left Oppenheimer to join Lazard Frères, we protested, even though we had no financial interest anymore. I saw it as completely unethical. Maybe I'm old-fashioned, but Lazard had represented us on the sale and done due diligence on Oppenheimer before they took in those three partners. I really think that was immoral. Maybe today it would be more commonplace.

Our own goals with Odyssey were to be able to build up a first-rate group to invest our own money—in bankruptcies or securities or leveraged buyouts, whatever we understood. One of the good ones was when we bought into the Chicago Milwaukee [railroad] at about $10 a share. That must have been in 1982 or so. The holding company was solid and had some other operating businesses, but they carried the railroad on their books at $1 and their board claimed the railroad was worthless. In fact, the board didn't speak to the trustee and didn't get along with him. We went and saw him and the board. I was convinced, because of the need to haul coal [after the OPEC price shock of 1979], that conditions were changed and the railroad would eventually acquire value. We started at $10 a share—actually, first we owned the bonds at 15, 25, 30 cents on the dollar. They were paid off at par, and the stock now sells in the 130s.

We didn't always succeed, though, and we did run head-on into The Establishment once. That was on our TWA fight, which was a very sobering experience for me. We had had Booz, Allen and Hamilton make a study that suggested that TWA could be divided into separate companies and those companies would be worth about $60 a share versus the $20 a share TWA was trading for. This was in the early '80s, at the very beginning of deconglomeration. Ed Smart, who was the chairman of Trans World, suggested that this would be a good strategy and that he should become chairman of each of the separate companies and that he would discuss it with his board. He said, in effect, don't call us, we'll call you.

We didn't want to take over the company. We only wanted to participate by buying the stock. We had formed a group, and we owned a little over 5 percent of the stock. And the proxies went out; several heads of the trust departments of leading banks called us up and said, "We're obviously going to vote for the board to consider your proposal." Later, though, it turned out that the TWA board had gone to all their pals who were running companies like General Dynamics, and those firms called up the banks and warned that if they voted for the proposal they would withdraw their money. TWA also sued us and ran ads against us, and we then sued them for harassment and were awarded costs by the courts—which is unusual. It was a profitable experience for us because the stock went up, but unpleasant.

The atmosphere in recent years has been so much more unbridled. Look at the advertisements for mutual funds today and how they tout performance. Maybe in the '60s everything was too puritanical and the SEC was old-maidish. I believe they were. But certainly, a great many ads today can be described as misleading. I just wonder when there's another sea change, as there inevitably will be, how many people will be vulnerable to lawsuits.

Editor: Lenny Glynn

Robert Mnuchin

Partner GOLDMAN, SACHS & CO.

Institutions now so completely dominate equity trading that it's hard to recall that not so long ago individual investors accounted for the bulk of stock market transactions. The block trading era didn't just arise spontaneously, however. Goldman Sachs equity trading head Robert Mnuchin and the firm's legendary chief, the late Gus Levy, played a vital role in creating the current institutional trading climate. At 53, Mnuchin remains one of the most senior, still-active pioneers of the block trading fraternity.

I joined the firm in September 1957, and became a partner on January 1, 1967, right at the height of the go-go years. Remember, now, we're talking about an environment in the '50s and into the '60s in which individual business, as opposed to institutional business, accounted for most of the activity. Today the market is perhaps 80 percent institutional and 20 percent individual.

What really contributed to the change—and to Goldman Sachs becoming an important factor in the trading of securities with institutions—was our ability to create supply and demand by making bids and offers for blocks of stock. The block trading firms created the ability for institutions to execute a significant percentage of their business with a limited number of firms that excelled in execution and at the same time to create commission dollars for firms that contributed important research or other services.

Gus Levy was certainly the architect of our efforts to become a factor in block trading. He was a very significant trader both before the war and when he came out of the army. His forte was arbitrage, and those years provided lots of opportunity. All the way back to the '30s there had been a series of corporate restructurings—mainly involving the railroads—in which shareholders typically got a group of securities in exchange for the parent stock. Gus was in the business of buying whatever outstanding security was becoming extinct, then trading what would be the new pieces on a when-issued basis. There was a spread between the whole and the parts. He was going out offering the new securities to different institutions in an effort to create demand. So if he bought 5,000 shares of Missouri Pacific, he would try to sell the underlying pieces for more than he paid for the stock.

In the course of showing them offerings of these pieces, Gus would say, "If you want to sell something to raise the money for this, I will take it off your hands," or, "If you don't want to buy Missouri Pacific, is there something else you'd like to buy?" And that was the beginning of Goldman Sachs talking to institutions on a transactional basis as opposed to contacting them on the basis of research ideas.

The equity trading desk was very different in the early days. It consisted of three people—myself and two others. We didn't have Quotrons. It was essential to watch the tape to know where the last sales were and what markets were doing.

Trading in size was a relatively new phenomenon in the '60s. I mean, we were past the point when 10,000 shares was a big block, but 50,000 shares was important and 100,000 shares was a very significant piece of business. Both we and the institutions were really just learning that bigger transactions could be done. Actually, since NYSE volume of 5 million shares was a big day, many of the pieces of business we did then were larger relative to the market than those we do today—even though some blocks today are humongous, so is the volume.

The entire habit or process of active institutional transactions—of their revisiting their portfolios, making changes—was in its earlier stages. Consequently, if you had, for example, a block of Lockheed for sale, it was very unlikely that you would at that moment find an institution or institutions that were prepared to purchase all or part of the block. The frequency of finding the other side of a trade was smaller—much smaller.

It was a long time before institutions found it as natural to ask for a block offering when they wanted to buy stock as they did to ask for a bid when they wanted to sell. They just tended to use block trading or liquidity when they were selling and that tended to be in down markets.

Once block trading became a product with a relatively broad base, as opposed to an occasional pick-your-spot situation, the positions we wound up holding were not a profit center in themselves. The volume we created and the aggregate commissions we generated minus a loss on positions for the most part became a profitable business. This was certainly the case with fixed commissions in the '60s, which were much greater than those of today. Of course, the volume now is infinitely higher and the average transaction is far larger, so direct comparisons are hard. But the positions themselves were not profitable—and that's been the result right up through today.

Another difference is that in the '60s a factor in block trading was, What price would generate retail or public orders once you printed the block? The print per se was a much more significant part of the business than it is today. You hoped the price at which you bought something or the price at which you sold something was going to create retail supply or demand after the fact.

Fortunately, we didn't have to depend entirely on retail, because the '60s was a time when mutual funds were blossoming. Bank trust departments were becoming more active, and you had a climate of institutions more actively and aggressively reviewing their portfolios—not just how many dollars they wanted invested in stocks or even in which industries they wanted to invest but, within industries, which stocks to buy. To what extent block trading developed because of institutional needs or because the existence of a block trading facility created that interest is an unresolvable question.

The hardest aspect of this business is the problem positions. When you can get out of a stock that you're long at a small loss or buy back a stock you're short at a small loss, that's an easy decision. It is painful when there isn't an apparent opportunity or the price is very far away. Then you hesitate. Then you pray. You hope that it will get better or you use the wrong judgment that it *will* get better. Those were the situations when it was absolutely fantastic to work with Gus Levy.

I remember him very well during the hardest single time I had before becoming a partner, in 1965, I think. One of the institutions called and wanted an offer on Motorola. I offered what was then a very large block—I think it was about 100,000 shares. I offered up a half or three quarters of a point—maybe even a point—from the last sale, and they said they'd buy it. Well, you never know which trade is the one that will not create supply and demand. On this particular transaction no supply of Motorola filled in. We were short it all.

I handled the position very badly, and the stock was just a steamroller. It wouldn't stop. We did this transaction at a price in the mid-$60 range, and, if I recall properly, we covered the last shares of the short at 109 or 110. It was a monumental loss—significant seven figures. I wasn't thinking about my partnership prospects—I was worried about my employment prospects. I had some genuine concern that I'd be fired as a result of this Motorola deal. Well, Gus was absolutely terrific about this one. Instead of getting fired, I was shortly thereafter made a partner.

The block business has been growing ever since the abolition of fixed commissions at Mayday in 1975, and it's here to stay. I remember the day itself, Mayday. Almost from the moment the bell rang there were all kinds of discussions: "This firm is doing it for so much!" "Somebody else is offering lower prices!" It was in the air. But I also remember a number of people calling to say, "We appreciate the effort that you [Goldman Sachs] have made to create a dialogue on this subject; you're good at your business, and we want to do our first transaction of the new era with you." It only took a few months, really, to sort itself out into a new general approach.

There's still no book, though, that sets down what is a good bid. If you're taking somebody's blood pressure or their weight or their cholesterol count, there are charts to tell you what's acceptable, what's very good, what's normal, what's abnormal. But equities are a moving target, and the conditions are always different; and no two moments in time are exactly alike, and many moments are very different. But block trading is here to stay.

Editor: Lenny Glynn

Hans-Joerg Rudloff

Vice Chairman CREDIT SUISSE FIRST BOSTON

Hans-Joerg Rudloff, 47, is widely considered to be among the greatest syndicate strategists in the Eurobond market. Born in Germany, he started his career in 1967 with a one-year stint as a trainee at Crédit Suisse and then joined Kidder Peabody in New York for $60 a week. After returning to Geneva as an equity and bond salesman for Kidder, Rudloff moved to London and took charge of the firm's European operations in 1975. Four years later, he accepted an offer from then CSFB chairman Michael von Clemm to head CSFB's syndicate department. In 1980 Rudloff introduced the bought deal, and the Euromarkets have not been the same since.

Before 1980 the investment banker was the intermediary between borrower and investor; he did not have to judge the market, because he took no risk whatsoever. Everything was based on an open pricing after a ten-day selling period. One had a feeling an issue should come at, let's say, 7 percent. So you indicated 7 percent, open priced, to the market. Then you let the market respond; the underwriters came back, the co-managers replied. Then you found yourself with a book; either it was oversubscribed or it was undersubscribed; or you had a lot of comments that the price was too tight or too generous. And in the end you took all that information given to you by the market, and you presented the borrower with the overall picture. Then you made a price recommendation. The sizes were anywhere between $25 million and $100 million. There was a simple rule: An issue had to be oversubscribed by 100 percent to be considered successful.

Success in those days meant the bonds should be selling around par. In other words, all of the firms who had worked on it, the underwriters, the co-managers and so forth, got their full fees, more or less, plus or minus half a point. Issues that opened at a discount of 2 percent, just around the fee level, were considered total disasters. It happened from time to time, but not too often. Unlike today, you had a lot of problems bringing the next issue.

Don't forget one other thing: Markets were not very volatile. Interest rates changed by a quarter of a point in a three-month period. So the only things you were dealing against were supply and demand factors. It was easy to be an investment banker.

New issues were run entirely by corporate finance people. Every investment bank was structured so that the primary business was done by corporate finance, while trading and sales were done by other people. The deals were cut and constructed by the investment bankers and syndicated by the investment bankers. Hopefully, the salesmen would sell the paper. The salesmen had no input on the deals. Actually, a salesman wasn't allowed in the room.

Investment bankers were a different breed of people—from Harvard, Yale, Princeton, whatever you like. It was a huge cultural gap. The traders and salesmen played a very, very inferior role, and the salesmen resented it. All decisions were taken by the investment bankers, who assembled at 9:00 in the morning and made the decision on underwriting commitments and so forth. Nothing to do with sales and trading. Syndication was pure execution: You sent out the telexes and wrote down the demand indications from the telexes that came in. Purely clerical work.

Kidder was different. It was so small that we built investment banking out of our selling and placing and trading capability. Other firms had built it the other way around. It was an accident, in a way, in that there was Stanley Ross who had built, out of his own ideas, with his own initiative and his own imagination, a huge trading operation. And I think we did likewise on sales.

Stanley and I both got started back in 1969. I was basically his salesman for years. I learned a lot from him. He was an excellent trader and an excellent manager. But Stanley never liked salesmen; he thought they were a necessary evil. But we still got along, though I guess we did have our ups and downs. He was the first one who introduced research into the market, with the famous Ian Kerr. For years Ian wrote his own weekly letter for Kidder. And it was the only one around the world handling Eurobonds.

I think we did three prepriced deals at Kidder back then. The differences between prepriced and bought deals was quite substantial; in a prepriced deal I contacted the proposed co-managers and got their commitments before we made the bid to, for example, New Zealand. In other words, we bid a fixed price. But the lead managers did not carry the entire risk. The risk already had been syndicated among a core group of five or seven banks.

Now, in a prepriced deal or in a bought deal, the investment banker has to make his judgment up front. He has to know his market well enough to say it is 7 percent at par; his skills are on the line. If he makes a mistake, he sits with a huge position; he can sell it, but maybe only at 96 with a respective loss, or he can sell it at 102 with a respective gain.

I had learned from my father, if you don't know the market, you will never be able to make a career anywhere. You have to know your market. And once I knew the market, I could turn to structuring, from structuring to making decisions, from making decisions to prepricing, and from prepricing to buying entire transactions. I knew how investors reacted very often. I was running a big sales operation, pretty big, so I had all the input. And I was a trader and running a trading operation, where you see all the flow. If I ever had an advantage, it was that I was probably the only person in the market who came from sales and trading and not from corporate financing.

Maybe I would have jumped from the prepriced to the bought right away. But there was no way to convince a firm like Kidder Peabody to make a $50 million commitment. Nevertheless, I was always ready to take the entire commitment. I thought Kidder was in excellent shape, perfectly organized in Europe to play a major role. But I had a feeling Kidder wasn't ready. At the same time, there was a change in management, and the group who had built Kidder International was gone. And there were more and more people put in charge of international business in New York who were totally inept.

[Michael] von Clemm from Credit Suisse First Boston called me, I guess it was July 1979. That year Credit Suisse First Boston did, I think, twelve deals, and most were placed with Crédit Suisse. When I joined, Credit Suisse First Boston had three salesmen;

Kidder at that time had 60. I insisted on a syndicate job because it was all I wanted to do; the selling, the structuring and the pricing are basically what I know best technically. There was no real discussion of what I would do or where I thought the markets would be going. I took the job at Credit Suisse First Boston because I thought it was a platform where one could do certain things for which Kidder was too small. I felt very clearly that the market would explode and become much bigger.

In 1980 the entire environment changed because of the volatility of interest rates. And one reason I developed the bought deal was that I saw borrowers had to be isolated from the market risk of that volatile environment. I think GMAC was the first bought deal we did. Or maybe it was J.C. Penney. I do remember we went to J.C. Penney and said, "Look, we'll just buy the whole thing. There is a huge opening to do a good issue." J.C. loved it! For an issue that big—I think it was $100 million—I needed to get authorization. I found [Crédit Suisse chairman] Rainer Gut somewhere in New York, and I said I want to buy a J.C. Penney overnight. Now Gut is an investment banker; he makes very rapid decisions. He just said, "Do you think you can place it?" and I said, "Sure, it's the right time to do it." So he just said, "Then go ahead and do it." We sat there all night writing the offering telexes. So by the morning at 7:00 we had an offering telex, and then we syndicated it and got rid of our risk. It was the first million dollars we ever made. Profit. Overnight.

Huge upheavals resulted from the bought deal. You have shifted the entire decision-making structure from the investment bankers to the syndicate department, because now it became risk management. Now you tell the investment bankers the time is right to do a deal because you feel comfortable with the market. We flipped the whole relationship between investment banking, syndicate sales and trading. It was a very difficult change, because it changed 25 years or 50 years of investment banking. But they had to do it, because the borrowers wanted only one thing: firm bids. It was clear the borrowers loved it.

The other thing which changed—and that's where you had the so-called gray market operators, of whom Stanley Ross was the first—is that they immediately could put a price on a deal. Before, it was sort of unprofessional—some people said unethical—to make prices in deals that hadn't been priced. And all that argument about the gray market from '78 to '80 fell apart, because now you had a deal that was priced and bought and a security that would be issued; therefore it could be traded. As I said, I bought J.C. Penney at 10:00 at night, and at 8:00 in the morning we started selling. And thereafter Stanley Ross started making a market. Everyone had a checkpoint.

I was always in favor of the gray market, because the need was obvious. If you preprice a deal or you buy an issue, the deal is in the market. It's a security that exists. Now, if you put the wrong price on it and someone calls you and says, "Your price is wrong, and I'm quoting at 97½ to 98," then either you were right or he was right. And then the market will decide. He doesn't have the bonds, but he was trading in them. You could go for a short squeeze and keep all the bonds, but then you're stuck with the entire deal. If he is right, it's stupid to go against him.

We later lost a lot of money on a bought deal for the Canadian Export Development Corp. After we bought, there was a dramatic change in the market during the selling period. We had totally syndicated it and were left with $30 million out of $150 million. But after four or five days, the market fell apart totally. So we decided to protect the underwriting group and the co-managers by taking all the bonds back. We had a reputation that our deals would sell well, because we were usually right on the pricing, and I didn't want to lumber people with a two-point loss within a day. If I allot the bonds, everyone has a loss. What would they do? They sell. So the bonds, in fact, would have gone down to 95, far too low. So I said, in protecting our own position, "Let's not even allot them, because that's a temporary situation." If it was temporary, it wouldn't have worked. Now that turned out to be a pretty stupid decision.

We told them they had the choice of taking the bonds back, knowing that it would be two points under water—and I still remember there were a few banks that took it. Westdeutsche Landesbank took it in full, even though they knew it would only be worth 96½, out of friendship and sort of solidarity with the bond and with us. It was a very dramatic week. There were about fourteen or fifteen issues. And all these issues went within two weeks to 92. Now at that time, we had the opinion that the market would recover. As it turned out, the market never recovered. Interest rates went from 9.5 percent straight up to 17 percent without any recovery. We took an enormous beating. I think we lost something like $20 million.

The investment bankers were horrified, needless to say. I am sure people used [the Export Development Corp. deal] against von Clemm and myself. If you go for the bought deal and you are right, you make a lot of money. Of course, there would be a few times when you would be wrong, and you lose a lot of money. But you can't have only one side and not the other side. That the EDC issue turned into a disastrous transaction for CSFB had a lot to do with our decision-making process, which was consensus decision making. I wanted to sell CSFB's position at 93 to 93½—maybe even 94—which turned into about a $2 million loss. But other parts of the firm decided, no, they wouldn't take a loss like this, they wanted to keep the bonds. So, needless to say, they finally lost their nerve and sold at 81.

Our entire decision-making process was at stake. It was a secondary decision we made—to relieve the underwriters and co-managers of their commitment. We made a mistake in taking these bonds back from the market. But that was a trading decision. No, I never had any doubt about the bought deal. Von Clemm also still believed in it. After EDC we changed the decision-making process. From that moment on, I decided whether we would stay long or not, whether we would blow bonds out or wouldn't. When it comes to trading decisions, you can't discuss it with a lot of people. As you make up your mind, you do it. I was always willing to take on that kind of responsibility. Whenever I start talking to other people, I lose all my convictions because everyone has his case. But you have to follow your own judgment, and judgment cannot be discussed.

Now that means you could be wrong. And, needless to say, I always expected that if you are wrong two or three or four times, you have to change the person—not the system, the person. After all, why did the other banks fall in the league tables? Because commercial banks were not used to vesting decision-making power in one person. It always had to be a consensus. And when it was a consensus, how could anyone in that position go against a general management view? If the general management just whispers and says, "Be careful," is he going to take the risk? No way.

I was very lucky that this decision-making power got vested in me, but at the same time, I think CSFB was lucky as well—for the simple reason that it gained us two years on our competitors. Only the very good firms that had the right people after one or two years stayed in place. And in those days, four or five firms shared 85 percent of the market.

Salomon was very competitive. I remember they had a very good Tokyo operation, which we didn't have. Salomon did at least five or seven zero-coupon issues in late 1983 or so, because they felt that demand. It was the one thing we missed in the biggest way ever. I had it, you know; I felt it was good, I felt it was ideal, but I didn't have the placement in Tokyo. We did a lot of zero coupons after that, but we were late.

Back in 1982 and 1983, it was a very close crowd; people felt very close to one another. Sheldon Prentice from Salomon, Theo van der Beugel from Swiss Bank Corp., David Craig from Morgan Guaranty, Archie Cox from Morgan Stanley and myself. We were making decisions that were unusual in banking on commitments for anywhere from $200 million to $300 million and more in those days. You had to live with that burden. No consensus decision. No committee support. And knowing that if it goes wrong, everyone will forget the 50 deals before and will only talk about the $10 million loss and nothing else. When CSFB won a deal, ten people called up and said, "Gee, well done." And when they won the deals, most of the time we threw our support behind them. It was a sports event. You were still gentlemen then. It was fun, it was competitive, but at the same time we supported each other.

After Jack Hennessy arrived as chief executive, we consolidated the new-business department with the syndicate department, because the two belong together. And again, we were far ahead of the competitors, who, in fact, usually did something else. They usually merged their syndicate operations into the trading operations in order to shift the commitment power and risk management of their positions to the people they thought were able to make these decisions. That was a mistake. Because a trader, by the nature of his dealing day in and day out, has to judge a market from the secondary side. And he usually, at least in those days, was thinking in terms of $1 million or $2 million trades. He couldn't combine the syndication process with the trading market; to go from 1 or 2 million to a 100 or 200 million was a different world.

The key element in these developments was simply that you have to know what you are doing. You have to enter a transaction knowing that you want the transaction. Most firms were pushed into transactions through market developments or for competitive reasons—"Oh, CSFB just did three deals; now we have to do one." And they always came in at the tail end of a window.

CSFB has never hedged a deal. I once hedged the market, in the big '80–'81 disaster. I believe firmly that new issues are there to be distributed. At the right price, whether that price is 97½ or 101. The other thing is that—which was sometimes CSFB's advantage—you should always have clear books. In other words, when the next round comes around, you can be more aggressive and you can take a much bigger risk than your counterpart at another firm, because I have no bonds, when he already sits on $300 million. How can he be aggressive?

Likewise, we never position. Positioning is the job of the trading department, not my job. Sometimes there is a flow-over because we can't sell it. But the intent is always to sell. If and when I were to allow people to position, they would never feel responsible. Now that's a big difference in our operation compared with our competitors. And that's why I, at least, feel that there is more skill in doing issues at CSFB.

Looking at CSFB, what I have changed is not just doing deals. We were doing risk management, and there were many months where we would decline to participate in issues or bid for issues because it wouldn't fit our risk patterns. CSFB has a seven-year record of increasing capital market earnings. If my job had just been to do the maximum number of issues, probably I would have taken many more risks. Maybe they would have worked out, maybe they would have gone wrong. You don't know. If anyone takes the trouble to check CSFB's performance, they will see that we have a very, very slow start in January and February. We are very careful in January and February—for the simple reason that I know my entire mentality would change if I had to work against a loss in January.

566

By 1985, I think, a third stage in the market had arrived. Clients began to use competitive bidding to ruthlessly play one firm against the other. A big league table game started. It was no longer competitive bidding, but negotiated competitive bids. Here are four or six banks before the client. The client tells you: "You are one of the chosen ones. But XYZ tells us so and so much; you have to be better." The moment you are better, you're told, "No, now I've got a better bid." It continued until it got to levels that were unrealistic.

What happened was perhaps an inevitable consequence. First, the initiative was with the investment banker. In the second step, with the bought deal, we took the initiative; we told clients, "If you need money, now is a good time." Now, in the third phase, the borrowers took the initiative. They said, "We made up our own mind and now is the time we want to borrow." So they then called in the investment bankers and had them bid against each other. It became an issuer's market.

But it is still a fascinating business. You do need to let the steam off in some way, say a lot of physical activity. I'm playing tennis, I'm skiing, I have a lot of fun all the time. I've so many other interests—intellectual interests—that usually I think it helps me to have pretty good judgment. From history to God knows what. I am reading everything. If I read a newspaper, it's not the financial page I start with.

At one time, I was only reading about Venice; it was all Venice, Venice, Venice. I have a whole collection about Venice, because it best reflects what I think this world should look like. I think Venice managed through its particular system to combine political power, military power and trade power in a way that no other civilization has ever reached in this world. And they dominated world trade and they had what we consider global markets today, and they did it with such skill it was unbelievable. And that's why it lasted for 800 years.

Editor: Kevin Muehring

Stanislas Yassukovich

Co-Chairman MERRILL LYNCH EUROPE

"Stani" Yassukovich has long been known as perhaps the Euro-market's most articulate, unruffled and effective spokesman. After a brief training period at Samuel Montagu, he joined White Weld in 1961, and for four years was managing director of the firm's London affiliate, during the years when it developed into a sophisticated underwriter and active market maker. In 1973 Yassukovich left White Weld to start up European Banking Corp., the consortium bank sponsored by the EBIC group, and in the '70s he served two terms as chairman of the Association of International Bond Dealers.

You know, there's always an argument about what was the first Eurobond issue, and several people will tell you different things. But I think that the generally accepted pioneer deal was the issue for the Italian Autostrade company, which was being worked on by Warburg. The original intention had been to file it in the U.S., to have an SEC filing and to sell it as a normal foreign dollar bond in the U.S. market but with a lot of European demand, as was then the pattern.

But I suppose through the sheer exhaustion of watching the legal bill go up day by day on an SEC registration, a light bulb went on and somebody said, "Why are we going through all this expensive and time-consuming trouble, since probably 80 percent of this issue is going to be placed in Europe anyway? Why don't we simply totally bypass the U.S. market and the registration and all the rest of it, and just launch it here in Europe where we have no registration requirement, where we can form the same sort of syndicate that would probably participate as underwriters and selling group members in a U.S.-registered deal, and—Bob's your uncle—the deal will be done." Which is exactly what happened.

When I transferred from New York to White Weld London, the Eurobond market was still a public sector market. White Weld managed one of the first non-public sector issues for a Finnish cooperative company called Kesko, and I did the whole syndication procedure. In other words, I wrote out telexes to the twelve underwriters we had, sent the telexes out myself and kept the book and did everything. It was just a one-man show. There was no need in those days for large departments or debt transaction groups.

The issue raised questions because the market had previously been confined to public sector borrowers, but the bank which was the guarantor was the best-known bank in Finland, Kansallis-Osake-Pankki, and therefore, obviously as far as the underwriters were concerned, the KOP guarantee made it immediately a triple-A issue. But the concept was a bit novel and people had to pause for thought, because they had never really confronted a financing for a private sector company in this way. But no, the deal went very well.

In those days the process was much more laborious. The gross spread on the deal was 2.5 percent, which you normally divided into 0.5 percent management, 0.5 percent underwriting and 1.5 percent selling group, and out of the 1.5 percent you were permitted to reallow a half percent, the so-called reallowance. There was an argument about whether the reallowance should or should not be given to nonunderwriting banks or nonselling group banks and so on. It was just unbelievable. Of course, the volume was so much smaller; I mean those margins sound ridiculous now, but you have to look at them in the context of the volume then. I mean, that issue was $15 million.

The selling period would be ten days or two weeks, and issues would very often be road-showed. Morgan Stanley, until a very late stage in the proceedings, had the habit when they were bringing an issue of personally visiting every one of the underwriters to explain what their thinking would be on the conditions, because these were open-priced issues. They would answer any questions about the borrower. They would travel for every issue.

Then the whole process began to speed up, leading toward the introduction of the bought deal. An acceleration of the velocity of the market began to develop at such a pace that obviously some of the old practices had to fall by the wayside. Really about the only market practice which has not been abandoned is the signing ceremony.

I remember being very pleased to get the lead management of a Norwegian deal for Sira Kvina, one of the big hydroelectric power projects in Norway. At the time, Hambros had an iron grip on the Norwegian market—lock, stock and barrel—so getting the Sira Kvina mandate was considered, at least by us, a great victory. Funnily enough, we got it largely by cooperating with the Norwegian banks, who were feeling left out of the process. Because Norway had exchange controls, they were excluded from participating in the foreign currency borrowing of Norwegian entities. It was thought, "What would be the point?" After all, they and their Norwegian clients could not buy these bonds, and therefore they would have no role.

Since the Norwegian banks were really frustrated that they were on the sidelines, I thought that one obvious tactic was to seek their cooperation and work jointly with them. I got rather friendly with Andresens Bank, which was subsequently merged with Christiania Bank, and with them we approached Sira Kvina and got on well with their people. I then lobbied intensively on their behalf with the Ministry of Commerce and Shipping, which was the responsible authority in Norway, and ultimately, I think, convinced it that Norwegian banks should be allowed some role in syndication of Norwegian issues.

The big breakthrough for White Weld came as a result of the entry of U.S. borrowers into the Eurobond market, which at the time was considered to be a ridiculously eccentric idea. Why would a U.S. borrower sitting in the world's largest capital market want to come to this rather exotic, obscure, slightly homeless market called the Eurobond market?

And, of course, what prompted them to do so was the voluntary restraint program in which President Kennedy directed U.S. companies to finance their foreign investments with foreign borrowing, in order to stem the very considerable capital outflow from the U.S. And that opened up the Eurobond market tremendously

571

because it introduced private sector borrowers in mass, in volume, for the first time. For really well-known U.S. names, top U.S. names. I think pretty much the first one was an issue for American Cyanamid, which was led by White Weld.

It was really at that stage one began to see the pattern where certain U.S. names, because they were particularly well known and their products were well known, were accorded, relatively speaking, a higher credit rating by the Euromarket than they had domestically. Investors just knew the name, and the fund managers in Switzerland felt that they were ideal names to put into clients' portfolios. I remember Gillette was a very good case in point. Honeywell was another one. When Honeywell came, it was just a very well-known name because everyone had a thermostat that said Honeywell, and it certainly came with a, relatively speaking, better rating in Europe than it would have enjoyed in the U.S.

I must admit I was brought up in an environment where the relationship was all and could frequently supersede even a particular competence in any area, because clients wanted first of all to feel confident about their investment banker. I think the pendulum, like all pendulums, swung violently at one point and is now beginning to settle back somewhere in the middle. Clearly the days of the exclusive and sole investment banking relationship began to be numbered when the identity of particular houses became somewhat blurred by the amalgamations, by the mergers in Wall Street that followed Mayday. The concept that one investment bank could not possibly be best at everything began to be clearly understood, and so there was a sudden swing away from exclusive relationships to no relationships. The transaction was all.

I think that is now seen as an equally extreme approach, as was the traditional approach of always relying on the same investment banker. Therefore what we are seeing now is the perfect and obvious compromise, where companies establish a select core group—might be two, might be three, four or five—which is designed to produce a spread of primary expertise.

Certainly I have never felt comfortable with the impact on investment banking technique and, if you like, quality control of the period of total transactional dominance, because I think the

572

companies in the end were very badly served. They were no longer getting investment banking service; they were getting people coming with huge laundry lists, and they were then having to pick out of the laundry list whatever they felt was appropriate. It led to a very sharp drop in the quality of research and client knowledge on the part of investment bankers. What was the point of really getting to know a client if really all you had to do was call him on the right day with the right basis-point spread over Treasuries?

As a result, clients were hoping to cope with a much greater flow of time-wasting solicitations, because, you know, you ended up with the shotgun approach. But in the Euromarket, of course, you always had a mix, in the sense that the more active public sector issuers began increasingly to adopt the transactional approach as they built their own capabilities in-house to perform the market advisory function and to track the market and so on. Of course, the first to do so was the European Investment Bank under André George, who was the first Euromarket borrower to invite competitive bids, to the shock and horror of the community.

The other, more interesting development, going back some years, was the introduction of a money market instrument in the Euro dollar area, which was clearly lacking. All other capital markets have a structure that involves money market instruments, which set base money market rates through the medium of a tradeable instrument. And then, of course, they all tend to have a base government bond market that sets the rate structure, which the Euromarket never had and probably never will have. But clearly there was a need for a money market instrument, and there was a tremendous untapped source of short-term funds for the Euromarket system, because investors were using domestic instruments to reflect that portion of their portfolio that they wanted invested in highly liquid short-term instruments.

And so the concept of the Eurodollar certificate of deposit was born, really through some conversations and late-evening exchanges of ideas that I had with my very old friend, Michael von Clemm, who was at that stage at Citibank here in London, while I was at White Weld. He and I grew up together, we were at

573

school together, our fathers were in fact friends in New York in the '20s, and we would sort of throw ideas around as to how we could make life more interesting and amusing.

Citibank had been the pioneer issuer of tradeable CDs in the States, so they were an obvious introducer in Europe. But there were endless technical and legal difficulties relating to the issuance in London of an instrument denominated in U.S. dollars. The problem actually went back to a famous case involving what was then National City Bank, in their St. Petersburg branch in Russia, where they had been taking deposits from the locals. Of course, when the Russian Revolution occurred the branch was closed down, as were all foreign bank branches. And many of the emigrés turned up in New York to collect on their deposits. The question was, under what circumstances is the head office liable for the deposit obligations of its branch if there is a force majeure in that country that closes everything?

We tried to get this thing launched, the idea being that Citibank would be the first issuer and White Weld would be the first market maker. And I remember the press conference at which the concept was introduced, which took place at the Great Eastern Hotel, Liverpool Street. The press asked immediately, what sort of volume do you expect to develop in this market? A terribly "wet-finger" guess had to be thrown out. I can't remember what sort of figure we bravely gave as a possible guess of what the volume would be in two or three years' time. But I think that the figure was reached within a month or so.

Then in the early 1970s, the natural follow-on I always felt was Euro-commercial paper. Could I get anyone interested in Euro-commercial paper? No. In fact Michael von Clemm, who at that stage was a professor at Harvard Business School, was taking on consulting assignments, and he had one with White Weld specifically to develop the Euro-commercial paper product.

We could not get issuers to take it seriously. They had very easy and convenient facilities for their Euromarket needs with Euro-market banks, where they would be quite happy paying a quarter over LIBOR. Can you imagine: Prime companies were paying a quarter, three eighths, sometimes a half over LIBOR? We kept arguing that if they issued paper, which would be addressing exactly the same market where the banks were picking up their deposits, they could disintermediate the banks and we could do it for them at an eighth over. Wasn't that interesting? Well, they said, that's a lot of trouble, and we have to issue bits of paper. In the States it's all right, because we've got the whole machinery in place, but how would it work here?

Schroders was very actively pursuing the same concept, and I think maybe five or six borrowers were beaten and dragged screaming into the arena as pioneers. We had a couple of issuers but they were almost all people doing us a favor. But, of course, it fizzled out because there wasn't enough volume created. Everybody thought it was a great idea, it just wasn't right. Well, it was just before its time, because look what's happened now. It's become a huge market and growing like Topsy.

The next area that I became very intrigued with, again without any success at all, was the Euroequity area. In fact, I gave a speech at a conference in about '71 or '72, in which I said that the problem of venture capital in Europe was that there was no exit mechanism, and clearly what was needed was a much more broadly based European equity market so the venture capitalists could look forward to some ultimate liquidity. And I said that given what has happened in the Eurobond market, clearly the introduction of a Euroequity market was imminent; therefore don't worry, this exit mechanism would be here any moment. Not much happened for a while, but now we have definitely just that pattern.

I think that it was really necessary to establish the legitimacy of the Eurobond market in the minds of both issuers and investors, because a great many people treated it as possibly a flash in the pan, as a market which was exploiting merely a short-term aberration, one that would immediately collapse and return to New York if the interest equalization tax was removed.

There was a feeling in the minds of some that a Euromarket operator was a kind of second-class citizen in the world of high finance. And therefore there was a great effort to give the market a mystique, to stress its unique nature and the fact that it was a phenomenon that was of truly international consequence. One did that in various ways: by trying to raise the quality of operations in that market, trying to give it more visibility, participating in lots of conferences that were beginning to be arranged, spending a lot of money on advertising, as we all did, and generally giving the market status. That inevitably led to a concept that there was something special about the Euromarket, which I think was necessary at the time.

Now we're a little bit stuck with that, because, if you look at it in a much broader perspective, there isn't anything special about the Euromarket anymore. Indeed, it is now no longer possible to define what the Euromarket is or even to say that there is something, a series of operations or a series of issues or a series of secondary market transactions, which are clearly and obviously purely Euromarket.

Editor: Suzanne Wittebort

Wilfried Guth

Chairman DEUTSCHE BANK

Few international banks, if any, can measure up to the postwar
success of Deutsche Bank. While the foundations for that success
were laid by Deutsche's legendary chairman, Hermann Abs, a good
measure of the credit for its perpetuation belongs to Wilfried
Guth. He joined the bank in mid-career, having previously served
as an International Monetary Fund executive director, but soon
was spearheading Deutsche's formidable efforts in the international
capital market. Guth was co-speaker of the managing board from
1976 until 1985, when he became the bank's chairman.

When I came to Deutsche Bank in 1968, we were in keen
competition with Dresdner and Commerzbank, and also
with Westdeutsche Landesbank. But our position in
Germany was very clearly first in size and, I dare say, also in
reputation and quality. Internationally, on the other hand, we
were a relatively small player; we had not fully entered the international field. So the gradual strengthening of our international
position coincided with my career at the bank, so to speak—but I
would certainly not want to say that I was the pioneer or the
architect of the strategy. It is primarily Abs and Ulrich [Hermann
Abs and Franz Heinrich Ulrich, Guth's predecessors as Deutsche
Bank chairman] who deserve this title.

It was Abs and Ulrich who brought me into the bank; I guess
they had to reflect on it quite a bit because it was highly unusual
to bring someone into the highest level of the bank from the
outside. It was my first experience with private commercial
banking, and it took a certain while before I felt at ease. I

remember one of my elder colleagues telling me, "The advantage of a management board of twelve is that you need not express an opinion on everything. As a junior on the board, express your opinion on the things you know best, and the rest of the time, listen."

We all agreed that the bank had to assume a greater international role. On that there was no dispute. But the Euromarket question was another matter. Here, especially, Abs was very skeptical—and we might say today he was right about his skepticism, at least as far as syndicated roll-over credits are concerned. It was partly due to these internal discussions that Deutsche Bank never jumped into the syndicated loan business with the enthusiasm that other banks have shown. Over the years, we were very proud that we maintained one of the top three positions in the league tables for international issuing business. But we were almost equally proud that in the syndicated loan tables we stood at, I don't know, No. 60 or so. On the other hand, it would be a lie for me to say we had foreseen the kind of trouble banks got into regarding country risks.

As I said, the Eurobond market was a different matter. It was always our ambition, and *my* ambition also during the time when I was responsible for the business, to be a dominant force. Not because it was crucially important from a profitability point of view; in a universal bank like ours the profit contribution of the bond business was rather marginal. But there were other elements that counted.

First, it had to do with the fact that issuing business was considered a very classic task of our bank. Abs was the pioneer of the international bond business in our market after the war. At the same time, there was—and is—the element of prestige; not personal prestige but prestige for the bank. And the issuing business helped us build up relationships: with governments, with important institutions, big corporations, institutional investors. In that way it contributed quite substantially to the commercial business of the bank.

We had many tough competitive fights with other investment houses or merchant banks with whom we had long-established friendly relations: in Australia, in Canada, in almost all the places where we did business. It was not that we made a decision that we wanted to outmaneuver Morgan Stanley or Warburg or anyone else. It was just a fact that by prudent and clever positioning of ourselves, by establishing good relationships—and probably also by creating the feeling that we were a powerful house that had a good placing capacity and could absorb something—that a number of important borrowers chose us as lead managers.

Fortunately, it is the basic tradition and the spirit of investment banking that you do not become enemies if you take away a deal from each other. And the best example of that is probably our relationship with the three big Swiss banks. We had some very competitive fights with the Swiss—so many instances that I cannot recall all of them. I remember one occasion when I invited to lunch [Crédit Suisse chairman] Rainer Gut—my namesake without the "h". We had a luncheon in our bank and talked about business, and in the middle of the lunch we were both called outside to the telephone because both our banks were bidding for the same deal in Canada. Toward the end of the lunch we were informed that they had won the deal. I congratulated him and we continued in a truly pleasant atmosphere.

We became known, with the big 1976 issue for the EEC and others, as a bank that imposed great discipline on its syndicates. This was unusual, and it was looked upon by some in the market with respect and by others, I assume, with resentment. But most people had a feeling at the time that some discipline was needed in the market. I remember Siegmund Warburg talking to me about whether we couldn't establish some greater discipline in the dollar bond market along the lines that were followed in the deutsche mark sector. We felt that this couldn't be achieved in this huge market with so many participants, but, where we had the lead, we always tried to maintain orderly markets in the sense of making sure that each participant in an issue met his responsibilities. It was an effort born out of our philosophy and out of the style of personalities like my colleague [Robert] Ehret, who was very strict about market behavior and kept a firm hand on the syndicates. Today procedures have become much more liberal and the market is much more diverse, so you probably couldn't do such a thing.

Back then there was a feeling—not only in our bank but in the market—that more and more the great powerhouses would dominate the field, because, apart from their placing capacity, they

579

were in a position to absorb an issue, to buy a deal, as you would say. They would, in fact, push the merchant banks aside, unless they, too, became very powerful. And I think this has been proven right. If you think of Salomon or Warburg or other houses that play a big role, you see that they are very strong today; the smaller players have more or less disappeared from the league tables.

In the course of the '70s, we felt the bank needed a more systematic strategy toward international business. By that I mean, in the first place, that we had to assess and compare the profitability of the group's units in relationship to capital and risk. I remember the shock when we told our branches, say in Paris or London, that if they had good earnings as a result of a tremendous volume of money market transactions at small margins, it was not satisfactory, because the capital committed to this volume was so big that their earnings did not cover the cost. We told them that "in a correct analysis, you have no profit." You may imagine it was a difficult educational process.

The other important strategic question was how to resolve this EBIC dilemma [the European Banking club, whose offshoots included New York's European American Bank and London's European Banking Co.]. We had formed EBIC for two fundamental reasons. One was our feeling that as European banks we lacked the size and strength to compete with the American banks. It is interesting to say that today. The other was our anticipation of closer and closer integration of Europe. In both cases our assumptions proved correct. We became stronger vis-à-vis the American banks, and European integration proceeded very slowly, with great setbacks in between, so the idea that EBIC might become the first European bank evaporated in the air.

So for a while we followed a parallel strategy: to build our own branches and also to play our part in EBIC, mainly in the various joint ventures. Why didn't we leave EBIC? I think the main answer is loyalty to our partners; we had a feeling that as Germans, we should not be the ones to break the club up. But we gradually put this feeling aside as we began to accept the fact that consortium banking was probably not the brightest idea. We also discovered that things weren't going so well with some of the joint ventures.

Why did we run into such a disappointing situation: First, as consortium banks, they were not closely enough integrated into our controlling system, so there was no adequate "early warning." Another reason, I think, was that we were too polite with each other, which again seems to me a typical element in consortium banking. Here on the board of Deutsche Bank, if something goes wrong we criticize each other and say, "This has to be changed tomorrow." In consortium banks you are more inclined to take it in stride and be patient for quite a while.

Because of our loyalty to EBIC, we were also for a rather long time reluctant to open branches in places where EBIC or its partners were present. It was a big decision to open a branch in New York. And I remember the trip Ulrich and I made to Paris to tell Société Générale that we would be opening a branch there. It was a very painful discussion. How different things are today!

You sometimes hear that Deutsche Bank only wants a certain type of person in its management. I think that's too simple a description. If you look at the twelve people who were there when I was on the management board, or the twelve who are there now, you see some very different types. Also, their talents differ widely, which makes for a very efficient complementarity. I would agree that we have a traditional style that influences our choice of leading personalities and makes them not too dissimilar. Of course, integrity of character, high intelligence and competence in banking, as well as physical and mental stamina, are basic prerequisites for being considered as a candidate, but a member of our managing board must also be a convinced teamworker, ready to accept our basic principle of unanimous decisions without ever taking votes. We also assume they have knowledge of things other than banking—although I wouldn't want to say that I ask someone whether he knows all the operas of Mozart or anything like that.

Teamwork is very important. There is, of course, the example of my relationship with my former co-speaker [F. Wilhelm Christians]. We were certainly not always in agreement when we discussed pending problems, but there were never what I would call trying moments. I think there were two main reasons why the relationship worked so well. First, we had known each other long enough before we became co-speakers, so we had mutual respect

581

and basic sympathy for one another. Second, we both knew that sharing power helped our efficiency; it was a great relief to have a partner who could go to Washington for a high-level visit while you had to be in Australia.

I think the co-speaker arrangement was—and in my opinion is still—a good solution. But I would certainly not want to make it dogma. It depends on the persons and on the constellation at a given moment.

In 1979 there were reports that I was a candidate for succeeding Otmar Emminger as president of the Bundesbank after he retired. When Chancellor Helmut Schmidt talked to me about it, I told him that while I realized that the Bundesbank presidency would hold great responsibility, I preferred to stay where I was, since I considered my current task equally challenging. I remember that very clearly; he called me back from a vacation to talk to him in Bonn about this crucial question. He said: "I am sorry. Maybe you are making the wrong decision." I said to him, "If you would allow me to say this, I am convinced that Mr. Pöhl, who, I know, is under consideration, will be an excellent choice for president of the Bundesbank." Having this in mind, I felt I need not have a bad conscience for not making myself available as a candidate.

Helmut Schmidt sometimes took my advice, just as [Chancellor Helmut] Kohl takes the advice of [current speaker Alfred] Herrhausen. But that, in my view, has nothing to do with the great power of Deutsche Bank that people speak about. Our influence with politicians has been very limited; besides, most politicians are much too self-confident and self-assured to be strongly influenced. I mean, you express your opinion, and sometimes they listen to you very carefully, sometimes less so, but what they decide is a different matter.

We have been, and still are, of course, conscious of the allegation of having too much power. Certainly, Deutsche Bank as well as other banks have a certain amount of power, although I prefer calling it influence. Many other groups or institutions of our society have similar power or influence—think only of trade unions. But our potential power is often much exaggerated by the media, for whom the power of the banks and of Deutsche Bank in particular is a pet subject. But the media are there; there's no use quarreling with them. They are a fact of life, and therefore we have to be conscious of this phenomenon.

Look at what happened in 1986 with the big Flick deal. [Deutsche bought the whole block of Flick shares and then resold it in the market.] It was a very important and useful transaction from an economic and a political point of view; the fact that we could place it broadly meant that there was a dissipation of industrial power. But some people said, "You see, there is the all-powerful Deutsche Bank again; only Deutsche Bank can do that." We then placed the Springer [publishing empire] shares and the same thing happened.

When you boil it down, where exactly is all this power? If you look at the big firms like Siemens and the chemical companies, they would never think of being dependent on us in any way; if we do not offer them what they want in terms of finance or services, they will go next door. Then there is the argument about all the supervisory board positions we hold. If you are a member of a supervisory board—as I was, for instance, in Thyssen, Schering and a number of other companies—you are one among twenty people and have just one vote. Yes, power comes into play when you are chairman of the supervisory board, as I was in Daimler-Benz or Philipp Holzmann, but in what sense is this position powerful? It is only powerful when it comes to selecting the top manager and the chief executive. Even then, you don't have a unique voice.

Looking ahead, there are some things that worry me—not in our institution but in the banking world at large. There is a danger nowadays, in young people in particular, in believing that banking is the art of making a quick profit and selling whatever product seems fashionable. That is not the true spirit of banking. You must cultivate a permanent relationship with your client and be aware of the potential risks in a changed general economic climate. The long period of declining interest rates and great liquidity that we have experienced was the ideal time to try all these new instruments and new technologies. But if we get into a period when interest rates would go up again, all these new instruments would be put to a severe test.

I see two potential dangers. One which is already evident is that the quick profit mentality will bring about excesses—in a way, the sort of excesses we have seen in Volkswagen's foreign exchange operations recently. These are the excesses of people who are not really responsible enough to cope with the new possibilities. Here only education can help.

The other is the system danger, the accumulation of too much potential risk in the system. A few years ago I warned that our margins on Eurolending were too small to cover the risks. I think the same is true today with respect to RUFs, NIFs and swap transactions.

But, I am afraid, in most cases we only seem to learn through painful experience.

Editor: Cary Reich

Donald Marron

Chairman and Chief Executive Officer PAINE WEBBER

Donald Marron's two-decades-plus career on Wall Street is the history of the institutional brokerage business in microcosm. In the late 1960s Marron helped develop Mitchell Hutchins into one of the pure institutional research boutiques, and in the hard politicking that led up to Mayday, he was one of the few Street executives urging the abolition of fixed commissions—although he also reportedly predicted Mayday itself would be a "nonevent." Then, in the shakeout that followed Mayday, Mitchell Hutchins, like many other research boutiques, was absorbed by a big retail firm. But Marron, unlike his other research-firm counterparts, came out on top.

In 1967 Mitchell Hutchins was a retail firm, and we decided to transform it into an institutional firm. What we saw was all this money going into what was then a relatively small number of places—the mutual funds and pension funds. And all of them needed help, because they hadn't been used to dealing with sums of money of that size.

There was a little core group of about three or four people in Mitchell Hutchins doing institutional work. And that was clearly the business that was going to be the one to provide the great leverage. So we set out to do it. High-caliber, highly paid analysts just didn't exist back then. So it was partly a case of going out and finding people who you thought would be good as analysts. One of the best places to go in those days were the institutions themselves, like Waddell and Reed or Fidelity or Capital Research. And so we built a small team significantly from the clients. But that was before this whole idea of stealing and raiding. Everybody was very friendly, people talked to each other, people helped each other.

The other thing that we figured out was that the kind of business wasn't just restricted to analyzing stocks. It was understanding the environment and everybody out there. So that prompted the start of our consulting program. We got Otto Eckstein, Henry Kissinger and Bill Moyers, because we thought economics, international affairs and political affairs were the three major forces in the world to be superseded only by the press. So a couple of years later we got David Broder, who eventually won a Pulitzer Prize. And, of course, then Otto Eckstein and I started Data Resources, based on the same idea: that all these people with these growing amounts of money were very interested in other ways of looking at the environment in which they were managing it.

It was very clear to me in the early '70s that Mayday was coming. That was in the days of give-ups. I mean, you made so much money that you could afford to take part of your income and just send a check to somebody else. I can't remember when it was that the stock exchange had to go to a four-day week, but I think it was in that period, too. There was so much business they couldn't handle it. Well, the one thing you can be sure about in terms of excesses is that someone has to come along and correct them. At one point I was advocating that we ease into negotiated rates with a system tied to volume. I didn't feel much pressure from other Street firms for my stance. But the pressure came a lot from my fellow employees, because they were worried about the impact on the economics of the firm, not just our firm but other firms in the same position. And I was saying, "Well, if we could do this gradually, we can certainly make the shift and we'll all be fine." What you don't want is to fight it and one day wake up and find they've imposed some radical change on you. The options were us managing the change or Washington managing the change. Those are the two choices. Which would you prefer?

It's just clear to me that if we had worked more closely with Washington then, probably the whole relationship between the two communities would be better and probably the transition would have worked even better.

Somebody said that I predicted that Mayday would be a "non-event," but I don't actually remember saying that. What I did say was I didn't think that there would be enormous discounting on day one, and the discounting did come much faster than I would have thought. The biggest thing at work in bringing down commissions was the growth of the industry; there really was an awful lot of business, and more coming, and when it was freed up from this artificial structure, it just encouraged more people to do more trading. Things changed very, very fast.

In the end, the huge volume in effect permitted the economics of the industry to be maintained—not at the same extreme levels as before Mayday, but they could be maintained. One of the reasons I had thought that discounting wouldn't come faster was that you couldn't change the economics of the business that radically. Well, the business increased a lot, so if you discount it by 25 or 30 percent, there was a lot more business to make up for an awful lot of that. And, of course, the other thing that happened was that the value of research started to broaden beyond just a narrow institutional market, to individuals and eventually investment banking. People started to see these were very valuable services. And, in fact, what happened was that firms, including Mitchell Hutchins, merged with bigger firms that had different client bases, and thereby you could spread the impact as well as the cost of the research over a much broader base.

We very much wanted to keep Mitchell Hutchins going. It was fun and it was doing very well. I remember sitting there, saying we really think we're fine as a firm and that we'll get through this and do well, but we said it would probably take five years for us to restructure our own business and reestablish priorities, and that's a long time.

And it became clear that we were better off as part of a bigger operation. In retrospect, we probably should have speeded up and invested more time in developing investment banking and money management much earlier.

After Paine Webber bought us, it was a very big adjustment. I think the biggest thing that I learned quickly—not quickly enough, I wish it had happened even more quickly—is the amount of time in a big firm between deciding to do something and getting it done, and, on the other hand, the difficulty in changing your mind. In a small firm, you have six, eight key people in the room and you're all deciding what to do, everyone knows what everybody else thinks, and off you go and do it. And you make adjustments as you go along; you can make adjustments very easily. In a big firm, it isn't as simple as that. It goes through a lot of processes and doesn't always come out at the other end the way it started. I will always remember going somewhere in the firm and asking someone, "Why are you doing it this way?" And them saying to me, "Well, because that's the way that you want it done." And I said, "Well, it isn't the way I want it done." And then going back and finding that we had some meeting and I had mentioned something, and by the time it got through the process, it became something totally different. It just never would have happened in a small firm.

What if Mayday hadn't happened? There is an example that tells us the whole story, and that's Japan. Because if you look at the economics of the leading Japanese firms, they had no Mayday. They're dealing with fixed rates, huge numbers of individual clients, gigantic profit margins. They've been able to take those profits and reinvest them back into other aspects of the business, run them on very thin margins and build up world positions. However, this is not Japan; there's no United States, Inc. So what was allowed to happen in Japan wouldn't have been allowed to happen here, and, I think, appropriately. Japan could justify those revenue streams by saying they're going to reinvest this money in order to strengthen the position of the country in the world. So my guess is, if there had been no Mayday, the excesses would have been so staggering that they would have really threatened the system.

Somebody did a little study of what would have happened to Mitchell Hutchins if fixed rates had stayed, and we would have been 50 times the size five years later or something in terms of profits. Another thing that would have happened was that the customers would have come into our business because they wouldn't have wanted to miss out on that big opportunity. But then you have to go farther and say, well, maybe if there was no Mayday, volume *wouldn't* have gone up because of the high, fixed rates holding people back from trading. We certainly wouldn't have had program trading or index funds and all those things.

I suppose my greatest regret is that I didn't make a big bet on the growth of mergers and acquisitions—because it encompassed so many different aspects of the financial business. It's junk bond financing, globalization of money, investing, restructuring, new business alliances. It essentially represents a whole class of new opportunities. Who knows how things would have gone?

Editor: Nancy Belliveau

Jack Bennett

Chief Financial Officer EXXON CORP.

As a senior Treasury official in the early 1970s, Jack Bennett introduced the controversial Dutch auction to Treasury borrowing; later
he did the same at Exxon Corp. This scholarly, innovative and
very demanding CFO is considered by many to be the presiding
senior statesman of American corporate finance.

The notion of the "good old days" in the late 1960s, when we
were trying to peg the dollar and were forcing American
soldiers in Germany to buy American lettuce and forcing
American investors not to invest abroad, is silly. These things
hampered the economy.

When we wanted to borrow some money then, we had to go
through a very convoluted process, a long registration statement
and whatnot. Back then the financial system was tottering, and the
whole mind-set of the government was toward controls to try and
prop it up. We had foreign exchange controls, a foreign investment review agency. Finally, in 1971, there was a clear break. I
had been invited down to Washington to be deputy to Paul
Volcker, who was then under secretary of the Treasury for monetary affairs. Given the circumstances of the financial system, I
had no desire to go to Washington. But when August 15, 1971,
came along, and President Nixon said that the U.S. would no
longer take any actions to try to peg the dollar to anything, and
the link to gold was finally broken, I thought it would be a much
more interesting period. And it was.

Some people say we didn't go floating until 1973; in fact, after

591

August 1971 the U.S. no longer took any actions to try to peg the dollar to anything. It spent its time trying to persuade other governments to *stop* doing things to try to peg the dollar. After that August 15 speech, a lot of the other governments sort of announced that they still had a price relative to the dollar. In February 1973 these other governments announced that they had abandoned efforts to peg their currencies to the dollar. We moved to a freer exchange system, and that, I think, facilitated the freeing up of the markets.

U.S. companies could now borrow abroad, and we moved toward a *world* interest rate rather than a bunch of segregated rates. Ultimately, the freeing of the dollar permitted the removal of the foreign investment review controls, and that contributed a lot to the development of the capital markets and the resurgence of New York as a trading capital. For years our regulations here had been wonderful for London. They had hampered the U.S. market and facilitated London's. While I was living in Washington, one U.S. financial institution wanted to lend some money denominated in a foreign currency, and the chairman of the Federal Reserve effectively blocked it. He didn't think it was appropriate. It's a different world now.

I ended up succeeding Volcker as the under secretary with responsibility for Treasury borrowing, international monetary relations and assorted things like East-West trade. It seemed to us the Treasury was borrowing a great deal; compared with today, it doesn't look quite so large. But we still managed to do some innovation. For example, we introduced the Dutch auction [in which several firms bid on an offering of securities, and the lowest bid that accounts for all of the securities becomes the price for all participants]. Then we used it here at Exxon back in November 1976 on a $54.9 million pollution control bond.

In the 1960s the major corporations had a chosen investment banker, and that was an expected, normal relationship. We at Exxon thought, well, maybe investment bankers could compete for our business. We popularized the notion that competition was probably beneficial to the borrower. That was the essence of doing a Dutch auction. It could have backfired, but it didn't. That doesn't mean that everyone was thrilled with the idea. A friend of mine, John Whitehead, who was chairman of Goldman Sachs and is now deputy secretary of state, made speeches inveighing against it as unpatriotic and un-American. And some employees of a few small investment banking firms around the country sent in their Exxon credit cards. But most of them took it in stride, and the initial issue was successful despite the fact that it was on a pollution control issue. We would have preferred to introduce the concept on a larger, normal deal, but we just didn't happen to need any larger normal borrowing at the time.

That was just the first step in making bankers compete for our business. We decided that any time a banker came up with a good idea, we'd talk to him. We've had lots of ideas come to us from different firms. That was considered unusual then, but now it's the norm. That's the major change. We used to have a formal system of arranging for financial institutions to buy our debt. Now that's hardly necessary. You hardly need an auction; it's sort of a continuous auction. Institutions are calling up every day, or we call them, and they're willing to do deals.

Raising money for corporations has become a lot more efficient. You use a lot less of the time of accountants and lawyers and others with shelf registration. We took a leading role in supporting the idea. Bankers opposed it, saying there would be great problems from a lack of due diligence. I don't think those have ever arisen, though I doubt there is as much due diligence as there used to be. For major corporate underwritings, I suspect due diligence procedures are adequate. With shelf registration, we also don't need to have as large a treasury staff.

But there's one thing that goes on all the time—it's not new— and I don't think it will ever stop. That's the continuing battle with the tax man. The government will think of some unjust aspect of taxes, and the people will try to find a way around it. Then they'll change the laws—that's the battle. We still have the basic problem of double taxation on corporate income—the corporate tax plus the individual tax on dividends. There's always some inequity, and you simply try to find a way around it. Find one way, though, and something else will crop up. The availability of more sophistication and competition in financial markets at least facilitates finding new ways. I mean, for a while we were able to use strip bonds, and it was nice to sell them to the Japanese and so forth. So that helps.

I guess the other thing that the greater sophistication in the markets can facilitate, in some cases, is to put pressure on financial transactions. For example, we sold Reliance Electric, our electrical equipment subsidiary, in an LBO. So when I hear people now inveighing against junk bonds, I think to myself, well here was a transaction in which there was nothing wrong with somebody taking the risk on bonds and financing the purchase of this operation from us. There was no reason why Reliance had to stay with us. It could have, but maybe it'll be more efficient in independent hands. So that makes me a little suspicious of people who are down in Washington, trying to put constraints on leveraged buyouts.

There has been a restructuring of the oil industry, of course. A lot of the major oil companies made major acquisitions—Texaco, Getty, Chevron, Gulf. Exxon didn't. Instead, we undertook a major share-repurchase program. Now, whether Exxon shares were a better buy than those companies' acquisitions remains to be seen. We're not regretting our decision at this point, but it'll take ten years to see how things work out. We had a chance to make those investments and chose not to—we had the feeling somebody else was paying more than they were worth, that's all. We have, though, made some acquisitions. Last year we made a 50 percent investment in the Hunts' activities in Yemen, for example. We thought that was a good investment. And we bought a fair number of smaller properties in the United States, but we haven't made any of these very large ones. This wasn't because we were opposed; in practice we just thought the prices were too high.

The major things I've noticed during the past decade are the increased competition among firms for underwriting business, the increased internationalization, some unfreezing of the capital markets—that is, the elimination of investment controls—and the availability of shelf registration. And if a particular company is not doing well in managing the assets under it, the market is more efficient in putting pressure on that company. I think that's useful.

In the early 1970s it was a simpler time; there was a smaller variety of securities one potentially could issue. But I don't know any reason to think it was better. I still think, though, we have an antiquated financial system.

Editor: Beth Selby

Arthur Cashin

Floor Broker NEW YORK STOCK EXCHANGE

Amid the 50-point swoons and surges of the late '80s stock market, one group of players remains largely the same as in the go-go years of the 1960s: the floor brokers. At the cutting edge of transaction flow, they have adjusted—sometimes reluctantly—to technological changes that permit 200-million-plus trading days. Arthur Cashin, one of the NYSE's sixteen governors and a floor broker for more than two decades, discusses life in the maelstrom, where bids meet offers.

The most basic change in the last twenty years has been the growth of volume. In the late '60s a 30-million-share day would probably have riveted everyone's attention. We have that type of volume today in the first hour. In fact, on one of the recent record days, we traded more shares than in a whole year around 1940.

The business on the floor has always been pressure-filled. People have used the analogy that it's like being in the engine room of a battleship. On short notice, people call in and say "more steam" or "less steam" or "all astern." The shifts can be rather dramatic. But in today's volume the floor is less and less conducive to reflective thought. You've got to just keep moving all the time. And the technology has brought in additional factors. Program trading, for example, is both a blessing and a bane.

The programs tend to add to the volume, so that adds to the demand for the independent subcontractor or two-dollar broker's services. But you can spend four hours trying to determine what would be the fair and right price for a client to get; you can be watching everything from the commodities markets to the bond market, the futures market and the news ticker, and then you reach a determination. Shortly thereafter, based on a minor glitch in the interest rate picture, programs can come in, and what looked like an eminently logical sale at $47 can turn into something abominable.

But a lot of things haven't changed. There's still a lot of paper, even if there's less than in the '60s. Guests often don't understand why we throw all these papers around on the exchange floor. But the reason is that if you cross out or scratch over an order and a clerk reads it wrong, it can cost you $50,000, but if you rewrite from scratch, it costs you the price of the paper.

Another change now is that a lot more seats are active that used to be unused, and the floor in some ways is more crowded. The information flow is richer, too. In the '60s there was ticker tape, and they were just beginning things like Bunker-Ramo and Quotron, in which prices were dispensed to the public. Twenty years ago, the tape was rather limited and would run late on a 30-million-share day and make prices "stale" by fifteen to twenty minutes. Now the tape can still run late, but it's because of human limitations. They can record trades as fast as we make them, but no one can read that fast.

Generally speaking, day-to-day activity was considerably slower in the 1960s. Legwork used to be a lot less. We have put pedometers on brokers recently, and the standard, if there is one, is that on a quiet day the average broker walks six to eight miles while on a busy day he clocks between twelve and fifteen.

The periods of lapse in trading during a day tended to be longer. In my twenty years, the floor has always been the financial equivalent of being an airplane pilot: an hour of boredom, ten minutes of sheer terror, then half an hour of boredom again. But the periods of boredom have grown shorter and shorter—and the terrors last a bit longer.

There's always stress. I heard of a two-dollar broker who went in for a checkup and the doctor put a portable pacemaker and stress tester on him, and after the first day he got a message to call the doctor. So he went back, and the doctor said, "What is it that you do?" And he said, "I'm a broker on the floor of the exchange." And the doctor says: "That explains it. Your stress test resembled that of a man having four to five mini-heart attacks every day."

The technology hasn't reduced the need for human beings down here. If you have a machine, it can only process so many things. A human being can exceed that at times. Probably at no time in the exchange's history did the execution process fall behind. The problems were in the reporting process because the machines couldn't handle it. Frankly, though, if there were no electronic routing systems, I doubt the exchange could handle 200 million shares a day.

The greatest problem for floor brokers is a market in a runaway stage—whether it's bad news or good, like the sudden change in interest rates in 1982, when the Fed decided to ease because of Mexico. When you get into such a situation, your market expertise gets tested and used, and that's where it's most valuable. You can sense when a market move has reached critical mass. We talk on the floor about smelling panic in the air. And if you smell panic, that's probably the time, if you can, to suggest to a client that he limit his order, step back a bit.

Brokers say they know they've done a good job when they can explain it to other brokers. But to explain it to a client is not easy. Because if you don't sell a stock down to a certain level and you say, "I held back and waited to sell it at $48 instead of $47," the client may be skeptical because the $47 tick never appeared, so you really can't prove that you avoided selling at a panic bottom.

Independent brokers have had to evolve along with the industry. Some have developed expertise in such areas as arbitrage, utilities, banks or even technology stocks. They read the research reports and the annuals, the daily news bulletins, the trade publications and watch exactly how the group is trading. Those with such expertise live on perception, available information, their sense of the market. Often they're aiding an upstairs professional to evaluate circumstances. Those who deal in the large volume orders are called on to evaluate such things as timing.

Some develop near-legendary feel. There was a fellow named Bob Oscher, for example, now deceased, who was so good at arbitrage trading that he became the broker for other brokers. Rather than try to do battle with his expertise in that area, other brokers recognized him as a very fair man who would get their clients the best price—and probably a better price than they could get coming in cold.

The crucial thing for a broker, though, is that you try as hard as you can to get the best execution, given the time and place that you received the order. The client, like all of us, doesn't like to be duped or defrauded or sell for less than he should get.

That becomes especially valuable during panics, like the one that occurred on the day of John Kennedy's assassination. The market was already turning weak when information began coming out piecemeal. The clients' anxiety level increased steadily. The first reports were shots fired at the motorcade; then the headline that "the president is reported injured"; then the report that he was en route to the Parkland Memorial Hospital, to the operating room; then the report of his death. By that time, the market had closed because the selling was tremendous.

Another example was the day of the collapse of the Hunt brothers' silver corner. It was a very edgy day. There had been some noticeable drops in commodity markets, and silver had begun to slide. There was gossip and stories of margin calls and people unable to meet them in silver. Brokerage names were being bandied about as being at risk, and the market began to border on being unwound. Selling became less and less logical. The smell of panic was everywhere, and the market did sell down very sharply in what was seen as a selling climax before recovering at the close.

That's an example of the need to think ahead. I mean, floor brokers are trained to think almost instantaneously. If there's a unique piece of good news on General Motors, you don't rush into GM—everybody knows about it. You think: "What's this mean for Ford? For Chrysler? For American Motors? For GM's suppliers? Does it have any impact in international markets?" And since you've got to rapidly think ahead and turn your mind on a dime, it breeds a minor cynicism.

During the Cuban missile crisis in the early '60s, the market had a very bad day. One young broker said, "Well, no one can blame anybody for feeling bad today, because the missiles almost flew." And one of the old brokers said: "Son, if you ever hear they're flying, buy and keep buying. If you're wrong, the trades will never clear anyway, and if you're right, you'll be buying on everybody else's panic."

Editor: Lenny Glynn

Martin Turchin

Executive Vice President EDWARD S. GORDON CO.

> From his office on the 22nd floor of the Chrysler Building, real
> estate broker Martin Turchin can see a whole panorama of build-
> ings he has helped buy, sell and lease over the course of his seven-
> teen-year career. He has not just observed the parade of Wall
> Street firms growing around the financial district and moving up-
> town, he has helped plan the parade route.

A lot of the major players in the investment business of the
'60s disappeared from the face of the earth in the '70s.
The Goodbodys, the Hayden Stones, the old Shearson,
the Hallgartens, Hentz & Co.—all of these firms were very major
office users in the marketplace. Hayden Stone was a big celebrity
situation. They had made a 300,000-square-foot commitment to a
building known as 2 New York Plaza at the tip of Manhattan. The
firm was going to go under, and when Sandy Weill agreed to buy
them out, it was on the condition that he would not have to absorb
that lease obligation.

The owner of the building was confronted with a choice: take a
couple of cents on the dollar to let Hayden Stone walk away from
the lease so that it could be bought by Shearson—at that time,
Cogan, Berlind, Weill & Levitt—or deal with the tenant in bankruptcy and get nothing. And so he opted to take a small consideration from Hayden Stone to let them off the lease. That building
stood on the market for two or three years before American
Express finally purchased it as its headquarters.

In the early '60s, before Chase Manhattan Bank committed to

building Chase Manhattan Plaza, the downtown market was perceived as an old, tired market that would ultimately revert to a
second-class nature—the way Park Avenue South and upper
Broadway had. But at that time downtown had a much more
diversified tenant mix than it has today. At that time downtown
still had all of what were then characterized as the Wall Street law
firms. There weren't really Wall Street law firms in midtown. You
also had a very large corporate headquarters population downtown. U.S. Steel was still downtown, and Mobil, Phillips Petroleum
and Anaconda were all still downtown. You also had a vibrant
shipping and insurance industry there. The initial thrusts to midtown came first from the corporations, followed by some of the
law firms.

Chase Manhattan Bank turned that trend around by making the
commitment in the early '60s to build Chase Manhattan Plaza.
That created a renaissance downtown. From 1950 to 1965 there
had been very, very little construction downtown. And most of
what had been built were back-office-type buildings, secondary-
type products not geared to headquarters-type facilities.

But with Chase Manhattan Plaza, you saw a building boom
begin downtown. It resulted in a tremendous amount of new
construction in the late '60s and early '70s, buildings like 1 New
York Plaza, 2 New York Plaza, 4 New York Plaza, 1 State Street,
55 Water Street—all of the Water Street buildings—7 Hanover,
77 Water Street and the World Trade Center. So you had all this
new construction occurring in the post-Chase era, primarily tied
to the rapid expansion in financial services, not corporations. For
the most part, they were already gone.

The market collapsed in 1971—for two reasons. Not only did
you have tremendous office supply coming into the market, but
you had a tremendous shakeout in the brokerage business. What
happened was that the banks' growth stabilized; they weren't
contracting, but they weren't growing. After the early '70s, you
saw nothing in downtown for eight or nine years. And that was
when a lot of the downtown law firms started their migration to
midtown, along with the accounting firms. It took nearly a decade
for the market to absorb all the space in the World Trade Center.

Prices collapsed in downtown. Between 1970 and 1972-73, they went from a high of $15 a square foot to 50 percent of that level. The rental values were cut in half. Today we are looking at numbers in the high 30s and low 40s.

What happened was that firms actually contracted their use of space. They might have had a total of 200,000 square feet at several locations, resulting from their acquisitions of other firms, and they really only needed 150,000 square feet if they put it all together. There was no net absorption in the marketplace during the early '70s.

But in the last three years, we've seen tremendous, tremendous surge in demand. The whole climate of investment banking has changed, primarily because of all the new products that have been generated—both in terms of their investment banking services and in terms of their competing in banking services.

So all of a sudden, you see a firm like Salomon or Drexel or Goldman or First Boston going from being a 200,000- to 300,000- square-foot user to a million-square-foot user in a matter of two or three years and projecting that they are going to need another million square feet in another couple of years—which is making them look more and more like banks in terms of their facilities requirements.

Anybody who bought a building in the late '70s, if he made every wrong decision, still turned out a winner. I mean, if you ask Paul Reichmann [president of Olympia & York] about his acquisitions in the U.S., everybody says, "Paul, you are an absolute genius; you bought it when the market rents on those buildings were $10 a square foot, and eighteen months later they went to $25." I mean, he says, "That's bullshit. When I bought those properties at $10, I figured it was going to $12 a foot. I had no expectations that in eighteen months I was going to be able to rent it at $25." I don't think anybody did.

Currently in downtown there are only two options for the really big user. There is the old Merrill Lynch building at 1 Liberty Plaza; and Larry Silverstein's 7 World Trade Center, the building that Drexel Burnham was going to move to. Beyond those two buildings, if you look at the downtown market you will find a very interesting situation because there are only two sites that are available in which you can build a new building with large enough floors to be applicable to the big user—only two. One is the site that Olympia & York apparently has at Battery Park City, and the other is the South Ferry site that was just awarded to a group headed by [developer William] Zeckendorf. That's it. And neither one of those buildings can come on-stream before the early 1990s. So if the two existing buildings get leased, there will be no other product available downtown to meet large users' requirements in '88, '89 or '90.

The name "Wall Street" used to have a connotation of investment banking as well as a special connotation for law firms. Look around today. Except for Brown Brothers Harriman, I can't think of a major investment banking firm that has its headquarters on Wall Street. You've got a lot of them, however, that have made commitments to stay downtown—Oppenheimer, Merrill Lynch, Thomson McKinnon. At the same time you've had commitments by Paine Webber, Hutton and Bear Stearns to move to midtown. So you don't have any clear, definable pattern as between midtown and downtown in terms of headquarters facilities anymore.

A lot of the decisions to relocate to midtown have been predicated on personality. A lot of the executives come from midtown or from Westchester, and, therefore, they find it more convenient to be in midtown. Also, you've had the investment banks saying that all their customers are based in midtown. But on top of that they've had to compete in attracting high-producing brokers. That entails, you know, lifestyle and convenience—where the office is and how high up in the building it is. Money alone is not necessarily the driving factor.

Historically, the prestige market for relocations from downtown to midtown has been on the east side. Some moved to Sixth Avenue, but most stayed east of Sixth Avenue. That is totally changing now. European American Bank's headquarters will now be west of Sixth Avenue; U.S. Trust will be west of Sixth Avenue; Morgan Stanley is considering going to Broadway; you've got Salomon Brothers going to Columbus Circle.

You are going to start seeing a shift in the historical pattern of what have been considered acceptable locations in midtown. I mean, the first generation went to Park Avenue, Rockefeller Center, some to Avenue of the Americas. Now we are seeing a whole migration going west.

Editor: Erik Ipsen

Paul Kolton

Former Chairman AMERICAN STOCK EXCHANGE

Equities trading was in the doldrums, and a crippling number of American Stock Exchange members might well have drifted away during the 1970s if the exchange had not developed its highly successful options trading program. But it was a long, often frustrating fight, as former chairman (1972-77) Paul Kolton relates.

The equities market in the mid-'70s, as far as the Amex was concerned, was laboring. Floor members and sole members were having a difficult time. In addition, there was a constant, competitive battle to keep Amex-listed companies from transferring to the New York Stock Exchange and to urge new companies to come to the Amex from the over-the-counter market or from initial public offerings.

The question used to be: Can the Amex survive? To me, that was never really in question. The Amex had a liquid reserve, and even if it were losing $1 million a year, it could have gone on for eight, ten, twelve years. The issue was that the infrastructure of members, of floor people, was coming under increasing pressure. And I think it's safe to say that unless there had been a turn in a relatively short time, they would have drifted elsewhere.

We developed several new products at the time. In the past, if a public customer wanted to buy government bonds, he had to go down to the Fed or call his bank and buy them in $25,000 units. We saw the possibility of making odd lots available—one bond, two bonds. It was a very good program, but it was a relatively small one, because bonds at the time were not part of our trading culture.

The CBOE had pioneered options, and our early surveys indicated there was a market in New York with the disciplines that an exchange could bring to it—with the paraphernalia of trade reporting, specialist systems, audit trails and the ability to reconstruct the market. But getting the thing on-line was the single most extended and difficult period that we had in terms of satisfying the various constituencies. It represented a new instrument in a territory that only the CBOE had been in—but with specialists rather than competing market makers. That raised a whole series of questions about the disciplines that had to be built into the system, the kind of markets that were to be made. And we thought of options in terms of an equity background; you bought them or you sold them. What developed pretty quickly was that it was a much more sophisticated device that had to be looked at more as a commodity product with the kind of transactions we now see are commonplace.

An enormous number of legal problems surfaced along the way. The SEC expressed concern about the potential for abuse. How can you be comfortable and certain that this whole unregulated put-and-call market can be brought under control? How can you be sure that public responsibilities are going to be fulfilled? Those were difficult questions and what we would have expected from the SEC. When we went over into the commodities area, to their regulatory authorities, the first question that I remember receiving was whether we were going to time-stamp order tickets. For a moment I was speechless. Time-stamping was so much a part of an exchange's operation that we hadn't given any thought to it. I mean, it was built into the procedure as mechanically as buttoning your shirt or tying your shoes. I really had to focus on the question and then went on to explain that all the principals involved did it routinely; it never occurred to them not to stick a trade into a time-stamp. But the question does show what the CFTC's sensitivities were.

When we were all set to go, the question was whether the Amex would set up its own clearing corporation or whether we should buy a piece of the CBOE clearing corporation. There were a lot of good reasons for doing either one. The SEC took a look at the various alternative plans and said, "There really ought to be one clearing corporation." It was clearly the right decision for the SEC to make, but here is the political problem: There were dozens and dozens of business reasons for the CBOE to want us not to get started. They wanted to establish themselves as a market; the longer they continued as a monopoly, the greater the market share they would have. And here was a competitor ready to open the door and sprint out of the gate. But we couldn't get started until we had a clearing mechanism. And they were being told by the SEC, "Make it a combined clearing operation, and sell half your interest to the Amex."

An agreement had to be reached. Provisions were also made, either then or shortly afterward, for the NASD to come into it, which further complicated the arrangements. And the CBOE was in no mood to hurry. Why should they be? I remember Joe Sullivan, who was then at the CBOE, was nifty at deflecting our proposals. I was on the phone yelling, pleading, cajoling, calling the SEC, calling our senators, calling our friends in the Street (who were all interested, but kind of bemused at the struggle going on). The SEC finally said to the CBOE, "You're not going to get more options to trade until this is all worked out." So it went along. But the trade-off, in perspective, was not exactly even.

There was another problem. New York City and New York State discovered the stock transfer tax, and the way they read the law was that it applied to options. Of course, the transfer tax law had been written before options were created, but if you make the leap that options are equities—which they are not—and it's not hard to see how you could, then options come under the tax. And the minimum stock transfer tax, which was $5 a trade, could in effect double the cost of a trade. So we went to the governor, we went to the mayor, we went to the New York State attorney general, we went to the city council of New York. People in the city council's office asked, "Has the SEC approved trading in options?" We said yes. "Were there hearings?" We said there were long hearings. They said, "Well, we'd like to see your testimony." We said there are 7,000 pages of testimony. "Well, we want to read it all."

There are a lot of times when people, confronted with a major issue, say, "This is the end of the world." And you become hardened to that. But I remember thinking, "There is *no* way around this." For low-priced options, given what they were trading at—sixteenths and thirty-seconds—you multiply that by 100 and add a $5 transfer tax and you're out of the box. No business was going to come here if they could go to the CBOE. Finally, Governor Malcolm Wilson told Attorney General Louis Lefkowitz: "You'd better take a look at this. These fellows aren't kidding." Lefkowitz and the head of the state tax commission, Mario Procaccino, examined the rule and the history of the stock transfer tax and concluded that options weren't equities and didn't come under the transfer tax.

It's interesting that we talk now about extended trading hours. We had a project in the early '70s called "Amex West," where we had discussions with the Pacific Coast Stock Exchange about a linkup or merger. The idea was that at the close of the trading day in New York, which was then 3:30, we'd press a button and the specialists' books would then be flipped to the Pacific Coast, and trading would continue. They weren't interested for a variety of reasons, so then we looked at a stand-alone project, to see if we could set up our own floor on the West Coast.

We had four or five study groups looking at trading, the brokerage community, demographics, order flow, technology, costs. Each group that came back had its set of numbers, and as they were put together someone said, "You know, there's one group that's missing in all this: the group studying lifestyle." Lifestyle in the sense that the securities industry on the West Coast in those days was very much geared to a closing in New York of 12:30 or 1:00 their time. They used to come in early and put in a vigorous day. But at 1:30, or whenever they went to lunch, that freed them in the afternoon. That was one of the most difficult things to crank into the Amex West equation. In any case, the bottom line was that the economics of it were not there at the time. But the pattern really was very clear: There was no reason you had to be bound by a 10:00-to-3:30 trading day.

Looking back, I am most pleased with the steps we took that

helped position the exchange for what turned out to be a much more strikingly different environment than we'd anticipated. We recognized the need for new financial instruments, recognized that greater computerization was coming, recognized that new kinds of publics needed to be attracted to the market. There was enormous ferment going on even then. But I don't think we had any idea of the speed with which it was going to evolve.

Editor: Clem Morgello

Gedale Horowitz

Managing Director and Head of Public Finance
SALOMON BROTHERS

In 32 years at Salomon Brothers, Gedale Horowitz has seen the
public finance industry leap from the Stone Age to the computer
era. When he started as an associate in Salomon's eight-member
muni department, he held down a 9:00 to 5:00 job—with lunch
breaks. Even as late as 1966, the muni department boasted only
one full-time finance specialist. And the long hours and cutthroat
environment of the negotiated bond business were virtually unknown. Now a member of the executive committee at Salomon and
head of its 190-person municipal department, Horowitz says the
turning point for his industry was New York City's near-default in
1975.

U p to that point, up to New York City's time, nobody worried about disclosure or anything else like that. Well, that's
not fair. Some of us worried about it but didn't express
great concern. To sell the bond issue in those days, you put out an
official statement of one page, and on the back of the page you
published the latest figures, and people bid and that was the end
of it.

When you bid on a competitive deal, the need for a finance
department is less because you don't have to chase the business.
What you need is a very good syndicate department and sales
department and trading department. All that happens is, somebody says, say in San Antonio, they're going to sell on such-
and-such a date $150 million worth of bonds at competitive
bidding. And they'll tell you what the terms are, what interest

rates you can bid, what the basis of the award is. You form an underwriting group, if you don't bid alone, and on the appointed day, you submit a bid.

Competitive bidding time was in one sense a lot of fun. Nobody had the capital to really bid by themselves in 1966. So it had the effect of getting people to bid together in syndicates. Now, if you're going to bid with somebody, you've got to work with them. So a certain amount of friendship occurs, as opposed to negotiated business, where it's every person for himself.

We changed the business—Salomon Brothers, Morgan Guaranty, Merrill Lynch, Citibank, plus a couple of other firms. The competitive bidding had been dominated by a lot of the firms that did the few negotiated deals, and while the capital of certain of our firms had grown considerably, other firms had not. We suddenly saw that we were bidding with these other firms, underwriting 300, 500, a million bonds—or I'll put it a different way, in a $100 million deal, underwriting half of 1 percent, three quarters of 1 percent—and there's little percentage in it for us.

So we decided that it was ridiculous. We were in two separate accounts, Citibank was in one account, and Morgan and Merrill and Salomon were in the other. We got together, formed a third account and started to bid on housing bonds. The housing accounts led to other groups—the so-called guerrilla groups—and the business really started to change. People started to use their capital. Instead of underwriting 1 percent of an issue, a $100 million issue, we'd underwrite 25 percent, or $25 million.

❦

But what happened with New York City was that, unbeknownst to us, they borrowed to pay their current expenses, and we went right on bidding and underwriting their notes. And basically, the music stopped. In February of 1975 one of the lawyers discovered that the city was selling tax-anticipation notes for taxes that may have never existed.

You can't appreciate the uncertainty—I guess that's the right word—for the condition that existed in April and May of 1975. And you have to appreciate that there was an ancillary event. In February of 1975 the New York State Urban Development Corp. defaulted on some notes. Defaulted. And did not, for a couple of weeks or so, pay these notes. Finally, the legislature appropriated some money to pay the notes, and that default was one of the catalysts for the city problem.

Nobody thought any of this would ever happen. People knew the city was borrowing a lot. But you know, the city had always paid its bills. We all lived through Penn Central in 1970, but that was a corporation; that was different. It didn't have taxing power and everything else; the city did.

And the other thing was, nobody knew the breadth of the problem. I don't think the city officials knew. I can remember in the first Municipal Assistance Corp. discussions to bail out the city that the amount of money that they thought they needed was $3 billion. It turned out, as I remember, MAC eventually issued $9.5 billion in new money.

In the very beginning of July, the first MAC issue was sold, $1 billion. Two thirds of the deal was done on a pro bono basis with thrifts, insurance companies, commercial banks; and $333 million was attempted to be sold to the public. I think that's a nice word, "attempted" to be sold. Let me just give you an idea. I would guess that the Bond Buyer municipal interest rate average in 1975 on July 1, right around when we sold the first bank issue, must have been somewhere around 7.25 percent; MAC sold bonds due in fifteen years and in ten years, I guess it was, at 9.5, 9.0 percent.

Now, you have to realize that the city put great weight on the entire market, particularly on the state of New York. There was also a moratorium on the city's short-term debt. The state legislature passed a bill declaring a moratorium, and the notes that came due in, I guess, January, February, March of 1976 didn't get paid.

Because of New York State's commitment to New York City, the market began to close to the state. In 1976 there was no public spring borrowing for the state of New York. A task force was put together, and the state notes were placed with commercial banks all over the country, with the residue—I would say over $1 billion—being placed with the pension funds in New York State.

And this was not the only thing that was in effect. The state had all these moral obligation bonds, all these notes that they couldn't roll over for which they had to get money from other

613

places. You had the HFA, you had the Dormitory Authority securities, among others, that were thrown into the mix. When the state was closed out in April of 1976, that was a much bigger crisis time. Of course, nobody remembers. Everybody remembers 1975.

In September of '76 the city owed the state $250 million. In October they owed them $250 million. In November they owed them $250 million. The city had the $250 million in September and October; I don't remember how the heck they paid it off. And in November the New York state comptroller had taken $250 million worth of MAC bonds as security for his loan.

You know, I believed in MAC from day one. Very few other people did. When I tell you bonds that came at 98 in July of 1975 traded at 71—they may even have traded at 69, I don't know—when I tell you that, it tells you that it was not a question of price. It was a question of the availability of money. Because most people didn't believe in it. They thought it was going to go down also.

So we had to sell $250 million of MAC bonds. They had an 11 percent coupon—State Comptroller Arthur Levitt wouldn't take any loss, and they'd been sold to the state at 11 percent. And I remember saying to Arthur Levitt, "Well, we think maybe we can do $100 million. Can you get some of your pension funds to stand by to take the other $150?" You realize, the $250 million were owned by the state itself. As it turns out, we were able to sell all $250 million at 10.5 percent, which is one financing I'm proudest of.

✦

The deal was delivered on a Friday morning. On Friday afternoon the Court of Appeals, which is the highest court in New York State, ruled the moratorium on city notes unconstitutional. And now all the New York City notes became due and payable. There were billions of those things, and we had just done this deal. The MAC bonds, which were trading probably above par, went down five, six points. I said, "We have to buy," which we did; we didn't buy many bonds because nobody would sell, but we bought bonds at 95, I remember that—bonds that come at par and were trading at 101. But it worked out.

In retrospect, I loved every minute of it. I used to complain all the time, but my wife will tell you that it was probably the most

614

exciting time for me. It was. We got it done. Got it done. And the next year, we did the entire short-term finance thing for the state of New York publicly at a rate of about 4.25 percent.

You know, I was born in New York City; this is the place where my grandparents got off the boat with nothing. This is the place that gave them a great opportunity, that gave me an opportunity to be part of Salomon Brothers in 1975. It may sound hokey, but it's a fact. This wasn't just another piece of business.

Editor: Fran Hawthorne

Pierre Haas

Former Chairman PARIBAS INTERNATIONAL

Relationship banking may be passé today, but in the Euromarket's early years it was everything. Indeed, the market probably would never have reached the heights it did without the tireless globe-trotting of the early Eurobankers. Perhaps the consummate example of the breed is Pierre Haas. He joined Banque Paribas in early 1965 as a senior vice president in charge of its budding Eurobond activity and quickly positioned the bank among the top ten managers in the market. After retiring from Paribas at age 65 two years ago, he became senior vice president of the Groupe Pargesa-Bruxelles Lambert, led by his ex-Paribas colleague Gérard Eskenazi.

I regretted very much that I didn't keep some kind of diary, because looking backward you realize that you lived in a somewhat revolutionary period, but when you're in it, you don't realize that. And, of course, everything was innovation at the time. Everything is innovation today, but in a different way. We were doing something with a skeleton crew, no background as far as files are concerned. We had to create everything along the way. And consequently, the pressure of daily events was absolutely tremendous. There was this joke that I had a packed suitcase under my desk; this is not true, but it reflects how we had to move at an incredible pace.

At Paribas, Jean Reyre, then the chairman and chief executive officer had the foresight to see that the international business was going to be something big. That was in January 1965; the first issues had been made in the Euromarket just a few months before. There was only one man who was working for me; it was Michel Francois-Poncet, who is today the chairman. The two of us were in one office, and we were the whole international financial department of Paribas—but even that was much more than any other French bank had. All the other banks in France had no inkling, no inkling for years, as a matter of fact, and that gave us, at least in France, a head start. (At that time the bank was not called Paribas, mind you, but Banque de Paris et des Pays Bas— which is a mouthful when you give that name to the secretary of a treasurer of a Middle East company.)

Paribas had quite a few things we could sell. First of all, there was a tradition in Paribas. Paribas was one of the most active banks in selling international deals before the First World War. Norsk Hydro in Norway, I think, was created by Paribas. I think we even participated in the creation of Stockholm's Enskilda Banken, although they would be surprised to hear that. And we had as our leader Reyre, who was an outstanding international financier. After having contributed to the financing of the reconstruction of France after the war, he looked at the world and saw that in the nascent Eurodollar market, we had to play a role. Then what did we have to offer? We had to offer our really strong Swiss subsidiary, because Switzerland was the repository of enormous liquidity after the war, and this liquidity was looking for employment. And Reyre had strong international connections with people like Sir Siegmund Warburg, Hermann Abs, Bobbie Lehman and Alfred Schaefer, the chairman of Union Bank of Switzerland. These men were in constant touch. So we had the friends and we had the liquid deposits in Switzerland, where we could place bonds.

The only thing which was lacking in Paribas at that time was knowing the technique of these new operations. And this is why Reyre, when he hired me in 1965, sent me for three months to Warburg. When I started to sell bonds and Euro-issues for Paribas, people were questioning our know-how, and I would say we have the know-where: We know where to place the bonds. And we very quickly proved it.

We became a valued member of a very small community of investment banks, in which there was no French bank except us. There were the major U.S. banks—Morgan, Stanley, Lehman—

then the U.K. merchant banks, where Warburg was far ahead of the lot, the Deutsche Bank, the Union Bank of Switzerland. But it was not easy because we had a lot of problems persuading the U.S. investment banks who were leading the game that they should deal with us. At that time our relationship with Morgan Stanley was sometimes difficult because they didn't recognize immediately what we could bring to this business.

When that business started, one has to remember, it was not at all at the pace which we have known since. At that time there were three, four, five deals a year, maybe ten deals. You started to do these deals in a very orderly fashion; when you wanted to make an issue, you worked on it for two or three months. The managing group decided at a leisurely pace who would be the underwriters and then who would be the selling group, and we exchanged lists and discussed it for weeks. One cannot even imagine that today, where you sometimes don't know that you're a co-manager in a deal until a minute and a half before the deal goes on. For months we had meetings, and there were hundreds of telephone calls from banks who were disgusted to be left out. You used to have almost the same fight to be an underwriter as you had later to be a manager.

In those days you could even make a little money as an underwriter, which today is incredible. And then after a few years the business became such that you could only make money by being a co-manager, but then as a co-manager you made good money for a few years. And then it became such that you could only make money as a lead manager. Today the question is, can you make money as a lead manager? No, you can't, if you don't have a swap or something else underlying the business.

I had decided that our priority should be underwriting the issues of American businesses, and we were on the right track, because the biggest borrowers were to be American businesses. I started to commute to the States and see businesses that were clients of Morgan Stanley or Goldman Sachs. What we tried to explain to these people was that Paribas would be a valuable asset for your issue, because it's going to be better placed, and your credit is going to be enhanced by good placement because your bonds are going to go at a slight premium, which means the next time you borrow you will pay less. We also said we cannot use that placement ability if the underwriting position is too small: We need a big allocation of bonds. What we called a big allocation of bonds at that time was $1 million, because we had $20 million issues, $15 million issues—that's the game we were playing.

For our part, speaking for myself, I would say I never had the fear others had, that the Eurobond market would disappear. Never. I always took the line that the market is going to endure as long as the dollar is accepted, and if the dollar is not accepted, as long as we have a multiple convertible currency market. I never feared that the market would go back to the States, because there were always reasons, good reasons, why the market should continue in Europe: for instance, the absence of regulation, the existence of this reservoir of dollars outside the States and so on. And the English have maneuvered superbly well to keep the market in London. It's a master coup the way the City of London has reacted to the whole situation and that you now have more than 400 foreign banks in London—and that most of the French operations in the Euromarket have moved to London. Immediately after [former chairman Jean-Yves] Haberer came into Paribas, I gave him a memo saying we must move our capital market operation to London. He didn't do it immediately, but he finally did it. Today it's in London because most of the operators are there, and it's by scratching the backs of each other that you get the deals.

I suppose the most difficult deal I have done, for personal reasons, was the first Eurobond deal of the World Bank, because I wanted the Deutsche Bank to share the honor with us, as we considered them our closest friend in that business. But they were dismayed not to have the deal, and they refused to do it with us. That made life very difficult for us because it's very tough to put together a deal in uncharted waters when you are fighting not for the deal itself but for the appearance of the deal; it takes away your concentration from making the deal a success. It was a very big deal, and it was the first of that kind with the biggest borrower in the world. So then, if one of your powerful friends is missing, and when you attach so much weight to the friend's being there and you have only a few hours to put that deal together, and five minutes before closing time he has not said yes and you have kept his seat warm, it complicates things and takes your attention away from the structure of the deal.

620

The first EEC deal was also difficult. There we were with the Deutsche Bank in the management group of the first deal. There, it was not the Deutsche Bank with which I had a problem; it was Sir Siegmund Warburg. He was a close friend and a man I respected so much, and he was very unhappy not to be in that deal. He said nothing, but I remember that afterward he was unhappy with me that I couldn't pull him in. I was disturbed, if you will, not to be able to pull them in. But there were so many political considerations in the construction of that deal that we spent more time on the construction than on the deal itself.

You never know why someone is not there. Probably Warburg didn't play its cards the way they should have played them. You know, there were no English banks in the top tier of the management group, because I think the English had applied so much pressure that the head of the EEC was upset. It's very difficult, because to be in a deal of that kind you have to press enough but not press so much that people at the end are upset. And how they did it I don't know, but I know that the English pressed too much—probably not Warburg, who is very, very attuned to what should be done and not done—but probably others, and Warburg suffered from that.

Relationships were not just important; they were fundamental. Today, the relationship is less important because the deals have become more technical and the game has completely changed in the last four years. But in the old days, you see, you had contacts; you had to be trusted. As an example, I would go back to this World Bank deal. I was in London for a bond meeting, and my colleague Olivier Brunet called me just before I went out for dinner, at 8:30 P.M., to tell me, "The market has moved, and I think we can do the World Bank in Europe cheaper than in the States." Two minutes later I called [World Bank treasurer] Gene Rotberg, and there was silence: He couldn't believe what I said. Now, he knew me, and he knew I was incapable of giving him a cut rate just to get a deal. He knew I was going to give him the market rate, not a cheap credit to attract his attention. Then he was very pensive, the way he is on the telephone, and said, "All right, let me think about it. Where can I reach you tomorrow night at the same time?" I said, "I'll be at the big dinner at the

621

Ottoman Bank," of which I am vice chairman. Then the next night, a Thursday night, at the banquet for the directors of the Ottoman Bank, I was called out, and Gene says, "You have the deal if you can stick to that rate. I'll give you till tomorrow, our opening"—which gave me the whole morning in Europe. And I took a 6:30 A.M. plane to Paris.

So then, to come back to trust, I knew that for him this deal was as important as it was for us, because it was the first time the World Bank borrowed dollars outside the U.S., which was something the board of directors was not very keen on. So what was at stake was his reputation and his job, and my reputation and the reputation of our bank with him.

Gene trusted that we could deliver. You see, it's a very difficult business when you offer the same thing as everybody else. You offer the market rate. Then how do you, the treasurer, decide that you'll give the deal to the Deutsche Bank, or to Morgan Guaranty or to Morgan Stanley or to Salomon or to Paribas? How do you choose? If you're a good treasurer, you know well the personality of each of the firms and of each of the operators, so you deliver the deal to the firm best positioned for it. In that sense, the relationship is very important.

In '67, '68, when we went to the States to see, say, the treasurer of Burroughs, how was it that he told Morgan Stanley, who was their banker, to put Paribas in as a co-manager? Why would he do that? He would do that because of something which doesn't exist today. We took the trouble of traveling there, and we arrived with first-hand information on the market, which today they get on their screens.

In those days your personality had a lot to do with it. You won trust by giving good information, not by saying, "I want the deal at all costs, and I am doing everything to get that deal." My technique was completely different. Very often I told these people, "You should not make a deal now," and nevertheless they went into the market, or I said, "You should not go into deutsche marks and Swiss francs," and they wanted deutsche marks and Swiss francs because they were cheaper than dollars; then the dollar went down and they lost a fortune. Then they came back to us: We had given them good advice. There is only one thing—it's to win trust. You play the long term; you may miss a deal, but you may win a war.

It was for that reason that the IMF meeting was so extremely important at the beginning. Because, you see, at the beginning there were not many more bankers than there were governors and ministers. They were looking for information, these ministers and governors, so they were seeking us the same way that we were seeking them. They were glad to see us. Sometimes they even entrusted us with a message for another governor, another minister. And then the meeting became progressively larger, with hordes of young men they didn't know, and they started to hide, the ministers and the governors; they didn't want to be in that crowd and to be hassled, to be part of the hustle, and the meeting lost some of its interest.

I found my banking life extremely stimulating. And I think that today, to be in the financial field is still probably one of the most exciting and stimulating things one can do. There is room for initiative, room for innovation. Despite the screen, there are still ways to be creative.

Editor: Cary Reich

Nikolaus Senn

President of the Executive Board UNION BANK OF
SWITZERLAND

Nikolaus Senn, CEO of Union Bank of Switzerland for the last
seven years and a member of the UBS executive board for more
than two decades, is the individual probably most identified with
the bank's phenomenal growth from a virtual also-ran among the
Swiss Big Three in the years following World War II to an international underwriting powerhouse. A former lawyer and an officer in
the Swiss army, Senn became head of the bank's investment banking division in 1966; his leadership in this sphere led to the creation of Union Bank of Switzerland (Securities) in London, UBS
Securities in New York and such acquisitions as U.K. broker Phillips & Drew. For these accomplishments and for UBS's comfortable
lead over its Swiss rivals in both total profits and assets, Senn was
named one of this magazine's bankers of the year in 1986.

T here are quite a few reasons why we achieved this rapid
growth and the expansion of the last two decades. One of
the main reasons is that we have a good management, a
motivated management, and not only on the top, but also in the
upper and middle ranges. Then, we set—well, more than twenty
years ago—clear goals as to how to expand in Switzerland into a
leading position (we were No. 3 at that moment, more or less) and
to become one of the leading banks internationally. Not on the
retail side, similar to the American banks, but in the wholesale
sector, so concentration was on financial centers and on getting
there, not a little bit but full speed.

The figures are crazy. After the war we were by far the smallest, the newcomer or the runner-up to Crédit Suisse and Swiss Bank Corp. at the time. If you look back—we have to look back because we are in our 125th-year jubilee—25 years ago, I remember we had a balance sheet of about Sf6 billion. In 25 years it went up to Sf150 billion, just like that, without affiliate companies included. The whole world made huge steps, of course.

I would say that one of the very decisive discussions was if we should go outside Switzerland. The elder generation had had some really bad experiences just before the Second World War with all the debts and problems, so they were hesitating. We were building up our trust business with an international clientele. But to really go out with credits and loans on the foreign market, that was quite a decision. There were strong arguments from the older generation not to go to New York or London. We, the younger generation at that time, had more or less to batter our heads against the walls, to come finally to the conclusion that we make the bank an international bank in the main financial centers.

The older generation said, "We are a Swiss bank. We want to do our ordinary banking—getting money and lending money—in Switzerland." The objections were, "If you go to New York you are submitting yourself to American law; if you go to London you are submitting yourself to English law. Who knows what that brings?" But we had the impression that the world was becoming smaller. It was a hard discussion, but, I would say, in a friendly atmosphere. You know, we had people who really knew something about the world and banking, like Dr. [Alfred] Schaefer [then UBS president], and we had to convince him. Finally, he said, "Well, you are the next generation to lead this bank. If you think it is indispensable, then you go." Finally, youth got it right. It is usually so.

We saw that when the Euromarket opened, after the interest equalization tax in the United States, that it would be one of the main markets of the world and that to be really international a bank had to be as strong as possible in this place. We first opened a Bermuda securities company, but then we transferred it to London. We reflected very long if we should combine with an investment bank, as Crédit Suisse did later on. We came to the conclusion that we wanted to build up by ourselves, even knowing that it would take more time; but we would then be our own masters, 100 percent.

Perhaps somebody may remember that in 1971 we started in New York, first with a combination, the so-called UBS-DB Corp. We tried to go together with another big European bank, Deutsche Bank, strong in investment banking. The original idea was that we, with our strong placing power at that time, should combine with a bank which had excellent relationships with international companies. But we finally came to the conclusion that we had to separate again. They had become a strong placing power, and we had gotten excellent relationships with the international companies, so we were competing in the same company. From there on we developed our investment banking ourselves, with the securities company in London, the securities company in the United States, and in Tokyo with the trust bank and the combined securities company, UBS-Phillips & Drew International.

It was rather difficult at the start because internationally we were not well known. We had no experience in managing or lead-managing big issues. So we not only had to build up physically, we also had to hire and train the staff, and that took quite a period of time.

On the Euromarket the breakthrough came when we were the lead manager of the first international loan for Volkswagen. That was a kind of sensation, because it was a German company very closely connected with German banks. The second breakthrough was when Bell Canada came for the first time to the European market—not with an American investment bank, not a Canadian bank, but with the Union Bank of Switzerland as lead manager. And it was a big one—about $200 million, at that time a huge issue.

In order to get those deals, we first started to exploit our relationships with companies. I was traveling in Canada—I think as one of the first Swiss bankers in Manitoba—making Swiss franc loans in this market. We did not have to go to the Euromarket because we had, contrary to the German solution, the possibility of making international loans in Switzerland. So in bringing Canadian companies over here, we were making the acquaintance of all these companies, and we finally got the lead management on the Euromarket.

You had to travel once or twice a year and make the acquaintance of everybody—*personal* acquaintance. To get lead managements, you first of all have to be competitive. And you have to know the needs of your clients. It is not purely a transactional market. It's long-standing relationships. But very often a company may have excellent relationships with different banks, and then it's a question of, well, if you just hit their needs and if you are competitive with what you offer.

Therefore, on the question of aggressive competing in the market, I would say we are not a sleeping giant. And if we think we can handle a deal at the conditions that we offer, then we do it. That may go very close to the point where it is yes or no, it can go or not go. But before you do things like that you have to be strong so that you can support it if it goes the other way around.

Second, you have to make an evaluation of the market. If you are in a sinking market interest-wise, then you can be much more aggressive than when it goes the other way. It's very often a judgment of how you look at a market. Usually it goes for one basis point or a half basis point or something like that, and there we are competing. We are playing with the strength we have. Well, some like it, some don't like it, some do it the same way.

Three or four years ago there was some discussion of our being tough on co-managers, and especially my colleague, Armin Mattle [head of UBS Securities, London], was attacked on that point. But if we make a syndicate, the members should work as a syndicate. And we very often got the impression that they liked to be members of our syndicates just because of prestige, instead of really placing the things. So sometimes, when it became hard, we had to press them a little bit. Well, I know that a lot of people didn't like it. But it was wrong that just anybody, without any placing power, was jumping into our syndicates. If the syndicate member was good he would place the issue to the benefit of our investing people; if not, then he went to the market and destroyed the issue because he had no placing power. And we tried a little bit to have banks in our syndicates that are really able to fulfill their role as syndicate members.

Things are now so competitive that somebody who is not able to be a syndicate member with some real placing power is sooner or later out of the picture. This kind of competition, especially now in London, at least as I see it, is such that there will finally be quite a few deaths on the battlefield. It's somehow similar to what happened in the U.S. when they removed all the regulations from the stock exchange. Remember, it was a hard time for everyone, but finally the strong survived. And I wouldn't be surprised if something similar happens in London. It's already on the way.

Deals have changed; they became much more technical. You had first the fixed interest rates on the Euromarket. Then the rollovers came, and since then, a lot of possibilities came up—with all the futures, the swaps, with all these combinations. And it's very often hard for the investor to understand what he really buys. There have been some necessary new innovations on the market because of the floating of currencies, but there have been a lot of innovations that I think will disappear. We will come back to the things the investor is able to understand: fixed-rate issues and rollovers combined with swaps, options or futures because of the currency situation. I wouldn't be surprised, if and when the market should change a little bit, that the credit sector will come much more to life again. Until the last few months, we were able to sell anything to anybody at any price. And I wouldn't be surprised if this climate would change sooner or later.

The things that will endure include everything which is connected with the possibility to swap or to secure swings in currencies or interest rates, because that is a really unforeseeable situation for which you have to find solutions. At the beginning, currency swaps were very short-term, but then they became longer and longer. That is sensible. I think it is also sensible to make some kind of provision against big interest swings that either may be in the interest of the investor or in the interest of the issuer. These things will certainly go on at least as long as we have the floating rates, which were a very decisive event in the whole development of the market. But for the other things, where only a few specialists know what they are, I make at least a question mark.

A different kind of a breakthrough was when we lead-managed the first U.S. internal loan for Allied-Signal, last year, because nobody had dared to do that up to then, no foreigner. And that went quite well; now we have done quite a few of them. And it

629

seems that this globalization and internationalization is not only coming to Switzerland, it's also going to the U.S. Just as now the American banks and the Japanese banks are lead-managing here in Switzerland, we start to lead-manage in the U.S. and sooner or later we will also lead-manage in Japan.

I still like to make deals, but the real deals done daily in the operating sector are now done by my colleagues. The most personal business I was involved in was the takeover of Interhandel, the famous case that is now before the German judges. But the takeover of Interhandel was for me, I would say, our start as an investment bank; it was a very important thing. There was E.G. Chemie, the big German firm, which had General Aniline and Film Corp. in the United States as a daughter, as an affiliate company. And before the war, perhaps foreseeing that the war could come, it sold this company to a Swiss company, Interhandel. When the war broke out there was a dispute between Switzerland and the United States over whether General Aniline and Film Corp. was enemy property. Finally, the Americans said, "Perhaps it's not enemy property, but it's enemy tainted," because there were suspicions that there were still connections between the Swiss company and the Germany company.

Well, that had to be cleared up after the war. There were long discussions, and the Interhandel administration finally came to a kind of settlement with the United States government, with [Attorney General] Bob Kennedy and his successor Nicholas Katzenbach; we sold General Aniline and Film Corp. together to the public and divided the gain coming out. In 1965 Interhandel got half and the Americans got half; finally we have in Switzerland a company called Interhandel, with all the money on the active side, the cash. And then UBS took it over. It was quite a transaction at that time, because it increased our capital by about 70 percent and gave us, of course, a lot of possibilities to expand in Switzerland. Our total capital then was roughly around Sf600 million, and after the deal it was almost Sf1 billion. I had to make the concept— at that time I was first vice president—I had to find out how we could bring it together; it was rather complicated. We had a lot of discussions, and I would say the final talks were made by our chairman at the top level.

I remember well when I arranged the contract to rent the offices for the new branch in London a bit more than twenty years ago. Dr. Schaefer, at that time the chairman, told me, "Look, don't take more than space for about 70 people. We will never have more than 70 people in London." Now there are, together with Phillips & Drew, about 1,400. And in New York it's the same. We signed a contract for a skyscraper many years ago; we got half in the form of a mortgage, which we can convert into property, with an option on the whole. If you go to New York you will find that a big part of the skyscraper is already occupied by Union Bank of Switzerland and UBS Securities. And that at the beginning was a small office on Wall Street.

Of course, we had problems with growth. We had problems especially with bringing in good staff. That is for me the main point, to have an excellent staff, well educated and motivated; that's the A and Z of the whole story. If you have that, and of course a technical and financial basis, then you have a fair chance to be successful. We have eleven educational centers in Switzerland for the ordinary staff, where they have a chance to learn foreign languages, typewriting, computers and I don't know what all.

Apart from that, we have the management center, which is in Wolfsberg. More or less everybody who is selected for management has to go through there; we have 2,000 people trained annually at this center. The basic training is four times for four weeks each. They have to learn on the job and then go back to the center—and then come back again. There are three main things they study there. First is general education—politics, literature and so on—then management and finally banking. And our managers, even executive vice presidents, each have to go every second year for one week for a repetition course. The center is eleven years old. Before, we hired staff from one school or another, all different types of schools, but we found out that this didn't correspond to what we really wanted, that is, for them to be informed in management. (Of course, we do want them to be interested, not only in banking, but in a little bit broader range.) And finally they become bankers by training at one of our branches.

I think without Wolfsberg we would have much more trouble developing the staff which we need for a bank of the size we are. The other side is training on the job, which is still the most important thing. To learn to be an investment banker, you have to go into the middle of the battle and make an issue or make some mistakes and learn from the mistakes till finally you get it.

We did have problems with computerization; we once had a big failure. We were the first to start with real time online; we thought we would be ahead of our competitors. But it failed because the company that we chose wasn't technically able to fulfill what we had planned as hardware. So we had to start again, and that was quite a critical period, in the middle of the '70s. But since then we have had engineers on our executive board. In modern banking, it depends completely on how you are technically equipped. Of course, it is mainly human-to-human relationships, but without top technical equipment you are lost. That's a very important change, and it's one of the main reasons we have this internationalization and globalization. You work in one second with London, you work with the U.S., you work 24 hours just on the screen. The deals are done immediately. A company or a bank not able to have these logistics will sooner or later be out of the battle.

Yes, this has been a fascinating time. And it's a challenge, too, because there are risks; you don't know if you really will finally perform in this international market, which is very competitive. And you invest quite a part of your earnings in this buildup. But we are optimistic.

Editor: Suzanne Wittebort

Yusuke Kashiwagi

Chairman BANK OF TOKYO

Yusuke Kashiwagi spent most of his working life at Japan's Ministry of Finance, where, as head of the international finance bureau, he had a significant impact on his government's monetary policies. Here Kashiwagi recalls the decisions that contributed to the rise of Japan as an economic powerhouse, as well as the move to and consequences of floating exchange rates.

In 1967 Japan was still a very small country; the GNP was then $173 million. Today it's $2 trillion; I never expected the figure to be so impressive. Beginning in 1967 we entered a period of growth with stability, though we had a series of balance-of-payments deficits in connection with the oil crises. As a result, Japan could devote itself to expanding its own economy, though it is export oriented insofar as we always had to export something to obtain our raw materials and our energy. But that our economy is completely export oriented is a misconception. If you look at the figures, you will find that Japan's dependence on the export sector is very low; even today it's a little beyond 15 percent of GNP. It's almost the same as the United States. We have been more domestic oriented.

The consistent policy of the Japanese was to defend the $1-to-¥360 rate that was set in 1950 and to never devalue the currency. That was to be the key economic policy. So I think Japan is the only country in the world that has never devalued its currency. Fixed exchange rates exercise a kind of international discipline on the economy, and that is, I think, the basis on which we could keep our economy moving fast and on an even keel. You can have growth with stability with a fixed exchange rate.

But events did not turn out that way. The Nixon shock [when President Nixon, in 1971, first adjusted the dollar against gold and then floated it] came as a real shock to Japan. For about three years before that, I was vice minister for international affairs, and there were many occasions when we had discussions with so-called academics. On the government side we had Paul Volcker and Otmar Emminger [from West Germany] and myself. And at these meetings we discussed exchange rates so often, and I recall the academics were always arguing about why governments stick to these rates when you have these perpetual crises—sterling, French franc, deutsche mark crises. So why don't you move to a floating, flexible exchange rate system, where the so-called invisible hand would control the economy?

Anyhow, I heard about Nixon's decision in a phone call from Volcker. I was at home, and I called him back when I got to my office, and he said, "I'm leaving for Geneva right now; I only have 30 minutes to talk to you." He explained to me the action that the United States was going to take. He was basically saying that under Bretton Woods, there was no way for the dollar to be devalued, and he wanted the other currencies to appreciate against the dollar. And then a year or so later—I remember very well it was in early '73, rather early in the morning—I had a telephone call from Takashi Hosomi, the head of international at the Finance Ministry, which I had already left. He wanted my advice on what to do with the yen. He wanted to float it. I had advised the ministry in, I think, September of '72 that Japan should revalue again, and I advocated ¥260 to the dollar. But even then the economy was booming. I said, well, the situation may be very critical, and you may have to float the yen.

The journalists also favored floating, and the mood was perhaps going for floating. But I told this gentleman, if you once float the yen, it is very difficult to return to a fixed exchange rate, so this must be a very careful decision. You might have to float it, but never do it unilaterally. You should always do it together with the Europeans. Don't let Japan float alone. That was my recommendation.

I didn't know that Paul Volcker would be visiting Japan in a few days' time, and he did come on a secret mission to Tokyo. The dollar, he said, could not be maintained at that level, so won't the Japanese revalue, raise the yen? Or what would they do? I don't know the answer he got from [then finance minister] Kiichi Aichi. But Aichi must have told him that he would prefer floating, if the Europeans would float. And on that basis, Volcker went to the Europeans, and they all agreed to float. So in February of '73 we entered the age of floating. That was really a dramatic change. So all the currencies floated and the academics didn't realize that what would happen with exchange rates would produce greater volatility and larger imbalances in terms of surpluses and deficits.

In 1973 there was much concern about what would happen. We had been living with fixed rates very successfully; they were a good yardstick to measure the economy so we never went to excesses. And then we had the oil crisis.

But Japan was a country that had survived so many crises, and if you are faced with a crisis, you must adjust. You must reduce your import demand and try to promote exports. That's why we went into a very restrictive fiscal policy and a very tight monetary policy, and that is why we recovered quicker. And we did not try to borrow money to finance ourselves through the crisis.

In Europe, though, many felt that this was a crisis that is outside individual countries, so it wasn't a question of adjustment, but how to finance themselves until the storm had passed. But in Japan we took it more seriously. Then, during the second oil crisis, they went into a recession because all the countries tightened up and reduced demand, and this caused the industrial world to go into recession. But we were successful, because we had been able to prepare our country.

By then, though, I was no longer at the Ministry of Finance, so I didn't have responsibility for the whole economy. Industry people were groping to live with all this. The average movement in the exchange rate from 1973 to 1980 was about 20 percent a year, up and down. But by then I was at the Bank of Tokyo, and our bank would have to live with all that. It was our bread and butter.

Now people are still arguing that exchange rates must be stabilized, and I've been asked many times, why don't you suggest how to get more stable exchange rates? Intervention will not help very much. You must have better coordination of macroeconomic policy between the U.S. and Germany and Japan that will be conducive to stabilizing the exchange rate. The U.S. has a particular responsibility.

Paul Volcker is my hero; I've known him more than twenty years, and I really like him and admire him. He understands that we live in an interdependent world. I think that when we used to have these meetings in the late '60s, there was a certain kind of political camaraderie; people got to know each other and help each other in difficult times. But unfortunately, it looks now as if you don't see this going on as before. I think if we could revive this kind of close friendship among these mandarins of the financial world, then we might be able to work out a better solution to many things. In the '60s, we always thought in terms of defending the international monetary system. But today we always agree in abstract terms, but not in terms of what must be done. Politicians have become so concerned with their own economies that they are not so concerned with the stability of the world.

In August of 1982 we had some understanding of the problem of the Mexican crisis, but it came as a surprise that the Mexican situation was as bad as it was. We thought that this was a problem not only of Mexico but of all the countries, because part of this question was that the economies of the world were going through a kind of recession. Of course, the developing countries had poor management of their own economies. Or perhaps they had mistaken the world economy, in that they thought there would be prosperous times forever. But on the other hand, many people said it was the greedy banks that lent them money they didn't need. So where is the fault? I don't see it that way. We never asked them to borrow the money; they came to us. I think the banks did a service to the world at that time.

Now the leaders of each country must think more in terms of how to achieve greater growth for the world as a whole, maybe at some sacrifice to their own economy. We in Japan must move our economy faster; we must expand domestic demand. Perhaps we should have a stronger fiscal policy, in the sense of more incentives, tax cuts that would stimulate the economy by favoring housing and certain kinds of consumption and investment. I am always of the view that Japan lives with the world. As Japan gets bigger and bigger, we must share the prosperity. We benefit because the world is prosperous. And we must also help the developing countries. Today, I also think, the IMF should go into this matter of seeing what is the proper relationship of currencies. I am an idealistic internationalist.

The international financial world is changing very fast. There may be more risks, but there are also more ways to cope with risk. The U.S. dollar cannot be the single reserve currency anymore. It will have to share the responsibility with a number of other currencies, and I think the yen will be one. We never believed the world would collapse. We all believed that we must compromise for the good of the whole. Each one must give something. If we can have the camaraderie we had before, we can try to work out a better solution.

Editor: Henny Sender

Christian Hemain

Former Publisher INTERNATIONAL FINANCING REVIEW

> Not all of the Euromarket's great success stories involve bankers.
> In 1967 a French financial journalist named Christian Hemain ar-
> rived in London on a routine two-week assignment and ended up
> hanging around the City for the next two decades reporting—inci-
> sively and straightforwardly—on the burgeoning Eurobond mar-
> ket. Eventually, Hemain founded a highly regarded weekly market
> newsletter—*International Financing Review*—that he sold in 1986,
> purportedly for the sort of sum that even a thriving Eurobanker
> might envy.

In 1967 I was working on the foreign desk of a group of French
financial papers called *Agefi,* and one day they asked me to
write something about Eurobonds. I hadn't a clue what a Eurobond was. So I made some inquiries, and among the first bankers I met was Hélie de Pourtalès [now a partner at Lazard Frères
et Cie.]. He was very nice and took his time to explain what a
Eurobond was. I went to see three or four people like that, and so
I started to write—in French—about the Eurobond market. A
year later I was sent to London by *Agefi* for two weeks—and I'm
still here nineteen years later.

In those days there was only a column in the *International Herald
Tribune* and, of course, the *Financial Times* that covered Eurobonds. At the time, the City was ruled by the traditional London
merchant banks, with kings like Sir Joclyn Hambro. And they *were*
kings! They *ruled* the City.

The reaction of the bankers to me was very cool. The continental banks were mostly operating from the Continent, and

there was very little Eurobond issuing done from London. The City had started to be a center for Euroloan syndication a few years earlier, with big banks like Lloyds putting syndicates together. But at the time, it was still a very tiny, provincial market. It was very sophisticated, of course, because of the merchant banks. But they were all living their own lives, cut off from the rest of the financial community, really. They worked in a very closed way. If you phoned somebody at Hambros to say, "Hey, by the way, I hear you're putting together $20 million, won't you tell me about it?" It was like asking the pope the name of his latest mistress. It was awful, and it went on like that for some time.

Then the American banks started to develop in London at the end of the 1960s, and so life started to change. These people were much more open to talk to. They were foreigners, and that was the big difference. Whenever I needed help it was the American banks I turned to, much more than the French. The first were the big commercial banks. Citicorp, of course, was No. 1. When Citicorp decided to come to London, they chose the best guys from U.S. universities and they gave them higher salaries and Porsches. They were a bunch of young wolves, as the French would say. And that started to change the whole pattern.

The investment banks came later. Then the very first Japanese came. They were very, very shy, not at all sure of themselves. I remember meeting a guy from Yamaichi, who said: "Listen, I'm coming to London, but after that we will open up in Paris. Will you teach me a little bit of French?" Now, my English has never been tremendous, and my accent has always been what it is. But *his* English and *his* accent were awful. So to talk together in English was quite something, and to try to teach him French was something else. They were just trying to get their name known and to introduce themselves.

So with the backing of the Americans and a few Japanese, I started to make my way in the City. But I couldn't ignore the merchant banks like S.G. Warburg, because they were so very good—also very powerful and very secretive. Some of the people who came to work for them came from Oxford or Cambridge, but many got there because of family relationships and things like that. They were very nice, though not the greatest bankers in the world. They wanted to be City gentlemen, that's all.

They were so badly paid. I'm sure my salary was much higher than any of these guys'. They could only afford sandwiches. But they were happy because they had social status. Me? I didn't have any social status, but at least I was getting decent meals—which is much more important.

At the time, the continental banks—the Swiss and the Luxembourg banks—were much stronger on Eurobonds than the British banks. So I did have a big advantage. My competition was doing much better at reporting on syndicated Euroloans, which was most of the business of the City of London. But I was better at reporting on Eurobonds, which came from the Continent.

Around this time William Low left the *Financial Times* to start his own newspaper, *International Insider*. He was a very good journalist—a very nasty man—and I liked him enormously. His newsletter was very punchy, very aggressive. So the continental bankers, like Kredietbank in Luxembourg, said to me: "Listen, there is the *Tribune* and the *FT*, but they're all Anglo-Saxons and their main contacts are always Anglo-Saxon bankers. We would very much like to have our own point of view put across, because we are quite active, too. Could you write in English?" I was writing for another paper, and I could not start an English newspaper because I didn't know how. But I had met a guy who was working for the *Sunday Telegraph*, named Donald Last, who had started a newsletter for a German group. He said that he could help me, and today he is working for us.

So I launched the newsletter in 1974, I must say against *Agefi*'s will. I started it for them but I didn't tell them—I just did the first issue—No. 1—and I phoned them afterward. Donald Last was working for his German group, and they printed the first issue and did the mailing, so I didn't have to pay for anything. But when *Agefi* saw it they started shouting: "Oh God, what have you done? You are raping us." But it was done. So in a hurry they set up a £100 company [for the newsletter venture], in which I had one share.

Donald Last helped me very much because he provided me with printing facilities in Sevenoaks, Kent. I was still working every day for *Agefi*. But when I finished work there I used to take the train from Charing Cross railway station to Sevenoaks every Friday, and from 6:00 in the evening until 6:00 the next morning

641

we wrote the newsletter and then printed it and sent it out by post. It was four pages long and it went out every week.

⁂

The subscription was £40 a year, and our first subscription came from a British bank. For me that was very important. I hadn't tried to approach a French bank because, being French, I knew the pressure that can be put on a journalist. You see, the French press has never been very free. My own paper, *Agefi*, was owned by the French equivalent of the Confederation of British Industries. That meant that all the banks except the ones that were nationalized owned my newspaper.

I remember once writing in *Agefi* about an issue for Denmark lead-managed by Crédit Commercial de France and saying it was not the best issue in the world. That was like saying it was a flop. Even before it had gone out I received a phone call from the chairman of *Agefi*, saying, "What have you done?" The guy had received a phone call from the chairman of CCF, who was one of the main shareholders in *Agefi*, so it was a big drama.

I still had my office at the *Daily Telegraph*, whose City staff was on the top floor of the *Financial Times* building. This gave me the advantage of being where I could use the *FT*'s common dining room and so on. The *Telegraph* people didn't like having a French journalist among them, so they put me with the switchboard girls. But I was very happy because the girls took care of me and did my laundry.

I went to the *Telegraph*'s daily editorial conference, but I just sat by the entrance and said nothing. One day, though, I think in the late '60s, they said at the conference that they wanted to publish something on the front page about the French franc, because they thought it was going to be devalued. But I said it wouldn't be. It made those people wild. Nevertheless, there on the front page of the *Telegraph* the next morning was a piece predicting that the French franc would be devalued. But over the weekend de Gaulle came back saying the French franc would never be devalued, and the French franc was not devalued. When I came back to work after the weekend, I had my desk among the journalists.

Since *Agefi* had been a journal of record, I also recorded everything in the newsletter. I was the first to write about exotic currencies—and don't forget that at the time an exotic currency was the deutsche mark or the Swiss franc, not to mention the French and Luxembourg francs. I was the first one to write about the first Luxembourg franc international issue that was done by a non-Luxembourg borrower. I was the first person at the beginning of 1974 to write on this side of the Atlantic about M3 and the money supply. In every English paper that was a joke. They didn't think it could have any impact on interest rates. I was the first one to write about [Salomon Brothers economist] Henry Kaufman, and in 1974 there were not many people quoting Kaufman.

I think I have excellent French, and I'm not modest, but in English I'm not Shakespeare, unfortunately. So I was forced to use very simple sentences in my newsletter. But that was good, because the Japanese who were coming to London were not very good in English, either, and they could understand what I was saying. The newsletter was different in other ways, too. Bill Low [of *International Insider*] was very witty, and he would always write about one subject in a very brilliant way, but with a point of view. I tried to remain a bit more neutral or less personal than he was and to make *International Financing Review* a journal of record and one with broader coverage, because I got many tips from the Continent.

When I wanted to tell my people—I had 80 people working for me when I quit *IFR*—what a bad piece of journalism is, I often showed them the *FT*. A story is happening, but if you read the *FT* you have to read the whole blooming article, and in the middle of it you will discover what it is. I like an American first sentence: The problem is this and that and that. You don't have to spend 30 minutes reading the paper to find what the problem is.

I'm sure I was one of the first journalists to be queuing with bankers to see the central bank in Saudi Arabia when the oil crisis broke. The same with Kuwait. I knew quite a lot of the Arabs because my family was in glass manufacturing, and I had spent a lot of time in the Middle East. So I managed to get a lot of tips.

I was the first to publish a list of blacklisted banks. Most of them did not even know they were blacklisted. There was Rothschild, and Banque Bruxelles Lambert in Belgium, and some of the Lazards but not all. This kind of thing boosted my readership.

We still weren't making any money, but I didn't give a damn

because I still only had one share. We were still typing on type-writers until 1977, when there was the big switch to computers. First there were two divisions, syndicated loans and bonds. "Eminence Noire" [IFR columnist Ian Kerr, who heads Eurobond research for Kidder Peabody International] came to work for us four or five years ago to add some spice, because the newsletter was so boring.

We also started carrying cartoons. The very first one was about Brazil. You see, Brazil was the same as today even fifteen years ago—too much tax and too little money. The cartoonist [David Langdon] told me about a song from before the war called "There's an awful lot of coffee in Brazil," so we started on this theme. We had [former Brazilian economic czar Antonio] Delfim Netto with a huge sombrero playing on the guitar and singing, "I have not an awful lot of money in Brazil."

The caricatures by David Smith came later on. You see, the market has always been made by individuals. In the beginning there were the continentals. You had guys like Armin Mattle of Union Bank of Switzerland or André Coussement from Krediet-bank in Luxembourg. I always said it was Coussement who made the first Eurobond issue. He was a salesman—he could have sold anything, the Eiffel Tower or socks, sugar, anything. People al-ways say the first Eurobond issue was done by S.G. Warburg, but it wasn't; it was done by Coussement for a Portuguese borrower, Sacor. A true Eurobond issue is one made by a borrower outside his own market via a listed public issue with bearer shares and an international syndicate. In all the issues before Sacor there was always one of those things missing. This first real one was made in units of account, which was a composite currency unit set up by Kredietbank and a Belgian professor long before the ECU was used to denominate Eurobond issues.

The Euromarket started to change around 1978–79. The peo-ple became very worried. When the shah of Iran was deposed and the ayatollah took over, for the first time people began wondering what a risk really was and what they stood to lose. For the first time assets were frozen—something nobody thought could hap-pen. And soon after Iran came the Latin American debt crisis.

Before that it had been so important to be high on the league table. It was always a fight between Citibank and Chase Manhat-tan. At the end of the year, Citicorp would phone up and ask, "How much has Chase done?" If I said Chase was No. 1, then

Citicorp would say, "Listen, there are some loans we forgot to tell you about." They would say they lent $600 million privately to Mexico, but there was no tombstone. It was amazing—they always wanted to be No. 1.

Then there came a big change. The investment banks arrived in London and started making new instruments that completely changed the pattern of financing. Among the investment banks that were at the forefront of change were Crédit Suisse White Weld, later Credit Suisse First Boston, Goldman Sachs, Salomon Brothers, Merrill Lynch and Morgan Stanley. But for me Morgan Guaranty has always been at the top—even if they are not No. 1 in the league table—in skill, sophistication and knowledge. If I were to put my money in one bank, it would always be Morgan Guaranty—no problem.

The coming of the Japanese also made for a big change, because they could buy everything and put a lot on their books. The Japanese will take a watch from the Swiss, and three years later they'll come back with a better watch at a cheaper price. So they looked at what the U.S. investment banks were doing and they are trying to do the same.

But it was the U.S. investment banks that completely changed the face of the market. They came at just the right time. People were going away from the syndicated Euroloan and into other instruments, like floating-rate notes and floating CDs. Later on the American firms were the first to introduce securitization of everything.

The whole trend in the Euromarket has been toward globalization, universalization. There's more and more the view now that the Eurobond market as such doesn't exist anymore. We still use the word "Eurobond," but what's the difference now between Eurobonds, foreign bonds and international bonds? It's a global market, and it's changing so fast that it's difficult, even for someone who's observed it firsthand for almost twenty years, to see where it's going.

Editor: Fiammetta Rocco

Carl Icahn

Chairman ICAHN & CO.

Carl Icahn left medical school for Wall Street at an opportune moment: The year was 1961, and the market was on a tear. The neophyte Dreyfus & Co. broker quickly made a bundle, only to lose it all in the crash the following year. Having learned a painful but pertinent lesson about risks and rewards, Icahn went on to flourish as an options salesman and then classic arbitrageur, founding his own firm in 1968. But it was as a corporate raider—an arbitrageur of corporate assets—that he developed his fearsome reputation as a scourge of American management.

Takeovers are, to my mind, almost as risk-free as [classical] arbitrage, in that you're buying assets, you're buying value in the marketplace, and what stands between you and the value is management. So if you can take control of a company, it's the greatest thing in the world. And, you know, there's a certain enjoyment in the chess game—the fighting to get control.

In this game the most successful and the best way to come out, I've said over and over, is not to sell your stock to another buyer but to take the company over. Those are the most successful. By and large, ACF and TWA are by far the most successful of our deals, because we were able to go in there and sort of prove what I've been saying, and they're going to be the most successful financially. I think we've done a good job of running these companies.

When we were doing arbitrage, we'd see a big profit and say, "Okay, let's grab it." But now I say: "Wait a minute, let's look at

647

the value of this company. Why not buy it and fix it up and really accomplish something? Then sell it, if we want to."

My opinion is that, philosophically, I'm doing the right thing in trying to shake up some of these managements. It's a problem in America today that we are not nearly as productive as we should be. That's why we have the balance-of-payments problems. It's like the fall of Rome, when half the population was on the dole.

There was a time when I got on this board, in a proxy fight. I'm the biggest shareholder, but I only got one seat; it was cumulative voting. So I'm trying to be a nice guy and I'm watching what's going on, and this [CEO] gets up—he waits till the end of the meeting because everybody is looking at the clock and none of the board members really give a damn what's going on—and he says, "I want to buy this other company." And he shows us this company that's been losing money for five years, you know? Garbage-disposal business. And he wants to pay 40, 50 million bucks for it. The sales are down, and, you know, it looks terrible, but nobody says anything about it. Everybody is going to vote for it. I'm looking amazed.

Finally, one little guy there who had some stock—the only other guy on the board who had some stock—said: "Well, wait a minute. I don't want to argue with you, but how the hell can we buy this company?" And [the CEO] starts glowering at this guy, and he says, "Are you doubting my ability to turn a company around?" Then the little guy said: "Wait, we haven't heard from Mr. Icahn for three months. Mr. Icahn, what do you say?" I say: "I think this is the worst deal I've ever seen. This is insanity." Then I said, "And furthermore, I think every one of you board members will be held personally liable if you do this." As soon as I said that, everybody looked up from reading the papers, and they voted it down. Now, *that's* what goes on at these boards.

In this game, if you have the stock, you should win. The guy who has the most stock *and* the fortitude to hold on to it can go ahead and can win this thing. But it's a tough game. When I first started in, I remember telling an old-timer who had been around a long time: "They're hitting me pretty hard on these first deals. They're killing me with lawsuits and this and that." And he said,

"You know, Mr. Icahn, there aren't many that can play this game."
That's still true today.

My favorite poem—unfortunately, I don't fulfill most of the
things said in it—is "If" by Rudyard Kipling. Well, in the middle
of the takeover game, there's a lot of that in there. If you can risk
everything you've got, and if you can keep your head when all
those around you are losing theirs and blaming it on you. . . .

This game gets in your blood, though, because when you're in
it, it's like being in the middle of a tiger hunt, and the tigers are
coming at you and you've just got a spear. At times you don't get
sleep for three, four days. You just keep going, and you're not
even tired.

The chairman of ACF was very fair, even though they didn't want
me. Maybe that was because we had so much stock anyway, and
they figured the hell with it. They said, "Okay, you've got this
much stock, and you say you want to buy us." The stock was only
at 35, 37. I said to them: "I'll stop buying the stock for six months.
You go out and you can find another buyer for the company, and
I won't bother you. I'll give you a standstill. But I want the right
to compete with any bid you get." They said: "Okay, but you have
to have cash. We're not going to take paper from you, Icahn." I
figured okay.

But we loved the company. Later on there were a couple of
buyers, and one of these buyers offered me a high price to get me
out. I didn't want to get out. I wanted the company. Well, this guy
comes into my office from Cooper Industries and says, "Carl, if
you buy ACF, we'll buy the W-K-M division from you."

ACF wasn't too pleased, I guess, that Cooper Industries was
helping me. With Cooper's agreement to buy W-K-M for about
$200 million, I obtained the financing to buy ACF. Right before I
bought ACF, the company went ahead and sold W-K-M to Joy
Manufacturing before I could buy ACF. Of course, the money
was in the company already, so I still got ACF.

All of the companies—I would have bought them all if I could
have, and, in retrospect, I'm sorry I didn't buy a few more of
them. I'm really sorry. If you look at the market as a business and
not as a gambling casino, I think you can do very well. The big
thing in a lot of this is never to let your ego get away from you.

649

I've seen a lot of successful people who start believing their own press clippings, believing all the stuff that people say about them because they've made some money.

There are certain creative things I'd still like to do, though. I've always been interested in producing a movie. I have certain artistic bents that way.

Editor: Firth Calhoun

Brenda Gall

Apparel and Household Products Analyst MERRILL LYNCH

Brenda Gall joined Merrill Lynch fresh out of college in 1961 and gradually became one of the most respected and successful securities analysts on Wall Street. She has been a member of the *Institutional Investor* magazine's All-America Research Team in apparel since 1974 and in household products since 1976.

When I was a senior in college in the early '60s, I decided that it would be nice to work for a brokerage firm. I wrote a series of letters to a number of brokerage firms, saying I was graduating with a BA in economics and that I would be interested in any training programs that they offered. Merrill Lynch was the only firm that wrote back.

At that time Merrill had a program that ran for about two years. Trainees started out in the research room answering requests about this stock or that stock wired in by brokers in the field. Then we ran around to the individual specialists in the booths who answered the wires. At that point we were just messengers. After paying your dues in that area and in the statistics department, you moved on to portfolio analysis, which at that time involved dictating letters to clients, providing opinions on the issues in their portfolios.

If you were interested in moving into securities analysis, you took your chances on where an opening might pop up. In my case it happened that an opening occurred in the chemicals, textiles and apparel booth. The two men I worked with there were both chemical engineers. Since they were interested in chemistry and I was not—it was one of my worst subjects in school—it was natural for me to lean toward the textile and apparel companies. Also, I preferred reading *Women's Wear Daily* to *Chemical & Engineering News*.

A lot of people wouldn't have wanted the apparel group, since it was regarded as a secondary or tertiary industry. Most wanted to get into technology or some other important industry where the compensation was higher. I felt it was important to get into an area that I would enjoy, and also, I wasn't in a big hurry. I had just gotten out of undergraduate school and didn't have the confidence that a lot of the MBAs have today. I was willing to pay my dues, and learn, and gain confidence.

Merrill Lynch was certainly not recognized for its research in the early '70s. We were really providing information for our retail brokerage system. It was a much different business—very short reports, much more superficial than it is today, in my mind. I think a lot of the change had to do with *Institutional Investor*'s emphasis on research. Our top management was concerned at the time that Merrill Lynch wasn't being recognized at all in that area. So they made a decision that we were going to become No. 1 in that category. They went out and started hiring. There had been a lot of analysts at Merrill Lynch who were fine under the old system, supplying our retail network with information, but when marketing became a much bigger element in the analyst's job, they realized they had to have a different type of analyst.

When I started, there were already numerous women securities analysts. In fact, Merrill Lynch probably had more than most firms. I've never felt discriminated against at Merrill because I'm a woman. I've always been treated fairly. However, I never wanted to go into management. Perhaps if I had, it might have been more difficult. I believe it's a disadvantage being a woman in management because it's hard to be "one of the boys." I don't think that's expected of a research analyst. Our job is strictly professional.

If I take a male client to lunch, there's no problem about picking up the check, in this day and age. As an analyst, you're recognized for your performance, whether you're a man or a woman. I would have to say there are some industries where it's actually an advantage to be a woman. I think apparel is probably one. Women seem to understand the fashion business better than most men, and I have a greater interest in that industry than male analysts might have.

Where I think women are truly at a disadvantage is that most men have a wife behind them who is taking care of a lot of the details of everyday living. If you're a single woman who is trying to run an apartment and a weekend house, get your meals cooked and the laundry and grocery shopping done, it's a lot tougher, doing it all yourself. Plus, you have to be willing to commit yourself to the job, virtually around the clock. You have to be willing to think about it all the time.

Until five or ten years ago, the apparel industry was the consumer group's stepchild. Most people didn't even want to hear about apparel stocks. Seventh Avenue had a tarnished image, an image of volatility and unpredictability. Portfolio managers would say: "The capitalizations are too small. We're not interested. They're too volatile. We can't keep on top of the constant changes." I picked up the soap stocks in the '73–'74 period so that I'd have a group where there was institutional interest. The soaps were very different. They were huge companies with big capitalizations that had defensive characteristics.

It became evident in the '70s that demographic trends could determine what segments of the apparel industry were likely to do well. And the well-managed companies that positioned themselves in the right segments would benefit from emerging lifestyle and demographic trends. Liz Claiborne's astute positioning as the designer for working women was evidence of that. Oshkosh B'Gosh homed in on the better children's wear market, just as the baby boom developed and working mothers were willing to spend more on their children's clothes than they had in some years.

Reebok identified the fact that 80 percent of athletic shoes were worn for casual wear, not for performance. So they moved into that category and positioned their product with fashion and comfort features to appeal to the 80 percent, not the 20 percent. They introduced a product with soft garment leather, a new material for athletic shoes, and now, because they read the market properly, they dominate the athletic footwear market. Women started wearing athletic shoes to work in place of their dress shoes. It made sense to wear a less expensive shoe to the office so the more costly dress shoe would last much longer. It had an economic as well as a comfort appeal. If you need performance shoes for running, you'll buy one pair, but if you need shoes to go with different outfits for different purposes, you'll buy multiple pairs.

I don't just use my own judgment. I seek input from a lot of sources. I talk to my companies' key customers to make sure that what they're doing is on target. I have to confirm input with professionals who are in the market every day. You have to know whether the product lines are selling well at retail to clue you in if something's wrong. They really have no reason to talk to me, but everybody likes to discuss what's happening in their business. You get one source at a buying group, and they introduce you to another. If they tell you something's not selling, you go back to the company.

The job entails much more marketing now than it did in the early days. The amount of time spent on the phone and traveling has grown dramatically. We instituted an annual textile and apparel seminar ten years ago, and it has expanded each year. I travel to Europe every couple of years on a marketing trip and to the West Coast, Chicago, Boston and numerous other cities once a year to keep in contact with my institutional counterparts. Those counterparts keep changing, so you have to reestablish your relationships. That's probably the most frustrating part of the job; just as you get a relationship developed with a client who depends on you or respects your judgment, then that person is gone.

The job entails more investment banking work today, which I enjoy. In research you often never really know if an order evolves from your efforts, but if you work with investment banking on bringing in new business, it's gratifying when you get the assignment, particularly if they indicate that your understanding of the industry played a key role. You get to know the management well and can call on them as a source of industry trends and information.

The toughest thing about this job is it never stops. If you go on vacation, you have to know everything that happened to your companies while you were away. When you get back, your desk is piled high with all the trade papers, requests from people who called that you have to answer. It never lets up. It's a very demanding job, but it's very rewarding, mentally and otherwise.

Editor: Joe Kolman

Charles Minter

Former Institutional Salesman MERRILL LYNCH

> Charles Minter began his career on Wall Street in 1966 as a retail broker in Miami, then moved to New York in 1970 to join the Merrill Lynch institutional sales team. For better than fifteen years, he was one of Merrill's top salesmen, during some of the headiest and most freewheeling times for his profession. Early in 1987 he and Merrill's former chief investment strategist, Stanley Salvigsen, and senior market analyst, Michael Aronstein, set up Comstock Partners, a money management firm with an office on lower Broadway.

With Mayday, many of us thought that the good old days would be over. There were quite a few brokers who thought that they would never again live in the lifestyle they had lived in in the past. However, as the paychecks started coming in months and quarters later, we realized that things were not slowing down. Trading was increasing, the institutions' percentage of the market was increasing—to such a radical extent that most of us ended up with a higher remuneration than we had had.

As it turns out, the market was just starting back up again, so it didn't have much effect. In '74 we had had a pretty bad crunch, and that's when you had some institutional brokers switching either to the retail end of the business or to driving cabs. It had also happened in 1970. But after Mayday, when the institutional salesmen saw the volume coming in, there was just no problem.

The first and probably the most significant change of the last ten years or so concerns research. It had been the key to doing business in the old days, while execution was secondary or, in some cases, nonexistent for the firms who never used capital. This has been reversing ever since.

Institutions are now such a high percentage of the volume that when they want to buy or sell a large block of stock they expect a broker to step up to the plate and commit its capital on the block desk.

Entertainment has been the second big change. Brokers entertained their clients a lot more in the past. Some of this might be a reflection of the fact that so many portfolio managers have become independently wealthy and no longer feel that it is a great privilege to attend a Knicks or Rangers game with the salesman covering the account.

I used to go to Knicks games. Now I don't think I have attended a game in at least three years. Merrill Lynch had a great box seat at the Garden—this is in the old days, when Walt Frazier was playing, Willis Reed, Earl "the Pearl" Monroe. It was just common practice that one of the salesmen in our office was using that box. Some salesmen went nuts over entertainment. There were an awful lot of salesmen in New York who entertained quite a bit with limos, $500 dinners at the Côte Basque. I do so little entertaining now that I don't even know if that place is still open.

I have gone on trips with accounts. I once went on a trip to Switzerland with an account. I have even raced my Porsche with an account. We still have the social engagements, and today we are more like friends. If I started up new in institutional sales right now, I would probably find it much more difficult to make those friends.

Right now the salesman's time is largely taken up just trying to keep track of all the deals that the brokerage firm he is working for is doing. I mean, there are so many companies that are issuing stock or bonds or convertible bonds or Australian bond deals that your time is taken up just trying to read prospectuses and understand what the company does and why it should be bought and which clients these deals are appropriate for.

In the early '70s, to make money for people you had to try and determine which analysts at your firm were the most significant as far as making money for your clients went. Now you still have to do a lot of that, but it no longer takes anything like 90 percent of your time. Now you spend about 70 percent of your time on the deals that your firm is coming out with and on sales execution type of work.

Execution and the calendar have come to overshadow research. Not completely, but in terms of time we devote to these different aspects, there has been a great deal of change. The calendar of offerings has grown not only a lot more crowded but also more complicated. Not only do you have to keep track of every deal, but you have to keep track of all of the various forms of deals and forms of financing.

Government bonds went from straight government bonds to TIGRs and CATs and stripped governments. From common stocks, you went to convertible exchangeable preferred shares. You have LYONs now—liquid yield option notes—and there are zero-coupon convertible bonds. You not only have to understand the instrument, but you have to understand what makes the company tick and what could potentially make the company's stock prices go up. And then, with a combination of those two, you have to fit that to the investor's requirements.

Another big change is in the way salesmen are looked at by the management teams. It was a lot more freewheeling in the early '70s. If an account generated a lot of commissions, it was usually assumed that that business was due to the efforts of the salesmen covering the account. Now the salesman is treated more like a commodity that can easily be replaced with other experienced institutional salesmen or hungry and bright MBAs.

There used to just be research salesmen. Today it's hard to figure out who accounts for the commissions generated. Is it the research salesmen, the sales trader, the trading desk and the capital that the trading desk is putting up, or is it the underwriting and the ability of the investment bankers to come in with very good deals for the firm?

So the business has become more sophisticated, and the managers have to try to determine where the value added comes from. It has been a slow, gradual process that is probably now, if anything, accelerating. It's on an exponential curve to where there are more and more sophisticated evaluation techniques to determine compensation of institutional salesmen.

A lot of the computer runs are part of a survey that the manager has the staff do. I'm sure the biggest factor would be the amount of assets under management, how much in commissions is paid out to the Street and what percentage of those commissions the brokerage firm receives. It would measure if there is trader-to-trader or direct analyst-to-analyst contact, and, if there is, how much in actual computer-measured time the account spent talking to the analyst.

Before, the institutional money manager felt more like he was dealing with an individual than with a firm. Now in most cases he probably feels more like he is dealing with the firm, and I believe that the firm would like him to feel that way.

I believe strongly that management will try and discourage clients from dealing just with the institutional salesman and will try to get as many contacts within the organization as it possibly can. It makes sense. You don't want him to get tied into one person who may leave or go with another firm.

It's my opinion that the business is less fun today than it was in the early '70s or even the late '70s. The trend in the last few years has been toward the parroting of research and away from initiative. If I were an institutional sales manager right now, I would probably only hire the guys I could trust to stick with the recommendations from the analysts. But the really successful salesmen are salesmen who take a stand, and the accounts like them to take a stand—usually. Many times I utilized resources outside Merrill Lynch. But a manager is taking a real chance with a guy like me.

Accounts also like the salesmen to understand what they want. My goal was to constantly seek out various ideas or financial instruments that I could utilize to make money for my clients. If I did that, then I expected to get paid. And that's the way I looked at it in the early '70s, and that's the way I looked at it in 1986. And if I recommended zero-coupon Treasury bonds in '82—even though we might have had a tough time in '84—if the individuals and institutional accounts that I recommended them to held on, they made a lot of money and I made a lot of money because I took the stand.

Editor: Erik Ipsen

Charles Ellis

Partner GREENWICH ASSOCIATES

> Probably no one has had a better vantage point on the institutional
> money management game than Charles Ellis. Fifteen years ago,
> after nine years in research and institutional sales at Rockefeller
> Brothers and Donaldson, Lufkin & Jenrette, he founded Green-
> wich Associates, a consulting firm that has helped reshape the in-
> dustry by giving institutions and brokers detailed information on
> how their clients perceive them. A published novelist and frequent
> business school lecturer, Ellis wrote an article for the *Financial Ana-
> lysts Journal* in 1975 entitled "The Loser's Game," spelling out why
> institutional investors have not—and will never—outperform the
> market. The money management game has never been quite the
> same.

I was not one of the originals in the investment management
field. I just came along in the early 1960s looking for a job.
Retail investors were 80 percent of the market then; the institutions, for the most part, were formally structured and they
made their decisions slowly.

Beating *that* market wasn't hard. Retail investors make certain
characteristic mistakes repetitively. Large, structured institutions
that make ponderous committee decisions make repetitive mistakes, too. So if you had more information than they had or got it
faster or acted more boldly, then it was not hard to beat competition in those days. And if you couldn't outperform the traditional trust company, you didn't deserve to be in the business.

But today over 80 percent of the transactions are done by
institutional investors. Now, these people are different. Smart,

competitive, tough, they work all day, every day—weekends and nights—getting ready in advance to be on the other side of each and every one of your transactions. The securities and the investment management firms are recruiting a large percentage of the best business school graduates, and they are going to work hard to make a real difference by being smarter.

So when you step up to play against *them,* it's a completely different experience than it was in the 1960s. And when someone says, "I intend to beat the market," the market he is talking about is not some neutered beast; it's the sum of all the smartest, toughest minds in this business. When you come to market to sell, the only buyers you'll find are the ones who are thrilled that you just came into the cross hairs on their sniper scopes.

There are a lot of people out there who somehow still think they can outperform the market, but there are fewer of them who can actually do it. Moreover, it's harder and harder for the rest of us to find them. The reason is, many of the guys who do very well stay small. This line of work is a team effort. In sports if a team has eight or ten guys who know how to play together, that's pretty exciting to watch. But there aren't any team sports where you have 50 guys who can play together, let alone 150.

Given the concept of the loser's game, there are two ways in which you can do some good for yourself. One is to be smarter than the other guys or work harder or whatever, just beat 'em. The other is to not get caught up in excitements and depressions. Compose a long-term investment policy that is right for the market and right for you and settle into it and stay there forever. When you think the market's too high, don't do anything. And when you think a particular stock is a hell of a buy, don't do anything.

And if you keep from making those decisions, it allows you to concentrate on the one thing that might make a real difference: Do you really own the right ratio of equity to fixed investments for you?

My favorite investor, and everyone else's, is Warren Buffett. Others include John Neff, Bob Kirby, Ben Graham, Dean Le-Baron, Ned Johnson, Claude Rosenberg, Joe Reich, Henry Singleton, Ed Hintz, T. Rowe Price and George Ross-Goobey.

Warren really understands the difference between one kind of investment situation and another more deeply than most. He does a tremendous amount of homework, and he's got great network contacts. He's so highly regarded that people reach out to him. And he's extraordinarily patient both in not acting and in acting. Warren's the guy that says when you get to the plate in baseball, swing at every pitch coming over that you want, but don't swing at any you don't want. That's a very different attitude than most people have; most people feel that you've got to be in there doing something. John Neff is, I think, very much the same.

The biggest changes, besides the institutionalization of the business, have been the growth in technology and the increase in fees. Eleven or twelve years ago, I took over the course directorship of the investment management workshop sponsored by the Financial Analysts Federation, and we had computers installed on every floor of the dormitories at Dartmouth. Two or three of the participants out of a hundred sat down and played for fifteen or twenty minutes, but that was all. Next year we dropped it. Now almost all of those people have terminals in their organizations and use computers as a regular thing.

Will investment fees ever come down? Maybe. Low-fee managers have been raising fees every year since I can remember because clients care less about fees than anything else. And where you once might have had one manager, you now have maybe ten. If you have five $20 million accounts, you pay more than if you had only one $100 million account. Then, too, there's been a movement toward high-fee types of investments, like venture capital, real estate and international. The evidence in the marketplace is overwhelming that if you are charging little, you should charge more because a low fee predicts low value, and in this field hope is very, very important. Now, for the first time, we're getting indications that the era of big increases may be behind us.

Performance fees, on the other hand, could have a negative impact at the wrong time and a positive impact at the wrong time. When an investment manager most needs his clients to say constructive things, to be helpful and supportive, is when he's really down and disappointed because his kind of stocks have fared poorly. I'm afraid that when your kind of stocks have been doing poorly, you'll get hit with a cut in fee income when you surely don't need it. And when your stocks have been going great, when you have superb results and everybody loves you, then along will come a huge increase in fees when you don't need it. Your work may be just as good in both cases. First-class investment performance cannot be measured on a quarterly or annual basis. Outstanding investors don't work that way.

The pension officer has come into his own. Twenty years ago very few people considered pension fund responsibility a serious job. Ford had Bob White; AT&T had Tommy Thompson; the Ford Foundation had Tom Lenagh, but there were few others. Today most corporations have someone who is in charge of the pension fund—either full or part time. And companies like AT&T have up to 50 people and very able professionals on their pension staffs. But in most companies it's still a rotational position: You hold the job for three, four, five years, then get rotated on to another financial job.

The problem is that it takes fifteen years to learn the real truth about investment management. So most pension executives are in the awkward position of being amateurs—relatively new to the field—and so are dependent upon others, the so-called professionals.

Investment consultants—I call them selection advisers—have made a great difference in one dimension of the business and no difference at all in another. They have made a difference in terms of increasing the speed at which some investment managers accumulate or lose assets. They have had a large influence on the redistribution of assets from larger organizations to smaller ones. They have not made a difference in terms of adding value for the clients. They are not able to prove that they choose better money managers. They've gotten a lot of investors to pay attention to more data, but I think they have a pretty short time horizon.

You know, there's a wonderful sign in Vail, Colorado, that all investors and clients of investors should contemplate. It's near the children's ski slope. It says: "Leave your kids for the day—$15. You watch—$20. You help—$30." The same sound interest in benign neglect should apply to investment management.

Editor: Edward E. Scharff

André George

Former Financial Director and Treasurer EUROPEAN INVESTMENT BANK

The career of André George in international finance has spanned not only the last twenty years, but most of the three decades since World War II. In addition to having had a long career with the French Treasury and Finance Ministry, George spent ten years with Société Générale in Paris, where he was director of external affairs. During his 1974-to-1982 tenure at the European Investment Bank, which corresponded with some of the most bruising competition for mandates in the Euromarkets, George negotiated an annual borrowing program of approximately $3 billion in virtually every major currency and oversaw a $1 billion treasury operation; his tough, no-nonsense approach to his lenders became something of a legend. George is now a partner at Price Waterhouse and Partners in Paris.

The 1970s were certainly a period of very exceptional agitation in the market. There was so much fluctuation of every sort that we at the EIB had to be very vigilant. And as the biggest European borrower in the international market, we had to look at every possibility for borrowing. We were also very proud of our triple-A rating; it was not awarded to every large borrower. So we tried to get conditions we considered normal for our status as one of the best credits in the world and for our mission. And we were also regarded as a sort of leader in new techniques and new instruments. After all, someone had to open the market.

We tried to venture into some segments of the market which were perhaps not considered among the most promising in the world at that time. These were opportunities not only to tap different markets, but also to show that even some banks in these remote parts of the world were able to raise funds for a European institution. We placed several Asian dollar issues in the Far East, for example, with local syndicates led by banks in Hongkong and Singapore. We also tried to develop the possibility of raising funds in the Middle East to try to get our name known in the region. We organized special Arab syndicates to underwrite and place our issues, particularly in the Gulf. Perhaps this has proved to be a short-lived experiment, but it was an occasion to show there were effective, if perhaps limited, ways of tapping the market beyond the classic way of European syndicates.

The difficulty in the Middle East and Far East was mainly for the banks to find clientele to place what they had underwritten. But this was not because of the signature of the EIB. The Arab and Far Eastern investors were really not all that interested in bonds; they were more attracted to direct investment or shares or venture capital—things they could see and touch, ships, hotels, merchant banks.

It was not so easy in this market at the time of the oil price shock. And I remember when, in 1973–74, we obtained a private placement from one of the oil-producing countries for $600 million, at that time a huge amount. Even in the difficult market of that time, we had to overcome some hesitation on the part of some members of our board, who were apprehensive about paying 10 percent for this huge amount of money for ten years. But when, perhaps five or six years later, I met the Arab signatories of this loan, they themselves complained about the loss of value of their money in that loan, because at that time the 10 percent interest rate was in reality much below the inflation rate.

When you are coming regularly to the market, you have to follow carefully the evolution of the rate of interest. But I was doing at the EIB exactly the same thing as Eugene Rotberg at the World Bank: trying to push our borrowing in the international market. The market for us was mainly long-term, and we were looking at our borrowing needs six months, one year ahead in order to be prepared. But interest rates were changing so rapidly that even if you were expecting to come to the market at the right time, you could arrive just three or four days late, and that was sufficient for a failure. We made some mistakes, mainly errors of timing.

I must add that we went first, of course, to the national markets in Europe; our first issues were placed mainly in Germany, France and Switzerland. Then we did issues in Eurocurrencies—the dollar to start with, but also in sterling, French francs, deutsche marks, even Euro-Canadian dollars and Eurolire.

When we went to the United States for the first time in 1976 or '75, we were not known at all in that market, and we had to give a number of presentations and road shows around the country to demonstrate that the EIB's creditworthiness was in reality what it was in the international market in Europe. We had to prove to the U.S. rating agencies that we should be awarded a triple-A. It was not totally easy, and we had to wait for a year or two; but once we had obtained the triple-A rating from Moody's and Standard & Poor's, we came to the market without meeting any hesitation or difficulties. In fact, we moved from the international market to the U.S. market very easily and sometimes were even retreating from one market and moving to the other.

When we came to the yen market in Tokyo, we had already established our rating and our position as one of the best borrowers in the world, and we had no difficulty at all accessing the market at the best conditions. There was no need to make a presentation to the public; we just had long discussions with the syndicate and the stock exchange. And the Japanese, when they want to, can respond very quickly, in two or three hours. I remember negotiating a private placement directly with [president Kisaburo] Ikeura of IBJ; he went over each point, one after the other, and signed the document right there and then.

We perhaps could have raised the same amounts in the same currencies close to the same conditions, staying simply with the very classic way of raising funds. But I thought it was our mission, as the biggest borrower in the market, to consider ourselves an explorer of new possibilities; that was the reason why we had to be imaginative. It was the mission of the EIB and of the European Community in general to try to push the borders of this market, to enlarge the possibility of raising money through other instruments. I have often been told, in fact, that we were too aggressive, were trying *too many* techniques. I don't feel, personally, that we were going too far and too fast. And even if we had not succeeded

665

in a number of experiments, it still would have been necessary to make the attempt, to prove that there were funds available through other than traditional instruments.

I suppose we probably had the biggest difficulty with our Dutch auction deal in June 1978. We had expected to have a special response from a number of banks which were not normally members of our syndicates; it was an opportunity for them to prove their capability. But perhaps we hurt the lead institutions, and we were not really rewarded by this attempt. The final result was similar to a classic issue.

The bankers in Europe who did not want to go into this type of competition preferred to continue working on their normal type of issue—through a classic syndicate or their traditional partners—without trying to get a special position with us through a new technique. This technique had also been attempted by a certain number of borrowers in the United States; some succeeded, and others were not completely accepted. In the final analysis, I suppose it's a marginal technique on the market, even now.

As you can imagine, the Dutch auction idea did not come from our bankers. But we did notice that some of our traditional banks were ready to show that they were able to serve the interests of the EIB through new instruments. Some frequently presented new ideas to the Luxembourg headquarters, though we did not accept all of them. In fact, the competition was very, very aggressive, and I agree that sometimes bankers approached the EIB with conditions that were not very realistic. But we were in a position to judge what we could obtain from the market and when these conditions were too aggressive, and I don't remember ever having accepted conditions which were not possible in the market. Because the market changed so rapidly between the time of a proposal and the launch, it would have been bad for the EIB to go to the market with all the indications of a failure.

We always considered that we were offering the world's bankers the best guarantee, the best stability as a borrower, and we put them in competition for our mandates. In fact, we didn't rely only on big, established international banks; we also looked at the possibility of giving chances to smaller institutions or those with special market niches. Sometimes we were told that we were perhaps too heavily committed in our lending to one of the countries in the Community. But every time we went to ask our member states to increase our capital to follow up our increasing activities, we got satisfaction rapidly; we did not have any pressure from any country to distribute our borrowing activity among banks in Europe. Everybody knew that some of these banks were very active in the market, not because of their nationality but because they were technically prepared and had the clientele to place the issue more easily than others. Even in a smaller country, we could find very active banks; and in a bigger country there could be less active banks, perhaps because of tradition or foreign exchange controls or lack of clientele or competitiveness.

Of course, it's different if you are talking about the lead manager of international syndicates compared with the lead manager of a syndicate in domestic markets. Domestic issues in Europe were mainly conducted by the same bankers each time. We had Deutsche Bank in Germany, Amro in the Netherlands, so we were served in the best possible way by these two in their national markets. But when we were in a position to give a bank the possibility of showing its real interest in the issue, its capability and placing power, perhaps we had a better response from the merchant banks in London and from the American banks, which were looking not only to serve our interests in the New York market, but also to act as lead manager of our issues in Europe. I was very impressed by the people of First Boston in New York and CSFB in London, who were aggressive and always ready to do an issue when we were. We were also impressed by some bankers from traditional merchant banks in London—Warburg, Kleinwort Benson, Morgan Grenfell.

Perhaps we dealt in a more classic way with Belgian, Swiss and French bankers. The French and the Belgians were limited by their financial situation at that time. We were regularly in the market in Switzerland, which was well regulated, and with a rotation of lead managers; so there were not as many possibilities for choosing specific conditions. But in the freer international market, mainly in London, we *were* in such a position, and there we built up some very special relations with a number of these banks because of their aggressiveness and willingness to come to the market any time we needed.

I have been told that I was particularly tough in the negotiations. We didn't bargain with a knife in our hands, but we negotiated the best conditions because we felt that we *had* to. In any event, we were a client which deserved the best terms. We were always furious when we saw a newcomer on the market—particularly a multinational or even a corporate from the United States with a double-A or even a single-A on their market—and because it was a new name, because it was a corporate, because it was American, it obtained better conditions than we did. We could not accept the fact that, because of a psychological reaction of the market, the basic principles of creditworthiness and solidity were not considered the primary conditions for determining our access to the market. Perhaps because of that I was considered particularly difficult by some of our bankers. But I continue to think that a rating is significant, and when you have a triple-A rating, you should get the terms of a triple-A rating. Rating agencies are normally the best financial analysts; unfortunately, the market reacts to factors which are not always rational.

When you are in a position to obtain the services of every bank in the world, and you are also in a position to choose the best conditions offered at a particular time, I don't think there is any reason to develop a special relationship with any particular institution. This would not be fair to the banks, either. After all, they are all competing, and it would not be fair to say to one of them, "Sorry, we have another proposal from a particular institution, perhaps not the best terms, but we have been working with them for so long that we feel we should stay with them." There is no service being rendered, either to the special-relationship institution or to the other banks trying to develop business with you, perhaps offering better terms. Several times I was told that I was unreasonable, that if I were giving a mandate to a new syndicate, then this syndicate would make a special effort once, but next time I would have to give the mandate to someone else. But there was always somebody around to make a special effort at a particular time. As a borrower, why not take advantage of it? Except if the terms were not realistic, and we were in a position to judge that.

Nowadays, is there really a Euromarket? The international market now has no real borders. When we tried to develop our activities ten, fifteen years ago—in the Far East, the Middle East, offshore in some part of the world—it was certainly compartmentalized like that. It's a worldwide market now. And I don't think the EIB or any other European borrower attempts special issues today, mandates a syndicate of Hongkong and Singapore banks or Arab banks as we did in the past. There is more and more penetration into the domestic markets by foreign issues. Today you have ECU issues led by American syndicates in New York or Euroyen issues going back, for the most part, into Japanese portfolios. Where is the border between a foreign issue in deutsche marks on the German market and a Euro-Dm issue outside? Or between a Euro-French franc issue and a foreign French franc issue in Paris?

It's a freer market, but are we going too fast? Perhaps we are reaching the point where there should be at least some general international standards for all these issues—not only for comparison of terms and access to the market, but also for clearing and settlement all over the world and for the regulation of stock exchanges and new instruments. I imagine that at present, in a number of banks, the specialists and the staff have perhaps not yet entirely mastered a number of these new techniques. And it could be dangerous if they are not fully understood by not only the bankers, but by the investors themselves. The market needs to be educated.

I remember when LIFFE first started its futures and options operations in London. It had to develop a number of presentations—documentation and training—so that everybody understood its function. We have the same revolution now in Paris—not such a big bang as in London, but at least quite an opening-up of the financial institutions and brokerage firms. They are doing the same thing in the Swiss market, and Luxembourg or Frankfurt will probably do the same. I am a little afraid of seeing new instruments go into the market without enough knowledge of the potential risk.

I also think that the back offices of a number of banks, particularly here in France but also in the rest of Europe, are rather submerged by these operations. If the institutions are not able to follow the issues and settle on time, this could be a very disturbing factor for the market. I remember fifteen years ago Chase itself was completely submerged by their settlement problems at a time when they had not quite decided on their new computer technology; their business was completely blocked for three or four months. Probably now there should be new clearing organizations throughout the world, some sort of international network, not really centered in one place or another. London, of course, aspired to that role, but I see something more along the lines of multipolar centers, making possible 24-hour business around the world. They will certainly need some development of new computer technology and the training of a new generation. This is on the way, but far from completion.

Editor: David Cudaback

Paul Miller

Partner MILLER, ANDERSON & SHERRERD

Paul Miller stunned the investment world eighteen years ago when he quit as CEO of the investment banking firm then called Drexel Harriman Ripley to start his own small firm for the discretionary management of major accounts. He seemed to sense some handwriting on the wall that no one else had yet recognized. And Miller, Anderson & Sherrerd, one of the first money management "boutiques," grew slowly, then more rapidly, until today it manages some $12 billion in stocks and bonds, making it the largest pension management partnership. The firm has a record, and a culture, that's unique among institutions.

We started up on a shoestring in the fall of 1969. I remember visiting the offices of some other money management firms at the time and feeling very inferior. One firm in particular that opened around the same time we did had spent about a million-and-a-half bucks on their offices, as I recall. They had a winding stairway going from one floor to the next and some nice paneling. I'd come back to the orange crates in our offices and think to myself, "Are we dumb, or are they dumb?" Because we were spending nothing like that. We didn't have it to spend.

We didn't need great surroundings because we didn't have any clients when we opened. Not a single account. And here we were, asking for a minimum account size of $20 million, which was pretty audacious in those days. But the business came in, especially once we established a record. A lot of the clients we got in the early 1970s never even came to our offices to kick the tires before they signed up. Actually, a couple of them never even interviewed us. We knew they were looking at us and we sent them some written material and, lo and behold, we got the business. One account for $200 million came to us that way.

We were approaching a billion dollars in assets by 1980, but then in 1981 we decided it was time to market ourselves. We brought a new man on board to do that. It was agonizingly slow at first, dealing with the consultants. And then, suddenly, the dam broke. We had one of the best five-year records in the business at that point. And like it or not, five-year records still sell pretty well. I think it's ridiculous, but they do. Basically, what you're doing is buying people—people with whom you're comfortable, people in whom you have confidence that they're going to do a workmanlike job. You have no remote idea how well they're going to do in the future. You know how many five-year records have been blown apart?

Anyway, we just sort of exploded. And one other thing happened: We began an intensive fixed-income effort, which was one of our better business decisions and has been very successful. All good fortunes just came together. I can't remember precisely, but I think we went from $1 billion to $3 billion to $7 billion to $9 billion to $12 billion in assets.

We've always been caught by surprise that we got this much money. I grew up in Philadelphia, and Penn Mutual Life Insurance Co. was always a tower of strength in the city. It stands right behind Independence Hall, and I've always regarded it as a huge institution. The other day in the paper I saw their assets are something like $3.8 billion. And I thought to myself, "We've got 75 people in Bala Cynwyd managing $12 billion, and there's this huge building behind Independence Hall managing $3.8 billion?" When you think that here we are damn near as big as the Morgan trust department was when I first started in the investment business, it's incredible.

If you look at our record, and I think this holds true of other firms that are also more durable in the business, we never shoot the lights out in up markets. We tend to be very good at preserving capital in down markets. And we tend to beat the modest up markets and the modest down markets by bigger amounts. I think that's a comfortable style.

When you go back and analyze our successes, so often they were the result of strategic decisions rather than deciding to invest a bundle of money in some hot stock. Being very early to spot the disinflation of the early 1980s was the biggest single contributor to our record of the last ten years. Around the same time, oil prices were in their second explosion, and we just said, "Hey, that's not going to last." From 1983 to 1985 it was the fact that we were not hanging our hats on a continuing cyclical boom in the economy. And more recently, it's been that we were early to see the dollar's decline and have been steadily willing to say that it's going to continue.

There's something else that has contributed to our success. We've bred an atmosphere where people don't feel as though they're in competition with each other. I've seen a lot of organizations that are just blown apart by incentive systems that pit one investment manager versus another. We've never had any of that. I don't think it pays off because inevitably people begin to hate each other. We have a culture in which people make investment decisions as part of a group but also give some independence to make decisions of their own that aren't measured against everyone else's. The main thing [our structure] has done is to let people be creative on their own. They have a portion of every portfolio to manage, plus an optional portion to manage. They aren't sat on by a committee, and yet they're part of a group decision.

I think it's important that we don't have a hierarchical structure. I don't like hierarchies. We've always had equals here. When we started this business, Jay [Sherrerd] and Clay [Anderson] and I had equal percentage interests. Everybody probably thought Miller owns the damn thing. Well, Miller didn't. I made the decision that the firm wouldn't prosper as well if I did. We started off with that philosophy and we've always kept it.

Generally speaking, I believe in the perfect-market hypothesis. But over the past twenty years some people have accumulated very durable records, so durable that it's more than accidental that they have done so well. I think there are three things behind this kind of success. First of all, many of these people use a valuation model of some kind, so they never tie their judgment on a stock's price to intuition or light bulbs flashing. That doesn't

673

mean they necessarily buy value stocks, but just that they use a model to judge whatever stocks they buy.

Second, many of them draw from a part of the market that gives them an advantage. John Neff [of Wellington Management] fishes in a low-price-earnings ratio pool. So he starts off with an advantage and, in turn, gains some advantage over it. As much as I admire John Neff, I would claim that most of the advantage he has comes from the pool he fishes in rather than from how good a fisherman he is. And the third thing I'd say is that most successful managers aren't frantic. A decision doesn't have to be made every minute. That's certainly true in our own case. Phones aren't jingling off the hooks all the time.

I think one of the things that has changed about this business is that we've all become a little bit more sophisticated and confident of ourselves. I mean, for those of us who have grown up in these markets, there's not much new to be heard. Also, communications have improved so much and so much stuff is being written. Most experts have been discredited, no matter what field they're in, and have proved they're not worth listening to. Economists especially. Ninety-eight percent of them have been dead wrong 98 percent of the time. They've never been able to identify the most important things for us as investors.

Even so, there have always been a lot of people in our business who need security blankets, who aren't quite able to make their own judgments, and I suspect there always will be. As you get older, more established, wealthier, and don't have to worry about it so much anymore, it changes your perception of what an expert is. The world appeared to be predictable for some time, the funds were so solid and so long term. But nobody believes in experts anymore. You believe in yourself, I guess.

In some ways, the old days were better. I really believe that never have so many people made so much money for contributing so little to the world as Wall Street is today. For that matter, I'd throw ourselves in that boat, too. I think Wall Street is in for a comeuppance beyond the insider trading thing, maybe the next time the market turns down. Money is simply not as easy to make as it has been. And if it is for this small group of people, then there's something very wrong with the system.

I'll be 60 this year, and I've told my partners I'll retire when I'm 65. And I've been withdrawing, bit by bit, year by year. I've tried to get to the point where this isn't Paul Miller's firm anymore. At this point, my main role here is one of a spiritual leader of some kind, a cheerleader, the one who will, once in a while when somebody gets a little feisty, take him or her aside and give them an avuncular talk.

Editor: Peter Landau

Stephen Paradise

Former Assistant Counsel U.S. SENATE BANKING
COMMITTEE

As assistant counsel to the Senate Banking Committee and one of
Senator Harrison Williams's top aides, Stephen Paradise was a major architect of the Securities Acts Amendments of 1975, which
gave the SEC greater control over stock exchanges—and impetus
to Wall Street's historic unfixing of commission rates. Paradise is
now a vice president for congressional and regulatory relations for
the New York Stock Exchange, but back then he was known as
"the man behind the senator."

Oh, it was a wonderful time. We were really doing something—enacting a bill that would actually be the law of the
land. If you believed in it, believed you had something
that was going to be good for society, the experience gave you a
wonderful feeling.

The main problem that ultimately led to the '75 act amendments was the paperwork crunch on Wall Street in the late '60s,
where firms were choking on the volume, which was about 10
million shares a day. Then the market turned down, and we had
a rash of failures. A number of securities firms, and the New York
Stock Exchange in particular, came to Congress and asked if an
insurance fund similar to the Federal Deposit Insurance Corp.
could be set up to cover accounts at brokerage houses. At the
time, the exchange was making customers whole out of its own
funds.

Congress did pass legislation in 1970 to start the Securities

Investor Protection Corp., but as they looked at it they decided that a lot of discriminatory practices such as fixed commissions and exchange membership should be more closely scrutinized, so they created a special task force to do a study of the securities industry and report back the legislative findings. I was already on the staff.

We hired a staff of experts, including a number of people from outside the Congress. And Senator Harrison Williams, who was chairman of the Senate subcommittee on securities, told me to let the chips fall where they may: "I want you to do an objective study of the regulations and the '34 act. And then you come back and make recommendations. Write a report, and you do what you think is right. I'll devote the time to hold hearings and work on this."

We put our recommendations into legislative form. Two big issues emerged on the Senate side. One was what would happen if the industry goes under because of negotiated rates: Can we go back to fixed rates? And we put some language in the committee report—it might have been in the statute, too—saying that if there's a debacle, of course you can go back. I mean, we didn't want to put the securities industry out of business. Hell, nobody wanted to be punitive.

The second issue was the national market system, which the act was intended to bring about. How were you going to do one? There were all kinds of crazy ideas floating around. Working with Jim Walker, who was on the Securities Industry Association staff at the time, we came up with what I thought was a good solution. A national market system would be developed and governed by a new body made up of the self-regulatory organizations—the exchanges and the industry. And the SEC would oversee it. We put that in the Senate bill, and the Senate passed the amendments in 1973.

The industry, of course, was upset. Commission rates were an issue, although, you know, we didn't legislate an end to fixed rates. The SEC finally did that under heavy pressure. The bill that was reported out of the Senate subcommittee did do away with fixed rates, but by the time it got to the Senate floor, fixed rates were already on their way out. Bill Casey was heading the agency at the time. It was getting pressure from the Hill, pressure from the Justice Department, pressure from everywhere. The agency was doing it gradually—it was already doing it on the biggest transactions—just doing it slowly.

The New York Stock Exchange and the other exchanges wouldn't support the national markets provision, either. Anyhow, over in the House, the bill couldn't get a rule from the rules committee and it died with the Congress.

So in 1975 we had to start all over again. I guess by now the industry realized there was going to be legislation and decided it was not wise to fight it tooth and nail. The Senate passed the bill early that year, and the House finally passed its version. We went to conference where most of the things in the Senate bill prevailed. And it was finally enacted into law.

You know, when you look back on it, I think the demise of the third market was due to the '75 amendments and the abolition of minimum commission rates. The third-market firms were able to trade at a cheaper rate because they didn't have a fixed commission schedule. They lobbied to end this thing but really cut their own throats because they couldn't compete the way it ended up. They thought: "The New York exchange guys can't compete with me. They are old and stodgy." They were wrong.

There are also a couple of things I wish we hadn't done. The national market system is something that is really in the eye of the beholder, and I wish we hadn't been so specific on that. I think it's something for the industry to accomplish. The SEC can't impose that. It's something that evolves through technology and through time.

The second problem is one that appears to be coming up now. Today you have this one-share, one-vote debate. That's a corporate governance issue, yet we never went into this area in the '75 act, never had any hearings on it. We were working on an entirely different set of issues. The SEC is saying it has power over corporate governance under the '75 act, and it does—if you read the act literally. But Congress never intended to give the SEC that power. The '75 amendments were about the exchanges and rules of the marketplace.

But the act was still a good law. It has brought us today a much stronger self-regulatory system, where before a rule is changed it is gone over again and again and the SEC must approve it. It really makes it a much more thoughtful process.

I also think Wall Street realized after the '75 act that Washington wasn't a foreign country, that Washington was a place that affects everyone's lives. People have become less myopic. And so there is more of an interchange now between the Street and Washington.

Editor: John W. Milligan

Benjamin Holloway

Chairman EQUITABLE REAL ESTATE GROUP

> Benjamin Holloway, 62, has been one of the leading figures in the
> U.S. real estate industry for more than three decades. In the early
> 1970s he was instrumental in steering Equitable Life Assurance
> Society—and other large financial institutions—away from pure
> mortgage investing toward direct ownership and development of
> properties. Holloway currently oversees some $28 billion in real
> estate assets for Equitable.

Twenty years ago the real estate business was generally run
by individuals. The institutionalization of real estate was
just beginning in those days. The traditional way to finance
real estate was through the life insurance industry, basically
through first-mortgage loans. Very few life insurance companies
were buying and owning real estate at that time.

It was a simpler business then, and what you really needed were
good appraisers. We were making a lot of loans on shopping
centers, on regional malls. The big hitters in that field are still
around—major owners like Edward DeBartolo, Al Taubman and
Mel Simon. They were all in the business in those days, dominating the shopping center field. And we were lenders to them.

I always wanted Equitable to own real estate, because the rewards were greater. If you were a lender, it seemed to me that you
had the worst of all possible worlds. If the real estate was successful, then the owner reaped all the benefits and would pay you off.
If it wasn't successful, he'd give it to you and you ended up
owning the poorest real estate through foreclosure.

During the 1960s there had been a growth in what you call participating mortgages, sort of a first step toward ownership. When rates were rising, you were able to get kickers on a lot of deals. Later on we would make a loan and get a participation in the actual loan. So that was how we kind of backed into buying real estate.

We got into real estate equities through two joint ventures in Florida in the early '70s. The pattern was that we put up all the money, and the developer put his development and marketing skills into the deal. Since that time there have been a lot of variations on that formula, but it's still the one that is most widely used.

It was considered a daring thing to do at the time, to put up 100 percent of the money and take all of the financial risk in a transaction. But for that you got priority on the returns. It was a breakthrough for us. We were willing to take the risk. The deals weren't a lot of money by today's standards—$15 million. But as it turned out, they were very, very successful ventures, and it was probably fortunate for us that they were successful because they led us into more development.

In the early 1970s we had sort of been forced into becoming developers as well. We found that we owned real estate through foreclosures and had to actually manage it in an aggressive way. We just couldn't be a passive manager because if you were, you didn't maximize the income. You had to rehabilitate it or add on to it to make it work. So we became developers ourselves. We had to. But after we learned something about the process, we started doing a little development on our own. We were doing industrial buildings, and office buildings for our own use.

Later on, in the mid-1970s, we thought we could probably compete better if we could create a downstream subsidiary, a fully integrated real estate company that was divorced from the life insurance company. We could pay the kind of salaries and incentive compensation that would allow people to become more entrepreneurial and compete with some of our former customers, the developers. It was difficult. But much of the legal ground was broken first for us by the Equitable sub that was managing common stocks, mostly for pension funds. In 1984, a year after they went downstream, we started taking all the steps to qualify in the 50 states to do business. There were a lot of legal problems. In Puerto Rico a lot of us had to be fingerprinted to do business.

Another breakthrough came in the latter part of the '70s, when the Tishman companies split up. To make that split-up work, they had to sell the real estate. We made a deal with New York Life to buy all of the property together. They were to buy half, and we would buy half. When it came down to the short strokes, New York Life backed out and we were able to convince Equitable on the idea of picking up their half. It was probably the largest real estate transaction we'd ever done, about $275 million. It turned out to be one of the real genius moves because we bought the real estate at 1970s prices and very soon after we closed the transaction property values suddenly began doubling and tripling in the New York area.

We were lucky in the sense that during this period a lot of companies decided to do away with a big field organization. We made a decision to keep ours. So when the great big purchases came along, like twenty shopping centers, we were one of the few organizations that had a staff that could handle a transaction that size.

Despite the growing institutionalization of real estate, there are still some big strong entrepreneurial types out there in the marketplace. Ed DeBartolo, for example. He owns more shopping centers than Equitable does today. He can build shopping centers without borrowing money. He builds them with cash flow.

And Al Taubman. He recently used his properties to raise $645 million. In doing that he lost some of his entrepreneurial control, but he's been able to diversify his investments and get into other kinds of businesses. Al bought Sotheby's, for instance.

I think one of the most interesting people that I've ever known in the business is Trammell Crow. His biggest innovation was hiring people from good business schools and putting them in marketing. That has turned out to be a very, very wise way of teaching somebody the real estate business, because to understand real estate you've got to understand the people who use it, and the best way to understand that is to be in the rental business. Starting from a marketing base, you get a sense of what to build because you know what people want and what they're willing to pay for it.

Men like DeBartolo, Taubman and Crow—they're solid, a real credit to the industry. Not everyone in the business is like that. Some of the syndicators in the '70s had a tendency to oversell. They bought a property for $100 million and syndicated for $150 million. It wasn't worth $150 million. So those syndications were doomed to failure as far as the buyers of the syndications were concerned.

But there still is a need for an honest way of doing a retail product. The real estate investment trust was one of those ideas, although they had a lot of problems in the '70s for the simple reason that they tried to leverage them too high and they were caught in very violent swings in interest rates, which caused a lot of problems.

But overall the real estate investment trust was a successful vehicle and still is. We've learned how to deal with them a lot better than we used to. In the first place, the first round of them was dominated by big institutions that used big institutional lawyers who put a straitjacket on them so they couldn't operate in a way that made them competitive. The smaller REITs didn't use those expensive lawyers, and they were much more successful.

The old rules in real estate financing are also changing rapidly. Investors are now looking at cash flow and internal rates of return. These measures have been around for a long, long time but we're starting to think about property the way people think about common stock. It's the combined rate of return, the increase in values as well as the dividend that tells you something about what you're getting for what you buy. Modern investment analysis tells us to look at all investments the same way, and real estate is being looked at like all other forms of investment.

Real estate will become even more institutionalized in the next few years because the numbers are driving the industry in that direction. There's also going to be some technological advances in how we build because construction costs are getting much more expensive.

After these years in the business, it's clear to me that real estate will outperform other kinds of investment—in an inflationary, stable or disinflationary period. It will outperform any other kind of investment over a short period of time. And over a longer time frame, there's just no contest. Real estate will win the battle. This is basically due to the fact that there's a finite supply of property on the surface of the globe. And there ain't going to be any more of it.

Editor: William Meyers

Enrico Braggiotti

Managing Director BANCA COMMERCIALE ITALIANA

Born in Turkey, educated in France, trained in banking in the
U.S. and Great Britain, Enrico Braggiotti is arguably the most
thoroughly international of Italy's bankers. Named the head of
Banca Commerciale Italiana's securities department in 1968,
Braggiotti—to the initial dismay of many of his colleagues—turned
the unit into an active, aggressive Eurobond underwriter. In 1980
he took over the bank's international division and since 1984 has
been *amministratore delegato,* one of BCI's top three officers.

In 1968 I was appointed general manager to head *titoli e borsa,*
the department that handles all securities matters, stock exchanges here and abroad and the Euromarkets. At that time I
was one of the youngest of the bank's seven or so general managers; they used to retire at 70, and I was 40 or 41. Today that is
not so young, but then it was. Before becoming general manager
I had been in the department for some time, and the normal
business in that department was domestic securities. The new
activity that I started in the bank—I think in 1960—was helping
foreign investors invest in Italian equities.

And from there we went to the Euromarket. We managed the
first Eurodollar bond by an agency of the EEC, the European
Investment Bank, in 1966. Then the Coal and Steel Community
followed. I enjoyed helping to make BCI a lead manager in the
Euromarkets because it was a new business, and when you are
young you are always attracted by a new business. We succeeded
in part because we had enormous placement power in Italian

securities, so we used this power to place foreign bonds as well. It was a natural development; we didn't have to push very much. We already had a dominant position in the Italian market.

BCI has always been the most international Italian bank. We were born that way; we have an international network dating from the turn of the century, and our specialty is to finance trade. Our share of that market is 14 to 15 percent, versus our share of deposits, which is perhaps 4 percent. Still, my colleagues in the bank were not very happy with the Eurobond business at first. They were convinced that it would have a very short life and that the risks were very high. One of the first issues we managed was for the Spanish company Autopistas. It was not very successful, and we had to keep a good part of it in our own portfolio, so this seemed to confirm my colleagues' view. So I was not in a very happy situation. They thought, "This young man is too bold and aggressive." But after a period of time we managed to sell [Autopistas] in the market—and it has been an excellent debtor, by the way. We had worse debtors after that.

For the period 1969–72, we were the fourteenth [Eurobond] lead or co-lead manager in the world. And in the early '70s, our syndicated loan business intensified. (It was an obvious thing to develop; I deserve no particular credit.) But then came the mid-1970s, which were very difficult years in Italy. It was a bleak period of abductions and crimes. The quadrupling of oil prices caused such capital outflow that the Banca d'Italia imposed a requirement that any Italian resident purchasing a foreign security had to put up 50 percent of the amount in a non-interest-bearing account with the central bank. This was a death sentence for the Euromarket in Italy.

Another problem for the Italian banks in the mid-'70s was the [Michele] Sindona scandal. We did very little business with him and we were not involved in the bankruptcy. He was a curious personality. He didn't really care about money; he didn't have a yacht or an airplane, and he lived very modestly. But he had a dream of becoming a Morgan, a Rockefeller; he thought that with money he could have big power. But he failed because he made big mistakes. His fundamental mistake was that he thought the dollar was too weak, and he speculated against the lira and other currencies. A few years later he would have been right. I don't think he was a dishonest man at the start. But you know, if, when you lose money, you are not surrounded with proper people, you can become dishonest. [Central bank governor Guido] Carli had great respect for Sindona. You see, Sindona was a very clever man. He was a lawyer who knew the law pretty well, while there were all these other crooks who were not as clever. I didn't know [Roberto] Calvi, for instance, but I'm sure that Sindona was much more clever. We didn't put money into Banco Ambrosiano deals because the situation was not clear, and we do not like that which is not clear.

The period from 1974 to 1978 or so was a great lesson for everybody. The most difficult thing for Italian banks during the last twenty years has been to be an international banker when your home country can be a country at risk, with a weak economy and a weak political situation. It is a challenge; when you try to have a better rating than your country, even though creditors can recognize that you do, that is difficult. I remember back when BCI was 80 percent controlled by [Istituto per la Ricostruzione Industriale], a government agency. For a very long time IRI didn't go into the market because they were in a lousy position, with a lot of debt. When, toward the end of the '70s, they sought financing, Deutsche Bank provided it, but to make the loan to IRI, they asked to have *our* guaranty.

I remember a very funny meeting of EBIC we had a few years ago. There was [Maurice] Lauré, who was at that time the chairman of Société Générale, and [Deutsche Bank co-speaker Wilfried] Guth, who was making speeches with the usual German *como se dice sicurezza*—self-confidence. And Lauré grumbled to me, "If I had the German mark I could sound pretty good, too." You know, if you have the deutsche mark or the Swiss franc or even the yen, it is another life than having the Italian lira or the Belgian franc. Or even the pound. And now even the dollar.

In the late '70s many Italian banks had to pay a premium to get dollar deposits. Fortunately, BCI never paid such a premium, because we were probably the best-known Italian bank. Our correspondents knew that we had huge investments abroad and that the management was rather severe and competent. And at a time when many commercial banks took deposits out of Italian banks, we had quite huge deposits from central banks. At this time we had to just take care of the shop and not take any particular risks.

687

It was a stormy period. I had been very aggressive until 1973; in the 1973–78 period, I was definitely for great caution. Ironically, the need to cover the commercial imbalance of Italy prevented Italian banks from helping to recycle funds from oil exporters to high-risk oil importers. And this was a great lesson for us when the second petrodollar flux arrived. We didn't rush in, so when the Latin American crisis came, we had very low exposure to the LDCs. And this is why today the Italian banking system may be the soundest of all. BCI's consolidated capital, with reserves, is $3.5 billion, and our whole exposure to LDCs is $500 million, or about 15 percent.

Things began to improve for Italy in 1978–79, and I moved over to head the international department in 1980. We set about to open a number of new branches, and I personally opened the representative office in Peking in 1981. It was a very funny experience. The central bank governor was I don't know where, so his deputy, a woman, met with me. And while we were talking gently, she would stand up suddenly, make a speech against the Gang of Four and then sit down again and go on calmly discussing our business. Then she told me that it was very difficult to have a representative office in Peking and that there would probably be a very long wait. I was upset and very cold, so I left. Our people there, Chinese from Hongkong, were very upset to see that I had this attitude. And they said, "What now?" and I said, "I want to leave China with a written statement that we can open the office." And we got it. After that, I had an excellent relationship with this lady. She doesn't make any more of those political speeches.

Becoming one of the first foreign banks to open in China comes from the international history of the bank. When we reopened our branch in London after the war, five minutes before the branch opening a Chinese gentleman came to us with a check for several million dollars. "Here I am from the Bank of China," he said. "We want to have account No. 1." It was touching and an honor. In the early '80s we opened a good many branches, for instance, in both Rio and São Paulo, even though we already had a big network in Latin America through Sudameris [a BCI-controlled consortium] since the beginning of the century. Banco do Brasil opened in Italy, and as an exchange the Brazilian authorities gave us the chance to open direct branches. We were the only Italian bank to get permission. Through Sudameris we had very old relationships with the Brazilian authorities.

We had very old relationships in the U.S., too, and they led to our acquiring 15 percent of Lehman Brothers in 1974. When [former BCI chairman Raffaele] Mattioli set up Mediobanca after the war, he chose Lehman to be probably the only foreign partner. And so there was a very good relationship between BCI and Lehman Brothers. I had a lot of good friends there, starting with Bobbie Lehman. George Ball, also a friend of mine, joined them when he left the government, and they were in a very bad situation at that time—first, because of trading losses made by my friend [former chairman Lewis] Glucksman plus a little bit of internal fighting. So Ball joined as de facto, though never official, chairman and tried to pull these people together and get out of this mess.

He hired Pete Peterson, who came to see me and said, "We have to recapitalize Lehman, because the firm is on the eve of a tragedy. Are you prepared to help?" This was at the start of a very difficult period for Italy. So we talked to Guido Carli, and he said, "Out of the question." But we were convinced that it was a good business, so we asked Sudameris and Banca da Svizzera Italiana, both of which we controlled, to take the participation. Then when things were more relaxed, in 1978, we took the position back into BCI.

We took 15 percent of the equity in return for a loan of $7 million. But the capitalization of Lehman then was $16 million. *Nothing!* I was sure that Lehman would not go bust, because it had such a prestigious name then, and somebody would have bought it. And people inside the firm were willing to work to get it back on its feet. This was a very personal involvement. I was on the board for many years; I used to go there once a month, but I had no problem of jet lag because I was young. I could go for one day.

Lehman was sold for $350 million. We made a great deal of money, but not 15 percent of $350 million, because, although we invested more money over time, slowly we had brought down our ownership percentage as Lehman became more and more successful under the leadership of Peterson and needed more and

689

more shares to bring on partners. We could have kept our participation when Lehman was sold to Shearson, but I was not interested in having 4 percent when someone else had 90. So we sold. It was another animal. We had wanted to be with Lehman because they had very strong personalities: Peterson, Ball, James Schlesinger. For our PR in the U.S. it was fantastic.

When Lehman decided to move from its landmark building at 1 William Street in 1981 because there was no longer enough space, I was against that. It could have been a representative office at least; they could have kept that beautiful building, with its partners' room. I had a desk there; I loved to be there. When they decided to sell anyway, I said, "At whatever price you find a buyer, we'll pay that price." And the price they found was $8 million. I said, "It's absurd, but if that's what you want, here it is." It was very cheap; we paid more to renovate it.

In 1984 I was appointed *amministratore delegato* of BCI. There are two of us, and we serve under the chairman, who is the CEO. I think it's going to be necessary for every Italian bank to undergo radical change, and so in my present role I have tried—and am still trying—to modernize the bank. Adapting a 100-year-old organization to something completely new is quite traumatic. We have 20,000 people, and we have to modernize everything.

In the last three years the noninterest income of the bank has grown to 45 percent of the total. But the bank was *built* to make its money from taking deposits and lending money, and the number of our people working on deposits and lending is very out of proportion to its importance in earnings. So it is quite a big reorganization I am now facing, which starts at the top. The treasury department, for example, was administered in a very archaic way, and so the other banks and financial companies were robbing us of the float. By changing the system we have saved a lot of money.

I created a capital markets group, which is just starting to work. From the time you decide to do something, you have to argue with a lot of people, so it takes you two years until it works. You have all the telecommunications and other information systems to get into place, and you have to educate people to adapt to new environments and to understand what different enterprises need. One big difference in Italy is that big companies have been successful in increasing their capital stock, which means they are getting less money from the banks. So we have to lend money somewhere else and meet the needs of the big companies in some other way.

We have to get prepared in the bank for the time when movement of capital will be free, which is coming soon. In 1992 foreign banks will be allowed to open branches freely in Italy. Our competitors are not Italian banks anymore, which would be easy for us. It's the Deutsche Bank, for instance, which is buying banks here. So we have to act quickly, and as we started late, we must accelerate. But it is not only our problem. When I see [Chase Manhattan president Thomas] Labrecque or [chairman Willard] Butcher in the United States, they have exactly the same problems we have.

I think we have generally moved earlier than our competitors in the Italian banking system. When the buoyant Italian stock markets began in 1983, we had 80 percent of the new-issue market. We couldn't keep 80 percent, of course, but we still have 50 percent. So we are already investment bankers. And I think we are moving also quite fast in the reorganization of our branches.

I don't think that the next twenty years will be like the last, so I am not convinced that the lessons of the past are useful for the future. As a banker, if you are not aggressive, you don't acknowledge that things are changing. But you have to be cautious in making the change. These times will require very great bankers. I have had the fortune to know some of the great bankers of the past. Bobbie Lehman, of course, and we were close to Siegmund Warburg. He used to invite me to lunch twice a year, generally in Zurich at the Dolder Grand. He was a charming man. [Former Deutsche chairman Hermann] Abs, [Mediobanca chairman Enrico] Cuccia, our postwar chairman Mattioli—these have been very great bankers. They share, above all, intelligence, the capacity to judge events and people, and determination when they decide to do something. I hope I will find these qualities.

Editor: Heidi S. Fiske

Joseph Flom

Partner SKADDEN, ARPS, SLATE, MEAGHER & FLOM

For almost 40 years Joseph Flom has been a pioneer in securities law, introducing novel proxy-fight tactics and tender-offer strategies. Indeed, it's been said that companies have put his firm on retainer in the hope that prospective raiders would shy away from a fight, although Flom says that's apocryphal. Flom joined Skadden Arps as an associate, after graduating from Harvard Law School in 1948, because "it sounded more challenging" than working for a large firm. He became a partner half-a-dozen years later and stayed as the challenges, and the firm, grew larger.

The firm had about twelve lawyers in the early 1950s. At that point William Timbers, who had been general counsel to the SEC, joined the firm. He had tried a major proxy case just before he left the SEC. It was natural that when he went into private practice, somebody came along with a proxy contest. He turned it over to me. Not having a heck of a lot to do, I had time to study what it was all about.

The next year I was recommended by Arthur Long, a son of a then-client who was in the proxy business, to handle the counting of proxies for the Alleghany Corp. proxy fight—just the counting, not the whole thing. Again, I was obviously building experience, and there was not a lot of proxy expertise around in that area.

Then I got to handle a potential proxy fight with a well-known investor named Victor Muskat, who owned about 33 percent of the stock of American Hardware. The case was a real challenge early in my career and it was my big break. Several times I was walking up and down the streets of Hartford at 3:00 A.M., looking for a diner—I was too excited to sleep.

It was one case where I thought lawyering had a very significant effect on the outcome. When Muskat sued for the stockholder list, instead of just saying, "I have 33 percent, give me the list," he said, "This company is mismanaged and I have to go for the company or else the stockholders are going to be disadvantaged."

The headlines in the newspapers were saying "Mismanagement of American Hardware," and my client was dragging me by the coattail and saying: "What the hell are you doing? Go home. I'm finished."

I said: "Look, Muskat's accusation is the best thing that happened to you. The judge is not going to start with the stockholder list; he is going to decide whether you are mismanaging the company." And, sure enough, the judge wrote a lengthy opinion about how this is one of the best-managed companies in the United States. The other guy didn't get the list.

But we still had someone with 33 percent of the stock, and how the hell do you keep him from getting 50 percent? You start looking into his sources of financing. Some of the 33 percent came from a related insurance company that may have exceeded applicable insurance investment rules. The state of Texas then became involved. Then you started to look at some of the other sources of his financing. Ultimately, the question was how did he get enough money to keep the stock, rather than how is he going to get the money to buy more shares.

So then you say, "Okay, what do you do for an encore?" Suppose he sells the block? Eventually, that's what he had to do. So the whole block was sold to Albert List, a noted entrepreneur. List went up to 40 percent. And obviously, List was a different kind of guy to deal with. We finally got to a situation where we could find somebody who was willing to merge on a fair basis with us and as part of the transaction take List out and share the management. A year later the board chose American Hardware's as the ultimate management of the combined company. American Hardware is now called Emhart and is now a much bigger company. The case was very well publicized.

With that kind of expertise, when takeovers were being done by only partial stock acquisition in the 1960s, it was natural that we were brought in because control fights were apt to be involved. I mean, we were involved in one after the other at a very rapid clip.

It started with small companies acquiring large ones with paper. Then the Williams bill passed in the late 1960s, which imposed federal regulations on corporate takeovers. For three or four years thereafter, we were on the defensive side. During that period litigation stopped almost every unfriendly offer that came along.

At the end of the 1960s you ran into a confluence of forces that really slowed down hostile takeovers. Due to the stock market crash, you couldn't really issue paper, and the changes in accounting rules made transactions less attractive—previously, you could almost choose accounting gimmicks that made 2 plus 2 equal 5. Then antitrust enforcement got fairly rigid, and money was practically rationed by banks. The net result was that from 1970 to about 1973, there were no significant hostile takeovers.

In the 1960s the "respectable" banking houses wouldn't touch any hostile takeovers. However, in 1973 Morgan Stanley approached me about a takeover. We never had to make an offer, because it turned friendly. After that, we started on the hostiles. Some blue-chip companies were involved, and once that happened the logjam was broken and everybody was starting to do these things. So I was lucky to be there at the beginning with Morgan Stanley. A year later, I started working with First Boston because it had been cobanker on one deal and apparently liked what it saw.

Early in the mergers and acquisitions era, one investment bank wanted to charge a significant fee. Some of its partners threatened to resign because they thought the underwriting business was their real business and that mergers and acquisitions should be done for clients for free! If you think of how much they made at M&A and how much they made on underwritings over the recent period, it's no contest.

Once these takeovers got started again in the 1970s, we were off to the races. I remember in '73 or '74 I had taken a house in Spain for two months with the family, but I ended up making seven trips back and forth during that two-month period. I had a little explaining to do at home for a while.

As takeovers grew during the 1970s, the transactions got bigger and bigger. We represented Morgan Stanley and Belridge Oil when Shell Oil took it over, and that was a friendly $3.6 billion deal. That was the biggest one until then. The oil patch tended to have very big deals.

From 1973 on for a long period of time, there were a number of large industrial deals, but it was nothing like what we had just recently. What has happened is the financial entrepreneurs got into the act. You had not only the availability of traditional financing, but in the early '80s there was the availability of junk bonds, or high-yield bonds—the terminology depends on one's bias. The transactions escalated to an entirely different level.

An overlay on this whole thing was another form of merger and acquisition activity—the leveraged buyout. We represented Kohlberg Kravis Roberts & Co. when they were getting started. Jerry [Kohlberg] is a very close friend. We've been working together for a long time. The whole concept of a leveraged buyout, which he pioneered, took a lot of imagination. Remember that in the early days the law on LBOs was in tremendous turmoil. This was a new field, but I love the chance to help pioneer. I'm delighted to have been involved in the three major areas of financial change—the growth of nonconsensual transactions, leveraged buyouts and high-yield bonds.

I used to say the proxy area and tender offers were so intense that you couldn't spend a lot of time clearly defining which disciplines were which. You'd have the lawyer acting as a public relations man, and the investment banker acting as a lawyer, and the PR guy second-guessing everybody. You had to have a little of everything. You also had to second-guess the accountants or be creative to get the deal done, to determine what kind of crazy paper could be issued to fill in the gaps.

Now, as time went on and as the issues became more complex, no one person could be an expert in all those areas. You had to build the expertise to go with all the different periods. A firm that was four lawyers and one associate is now more than 700 lawyers and 130 paralegals. What we've done—and it's the same advice I give a guy in the takeover area—is you have to have your systems in place so that you can take advantage of opportunities.

Among the cases I've been involved in, Pullman was fascinating. This was where Wheelabrator-Frye came in as a white knight, fighting with whoever made a bid for 20 percent of the company. It was necessary to change the offer, and then on the last day, the last-minute change was challenged. We first learned of the challenge on Yom Kippur Eve, when the lawyers working on the matter were no longer around. We finally got somebody to the courthouse that evening. The judge insisted on going forward with a hearing that evening and enjoined the transaction. Fortunately, the court of appeals reversed the lower court early in the following week.

Another exciting case was the Conoco transaction. We had a three-ring circus going. We were representing Conoco. There was a bid for Conoco from Seagram, and then there was a second bid from Mobil. Conoco ended up going to Du Pont, but it was a very tense three-way fight and very complex. Du Pont had never been in this kind of an arena before. There was litigation all over the place, and the litigation that finally settled the outcome was argued in 24 hours.

I have yet to see the same situation twice. The important thing is, you build a backlog of information that may cover 80 percent of the maneuvering in the law. So you don't have to look up all the cases, because you've got them all. You can have your papers out overnight. That's important because everything gets done on an emergency basis. It's a situation where everything gets truncated into three months if you're lucky, and maybe three or four weeks. It's very intense, but that's the fun of it. If you try doing several of them in that period of time, you really have some fun.

It's also intensely competitive. A number of cases have involved Marty Lipton. I never took things personally, and by and large he never did, except for one case about which he felt very strongly. Relations between us cooled off for a while, but we're friends again. I like the guy. I would say that we were in this thing for a long period of time before he got in. The case in which he really came to prominence was one where we had a conflict of interest so we couldn't get into the fight. It was the CNA case, and he got control for Larry Tisch. We were representing some CNA directors on another matter.

I'm very intense when I'm working for a client. My wife always says about me, "My client right or wrong." I hope I have more perspective than that, but I always felt a personal challenge, and I still do. You get involved; you're dealing with people's lives; and you really do have to bust your tail; so if you don't get involved, then you really don't have anything.

I think about the broader implications of what we're doing a great deal. I take the view that there are abuses that have to be dealt with. During the late 1960s I went down to Washington and talked to the powers that be in the White House about why I thought things were getting totally out of hand and what ought to be done about it.

I guess if you are an advocate, you take your client's position, but there is a balance to be struck. The hardest part is to define the mechanism to strike the balance, because whatever you do, you're going to cut something too deeply. Nobody's ever written a law that didn't sweep within it some innocent activities or socially beneficial activities.

Take a thing like the poison pill. There are extreme positions on that. Our position was that if the pill [concept] in its pristine form were allowed to remain, there would be no takeovers on a hostile basis. The courts said we're not going to talk about that—we'll deal with it on a case-by-case basis.

Look at the cases since that time. Half of them sustained the way the pill is set up, and half of them knocked it out. The courts are coming in and saying there is a balance. We're not going to make a broad law—let the legislature do that. We're going to deal with the pill on a case-by-case basis.

Like anything else, there are some takeovers that are good and some that are bad. When you start looking at the financial take-overs, the so-called financial entrepreneurs often don't succeed in getting the companies. They just force them into somebody else's hand. So to the extent that they end up making a good marriage, they're probably doing something socially constructive. There are also a lot of corporate restructurings, and are those good or bad? The stock market is telling us that they are terrific. They've out-performed the rest of the market. The values created for the shareholders are mind-boggling.

Now, if you want to be negative, you say these companies are so loaded up with debt that the stuff can hit the fan, and we'll all go

698

under. But some of that debt is really quasi-equity, and if they get into trouble, some of the subordinated lenders that were looking for 30 percent or 25 percent returns will restructure that debt and it will be taken care of. So again, it evens out.

Now, as far as takeovers where the guy actually succeeds in taking over a company, some of them have been sold off in pieces. The [Reagan] administration says that's good because then they are moving these individual units to the most economically efficient areas. And a lot of these deals have shown that if you take the LBO route, suddenly management has an incentive to start cranking out earnings where they wouldn't before. Or they start worrying not about how many people report to them but about how many dollars are going to be left at the bottom line. And that's socially constructive in many ways. The guys who are actually trying to run a business have shown some good results, but then you have to ask yourself if we have the ultimate answer. Are they going to show good results for three years, and then is there going to be a fall off a cliff? Nobody knows the answer to that.

Editor: Harvey D. Shapiro

Stanley Sporkin

Former Director of Enforcement SECURITIES AND EXCHANGE COMMISSION

> A former accountant and lawyer and currently a U.S. District
> Court judge, Stanley Sporkin joined the SEC in 1961 to work on
> the congressionally mandated special study of the securities indus-
> try. In 1974, shortly after the watchdog activities of several SEC
> units had been consolidated into the Division of Enforcement, he
> became its second director. Over the next seven years, Sporkin
> earned a reputation as a tough cop and oversaw the division's
> emergence as a powerful force regulating the nation's corporations
> and securities markets.

We could make cases. You never would believe the kinds of cases, and quickly like you couldn't believe. For example, one of the finest investigators you would ever find would call me up from Canada. One day he says, "Stan, there's an unlawful distribution of Canadian stock being made by a prominent broker in Washington. I want you to immediately suspend trading and get an injunction." This is one of my guys giving me orders. Because he was twice my age, I would say, "Okay, Ed, that's all very good, but I can't go on your word." He says, "So what do you need to verify it?" I said, "What do you mean?"

He says, "Look, suppose I get you the executive vice president of this brokerage firm to confess on the phone." I said, "Well, that will do it." He says, "Okay, stand by." Five minutes later I got a call from this guy who I knew because he used to work with the commission. He says: "Everything Eddie told you was true. We did everything. We'll be in with our lawyers. We'll confess." I had the case right in my pocket.

We had instincts. We could spot things. Over all those years, we made very few mistakes. I think it was less than one and a half of 1 percent. Our quality control was higher than the Japanese when they make their cars.

I remember one case where I got a tip that XYZ Corp. was involved in unlawful bribery. I assigned it to some of my people, and they brought the corporation's executives in to get them to confess. The executives didn't know what the hell they were doing. They said, "Come on, you must have something." They hired an accountant; then they came back in and they said, "You're right." "Would you," the executives said, "would you tell us how you knew about this? Nobody knew. Our accountants didn't even know about this! How did you people, how could you know, conceivably know, about something like this!" We brought the case and my informant then calls me, and I said, "Well, we brought the XYZ case." He says: "What are you talking about? That's the wrong XYZ company. There's another XYZ company operating out of so-and-so." So we had gotten the wrong company. We had a twofer in that case. Those were fun days.

Equity Funding was an excellent case. That case came to my attention on a Friday night. I got a call from a fellow who was a reporter for *The Wall Street Journal*. He called me and he said a fellow named [Ray] Dirks had just been in to see him and was telling him this story about Equity Funding, a New York Stock Exchange firm that had manufactured a lot of phony insurance policies. And he says do I know anything about it? And we both agreed it sounded absurd, but there was something about that call that caused me to think a couple of times, and I was disturbed that whole night. I was out having dinner. I think we were celebrating either my birthday or somebody else's birthday, but I was bothered by it. On Monday when I came in, I went and told the chairman about it and told Irv Pollack, who was the director [of enforcement] at that time. The thing didn't sound right to me. And finally, we decided to recommend to the commission that they suspend trading in the company stock.

Now, that's a very drastic thing to do. And I had to prepare myself for the questions: suspend trading, based upon what? And what Pollack and I had figured out was that we didn't have to know what the true facts were at that time. All we had to know was: either the facts were true, and if they were true you would suspend trading; or the facts were untrue, and if untrue you would suspend trading because it meant that somebody was circulating these awful rumors in order to have a bear rate on the company stock. We then called the company. The guy was very upset.

We told the lawyer that they could release the trading suspension very easily. All they had to do was to put out a statement that says there's no truth to these rumors. After two days we got no statement. I called back the lawyer and said, "What's the problem?" He said, "We're having trouble drafting a statement." Well, the next thing that happens, I get a call from a prominent lawyer in New York, with Shearman & Sterling, who said, "I got to see you right away; I got to bring a client of mine. I can't tell you on the phone."

So he came down to see me, and he brought a vice president of Citibank, who told me that the No. 2 guy at Equity Funding had been in to see him and he had spilled the beans. He told him it was all true, and I got him to get on the next plane out to the West Coast and to call my regional administrator out there, and I said [to the administrator]: "Start preparing your papers. I'm sending a guy out who'll give you an affidavit. Let's get into court." We got into court that weekend and put the company into receivership.

Dirks beat us badly on the insider trading case. We sued him on the basis that, besides going to *The Wall Street Journal*, he was an investment adviser, he had clients. See, what happened was, an [Equity Funding] insider came to him, the controller, and told him that they were phonying up these books and records. And what he did was, he went to his clients and said, "You better sell Equity Funding because there's this problem." We thought that that wasn't the right way to do it, and the commission brought a case against him, went to the Supreme Court and the Supreme Court said, No, there's no duty. So we lost a few.

In the late '60s we had the tremendous back-office problems that emerged on Wall Street. That was a very trying period for everybody, because the industry had not prepared to deal with the increased volume of business. They were not automated. They were being run as a bunch of partnerships, which meant that because of the tax law all profits got paid out during a year, so there was no building up of money to put into long-term projects such as EDP and things of that kind.

We were faced with a number of firms failing because they couldn't keep up with the business. The SEC was told not to come into the problem. The industry said it would take care of it. The exchanges would take care of it. Well, we were lulled into a false sense of security, because they didn't take care of it. And when we finally did come in, things were almost out of control.

The whole industry was ready to come down. There was complete chaos in the back office of these major firms. We had to get their attention. We had this one case, Lehman Brothers. They were $600 million out. We went in and I determined that we couldn't go in and sue them in a federal court, because the whole Street would come down.

We brought a private proceeding. We called them in and told them that unless they cleaned up their place within a short period of time we would take their broker-dealer license away. Lehman was very disturbed. They said, "What do we do?" We told them to go out and hire accountants to research these differences. They did that. Within six weeks, they came in and they were in balance. We then announced the proceeding. We censured them, but we were able to do that by using some imagination, by treating it in an unorthodox way. We were lucky. We came out ahead. If we were unlucky, I wouldn't be in this position today and I would be some flunky on the Street.

One of the things I enjoyed doing was to try to bring some sophisticated kinds of concepts to the enforcement area. For example, we started with the access theory. The theory there was, look, we used to always have more cases than we could handle. Now, a normal organization would say, "Okay, we're budgeted to handle 25 cases this year. We'll do 25 and that's it." That wasn't enough for me. The way you maximize it is, you get the private sector to come in and do the investigations.

And the way you did that was to put emphasis on the access areas. Some professional groups have access to the marketplace: the lawyers, the accountants, the brokers, the banks. They're going to be around after the two-bit promoter leaves, and their ticket to practice is going to be important. And so we said that we're going to have enterprise liability and we're going to require that the enterprise be responsible for the acts of its people and they must supervise. And we started, therefore, to bring these cases against the access people; that meant they had to respond.

How did they respond? They went out and brought in compliance directors and people. That meant an in-house police arm that the government and the stockholders didn't have to pay for. We started something that is unique in all of U.S. business: an internal consumer group that is going to be there to prevent the corporation from violating the law. Maximizing the use of the private sector, holding enterprises liable for the acts of their people—those were new concepts.

We were like pathologists with respect to American business. We were able to put American business on the table, and open him up and see how he was really operating. It was the first time that ever happened. Growing out of the Watergate mess, we found that there were numbers of corporations that had given political contributions that were illegal. We decided to go into these corporations and see if the accounts these monies were coming from were pools for doing other nefarious kinds of activities. We watched the [Watergate] hearings on TV. We saw these people all coming before the committee—it was on the last day or so—saying, "Yeah, I gave a hundred thousand . . . yeah, I gave a hundred." And we just picked up those companies and we went in and we said, "Okay, show us how you did it." And that disclosed it all. They were in effect using funds to buy business overseas. There were over 700 companies at the end, so many that we went into a voluntary disclosure program. We actually brought about 70 cases. And then we got a new law, the Foreign Corrupt Practices Act. It was a requirement that public corporations keep honest books and records and have a system of internal controls. There was never any requirement. I couldn't believe it.

We also saw that insider trading was big stuff at that time. And who did I bring in but Ted Levine. Ted is Boesky's lawyer now. And Ed Herlihy, who is now a partner at [Martin] Lipton's firm. And I said, "Okay, put in an insider trading surveillance program"—and they did.

The difference between then and now, why we're seeing what we're seeing, is because of the tremendous amount of takeovers

705

taking place and the fact that the options market has only been in since the early '70s. It used to be when you traded on inside information, you bought the stock. And that meant that the price would go up immediately. So you couldn't really make a whole lot of money, and it cost you a lot of money to do it. But with the advent of the options market, your leverage is tremendous and your impact is very limited.

The SEC just doesn't do hard-core kind of enforcement—that's done through the U.S. Attorney's Office. We were asked at one time to set up a phony brokerage firm to bring people in to do manipulations. My answer was, there's so many crooks out there that we're after, we didn't have to engage in that kind of tactic. There were too many crimes that were already being committed to *create* crimes.

Some years back a producer came to see me. He wanted to make a movie, and we had dinner together one night and he got so turned off when he found out we don't carry guns. He couldn't understand how he was going to portray the fact that we're doing this with pencils and eyeshades and he said, "That's not going to sell." A lot of it was the fact we knew how these things operated, knew how to press the right button and did our work.

Editor: Suzanna Andrews

Frederick Joseph

Chief Executive Officer DREXEL BURNHAM LAMBERT

Frederick Joseph spearheaded Drexel Burnham's aggressive moves
in corporate finance, encouraging the pursuit of the high-yield
bond market starting in the late 1970s. His background in corporate finance stretches back to his work at E. F. Hutton & Co. in the
1960s and later at what was then Shearson Hammill. Shifting gears
for two years, Joseph ran Shearson's retail system and then
stepped up to chief operating officer. He arrived at Drexel in 1974
as co-head of corporate finance and became CEO in 1985.

In 1974 I decided that I had an interesting combination of a
line corporate finance background and fairly high-level administrative responsibility and that I'd like to try to combine
them by seeing if I could manage a corporate finance department.
It seemed to me that if you wanted to do that, you really wanted
to join a major firm, because the business was increasingly controlled by the majors. Since neither Shearson nor Hutton were
major firms, and since I was at that time only 36 years old, it
seemed to me that I really needed a major investment bank that
had a fairly weak franchise in investment banking if I was to have
a chance of getting a job running a corporate finance department.
I found there were four of them at the time: Loeb Rhoades,
Wertheim, Reynolds and Drexel Burnham. Of those four, I
thought Drexel was the firm I'd most like to join.

I arranged for a meeting with Mark Kaplan, who was then the
president, and I. W. Burnham—"Tubby" Burnham—who was
chairman. I had known both of them before. They had just

merged the Burnham & Co. and Drexel corporate finance departments and thought an outsider might have a better opportunity to bring the two together. I came over, interviewed, and within a month they and I agreed I would become co-head of the corporate finance department. It turned out my analysis had been pretty good, because each of the other three firms also selected someone new to run their corporate finance departments during the next eighteen months.

The reason the franchise here was not all that well developed at the time—but had very good upside potential—was that it was a fairly recent amalgamation. Harriman Ripley and Drexel had merged in the late '60s; then there had been some political and market turmoil. So that firm became Drexel Firestone and then was acquired by Burnham & Co. in 1973. Burnham had not been a major firm prior to that time, so you had a pretty young, not yet fine-tuned, amalgamation of three different corporate finance departments.

Nineteen seventy-four was an extraordinarily difficult year, maybe the most difficult year. You had very bearish markets, almost no initial public offerings—I think there were three IPOs in the whole Street that year—great scarcity of capital, interest rates skyrocketing and a real malaise. Just a very tough time. So you had an opportunity to take a fresh sheet of paper and figure out what you wanted to do.

Now, we had some interesting special capabilities. Burnham & Co. had a very strong research capability and good knowledge about a few industries. We had a number of very bright people and some special expertise in utilities and small companies. We had a couple of strategy sessions. Our conclusion was that the investment banking business is very competitive and that we were among the weakest of the major firms. Well, given our overall weaknesses in size, recent loss of accounts and turnover of people, it seemed to us that the only way we would get an order was if we had a bona fide competitive advantage that would stand careful analysis. That would be where you would put your effort and get your deals.

My view was it didn't matter an awful lot what your edge was. So we began to search for competitive advantages and designed a bunch of them. For example, we decided we were willing to do issues for smaller growth companies that the other major investment banks might not be willing to do. We decided that we had some special expertise in REITs; there were a lot of them outstanding, and they had great difficulties. We had a number of people that worked on underwriting them in the past; I personally had done a lot of them. And our high-yield bond department, which was being run by Mike Milken, was the dominant market in the after-market of REIT bonds because they were deep-discount high-yield bonds at the time.

Mike's department was already the leading high-yield bond operation in the country. Shortly after I joined Drexel, a number of good professionals in the industry said, "Boy, there's a fellow in that firm who is brilliant, and you ought to meet him." So I made it my business to go introduce myself to Mike and get to know him; I went down to the floor, and someone pointed him out to me. He impressed me as very bright and very knowledgeable. The first thing that we did together with the high-yield department was a number of REIT debt-restructuring and consulting assignments; we also did some high-yield bond fund underwritings and maintained a good presence in the utility business. But it wasn't evident that our major edge was going to be in high yield.

In 1977 a few high-yield bond issues were done away from us. Mike pointed out to me that the underwriters did not understand the market very well and were not selling the bonds to buyers that really wanted to keep them. They were selling them to high-grade buyers, and then the bonds were retrading in the aftermarket, and he was replacing them. So we went to work trying to find prospective issuers of high-yield bonds. The first one was Texas International. They had done their last deal with John Kissick [currently Drexel's director of West Coast corporate finance] when he was at Shearson, and when he joined us at the end of '75, he brought the relationship with him. We knew they wanted to raise money, and we proposed the high-yield approach once we realized that was a market. The second was Michigan General.

Nobody had done this before; there had been no new issues in straight, less-than-investment-grade debt in any magnitude prior to 1977. We found that Mike could sell them and that companies liked raising money that way. His group was the strongest trading and sales organization in the high-yield market. Mike by then had gotten fairly well established as the person who best understood

709

the economics of the high-yield business. He had promoted the concept [that the higher premium more than compensated for the higher risk] and the idea that you had to tie that to good in-depth research and the ability to have a diversified portfolio. We sold that idea to institutions, and we developed a steadily growing constituency of buyers. The high-yield department was already a pretty good-sized operation. We probably had a dozen professionals in it, and it was a real profit center. So as we got into 1977, we began to issue new bonds into that market—matching our new issues with the buyers we already had, making markets, providing aftermarket research and new underwritten products.

In 1977 we were the No. 2 underwriter in that market, behind Lehman. Lehman did more dollar amount than we did; we did the largest number of deals. They did the first few, the LTV and Pan Am and Zapata deals that were done in '77. We became the No. 1 underwriter in 1978 with about a 35 percent market share, and we maintained that share right into 1980–81. Then, as we got into the very tough markets in 1981, when it was tough to sell high-yield bonds because the bond market was in such disarray, our market share increased. It got as high as maybe 75 percent by 1983 or '84.

The first billion-dollar deal we did was for Bill McGowan of MCI in the summer of 1983. The first time I met MCI—in the '70s— we were being asked by its banks to see if the company was viable. For financing, intially MCI came in to us; but we worked pretty hard to solicit their business by the time we began to do financing business for them in the early '80s.

Since then, I think there have been maybe fifteen billion-dol-lar-plus deals, and Drexel's probably done 80 percent of them. One of the best was Metromedia, a refinancing of a leveraged buyout where we raised $1.4 billion for the company in late 1984. I remember the prospectus had to point out that the prior year's cash would not have covered the interest on the debt. And I don't think the company had any tangible net worth at the time. But we knew that the cash flow was going to increase and that we'd raise some extra cash and that the properties were very liquid and had a fair market value of hundreds of millions of dollars in excess of what we were raising. So the credit was, in fact, really quite strong.

The press ran a lot of articles saying this was a disaster for sure. We did the deal successfully, and within a couple of years the company sold these properties to Rupert Murdoch on a basis that left, I think, $500 to $600 million of equity after all the bonds were paid off. Then the press ran more articles, and we financed Mr. Murdoch's acquisitions for another $1 billion-plus. So everybody went away happy—except for the press.

Flight Transportation qualifies as the one that was the most shocking. It was as bad as they come—in fact, an unmitigated disaster. We raised $25 million for the company in 1982, and the SEC and FBI shut them down two weeks after our financing. I remember I was at my mother-in-law's house in Concord, Massachusetts; it was a Friday night. Stan Trotman, who had handled the deal in corporate finance, called me. I was horrified. My immediate reaction was to try to get more facts. The SEC and FBI had sealed up the company's files and said there was a major fraud. It turned out that one of the company's businesses *was* essentially a total fraud—a massive conspiracy by the principals of the company that was awfully tough to discover. But, nevertheless, Drexel became very actively involved in filing lawsuits right away to preserve as much of the money we'd raised as we could; we participated aggressively in the negotiations in the settlements, and it cost the firm several million dollars. But when we were all done, investors—bondholders—got back 95 percent of their money and I think have a chance of essentially recovering all their money.

Everyone talks about LTV and the junk bond market in articles about Drexel. But that was not our client. The fact is that we've done about 50 percent of the high-yield bond underwriting, and our issuers only account for about 16 percent of the problems in the market. So the other firms have done 50 percent and get 84 percent of the problems. We have developed a very strong reputation among our institutional buyers for staying with our issuers and working with them; if they have a problem, we try and help solve it. There are a number of companies that we underwrote that, when their fortunes deteriorated, we remembered them—in the oil patch, for example, companies like MGF Oil and Petro-Lewis.

The [high-yield] market kept growing fairly steadily year by year in the new-issue market, and we began to develop new products. For example, in 1980 or so we began to do high-premium

convertible bonds, which were being sold as fixed-rate investments with a long-term inflation hedge, as opposed to low-pre-
mium preferreds, which typically sold as equities with some
downside protection. Then a couple years later we began to underwrite notes-with-warrant issues, which was just taking converts
and breaking them into their component pieces—an equity kicker
and a straight debt instrument. And in '84 or '85 we did several
billion dollars in variable exchangeable high-yield bonds. We then
created an unrated commercial paper business, which was very
short-term high-yield bonds.

This is an archetypal example of an extension of a product line.
We didn't concentrate on one area as much as the world has
believed. In the meantime, we were developing quite a bit of
industry expertise. For example, we decided at one point to go
after the cable industry and became the leading underwriter of
cable company stock and bond issues. We developed a pretty
strong energy department. We did some geographic diversification, developing strong Los Angeles and Boston corporate finance capabilities. We began to grow our private placement
business to where today we are one of the top in the country.

At the end of '83, we put a very large push on merger and
acquisition activity. I was sitting in the bull pen [as head of corporate finance]. David Kay, who was running the merger department, came over to me, and we just started bantering. He said that
his department had done great. And I allowed as they had done
good—not great—because they were still providing only 10 percent of our corporate finance fee income; most merger departments were providing more like 30 to 40 percent. So we had a
brainstorming session and concluded that we ought to use our
financing muscle to help us do merger business by arranging LBO
financings. And we figured out that we also could do the financings of large, unfriendly tenders.

Even at that first strategy session, we talked about the heat that
would generate; but that was fine as long as the deals made sense.
We concluded that takeovers were, in fact, serving a useful economic purpose and that we had a competitive advantage in our
ability to finance them.

Boone Pickens's run at Gulf Oil [in 1983 and 1984] was a pretty good watershed for us. After we decided that we could do high-yield-finance unfriendly acquisitions, within a matter of months Pickens came to us to help finance the next step of his Gulf transaction; he had been having trouble financing that step. So a couple members of his partnership, Gulf Investors Group, who were clients of ours, brought him in to see us, and he was pleased to find that we could do the financing he wanted. And that got the attention of the world.

Financing unfriendly acquisitions is difficult to do in advance of the announcements. Even though the securities laws do permit you to talk to sophisticated institutions about financing in connection with an unfriendly acquisition, we were doing some very large deals, and, while we never had any evidence that institutions we were talking to were using the information, we still were concerned that they might be. Once people realized and we realized that we could do multibillion-dollar transactions for sure, we developed a technique of not doing a deal until it had been announced, of just telling our client that we were "highly confident" we could do it. And then he could announce his deal without us having to talk to any institutions. Then we could go to work raising the money.

I think one of the best takeover financings was Coastal Corp.'s acquisition of American Natural Resources [in 1985]—an initially unfriendly takeover. We had provided several hundred million in financing to Coastal before the deal, and then in connection with the deal we raised $600 million. When they acquired American Natural Resources, they paid a premium way over market. Those shareholders integrated the companies, and the Coastal stock rose very handsomely.

We have an absolute policy that when one of our clients attacks another client, we are opposed to the attack. If asked, we will defend the attacked company. We will never work with the attacker—very important. We had done a financing for TWA before Carl Icahn began to accumulate the stock [in the spring of 1985]; we had also done some prior financings for his company, ACF. So when he went after TWA, we offered to help TWA. They initially did not want us to because of the potential conflict, but we told Carl from the very beginning that we could not and *would* not help him. I, in fact, did not think that was a good deal on the merits—the political environment was negative at the time, the airline industry is a terribly difficult industry to manage—and I tried to dissuade him. It turned out I was wrong, but at the time I just thought it was too risky. He proceeded with the attack. TWA then asked us if we could bring in a white knight and we actually represented Texas Air, which did try to do a deal with TWA to keep Icahn from buying them. Ultimately, Icahn won that battle.

During the battle he retained another firm [Paine Webber] to do his financing once he finished the acquisition. After he owned TWA, [Paine Webber] was unsuccessful in completing the financing. He then came to us—he was now representing TWA—and asked us, now that there's no longer a conflict and since the other firm couldn't do it, would we help? And he is a good client, it's a good management, the deal made sense—and we did do it. I still had some concerns, but the way we structured the deal made it make sense; we did a lot of equipment trusts. I wasn't telling him whether it was a good acquisition for *him* or not; what made sense when we did the financing was that the debt we sold was good debt. That's a different issue.

We refuse to represent someone when we think a major objective is greenmail. Sometimes they'll say it isn't, and the way to resolve that discussion is to tell him, "Fine, we'll need a commitment from you not to accept greenmail." We often do it when a raider's involved. In the Phillips Petroleum case [in 1985], Icahn signed the agreement. We did not ask Saul Steinberg on Disney [in 1984], because it was clear to us that he really wanted to acquire the company. If the company's going to really hurt the values on the one hand or pay you a premium on the other, maybe the only viable alternative for the investor is to accept it, and that appeared to us to be the case in Disney.

Our association with raiders is overblown. The firm has 800-odd corporate finance clients, of whom maybe a dozen are characterized as raiders by the press. From 1984 to 1986, Drexel served as financial adviser or arranged financing for 306 merger transactions, of which ten were hostile. And the fact is, in the last three years Drexel has provided 10 percent of the funds for unfriendly and unsolicited takeovers; commercial banks have provided 58 percent. So we're not the main source of funds by a long shot in unfriendly takeovers.

Based on the fact that we do the high-value-added, more difficult transactions, that we know a lot about doing sophisticated credit analysis and equity value analysis and that we've got the capital to invest—we'll get to $2 billion in capital this year and now have about $1 billion of excess net capital—we decided years ago to invest our money with our brains. We began to take interest in venture capital deals back in the '70s and in leveraged buyouts and merger transactions beginning in the early '80s. We took equity in companies we were working with when we could, again back in the '70s.

We've been the fastest-growing firm on the Street. We've grown probably 20 percent compounded in personnel over the past decade. The fact is, we have a very long-standing, solid infrastructure of very experienced people. Take our executive committee. You start with Tubby Burnham [honorary chairman], who has been here 52 years; Bob Linton [chairman], who's been here over 40 years; Mark Edersheim [deputy chairman] has been here over 35; Eddie Kantor [vice chairman], over 30; [senior executive vice president] Howard Brenner's been here 24 years. I'm a newcomer; I've only been here twelve years. [Vice chairman] Jim Balog's a newcomer; he's been here eleven years. It's a very solidly established management team that's been working together for decades—like the old Celtics: [Bob] Cousy could always throw the ball behind his back and know where [Bill] Sharman was.

I found out about Ivan Boesky's [involvement in the insider trading scandal] while I was at a firm training session with 40 of my senior people. My reaction was surprise and dismay. There's no question that something went wrong in the securities business. I think the majority of the major firms have all found that they have a problem. I have some ideas; for example, I think it might make sense for it to be a federal offense to lie on an employment application for a securities firm or any financial institution. At Drexel we've recently gone to 100 percent background checks. We used to do background checks only for certain jobs or if there was a specific basis for one; now we do checks on all applicants. We all need to pull together to improve the business, and I think we may need some help from regulators and legislators.

Editor: Hilary Rosenberg

Toyoo Gyohten

Vice Minister of Finance for International Affairs JAPAN

Toyoo Gyohten is the seniormost official in the Japanese Ministry of Finance dealing with international affairs. As an MoF official for three decades, he has been deeply involved in the deregulation of Japan's internal and external markets as well as in its negotiations with the rest of the world on such matters as export credits and exchange rates.

In the late '60s, when Japan was still more or less in a period of recovery and reconstruction after the war, the Japanese financial industry played a great role in encouraging high economic growth by channeling financial resources to the most productive sectors. This was done under rather strong regulation.

I was with the Asian Development Bank until 1969 and was assigned to the banking bureau [of the Ministry of Finance] when I returned. Those were the very early days of deregulation; looking back, it was very primitive. Until that time, we exercised very rigid control over banks' branching out; every year we decided which banks could open branches where. We also had strict controls over banks' dividends. So we made initial steps to reduce those controls.

The year of the so-called Nixon shock [the end of the dollar's convertibility in 1971] produced really remarkable activity. I was assistant to the vice minister for international affairs, [Takashi] Hosomi. Both of us were newly appointed in mid-year, and the shock came in August. Very hectic days followed until December, when final agreement [on exchange rates] was reached in Washington at the Smithsonian Institution. Between August and December we made about six or seven trips abroad. We had bilateral meetings and Group of Ten meetings and IMF meetings. Finance Minister [Mikio] Mizuta was still alive at that time, and the Bank of Japan was headed by [Tadashi] Sasaki.

Probably the greatest lesson we learned was the appalling gap between domestic and international perceptions of the strength of the yen. In those days the yen was fixed at 360 to the U.S. dollar. We had lots of international discussions about appreciating the yen by 15 percent, 20 percent. Those kinds of arguments were absolutely unacceptable at home, where the almost unanimous view was that appreciation of more than 10 percent would definitely kill the economy. So when Mizuta had to accept yen appreciation by 16.77 percent to 308 yen, he thought that upon his return to Japan he'd be really treated as a traitor!

When the meeting was over, other participants were more or less relieved by the at least temporary solution. President Nixon came to the meeting hall to greet the finance ministers, but poor Mr. Mizuta, he was so downhearted, he didn't wait for President Nixon. We came back to our hotel and had to face the Japanese press reporters who accompanied him from Tokyo. As we expected, the questioners accused him, asking, "Why did you accept this kind of humiliating result?" The minister had a hard time responding. However, I remember during the bombardment of accusing questions, one Japanese reporter stationed in Washington said in a rather cool voice, "Sir, well, from what I understood here in Washington, I don't think this much appreciation is enough." That was a very revealing moment for me, because I learned that even among Japanese, there was such a really appalling gap of understanding. And I thought, well, we have a long way to go.

Popular opinion in Japan was so convinced that appreciation of the yen of more than 10 percent would immediately bring about recession, stagnation or depression. In hindsight, there were many people who actually did not believe this—because the stock market went up upon the news that the yen would settle at 308. But such people did not speak up. After the war Japan had enjoyed the 360 yen rate. I think the currency was undervalued, but this undervaluation enabled Japan to export and therefore boost economic growth, increase employment, increase income— so people instinctively knew that this relatively weak yen did help and would help if it could be maintained a bit longer.

The star of the [Smithsonian] show was [former U.S. Treasury secretary] John Connally, and you know his style. He is a very hard bargainer. I think he believed in conducting the negotiation in a high-handed posture. Throughout the meeting he displayed that ability. It was not only Japan that came under his pressure. Judging from the discussions, there was an impression that Connally won. But later, if you look back, you are certainly sure that Connally didn't get very much. Mizuta was the main negotiator for Japan. [Yusuke] Kashiwagi [now Bank of Tokyo chairman but then special adviser to the finance minister] was there, but in those ministers' meetings it was very difficult for officials to participate. You have to leave your minister to do the job.

I don't know how much Mizuta understood financial affairs, but who else did? You can imagine at the later stage it was not pure economics they were discussing; it was more political, so final agreement was reached between Mizuta and Connally bilaterally. Other countries also made deals. At that time the U.S. agreed to devalue the dollar by raising the price of gold. Some currencies were to stay neutral without any move, and other currencies were appreciated. Each country was fighting for itself. So we found no enemy in that sense, but no friend. There was no clear and explicit sentiment that the yen's appreciation should be smaller, so in that sense there was no friend.

We stopped over at Anchorage on the way home, and we got the first news from Tokyo that the stock market had soared. So in many ways that was quite a revealing time. I learned what the market was. I was also interested to watch ministers, particularly the Europeans. You knew they had experienced ups and downs of their currencies so many times, and I think through those experiences they had a certain amount of respect and also resignation toward so-called market forces.

In the Smithsonian agreement the tentative provisional rate for the yen was agreed at 308 to the dollar, but it couldn't be held too long. In early 1973 some European currencies came under pressure. Everything started to be chaotic again, and finally we decided that we had no way but to float. That decision was made in March, and Hosomi, by then adviser to the minister, was asked to visit Europe. I was the customs commissioner at Haneda Airport, and I was later told that Hosomi insisted that he should take me with him. It was a very unusual assignment for a customs commissioner. I got a phone call from the director of the chief secretariat, Michio Takeuchi, who is now the chairman of the Tokyo Stock Exchange, and he told me that I had to leave tomorrow with Hosomi for Europe.

We had meetings in Paris and Bonn; I think the final decision was made in Bonn. We were talking with Paul Volcker, then under secretary of the Treasury, and then Sam Cross, who is now vice president of the Federal Reserve Bank and was then Volcker's assistant. For Japan there was Hosomi and myself. The decision to float the currency was recognized as inevitable, but even after we made the final agreement we were told not to come back to Japan too quickly, because it might excite the mass media. So we tried to hide away for a couple of days. Hosomi asked where we should go. At first we thought Mallorca or some very remote, inaccessible place; but then we thought that although we would be disappearing, we shouldn't disappear completely. We finally settled on Athens, Greece, because Japan Air Lines had just opened the Athens-Tokyo route; we thought if something happened we could get a flight quickly. We drove around the country and that was fun. It was snowing heavily in Bonn, but in Athens the cherry blossoms were blooming.

Immediately after the floating-exchange-rate introduction, the Japanese economy showed no signs of a serious setback. I went back to Haneda to be customs commissioner, but I didn't stay long. In mid-1973 I was back to the international finance bureau and went to Nairobi, Kenya, to the IMF meeting in September, where news of the oil crisis arrived. First the Gulf war broke out. We didn't realize the actual impact [of rising oil prices] on the economy until after we came back. That time there really was a shock, an actual shock. Hoarding started, inflation gathered speed, the trade balance deteriorated quickly, we ran out of reserves. There were many arguments that the Japanese economic myth had finally collapsed.

You learn that when you are badly hit you can't really expect any friends to extend their helping hand. Japan pulled around.

720

We begged the Saudis to lend us $1 billion. [Masao] Fujioka [then at the MoF international finance bureau and now president of the Asian Development Bank] did the negotiating, in cooperation with Kashiwagi, who had gone to the Bank of Tokyo. That borrowing was formally made between the Saudi Arabian Monetary Agency and the Bank of Tokyo, and the funds were put at the disposal of the government. The Japanese government marketability is much higher now. We didn't want to make a big political issue out of it, so the government itself didn't do the borrowing. The deal was kept confidential until it was finalized.

By 1975, at the time of the Bonn summit meeting, there was a unanimous feeling that Japan and Germany had recovered from the oil shock. Advocates of the famous "locomotive theory" began to be heard, urging that these surplus countries should play the role of locomotives in the world economy. We started to implement a very expansionary fiscal policy with a supplementary budget in the fall of 1975. I don't regret the decision myself. What we should regret is the process that followed. If we could have maintained a substantially more prudent fiscal policy, then the situation wouldn't have deteriorated that much. Maybe it's no use to regret that once you open up the floodgates, you really cannot control the water. That is partly why the Germans and Japanese are so reluctant to do that over again, because they know once you start borrowing money there will be no end. We have seen a recent victim of that in the United States.

The second oil shock came in 1979, but we Japanese were experienced now and knew how to cope with this kind of thing, so handling of the situation was much better. We learned that we shouldn't try to control the oil price, so we let it go, and we tried not to introduce any rationing of oil. We let market forces work. That was the quickest and best way to reach the new equilibrium. At the same time we started very intensive conservation policies.

Until a couple of years ago I was deeply involved in negotiations on export credit guidelines. Japan, as a low-interest-rate country, had a really hard discussion. The meetings were held in the OECD, which has 25 members, and quite often I found myself one against 24. Well, I'm accustomed to that to some extent. I wouldn't say I enjoy it. I found that in these international meetings, it doesn't pay to play gimmicks, because it can work once but you cannot maintain a minimum amount of credibility. I try to be as honest as possible when I say what the Japanese position is, what our interest is, why we argue this way. Of course, I have to bargain sometimes—for instance, if you are talking about figures, of course you have to bargain—but I am not terribly fond of bargaining.

[Prime Minister Yasuhiro] Nakasone's leadership has been very instrumental in enhancing Japan's international image. But Japanese businessmen were internationalized even before politicians and civil servants. After all, in the world of business, profit-making is the only axiom for everybody. National boundaries do not matter very much for them as long as they can share the profits in a reasonable way. But politicians, civil servants, they don't have this kind of common denominator like profit-taking. As an international player we have a long way to go.

I am aware of foreign resentment about the growth of Japanese financial institutions' assets abroad. But this recent situation is certainly somewhat unusual, because there is such a huge accumulated surplus in this country. Japanese financial institutions do have funds to be invested, so they bring that money to London and to New York, so that certainly increases their share in that type of business. But if you are talking of collecting deposits from local residents, Japanese banks in London and New York are not doing much better than foreign banks in Japan. So those monies that Japanese banks and securities firms are deploying in foreign markets are those funds created at home. I say that is not a very unusual situation.

The lesson of recent financial history is that personalities count for a certain period of time, but they don't change the whole picture over the long run. For instance, John Connally did an outstanding job; he certainly made a show. Who else? There are not many stars in this field; it's not diplomacy, after all. On the Japanese side, certainly Mizuta did his job. [Noboru] Takeshita had the Plaza agreement; [Kiichi] Miyazawa had the Baker accord.

There have been two pushes for Japanese deregulation, one external and one internal, both of them indispensable and inevitable. Even without external pressures, internal pressures would have mounted to force deregulation. For instance, take the case of interest rates: Even without any external pressures, internal changes in the flow of funds did force deregulation. The huge and explosive expansion of the secondary market for government bonds really negated the efficiency of interest rate controls. But we cannot separate external factors and internal ones; they interact. The Japanese economy grew big, and its trade relations have permeated into all markets. Along with this, Japanese financial institutions have started to become very active in other markets. Foreigners also saw the growing potential of the Tokyo market, so they naturally wanted a bigger share. All these factors combined. Certainly those external pressures accelerated the process of deregulation to a considerable extent.

In many respects, the Japanese process of deregulation is much more, what shall I say, thorough, orderly. We do a much greater amount of ground-leveling work before we do something; for foreigners the work of ground-leveling seems to be totally unnecessary. I remember [then U.S. Treasury under secretary] Beryl Sprinkel once told me that back in his country home, they have these sheep dogs. For some reason the sheep dog should have a short tail, but when they cut the dog's tail, they do it in one chop rather than cut it off inch by inch every day. He complained that we were [deregulating] inch by inch, lump by lump. For the British it is totally inconceivable why we are taking so long to deregulate interest rates. The reason is that we have to convince those who are going to be affected by deregulation that this is inevitable.

Total interest rate deregulation is coming, but we are still arguing about the timing. There are two problems: the postal savings and small institutions. There is resistance because people are facing a new situation, and when you have no experience at all you overreact to the possible change. I still remember vividly when we first tried to allow foreign banks to set up trust banks here; there was such a strong opposition from traditional trust banks, but they very quickly adapted themselves to this situation. I think people need to be convinced that, okay, some small institutions will have a hard time, but this problem will be solved by merging or acquisition or help by the central bank. Once this experience has been established, fears of the unknown will simply disappear.

I think that things could have been done much more quickly, but the fact that I myself think so doesn't count very much. It is easy to exaggerate the power of the Ministry of Finance. I don't think we have made mistakes in deregulation, but maybe lack of uniformity was a drawback. We had a uniform process in the Euroyen market, but not in the domestic market. If we could have carried out this deregulation on a more across-the-board basis, things would have been smoother. In hindsight we could have done things more quickly or much earlier.

Editor: Kevin Rafferty

Maurice Greenberg

President and Chief Executive Officer AMERICAN
INTERNATIONAL GROUP

> Iconoclastic, aggressive, visionary—Maurice Greenberg of Ameri-
> can International Group has been a primary force in commercial
> insurance since becoming CEO in 1967. He has made AIG into
> one of the most successful insurers in the world—and changed an
> industry in the process.

Starting in the '60s at AIG, we set out to build a completely different organization. And when you do that, you do have some believers—but you also have some who are going to sit back and question whether or not it's wise. We had those both within and outside the organization. It wasn't as if everybody in AIG woke up one morning and said this is a great idea, and we were all going in one direction. It wasn't that at all. Many of the things that we were doing were a hell of a change.

The insurance industry, going back twenty years, was never noted for its creativity. When one thought of writing an unusual or difficult risk, Lloyd's of London was the market one turned to. And I think we helped change some of that. We have been prod-uct-innovative, marketing-innovative. And certainly in the late '60s and throughout the '70s, we became a growing force in the industrial-commercial sector, whether it be casualty or property.

Many of the brokers were excited by what we were doing. They felt a new market was being created that would fit very nicely with what they were trying to do. I think that Marsh & McLennan, Johnson & Higgins—the corporate brokers—were very support-

725

ive. And we were fortunate in having a great group of people with the right talents at the right time.

So you could almost say the industry was split. There were the traditional companies that looked at us like we had some kind of disease. And there were those who believed that change was in the wind and that we were in the forefront of that change, and that there would be others following in our path in a few years once some of the risks were proven to be reasonably sound. And that, indeed, has happened.

We also set out to be different in our emphasis on underwriting. Over the years the industry became enamored of the financial part of its business and, to some degree, disregarded or felt less inclined toward the underwriting side. What gave rise to that, I suppose, were a lot of factors. Some people came to the top from the financial side of their company, were more financially oriented and certainly became mesmerized by interest rates of 18 to 20 percent, believing that would cover all problems.

There was also an attempt to emulate a lot of other companies. "If company A is underwriting directors and officers liability insurance, we can underwrite directors and officers liability insurance." They began to step out of their historic culture into areas of underwriting that were alien to them, simply by copying somebody else's policy form and cutting 5 or 10 or 20 percent from the rates. They got caught up in that frenzy—like a feeding frenzy. That's almost the way it was done.

There was also a feeling that they could succeed by simply hiring somebody from another company that was doing it successfully; the belief was that these people would take that culture with them to an alien culture, a different culture. But it never works that way. Every company has its own culture, and one or two or three people injected into that find it very difficult to change it.

This has been one of the things that have added to the volatility of the industry in the last twenty years. Another is the rise of the risk manager. Risk managers put pressure on the brokerage community to find what they felt was the best price. To some degree this pushed aside concerns about the *quality,* the *durability* and the *service capabilities* of that security. Price was the No. 1 issue, which turned out not to be the wisest policy for many. Some chose underwriters who walked away when things reached the bottom.

There was a period in the '60s when there was more stability in the business, when a risk didn't move at the slightest drop of the hat, where a broker was able to influence the account more than they can today. Moving from company to company in the long run has not done anybody any good. It certainly has added to the volatility that we've been speaking about. But it's a fact of life and, you know, we can sit around and preach about it all we want but that's not going to change it.

Then there are the reinsurers. Twenty years ago reinsurers were fewer, more professional, more stable than during this last underwriting cycle. For some reason there was a belief that reinsurance was a great business to be in. And it attracted players from all over the world. Some of the third-world countries got into reinsurance with their national insurance companies. A whole, almost subculture in reinsurance emerged. And it added to the lack of discipline that the market experienced. It turned out that for many insurance companies, reinsurance was illusory. Many reinsurers were simply blown away. It's unlikely there will ever be a return to anything like the number that existed before. I think we're back to a more professional industry with fewer reinsurers, and that will impose a discipline on a significant part of the market for some time.

Certainly, the legal system has also made the industry more volatile. Look at the risks that were underwritten twenty years ago—asbestos, for example. When one underwrote a risk back then that happened to have asbestos in it, the state of the art in both science and medicine was that it wasn't hazardous to your health. But now you're held accountable for standards years after the event. You know, like any other industry, we have to show a reasonable return on equity that's competitive with other industries, or nobody is going to invest in insurance companies. And if you don't invest in insurance companies, you haven't got the capital to underwrite anybody.

The industry's ROE has been pitiful in the past five years. And I'm not suggesting that it's all because of the tort system, but a significant amount of it has been. And until we resolve this issue, corporate America won't be able to buy all of its coverage at prices it considers to be affordable. I don't know what affordable means in any event. What's affordable is what you have to charge for the product, whether it's a bottle of milk or an insurance policy. I don't hear anybody saying that automobiles are not affordable. If prices go up, it's because costs have gone up.

I don't think we've addressed the issue in this country yet of the legal system. The debate has been a bit stilled in the last six months because of the partial recovery of the insurance industry and the flowing back of some additional capacity in many classes. But the problem is still there.

What has changed for the better, I'd say, is the quality of people the industry is attracting. There's certainly more of a recognition that you're competing with other financial institutions for talent. The investment area certainly has attracted brighter people. Underwriting, claims, the legal area—yes, I would say we are seeing better people. Better educated, more inquisitive. The industry had a reputation twenty years ago of being really sleepy. The image was one of knocking on doors, selling a debit account. There are some who still think of it that way.

You wouldn't dream of hiring anybody today out of college who hasn't had some experience with computers, who is not really acquainted with some financial aspects of the world we live in. If they want to go on the international side, they've got to have more than just desire. They've got to have some experience in that, too. There are also more women in business today. Twenty years ago you wouldn't have seen any women, or minority groups, in the insurance business in any managerial roles.

❦

One of the reasons I suppose the industry didn't have scandals twenty years ago was because it was sleeping. You didn't attract aggressive, entrepreneurial types who were looking for an edge.

And, yes, I suppose there is a person that we would say fits better in AIG than they would elsewhere. I think you would probably recognize the type. We do want a more entrepreneurial type, one who is willing to take chances, who is a risk-oriented person, one who wants to succeed and is willing to pay the price, who will accept responsibility at the drop of a hat and, obviously, is endowed with a good deal of brains.

AIG makes the person; the person doesn't make AIG. Some people become very impressed with their credentials and believe they can easily transport that elsewhere. There is a great support organization at AIG that makes people look pretty good. Take that away and it's like taking away the surgical team from the surgeon. It's hard to do it all alone. And it is a team that makes AIG succeed. There's no one person that makes this company succeed. It's a team. And it has worked very well.

Some people may leave because they lose the fire in their belly to continue in an organization that is performance-oriented. In a way, that's a cleansing process. We *do* have a strong culture at AIG, and when somebody leaves it reinforces the culture by taking out some of the impurities. It makes more opportunities for younger people who want to grab on to that ring and make it very high up in AIG. And if they don't have that desire, we would rather know that, and I hope they know it, too.

Do they leave because I'm too tough with them? I don't know if "tough" is the right description. I'm not making excuses. I am what I am. You don't have to guess what I think. I'm reasonably outspoken. I think it's best. What I regret is that people in this company and elsewhere read and think that fire and brimstone comes out of this office and nothing else. I think that's an unfair characterization.

You don't build an organization with just one simple theory—that you're going to have everybody in fear. That doesn't make any sense. But I don't make any apologies for how I am.

Have I accomplished everything I wanted to? There are some areas of AIG that I would like to see do better. Sometimes you're disappointed in somebody who you thought would be able to do something that was delegated to him and didn't. I suppose some of the biggest disappointments have been some people. On the other hand, some of my greatest feelings of achievement have been because of people. By and large, there has been more right than wrong.

And no matter where they are, we back our people up. Look at what happened to us in Iran. When we first started there, we looked around our own company to see if we had anybody who had any experience in that part of the world. We had, of course, been doing business in the Middle East for many, many years. And we found a chap who was with our New Hampshire Insurance Co. subsidiary out on the West Coast—K.C. Shabani—who was born in Teheran and had family there, was well educated and knew everybody.

So we lifted him out of California and sent him to Iran. He

helped establish our company there. Within a very short period of time we built the largest private insurer in the country, both life and non-life. It was a joint venture with the Iranians.

Well, when Khomeini took over in 1979, Shabani got detained and was incarcerated for almost a year. He was tortured and they threatened his wife with violence. The pressure they lived under—the threat of being killed—was constant.

We finally got him out of prison and out of the country with his wife and child. They had a bad experience, but we never gave up for a moment. We got them out through means and devices that even today I would rather not publicize. We worked at it. We've never abandoned our people, whether they were in Vietnam or Cuba or Iran or anyplace. We've always had a policy that we'll go to any ends to get our people out, and we have. Shabani's back in California, and he's still working for AIG.

You can't be global and not have these things happen almost as everyday problems. You have to live with it and adapt and, again, it's part of our culture. It's something we take as an everyday event, where others, you know, would consider it kind of unusual.

Editor: John W. Milligan

George Russell Jr.

President FRANK RUSSELL CO.

> George Russell Jr. launched the pension consulting industry eigh-
> teen years ago, and today his firm's more than 600 employees
> serve clients in thirteen countries, including companies that repre-
> sent an estimated 10 percent of the assets in U.S. private pension
> plans. Russell is also chairman of Frank Russell Trust Co. and
> Frank Russell Investment Management Co., which choose manag-
> ers for some $8 billion in assets of smaller retirement funds and
> bank trust department clients.

The Frank Russell Co. has really had three lives. It was my grandfather's first, from 1936 to '58, when I came in. He died 60 days after I got here, at the age of 80. My father had never been in the business.

So the second life was from 1958 to 1969. I carried on my grandfather's business, a retail business. We sold mutual funds, life insurance, real estate syndications to mom and pop around the kitchen table in Washington, Oregon, Idaho and Alaska. We had 300 salesmen, 80 percent of them part time. I also managed a mutual fund that my grandfather had started in the '30s, one of the early funds.

My grandfather had fourteen investment consulting clients he ran portfolios for. When he died, I looked in the Yellow Pages of the Seattle phone book and identified the three investment advis-ers that were over there and gave those names to the fourteen clients. As I look back on it, it was my first manager search.

About 1967 and '68 I started getting interested in pension

accounts, the possibility of mutual funds for pension funds. I actually developed a presentation and, by some fluke, sat next to the assistant to Jim Ling [then chairman of Ling-Temco-Vought] at a Harvard Business School conference in Seattle—I had gone to the business school. Out of that twenty-minute conversation, a month later I was in Dallas talking to Mr. Ling, and within two or three months I had sold $50 million worth of mutual funds to three major corporations.

But all that did for me, really, was to give me more information on what pension funds needed, and I realized that mutual funds weren't what corporations were looking for. They were looking for information on money managers. So in 1969 I developed an approach to service the industry and made a call to J. C. Penney in New York. I really will never know why it was J. C. Penney. I picked up an S&P sheet that had the chief financial officer's name and telephone number on the back of it and phoned him. He wasn't in, but the treasurer, Paul Kaltinick, was, so the call got referred to him. He told me later he took the call because he was wondering if I was calling from Penney's Tacoma store. Anyway, he'd been put in charge of retirement assets some months before, and I made arrangements to visit him in New York. Penney became our first consulting client. We basically gave the sales force away to the fellow who was running the insurance part of it and changed the direction of the company 180 degrees.

I made some decisions at the outset that I think have been proper for this organization. I figured if we were the first ones to be a consultant in this field, then we could probably set our own rules. If it works, it works. And if it doesn't, so what? So I said, look, we don't really want to provide a service and then start diluting it by adding clients on top of clients. Let's limit ourselves to a number of first-class clients. That way we won't dilute the quality of the work we provide. That meant we needed ongoing relationships. So I told Penney and everyone since then that we weren't in the business to provide a recommendation for the solution of a problem. We were on for life, as long as we did our work. They could fire us anytime they wanted. And we could leave anytime we wanted. There was always just a handshake, until the federal government required contracts for soft-dollar arrangements. We were up to our client limit of 40 by 1974. It seemed to be a vacuum that needed filling.

It's been a very stable business. There have been only nine changes in that client lineup in the eighteen-plus years, some prompted by clients, some by us. When the team players change on the other side of the table and these changes don't result in good chemistry, it's not good for us and it's not good for the client.

Our second client, I think, was Burlington Industries, which sat on Sixth Avenue between the Hilton Hotel and Penney. Paul Kaltinick said something to his counterpart at Burlington, and they became a client overnight.

Many years later I was sitting in the office of Burlington one day, and they said to me, "We've got this $25 million piece over here that's not part of the master trust and what are you going to do about it?" So I said: "Why don't we set up an organization with some commingled funds, one equity and one fixed and one international and one real estate, and then you only have an asset allocation problem, because we'll hire a bunch of managers to manage each pool. If there are other people with your problem, it will work." And that's how I found the answer to the small sponsor—the $100 million, the $50 million sponsor—who, because he doesn't have enough assets, can't get multiple managers and cover asset classes properly. I formed the Frank Russell Trust Co. in 1980.

Then a few months later Paul Kaltinick—he was a senior financial officer by that time—was out in the Northwest, and I asked him to help me pick the president of the trust company. He said, what's that? So I explained the concept to him, and a few minutes later he asked me how I would rank him for a job like that. And I said, "Well, on a Bo Derek scale, around a 9.5." So he came to us in October of 1980, and he's been the president of the trust company ever since. We have about 150 clients, with about $5.5 billion in the trust company now, and use some 45 managers.

The Frank Russell Investment Management Co. is a mutual fund operation. There are seventeen funds and 30 or so money managers there. The funds are marketed through some 50 regional banks. We supply the banks with asset allocation models to use for individuals and small sponsors. We started that a year after the trust company and now have about $2.5 billion.

We really introduced, I think, the concept of getting away from the balanced-bank-manager theory that one organization has all the answers. Over a period of three or four years, we persuaded all of our clients to go to a multimanager mix, diversified by style, which makes sense in an efficient market, where it's quite important to spread your bets.

In the first few months after getting into manager selection, we said we didn't want to compete with A. G. Becker in measuring performance. But it became evident, very quickly, that we had to measure performance—for the managers we were researching and for our clients. Peter Dietz, who was at the University of Oregon, published the first book on how to measure pension performance, and he worked with us part time to help us set up our system. He then joined us full time in 1971. Our measurement system and audit system have become a rather large part of the organization.

We also sell performance information to money managers. The basic difference is that we give our clients the names of all the players, and when we sell that information to the investment community, they see where they are in the universe but they don't know who the rest of the players are. We got the consent of our consulting clients, because it creates a potential conflict of interest when you're selling something to a money manager and then recommending money managers. From time to time we would get a potshot from the press that would attempt to indicate that there might be something fishy there, but, to our knowledge, we never took advantage of the situation, and nobody from the press has asked us about it in years.

The information we had twenty years ago we would be embarrassed to show anybody today. For example, we can now take the eight managers you have, give their combined portfolio results and put whatever index you want next to it. Suppose you don't like manager No. 3; we can pull him out in about one second, put another manager in and see what that does to the composite. I mean, that kind of technology and accessibility blows your mind.

If you're looking for the most important thing that we look for in a money manager selection process, it's continuity of good managers. That's 10 on the scale, and the next most important item would be a 5. It's the common denominator of success in money management—a dedicated group of professionals who have worked together for long periods of time. So that when they do fall into the tank, they work themselves out of it together. And if you have confidence in that group of people, then you don't terminate them when they go into the tank. You know that in due course they'll get out. Paul Miller [partner at Miller, Anderson & Sherrerd] has been in the tank before. Did we ever think of terminating him? No. Miller, Anderson, by the way, is the first manager we selected for our first client, Penney, and they're still there. Generally speaking, I think size does have a negative impact, but there are firms—they're rare—where size has not had a great impact, and Miller, Anderson is a good example.

Not too long ago somebody asked me why we've been as successful as we've been. The prime reason, of course, in a business like this is that we've been able to hire and keep bright people. But I think another important reason is that we found out a way early on to finance R&D. We were fortunate, I think, in being able to identify ways in which our intelligence base and data base could be leveraged. I see the consulting practice here as the greenhouse, the think tank. That's where the R&D resides, and we have a large R&D budget.

R&D to us is the ability to access data and to prove or disprove multiple correlations—to find out, for example, if we have an efficient market or not. Because if we do, it means one thing. If we don't, it means a totally different thing. And our responsibility to our clients is to help them improve returns and, at least, control or modify their risk. And if that's the case, then it seems to me that we have to continue to poke at the frontiers. I've been saying to our clients for almost twenty years, and certainly to my own people, that there are no answers in this business. There's just a hell of a lot of information.

And it's gone way beyond just the efficient market concept. We would classify as R&D the work that Bill Sharpe [on leave from Stanford University] is doing in the Sharpe-Russell Research unit that was set up in September 1986. To start with, its prime focus is to push substantially the state of the art on asset allocation for defined-benefit plans. And they're working on benchmarks for specialized styles and normal portfolios. We've come up with a lot of things over the years. Like our indexes. We've worked up the Russell 1,000, 2,000 and 3,000 U.S. stock indexes, because we found that our clients' small-cap bet average is about 18 or 19 percent of their equity portfolios, and the S&P 500 covers only about 2.5 percent of that bet. And we're doing an international index, because the EAFE has too many stocks in it that you can't buy. And there's the FRC Property Index. It isn't paying off from a P&L point of view, but it is from a need point of view. It's the only real estate index there is, and it took us seven years to develop.

In 1969, of course, the only two asset classes that you could find of any significance in any pension account were stocks and bonds. I raised the question with Penney that year: Why don't you use real estate? They didn't even consider that an asset class. Besides, how would they invest in it? So I made calls on six organizations in 1969—Landauer, Prudential, others—and queried them about why they couldn't be responsible for setting up the product that a pension account could invest in. And they looked at me kind of strangely, I think because I was from Tacoma, Washington. They would say something to the effect that, "Young man, real estate is for taxable people, not for tax-free people." And I kept persisting, and it is to Meyer Melnikoff's credit at Prudential that he saw the need and PRISA was formed as the first vehicle. And that was when I hired Blake Eagle to be our adviser.

International started for us about the same time. I think it was 1970, in a talk I gave to some treasurers in New York, that I said that in a decade our clients would be investing rather seriously in international markets. They sort of laughed. But we got started. It turned out that Peter Dietz, who was then still at the University of Oregon, had an exchange teaching assignment at the University of Amsterdam with some free time. So he researched money managers in the U.K. and Scotland, and we developed our first file. Then I went over every year after that to follow up.

When the oil crisis hit, it occurred to me that Frank Russell Co. might be able to help the pools of capital in the Middle East. I made six trips there from 1975 to '80, but I was unsuccessful. It was ten years later that we got clients in the Middle East. I was asked by Citibank in London to give the wrap-up talk to a Bahrain

736

conference they were sponsoring in January 1986. But with all the hijackings, we figured that probably wasn't in our best interest. So I phoned Citibank, and they agreed to a videotape. Five or six of us said what we wanted to say on the tape, and, as a result, we have two very fine consulting relationships in the Middle East. And I've decided not to give any more speeches. I think videotapes are a whole lot more effective.

I had thought the Middle East would get us going internationally, but after our first false start, I decided we'd just finance our own effort. Jan Twardowski, who was a senior vice president at Vanguard, joined the company and went over to open our London office in 1979. From that office we service U.S. companies investing internationally that need research on managers and some Bermuda offshore captive insurance companies, mostly helping them select fixed-income managers and measure their performance. And then we have the domestic corporate clients, like Rolls-Royce, Rank Xerox, Vauxhall. We've limited ourselves to 25 clients in the United Kingdom. I think we have twenty now. Since 1986 we have a Tokyo office, and we'll be doing the same thing—exporting our technology and our business.

I have stood in front of a tremendous number of committees and boards trying to persuade the members to go international, and in those situations where some strong voice on the board says no, half the time I've been able to get over that hurdle by asking him what kind of car he drives. If that doesn't work, then I ask him what kind of a stereo system he has at home. I almost always win that one. I get him to start thinking about how internationalized we live every day and we just haven't translated that to our portfolios. For all practical purposes, that battle's now won.

In the U.K. the pension market was pretty much held by the merchant banks, and they really weren't too interested in sharing information. The main switch came when they realized they could start managing U.S. money. In order to qualify, they had to play it our way.

ERISA had its impact, though it didn't change my business a bit. But it got corporate officers and the boardroom to pay attention to the fund. And if the boardroom is paying attention and you want to up the salary levels of your people so you can hire better people, the answer will be, "Yeah, you'd better do that." So ERISA raised the professionalism of the whole effort.

We use a passive approach for some of the assets of our accounts. I mean, anybody with assets of $10 billion or more, you have trouble finding enough active managers. But all the assets can't be run passively. It's about 18 percent of all pension money now. When it gets up to a somewhat larger percentage, then some active managers will fall out and the better ones will survive, and you'll start seeing an alpha develop. There have been several times since I've been in the business when the S&P has beat the pants off the active managers. The period that we have just come through, and which might be ending now, has been the longest I've seen. But if you look at a fifteen-year time frame, using mutual fund data, mutual funds basically outperform the S&P. We are of the opinion, as are most sponsors, that over a long period of time, active managers can add value.

Editor: Everett Mattlin

Peter Vermilye

Chairman BARING AMERICA ASSET MANAGEMENT CO.

Peter Vermilye is one of the deans of the money management industry. His perspective of how money is managed at large institutions spans almost a half century. After spending 24 years at J.P. Morgan and Morgan Guaranty Trust, he was subsequently a partner and vice chairman of the investment committee at State Street Research & Management, president of Alliance Capital Management and senior vice president and chief investment officer of Citibank. Currently, he is chairman of Baring America Asset Management (until recently known as Endowment Management & Research Corp.), a subsidiary of Baring Brothers.

This activity that we money managers indulge in has a lot of the characteristics of a profession. It resembles the legal profession, the medical profession, the accounting profession, in that we go through a great deal of training and education—actually, it's a lifetime of learning that we have to do. We are fiduciaries dealing with our clients' financial health just as doctors are dealing with their patients' medical health or lawyers are dealing with their clients' legal rights.

In the old days the pension trustee or the pension manager was a fiduciary representing the employees, not the corporation. Throughout my Morgan days, we had that very clearly in mind. Now that distinction has been very badly blurred. Corporations are guaranteeing the pensions, making up the short-fall, so there has been a blurring of fiduciary responsibility. It was, I think, in the early '70s that people began to talk about the pension fund as a profit center for the corporation rather than as a pool of assets there for the benefit of employees.

What's different in the investment management profession as opposed to the medical profession or the legal profession is that investment managers who are superior can make an enormous amount of money for their clients. And if you can do that, you can expect to get paid a significant amount of money. In the old days the banks never charged more than an eighth of 1 percent for their assets. It took a while for Morgan, on any substantial sums, to get up to a quarter. It took a while for Citibank to get up to a quarter. Then along came the counselors, who said we can do a lot better than the banks. We can give you a 5 percent better return and therefore we're going to charge you 50 basis points, and some of them said we will charge 75 basis points, or 100.

At the same time, of course, the assets under management have grown enormously. At one time, say in the early '60s, when half-a-dozen banks had half the pension fund business in the country, the total pension business was less than $50 billion, and now it's well over a trillion dollars or whatever. Here in Boston, Fidelity, which had a few hundred million, is now tens of billions, and State Street Research, when I went there at the beginning of '65, had a few hundred million in mutual funds and Harvard's endowment and now has more than $10 billion of pension fund business. It's the same with outfits like Mass Financial and Putnam and Batterymarch.

And the profession, reflecting these changes, eventually became a business. The stream of earnings that was generated from higher fees on a larger and larger asset base enabled money management to become more and more of a business. And then you could sell that business.

Now, you never hear of a law firm or a medical group selling stock to the public. An investment firm's assets are its own people and its client relations. It has no other assets. Theoretically, at least, your people can leave at any point; it's not like a manufacturing firm, where you have plants and patented products and a very clear franchise.

That's one reason why I have difficulty with investment firms selling themselves. But that's what's happened. It is one of the basic developments of the time we're talking about, and it's now in full bloom. There are a few firms left—Capital Guardian, Fidelity—that are still in private hands, but most of the others have sold out. A number of the smaller firms have sold to Norton Reamer's United Asset Management. His approach puts the firms together in a fairly independent, autonomous structure. His approach, I think, assures a degree of permanence in that he ties up the principals thoroughly in a compensation stream more so than is possible for Alliance Capital or State Street Research & Management.

I think that over time when a firm sells out to, say, an insurance company, it has to take its toll. You are no longer the master of your destiny. Your opportunities to build equity or to earn very large returns are sharply diminished, and the incentive for younger people to come into these firms has to be a lot less than it was. Then you have a situation in some of these firms that sold out that the buyer assigned its senior people to three-year contracts. The senior people have control of substantial assets within those firms, and they have the option of going out on their own at the end of the three-year period. In order to try to retain them, the parent has to rewrite those contracts in a very generous manner, and that may be difficult for a mutual insurance company to do. Can they justify paying millions of dollars a year to investment professionals in a mutual insurance company? It remains to be seen how they're able to deal with that and what that does to the ongoing business.

As I said, your only assets are your people. And only the top 10 percent of the people in this business add value. I keep saying average people are worthless and mediocrity breeds failure. A mediocre analyst gets between a portfolio manager and a good idea and obfuscates the situation. A first-class analyst, a top 10 percent analyst, will steer you to it and shine the searchlight on the driving changes. And the top investment people like to work with peers who have the same quality and character and background and empathize with them in a compatible culture.

That's why you've had a stream of people out of the banks throughout the history of the last several decades. Morgan Bank was a very successful investment operation in its heyday, but it has had its troubles, and Citibank has had its troubles, as have most banks. The chief problems are, one, the compensation structure; secondly, the culture; and thirdly, the management, in almost all

741

cases. It's important to have investment people running invest-ment management businesses rather than commercial bankers. Those are the reasons banks, almost all of them, have set up separate subsidiaries. And I think that at this point they are prob-ably, for the most part, holding their ground to a much better extent than before.

It isn't size alone that causes trouble. Morgan Bank was a very successful investment operation in its heyday. In the mid-'60s it was probably as fine as any investment firm around, with maybe $10 billion in assets. So it can be done. But you have to manage your growth and manage the way you do business to cope with size. If you restrict the number of clients, if you concentrate on larger accounts, if you try to run them in a similar style or if you try to run them in separate operations where you have different types of investments run semi-autonomously, you can do it. There are a number of outfits that are over $10 billion in size that are still growing in a healthy manner. But you have to have the structure to cope with it.

To manage money successfully, I think you need exactly the same skills and talent that you always have. Above all, you need invest-ment judgment. You need enormous curiosity. You need a sense of causality. You need to be able to identify the driving forces that make economies and industries and companies rise and fall and to sense the quality of managements and sense who moves the mar-ketplace. This is as true today as it was when I started out in the business and in Bernie Baruch's or Jesse Livermore's day.

What is different now is that there is an enormously greater amount of information available from Wall Street. There are a dozen analysts on each industry, each company, that can tell you all you need to know. There's the immense computer power to massage and recall all of the figures. You have a communications network so that we can see on a television screen what's going on in a securities analysts' meeting in New York, or we can press a button on First Call and get all the leading brokers' information on any company and print it out instantaneously.

But with all that, a successful investor has to apply the same investment criteria. And I think the quality of investment professionals today is no better than it was 30 years ago. They just have a lot more information available to them. And though it is obviously more difficult to get superior *information* on a company, the crux of the matter is superior *judgment,* to know what to look for, recognize it when you see it and know how to weigh it. Sometimes I feel that there is so much emphasis today put on massaging the infinite amount of data available that people get distracted from identifying the critical variables. The qualitative distinctions get lost in the computer evaluations.

The use of quantitative techniques in managing portfolios has obviously become very important, too, not just pure indexing but selecting certain criteria and screening stocks for those criteria and managing funds on that basis. We do that here with part of our funds—though that's a minor part of our investment activity—to help us focus on areas and companies, but then we do fundamental work on top of that to corroborate what we turn up. And I think it's important to superimpose fundamental research on top of what comes up on the screen.

I think the better investment minds are just as able to provide superior performance now as they did before. For example, way back in 1960 we had at the Morgan Bank a brilliant young man who came running down to me with a light in his eye and said, "You have to buy Xerox. It has made an enormous breakthrough in how you copy everything." So we bought Xerox, and it went up 100 times in value. Now here at this firm we have a very bright young lady who came to us a couple of months ago and said Apple Computer has a major breakthrough. She was able to see the significance of what was happening in their whole new product line. And Apple Computer doubled in a few months.

Our philosophy here is identifying change, anticipating change. It's been the philosophy I've had in every institution—Alliance, State Street. Change is what drives earnings growth, and if you identify the underlying change, you recognize the growth before the market and the deceleration of that growth.

One of the driving changes today, for example, is the decline in the dollar. You note that the dollar has declined vis-à-vis Europe, where we compete in the paper industry, but it has not declined

743

vis-à-vis South America or Africa or Australia, where we compete in copper and aluminum. And so copper and aluminum have not done much, but paper stocks have doubled.

And one of the basic changes over the period we're talking about has been the globalization of the investment business. We are now one business world, one financial world. You can no longer make a decision about the attractiveness of U.S. chemical stocks without knowing what's going on in Europe, nor can you know what determines the attractiveness of a drug stock without knowing what's going on in Japan or Great Britain. And the strength or weakness of the dollar is crucial to the profitability of a number of our industries, so you have to think in those terms. The world is awash with liquidity, and how that is going to slosh into this country is vital in appraising the U.S. stock market and what's going to happen from here. You have to think in those terms and not just in parochial terms.

Financial institutions have been slow to recognize that. Only 4 percent of pension fund assets are invested overseas, whereas in Britain it's well over 20 percent. Some of the smarter investors like John Templeton and Harvey Molé at the U.S. Steel pension fund were early at this. Fidelity has done an excellent job internationalizing. I tried to do it at Citibank. But it's an expensive thing to do, and there's a lot of parochialism that has to be overcome. Nowhere near as much has been done as should be done, but the momentum is inevitable and it's just going to keep coming and coming and coming.

Twenty-odd years ago the U.S. Dow was selling at 1,000 and the Japanese Dow was selling at slightly above that. Now the Japanese Dow is selling at over 20,000 and ours is selling at 2,200, which indicates the enormous dynamism of the Japanese economy in the last twenty years. Obviously, that was the place to have your money over the two decades.

It's my judgment that the Japanese market has crested. Japanese companies are hurting very badly from the strong yen, earnings are down by over half in many major companies, and Taiwan and Korea and Hongkong are eating their lunch because their currencies have not gone up 50 percent, so they're able to end-run and sell to all the Japanese markets. It's my judgment that in the next two decades you will have the same dynamic growth in the better developing countries. Well, my answer to the Taiwanese

744

and the Koreans is, if you can't lick 'em, join 'em. Put as much money as you can get into their markets.

As more and more money became institutionalized, it led to stocks moving up and down more, and corporate managements became very aware of this and managed their affairs with this in mind. They took a much more short-term point of view, tried to maximize short-term earnings instead of looking to the future, as the Japanese did. A lot of the restructuring was brought about by this. Restructuring is good insofar as it enhances the productivity of capital and labor. Restructuring is bad insofar as it lays a lot of debt on a company that it then has to pay interest on and pay off as opposed to developing products and plants and a more efficient operation over time.

The one favorable effect on investors has been that management today pays a lot more attention to return on equity than it did twenty to 30 years ago. Twenty years ago you had to be a growth stock to get any attention from Wall Street. Now if you can get a 20 percent return on equity, pay good dividends, buy in your stock, you get a premium in the market. And this is a way of encouraging efficient use of capital, which in turn provides a more vibrant economy.

One thing has not changed. Bear markets still correlate with tightening money more than anything else. If I ever see the Fed tightening money significantly, I'm going to sell stocks hard.

Editor: Everett Mattlin

Barr Rosenberg

President ROSENBERG INSTITUTIONAL EQUITY MANAGEMENT

> Perhaps no one better epitomizes the advent of the "quants" as key figures in investment management as Barr Rosenberg. Since the 1970s Rosenberg has had uncommon influence in shaping investor thinking about risk and reward and its application as modern portfolio theory. After spending fourteen years in academia and with his portfolio consulting firm, BARRA, he started Rosenberg Institutional Equity Management in 1985.

When I started to write my thesis at Harvard in 1967, I had funding to develop more realistic econometric models using large data bases. I wanted to apply these models, and it seemed to me that there were two applications: finance and medicine. I wanted to help people, and medicine seemed an awful lot more appealing than finance. But it was very hard to collect the data base in medicine, and securities price data became readily available from Compustat, so finance was the application that took off.

The theory about decision making in the face of risk was really strong by the time I went to graduate school. Before that, there was a theory of capital, but there was no portfolio theory at all. The only theory, going back to the '20s or '30s, was a common-sense acknowledgment of diversification. The typical bank trust department bought one big stock—one big, safe stock—from each of ten to twenty industries, and that was your job. Common law at that time said that prudence meant buying safe things, so an institution would never buy little stocks. It never occurred to people that you could get more safety by buying stocks of small companies.

Academic research was showing that you could build a portfolio of stocks in which each had some risk, but in the aggregate there wasn't necessarily more risk. Also, there were efforts by several people at the University of Chicago that supported the idea that it was hard to predict the stock market.

The capital market theory argued that a portfolio that reflected the whole market would be efficient for someone who held consensus beliefs. Furthermore, it also meant that the market portfolio had minimum risk, in the sense that it got rid of all the diversifiable risk. It was obvious that this was a simplistic thing, but people took it as a beautiful and elegant description of what it was about risk that really mattered. However, it shook all of us up: We graduate students had been trained to think of only a single random variable, with its own mean and variance, but now we had to talk about covariance.

Performance studies also showed that the institutional investors weren't beating the market, suggesting that they didn't have superior beliefs. Professor [William] Sharpe noticed, as anyone else could have noticed, that if you add up everyone in the marketplace, by definition their average return is the market return. That just overwhelmed institutional investors.

In fact, ten years later Professor Sharpe said at a seminar that all the big bank managers got together, sitting around a table, and agreed on what they were going to do that year in terms of performance. Everyone said, "Well, we're going to outperform the market by 15 percent next year." It never occurred to them that they were the market.

The availability of data made it possible for academics to do research on performance. People like Bill Sharpe were not saying that nobody can beat the market. They were saying the average person could not beat the market. But that just collided with the marketing pretensions and the illusions and, possibly a little bit, with the corruption of institutional investors—corruption in the sense that they knew, really, that their advertising was misleading about rates of return compared with a performance index, but it was part of their business. The indexes did not include yield, but their rates of return did. It took me years to understand why everyone was so mad at people like Bill Sharpe.

People went overboard on it, partly because they were mad at institutional investors for claiming they could do something that maybe they couldn't. It was almost a social tension, and there was also a tremendous naiveté because they believed in all these hero myths.

748

When I arrived in the financial area as a professor at Berkeley, I also started consulting for Wells Fargo. I knew I was a good economist, and I felt I could model investment risk. I built a model that had two claims to fame—it was very good at predicting beta because it was aware of the multiple factors in the market, and it also identified multiple factors of risk and return. It was a perfect application of my theoretical techniques. American National Bank also hired me as a consultant to build a risk model for them, and I was able to use that as bootstrap funding to start a consulting firm. People needed a risk model, and the alpha and beta ideas of Bill Sharpe were very strong. Several graduate students that I had worked with became partners of BARRA. We realized that we had the capacity to build more sophisticated portfolio-building software.

We weren't the first to do many of the things we did. There was the Q-Group—the Institute for Quantitative Research in Finance, supported by Columbia University—and the Center for Research in Securities Prices at the University of Chicago, but we did things more thoroughly than others. People could take our tools to their firm and use them via Interactive Data Corp. BARRA did very well.

I was both a professor and the principal of BARRA from 1975 until 1983, when I resigned from the university. I was very happy teaching and consulting at BARRA. But money managers won't rely on a consultant for their key active management ideas—it's got to be in-house—and I wanted to see all of my ideas applied.

When I was asked in 1980 if I wanted to go into the active management business, I said no. I didn't have the maturity to be an active manager in 1980. In 1985 I felt that I did.

The first thing to realize is that modern portfolio theory says nothing about which stocks you should buy. It talks about how you should build a portfolio based upon your expectations. The role of the theory is like the relationship between an editor and an author. The author determines the material, and the editor just makes it work better. And any money manager can be the author of the alphas and then use portfolio theory, portfolio optimization, to build a better portfolio out of the alphas. Portfolio theory doesn't take a position on market efficiency. People think it does—it doesn't. It just talks about how you should build a portfolio based upon your expectations.

If you look at people who've been ahead of the market for five

749

years, their chances of being ahead for the next five years are not very good—only a little better than random. So this is a very difficult industry. But we felt it was entirely realistic to lead our clients to expect that we'd be ahead over 60 percent of the time. And, in fact, in our own planning we thought the probability was a lot higher than that. We felt we could be ahead most of the time, and ahead by a lot.

Index funds are an honest expression of incompetence. It's a vote for the inability to choose a good manager, so you put the money in an index fund. It's not saying I don't believe there is such a thing as a good manager. It's not saying I believe in efficient markets.

You have to remember you're buying stock from the same market that you're relying on to pay you more later. So somebody's got to change their mind, and if you're right, then they're wrong: Either they're wrong now, or they will be wrong in the future. How can you ever know for sure that someone is going to be wrong at a certain point in time? That's presumptuous. And for us to say that we can out-perform the market involves the same kind of presumptuousness. But we believe that for the kind of opportunities we are exploiting, it's quite realistic that other people are going to be wrong—an error that we can profit from.

Investment management is a knowledge industry. So academics are well suited for it. The financial markets are very efficient in the sense of allowing someone who knows something to take advantage of it. I can talk about the tea trade in Nepal, but I can't always act on what I think. The tea trade is influenced by people's tastes and by the production function of tea. Financial assets are pure—they pay money—so there's almost no element of taste in which one chooses. It's all measurable.

The greatest culture shock for me is that academics really care about ideas being right and about achieving a certain logical perfection, but business people care about ideas being useful. Even though you may have to have an idea right in order to make it useful, the business people just aren't as interested. It's as if every footnote that I ever put into an article was counterproductive in a sense, and that's hard for academics to learn.

Editor: Harvey D. Shapiro

Yves Oltramare

Former General Partner LOMBARD, ODIER & CIE.

Between 1960 and his retirement in 1986, Yves Oltramare was instrumental in transforming Lombard, Odier & Cie. from a small, local firm in Geneva, serving primarily private individuals, into a major, internationally oriented bank with a significant institutional clientele. After giving up the study of medicine, Oltramare trained at Lombard Odier in the late 1940s, then worked in the U.S. at Dominick & Dominick and Lehman Brothers, returning to Geneva in 1956 to build up an American-style research effort at Lombard.

It was not tax evasion that brought clients to Switzerland; it was fear of war, revolution and inflation. Obviously, if you try to hide your fortune somewhere, you are not going to declare it, and therefore you evade taxes. But I insist that Switzerland is not a tax haven. Above all, bank secrecy should be seen as a kind of protection for the individual.

This can be abused, but governments are not always right, either. When the British government was taking 80 to 90 percent of their income, plus most of their assets at death, you could not blame wealthy individuals for finding ways to fight that kind of exploitation. A former French minister said: "Switzerland is a reflection of our mistakes," and another added, "It has saved the fortunes of the French." Basically, our banking system respects individuals in a world in which individuals are more and more taken up in a system where they have nothing to say on their own.

We had gotten the money that sought refuge, not because we were Swiss per se, but because we had escaped many of the accidents of history. But in the last few decades, war in Europe has grown unthinkable. Recognizing that we were no longer going to get our clientele from those seeking refuge, we asked ourselves, what else could we bring to the world which others do not have? Having been a country of refuge, we were also a country of international fund management. And so, in the '60s we set about to sell this worldwide. We had a hunch that we would be in the middle of a very competitive world, and we wanted to be part of that competition. And as we saw the markets becoming institutionalized, we thought that we could attract those funds based on our international ability.

I think the only country with which we had—or, even today, really have—a feeling of being competitive in this regard is the United Kingdom. Switzerland has always had to manage internationally, because our domestic markets were far too small to absorb the amount of money we were given. You still don't find many who are international-minded in France, Germany or Italy. It is coming very fast, because the rules of the game are changing. You cannot resist a fact; you can just delay it. You are going to be wiped out if you don't adjust. It's amazing the fantastic speed at which it goes. The Big Bang in London will lead to a world financial market and to deregulation, and the competition is going to be fierce and free.

But going back to the infancy of these ideas, in 1956 I returned to Geneva after spending about six years in the U.S., mostly with Lehman Brothers. Very often at that time in America, one had the feeling that the world belonged to the Americans. I love America and wanted to become American. I had applied for my first papers, and if it hadn't been for the fact that I was asked to come back to Europe and became a partner very soon after that, I probably would have made my life in America. At that time it was rare to have a European who had spent so much time in the U.S., and we brought something to Europe about which little was known here: U.S. methods of investment research. So I built the investment research department at Lombard Odier, which, frankly, didn't exist seriously at that time.

In past years, we had gotten lots of money, but it was not very complicated to manage; you put it in a limited number of shares.

There was a tremendous stability. One just owned the *titres de père de famille* [blue-chip stocks] then. In addition, the Geneva banks had a complete lack of new blood, since, from the 1930s to the 1950s there had been little growth and, consequently, little change in personnel. Then all of a sudden, business developed very fast, starting in the mid-'50s. So we of the new generation could write our own tickets. It was a fantastic feeling. You sensed that something important was changing in Europe, and America was a real model at that time.

In about 1960 a group of friends and I formed the Groupement Européen d'Etudes Financières to bring American research methods to bear on European securities. We were a small group: Frenchmen (Pierre Cabon from Banque Mobilière Privée, today president of DAFSA, the European equivalent of S&P, and Géraud de Labeau, today president of an asset management company); one German (Michael Hauck from Georg Hauck & Sohn); one Dutch (Baron Adolf van Grovestins from what was then Mees & Zoonen and today chief general manager of ABN Bank); one British (Brian Rowntree from Kleinwort Benson and today managing director of A.P. Bank, London); and one Spanish (Mariano Rabadan from the Banco Popular Español). We did this as individuals, not as firms; we were just a little handful of friends. We looked at companies as investments in the context of their international competition, and we were the first to do this anywhere in the world. We believed that the best company *worldwide* would win and that you could not just choose the best one in your own country. These ideas that today are *élémentaires* were not known at all at that time. We still meet unofficially once a year for two days, though the group was disbanded in the early '70s.

In the meantime, we came out with a few studies of electronic issues, computers, steels, motor cars, among others. It was very hard, really. At that time you had no computer to work with and very little information. We tried to build up a kind of "common market" of financial studies. This was my great activity at the time; I wrote and spoke about it at conferences a great deal.

Occasionally, our work led to some embarrassments. We visited companies, and though we did not get inside information, we were surprised at how much more information we got than we could get just by reading the papers. With everybody telling you something, you really get a kind of impression. So we tried to project their profitability and rates of growth and occasionally were very successful indeed.

But one time I had a problem because one of my partners was on the board of directors of a company for which we published an earnings estimate. It was so close to reality that the president said to my partner, a very correct man who never spoke about his directorships, "Look, there must have been a leak." And my partner said, "Absolutely not. The only thing I can do is to send over the analyst, who will tell you exactly how they came to these figures." We didn't use very sophisticated methods then, but nine times out of ten we came pretty close. So, more and more, the European companies complained to the partners of our various enterprises that we were putting too much pressure on them. To the credit of our partners, they often said to these companies: "Look, these young people are the future; we'd better prepare ourselves to be more open." I can tell you it really was great fun because we felt that we were doing something not just for our countries, but for a continent that was becoming progressively modernized.

I think we were among the first European firms to make trips to the U.S. to tell American institutions that someday they would not rely entirely on the dollar, but would have to be multi-currency and multinational in their investments. Then we had to fight to hire people with the right technical training. "Fight" is perhaps too strong. But in my experience, when you have the image of being successful, you get good people. We did not always have that image. Originally, we had the reputation of a good, solid, stuffy, local old firm. But when we built up aggressively, this brought us recognition as people who really wanted to be part of the game. The change occurred as Lombard built up its team of analysts, and also because we were pioneers. We had our first international investment trust in 1950; we were among the first to launch an international investment service in English and to develop institutional expertise; and we were the first foreign firm to join the New York Stock Exchange.

In any event, when we first went to the U.S., the demand among a small number of institutions—perhaps twenty or 30— for the information we could supply very much exceeded our expectations. They didn't do much trading through us, but they wanted the information. At that time you had an explosion of the European markets because of foreign exchange liberalization in December 1959, but then a collapse in 1962. First, the interest equalization tax ruined the business; then, when the IET was repealed in 1974, ERISA was enacted. It was three to five years before U.S. institutions invested overseas again. So from 1962 until about 1978 we served the U.S. institutional market without much result. That's a hell of a long time. In the meantime, the dollar collapsed.

The first, pre-1962 wave of international investing turned out to be a wave of vast speculation, just a short-term fad. American managers thought they were in for the long term, but when they lost a lot of money, they lost their jobs. The next managers were quite conservative and thought, "We lose nothing by staying in the U.S." It took a very long time before Americans came back into European markets. The mentality this time is totally different; they will not be dissuaded by short-term declines. I think that Americans—finally—are in the international markets for good. And today in Europe you are seeing two very exciting trends for the stock markets: the privatization of companies that had been nationalized, and then a lot of private companies going public. Together with Big Bang, I think, these events have changed completely the face of the financial system.

At the same time, the recent scandals could lead to our being surrounded with more legalities. We have seen this in Switzerland after the Investors Overseas Services episode that culminated in the early '70s. For example, before [IOS founder Bernard] Cornfeld, we had lots of investment trusts in Switzerland, and there was no real supervision because they were playing the game in a very correct way. In 1967 we got a special law regulating investment trusts. Each scandal brings additional regulations and laws. And the more laws you have, the more people believe that what is *not* prohibited is legal, so the more loopholes people find.

It is a shame about IOS for another reason, because it started with a very strong premise. As I understood it, it was a kind of network of worldwide investment trusts. This was an exciting idea. It's the way it was exploited that was disreputable. IOS went

755

to all the private banks here looking for cooperation in managing the money, and, you know, this is a small place. In one day firms had exchanged views, and I must say that immediately people decided it was not our cup of tea, according to our standards. They were inviting people to lunch or dinner, taking pictures of them, then pretending that they were your advisers, when it wasn't true. They held a conference, *Pacem in Terris*, which was a mixture of religion, finance and moralizing. It was really strange. I must say they were fabulous at publicity. When the banks here wouldn't cooperate, IOS reacted by saying, "Well, after all, they are very stuffy, conservative people," and so on.

When IOS went public, they approached the banks here again and tried to get them to participate in the syndicate. We wouldn't do it, so they instructed people to buy through us and the other banks so as to force us to cooperate. And members of some families who were against the banking side also chose to buy shares. One woman who didn't have very much money came to us to buy shares. I said, "You shouldn't touch it with a ten-foot pole." She said, "You're just prejudiced." I said, "No, no—look at the balance sheet." But she went ahead and did it and lost everything.

Since that time, the competitive lines in our little Geneva community have changed a good deal. I used to think the private banks should do more things together while preserving their individuality. Today that would not be my idea, because some of us have changed our character, in that we have come to be a very large private bank with international impact, while others have chosen to remain relatively local and concentrate on private clientele. In the competition for international business, one group here that probably attracts a clientele that is not by definition ours is the big American banks such as Chase and Citicorp. The mere fact that these banks have a reputation worldwide makes clients want to have an account in Switzerland. Middle East clients go to names they have heard of in the institutional business, which would include us and Pictet, for instance. And private banks that are not 200 years old and dominated by old Geneva families have significantly increased their competitive power; in this group you have banks which are doing an excellent job.

The notion that Swiss rates are high is a little bit of a legend. What struck most people were the double commissions charged— first the American and then the Swiss on top of that. But we have all started negotiating commissions, and now obviously they have become very low. The client is probably happy to pay a special rate if he can see that the firm is stable, if he meets with the same people he has confidence in. You don't go to a firm for a label; you go for the quality of the people. A good hotel is one where you have the same concierge for twenty years.

But in times like these, when business is good for all of us, one does not think so much about client competition as about people competition. I guess that the thing of which I am proudest is helping one of the oldest Genevese and European firms to handle the turn of the next century successfully, by leaving it in strong hands.

The game now is—and will remain—international investing. Interestingly, since the war, whenever Americans have invested overseas they have had a weakness for German companies. You see, we are in a business where we pretend to be objective; but in fact we start sentimentally to decide what we want to buy, and then we try to prove our own point. I don't want to underestimate the Germans' enormous qualities, but Americans had a tendency to overestimate them because they were hard workers, serious, with not too much of a sense of humor, and to underestimate people who they felt were a little bit lightweight, but who were full of sensitivity and finesse. We had great difficulty in convincing American institutions that the French market had a far better choice of companies, for instance. Even today, Germany is way behind France and England in privatization and opening markets to the public.

And what now? I think the world faces a crisis because America has problems that are absolutely staggering. It has lost its aggressiveness. It does not recognize that the world around it has developed and that in some ways America is being passed by. Then there is America's debt. It's like an astronomer's black hole, it is of such a magnitude and so complex. I think we will all go into the black hole—and I am sure that on the other side another light will come—but in the hole you will discover that the laws of physics are different.

It's like 1938. Everybody said there would be a war, but nobody knew what exactly would start it. The problems will create not only financial but psychological difficulties. The masses are not going to adjust psychologically; the political system will modify itself and become more of a dictatorship. It's very dangerous.

But you really don't need to run into a major crash. What you could very well foresee is the penetration of the best Japanese and European firms into the United States, taking advantage of cheap dollars and buying America. In fact, the Japanese could be preparing their own competition. You may very well see in the next century the opposite situation: an enormous deficit in Japan, a big surplus in the United States. America is a fabulous country; it has a capacity of absorption which is absolutely fantastic. So, long-term I have enormous confidence. But in the meantime, I am staggered. Americans have to go through a difficult period until they wake up to new realities—but it's fun, it's constructive, it's challenging.

Editor: Heidi S. Fiske

Haruo Mayekawa

Former Governor BANK OF JAPAN

A career Bank of Japan official who took time out to serve as deputy president of Japan's Export-Import Bank before becoming governor of the Bank of Japan in 1979, Haruo Mayekawa has had exceptional experience in international finance. After he stepped down from the bank's leadership two years ago, he was tapped by Prime Minister Yasuhiro Nakasone to head a distinguished group of business and financial leaders, which developed the so-called Mayekawa report. To date, the controversial report, which calls for a restructuring of the Japanese economy, has yet to be implemented.

In the past twenty years Japan has experienced three big economic changes. The first was the move from high to lower economic growth in the 1960s; then there were the two oil shocks—in 1973 and in 1978. Japan's economic growth had been based on low energy costs, so the huge rise in oil prices was *literally* a big shock. High energy costs led the economy to move from heavy industries to high technology, high-value-added industries—like electronics, automobiles and machine tools—industries that don't use too much in the way of raw materials or energy. Now again we are going into a new era of structural change. The Japanese economy still is export oriented, but it has to change.

The financial pace has lagged behind industrial change. While I was at the Bank of Japan, I tried hard to revitalize the financial sector and to remove restrictions as far as possible. However, financial deregulation has not been carried out so quickly. That's the case, of course, all over the world. Even in the United States, the removal of the regulations on interest rates and deposits took several years. So in Japan, too, interest rates, particularly of deposits, are still in the liberalization stage and are not fully liberalized yet.

I am not satisfied with the progress that has been made in this country. It's too slow, it seems to me. And among the things I regret most since I left the Bank of Japan is that this liberalization and deregulation in the financial field was not as fast as I expected. There is always a political problem or a tax problem or an administration problem involved. In this country financial institutions have been protected for many years. The big city banks are quite strong. They can compete with foreign banks and financial institutions. However, the smaller institutions have been quite immune in the past from such competition.

In addition, there is a trade-off of how to liberalize the financial sector while protecting small savers. In Japan the savings rate is rather high, partly because Japanese people are thrifty compared with those in other countries. Another reason is that small savers are protected by the authorities, which also promoted this high savings rate. People feel the government will protect small savers. It's quite different from the United States, where a deposit insurance system is well established. When the management of a financial concern is bad and the institution goes broke, that insurance will cover the loss. However, in Japan such insurance is not well developed, so the government or central bank tends to protect savers.

In the past, savers have put their money into financial institutions, and the banks in turn lent the money to business corporations. So relationships between corporations and the banks were very close. But more recently, the big, prime-name companies can easily raise money in the markets—not only in this country but in Europe and the United States. So direct financing has started to be very popular among these big corporations—although smaller-sized corporations and businesses still tend to go to the banks.

When I was appointed governor of the Bank of Japan in 1979, about the time of the second oil shock, I was very much concerned not to repeat the inflationary situation of 1973–74, when prices in

Japan jumped by 30 percent. Another factor I had to consider was that the yen tended to be weak. In 1984 people in the U.S. administration boasted that the strong dollar was good for the U.S. economy. That meant that the yen tended to be weak—and the balance-of-payments imbalance started to increase for Japan.

In the U.S. the Bank of Japan and the Japanese government were criticized for manipulating the yen to weaken it. One magazine editor, for instance, wrote several times that the Bank of Japan was manipulating the yen. I met with him and talked with him, and he seemed to be persuaded. But on his return to the U.S. he wrote it again. It made me mad. It's a kind of political propaganda.

Bank of Japan officials face a very difficult problem. I sympathize with them. *Nobody* can control the exchange market. The exchange market is influenced by market expectations. So as long as the basic economic policies of the leading industrialized nations do not converge, market expectations tend to produce quite wide fluctuations. From that point of view, the Paris agreement [of 1987 among leading industrialized countries] rightly suggested policy coordination was necessary.

From time to time, we central bankers got together in Basel at the meetings of the Bank for International Settlements. I myself attended such meetings three or four times a year, usually when Paul Volcker was there, and we exchanged views and information quite freely. There was no serious conflict between us. Every central banker is in a more or less similar situation. There should be a kind of coordination between fiscal and monetary policy; however, over the past ten years or so the fiscal side has reflected the inflationary trend all over the world, and fiscal policy has not been so well used. So the policy burden has tended to be very heavy on monetary policy. It's unfortunate that there isn't better coordination between fiscal and monetary policy.

To a certain extent, if central bankers were running the world, everything would work better. However, the fiscal and budgetary situations are influenced by politics. Every country has a similar problem. We cannot say too much. All central banks have to live with the situation.

Japan has faced another international criticism recently. As long as Japan's current account shows a surplus, that means—it's an accountant's rule—that Japan will export capital by that amount. As long as the current account accumulates, then Japan's creditor position will increase. It's inevitable. We are trying hard to reduce the current account surplus through structural adjustment of the economy. Just how soon we shall succeed I don't know. It will take several years because of the size of the surplus, $90 billion in 1986. It's very difficult to wipe out a surplus that big in a short period of time.

When Japan joined the BIS in the 1960s, Japan was a capital importer. Nobody ever expected a change. In fact, the vast balance-of-payments surpluses of Japan only started in 1982; before that the surpluses were not so big. In any event, the balance-of-payments problem is not one country's work. It is a bilateral, multilateral trading problem. In the case of the Japanese surplus, it can be seen as the mirror image of the U.S. deficit.

To do something about our surplus, we produced the "Mayekawa report." For this we have been criticized by famous Japanese economists. Such people criticized us on the grounds that the surpluses are not of Japan's making, but are mirror images of the U.S. deficits. Unless the U.S. takes steps to correct its imbalances, the Japanese surpluses will not decline.

Our idea, as explained in the Mayekawa report, is that Japan's economy is interrelated with other countries' these days, and Japan must bear responsibility for the functioning of the world economy. Although the U.S. has a certain responsibility about these imbalances, Japan does, too. The Japanese economic structure is export oriented. Nobody doubts that. So we have to take measures to correct it from our side. But it's also true that in order to reduce the imbalances in external trade between Japan and the U.S., Japan's efforts alone are not sufficient.

The Mayekawa report was presented to the prime minister in April 1986 and met with a mixed reception. In the year since then, the yen's appreciation has been quite rapid. In 1986 the yen stood at 180-190; now it's 145 or so. And this rapid appreciation has changed the mood of the economy in Japan. Most exporting companies no longer find it profitable to export goods from Japan, so they are planning to go outside to manufacture offshore. Such events have produced a growing recognition among businesses that adjustments are necessary. But there is also an awareness that the adjustments will cause lots of pain. A typical example is the coal mining industry. It has already decided to cut production in half, so mines are being shut down and miners have lost their jobs. Steel companies want to cut production by a quarter and lay off people by a quarter in three years. The shipbuilding industry has to close shipyards. The metal industry, too, is facing retrenchment. Although there is acceptance of the need for structural change, inevitably there is unhappiness.

The only solution is economic and industrial restructuring—and to enforce the Mayekawa report. I am not responsible for implementation of these policies. Their implementation, however, is a most important, very urgent need. Prime Minister Yasuhiro Nakasone really means business. He is quite anxious to implement the Mayekawa report as soon as possible. But its implementation will mean lots of difficulties.

Editor: Kevin Rafferty

Jean-Maxime Lévêque

Chairman CRÉDIT LYONNAIS

An eighteen-year veteran with Crédit Commercial de France, Jean-Maxime Lévêque was one of the most outspoken critics of the sweeping nationalization program adopted by the Mitterrand government in 1981, which included CCF. To dramatize his protest, he resigned as chairman in 1982 to campaign against further state intervention in the French economy. The following year, Lévêque and several former CCF officers put together a Curaçao-based holding company with a bank in Luxembourg. The formation of a new conservative government in 1986 brought Lévêque back to mainstream French banking with his appointment as chairman of Crédit Lyonnais.

In the early 1960s there were many people in France who did not have a bank account; either they had a small account at the post office or an account with a savings bank, but they did not go to the commercial banks with their deposits. And therefore the French banks had an enormous market to create—which is what they did in the period from 1965 to 1975. For ten years there was a fantastic development of banking activities in France.

Within the French market, all the positions of the different banks during this decade were in some way frozen. They were not free to open new branches, and all the conditions under which they were lending money—the level of interest rates, the level of the fees for services that they provided to the customers—were regulated by the monetary authorities. Each bank had to ask the central bank for its approval before granting a loan to any corporate customer. So when I arrived at Crédit Commercial de France in 1964, the situation of each individual bank in France was also protected. And for certain banks it was extremely bad because it was an incentive not to move but to stay as they were. And at that time Crédit Commercial de France was rather sleepy.

But this was also the period when the government began to realize that this policy of too much regulation was a very bad policy. And in 1967 the minister of finance and the government decided to grant much more freedom and to deregulate part of the banking activities. I knew that would happen rapidly, and what I did when I came to Crédit Commercial de France was to prepare for more competition and for that new freedom. I tripled the bank's network of branches, which was obviously insufficient in France, and created a new department for dealing in the Euromarket. And I think that these two big changes were the two main reasons for the success of Crédit Commercial de France.

Of course, banking is like all the commercial activities, an activity based on the use of human resources. And I think that I was also able at Crédit Commercial de France to create a situation in which all the people who worked there had a sense of conquest and of developing marketing techniques. Furthermore, as Crédit Commercial de France was one of the banks which had the luck not to have been nationalized just after the Second World War, it was easy for me to make all the people working at the bank understand that they could not rely on anyone other than themselves. This was necessary in order to create the confidence of the market, so that we could constantly increase our capital by issuing new shares.

And it was a kind of message that the big nationalized banks could not convey to their own staffs. I think that in emphasizing private ownership of the capital of Crédit Commercial de France, I helped all the people who were working with me to have a much better knowledge of what could make their own success. Because when an enterprise is owned by the state there is a feeling of safeness that expands among the staff and which is not favorable to competitive and aggressive behavior.

What I did not like about the system of nationalization was that the development of the nationalized banks was exempt from the constraints of the stock market. These banks have always been run by people who were appointed by the French government and who were not using the same policies as the managers of private banks as far as financial information about their banks was concerned. And I think that this was damaging to the functioning of the entire banking system in France.

But this has not at all created difficulty for their international activities, because abroad they were in the game of competition with all the banks in the world; all French banks have been quite free to elaborate their international policies. And I don't see any difference between the policy that Crédit Lyonnais followed outside France and the policy that other big, privately owned banks were conducting all over the world.

The difference between a nationalized company and a private company pertains to the relationships with the market and with the public. Nowadays the French government is reprivatizing many nationalized companies, and especially the banks. This means that the French people, the French financial market and finally the international financial market will be much more interested in knowing exactly the financial situation of the French banks. It is very important because people will understand more about banking and about the policy of the French banks; it will be much more a question of public interest than it was in the past. Furthermore, I think that there will be a change in the managements of the banks because they will become independent of the state.

I became an outspoken opponent of the Socialists' nationalization program because it was very dangerous for France that, step by step, all the big French enterprises should become state property. First of all, it is necessary in a modern democracy and in a modern economy to have enterprises as independent from the state and from political circles as possible. The second reason is that it's very dangerous in a country to transform everybody into wage earners and only wage earners, into people who have no savings invested in the enterprises. Because then the people are not interested in knowing where the money for the development of the companies comes from; they believe it comes from the state. On the contrary, when all the big companies are private, people understand that the development of the economy comes from the stock market, that the market will respond only if the companies are successful and that they must be interested in investing in the equity of companies.

In France since the end of the war, the state has nationalized—confiscated and kept for itself—a great part of the wealth of the French economy. Our stock exchange was therefore one of the smallest among the Western countries; French people were not interested in French shares; and there were a lot of people who did not consider possible or feasible having a certain capital of their own. It meant that they were completely dependent on the state, that is, on the policy of the state concerning social security and retirement schemes.

The main project that the leftist parties presented to the public in the presidential election of 1981 consisted of further nationalizations. And what was extremely curious was that the parties of the rightist coalition didn't seem to be concerned with this problem. They did not think that in fighting against the Socialists' nationalization program, they would gain any votes. And it was true at that time that public opinion was not interested. I knew why: It was because France was already in a situation in which the state owned too many enterprises, and there were too few private shareholders. Public opinion was completely uninterested in the question.

I considered it necessary to explain that if we French continued to be completely uninterested, one day we would discover that the state finally owned all the dynamic wealth of the country. And we would also discover that everybody was completely dependent on the state. It was necessary that someone *say* that. And I was backed by all the people who were working at Crédit Commercial de France; that gave me the possibility of dramatizing my departure from the bank. I am the one who first pronounced the word "denationalization" in France.

Nowadays there is only one thing that counts for me: It is to succeed in transforming Crédit Lyonnais, which is a very big French state-owned bank into a very big, privately owned bank. And I think already there are a lot of people inside Crédit Lyonnais who are interested in this project; they realize today that it will be a new chance for Crédit Lyonnais and at the same time a new challenge. They feel closer to their corporate customers because they will have the same constraints as the private enterprises. It is very important, because I would not be able to persuade the people *outside* the bank to buy shares of Crédit Lyonnais if the entire staff were not interested.

I'm not only encouraged by the success of privatization in France so far, I'm encouraged by my own ideas. I have always said that privatization of the big French companies would be an enormous success because the French public will discover something that is quite stimulating. French people are discovering what capitalism really is.

Editor: David Cudaback

Rong Yiren

Chairman CHINA INTERNATIONAL TRUST AND INVESTMENT CORP.

World War II and the Chinese Communists' seizure of power in 1949 thwarted Rong Yiren's ambitions to build a major textile operation in Shanghai. Having gained a measure of political stature during the 1950s, Rong suffered at the hands of the Red Guards during the Cultural Revolution of the late 1960s. Following Chairman Deng Xiaoping's formulation of a more open economic policy for China in 1978, Rong was tapped to set up China International Trust and Investment Corp., which was to serve as the country's window to the outside financial world.

After the liberation of new China in 1949, I served as deputy major of Shanghai and deputy minister of the textile ministry. For a long time I served as a delegate to the National People's Congress, so I had some political stature. Chairman Deng Xiaoping was only one of the state leaders I knew; other leaders included Chairman Mao Zedong, former premier Zhou Enlai, General Zhu De and President Liu Shaoqi. But for ten years during and after the Cultural Revolution, which started in 1966, I was a prisoner.

When Deng Xiaoping came to power, Marshal Ye Jianying, who is one of my close friends, reintroduced me to Chairman Deng. By the end of 1978 our party had laid down a policy to open the country to the outside world and to revitalize the national economy. In February 1979, Chairman Deng arranged a meeting attended by some former industrialists and entrepreneurs. He hoped that we could play a role and that I could contribute my share to this endeavor.

My ideas were formalized when Chairman Deng talked to me. The idea behind setting up CITIC is not something new; I drew on the experience I gained some years before 1949, when I ran enterprises. The state council also asked me to be in charge of the preparatory work, so in October 1979 CITIC came into being. The guideline the corporation follows is to become a window opening to the outside world. Immediately after the inception of our corporation, I traveled to the United States and Hongkong to make contacts with foreign partners. The purpose of CITIC is to attract financiers, bankers and industrialists to China for investment cooperation.

People still ask whether China's open policy can continue and whether the policy can be consistent. But the experience of the past seven years has proved that our policy has been well implemented, developed and promoted. CITIC's staff has grown from several dozen to close to 1,000, not including workers in CITIC factories.

Initially, the number of foreign business executives coming to China to set up joint ventures was limited. Both foreign business people and Chinese had their worries; after so many years of a closed-door policy, Chinese were afraid of having contacts with foreign partners. To lessen their worries we shouldered the responsibility; we took the initiative to contact the outside world, and through us the domestic enterprises did their business. We also took an initiative in floating securities and bonds in other nations. When we had explained this, other enterprises also saw it as a way of raising money. Other CITIC firsts were to start leasing and real estate businesses. You probably know that the word "landlord" is not a popular one in China. But we realized that foreign business partners, when they came to China, needed offices and apartments; so by launching CITIC Real Estate last year we helped them. The design of the CITIC building itself was started almost simultaneously with the establishment of our corporation. Another problem for foreigners coming to China is to get help on economic, accounting and legal matters, so we set up China International Economic Consultancy. We have also gone into overseas investment to help China achieve a stable supply of essential materials.

I don't want to compare the operations of my corporation with others. My essential idea is to let everyone give good play to their ideas, to let everyone blaze new trails in the development of business operations. In 1984 Chairman Deng Xiaoping wrote, "Be bold in creativity and make contributions." The idea can also be put this way: Some in China are worried about contacting the outside world; they are afraid of being labeled "capitalist management." My view is very clear: The methods and approaches in capitalist management, if they can survive for so long, must have their merits. So we can use those parts which are beneficial to the development of our socialist economy—and, of course, discard the bad things.

I don't want to argue, because each nation has the right to decide which kind of system it wishes to follow. I think capitalism has failed in China. In the past I tried, but failed. But during the past seven years, CITIC has grown to be a diversified conglomerate with investments in about 180 enterprises. "Conglomerate" is the concept or terminology borrowed from the Western world; we call CITIC a socialist conglomerate.

We are developing CITIC into a holding company. In addition to functional departments, we are making efforts to set up or establish subsidiaries. Very soon we are going to open CITIC Industrial Bank, CITIC Development and CITIC Trade. In addition, we are making preparations to organize CITIC Tourism, CITIC Travel and CITIC-Tianjin Industrial Development Corp.; in Hongkong we are making preparations for CITIC Hong Kong Holdings. The major task of CITIC Industrial Bank is to encourage investment. We will have branch offices in places where we are doing big investments. In Hongkong we bought Ka Wah Bank, so Ka Wah and CITIC will join their hands as we have to extend our business to other nations.

We have a dual purpose—to serve the national economic development and to improve the people's living standards. The question of selling shares to the public is being considered, but the percentage, the amount, will be restricted. The making of profits is only the ways and means for the extension of economic development through which people's living standards can be lifted, not our ultimate goal. I am proud of the fact that CITIC is following a correct road in opening the nation to the outside world and revitalizing the economy. Of course, there are also some unhappy things, because we are in the process of reform, and some things need to be improved. These include red tape and complicated procedures and time wasted on arguments.

I don't think that there is a chance that the Cultural Revolution will be repeated. It was a big waste of ten years, which need to be made up by several dozen years. The Communist Party has the huge merit that it always summarizes its bitter experience and corrects mistakes and continues making progress. I am not a member of the Communist Party; I hope someday I can be a member. Rank-and-file Communist Party members need only to reach the level of political understanding. To be a true Marxist-Leninist, a person of my status needs a deeper understanding of the theory of Marxist-Leninism. Of course, time is running out for me; I am sort of beginning to tire. It's more than just reading some Marxist-Leninist books; it is more important to have a clear understanding, an analysis of the international situation and of things developing in an economic world and to combine the objective situation with the real situation. It needs huge efforts to truly understand.

Of course, there are other people of similar background to mine, who were industrialist entrepreneurs. They are scattered to all parts of the nation. At present they are doing the same thing as I am doing: They are all working for socialism. Right after my graduation from St. John's University in Shanghai in 1937, I went to work in my own factory. At that time the Japanese imperialists invaded China. Our nation and my factory suffered a lot until 1945. When I left St. John's I had a very high ideal to devote myself to develop a big business, but I failed. Between 1945 and 1949, when new China was established, I had a hope that my family business would be restored, that the nation could develop and go ahead. But my hope vanished.

In almost the same length of time, less than eight years, I have already established CITIC. This is a big achievement, this is a big comfort. Whenever the policy the government is following is correct, the nation as a whole can advance. This will entail improvement of the living standards of the people. The people as a whole will never be against this, and they will give firm support. We don't deny there are certain people with egotistic ideas, individualistic to such a degree that they only think about themselves; they don't think about the nation's welfare. In the world there are a lot of nations, so everything cannot go in one way.

Editor: Kevin Rafferty

Stanley Ross

Managing Director DEUTSCHE BANK CAPITAL MARKETS

> The raffish, irreverent Stanley Ross has been a fixture in the Euro-bond market since its formative days. He traded the first Eurobond issue and went on to become one of the secondary market's most prominent, and controversial, figures. After a celebrated falling out with his superiors at Kidder Peabody, he founded his own firm, Ross & Partners, and promptly sent shock waves through the industry by popularizing "gray market"—preissue—trading. Today he is overseeing the Eurobond trading activities of Deutsche Bank Capital Markets in London.

W hen the Euromarket took off, I was working at Strauss Turnbull. I used to work in the settlement department there, until one day Julius Strauss went down to the basement where I was working. "Hello, my boy," he said. "What are you doing?" Then he spotted a book I had beside me. "What is this?" he said. "Is this *Proust?*" "Yes, sir," I said. I used to read everything and anything. "But," he said, "this is volume *six.*" And I said, "Yes, and I shall read the other six." "Goodness me!" he said. So he goes upstairs and calls in his partners. "There's a boy in the office reading Proust," he tells them. "I'm going to give that boy a chance." And that's how I came to work with Julius Strauss. The biggest stroke of fortune in my life was that that book happened to be there on the desk at that time. If it hadn't, I might still be a back-office clerk.

At Strauss Turnbull I traded the very first Eurobond issue, Autostrade. Julius Strauss came in one day and said, "Do you want some good news or some bad news?" And I said, "Oh, Christ, Julius, I'm too busy. I haven't got time. What is it?" He said, "The good news is we're going to be broker to a new type of issue—a Eurobond issue." I said, "Oh, yeah, that's great. Okay. So what's the bad news?" He said, "You've got to trade it."

So we had to trade this blasted thing. It really was a nuisance. But then suddenly it was followed by another one, and another one, and another one. And suddenly we had a whole new market building up. Then I remember we discussed whether I should stay on the equity side, and I said: "No, I think this bond side is really becoming very important, and I don't want to leave it. Everyone's trying to get into the game. It's the new game." So I refused to be put into the equity side. And I ended up going to Kidder in 1967.

Kidder seduced me with the usual American-type story. You know, "We're going to give you a huge amount of money to trade with, we're going to do this, we're going to do that." So I joined Kidder and they said, "Okay, now here's your capital." And it was Sf500,000, which I think was worth about $135,000 in those days. And I think, if you check today, you'll find that the capital of Kidder, Peabody Securities is still Sf500,000.

It was only the establishment of Euroclear that came to the rescue of the markets; otherwise, we would never be the market we are today. In those early days all the settlements were done in New York, and every firm in the business had a different firm settling for them. At Kidder we had Schroders. We had a situation where we were sending long telexes to Schroders: "Received, received, received. Deliver, deliver, deliver." Well, they received everything, but they didn't deliver anything. And when they received, they charged us interest on the money they paid out against the bonds. So suddenly we found ourselves with this huge overdraft and nobody getting any bonds.

I caught a plane to New York and went down into the Schroders vaults. A guy comes up to me—I remember him still. He had a big belt with all sorts of keys and things hanging down from it and a battery of pens in his shirt pocket. He said, "What do you

774

want, Mac?" And I said, "Well, I'm here to see the Kidder Peabody settlement records." He came back with this enormous thing and threw it down in front of me. When I opened it, all these dozens of delivery instructions fluttered about and I said, "Oh, my God, my God." I just sat there with my head in my hands. And ten minutes later somebody came up to me and put his arm around my shoulder and said, "Never mind, Stanley, I am here since three months." It was Wolfgang Kron of the Deutsche Bank. He had turned a $13 million debit into a $20 million credit. And that was real money in those days.

So I reckoned the best thing that I did for Kidder was to take my $135,000 to Brussels and see Charles D'Ursel of Morgan Guaranty, who I knew had been talking about setting up a clearing system. I said, "Look, I've got $135,000. I want to give it to you. I want you to take a million dollars of bonds in." And so we became the first people in Europe in Euroclear. I'm quite proud of that.

Then a group of us got together—about seven or eight of us—and we said, "Let's have a drink together every couple of weeks and talk about what we're doing." Because this market was all fairly new and we all had problems. It was late 1968, I think. We called up all the people who made prices—we found nineteen of them—and we all met at Rothschilds and we said, "Okay, let's form an association." And that was the start of the AIBD [Association of International Bond Dealers]. I'm proud of the fact that I was on the first board and that I wrote the first set of rules. I'm quite pleased that most of those rules are virtually unchanged today. The other day, in fact, I was asked to arbitrate something, and one of the parties was saying, "Okay, under this rule I can do such and such." And I said, "Well, I wrote the rule, and I know you can't interpret it that way, because that's not how I wrote it."

The floodgates opened in 1968 when the U.S. government decreed that if American companies operating abroad wanted funds they had to raise them abroad. You had an enormous number of convertible issues by all sorts of companies. I remember once we had an order on the telex from a bank in Zurich for ICC convertibles. ICC was Robert Vesco's company. And I telexed back, "We've stopped trading those." They asked me why, and I said, "Because I hear a rumor that they're not going to pay their coupon." There was a long pause and then—Ding! Ding! Ding!—the telex was going, and it spelled out very haltingly,

"This is Robert L. Vesco at the machine." And he went on to say that this was a totally bad rumor, that this couldn't happen, and how dare we report such a thing? Anyway, that night Vesco sent telexes out to everyone in the Eurobond market—anyone listed anywhere, saying, "There are rumors circulating in London, and they are totally without foundation, etc."

Everyone talked about the Belgian dentists in those days. I must confess I didn't know any Belgian dentists. The big Swiss banks were the takers of bonds. And they took them for accounts that were, maybe, hot money, where the accounts really didn't care, you know. I think those accounts often took a bashing.

Then we had the oil embargo in 1973, 1974. Things were really bad in those days. We even lost money trading on bonds. But we went into other areas; I took Kidder into trading the U.K. investment currency premium. You may recall that U.K. residents could only buy securities abroad if they were to actually purchase the currency, and there was only a certain pool of currency available. When everyone wanted to invest abroad, the premiums for the currency could be as much as 15 or 20 percent. In John Galvanoni I had a star player in this market. So when everyone else was really hurting, we were able to continue to show some big profits. I remember [Kidder chief executive] Ralph DeNunzio asked me to come over, and I brought John Galvanoni with me, and I said, "Look, here's the guy who's really been the key to it all." And Ralph said—he's a very greedy guy—"Okay, if we give you ten times the position, can you make ten times the profit?" And John said: "No, it doesn't work that way. We're already the biggest in the market." And we were.

We were also more involved in equities in those times, in the Japanese convertibles. In the mid-'70s we made some big turns every day on the yen, because at that time the yen was beginning to move. We had a tremendous time. We were selling shares, receiving yen, and we wouldn't sell the yen. I mean, every day the yen went up in value against the dollar, and we would never sell the yen. People like Nikko and Nomura used to send us frantic telexes: "If you do not sell your yen today, we shall sell it for you." We made a fortune for Kidder in trading a relatively small amount of Japanese convertible issues.

776

We also put Kidder in a much better position in Euro-underwritings. There was that big EEC deal in 1976. I remember Rudloff [Hans-Joerg Rudloff, then Ross's sales and syndicate counterpart at Kidder] called me and said, "Stanley, we have the opportunity to do an EEC deal." And I said, "Okay, what does it mean we've got to do?" He said, "It means we have to commit." I said, "Okay, I'll take $25 million." That was a big size in those days. So we did that deal. Full credit to Rudloff, but he did it because we said we would take all those bonds on the trading book and place them. He didn't do it any other way.

I've always been anti-salesmen; I didn't think they were doing enough for the huge monies they were being paid. You know, they came to me one day at Kidder with this thick wad of computer sheets and said, "These are the people you deal with worldwide, and you don't give the offices anywhere any credit. In the future you'll give them an eighth on all this business." The reason for that was that our profits were an embarrassment to them, the fact that our little group of 45 people could be producing so much and that I could stand up at the stockholders meetings and say: "Look what we've done for you again this year. And look what you've done for us. Zero." So they diluted those figures by handing them out gratuitously to salespeople.

I mean, when I joined Kidder, they didn't even know the UBS. "Oh," someone said, "that's my account. I've been working on it for a long time." I said, "Wait a minute, have you ever written a ticket?" "No, but I've been working on it. I'm taking him out to dinner." I said: "Bullshit. You've never done a ticket with him. As soon as I came, we started dealing with him every day. So get stuffed. I won't pay you a penny." I might have been a bit rough in those days. But you know, it was justified: I can't stand people who want something for nothing. I can't stand a system where people get a cut just because they have their names on something.

The top people at Kidder really didn't know what they were doing. They just knew they saw the profits coming in, but they didn't know why. Just to tell you a quick story: [Kidder trading chief Richard] Wigton sent me a telex one day. He wanted me to buy some bonds, and he put on the telex, "Please confirm that we can pay in Eurodollars." So I said, "Yes, please pay the dollars to so and so." But he kept sending the same request over and over. So eventually I rang him up. I said, "Dick, do me a favor. Take a dollar bill out of your pocket, will you?" He said, "Why?" I said, "Look, you take one out and I'll take one out. Now I've got a Eurodollar in my hand and you've got a dollar. Okay? They're all the same. They're not overprinted with the word 'Eurodollar.' They're all the same dollars. It's a question of geographical ownership." And do you know, they didn't know these things in the early '70s?

New York was not terribly happy with my weekly letter, "The Week in Eurobonds." I'm quite proud to have produced the first weekly letter in the market. But some of the things I wrote didn't sit too well with some people. I once criticized a deal for Finland. I didn't know the finance minister of Finland read the bloody thing, but one day [Kidder chairman] Al Gordon rang up and said, "Look, I have this letter from the finance minister. What should I do?" I said, "Well, tell him that you slapped my wrist." And Gordon said, "Can I do that?" And I said, "Well, of course you can." Gordon said to me, "I'll protect you against Ralph DeNunzio in the same way that Ralph protects Sam Nakagama [Kidder's economist] against me."

I was often taking a swack at Ralph and New York in the letters. There was the famous time when somebody rang me up from New York and said, "Stanley, you've got to sell all your bonds today. And you're not to buy anything." And I said: "Wait a minute. I've never heard this before. Why is this?" And he said, "Well, we think the market's going down." I said: "Okay, I'll mark the prices down. But I will not make a one-way price only. You do that in New York, they do it in Germany all the time, but we don't do it here." So he said, "Okay, but you better adopt a very low profile." Well, that evening I wrote in my newsletter: "I've been told by my superiors in New York that I have to adopt a very low profile. Accordingly, I've told my dealers in London that every time the phone rings they are to lie flat on the floor. I wonder if that profile will be low enough?"

You may think that that was pretty stupid of me to do. And upon reflection, I guess it was a little stupid. But I thought that as long as I was bringing in the money all the time, week in, week out, it didn't matter. I thought I was protected, really, by what I produced for them. Because there's no question that over a five-year period, we produced 35 percent of the net income of Kidder

Peabody—45 of us, in a company that was then 2,000 or 3,000 strong. And we were making Kidder into something internationally.

The way that they finally dealt with me—I mean, it was done in all the worst ways you hear about American companies. It really was. And I still hurt over that. I was chairman of Kidder Peabody International, and [Kidder international chief Richard] Coons and Rudloff took me to lunch and said, "We think it would make sense for Rudloff to be chairman of International." I said, "Sure, fine, I think that's a good idea, too." Of course, Rudloff couldn't believe it. When he got back, he called my colleague Bob Smith in and said: "Smith! What is happening? What is the matter with Stanley? He's just given up the chairmanship of International without a fight!" But what had happened was I had come back a week earlier from Tokyo, where I was taken ill with a blood pressure of 200 over 125. I came back to London and saw a specialist, and he said, "Okay, untreated I give you five years." My father had died of a stroke just a few years earlier. So I thought, well, I'm going to ease off, do less, take the tablets. So when Coons and Rudloff said this to me, I had this in mind.

But giving up power in an American-style company is wrong, because the other guy always wants the next thing. And the next thing Rudloff wanted was to be in charge of the whole thing. One day we argued about something, and he said, "Stanley, this firm isn't big enough for both of us." And I said, "Well, you know where to go." And bang! Down went the phone. Six months later we had a big row in DeNunzio's office with DeNunzio, Coons and Rudloff. And DeNunzio said to me, "Stanley, don't ever let me hear that you have said that the firm isn't big enough for you and Rudloff. Don't ever let me hear that you said that." And I said, "Now wait a minute, Ralph, do you want to know who said . . ."

He said, "I don't want to hear any more! That's finished! That's over!" And I said, "But just a mo . . . ." "No," he said. "I don't want to hear any more." And, you know, they both sat there, and they both know who said that. And I thought, "Honesty doesn't count for anything. It really doesn't count for anything."

Later, when Coons invited me to lunch, I had no idea what he was going to say. I wasn't fired, you understand, but I was told that I could have a year off with full pay. I could come in when I liked. My secretary would still be there. My office would still be there. My American Express card. My car. But I would no longer run the shop.

When I left Kidder I had 32 different job offers. That was really quite amazing. It was the most heartening thing of a very disheartening time of my life. And I thought to myself, "With 32 offers I must be worth something. Why don't I start something of my own?" So I started Ross & Partners. We did a few bits and pieces, and then we discovered the gray market.

One day a Japanese banker called me up and said, "Ah, Mr. Ross, I can offer you these bonds, less 5." It was a Japanese convertible he was lead-managing that had not yet come to market. Now, less 5 was something I'd never heard of in my life before. I mean, I'd heard of less 2 and less 2 1/2 and all that—I think the commission on a Japanese convertible in those days was 2.5 percent—but less 5, this was something incredible. I said to myself, I must wait and see how this comes out. The issue comes out at par, and I thought, I wonder where these things are going to trade? And the first trading price was not 97 or 95 or 90—it was 88. And this was the thing that the lead manager had offered me at less 5. I thought, "This is some f—g rip-off. There must be a way to make a turn here."

So I got in touch with Reuters and I said, "Look, I want a page [on Reuters Monitor]. I'm going to start putting out prices on an if-and-when-issued basis." One of the first issues we did it on was a Norway issue that the Deutsche Bank was doing. We put it on the screen less 2 1/2 to 2. I was away that day in Luxembourg, and one of my dealers gets a call from European Bank: "We want you to know that the Deutsche Bank is gravely displeased at this price on the screen." So the dealer took it off. When I rang up and they told me what they had done, I said, "Who pays your salary, the Deutsche Bank or me? Put it up 2 3/4 to 2 1/4." In other words, I put it even lower. So the European Bank called again, and I said, "Well, do you want to buy in?" And they said, "No, we don't, but we don't like to see you do it." So I said: "Well, that's too bad. If you want to change the price, then you put your money where your mouth is." And that was how it all began.

In 1980 we were interrogated something like 3,000 times a day on the Reuters screen. By 1982 we were sometimes interrogated 16,000 times a day. Did you know we had 72 pages on Reuters and we didn't pay anything for the pages? Our screen, it turned out, was Reuters' biggest selling point.

I got such abusive phone calls. I mean, people were screaming and shouting at me: "You're not going to get away with this! What the f—do you think you're doing? A tiny outfit like yours!" And I said, "If you don't like it, fine." And I made them "selected access," which meant they couldn't see my screen. In my time, I made Deutsche Bank, UBS, Crédit Suisse selected access. Such was the power of that screen that one day Reuters made an error and blacked out the whole of Switzerland and France by mistake. When people keyed in in the morning, they saw, "Selected Access." That day our switchboard was totally jammed by people I never heard of before, complaining about our making them selected access. I said, "Okay, what's your name? We should be doing business with you. Okay, we'll put you back."

UBS put a bear squeeze on us, and so did Crédit Suisse. I remember it very well: It was in their own issue, a Crédit Suisse convertible. We made our two-way price, and we were taken, and we were taken, and we were taken, and we were taken. I got a little worried about this, and I called one of my friends at another of the big Swiss banks. I said: "Look, I need to buy 5 million of this bond. And I'll pay you over the odds. But I've got to have delivery." He sold them to me, and I paid a bit more in price, but I delivered. They thought they were hurting me, but I wasn't really hurt.

At the AIBD meeting in London in 1979, they tried to prevent me from putting my prices up. They tried to bring in a rule. This was the only time that [then AIBD chairman Stanislas] Yassukovich—the urbane, the cool, the detached, the beautifully fluent Yassukovich—was stopped. He was trying to defend the indefensible. They tried to put me out of business, and they failed. I called for a vote and the whole assembly voted with me. The board had egg on their faces; I mean, they looked really stupid. But it was a pyrrhic victory, because from that point on it became a game that anybody could play. Okay, so I was still in business, but then everybody joined me. And so, in a way, it didn't really help me.

What we did, I think, changed the way the market did its business. We showed everybody what the real price was. It used to be this sort of comfortable club of people ringing up and saying,

"Hey, I can offer you some of this, but don't let the lead manager know." By putting them up on the screen less 3 to less 2 1/2, we really shattered that comfortable club forever. And we hastened the bought-deal concept.

The firm had begun to be profitable for the Marlon House group, which actually put up the £1 million of capital. But then another company in the group lost a fortune on gilts, and Marlon needed cash, and Drexel Burnham took us over for a song. We then began to have our problems with Drexel; they wanted to run things their own way. I had a hate-hate relationship with Mike Milken. He often wanted to buy these undervalued bonds, and he would call us and deal with us, but at the same time he would deal with everybody else around the Street. And we didn't always get the orders first. We most frequently got them last. I told him, "Don't pay us 142 when you pay the other people 144."

So I retired from Drexel and I went sailing and skiing. But there's only so much skiing and sailing you can do. Then Deutsche Bank called. I thought, well, I don't know, this might be something interesting. To see the other side of the coin. To see the mighty Deutsche Bank at work. It was interesting and it has been interesting. I can say things and do things and try to change things in a way that perhaps the existing Deutsche Bank personnel, whose careers are tied up in the hierarchical structure, can't do. I'm also working on the AIBDQ [a proposed automated Eurobond trading system], which could turn into a full-time job, it seems to me.

I have a photograph of J.P. Morgan in my office now. You know, he was the biggest bloody pirate of them all. It's one of the few full-plate pictures of him; if you go into Morgan Guaranty offices, you'll only see half plates of him. I'm just hoping that one of these days Morgan Guaranty or somebody will come in and say, "Hey, we should have that," and give me five grand for it or something.

I think he's rather nice. I like to look at him every day. He doesn't distress me at all. I just wonder to myself if he enjoyed his life as much as I've enjoyed mine. I don't think he did. And that just helps me to enjoy my life a bit more.

Editor: Cary Reich

John Slade

Managing Director BEAR, STEARNS & CO.

> John Slade's perspective on Wall Street goes back more than a half
> century. A refugee from Nazi Germany, he started as a runner at
> Bear, Stearns & Co. for $15 a week. Slade went on to head Bear
> Stearns' risk arbitrage department. After earning a Bronze Star in
> World War II and then playing goalie on the 1948 U.S. Olympic
> field hockey team, he reopened Bear Stearns' international depart-
> ment, which had been closed since the start of the war, and in the
> ensuing years was a pioneer in selling U.S. stocks abroad.
> Currently, he is honorary chairman of the executive committee.

I was one of the first to see the opportunity in Europe. When I
was a member of the U.S. Olympic field hockey team in 1948
in London, I received permission from my bosses to try to start
the international department. But when I ran around Europe in
my Olympic jacket, I found out that there was hardly any interest
in our market, because in many countries you had currency restrictions. One country that had no currency restrictions was Switzerland, but the bankers in Switzerland had their connections in
the United States already—Brown Brothers Harriman from before the war, Dominick & Dominick and Hentz & Co. So at that
time, there was no money available to invest in the United States.

The real urge to invest in the United States only came after
1960. At that time the Kennedy administration imposed a special
tax on Americans investing abroad. Meanwhile, because the dollar was so weak, like today, Europeans could buy American securities at very low prices. But there was one great difficulty: At that

time relatively few Europeans spoke English. So most of the Europeans concentrated on their own markets—with the exception of the British. The British were always interested in our market. During the war they had to pay all of their American securities to the government in order to finance the war, so afterward Great Britain had to start from nothing again to buy American securities. Also the Scots, who were the founders of investment trusts; they were among the first ones to invest in this country again.

Now, this business has grown immensely, and, of course, there are many new countries investing that did not invest before. The next ones in Europe were the Scandinavian countries, then Germany, Italy and France—and, of course, Luxembourg, which is to a certain extent a banking competitor of Switzerland and is becoming a greater competitor all the time. Also Hongkong. And, of course, now Japan. And I forgot to mention Holland. Holland was always very much interested in American securities and had a number of American securities always listed on its stock exchanges.

The types of investors and the types of investments have also changed. At the beginning we only did business with the banks and the mutual funds. We never did business with individual investors, because I felt—and rightly so—that the individuals are the customers of the banks, who were my customers. And consequently, I didn't want to compete with the banks.

Now you have more and more insurance companies and pension funds investing. Especially since interest rates were considerably higher here and the dollar was stabilized for a long time, more money came here, to invest in, in my opinion, the greatest country in the world. Of course, we went through many cycles. Whenever the dollar was weak, they could buy at a very low price; when the dollar was strong, interest in our market diminished. And, since the invention of the Eurodollar, the investment in dollar securities and dollar bonds and convertible bonds has increased tremendously, and the Eurodollar market is mainly in Europe.

When I started, I found that it was very difficult to get customers because you needed connections. So I had the idea to ask banks to send young people to this country as trainees. We would pay them; we would teach them the business; we would also teach them English. Over the years, I had at least 600 trainees from all over the world. And, of course, we established relationships with the trainees, and when they went back to their banks they became customers of ours.

I am a very proud American, and I believe in this country. I just went from bank to bank, showed them our product, and tried to convince them that the best investments are in the United States—that we know our business, that we are a great house and that they should buy the securities we recommended.

At the beginning they were buying blue-chip stocks—Exxon, U.S. Steel, Anaconda, General Motors, International Paper, General Electric—really, the Dow Jones stocks. That has changed considerably, and for a very specific reason. By now most of the foreign customers have their own research departments. And most of the members of their research departments trained in the United States, many of them with us. And consequently, they have many other sources of information and recommendations than those given to them by their U.S. brokers such as ourselves. And they decide on their own what to buy.

So today you get business in stocks you have hardly heard of—situations they like and that they discovered. They are today as well informed about our markets as any institutions here. The world is very small, really: They all speak English; they have access to any company we have access to; and they make up their own minds.

Furthermore, many foreign banks are members of the New York Stock Exchange, and consequently they transact part of their business on their own. You have to be in the bond business, in the Eurodollar business, in the merger and acquisition business, in the auction business, underwriting; you have to have a very strong research department in global securities.

The Japanese—they still buy mainly the Dow Jones stocks. We had a number of days now when we had orders from the Japanese to buy 50,000 shares each of 27 of the Dow Jones stocks, at our discretion. But they are still quite new to our equity markets. However, the Europeans are generally more aggressive, playing the so-called risk arbitrage stocks, etc.; they participate. The British are the most knowledgeable ones.

It's a younger generation abroad. Don't forget there was a war, and you needed young people to learn the business. And even 30 years ago the United States was very, very far away from them. When I lived in Germany before the war, my father would never invest outside Germany. It was too far away to invest in the United States.

Today, with the telephone and the plane, there's no distance anymore. Travel doesn't mean anything. Nor the time difference. Our market is open when it's 10:30 at night to 6:30 in the morning in Japan. We have one account in Japan that, whenever the market is up or down ten points, we have to wake him up. So these days he never sleeps!

When you are in a hotel in Geneva, you get *The Wall Street Journal* at 6:30 in the morning. That's 12:30 the previous night here. And they get the Dow Jones and Reuters, all of the news while we are asleep. So they are exceedingly well informed about the United States—much better informed than we are about Europe.

Now you have to work much harder because there are so many more people to see. You have to be willing to travel a lot—not only yourself, but send your analysts all over the world. You also need people to give you a review and preview about the political situation in the United States. If you want to be in the foreign business, you have to be willing to work yourself or have some of your people work round the clock. You have to have at least four offices abroad: London, Tokyo, Geneva and either Amsterdam, Frankfurt or Paris.

Besides, the potential is much greater. And they expect more. The world is much smaller. Today, when you are working in Wall Street, people are suddenly interested—"What did Tokyo do last night?" "How was the British market?" "How was the German market?" If it's an increase in the prime rate, the whole world's markets are influenced. And today it's a 24-hour market: trading stops here; soon afterward it starts in Hongkong and Japan, and then in Europe. We are all connected today and dependent on each other.

Editor: Fran Hawthorne

Pierre Moussa

Former Chairman BANQUE PARIBAS

During his three years as Paribas chairman, Pierre Moussa forged Paribas into the consummate French *banque d'affaires:* part commercial bank, part investment bank, part venturesome investor for its own account. But its very power made Paribas a prime nationalization target when the Socialist government took power in 1981. In a desperate effort to keep at least part of the empire in private hands, the French bank disposed of its interest in its Swiss and Belgian subsidiaries; the government, blaming Moussa for the maneuver, pushed for his ouster when Paribas was finally nationalized. Subsequently, Moussa was a defendant in a currency fraud and smuggling case that some felt was engineered by the government as a further act of revenge. Acquitted of the charges, Moussa went on to form a new financial base, the Pallas Group, and acquired a 50 percent stake in Dillon Read's London subsidiary.

W hen Jacques de Fouchier told me he was going to Paribas and said I would have a very good chance to be one day his No. 2 and his successor, I hesitated for only one reason. I had the same offer at the same time from another firm of the same size. But I accepted in the end the Paribas offer.

The image of Paribas then was extremely aggressive and maybe, at the limit, a little selfish, a little terrible. And the image was evolved by de Fouchier toward something more establishment—while keeping its great aggressiveness. I thought that the bank's greatest strength was the exceptional accumulation of first-class talents in all fields. I mean in all sorts of fields: international finance, industry, technology, economics.

It was really a pleasure and also a great source of efficiency to know that whatever the problem was you could just call somebody on the phone, have him over in three minutes and discuss with him how to play the game on that particular thing. If it was about gold, to have the people who knew most about gold; if it was South America, to have the best people on South America; if it was venture capital, to have the best people on venture capital. I think that has always been the greatest strength of Paribas. That, and our very informal approach to things, where a small number of people discusses something together, makes a decision and jumps, without the heavy approach of big institutions. Paribas was at that time becoming a very big institution but had really retained the energy and aggressiveness of a very young institution.

Our goal was not only to be quicker and faster and more sophisticated than most of the other French banks, but to be more international. We were already more international—this is a tradition of Paribas and even its name stands for it—and the international evolution was continued by de Fouchier and by myself very, very strongly during the three years of my chairmanship. We opened, I don't know, maybe twenty branches or subsidiaries in cities all over the world, in Asia, in Africa, in Europe, in America. But the important thing is not so much to have the big network; there is also a question of culture. And that is where I believe that Paribas has been ahead of the others. To be not only international but multinational. I mean by that not to have what you have in New York or in Hongkong or in Brussels as a kind of extension of the French bank, but to be really a Belgian bank in Belgium and so on.

I will always remember when I came back the first time from Hongkong after we had opened our branch there; to come back and to say, my God, I have seen, I don't know, 40 young Chinese officers, all of them extremely aggressive and all being Paribas. This was a Chinese Paribas, not Paribas in China but a Chinese Paribas. I think it is one of the characteristics of Paribas. When the Belgian government speaks to the four great [Belgian] banks, the four great banks are Société Générale du Banque, Banque Bruxelles, Kredietbank and Paribas.

The bank also had this industrial character. We had a strong team of industrialists, engineers and so on, people with a deep knowledge of French industry and world industry, and excellent specialists in the steel industry, in chemicals and so on. And in this area, we were always terribly opportunistic. I'll give you an example. One day I was at the Festival of Salzburg listening to Mozart, and I encountered there one of my excellent associates, Robert Lattess. And we walked together between concerts and he told me that we should launch ourselves in something which was really at that time not very much developed in Europe: venture capital for new technology. That was the origin of the development of the strong presence of Paribas in that field; in particular, that was the day that he talked to me for the first time of something called Transgen, a very good genetic engineering firm.

Did the companies in which we invested welcome our influence or did they resent it? It is difficult really to know what people think secretly. I had the impression that most of them were happy to belong to the big Paribas family and that we were for them a source of strength and a source of ideas as well as of money, but who knows? I mean, if they were angry with Paribas they wouldn't have taken me as their confidant.

In general, we were welcome, or we were even asked to join. I'll give you an example. Paribas had founded a company called Club Européen des Touristes, CET, which was a rival of Club Méditerranée, smaller but not much smaller. And I remember that one day Gilbert Trigano [Club Med CEO] came to see us and said, "Now we are beginning to be always in the same places, bidding against each other for the same locations, and it's becoming stupid. So either there will be a war, which I will win because I can outlast you, or we will merge the two—in which case we will do great things together." And we studied the matter and said, okay, we'll merge. And since then, Paribas has been a very faithful and I think welcome partner of Club Méditerranée.

Another example of this was our relationship with Paul Desmarais and his Power Corp. of Canada. I remember in the early '70s I first called on Desmarais, and I found him absolutely fascinating. I gave him my address and so on, but I was very offended when I learned a few months later that he had come to Paris, seen several people and not seen me. Then, one day a few years later, Lattess told me that there was a group that would be interesting for us—the Power group. I said to him, "Yes, that

789

would be great, but Desmarais doesn't like us." But Lattess thought I should try again, so I went to see Desmarais.

I found myself in his office and he said to me, "I have a proposal to make to you. I'm trying to get control of the group and I need three European institutions to invest with me. Would you be one of them?" I said, in principle, yes, but I asked to see his financials. Afterward, I remember I called him and I said, "I accept, but I prefer to be all three institutions myself. I'll take everything." He said, "No, no, no, you cannot. There must be at least two." Then he gave me the name of one of the greatest institutions in Europe and said, "It will be you and them. Do you agree?" I said, "Yes, but if they say no . . ." He said, "They will not say no. If they say no, I'll give you all of it, but they will not say no." They said no. And he gave me everything.

A similar situation happened with Empain Schneider. Didier Pineau-Valencienne, who was already the real manager of the firm, called one day a good friend of his who was also my right-hand man, Gérard Eskenazi, and told him he wanted to see us as a matter of extreme urgency. He told us that we could become a very substantial shareholder of Schneider if we wanted, but that we should make a proposal in a few hours. We organized a team that worked the whole night, and before 8:00 in the morning we had become a very important shareholder of the firm. And that could have been the starting point of a great development, if nationalizations had not taken place a few months later.

My personal conviction is that we were on a tremendous trend upward which was not undone by nationalization. After nationalization there were some very good people taking care of the bank, especially my friend Jean-Yves Haberer. But nationalization did make a difference.

It's not a matter of men, but it's a matter of . . . I mean, how can you have a government-owned *banque d'affaires*? It's so ridiculous, it's absurd. It is like saying, I want to be a jockey but I want to eat very heavy things at all my meals. A *banque d'affaires* has to be extremely energetic and extremely youthful, and whatever belongs to the state inevitably is something heavy and it cannot have the same kind of efficiency. For instance, a typical aspect of a *banque d'affaires* is that you can always offer to buy someone's company or part of his company with your own shares. How can you do that if your shares belong to the government? You cannot offer that.

I must confess that when it came to the possibility of nationalization, we at Paribas were blind and made some great mistakes. The main mistake I made was devoting a substantial part of my time to doing creative business instead of doing defensive business against that stupid nationalization idea when there was time. So that obliged me to do it when there was hardly time, and it was the origin of many difficulties for Paribas and for myself. I think to myself, why have we made that mistake? First, well, we thought that the chances of the left coming to power were less than they were. In that respect, all of the business class was blind. We had had this '78 experience where we had really thought that the left would win, and the left was beaten. And so that created a kind of belief that in the end, serious solutions always prevail, the French are reasonable and so on. Also, we considered that even if the left was to come to power, we knew some very intelligent people among them, and we thought that they would never do silly things like a complete 100 percent nationalization.

I can tell you that I knew not all but I would say two thirds of the stars of that Socialist government. They were good friends of mine or good relations of mine. I visited them one after the other and they all received me and listened to me very carefully, and I really had the impression that I had convinced them, most of them if not all of them, that nationalization was a mistake. But they could do nothing against this movement coming from the grass roots, in which ideological thoughts were taking the place of experience. People had no love for the successes of French firms except in certain things like cars or planes; when it was any other industry, insurance, banking, they couldn't care less.

What I should have done to prepare for nationalization was diminish the control of Paribas Paris over the Paribas network, maintaining the unity but making it impossible to take the whole network over. We thought it was better to have complete control, but in doing that we were exposing ourselves to a greater danger, the danger that it was sufficient to just take control of the Paris office and then be in this situation of dominating the worldwide institution. You cannot build a multinational without protecting yourself against the bad ideas of a possible government. And I failed to do that.

What was horrible was the possibility given to the French government of taking control of what we owned in Belgium, in Luxembourg, in Holland, in Switzerland, in Hongkong and so on through a political decision in Paris. And that could have been avoided by creating something more complex, instead of having Paris controlling this, controlling that. We should have had Belgium controlling Luxembourg and Switzerland controlling Belgium and Luxembourg controlling ... so that when Paris was threatened, well, anything can happen to the French assets but the rest of it can go on as private companies.

The excuse for not doing it that way was that we were so busy building things, creating things, that we had no time to construct this interlocking mechanism. This is really my mistake, not to have done it. I had the time in three years to do things which couldn't have been contested.

Incidentally, what I did in '81 could not be contested either. [Moussa divested Paribas's interests in its Belgian and Swiss subsidiaries prior to the bank's nationalization, arousing the Socialist government's anger.] I mean, it was perfectly legal. And in a country like the United States of America, nobody would have said anything—because if it is legal, a company can do what it wants. You cannot say, "You cannot do it because there is going to be a law in a few months which will make it impossible for you to do it." And second, you cannot say, "But you knew perfectly well that the government would not like it." My job is not to please the government. It is to do the best for my enterprise and my shareholders.

I did what I thought was my duty, even though I knew that would certainly cause some harm to me. To be quite frank, I did not think it would do me as much harm as it did. I remember I said to my associates, "We are going to have three very bad months personally." But it was not three very bad months. It was much longer than that. People in the government were saying, "Moussa has done something we don't like; no matter whether it was legal or not, we don't like it. It's a threat to our ideology, our great construction of the future. That man should be killed."

The Socialists considered their victory the beginning of history, the beginning of a new life, and that all the people who were against Mitterrand were against France. We had for a few months a real kind of temptation of totalitarianism. The Socialist Party is a very democratic party, but for a while they were tempted by totalitarianism, by fascism, whatever you call it. They were saying, "We are the good, and whoever is against us is the bad." It didn't last long, and I must say that Mitterrand himself never indulged in such things.

Some people on the Paribas board were upset with me, but I also had very good friends there. If I had not resigned I wouldn't have been ousted by eleven votes against one, I assure you. I resigned because I felt it was in the interest of Paribas to have a new chairman who would be considered an acceptable chairman by the government. Any other course would have been detrimental to the enterprise. So it was my duty to resign.

As for Jacques de Fouchier [who reportedly aligned himself against Moussa in the Paribas board and succeeded him as chairman], he did what he had to do and I think it's normal. It was useful to have him at that time to make the transition until Haberer was appointed.

At the end of '81 it was not impossible that I could have been sentenced to jail, even though what I had done to the ownership of certain subsidiaries was perfectly legal. So they came up with this old story, one year old, about an illegal action involving Paribas where they could say the chairman is responsible. The great difficulty for them was that something like 93 percent of the accounts referred to had been opened at a time when the chairman was not named Moussa, so it was very difficult to say that Moussa is responsible. [Moussa was ultimately acquitted.]

I recovered very quickly thanks to my friends. I would say my old friends and my new friends. You can't imagine how pleasant it has been to see not only that my friends were all faithful to me, but that people who I considered as good relations were behaving like friends, and people who I considered as relations were behaving as good relations, and people who I did not know behaved like relations. You see what I mean? There was a kind of upgrading of everybody. I was going to restaurants, and I remember I went to a restaurant one day with my wife, and somebody at another table stood up and raised his glass in my honor, just like that. And in the airport I was on the escalator, and people on the other side said, "Monsieur Moussa, bravo, merci."

And you know a great day was the day, two months after I resigned, when Gilbert Trigano called me on the phone and said, "I'm sure you have some time left now. It so happens that we are at a great moment of our international development. Would you join us in any way? Tell me what you want. You can become vice chairman of the company, working closely with me on all the international developments or you can also be a consultant, or whatever." About the same time, several American firms did the same thing, but it was more heroic for a French firm because he didn't hesitate.

Of course, not all my friends approved of what I did [with the Paribas subsidiaries]. I know that Siegmund Warburg disapproved. He was my great friend. I was his disciple to a large extent. I mean, he liked me, I think, and he liked to be listened to. And although I'm very talkative myself, when I was with him I really shut up and listened and even took notes. He generally offered me a remarkable meal with marvelous wines and so on, and we spent three, four, five hours together. And I learned a lot by listening to him. So my relations with him were exceptional. And I had the best relations at that time with Jacques Attali [a key Mitterrand adviser]; I introduced them to each other. Attali forgot to mention that in his book about Siegmund Warburg.

It's clear that Warburg was a very prudent man and he disapproved of what I did. He considered that the important thing was to be on good terms with the government. He had a different approach. On the other hand, when I founded my own little company, Finance and Development, in 1982, he wrote to me that he wanted to be one of the shareholders, one of the founders of my firm. When he died, his widow wrote to me that she knew of the intentions of her husband and offered to put money in my venture; I refused because I didn't want to trouble her. She died a few months later.

You know, we both had had great plans for the Warburg-Paribas relationship. My personal thought was that the best outcome would be more than a great alliance. It would be, if possible, a merger of the two companies. At the time, that was what I was

794

hoping, and Siegmund thought, I believe, along the same lines. It would have been one firm, one firm which would have been certainly one of the very few major actors in international financial activity. We talked about that; Siegmund was a man who liked to move very slowly toward great purposes. Unfortunately, nationalization and all the events that followed killed that; they killed many things.

As for our joint American venture, Warburg Paribas Becker, our plan might very well have been to merge with a big American institution. And mind you, we had a very long and serious conversation with one of the greatest names there, with a view to merge Becker and that firm and to have one of the greatest firms in the Street, with a minority but a very strong position for Warburg and Paribas. But that finally was not possible. We couldn't come to terms.

Starting out on my own was not easy. As my English friends have told me, "What you have done has no precedent. We have often seen people gathering $100 million for a very precise project, to take control of this, to buy that and so on. But getting $100 million just on your name and the idea that you wanted to create an international *banque d'affaires*, which was very vague— this we have never seen." I had decided that I wouldn't go ahead if I didn't get $100 million, and some people told me that you are completely mad because even if you have $50 million, the possibilities are great. But I said, I want $100 million. As a matter of fact, at the end I had 98.

Our investment in Dillon Read International came about out of the basic concept that the old notion of a *banque d'affaires* remains more effective than ever: that to have under the same roof a banker and an investor with a portfolio of diversified investments, this is great. And this is disappearing in the world.

We thought we would make one that would be completely international; a completely international one has never existed. Now, I admit this is not as precise as someone gathering money to take control of Lockheed or of such and such company in England. So it appeared to me that to succeed I had to give this concept a little flesh.

As for Dillon Read, they had a little team here, and they were asking questions of themselves about whether they should go on or not. The additional strength brought by Pallas, by myself, and so on, was something which gave them a chance to have better

795

development. So we negotiated that and came to terms, and that was done at the same time as I was gathering the money. I mean, the two things came to fruition at the same time. On a certain day, I forget which one, in April '84, Pallas was capitalized, and three days later we invested in order to get 50 percent of Dillon Read International.

How did I feel when Paribas was denationalized?

Well the first thing was that I was glad that this operation was made, that it was reasonable, and glad that it was a tremendous success. Altogether, I felt that this privatization thing so far has been handled extremely well. The selection of the first to go has been good, and the prices have been reasonable. The timing has also been good; of course, there was nothing which said that Saint-Gobain had to be the first, Paribas the second.

And for objective reasons, I think it was extremely good for Paribas and extremely good for France. And I would say maybe to a certain extent it showed that I was not that wrong in resisting nationalization and in trying to go on with the concept of a great, private French *banque d'affaires*. That showed that I had been to a certain extent a precursor.

I wouldn't say that I felt vindicated—because I didn't need to be vindicated. So "vindication" is not the word I would use. I was happy for my country, because I think this is the great sign of a complete change of our society. We are becoming adult. In France, on the financial side, on the economic side, we were medieval.

In France you have one-half right and one-half left, plus or minus one point. And the half left is the France of the workers, professors, civil servants, intellectuals. This France has really never understood the economy in concrete terms. The notion of enterprise, of a firm, of profit, all this philosophy which is common in the U.S., is traditionally ignored by that half of France. And each time the left comes to power, they come with their good merits, their knowledge of social things, but also with their ignorance of economic things. And after two years they're ousted and they have learned nothing, and when they come back to power later they make the same mistakes again.

So what happened? The government of the left learned. Most

of them are serious people, they're intelligent people, they are able people. And after two years they began just to learn something. They have understood especially what it means to have a prosperous economy, and that it finally boils down to having efficient enterprises and that these enterprises must be profitable and that they must invest. So now you have a large number of people who are interested in Paribas as well as in cars and planes. This is, in France, something completely new. So I consider that this is what the great success of Paribas in the stock market means.

The term "nationalization" has been utilized in the last 100 years or so to mean acquisition by the state or by the nation. But when 3 million of our compatriots own shares of Paribas, this is the *real* nationalization. This is a great thing. It was the philosophy I had when I was chairman of Paribas. A substantial amount of my time was devoted to that purpose: to make Paribas and its philosophy understood by the nation.

You can see the impact even here in London. The concierge of this building, who I didn't think even knew my name, two months ago told me, "Mr. Moussa, isn't it extraordinary what is happening to your Paribas? And by the way, do you think I can have some shares?"

Editor: Cary Reich

Irwin Jacobs

Chairman MINSTAR INC.

As a young man, Irwin Jacobs accompanied his peddler father when he made the rounds of grain elevators in the Minneapolis area to reclaim used gunnysacks and other cast-off "junk." That taught the young Jacobs a keen appreciation of undervalued assets that he has parlayed into a highly lucrative and also controversial career as a corporate raider and empire builder.

The first real deal I was involved in, back in 1976, was a little company called Grain Belt Breweries. It was a true leveraged buyout, and people didn't really understand the concept—not bankers, anyhow. I mean, leveraged buyouts are accepted today, but back then leverage was a very scary thing. It was a $4 million deal, and it seemed like all the money in the world to me, especially when I didn't have it. I was 33, and I wanted to get into "big business." It was a high-profile, local brewery and in the part of Minneapolis where I grew up. The management had been around for a long time and had pretty much given up. But the balance sheet was clean, they were publicly owned, and no one had control or even any major blocks.

I was able to borrow the money from Carl Pohlad [a Minneapolis banker and now a Jacobs partner]. I was nervous as hell, but as I look at it today, it was a no-brainer. I was a babe in the woods, but I could look at a balance sheet and understand that what I was buying was basically cash and assets. I never went to college, but I grew up in the family business. I worked from the time I was eleven or twelve years old with my father, who started out as a peddler. I drove a truck, picked up gunnysacks at grain elevators. It was a junk business, basically—scrap, barrels, bags—but it was identifying undervalued assets. We're buying oil service right now at really junk-mail prices. The game hasn't changed.

With Grain Belt, even though I've never drunk alcohol, I felt beer was a consumer-marketing thing and that I could go in there as some miracle man and develop something that they couldn't. I was wrong. I was losing about $200,000 a month in it. So I had to give up. It was very painful, because it was my first chance at big business—the company was doing about $30 million a year, and I considered that *big*.

As it turned out, I did very well on it financially, because I was able to sell the brands to another brewer. I had no money going in. I got out a year later, and I made $5 million and I said to myself, "My God, that's more money than I could ever spend in my life. And if I just put it in bonds, I could live the rest of my life with that." That idea lasted about three months, and I said, "I got the fever burning." And that's what got me going.

I got involved with Pabst next. I failed in the brewery business before; maybe now I could succeed. I started buying the stock, and I talked with management. They were terrible, just terrible. But the balance sheet was good, and it was a national brewery. It had the ability to be a strong competitor. So I went after it. As it turned out, I wasn't wong, because I started buying the stock at $11, $12 a share and ultimately it sold for close to $35. But it took about a year, year and a half—this was 1981–1982—and I didn't win.

Today it's common practice, but that thing lasted fourteen months, with about four tender offers, two proxy fights, one consent process. The litigation alone was in the millions. I wanted to put Schlitz and Pabst together. It made sense. But management wouldn't go for it. They just didn't want me around. I did go on the board, but after going to one meeting I said, "This is not for me." I mean, they were eating steak lunches, passing out checks and not facing up to their responsibilities. They were living off their past.

I made about $20 million on Pabst. But I didn't want ever again to go through that. That wasn't what I was looking for in life. I said, "You know, I'm going to buy something, and I'm going to run a business."

I *really* was looking for a business to own. But I was looking for undervalued assets, too, and Kaiser Steel was undervalued, so I went for it. We didn't get it. Somebody else paid more. I'm not a chaser of deals. I've got a number, and that's it. But we made $32 million on Kaiser.

Right in the middle of Kaiser Steel we made an offer to buy Bekins. The beauty was, they had a lot of real estate that they didn't need for their business, and my plan was to keep the operating business and pay off my debts with the sale of those excess assets. It worked like a charm.

In the meantime, we had built Minstar—that was our boat business that came out of the ruins of a snowmobile company that we organized in 1979—from nothing. In 1981 it was doing about $20 million; we do about $400 million today.

Sure, I've made mistakes. We're heavily involved in Tidewater; my timing was very poor in that. I bought it early—four, five years ago. We're on the board, we're helping them reorganize, develop the thing to what it is. I got in at the wrong time, but what am I, a perfectionist? If my timing was off, it shows we have patience. We have the resources to hold our investments.

Going after Disney was more an accident than anything else. We got a call on a Friday from Drexel Burnham, which was raising money for [Saul] Steinberg to go after Disney. I offered to put up $35 million or something, and I signed the papers on Monday before leaving for a vacation in Europe. When I get to Europe on Tuesday, I read that Steinberg had sold out. I called my office and said, "What's this mean?" They said, "Well, we just made six-hundred-thousand-something dollars on the commitment fee, and we didn't put any money up."

That was fine, but I went to Merrill Lynch's office in Athens that day and Disney had dropped ten points. I was intrigued by that. When I got back to Minneapolis, I said, "Why is this company worth $47 today if it was worth $62 two weeks ago?" So I bought the stock without knowing where it was going or what was going to happen to it. I kept buying and buying. I got up to 8 percent and management was going crazy. There were lawsuits all over the place, and finally, in come the Basses.

The rest is kind of history. We sold out—I never actually made an offer for the company—and we made a bunch of money. I could have gone and raised the money to take over Disney any time I wanted to. I could have gone to the high-yield market. I could have gone to our banks. I mean, I had the credibility to do it. And I dreamt about it, there's no question about it. But I wasn't prepared to do that yet.

After Disney I went after ITT. What I find unbelievable is, Rand Araskog [ITT's chairman] is doing today everything we told him to do. I give as much credit, if not more, to somebody who's said no to something and then changes his mind rather than stick his feet in concrete. But the guy didn't even have enough guts to sit down and talk to me then—he'd send somebody else to do it for him. I mean, it was a joke. Maybe we could have resolved the thing without all the problems. What am I going to do, kill him?

You know, people say to me, "Irwin, you've never done a really big deal. Why?" Well, hey, we buy a company every year. You know, let me tell you something, big isn't beautiful. It has to make sense. I'm not going to be motivated by some investment banker or the press saying, "Irwin can't do a billion-plus deal." So what? I'm still doing what I want to do, and when I can do the right deal at the right price, I'm going to do it.

I never said, "I'm going after the big guys." It just evolved. I'm considered a raider, a financial entrepreneur, whatever the term is. I used to be called a junk man because I grew up in the junk business. Then, when I got out of the brewery business and bought W.T. Grant's receivables, after the company went broke, *The Wall Street Journal* called me "Irv the Liquidator." I really was very offended by that early on, but now I don't care. We have tens of thousands of people who work for us. We have lots of companies: Minstar, Jacobs Industries, C.O.M.B., Jen-Mar. I don't go out and run ad campaigns and say, "I'm not Irv the Liquidator, I'm Irv the Operator." If I were to pay attention to what everybody said and did, it could drive me crazy.

I'm not Don Quixote, no question about it. But [raiding] does serve a purpose. I read a paper where [Ivan] Boesky made a statement at some university that greed is healthy. To me, that statement is sick—on those terms. But if you were to ask people what motivates them, and if they were being honest with you, they would say a form of greed is not unhealthy—in the sense of saying, "I've done this right, I feel good about what I've done. I was honest. I didn't cheat anybody." There's nothing wrong with that form of greed.

You know, Wall Street says, "Well, Irwin Jacobs doesn't seem to know what the hell he wants to do." I think that's great. When they can figure out what I'm going to do, then I have lost my forte. Wall Street will never be able to track me. And when they least expect me, I assure you that's when I'll strike.

Editor: Gregory Miller

Setsuya Tabuchi

Chairman NOMURA SECURITIES CO.

Setsuya Tabuchi began his three-decade climb up the Nomura corporate ladder in 1947. His near-legendary reputation as the consummate salesman won him his first major executive position—deputy general manager of the sales department—in 1958. Tabuchi became a Nomura director nine years later and by 1978, at 55, was named president. By the time he assumed the less strenuous post of chairman in late 1985, Tabuchi had made Nomura the most profitable financial institution in Japan and put the firm well on its way to becoming the most profitable financial group in the world.

I joined Nomura Securities in 1947, two years after the end of the Second World War, but even then all you could see in Tokyo was destruction. The Tokyo Stock Exchange had not yet resumed business, and all securities transactions were done over the counter. It would be two years before the exchange was reorganized and reopened. And when it did it was small and limited to Japanese domestic securities. Nomura's transactions on the TSE were something like 5 million shares every day. This is quite a contrast with today, when Nomura's average daily turnover volume is 1 billion shares. The major event which revitalized the Japanese economy and therefore the Japanese stock market was the Korean War.

In 1955 Nomura took a big step forward by being the first Japanese private sector company to install a mainframe computer. It was made by Univac and used vacuum tubes and occupied a whole floor of the Nomura Securities building. The floor was something similar to the atmosphere of an industrial plant: So many keypunchers were working on terminals, and there were also many workers running around to take care of it. Nomura has continued to invest in computer and computer-related facilities, and our cumulative investment in computers is probably the largest in the securities sector in Japan.

About fifteen years ago Nomura established a new subsidiary, Nomura Computer Systems Co.; it uses mainframes of various makes and has a big building of its own full of computers, something like a computerized plant. The business that comes from the Nomura group of companies would account for less than 50 percent of NCS's work; other clients include many of the 36 foreign securities houses with licensed branch offices in Japan. The man who initiated the computer investment ahead of anybody else in the private sector was Tsunao Okumura, the first president of Nomura Securities after World War II. He was a man of vision, and we owe much credit to his foresight for the success of Nomura.

Of course, domestic recovery came first, and only after that did Japan turn abroad. If there was a single milestone in the internationalization of the Japanese financial market, it came in 1961 when Sony issued American depositary receipts in the U.S. The next most important milestone was the financial revolution in the U.S. in the early 1970s, which had a significant bearing on the evolution of the Japanese capital market and the invention of money market funds.

On the other hand, not everything has gone smoothly. In 1965 and 1966, just at the time that I was elected to the board of directors of Nomura, the Japanese securities industry went through a depression. Yamaichi Securities was in such severe financial distress that it required the infusion of special loans by the Bank of Japan. This was really a major problem and caught me by surprise. The only precedent I could think about was the Great Depression in the U.S. in 1929. I began reading many books on the Depression at that time. There is an interesting parallel today in that we are in the midst of a period with stock prices at record highs in both the U.S. and Japan. Even in the unlikely event of a repeat of 1929, I am ready.

In my years in the securities business, I have made many friends from many countries. Of all of them, the person who impressed me the most was Don Regan, when he was chief executive of Merrill Lynch. I was really favorably impressed by his caliber as a businessman, and I give him top marks as a chief executive of a financial institution.

I think it was 1974 when Don Regan visited Nomura and met with senior executives, including myself. During the meeting he pulled out a credit card and he stated, "This is used in conjunction with money market funds. Through this card Merrill Lynch delivers new services to its customers which were not previously available." Until then I wasn't even aware of the idea of a money market fund or credit cards issued by securities companies. Regan's visit and demonstration certainly triggered our move to develop a Japanese version of the money market fund. It was also a catalyst in our move to develop a card services company.

Among Japanese, I most respect Tokushichi Nomura, founder of Nomura Securities. He was a man of vision. In 1923, the year in which I was born, Mr. Nomura made a trip to the United States—of course, at that time by sea—and visited Wall Street. He made a very interesting remark that Nomura should some day become an international financial concern. That was back in 1923, and I can't find anybody with such vision and foresight among the Japanese community.

The person who most influenced me in joining the firm was Tsunao Okumura. I was attracted to his personality, and it was a major reason why I joined this company. Among political figures I have known, Hayato Ikeda, former prime minister of Japan, impressed me most. He initiated Japan's income-doubling plan, the era of the high-growth Japanese economy. He had extensive knowledge about the economy and capital markets and every day insisted that his assistant report the prices of the Nikkei–Dow Jones.

What I have learned from my years in the international financial business is that unless you study the cultural, religious and historical background of a nation, you will not be able to enter into intimate business relations with the people working there. Suppose that I make a trip to Europe; unless I have background knowledge of the history related to Christianity in Europe, much of the joy of the European trip will be diminished. When I go to Arab countries, I make it a rule to read introductory textbooks about the Koran. This is necessary for a financial man, even in an era of global 24-hour markets. For every transaction or deal, the basis is human relations.

If a Japanese institution wishes to do business on a large scale, it cannot do so by employing Japanese nationals only. It would have to hire many professionals from local markets, and how local operations perform will depend heavily on the quality and expertise of the persons we hire. The fact of the matter is that Japanese cannot become non-Japanese, and non-Japanese cannot become Japanese. This is true even though in the financial industry there is a common infrastructure used everywhere, including computer systems and various monitors and screens. With the aid of this common infrastructure, it has become substantially easier for people of different nationalities to do business in the financial market.

In my 40 years in the securities industry I have seen many changes. When I joined Nomura, Japan was under the administration of General Douglas MacArthur's general headquarters. But looking at how MacArthur's government was changing Japan's economic and political systems, I was convinced that Japan's financial structure would become closer to that of the U.S. At that time Japan was heavily dependent on what we called indirect financing, with banks providing a very major portion of credit to industry. I was convinced that the time would come when investment bankers and securities underwriters would provide a larger portion of the credit to Japanese industry. For this reason I decided to join the securities business. If I were to rate myself, the best job I did as president of Nomura Securities was to reinforce the in-house training system for all employees of Nomura, both senior and junior. Each program was designed to meet the needs of various age groups, and the emphasis was not on the things directly related to the financial business. These could be taught on the job. I invited university professors and asked them to formulate a training program.

Looking back on my career, I can't think of anything I regret. One important reason is that whenever I made wrong decisions, there were people around to tell me, "You made a wrong decision." This may be special to Japanese corporations or to Nomura Securities in particular. I have made lots of wrong decisions, but always someone would appear and tell me the decision was wrong. Such people gave me a lot of chance to reflect. I am also not afraid of changing decisions. This may also be a virtue of this organization. The only decision I made entirely on my own was to step down from the position of president last year. Some Nomura managers advised me that this was a wrong decision, but that time I didn't even listen to their advice. My strong belief is that for a business to respond to changes effectively, it takes young blood. Based on this firm belief, I decided to step down.

Editor: Kevin Rafferty

Vicar Richard May
Msgr. Edward Mitty
Rabbi Meyer Hager

Though the New York financial district is dominated by towers dedicated to Mammon, it also harbors a few religious sanctuaries. The black spires of Trinity Church (Episcopal) have cast their shadows over Wall Street for 287 years. Our Lady of Victory, a few blocks away on Williams Street, is the parish church for the New York Stock Exchange. The Wall Street Synagogue is only a short walk uptown, on Beekman Street. Vicar Richard May of Trinity, Msgr. Edward Mitty of Our Lady of Victory and Rabbi Meyer Hager of the Wall Street Synagogue all spend considerable time pondering the effects that market swings, social changes and ever-present temptations have on their Wall Street congregants.

VICAR RICHARD MAY

There's a great change between the old-style money managers and the new. The older style quite often were dealing with their own money or the money of a family or a trust, like Brown Brothers Harriman. They were very conservative. They had more of a fiduciary responsibility, or, if they worked at the trading level, they were more mechanical in dealing with money and helping people to invest.

Nowadays there are more strivers—out to make money for themselves or to make a reputation. And that's where you get the insider trading. You know, information is power, but it's not power if nobody knows you have it. You have to use it in order to get a reputation or to be known as somebody who has power and influence.

I think in many ways that the competition in the schools, the desire to get ahead, makes the people who come to Wall Street peers. They're all very bright. They're all very energetic, and to stand out from the competition is very difficult. So you use every bit of information or every lever you can to raise yourself and get noticed. With some insider traders, I think the desire to succeed becomes a compulsion, even if they don't need the money. Their goals get set early, and they don't really question them until they get to the top: the big house in the country, the kids they never see and the marriage they find they don't have. They make the long commute, and it's not until they've made the million dollars that they find out that all these things really don't bring happiness.

One of the things that's grown tremendously during the last three or four years is our Alcoholics Anonymous service. We have also run a methadone clinic for at least ten years—and it draws from this neighborhood. One of the reasons it's in this building, at 74 Trinity Place, is that people you would not think have a drug problem come here. Nobody really knows that there's a methadone clinic here, so they can just come into a regular building and not stand out—you know, in their suits.

Achieving can become greed when you do it for its own sake and not for any useful purpose. There are many people—and I think this is the philosophy of the 1980s—who just set out to amass as much money or power as they can. That focuses here on Wall Street because it's easier to see here and do here. You're not dealing with a product that you have to develop, advertise and sell. Here you can just do it and get instant money, and you can affect the whole country. That's something that the people here need to be aware of—that in fighting the takeover, you may cause a plant to be closed and put people out of work. To people here, it's more of a game. It's paper, and they really do not think of what deals do to the people out in the country.

MSGR. EDWARD MITTY

The stock exchange just happens to be in the geographical bounds of this particular parish. Our parish started 40 years ago at the request of stockbrokers who wanted the opportunity to attend mass before work or at lunchtime and wanted a church close enough so that they could get there very easily.

A committee of stockbrokers spoke to Cardinal Spellman about it, and Cardinal Spellman agreed. Major Bowes—the Major Bowes of "Amateur Hour" fame—donated the property. Then the stockbrokers themselves had a fundraising campaign to get money to build the church. Stockbrokers and others have used it to great advantage ever since.

You know, the reaction of visiting priests here is that it's very edifying, very inspiring to see that we have eight masses a day attended by some 2,000 people—and more during the season of Lent. These are fine, religious people whose devotion goes well beyond the Catholic's obligation to attend mass on Sunday.

For many years I was the New York Archdiocese executive director of an office known as the Trustees of St. Patrick's Cathedral. And I came to know many of the prestigious or prominent Catholic businessmen the cardinal appointed to direct our finances—mainly for church and cemetery maintenance. That's one reason I'm here. The cardinal knew that my heart was in parish work, and he said to me that after twenty years he felt he should reward me by allowing me to go back to what is the first love of every diocesan priest: parish work. And he asked if I would be willing to come to a parish of this type because so many of my friends work in the area. [NYSE chief] John Phelan, for example, attends church here.

To me, the insider trading scandals of recent months represent a very, very small fraction of those who work in the area. I think it's been done by very few individuals. And what they've done is contrary to moral law, civil law, the regulations of the Securities and Exchange Commission, the New York Stock Exchange and the basic American values of fairness and honesty. I also feel that what they've done is a betrayal of the very institution that provided their livelihoods—and a betrayal of their fellow workers.

RABBI MEYER HAGER

This synagogue was originally founded in 1929, and its rationale was to serve the working people, the weekday businessmen and professionals who want to meditate or come here to say services for their departed or to study Jewish religious subjects. For many years we were geared exclusively to the business community.

When I came here in 1965, I remember, there was really a euphoria. There was a limitless sky, as far as the market was concerned. My distinct impression—of course, everyone's impressions grow vague over twenty years—was that, all of a sudden, things started to cave in. I know many people who were wiped out in the late '60s. The new stocks, the new ventures, began to wobble and fold.

My father came to this community and to Wall Street in 1929. He knew of many cases when there was very overt discrimination, blatant discrimination against Jews in banks and insurance companies. During his time many people came to him for guidance. They were afraid to say they were Jewish because they might lose their jobs. For instance, there were people who worked on Rosh Hashanah and Yom Kippur.

I myself did not see this kind of discrimination on Wall Street. In fact, I have noticed that the numbers of Jews who are working here has increased greatly, especially among those who are Orthodox. When I came, it was practically unknown to see men walking around with yarmulkes and working in banks or financial houses.

The synagogue has sometimes been severely affected by the market, especially when things went bad around twenty years ago. Many firms folded. And once there was a shakeout, our support disappeared as well.

As for the recent insider trading scandals, it's not the norm in Judaism for people to consult the rabbi about complex business issues. I'd just like to say that business and industry are subject to rigorous religious and moral obligations. There is no substitute for plain integrity. In Judaism our prophets denounced greed throughout ancient history. For the past year or two, I've been studying the Mishnah with the congregation. The Mishnah is the great commentary that deals mainly with ethics. One very striking saying by Rabbi Chanina is that man must first get satisfaction from his fellow man, and only then can he obtain satisfaction in the eyes of the Almighty. He means that one must be found to be acceptable in his dealings with his fellow man as far as business and worldly matters go before he can be acceptable in the eyes of the Almighty. And we have another teaching in the Mishnah: As Rabbi Yose said, your friend's property should be as precious to you as your own.

Given the moral climate we have today—and not only on Wall Street, but in, let's say, government, sports or probably any area—it is imperative that whatever wisdom and ancient teachings apply, we should try to espouse them as frequently as we can and to as many people as we can.

Editor: Lenny Glynn